Cross-Currents of Jungian Thought

A C. G. JUNG FOUNDATION BOOK

The C. G. Jung Foundation for Analytical Psychology is dedicated to helping men and women grow in conscious awareness of the psychological realities in themselves and society, find healing and meaning in their lives and greater depth in their relationships, and live in response to their discovered sense of purpose. It welcomes the public to attend its lectures, seminars, films, symposia, and workshops and offers a wide selection of books for sale through its bookstore. The Foundation also publishes *Quadrant,* a semiannual journal, and books on Analytical Psychology and related subjects. For information about Foundation programs or membership, please write to the

C. G. Jung Foundation
28 East 39th Street
New York, NY 10016

Cross-Currents of Jungian Thought

AN ANNOTATED BIBLIOGRAPHY

Donald R. Dyer

SHAMBHALA
Boston & London
1991

Shambhala Publications, Inc.
Horticultural Hall
300 Massachusetts Avenue
Boston, Massachusetts 02115

Shambhala Publications, Inc.
Random Century House
20 Vauxhall Bridge Road
London SW1V 2SA

9   8   7   6   5   4   3   2   1
First Edition
Printed in the United States of America on acid-free paper
Distributed in the United States by Random House, Inc., in
Canada by Random House of Canada Ltd., and in the
United Kingdom by the Random Century Group.

Library of Congress Cataloging-in-Publication Data
Dyer, Donald R., 1918–
    Cross-currents of Jungian thought: an annotated
    bibliography
Donald R. Dyer.—1st ed.
        p.   cm.
    "A C. G. Jung Foundation book."
    ISBN 0-87773-904-8
    1. Jung, C. G. (Carl Gustav), 1875–1961—Bibliog-
raphy.   2. Psychoanalysis—Bibliography.   I. Title.
Z8458.75.D94   1991
[BF109]   90-53379
016.15019'54—dc20   CIP

Contents

Preface

This comprehensive bibliography has been compiled and annotated in order to provide an extensive source of information on Jung's own writings that either were written in English or have been translated into English, as well as Jungian-oriented writings by other authors. The criteria used to determine what to include are somewhat subjective, though "objective" criteria include such obvious evidence as the name *Jung* or the word *Jungian* in the title or subtitle of a book. Also used was evidence of the comments about Jung made by an author in a preface or introduction or text giving significant credit to Jung as contributor to his or her thinking and writing. Evaluation also was made of the number of references to Jung given in a book's list of sources, bibliography, notes, and index. Writings by Jungian analysts and by Jungian-oriented therapists are included, though a subjective element is evident in my choices, and not all writings by all Jungian analysts are cited. Included are more than twenty books for which Jung contributed a foreword, an introduction, or a commentary.

Only books, not articles in journals, are included. (There are, however, books on Jungian subjects that are collections of essays by various authors.) Even with that limitation, the listing amounts to more than 780 titles. Jung's own productivity during his lifetime was very large, including original publications in German, English, and French. His works published in English number seventy, including the volumes of the *Collected Works,* along with anthologies of his writings. A notable statistic within the framework of the historical development of the overall writings that are referenced in this volume is that more than half of the books (including initial editions, new editions, paperback editions, and reissues) have been published since 1975. Another indication of the remarkable explosion of Jungian-oriented writings is that more than thirteen hundred titles (counting all editions and reissues) have been released since Jung's death in 1961. (See the graph on page viii.)

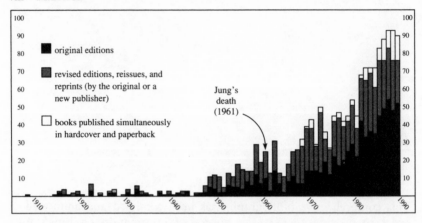

Number of Jungian Books in English (referenced in this volume)

Books that were forthcoming for 1990 publication at the time that this bibliography was being prepared have been included, although in some cases it was necessary to omit the complete annotation.

I hope that this publication may be helpful to close as well as more distant followers of Jung and to followers of other persuasions who want to become acquainted with the availability of Jungian writings. Cross-currents of Jungian thought may be likened to a river, wherein various energies are moving in a general direction but also are moving across, through, and alongside the main flow. The comprehensive and detailed nature of the book will make it an indispensable tool for graduate psychologists, psychotherapists, and all who study and work in the behavioral sciences. Moreover, it can provide a starting point for general readers who want to raise their consciousness and deepen their understanding of the theories and practices of Jung's depth psychology, as well as the amplifications and modifications by those who have been influenced by his valuable work.

Donald R. Dyer, Ph.D.
Chapel Hill, North Carolina

Acknowledgments

Although the energetic involvement with an almost endless number of details that is required in a work of this sort apparently suits my personality type, it is my anima, beckoning onward, that has been my ultimate inspiration.

I want to express special gratitude to Friend John Yungblut, who introduced me to the importance of the depth psychology of C. G. Jung within the triad that also includes the continuing creation of Teilhard de Chardin as well as the Cosmic Christ. His loving challenges that were garnered from his writings, workshops, and lectures have promoted my dedication to the search for truth, particularly as embodied by Jung.

I also want to express special gratitude to Marilyn Dyer, my wife of almost fifty years, who has given enthusiastic support to my effort in this project, particularly through her analytical talents. Her forbearance of my time spent on the project, which often entailed neglect of other matters, is greatly appreciated.

My endeavors have been aided also by expressions of support, interest, and even enthusiasm from Jungian-analyst friends and others who perceive the value of such a time-consuming effort to aid researchers as well as dedicated readers of Jungian thought.

Cross-Currents of Jungian Thought

Introduction

ON READING JUNG

Whenever a newcomer to Jungian psychology asks for advice on where to begin reading about this valuable and exciting field of knowledge, the most common recommendation is Jung's *Memories, Dreams, Reflections,* which is a kind of autobiography that was recorded and edited by Aniela Jaffé during 1958–61 from Jung's conversations with her and from his direct contributions to the book. It deals fundamentally with Jung's inner life, the self-realization of the unconscious, and the inward vision of his personal myth; it also presents a number of events of his outward life.

Many people report being attracted first by the colorful book entitled *Man and His Symbols* (published in an oversize format with nearly 500 illustrations), which contains chapters written by Jung and four of his followers. The chapter by Jung himself ("Approaching the Unconscious") is a model of clarity. It was his last composition, completed just before his death in 1961.

Other works by Jung written for the general reader include *The Undiscovered Self* (1958) and a collection of essays entitled *Modern Man in Search of a Soul* (1933). It generally is not recommended to start reading at random in the *Collected Works* (nineteen volumes of text) because many of the topics are very specialized and probably not of interest to the beginning reader. A plan for reading the *Collected Works* has been recently provided by Robert H. Hopcke in his *Guided Tour of the* Collected Works *of C. G. Jung* (1989).

In addition, there are significant collections of Jung's writings in the anthologies prepared by Joseph Campbell (*The Portable Jung:* fifteen essays) and Anthony Storr (*The Essential Jung:* fifty-three excerpts). C. G. Jung: *Psychological Reflections, A New Anthology* has nearly thirteen

1

hundred quotations selected by Jolande Jacobi (with R. F. C. Hull) from more than one hundred works.

The unique flavor of Jung's personality and writings can be sampled in *C. G. Jung Speaking: Interviews and Encounters,* edited by William McGuire and R. F. C. Hull, and *C. G. Jung: Letters,* selected and edited by Gerhard Adler in collaboration with Aniela Jaffé.

For the person who would prefer a short, systematic approach to Jung's psychology, concise introductions are presented in these two small paperbacks: *An Introduction to Jung's Psychology,* by Frieda Fordham, and *A Primer of Jungian Psychology,* by Calvin Hall and Vernon Nordby, both of which contain biographical sketches. Other, more extensive treatments of Jung's psychology are listed and annotated in chapter 3, "Jung's Psychology".

Impressions of Jung's work and particularly of his life may be gained from among nearly a dozen biographies, the most attractively presented being *C. G. Jung: Word and Image* (oversize format with 205 illustrations), edited by Aniela Jaffé, and *An Illustrated Biography of C. G. Jung* (oversize format with 231 illustrations), by Gerhard Wehr. The most extensive are written by Gerhard Wehr (*Jung: A Biography*), Barbara Hannah (*Jung: His Life and Work*), Marie-Louise von Franz (*C. G. Jung: His Myth in Our Time*), and Vincent Brome (*Jung: Man and Myth*).

The extent of Jung's own writings is strikingly demonstrated by the fact that they occupy eighteen original volumes of text in the *Collected Works,* with two additional volumes needed to contain a general bibliography (263 pp.) and a general index (735 pp.); a supplementary volume of lectures was added in 1983. Additional volumes have been published for his letters, seminar notes, and interviews. This comes to more than eight thousand pages of text and nearly three hundred fifty pages of bibliography. His published writings have appeared in eighteen languages.

FRAMEWORK OF THIS BIBLIOGRAPHY

This book is divided into three main parts, in which the works cited are arranged by subject, author, and title, respectively. Part One contains the bulk of this work, the annotated bibliography, in which books are arranged in twelve subject categories that have been selected in part from the categories used in Jung's *Collected Works* with some modifications and additions. Each reference includes complete bibliographic information on title, author, date and place of publication, publisher, editions (including paperbacks), as well as number of pages (distinguished by number of pages of text, pre-pages, index, bibliography, reference notes, and illustrations). These data, while providing information on the length and nature of the work by indicating the presence or absence of such "extras" as index and references, will not in themselves be a conclusive guide to the quality or seriousness of the writing.

The brief commentary on each book is neither promotional nor critical but rather descriptive, drawing from the author's own stated objectives in writing the book as gleaned from preface, introduction, or text, along with the table of contents. For readers who want critical assessments, I list the book review sources for each book. This listing also helps the researcher to assess the extent of the book's outreach by the numbers and kinds of periodicals in which it has been reviewed. (Identification of the abbreviations for periodicals appears in Appendix B.)

Part Two, which consists of books arranged alphabetically by author (except that the works of Jung appear first), may be consulted directly, if the author's name is known. The grouping together of works by author will be helpful to those who want to consult other writings by the author of a given book. Also, a brief identification is included for each author plus the page number to which the researcher may turn for complete bibliographic and annotated information in Part One.

Part Three, which consists of books arranged alphabetically by title, may be consulted if only the title (or a key word) is known. It serves, then, as an index because it lists not only titles *and* subtitles but also key words which form the basis for a subject index. As in Part Two, the page number to which the researcher may turn in Part One for complete information is listed. The author's name appears only with the complete title of the book in Part Three.

Finally, appendixes are included in order to provide useful information about (A) general abbreviations used in this book, (B) titles of periodicals given as sources of book reviews in Part One, (C) publishers of Jungian-oriented books, and (D) Jungian organizations, such as foundations, institutes, centers, associations, societies, and clubs.

Part One

Works Arranged by Subject

The major part of this book is dedicated to the arrangement of the more than 780 books under twelve subject categories that reflect the wide scope of Jungian thought, starting with books on the life of Jung and ending with the collective aspects of Jung's psychology:

1. The Life of C. G. Jung
2. Collections of Jung's Writings
3. Jung's Psychology
4. The Psyche
5. Psychological Types
6. Human Development and Individuation
7. Symbolic Life and Dreams
8. Feminine and Masculine Psychology
9. Religion and Jung's Psychology
10. Creativity and Jung's Psychology
11. Jungian Analysis
12. Civilization in Transition

Subjects with more than one hundred titles each are Jungian Analysis, Human Development and Individuation, and Religion and Jung's Psychology; while the smallest are Psychological Types, Collections of Jung's Writings, Civilization in Transition, Life of Jung, and The Psyche, with less than twenty-five each. The other four, namely, Jung's Psychology, Creativity and Jung's Psychology, Feminine and Masculine Psychology, and Symbolic Life and Dreams, have between fifty and seventy-five each. It may be noted that some books do not correspond neatly to a single subject. More than 150 books are placed under what is considered to be the major category and cross-referenced in other subject categories.

Within each chapter, books are arranged chronologically in order to provide a historical perspective for the writings. In cases where the book is published first in another language and later translated into English, the date of first publication is used in the chronology.

In order to facilitate locating a book, a listing of books alphabetized by author accompanies each subject-category chapter, with appropriate page references. (One may also consult Part Two for the author or Part Three for the title of a given book and thereby locate the annotated entry by subject.)

p   = paperback
p. = page
*   = book in print 1989

1. Life of C. G. Jung

These twenty-four books on the life of Jung (July 26, 1875–June 6, 1961) range from Jung's own *Memories, Dreams, Reflections* to more or less conventional biographies, as well as books on impressions of contacts with Jung.

Biographies written by close friends of Jung are those by Bennet, Hannah, Jaffé, van de Post, and von Franz. Others are those by Brome, Olney, Stern, Storr, Wehr, and Wilson—the most critical being that by Stern. Impressions of Jung from personal contacts are provided by Bennet, van der Post, Rolfe, and Serrano, along with collections of recollections about Jung edited by Fordham and by Jensen.

Jung: *Memories, Dreams, Reflections* [p. 8]
Bennet: *C. G. Jung* [p. 9]
_____: *Meetings with Jung* [p. 15]
Brome: *Jung: Man and Myth* [p. 14]
Fordham (ed.): *Contact with Jung* [p. 9]
Hannah: *Jung: His Life and Work* [p. 13]
Jaffé: *Jung's Last Years* [p. 15]
Jaffé (ed.): *C. G. Jung: Word and Image* [p. 13]
Jensen (ed.): *C. G. Jung, Emma Jung, and Toni Wolff* [p. 15]
Olney: *Metaphors of Self* [p. 11]
Rolfe: *Encounter with Jung* [p. 17]
Segaller & Berger: *The Wisdom of the Dream: The World of C. G. Jung* [p. 18]
Serrano: *C. G. Jung and Hermann Hesse* [p. 9]
Staude: *The Adult Development of C. G. Jung* [p. 14]
Stern: *C. G. Jung: The Haunted Prophet* [p. 12]
Stevens: *On Jung* (See Chapter 3, "Jung's Psychology") [p. 53]
Storr: *C. G. Jung* [p. 11]

van der Post: *Jung and the Story of Our Time* [p. 12]
———: *A Walk with a White Bushman* [p. 17]
von Franz: *C. G. Jung: His Myth in Our Time* [p. 10]
Wehr: *An Illustrated Biography of C. G. Jung* [p. 18]
———: *Jung: A Biography* [p. 16]
———: *Portrait of Jung* [p. 10]
Wilson: *Lord of the Underworld* [p. 16]

Memories, Dreams, Reflections by C. G. Jung, recorded and edited by Aniela Jaffé (Ger.: *Erinnerungen, Träume, Gedanken*. Zurich: Rascher Verlag 1962) London: Collins with Routledge & Kegan Paul, 1962; New York: Pantheon, 1963p; rev. 1973; New York: Vintage Books/Random House, 1965p; rev. 1989p*; London: Collins, 1967p; London: Flamingo/Fontana, 1983p* (430 + xiv, incl. 20–p. index, 8–p. list of the *Collected Works*, 12–p. gloss. of Jungian terms, 28 illus., 10–p. editor's intro.).

Stating in the prologue that his life is a story of the self-realization of the unconscious, Jung views his experience as his personal myth, as *his* truth. Therefore, he speaks chiefly of inner experiences, including dreams; and outward events of his life and work are illuminated by his deep understanding of the psyche. As an "autobiography," the memoirs are arranged chronologically, starting with his childhood and his school and university years, followed by psychiatric activities (first years of work as physician at Burghölzli Psychiatric Clinic and lecturer at the University of Zurich) and his friendship and break with Freud, followed by confrontation with the unconscious, the work (therapeutic practice, research, and writing), building his tower-retreat at Bollingen, and travels, concluding with chapters devoted to visions, life after death, late thoughts, and retrospect. Appended are three letters from Freud to Jung, six letters from Jung to his wife, Emma Jung, from America, a letter to Emma from North Africa, a memoriam to Richard Wilhelm, and Jung's "Seven Sermons to the Dead."

(Bk.revs.: AmJPsychi '63/120:616; ArchGenPsy '63/9:189–90; Atl Jn'63/311:130, AveM 8Jn'63/97:24; Blackf '63/44:531; BkMClubN My'63:16; BkRDig '63:540; ChrCen '63/80:619; Econ '63/208:268; LibJ '63/88:2506; Listen '63/70:85–6; LondMag S'63ns3:87–8; Midstream D'63/9:99–105; NewStates 12Jy'63/66:48; NYHerTrib 12My'63:1; NYTimesBkR 19My'63:3; PartisR '63/30:453–63; SatR Jn'63/46:23; SciAm '63/209:283; Spec '63/211:86; Time 10My'63:100; TimesLitSup '63:592; VaQR '63/39; cxxxix; IntJPsy-An '64/45:450-5; JRelHealth '64/3:289; NYorker 23My'64/40:156 +; PastorPsy '64/14:61; PsyanQ '64/33:561–74; AmJPsyth '65/79:153; BrJMedPsy '65/38:274–5; ModChman '68ns11:264; AmJArTh '72/11:68, BkWorld 1Ap'73/7:2; JAnPsy '79/24:82; JInterdHist '80/11:138; Leon '83/16:64; Tabl '83/217:841; BrJPsychi '84/145:220–1; PsyMed '84/14:477)

C. G. *Jung*, by E. A. Bennet. London: Barrie & Rockliff, 1961; New York: E. P. Dutton, rev. 1962p (165, incl. 6–p. index, 4–p. bibl.).

Reflecting on his long personal friendship with Jung, psychiatrist Bennet depicts some of the key aspects of Jung's work within the setting of Jung's personality. Because of Bennet's own career, he emphasizes the medical background of Jung's work. He provides an introduction to Jung as a person and then gives impressions of Jung's childhood and youth, Jung's first professional experience (at Zurich's Burghölzli Hospital) and his friendship with Freud. The remainder of the book highlights Jung's theories and practice on the subjects of introverts and extraverts, the mind (personal and impersonal), mental life as process, the mind in time (*Aion*), dreams, the interplay of opposites, and individuation. The appendix (notable occasions) contains an account of some of Jung's birthdays and the transcription of a BBC broadcast review.

(Bk. revs.: Econ 7N'61/201:36 + ; TimesLitSup '61:647; BksAbroad '62/36:214–15; JAnPsy '62/7:155–6; JMentSci '62/108:113–14; Spring '62:159–60; VaQR '63/39:lxiii)

Contact with Jung: Essays on the Influence of His Work and Personality, edited by Michael Fordham. London: Tavistock Publications for the Society of Analytical Psychology, 1963; Philadelphia: J. B. Lippincott, 1964 (245 + x, incl. 7–p. index, end-chapter references).

Originally intended as a memorial supplement to the Society's *Journal of Analytical Psychology,* marking Jung's death as the last of a generation of founders of a new science of psychology, this work is made available to a wider public in order to present not only the impact of Jung's scientific researches but also of the influence of his personality. Essays by forty-one contributors include thirty-one in English; the remainder are in German or French. Most essays are short (two- to seven-page) tributes or reflections on Jung's influence. Contributions by authors whose books appear in the present annotated bibliography are by Culver Barker, Barbara Hannah, Esther Harding, Joseph Henderson, Kenneth Lambert, John Perry, Marvin Spiegelman, Robert Stein, Jane Wheelwright, and Joseph Wheelwright.

(Bk.revs.: Blackf '63/44:533; BrBkN '63:477; BrJMedPsy '64/37:181; BrJPsychi '64/ 110:135–6; BrJPsy '64/55:233; JAnPsy '64/9:92–5; BulHistMed '65/39:590–1; Bul-MennClin '65/29:170; ContemPsy '67/12:253–4)

C. G. Jung and Hermann Hesse: A Record of Two Friendships, by Miguel Serrano. (Span.: *El Círculo Hermético.* Santiago de Chile: Zig-Zag, 1964.) London: Routledge & Kegan Paul, 1966; 1971p*; New York: Schocken Books, 1966; 1968p (112 + xi, incl. 9 illus.).

Serrano's contacts in Switzerland with Jung and with novelist-poet Hermann Hesse reflect his admiration that they had lived fully, expressing their very being in their work. His first interview with Jung occurred in May 1959 and the last in May 1961, less than a month before Jung's death. He characterizes Jung as having given new terms to myths that emanate from "mankind's eternal tradition." He records a dream following Jung's death in which Jung returns to receive Serrano in Jung's house.

(Bk.revs.: NYTimesBkR 12Jn'66:29; Observ 20My'66:27; BkRDig '67:1182; Choice '67/ 4:30; IntJParapsy '67/9:62; Spring '67:153–4; GerLifeLet '69/ns22:180–1)

Portrait of Jung: An Illustrated Biography, by Gerhard Wehr. (Ger.: *C. G. Jung im Selbstzeugnissen und Bilkdokumenten.* Reinbek bei Hamburg: Rowohlt Raschenbuch Verlag, 1969.) New York: Herder & Herder, 1971 +p (173, incl. 3–p. bibl., 5–p. ref. notes, 3–p. chron., 55 illus.).

Wehr, who has written biographies of such other famous persons as Jan Hus, Meister Eckhart, Martin Luther, Paracelsus, Jakob Boehme, Rudolf Steiner, Paul Tillich, and Martin Buber, characterizes Jung in this illustrated biography (fifteen photos of Jung himself) as explorer of the archetypes in the human psyche, that is, of "the collective unconscious," as well as interpreter of symbolism and the process of individuation in humankind. His topics include Jung's beginnings, the meeting and break with Freud, the elements of his doctrine, psychological types, psychology and religion, alchemy and the study of the psyche, Jung and Eastern thought, psychotherapy, problems of our time, and the importance of dialogue.

(Bk.revs.: Bklist 15N'71/68:255; LibJ '71/96:2763; LibJBkR '71:119; JPastorCare '74/ 28:213)

C. G. Jung: His Myth in Our Time, by Marie-Louise von Franz. (Ger.: *C. G. Jung: Sein Mythos in unserer Zeit.* Stuttgart: Huber, 1972.) London: Hodder & Stoughton, 1975; New York: G. P. Putnam's Sons for the C. G. Jung Foundation for Analytical Psychology, 1975; Boston: Little, Brown, 1977p (355 + x, incl. 31–p. index, 32–p. bibl., 3–p. biographic chron.).

Von Franz, close collaborator with Jung in alchemical studies, presents within a wide perspective the development of basic Jungian concepts, such as the collective unconscious, archetypes, psychological types, active imagination, and the process of individuation. In following the "basic melody" of Jung's inner myth, she touches on his influence on such varied subjects as anthropology, ethnology, religion, and atomic physics, as well as psychology and psychotherapy. Her subjects include the underground god (Jung's first great dream, at age three or four), the storm lantern (the guiding light in the psyche), the physician, mirror-symmetry and the polarity of the psyche, the journey to the beyond (experiencing the unconscious), the Anthropos, the mandala, *coincidentia oppositorum* (identification of opposites), man's morning knowledge and evening knowledge, Mercurius, the philosopher's stone, breakthrough to the *unus mundus* (unity of the world), individual and society, and *le cri de Merlin* (the cry of Merlin, the spirit in the stone).

(Bk.revs.: Bklist '75/72:479; LibJ '75/100:1427; LibJBkR '75:416–17; PsyToday D'75/ 9:114; AmJPsyth '76/30:690–1; BkRDig '76:398; Choice '76/12:1502–3; Econ 3Ap '76/ 259:133–4; InwLight '76–77/n88–89:61–3; NYRevBks 15Ap'76/23:26–30; NYTimesBkR 17Jy'76:7; PsyPersp D'76/9:114; Quad '76/9n2:60–1; RefServR Ap'76/ 4:92; USCath Ag'76/41:27; JAnPsy '77/22:190–1, 191–2; NYTimesBkR 24Jy'77:7+)

Metaphors of Self: A Theory of Autobiography, by James Olney. Princeton, N.J.: Princeton U. Press, 1972* +p*; London: Oxford U. Press, 1972 (342 + xi, incl. 10–p. index).

Pursuing his interest in the philosophy and psychology of autobiography, Olney uses Jung as one of his six examples of autobiographical types. In the 62-page chapter "Jung: 'My Personal Myth,'" he characterizes Jung as "nothing more and nothing less than a speculative metaphysician," adding that Jung's own autobiography offers a comprehensive statement of his profound experience in and understanding of the human condition.

(Bk.revs.: BkRDig '72:984; ChrCen '72/89:807; KirkR '72/40:566; LibJ '72/97:2843; LibJBkR '72:321; NYRevBks 20Jy'72/19:33; PsyPersp '72/3:187–93; PubW 5Jn'72/ 201:136; Choice '73/10:72; CompLit '73/25:164–7; Novel '73/6:190–2; PsyToday Ja'73/ 6:79; Quad '73/n14:22–4; QueensQ '73/80:135–6; SAtlQ '73/72:326–7; VaQR '73/ 49:152–6; GaR '74/28:159–63; JModLit '74/3:478–80; ModLangR '74/69:603; Bks-Abroad '74/48:217; Diacrit Wint '82/12:2–6)

Jung, by Anthony Storr. (American title: *C. G. Jung.*) London: Fontana/Collins, 1973 +p; 1986p*; New York: Viking Press, 1973 +p (116 + xii, incl. 4–p. index, 1–p. bibl., 2–p. biographical note).

In this short introduction to Jung's life and work, Storr emphasizes Jung's ideas on introversion and extraversion, a self-regulating psyche, the process of individuation, archetypes and the collective unconscious, and the concept of the self. He begins with a view of Jung's personal background and his early work and concludes with Jung's contribution to psychotherapy. He states that Jung's ideas are "profoundly valuable" and are necessary in order to counterbalance Freud, though as a psychiatrist with Jungian analytical training he prefers to be "unlabeled." He especially values Jung's contribution to the conception of human nature.

(Bk.revs.: AmJOrthopsy '73/43:492; BkRDig '73:1254; BkWorld 8Ap '73/7:13; Bklist '73/ 69:873; BksBkmen Mr'73:xi; BrBkN '73:213; BrJPsychi '73/123:364–5; Choice '73/ 10:1085; Econ 3F'73/246:86; Harvest '73/19:78; JAnPsy '73/18:176–7; JEurStud '73/ 3:81; NewBlackf '73/54:185–6; NewStates '73/85:91–2; NYTimesBkR 25F'73:31; Observ 28Ja'73:34; PsyMed '73/3:398–9; SciBksFilm '73/9:112+; Spec '73/230:75–6;

ContemPsy '74/19:208–9; Quad '74/n16:42; NYTimesBkR 27Jn'76:7; AmJPsychi '88/145:1311)

Jung and the Story of Our Time, by Laurens van der Post. New York: Pantheon Books/RandomHouse, 1975; London: Hogarth, 1976*; New York: Vintage Books/Random, 1977p*; Harmondsworth: Penguin Books, 1978p* (276 pp).

South African explorer-writer Sir Laurens van der Post's close friendship with Jung convinced him that Jung's importance to so-called normal people and societies was much greater than his gift of healing abnormal and psychologically ill persons. He is certain of Jung's greatness as an inspired psychologist and born healer and describes Jung as more than a psychoanalyst in the wider context of history. Following an introductory chapter on his own background and his first meeting with Jung, van der Post describes Jung's childhood and youth, his professional experience at Burghölzli Hospital, and his experiences with Freud, ending with a long chapter on Jung's contributions.

(Bk.revs.: Atl D'75/236:115–16; BkWorld 31Ag'75:2; Bklist '75/72:480; KirkR '75/43:1052; LibJ '75/100:1818–19; LibJBkR '75:139; Nation '75/221:504; NewRep 6D'75/173:256; PubW 20Oct'75/208:68; RBksRel(W) My'75/5:3; Time 1D'75/106:83; BestSell '76/35:389; BkRDig '76:1235; BksBkmen S'76/21:38–40; BrBkN '76:824; Choice Mr'76/13:141; ChrCen '76/93:500–1; Critic '76/34:74–6; InwLight '76–77/n88–89:60; LibJ '76/101:6; Listen '76/96:28–9; NYRevBks 15Ap '76/23:26–30; NYTimesBkR 27Ja'76:7; NewSoc '76/36:705–6; NewStates '76/92:248; Observ 20Jn'76:27; Quad '76/9n2:60–1; QueensQ '76/83:478–82; RefServR Ap'76/4:92; Signs Mr'76/55:44; Tabl '76/300:882–3; BrJPsychi '77/130:310; JAnPsy '77/22:79–80; PsyMed '78/8:729–30; SchLibr S'78/26:290; TimesEdSup 2Ap'78:20; JDocu '81/37:220)

C. G. Jung: The Haunted Prophet, by Paul J. Stern. New York: George Braziller, 1976; New York: Delta Book/Dell Publishing, 1977p (267, incl. 5-p. index, 4-p bibl.).

Psychotherapist Stern presents a picture of Jung in sharp contrast to most accepted views of his life and work, postulating that Jung was haunted by a prophetic revelation and spent a lifetime searching for the "reality of the soul." He characterizes Jung's life story as a "compelling parable that illustrates the creative uses of incipient madness." He interprets Jung's early life using such phrases as "a world he never made" (childhood), "ghosts" (college student), "the sense of non-sense" (work at Burghölzli asylum), and an "inexorable" marriage. This is followed by chapters on Freud (a mutual enchantment; and the break) and journey to the underworld, along with Toni Wolff ("Eros-winged muse"). There are chapters on the Psychological Club of Zurich, introversion and extraversion, Jung in America, alchemy, two well-tempered friendships (Richard Wilhelm and Hermann Keyserling), the flirtation with the Devil (Nazism), years of misery (1938–45), and the Institute (Jung's mystical body).

(Bk.revs.: BestSell Jy'76/36:120; BkRDig '76:1151–2; Choice '76/13:726; KirkR '76/44:182; LibJ '76/101:1281; LibJBkR '76:132; NewRep 15My'76/174:28–30; NYTimesBkR 27Jn'76:7+; NYorker 20S'76/52:136–8+; PubW 22Mr'76/209:39; Quad '76/9n2:60–3; Soc '76/13n6:80–2; ContemPsy '77/22:329–30; JParapsy '77/41:221–2; PsyRec '77/27:358; PubW 14F'77/211:82; SciBksFilm '77/13:32; ContemPsy '78/23:663; AmJPsychi '79/136:262–3)

Jung: His Life and Work; A Biographical Memoir, by Barbara Hannah. New York: G. P. Putnam's Sons, 1976; London: Michael Joseph, 1977; New York: Perigee Books/Putnam's, 1981p (376, incl. 11-p. index, 5-p. bibl., 10-p. ref. notes).

Presenting a "biographical memoir" of Jung, Hannah's point of view as student, analysand, colleague, friend, and neighbor makes his life come alive in this chronological account that reveals not only the complexity of this creative man but also his simplicity. She illustrates the common ground she had with him in her deep interest in psychological wholeness—the process of individuation. Her story begins with Jung's early impressions and then proceeds through years at Basel Gymnasium, Basel University, Burghölzli Psychiatric Hospital, the first years at Küsnacht, the First World War, after the war, travel (1925–26), storm clouds over Europe, an Indian intermezzo, the Second World War, creative writing, *Mysterium Coniunctionis* (his *opus magnum*), and the late years.

(Bk.revs.: Bklist '76/73:435; KirkR '76/44:1008; LibJ '76/101:1849; LibJBkR '76:105; PubW 23Ag'76/210:65; BestSell '77/36:393; BkRDig '77:559–60; BksBkmen D'77/23:48–9; 50–1; Choice '77/13:1664; InwLight '77/n90:51–2; NewSci '77/75:304; NewSoc '77/41:196–7; Quad '77/10n1:43–4; Tabl '77/231:1009–11; EdStud '78/9:82–3; JAnPsy '78/23:287–9; Month '78/11:105; BestSell '81/41:302)

C. G. Jung: Word and Image, edited by Aniela Jaffé. (Ger.: *C. G. Jung: Bild und Wort*. Olten, Switzerland: Walter Verlag, 1977.) Princeton, N.J.: Princeton U. Press (Bollingen Series XVII.2) 1979*; 1983p* (238 + xiv, incl. 6-p. index, 5-p. chron. of Jung's life, 5-p. technical terms, 1-p. list of the *Collected Works*, 205 illus.).

This beautiful, large-format picture book with explanatory text marks the occasion of a memorial exhibition in 1975 on the 100th anniversary of Jung's birth. Edited by Jaffé, Jung's personal secretary between 1955 and 1961 and an analyst herself, it serves as a companion volume to Jung's autobiography, which she also edited. Its contents reflect not only Jung's external life but his inner life as well. A wide collection of photographs, art work, and documents are included. Subjects covered are Jung's grandparents, childhood, and student years, as well as the occult and parapsychology, Burghölzli, Freud, confrontation with the unconscious, the mandala, alchemy, Paracelsus, psychotherapy, the transference, home and family, travels (North Africa, Pueblo Indians, Kenya and Uganda, India), the Eranos Conferences, the tower in Bollingen, religion, and life and death.

(Bk.revs.: PubW 11D'78/214:64; BkRDig '79:189–90; Choice '79/16:726; ChrCen '79/96:620; ContemPsy '79/24:1053; JAmAcadRel '79/47:700; LibJ '79/104:1465–6; LibJBkR '79:369–70; NewRep 4Ag'79/181:39–42; NewRBksRel S'79/4:13; Parab Ag '79/4:130–2; AmJPsychi '80/137:140–1; InwLight '80/90:48–50; JAltState '80/5:265–6; PsyanR '80/67:287; PsyPersp '80/11:95–6; Quad '80/13n1:116–17; RelStudR '80/6:127–8; Biog '82/5:271–3; BkWorld 15My'83/13:12; JAnPsy '84/29:202–3)

Jung: Man and Myth, by Vincent Brome. London: Macmillan, 1978 + p; New York: Atheneum, 1978; 1981p; London: Paladin Book/Grafton Books, 1980p* (327, incl. 11-p. index, 9-p. bibl., incl. list of the *Collected Works*).

An experienced biographer (of H. G. Wells and Havelock Ellis), Brome presents a sympathetic as well as critical story of Jung's life, characterizing him as an authentic scientist and artist whose philosophic temperament and training harbored a Renaissance-style humanist. Brome's research on Jung over several years and interviews with many people who had known Jung resulted in a rounded portrayal of "a sage—almost an oracle" in his later years. Brome's thirty-two chapters follow Jung's life chronologically from forebears to the last year. Appended is a 12-page recapitulation of Jung's theories in the form of a resume of the psyche, as well as an appendix on the psychiatric sources of Jung's work and a brief appendix on Jung's influence.

(Bk.revs.: Bklist '78/74:1651; GuardW 24D'78:14; KirkR '78/46:842; NewSoc '78/46:285; NewStates '78/96:551; NYTimesBkR 24D'78/83:2+; PubW 14Ag'78/214:61; Spec 11N'78/241:19–20; ArtPsyth '79/6:286–7; BkRDig '79:157; BksBkmen F'79/24:32–3; BrBkN '79:306; BrJPsychi '79/134:646; Choice '79/15:1724; ContemPsy '79/24:1021–2; Critic Jy'79/38:2–3; LibJ '79/104:396; LibJBkR '79:94; LondMag Jy'79/ns19:81–3; Month '79/12:72; NatCathRep Mr'79/15:12; Tabl '79/233:81–2; JAnPsy '80/25:205–6; JAmAcadRel '80/48:148–9; JInterdHist '80/11:138–40; PsyanR '80/67:287; PubW 30Ja'81/219:74; SFJInstLib '81/3n1:55–6)

The Adult Development of C. G. Jung, by John-Raphael Staude. Boston and London: Routledge & Kegan Paul, 1981* (134 + xxiv, incl. 4-p. index, 6-p. bibl., 4-p. ref. notes, 2 illus.).

Within the context of contemporary adult developmental psychology, psychologist Staude concentrates on Jung's mid-life transition in order to show how Jung developed his theory of the individuation process during the second half of life. Drawing upon Jung's own personal experience as well as clinical situations, he presents his own interpretation of what he considers to be the strengths and weaknesses of Jung's theory of that stage of the life process.

(Bk.revs.: Choice '81/19:557; LibJ '81/196:1741; TimesLitSup '81:1178; BkRDig '82:1284–5; ContemPsy '82/27:402; PsyMed '82/12:444; RelStudR '82/8:354; SFJInstLib '82/4n1:49–58; SciBksFilm '82/17:187)

C. G. Jung, Emma Jung, and Toni Wolff: A Collection of Remembrances, edited by Ferne Jensen. San Francisco: Analytical Psychology Club of San Francisco, 1982p* (131 + xi, incl. 4 illus., 1-p. preface by Joseph Henderson).

This is a collection of short reminiscences by thirty-eight people who knew Emma Jung, Antonia (Toni) Wolff, Jung's chief assistant, and Jung himself, along with memoirs by twelve members of the Club who had met Jung personally. The varied group of contributors, including mostly Jungian analysts but also authors, artists, editors, and clergymen, present a wide variety of remembrances.

(Bk.revs.: Quad '83/16n1:117–18; PsyPersp '84/15:105–6; SFJInstLib '84/5n2:31–2; JAnPsy '85/30:107–8)

Meetings with Jung: Conversations Recorded by E. A. Bennet During the Years 1946–1961. London: Anchor Press, 1982; Zurich: Daimon Verlag, 1985p* (125, incl. 3 illus., 3-p. introduction by Marie-Louise von Franz).

Having first met Jung in the early 1930s, Bennet made notes during seventy-one meetings with Jung between 1946 and five months before Jung's death in 1961. His background of psychological medicine as well as theology and philosophy provides a basis for understanding and valuing Jung's contributions. The notes present impressions of Jung's everyday life and his natural way of living and thinking. The sixteen short chapters are titled by season and year.

(Bk.revs.: JAnPsy '83/28:279–81; Quad '84/17n1:69–70; Tabl '86/43:316; IndPsy '87/43:19–20)

Jung's Last Years and Other Essays, by Aniela Jaffé. Dallas: Spring Publications, 1984p (Jungian Classics Series, 6) (172 + ix).

The first four of the five chapters are reprinted from Jaffé's 1971 *From the Life and Work of C. G. Jung,* the fourth essay being "From Jung's Last Years," which Jaffé supplies in response to requests from many who were more interested in impressions of Jung's personality than in his scientific writings. The last chapter deals with the creative phases in Jung's life, reprinted from the journal *Spring* (1972). Jaffé's observations of Jung's personality derive from her serving as his personal secretary during the last seven years of his life and before that as administrative secretary of the Jung Institute of Zurich from its founding in 1948. She met Jung in 1938 after fleeing from Germany and subsequently trained as an analyst. (See a new edition (1989) under the old title in chapter 3.)

(Bk.rev.: JAnPsy '83/28:79–80)

Lord of the Underworld: Jung and the Twentieth Century, by Colin Wilson. Wellingborough: Aquarian Press, 1984*; 1988p* (160, incl. 3-p. index, 1-p. bibl.).

Wilson, author of numerous biographies, characterizes Jung as an artist as well as a scientist, particularly in the way his painting (especially of mandalas) and his stone carving illustrated his "confrontation with the unconscious." His overview of Jung's influence on the twentieth century begins with a chapter on Jung's dual personality and continues with the topics of how to become a scientist, how to lose friends and alienate people, lord of the underworld, the invisible writing, and the sage—doubts and reservations. Appended is a discussion of active imagination.

(Bk.revs.: Econ 14Jy'84/292:87–8; SFJInstLib '85/6n1:47–8)

Jung: A Biography, by Gerhard Wehr. (Ger.: *Carl Gustav Jung: Leben, Werk, Wirkung.* Munich: Kösel Verlag, 1985.) Boston and London: Shambhala Publications, 1987*; 1988p* (550 + viii, incl. 11-p. index, 7-p. bibl. of the *Collected Works,* 32-p. ref. notes, 5-p. chron. of Jung's life, 27 illus.).

By far the longest biography of Jung, this is an attempt to present a somewhat conventional account of Jung's life, trying to do justice to both inner and outer dimensions in chronological fashion. Wehr closely follows Jung's own memoirs, providing a factual introduction with little new information. Following an introduction on origins and genealogy, he presents early experiences, a spiritual and religious awakening, studies in Basel, experiments in parapsychology, Jung's experience as a psychiatrist at Burghölzli, his encounter with Emma Rauschenbach, Sigmund Freud ("the first man of real importance"), the inevitable break, and transformation and confrontation with the unconscious. This is followed by traveling and tower-building, Jung's encounter with alchemy, the Eranos conferences, journey to India, the religion question, National Socialism ("I slipped up"), the Second World War, the Codex Jung, signs of age, creativity and growth, *Answer to Job,* and *Mysterium Coniunctionis,* ending with Jung's last days ("under the sign of wholeness"). Appended are essays on "Western Consciousness and Eastern Spirituality," "C. G. Jung in Dialogue and Dispute," and "Prolegomena to a History of Jung's Influence."

(Bk.revs.: AmHistR '87/92:925; Bklist '87/84:516; KirkR '87/55:1564; LibJ D'87/
112:105; LATimesBkR 27D'87:1+; PubW 6N'87/232:54; AmJPsychi '88/145:1311;
BloomR My'88/8:21; Choice '88/25:1315–16; BkRDig '88:1319; GuardW 21My'88/
139:28; HudsonR '88/41:575–80; NYTimesBkR 14F'88/93:22; QuillQuire Mr'88/54:82;
SFJInstLib '88/8n2:37–40; BkWorld 25Jn'89/19:12; JAnPsy '89/34:301–3; KenyonR '89/
11:154; PubW 14Ap'89/235:65; SciBksFilm '89/24:235)

A Walk with a White Bushman, by Laurens van der Post. London: Chatto &
Windus, 1986*; New York: W. W. Morrow, 1986*; Harmondsworth:
Penguin Books, 1988p* (326 + xxi, incl. 8-p. index).

The original idea for these conversations came from Jean-Marc Pottiez,
who, like van der Post, was born in Africa of European parents and shared
two cultures. They were intended as interviews for French television or radio,
but it was decided to publish instead. Covering the period 1982–85, the
conversations cover a wide range of subjects; and, as van der Post notes, "we
seemed to be talking around a camp fire in the vast natural world of Africa."
Such an overpowering feeling had occurred when he first met Jung in Zurich;
Jung took him home and they talked far into the night. Nearly fifty references
to Jung are made in the index, thereby revealing the close friendship these
two men had. In answer to the question, "Who was Jung for you?" van der
Post answered, "He was a friend who gave me much, to whom I owe more
than I can say, and who was also great fun. . . . But above all he was a kind
of lighthouse to me." The designation of van der Post as a white Bushman
refers to him as a white man with the Bushman's intuitive sensibility.

(Bk.revs.: Observ 14D'86:22; Spec 15N'86/257:29–30; KirkR '87/55:848; LibJ 15Jn'87/
112:67; PubW 12Jn'87/231:77; Resurg Mr-Ap'87/n121:46; TimesLitSup '87:93;
TimesEdSup 22Ap'88:22)

Encounter with Jung, by Eugene Rolfe. Boston: Sigo Press, 1989* +p* (232 +
xvi, incl. 2-p. index, 17 photos, 4 letters from Jung to Rolfe).

Rolfe weaves his "encounter" with Jung into his own autobiography, the
actual personal encounter occurring in chapter 31 (the last before the
conclusion), in December, 1960, six months before Jung's death. His first
"encounter" had been in 1946 when he happened to read Jung's book *The
Integration of the Personality,* which drew him from a deep depression and
caused him to reinterpret "God" in a meaningful way, in terms of the total
personality. Following his demobilization from the British Army in 1947, he
was inspired to write a book which he submitted unsuccessfully for publication; he then sent the manuscript for evaluation to Jung, who referred him to
Gerhard Adler. This led to Rolfe's acquaintanceship with Jungians in London
and to correspondence with Jung about Rolfe's writings. He writes in detail
of his nearly two-hour meeting with Jung in 1960.

(Bk.rev.: PsyPersp '90/22:174–5)

An Illustrated Biography of C. G. Jung, by Gerhard Wehr. Boston and Shaftesbury: Shambhala Publications, 1989* (159, incl. 1-p. bibl., 2-p. ref. notes, 4-p. chron. of Jung's life and work, 230 + illus.).

Drawing somewhat on his extensive biography of Jung (see above), Wehr provides the equivalent of about sixty-five pages of text to accompany the numerous illustrations (many in color, including eight drawings by Jung himself) that include photos of people, scenes, and documents such as Jung's notebooks, diaries, and letters. The first part of this large-format volume deals with the early years of Jung's life, and the second part deals with Jung's experience in depth psychology. The third and longest part covers "laying the foundations of analytical psychology" from a fresh burst of creativity to investigations of psychological types (1921), Jung's travels, tower-building on Lake Zurich, the encounter with alchemy, Jung's relationship with Eastern spirituality, confrontation with National Socialism, and psychology and religion. The fourth part is concerned with maturation and later work, last years, Jung's influence on the intellectual life of today, and a section composed of "voices and testimonies" that convey the diversity of his contemporaries' reactions from Freud to Steiner, Hesse, and more than forty others.

The Wisdom of the Dream: The World of C. G. Jung, by Stephen Segaller and Merrill Berger. Boston: Shambhala Publications, 1989*, 1990p* (A C. G. Jung Foundation Book) (211 + x, incl. 5-p. index, 5-p. bibl., 32 illus.).

As an accompaniment to a British television series, Segaller and Berger present this book about the supposedly difficult subject of psychology (science of the human mind), documenting their encounter with Jung through a journey in Jung's footsteps and interviews with Jung's students, followers, and family. They explain Jung's genius as belonging to a man who is "not an abstract theorist, but a doctor who liked to discover what was good for his patients," someone who dreamed and investigated dreams all his life in order to understand the wisdom of the unconscious. Following a brief introductory chapter on the life and influence of Jung, the authors discuss the reality of the psyche (Jung's research and methods, including a copy of his famed word-association test); the wisdom of the dream (reflections by Aniela Jaffé, James Hillman, Joseph Wheelwright, Mary Briner, Robert Johnson, Marie-Louise von Franz, Gerhard Adler, and Harry Wilmer); a creative life (reflections by Jung's grandson, analyst Dieter Baumann, Adolf Guggenbühl-Craig, and Dora Kalff); remembrances of encounters with Jung, the secret life of relationship (inner, outer, and collective), travels in time and space (through books and through visits to USA and Africa), concluding with a discussion of "the inner world of the outer world" and Jung's search for a meaningful life.

2. Collections of Jung's Writings

Among the thirty titles listed here is the set of volumes comprising Jung's *Collected Works*. Volume 18 *(The Symbolic Life)* and supplemental volume A *(The Zofingia Lectures)*, each of which consists of miscellaneous topics and writings, are annotated in this chapter. The other volumes of the set, in consideration of their contents, are annotated in the appropriate subject categories.

Listed here, but annotated under the appropriate subject, are eleven paperbacks consisting of Jung's writings excerpted from the *Collected Works* on such subjects as religion, dreams, archetypes, and psychoanalysis.

Collections of Jung's writings have been edited and published since 1916—first by Long, then by Jacobi, de Laszlo, Campbell, McGuire and Hull, and Storr, along with collections of Jung's letters edited by Adler and Jaffé.

A volume of abstracts of the *Collected Works* was published in 1978.

The general index of the *Collected Works* (volume 20) is annotated in this chapter. The general bibliography of Jung's writings (volume 19) is annotated in chapter 3, "Jung's Psychology."

Jung: *Collected Works* [p. 20]
_____: *Aspects of the Feminine* (See chapter 8, "Feminine and Masculine Psychology") [p. 160]
_____: *Aspects of the Masculine* (See chapter 8, "Feminine and Masculine Psychology") [p. 160]
_____: *Contributions to Analytical Psychology* [p. 21]
_____: *Critique of Psychoanalysis* (See chapter 11, "Jungian Analysis") [p. 206]
_____: *Dreams* (See chapter 7, "Symbolic Life and Dreams") [p. 132]

19

The Collected Works of C. G. Jung, edited by Herbert Reed, Michael Fordham, and Gerhard Adler; William McGuire, executive editor (from 1967). London: Routledge & Kegan Paul, 1953 +; New York: Pantheon Books, Bollingen, 1953–60; New York: Bollingen Foundation, 1961–67; Princeton, N.J.: Princeton U. Press, 1967 + (Bollingen Series XX) (more than 10,500 pages, incl. more than 600 illus.).

See Part Two, "Works Arranged by Author," for individual volumes.

General Index to the Collected Works *of C. G. Jung,* compiled by Barbara
Forrayan and Janet M. Glover. *(CW* 20) London: Routledge & Kegan Paul,
1979; Princeton, N.J.: Princeton U. Press/Bollingen, 1979 (735 + vi, incl. 9-
p. list of the *Collected Works).*

The general index to the *Collected Works* is exceptionally comprehensive
and detailed, following the principles laid down for the original volumes. It
employs paragraph numbers rather than page numbers to identify the location of an item, because subsequent editions often result in changed pagina-
tions, whereas paragraph numbers remain the same.
(Bk.revs.: Choice '79/16:648; AmNotes&Q N'80/19:57; AmRefBksAn '80/11:667–8;
JAnPsy '80/25:107)

Collected Papers on Analytical Psychology, edited by Constance E. Long. New
York: Moffat, Yard, 1916; ed.2 1917; London: Balliere, Tindall & Cox,
1916; ed.2 1917; reissue 1920 (492 + xxviii, incl. 18-p. index, 16 illus.).

This early collection of Jung's writings, which includes fifteen essays
originally published in German, English, or French, contains Jung's doctoral
dissertation presented to Zurich University in 1902 (psychology and pathology of so-called occult phenomena) and research articles on the association
method, as well as lectures and articles originally published in professional
journals on the topics of the significance of the father in the destiny of the
individual; the psychology of rumor; the significance of number dreams;
criticism of Bleuler's theory of schizophrenic negativism; psychoanalysis; the
importance of the unconscious in psychopathology; the study of psychological types; the psychology of dreams; the content of the psychoses; the
psychology of the unconscious processes; and the conception of the unconscious—all published between ages twenty-seven and forty.
(Bk.revs.: JMentSci '16/62:776–7; TimesLitSup '16:209; Bkman '17/53:132; Dial '17/
62:395–8; JMentSci '18/64:219–20; Nation '18/106:239–40; PsyanR '19/6:115)

Contributions to Analytical Psychology, by C. G. Jung. London: Kegan Paul,
Trench, Trubner, 1928; New York: Harcourt, Brace, 1928 (410 + xi, incl.
8-p. index) (International Library of Psychology, Philosophy, and Scientific
Method).

This selection is comprised of fourteen essays, including lectures in
German or English and articles published between 1919 and 1928, on the
subjects of instinct and the unconscious; the therapeutic value of "abreaction"; the relation of analytical psychology to poetic art; psychological
foundations of belief in spirits; analytical psychology and education; psychological types; significance of the unconscious in individual education; mar-

riage as a psychological relationship; spirit and life; and psychical energy. Also included are translations of German manuscripts on the topics of mind and earth; on the love problem of the student; and on analytical psychology and philosophy of life.

(Bk.revs.: Spec '28/141:999; BkRDig '29:495–6; Bklist '29/25:267; JPhilosStud '29/4:281–2; Mind '29/ns38:371–6; Nature '29/123:792; NewRep '29/57:329; NYTimes BkR 12My'29:23; PsyanR '29/16:352–4; TimesLitSup 31Ja'29:79; YaleR '29/ns19:211; Criterion '30/8:732–5; JNervMent '30/71:351–2)

Modern Man in Search of a Soul, by C. G. Jung. London: Kegan Paul, Trench, Trubner, 1933; Toronto: McLeod, 1933; New York: Harcourt, Brace, 1933: New York: Harvest Books/Harcourt Brace Jovanovich, 1955p*; London: Routledge & Kegan Paul, 1970p; London: Ark Publications, 1984p* (244 + x).

Most of these eleven papers were originally given as lectures or published in journals, six having been included in a 1931 German-language collection on "soul-problems of the present time" (the spiritual problem of modern man; a psychological theory of types; aims of psychotherapy; Freud and Jung contrasts; stages of life; and archaic man). Other topics are the problems of psychotherapy; psychology and literature; basic postulates of analytical psychology; dream analysis in its practical application; and psychotherapists or the clergy.

(Bk.revs.: AmR '33/1:623–9; BkRDig '33:498; Bks 12N'33:30; ChrCen '33/50:1377; Nature '33/132:767; NewRep 6D'33/77:108–9; NewStates '33/6:390; NYTimesBkR 26N'33:4+; SatR '33/10:105; Spec '33/151:530 AmJPsy '34/46:536; BrJMedPsy '34/14:89–90; Chman 15Ja'34/48:17; IntJPsy-An '34/15:349–50; JEdPsy '34/25:72–3; JMentSci '34/80:718–20; JRel '34/14:372–4; Nature 3Ja'34/138:27; Pax '34/23:270; Scrut '34/3:109–10; TimesLitSup 17My'34:354; BrJPsy '35/25:116; IntJEth '35/45:370–1; JNervMent '35/71:715–16; Mind '35/ns44:84–92; PsyanR '35/22:117–18; WorldAff '36/7:103; Philos '39/14:241; PsyMed '85/15:443)

Psychological Reflections: An Anthology of the Writings of C. G. Jung, selected and edited by Jolande Jacobi. (Ger.: *Psychologische Betrachtungen: Eine Auslese aus den Schriften von C. G. Jung*. Zurich: Rascher Verlag, 1945.) London: Routledge & Kegan Paul, 1953; New York: Pantheon Books, Bollingen, 1953; New York: Torchbooks/Harper & Row, 1961p (342 + xxvii).

The general purpose of this book is to provide an understanding of the inner forces by which people are changed—one of the most important aspects of ordinary human existence in the light of psychology. The 1945 edition, published in German, is associated with Jung's seventieth birthday. Analyst Jacobi presents a collection of short passages from a wide range of writings arranged in sixteen sections. She does not set out to assess Jung in any comprehensive way but limits selections to particularly characteristic, self-contained statements of a general nature in order to do justice to Jung's psychological outlook. (See 1970 edition.)

(Bk.revs.: BrJPsy '54/45:230–1; BulMennClin '54/18:268; JRelThought '54/11:178–9; TimesLitSup '54:489; IntJPsy-An '55/36:362; JAmPsyan '55/3:548; PsysomMed '55/17:83; PsychiQ '56/30:337; JPastorCare '57/11:174–5)

Psyche and Symbol: A Selection from the Writings of C. G. Jung, edited by Violet S. de Laszlo. Garden City, N.Y.: Anchor Books/Doubleday, 1958p*; Princeton, 1990p (363, incl. 12-p. bibl., 7-p. preface by Jung).

De Laszlo's selection from Jung's writings (published originally between 1929 and 1951) is presented to illustrate "in convincing fashion the objects of his symbol research and the manner of his approach." Jung in his preface characterizes these as some of his most difficult essays. Included are five chapters from *Aion* (on ego, shadow, syzygy, self, and Christ as a symbol of the self), along with the subjects of phenomenology of the spirit in fairytales; psychology of the child archetype; transformation symbolism in the Mass; foreword to the *I Ching* or *Book of Changes;* two chapters on synchronicity from *The Interpretation of Nature and the Psyche,* psychological commentary on *The Tibetan Book of the Dead,* and commentary on *The Secret of the Golden Flower.*

(Bk.revs.: SatNight 24My'58/73:26–7; InwLight Christmas'59/n58:41)

The Basic Writings of C. G. Jung, edited by Violet Staub de Laszlo. New York: Modern Library/Random House, 1959*; Princeton, 1990p (552 + xxiii, incl. 6-p. index, 2-p. bibl., 17-p. editor's introduction).

Intending this as a representative collection of Jung's creative writings, editor de Laszlo devotes two-thirds of the book to the nature and functioning of the psyche, taking excerpts from *Symbols of Transformation (CW 5), The Structure and Dynamics of the Psyche (CW 8,* "On the Nature of the Psyche"), *Two Essays on Analytical Psychology (CW 7,* "Relations Between the Ego and the Unconscious"), *Archetypes of the Collective Unconscious (CW 9,* pt. 1), and *Psychological Types.* The remainder deal with pathology and therapy (the nature of dreams; psychogenesis of schizophrenia; the psychology of the transference), the religious function (religious and psychological problems of alchemy; psychology and religion), and human development (marriage as a psychological relationship).

(Bk.revs.: InwLight Fall'60/n60:39–40; Spring '60:150)

C. G. Jung: Psychological Reflections, A New Anthology of His Writings 1905–1961, selected and edited by Jolande Jacobi in collaboration with R. F. C.

Hull. Princeton, N.J.: Princeton U. Press, new edn. 1970*; 1973p*; London: Routledge & Kegan Paul, new edn. 1971 +p; London: Ark Publications, 1986p* (391 + xvi, incl. 11-p. list of sources, 11-p. list of the *Collected Works*).

In this new anthology, appearing a quarter of a century after the original one (see above) and containing nearly thirteen hundred quotations from more than one hundred of Jung's writings, Jacobi expands the selection to provide a comprehensive view of Jung's non-technical work with an emphasis on religious and social problems. Among the topics are consciousness and the unconscious; archetypes; dreams; doctor and patient; man and woman; youth and age; the individual and community; awareness and creative living; problems of self-realization; between good and evil; life of the spirit; Western and Eastern points of view; development of the personality; fate, death, and renewal; and the way to God.

(Bk.revs.: JAnPsy '71/16:213; LibJ '71/96:947; LibJBkR '71:725; VaQR Aut'71/47:clxxxvii; BrJPsychi '72/120:462; Teilhard '72/7:28; BrJMedPsy '73/46:220)

The Portable Jung, edited with an introduction by Joseph Campbell. New York: Viking Press, 1971 +p; Toronto: Macmillan of Canada, 1971 +p; New York: Penguin, 1976p*; Harmondsworth: Penguin, 1985p* (659 + xlii, incl. 9-p. bibl. of Jung's works, 10-p. chron. of Jung's life).

Aiming first to acquaint readers with the elementary terms and themes of Jung's psychology and then to guide them through the treasury of the *Collected Works,* Campbell selects excerpts from ten volumes. Most of the selections range in length from eleven to twenty-eight pages. Longer ones deal with individual dream symbolism in relation to alchemy (113 pp.), *Answer to Job* (132-p. complete text), general description of psychological types (92 pp.), and relations between the ego and the unconscious (69 pp.). Other themes are stages of life; structure of the psyche; instinct and the unconscious; the collective unconscious; the ego; the shadow; anima/animus; marriage as a psychological relationship; transcendent function; relation of analytical psychology to poetry; spiritual problem of modern man; difference between Eastern and Western thinking; and synchronicity.

(Bk.revs.: BkWorld 21N'71/5:8; Life 31D'71:25; LibJ '72/97:507–8; LibJBkR '72:438; JPastorCare '74/28:312)

C. G. Jung: Letters, selected and edited by Gerhard Adler with Aniela Jaffé. (Ger.: *C. G. Jung: Briefe.* Olten, Switzerland: Walter Verlag, 1972–73 in 3 vols.) London: Routledge & Kegan Paul, 1973*, 1976*; Princeton, N.J.: Princeton U. Press, 1973, 1976 (2 vols.) (Bollingen Series XCV:A) (v.1: 596 + xxv; v.2: 716 + xlvii, each containing 11-p. intro. and 5-p. chron. of Jung's life; 76-p. index in v.2; 52 illus. in total).

From approximately 1,600 letters collected, the editors selected 522 for volume 1 (1906–50) and 463 for volume 2 (1951–61). They include Jung's correspondence with friends and colleagues, answers to those who wrote to him with problems or concerns, and attempts to correct misinterpretations of his ideas.

(Bk.revs.: KirkR '72/40:1298; BkRDig '73:669–70; BkWorld lAp'73/7:1–2; Choice '73/ 10:1284; Econ 19My'73/247:131–2; LibJ '73/98:1912; LibJBkR '73:110; Nation '73/ 216:822–3; NYTimesBkR 25F'73:31; PsyToday S'73/7:100; SatR 28Ap'73:62–3; Spec '73/230:817; TimesLitSup '73:1271; VaQR Aut'73/49:clxiv; ContemPsy '74/19:207–8; Harvest '74/20:26–7; JAnPsy '74/19:110–11; JRel '74/54:95–6; BrJMedPsy '75/48:87–8; JHistBehSci '75/11:96–7; KirkR '75/43:771; PsyToday D'75/9:114; AmJArtTh '76/15:90; AmJPsychi '76/133:1476; AnnSci '76/33:614–15; BkRDig '76:620–1; Bklist '76/72:1304– 5; BksBkmen Ag'76/21:30–1; ChrCen '76/93:841–2; Econ 22My'76/259:128–9; Harvest '76/22:144–5; KirkR '76/44:313; NewRep 15My'76/174:28–30; NewStates '76/92:248; NYRevBks 15Ap'76/23:26–30; Observ 20Jn'76:27; Spec 22My'76/236:25; ContemPsy '77/22:48–9; JAnPsy '77/22:195–7; VaQR Spr'77/53:52; AmJArtTh '78/17:118; JHist-BehSci '78/14:90–1)

The Freud/Jung Letters: The Correspondence between Sigmund Freud and C. G. Jung, edited by William McGuire. London: Hogarth Press with Routledge & Kegan Paul, 1974; Princeton, N.J.: Princeton U. Press (Bollingen Series XCIV), 1974*; 1975p; 3rd printing with corrections and additional notes, 1979p; London: Picador Books/Pan Books, abridged edn. 1979p; Cambridge, Mass.: Harvard U. Press, 1988p* (650 + xlii, incl. 58-p. index, chron. table of letters, 21 illus., 25-p. editor's intro.).

These 366 letters (163 written by Freud, 196 by Jung, and 7 by Emma Jung) record chronologically a very productive interchange of ideas from 1906, when Freud was fifty years of age and Jung was thirty-one, until the unhappy breakup of their friendship in 1914 with its attendant conflict. In spite of dissension and the inevitable break, each derived creative value from the encounter. This entire extant correspondence between the founder of psychoanalysis and his apparent heir (but founder of analytical psychology) contains references to more than 400 persons and 500 publications in the detailed index. McGuire's introduction contains valuable background information and comments.

(Bk.revs.: LibJ '73/98:3628; LibJBkR '73:436; BkRDig '74:397–8; BkWorld 7Ap'74:3; Bklist '74/70:1119; BksBkmen My'74/19:29–36; BrJCrim '74/14:414–15; Choice '74/ 11:1218; ChrSciMon 8My'74/66:F5; Commonw '74/101:41–3; Econ 20Ap'74/251:125– 6; Encoun(L) Jn'74/42:39–41; Esq Jy'74/82:53,55; GuardW 27Ap'74/100:20; Harper-Ag'74/249:88–91; JAmAcPsyan '74/2:393–4; JIndivPsy '74/30:114–17; JOttoRank W'74/ 9:67–70; KirkR'74/42:42; Listen '74/91:532–3; Nation '74/219:24–6; NewSoc '74/ 28:145–6; NewStates '74/87:516–17; NYRevBks 18Ap'74/21:6 +; NYTimesBkR 21Ap '74:1 + 32–5; NYorker 15Ap'74/50:151–2; Newswk 29Ap'74/83:95–6; Observ 14Ap'74:31; PsychiQ '74/48:298–9; PsyPersp '74/5:171–6; PubW 28Ja'74/205:292; Spec '74/233:515–16; TimesLitSup '74:489–92; VillVoice 15Ag'74/19:25; CanForum S'75/

55:66–7; Critic '75/33n2:56–8; HumContext '75/7:164–7; InwLight '75–76/n86–87:68–71; JAnPsy '75/20:79–80; JModHist '75/47:360–3; Manus '75/19:124–5; SnR '75/ ns11:926–32; Worldview '75/18:64; ContemPsy '76/21:336–7; EurStudR '76/6:160–3; JAmPsyan '76/24:669–83; ModStud '77/2:45–9; PsyanQ '77/46:514–27; RelStudR '79/ 5:309; ClinSocWkJ '85/13:91; NewIdeas '87/5:287; AmJPsychi '89/146:541–2; SciBks Film '89/24:131–2)

The Symbolic Life: Miscellaneous Writings, by C. G. Jung. Princeton, N.J.: Princeton U. Press/Bollingen Foundation, 1976; corrected 1980*; London: Routledge & Kegan Paul, 1977* (CW 18) (904 + xix, incl. 50-p. index, 20-p. bibl.).

Miscellaneous writings form the largest volume of the *Collected Works,* containing 135 items that deal with virtually every aspect of Jung's intellectual interests. Most numerous are forewords written for books by former pupils and colleagues, along with several reviews of books. Answers to journalistic questions are quite numerous, along with several letters in reply to questions. Lectures and addresses, many of which were published in journals, are also numerous. Longest is the series of five Tavistock Lectures (178 pp.), given in London in 1935 as the seminar "On the Theory and Practice of Analytical Psychology." The title of volume 18, *The Symbolic Life,* is taken from a talk given in 1939 to the Guild of Pastoral Psychology in London.

(Bk.revs.: NYTimesBkR 27Jn'76:28; AmJPsychi '77/134:1456–7; AnnSci '77/34:635–6; BksBkmen Ag'77/22:49–51; Choice '77/14:448; ChrCen '77/94:309; NewSoc '77/40:130; AmJArtTh '78/17:118; ChrScholR '78/81:190–1; ContemPsy '78/23:421–2; JAnPsy '78/ 23:196–8; PsyMed '78/8:175; PsyPersp '78/9:90–1)

C. G. Jung Speaking: Interviews and Ecounters, edited by William McGuire and R. F. C. Hull. Princeton, N.J.: Princeton U. Press (Bollingen Series XCVII:1), 1977; 1986p*; London: Thames & Hudson, shortened edn. 1978; London: Picador/Pan Books, 1980p (489 + xxii, incl. 19-p. index, 8-p. editors' preface).

This volume, outside the *Collected Works,* is a collection of fifty-five interviews and encounters selected from a large number of documents—some originally in dialogue style, some recast in dialogue style where appropriate. The earliest interview was published in 1912 in the *New York Times* when Jung lectured at Fordham University. The longest are transcripts of electronically-recorded interviews (the 1957 "Houston University Films" with Richard Evans and the 1959 BBC "Face to Face" television program with John Freeman) and of a 1958 tape recording of a meeting at the Basel Psychology Club. Also included are reminiscences by notable personalities of talks with Jung.

(Bk.revs.: LibJ '77/102:2437–8; PubW '77/212:64; BkRDig '78:189; Bklist '78/74:1462; CanForum Jn'78/58:24–5; Choice '78/15:297; ContemPsy '78/23:421–2; EdStud '78/

9:236; JAnPsy '78/23:368–9; ModAge '78/22:437–40; NewSoc '78/44:442–3; Harvest '79/25:88–90; SciBksFilm '79/14:205; RelStudR '80/6:127–8)

Abstracts of the Collected Works *of C. G. Jung,* edited by Carrie Lee Rothgeb. Rockville, Md.: National Institute of Mental Health, 1978p (136 + vii, plus 101-p. subj. index).

These abstracts, which cover volumes one through eighteen of the *Collected Works,* were prepared by the National Institute of Mental Health (DHEW Bull. No. CADM 78–743) as a sequel to the 1971 *Abstracts of the Standard Edition of Freud* in order to encourage wider scientific research and to be helpful to all who work in the behavioral sciences by broadening their knowledge of analytical psychology through the comprehensive scope and potential of Jung's theories.

(Bk.revs.: PsyPersp '77/8:227–30; ContemPsy '78/23:421–2; PsyMed '78/8:175; AmRefBksAn '79/10:710; JTranspPsy '84/16:244)

The Essential Jung, selected and introduced by Anthony Storr. (U.K.: *Jung: Selected Writings.* London: Fontana Pocket Readers/Collins, 1983; 1986p*.) Princeton, N.J.: Princeton U. Press, 1983 +p* (447, incl. 11-p. index, 10-p. bibl., 14-p. gloss. of Jungian terms, 7-p. chron. of Jung's life and work, 15-p. editor's intro.).

Storr presents the essential features of Jung's psychology by arranging extracts from Jung's own writings in the general chronological order in which they were developed. He prefaces each extract with explanatory remarks and furnishes an introduction for readers unfamiliar with Jung's way of thinking. The fifty-three excerpts are taken from the *Collected Works, The Freud/Jung Letters, C. G. Jung: Letters, C. G. Jung: Word and Image,* and Jung's *Memories, Dreams, Reflections.* Most range from one to five pages each, the longest being "On the Psychology of the Unconscious" (21 pp.), "The Practical Use of Dream-Analysis" (22 pp.), "Introduction to the Religious and Psychological Problems of Alchemy" (34 pp.), and the complete text of *The Undiscovered Self* (55 pp.).

(Bk.revs.: BrJMedPsy '83/56:397; Choice '83/21:194; Econ 12Mr'83/286:99; LibJ '83/108:1710; BkRDig '84:814–15; Quad '84/17n1:69; VaQR '84/60:160–8)

The Zofingia Lectures, by C. G. Jung. Princeton, N.J.: Princeton U. Press/Bollingen, 1983*; London: Routledge & Kegan Paul, 1984* (*CW:* Supplemental vol. A) (129 + xxv, incl. 9-p. index, 5 illus., 13-p. intro. by Marie-Louise von Franz).

These lectures were given during 1896–1899, when Jung was between twenty-one and twenty-four years of age, to his fellow student-members of the Zofingia Club at Basel University. They reveal his early passion for truth, communicated in a humorous-serious vein, and they represent the suppositions of his scientific thought and the bases of his religious views. His talks deal with the border zones of exact science, some thoughts on psychology, thoughts on the nature and value of speculative inquiry, and thoughts on the interpretation of Christianity with reference to the theory of Albrecht Ritschl, along with his inaugural address upon assuming the chairmanship of the club in 1897. The introductory comments by Marie-Louise von Franz provide valuable insights.

(Bk.revs.: BkRDig '84:815; Harvest '84/30:136–7; JAnPsy '84/29:383–4; LibJ '84/109:379; NewStates 20Ap'84/107:29; Quad '84/17n2:75–6; TimesLitSup 10My'84:803)

Selected Letters of C. G. Jung, 1901–1961, selected and edited by Gerhard Adler. Princeton, N.J.: Princeton U. Press (Bollingen Series XCV:A), 1984 +p* (218 + xix, incl. 5-p chron. of Jung's life, 2-p. index of correspondents, 2-p. biographical notes of correspondents, 5-p. editor's preface).

As an abridgement of the two-volume *C. G. Jung: Letters* (1973, 1976), Adler's selection contains 140 letters to 88 persons and is an attempt to demonstrate Jung's personality as manifested in his correspondence. Adler's intention is to give an impression of "the richness of Jung's mind and the scope of his immense knowledge, of his profound sense of responsibility and commitment, and of his deep compassion and reverent humanity."

3 Jung's Psychology

The psychology developed by Jung represents, like modern physics, a revolutionary advance in our understanding of the human and physical world. It is an approach to depth psychology which he termed analytical psychology rather than psychoanalysis; at one time he called it "complex psychology" in contrast to such psychological systems as the psychology of consciousness or Freud's psychoanalysis, which relates everything to instinctual factors. Jung acknowledged his debt to Freud as a pioneer, but he was not an uncritical follower, which cost him Freud's friendship.

Jung's psychology is not a kind of psychopathology; rather, it is a general psychology that recognizes the empirical material of pathology. It is a new scientific psychology based upon his own contacts with normal as well as neurotic and psychotic individuals. His own experiences, which included a turning point in his midlife period, resulted in a major contribution to psychology in the field of adult development, whereby his stressing of the spiritual aspects of human nature contrasted with and complemented Freud's emphasis on the physical. Jung insisted that people need to search for meaning in life and that the subjective experience of the individual is a vital counterbalance in a world dominated by objective, experimental approaches.

Instead of seeking to construct a complete, well-rounded system or dogma, Jung concentrated on his pioneering work, and his decision to do so left the way open for continually new developments. He viewed the psyche as dynamic and at the same time self-regulating, the inner or psychic process having equal value with the outer or environmental one. The psyche does not operate along the lines of accustomed rationality, since consciousness with its ego center grows out of the older, unconscious matrix, in which are found new potentialities of life. Jung's view of the unconscious is more positive than that of theorists who see it as merely the repository of all that is unacceptable to the ego. He distin-

29

guishes between a personal unconscious (stored experiences that fail to gain acceptance by the ego) and the collective unconscious (a deeper layer with a primordial reservoir of latent images).

Jung produced such terms as *extraversion, introversion, complex, archetype, individuation,* and *collective unconscious.* He drew attention to the possibilities of cooperation between consciousness and the unconscious.

This chapter includes primers and other introductions to Jung's psychology as well as surveys of basic postulates of "Jungian" psychology, along with some books that characterize Jung in relationship to the ideas of Freud and others. Of the nearly twenty "textbooks" on the psychology of Jung in this section, the most comprehensive are those written by Whitmont (1969) and Mattoon (1981).

The books are arranged chronologically within the twofold framework of books written by Jung followed by those written by others, in order to provide a perspective on the historical development of the writings.

Jung: *Analytical Psychology: Its Theory and Practice* [p. 33]

⎯⎯⎯: *Analytical Psychology: Notes of the Seminar Given in 1925* [p. 32]

⎯⎯⎯: *Collected Papers on Analytical Psychology* (See chapter 2, "Collections of Jung's Writings") [p. 21]

⎯⎯⎯: *Contributions to Analytical Psychology* (See chapter 2, "Collections of Jung's Writings") [p. 21]

⎯⎯⎯: *General Bibliography of C. G. Jung's Writings* [p. 33]

⎯⎯⎯: *Two Essays on Analytical Psychology* [p. 32]

Adler: *Studies in Analytical Psychology* [p. 35]

Adler (ed.): *Current Trends in Analytical Psychology* [p. 39]

Analytical Psychology Club of New York: *Catalog of the Kristine Mann Library* [p. 45]

Arraj & Arraj: *A Jungian Psychology Resource Guide* [p. 52]

Baynes: *Analytical Psychology and the English Mind* [p. 36]

Bennet: *What Jung Really Said* [p. 41]

Clark: *Six Talks on Jung's Psychology* [p. 37]

Cohen: *C. G. Jung and the Scientific Attitude* [p. 44]

Corrie: *A B C of Jung's Psychology* [p. 34]

Cox: *How the Mind Works: An Introduction to the Psychology of C. G. Jung* [p. 40]

Donn: *Freud and Jung* [p. 52]

Dry: *The Psychology of Jung* [p. 40]

Ellenberger: *The Discovery of the Unconscious* [p. 42]

Evans: *Jung on Elementary Psychology* [p. 40]
Fordham, F.: *An Introduction to Jung's Psychology* [p. 36]
Fordham, M.: *New Developments in Analytical Psychology* [p. 38]
Fordham, M., et al. (eds.): *Analytical Psychology: A Modern Science* [p. 43]
Gay: *Reading Jung* [p. 50]
Glover: *Freud or Jung?* [p. 35]
Goldbrunner: *Individuation* [p. 37]
Hall & Lindzey: *Theories of Personality* [p. 39]
Hall & Nordby: *A Primer of Jungian Psychology* [p. 43]
Heyer: *The Organism of the Mind* (See chapter 11, "Jungian Analysis") [p. 297]
Hillman: *Re-Visioning Psychology* [p. 44]
Hogenson: *Jung's Struggle with Freud* [p. 49]
Homans: *Jung in Context* [p. 46]
Hopcke: *A Guided Tour of the* Collected Works *of C. G. Jung* [p. 52]
Humbert: *C. G. Jung: Fundamentals of Theory and Practice* [p. 48]
Jacobi: *The Psychology of C. G. Jung* [p. 34]
Jaffé: *From the Life and Work of C. G. Jung* [p. 41]
Kaufmann: *Discovering the Mind: Freud versus Adler and Jung* [p. 46]
Kranefeldt: *Secret Ways of the Mind* [p. 34]
Laughlin: *Jungian Theory and Therapy* [p. 48]
Leichtman: *Jung and Freud Return* [p. 46]
Martin: *Experiment in Depth* [p. 37]
Mattoon: *Jungian Psychology in Perspective* [p. 47]
Meier: *Soul and Body: Essays on the Theories of Jung* [p. 51]
Mudd (ed.): *International Abstracts in Analytical Psychology* [p. 51]
O'Connor: *Understanding Jung, Understanding Yourself* [p. 51]
Olney: *The Rhizome and the Flower* [p. 47]
Oppenheim: *The Psychology of Jung* [p. 34]
Papadopoulos & Saayman (eds.): *Jung in Modern Perspective* [p. 49]
Progoff: *The Death and Rebirth of Psychology* [p. 38]
Samuels: *Jung and the Post-Jungians* [p. 50]
Schultz: *Intimate Friends, Dangerous Rivals* [p. 53]
Steele: *Freud and Jung: Conflicts of Interpretation* [p. 48]
Stevens: *On Jung* [p. 53]
Storr: *Jung* (See Chapter 1, "The Life of C. G. Jung") [p. 11]
Szemborski: *The Wisdom of Jung* [p. 45]
Tuby (ed.): *In the Wake of Jung* [p. 49]
Vincie & Rathbauer-Vincie: *C. G. Jung and Analytical Psychology: A Comprehensive Bibliography* [p. 45]
Whitmont: *The Symbolic Quest* [p. 42]
Winski: *Understanding Jung* [p. 43]

Analytical Psychology: Notes of the Seminar Given in 1925 by C. G. Jung, edited by William McGuire. Princeton, N.J.: Princeton U. Press (Bollingen Series XCIX), 1989* (179 + xx, incl. 5-p. general index, 4-p. indexes, 11 illus., 10-p. editor's intro.).

Containing sixteen untitled lectures given weekly during 1925 as the first of Jung's formal seminars in English and consisting of considerable interaction with the group, this book begins with Jung's personal account of the progression of his ideas from 1896 to his break with Freud. He then discusses the basic ideas of analytical psychology, including the collective unconscious, archetypes, typology, and the anima/animus theory, which are illustrated by diagrams and dreams. Appended are seminar discussions on psychological aspects of the novels *She* (Rider Haggard), *Evil Vineyard* (Marie Hay), and *L'Atlantide* (René Benoît).

Two Essays on Analytical Psychology, by C. G. Jung. (Ger.: *Der Unbewusste im normalen und kranken Seelenleben.* Zurich: Rascher Verlag, 1926; *Die Beziehungen zwischen dem Ich und dem Unbewussten.* Darmstadt: Reichl Verlag, 1928.) London: Balliere, Tindall & Cox, 1928; New York: Dodd, Mead, 1928; London: Routledge & Kegan Paul, 1953*; Toronto: Mc-Clelland & Stewart, 1953; New York: Pantheon Books, Bollingen Foundation, 1953; New York: Meridian/New American Library, 1956p; Princeton, N.J.: Princeton U. Press/Bollingen, ed.2 1966*; 1972p* (*CW* 7) (349 + xi: 35-p. index, 6-p. bibl.).

Brought together in 1928 as the foundation upon which much of Jung's later work was built, these two essays state the fundamentals of Jung's psychological system. He himself described it as being no easy task to try to popularize highly complicated material still in the process of scientific development. The first, "On the Psychology of the Unconscious," is devoted to the history of Freudian and Adlerian theories, the problem of the fundamental attitude-types of extraversion and introversion, the personal as well as the collective (or transpersonal) unconscious, the archetypes of the collective unconscious, and the therapeutic approach to the unconscious. The second, "The Relation between the Ego and the Unconscious," is concerned with the effects of the unconscious upon consciousness and the role of the persona, and with the way of individuation, the anima and animus, and the technique of differentiation between the ego and figures of the unconscious.

(Bk.revs.: Nation '28/127:664; Spec '28/141:999; BkRDig '29:496; IntJPsy-An '29/10:468–70; NewAge '29/57:329; NYTimes BkR 6Ja'29:16; TimesLitSup '29:79; Criterion '30/8:732–5; JMentSci '30/76:141–2; JNervMent '38/87:126–7; AmMerc S'53/77:139–40; CathWorker Oc'53/20:5; PsychiQ '53/27:712; Blackf '54/35:125; HudsonR '54/6:611–19; JRelThought '54/11:175; Listen '54/51:353+; QueensQ '54/61:132; Times LitSup '54:808; JPastorCare '55/9:121; PrincSemBul Ja'55/48:175; RMeta '55/9:71–89;

AmJPsyth '56/10:382–3; Person '56/37:182–3; PastorPsy Oc'57/8:57–8; IntJGroup '58/8:88)

Analytical Psychology: Its Theory and Practice, by C. G. Jung. London: Routledge & Kegan Paul, 1968; 1976p*; New York: Pantheon Books/Random House, 1968; New York: Vintage Books/Random House, 1970p*; New York: J. Aronson, repr. 1974; London: Ark Publications, 1986p* (The Tavistock Lectures) (225 + xvi, incl. 10-p. index, 3-p. bibl., 15 illus., 4-p. foreword by Bennet).

Five untitled lectures (under the general theme of analytical psychology) with ensuing discussions were given by Jung for the Institute of Medical Psychology at Tavistock Clinic in London in 1935 to approximately 200 doctors. He presents his own researches on the structure and content of the mind and on methods used in its investigation, as well as relationships between unconscious mental activity and the word-association test, dream analysis and active imagination, and a short survey of the transference phenomenon. Jung's personality is evident in the informal yet systematic talks.

(Bk.revs.: BkWorld 29D'68:5; NewStates '68/76:550; TimesLitSup '68:1151; BkRDig '69:680; Bklist '69/65:1030; BrJPsychi '69/115:246; Choice '69/6:144–5; KenyonR '69/31:285–8; LibJ '69/94:204; LibJBkR '69:518; NYRevBks 16Ja'69/12:4; Quad '69/n3:7–8; Spring '69:141; Tabl '69/223:59–60; JAnPsy '70/15:186–9; PubW 31Ag'70/198:282; BrJMedPsy '71/44:193; PsyMed '77/7:549–50; JPsysomRes '78/22:65; BrJPsychi '87/151:138)

General Bibliography of C. G. Jung's Writings, compiled by Lisa Ress et al. Princeton, N.J.: Princeton U. Press/Bollingen, 1979*; London: Routledge & Kegan Paul, 1979* (CW 19) (263 + x, incl. 23-p. title index, 7-p. personal name index, 4-p. index of congresses, etc., 6-p. index of periodicals, 9-p. list of the *Collected Works*).

This bibliography consists of a record (through 1975) of each original work written by Jung, as well as each translated and/or subsequently revised edition. It includes all books and articles written by Jung (including collaborations with others), forewords written for other authors' books, newspaper articles, book reviews, and published texts of lectures. Works written in German, English, and French, and those translated into English, French, Danish, Dutch, Finnish, Greek, Hebrew, Hungarian, Italian, Japanese, Norwegian, Portuguese, Russian, Serbo-Croatian, Slovenian, Spanish, Swedish, and Turkish are listed.

(Bk.revs.: Choice '79/16:648; AmNotes&Q N'80/19:57; AmRefBks '80/11:663-4; JAnPsy '80/25:107)

* * * * *

The Psychology of Jung, by James Oppenheim. Girard, Kans.: Haldeman-Julius Publ., 1925p (Little Blue Book, no. 978) (64, incl. 3-p. advertising of Little Blue Book Series).

Claiming Jung's psychology as "the psychology of the future," Oppenheim first presents in this pocket book a summary of the work of Freud and Adler. Then he describes Jung's theories, which "go beyond both." Writing soon after the publication of Jung's *Psychological Types,* Oppenheim describes the classification of types and the significance of the terms *introvert* and *extravert.*

A B C of Jung's Psychology, by Joan Corrie. London: Kegan Paul, Trench, Trubner, 1927; New York: Frank-Maurice, 1927 p (85 pp.).

Having been a pupil of Jung's for some years and distressed by the misunderstanding and ignorance of his work, Corrie offers a short and simple outline of Jung's principal theories. She discusses the mind and its structure, functions, and disturbances, and the significance of dreams.
(Bk.revs.: BrJPsy '27/18:235; Criterion '27/6:471; TimesLitSup '27:579; IntJPsy-An '28/ 9:127)

Secret Ways of the Mind: A Survey of the Psychological Principles of Freud, Adler, and Jung, by Wolfgang Müller Kranefeldt. (Ger.: *Die Psychoanalyse, Psychoanalytische Psychologie.* Berlin: Gruyter, 1930.) New York: Henry Holt, 1932; London: Kegan Paul, Trench, Trubner, 1934 (188 + xl, incl. 6-p. index, 16-p. intro. by Jung).

Introducing his theme by describing early studies of double personality and of the trauma hypothesis, Kranefeldt then focuses on the theories involved in Freud's psychoanalysis, Adler's individual psychology, and Jung's analytical psychology. In the long introduction, Jung characterizes his psychology as being different from the other two in the sense of being dualistic and possibly pluralistic, because it is based on the principle of opposites and recognizes a multiplicity of relatively autonomous psychic complexes.
(Bk.revs.: Amer '32/47:335; AnnAmAcad My'32/161:270–2; BkRDig '32:534; JNerv-Ment '32/76:417–18; WilsonLibB 28N'32:299; Person '33/14:217; BrJMedPsy '34/ 14:292–3; BrJPsy '34/25:115; Philos '34/9:490–1; Tabl '34/163:404; TimesLitSup 3Mr'34:167)

The Psychology of C. G. Jung: An Introduction with Illustrations, by Jolande Jacobi. (Ger. *Die Psychologie von C. G. Jung.* Zurich: Rascher Verlag, 1940.) London: Kegan Paul, Trench, Trubner, 1942 to ed.6 1962; Routledge & Kegan Paul, ed.7 1969* +p*; New Haven, Conn.: Yale U. Press, 1943 to ed.8 1973 +p* (203 + xiii, incl. 11-p. index, 34-p. bibl., 3-p. biographical sketch of Jung, 30 illus., 1-p. foreword by Jung).

Published two years after Jacobi left Vienna to study with Jung, her synthesis of Jung's psychology grew out of lectures presented to groups of psychologists, physicians, and teachers. Its concise yet overall view of Jung's findings is designed to "open up access to Jung's extraordinarily prolific work." She covers the nature and structure of the psyche, laws of psychic processes and forces, and practical applications of Jung's theory—all amply illustrated by diagrams. The book's values is attested by its numerous editions.

(Bk.revs.: JNervMent '41/94:658–60; BrJPsy '42/33:66; Listen '42/27:696; Spec '42/ 168:468+; TimesLitSup '42:232; Blackf '43/24:32–4; BulAnPsyNY Ap'43/5:5–7; ChrCen '43/60:1507; IntJPsy-An '43/24:81–4; SatR 25D'43/26:9; PsysomMed '43/5:109; PsyanR '44/31:353; PsyBul '44/41:496–7; SocForc '44/23:103; Thought '44/19:556; UnionSemR '44/55:259–60; AmJPsy '45/58:574; JBibRel '45/13:49)

Studies in Analytical Psychology, by Gerhard Adler. London: Kegan Paul, Trench, Trubner, 1948; New York: W. W. Norton, 1948; London: Hodder & Stoughton, rev. 1966; New York: G. P. Putnam's Sons for the C. G. Jung Foundation for Analytical Psychology, rev. 1967p*; Westport, Conn.: Greenwood, repr. 1968; New York: Capricorn Books/G. P. Putnam's Sons, 1969 +p (250 + vi, incl. 6-p. index, 19 illus., 3-p. foreword by Jung).

Basing this volume on lectures delivered in London during 1936–45, Adler presents the results of fifteen years of clinical experience as an analyst. He explains the fundamental concept of the psyche as a self-regulating system, describing the experiences of his clients who have worked on the integration of the personality by the process of individuation. Following a technical discussion of the methods of Jung's analytical psychology as they differ from Freud's and Adler's, he illustrates the fundamentals of the collective unconscious and archetypes by the study of a dream, which is followed by essays on the ego and the cycle of life, on consciousness and cure, on a psychological approach to religion, and on Jung's contribution to modern consciousness.

(Bk.revs.: BrBkN '49:116; AmJPsy '49/62:148; BrJPsy '49/39:172–3; BulAnPsyNY Ja'49/ 11:7–9; Listen '49/41:153–4; PsychiQ '49/23:178; PsyanQ '49/18:388–9; PsysomMed '49/11:180–1; BulMennClin '50/14:149; JNervMent '50/111:83–5; AmJPsyth '51/5:85– 7; InwLight Spr'68/n73:48–9)

Freud or Jung?, by Edward Glover. Oxford and London: Blackwell, 1949; London: Allen & Unwin, 1950; New York: W. W. Norton, 1940; Cleveland and New York: Meridian Books/World Pub. Co., 1956p; repr. 1958p (207, incl. 12-p. index).

Glover, an English leader in Freudian analysis, was asked to write a negative critique of Jung's psychology as being a religion rather than a scientific conception; but his investigation revealed no such bias. In trying to answer the question of whether Jung's concept of the unconscious bears any resemblance to or contradicts or is an improvement of Freudian theory, he discusses mental structure, mental energy, mental mechanism, character and consciousness, dreams and neuroses, individuation, alchemy, religion, and art, being very critical of Jungian theory.

(Bk.revs.: BrJPsy '50/41:199–200; Listen '50/43:997; NewStates '50/40:177; AmJPsyth '51/5:665–7; BkRDig '51:339–40; JMentSci '51/97:22; JNervMent '51/114:468; NYHerTrib 11Mr'51:12; NYTimesBkR 6My'51:7; PsyanQ '51/20:293–4; SFChron 1Ap'51:25; AmJOrthopsy '52/22:204–6; AmJPsychi '52/108:714; BulMennClin '52/16:76; PsysomMed '52/14:505)

Analytical Psychology and the English Mind, by Helton Godwin Baynes. London: Methuen, 1950; New York: British Book Centre, 1950 (242 + ix, incl. 4-p. index, 1-p. foreword by Jung).

Having served as Jung's assistant for several years and as Jung's traveling companion on the African expedition, Baynes offers this collection of essays, whose title is taken from one of the ten essays. He also includes the first three chapters of an unfinished book. He deals with complex psychic conditions and discusses such topics as the unconscious; the provisional life; psychological background of the parent-child relation; Freud versus Jung; importance of dream analysis; the structure of the personality in relation to physical research; psychological origins of divine kingship; persona; and libido.

(Bk.revs.: BrJMedPsy '50/23:224–5; BrJPsy '50/41:200; TimesLitSup '50/297; AmJPsy '51/64:313; PsychiQ '51/25:526)

An Introduction to Jung's Psychology, by Frieda Fordham. London and Baltimore: Pelican/Penguin Books, 1953p; Harmondsworth and Baltimore: Penguin Books, ed.2 1959; ed.3 1966p* (159, incl. 4-p. index, 7-p. bibl., 2-p gloss. of Jungian terms, 24-p. biographical sketch of Jung, 1-p. foreword by Jung).

Jung states in the foreword of Fordham's book that she "has delivered a fair and simple account of the main aspects of my psychological work," a by no means easy task. After an introductory outline of his psychology, she discusses the topics of psychological types; archetypes of the collective unconscious; religion and the individuation process; psychotherapy; dreams and their interpretation; and psychology and education. The last edition contains a long biographical sketch, "Jung on Himself," expanded from four pages in previous editions by drawing widely from his own autobiographical *Memories, Dreams, Reflections.*

(Bk.revs.: Blackf '53/34:503; Listen '53/50:313; BrJPsy '54/45:150; PsychiQ '54/28:166; TimesLitSup '54:489; BrJMedPsy '55/28:82)

Six Talks on Jung's Psychology, by Robert A. Clark. Pittsburgh, Penn.: Boxwood Press, 1953p* (84, incl. 4-p. bibl.).

Familiar with many schools of psychotherapy, psychiatrist Clark deems the analytical psychology of Jung to be most appealing because it lends itself to the application of religious concepts to therapy. He discusses the topics of Jung's libido theory; ego psychology and psychological types; the shadow and "how we know the unconscious"; archetypes and the collective unconscious; technique of analysis; and applications in psychotherapy.
(Bk.rev.: PastorPsy Ap'57/8:60)

Experiment in Depth: A Study of the Work of Jung, Eliot, and Toynbee, by P. W. Martin. London: Routledge & Kegan Paul, 1955; ed.2 1976p*; New York: Pantheon Books, 1955; New York: Humanities Press, 1955 (275 + vii, incl. 7-p. index, 2-p. bibl.).

Martin's experiment deals with the "mythical method," which explores the powerful forces from the unconscious depths (symbols, visions, ideas) that heretofore have been used chiefly by totalitarian ideologies but that now need to be used for more humane values and aims. He combines Toynbee's concept of withdrawal-and-return ("from the outer world of political and social chaos to the inner world of the psyche" and returning to the outer world with a vision of a new way of life) with Jung's creative ways of working out the psychological means of withdrawal-and-return and with Eliot's expression of it in "the greatest poetry of the age." Jungian topics include psychological types; archetypal images and themes; transforming symbol; the way between opposites; and the individuation process.
(Bk.revs.: BkRDig '55:612–13; LibJ '55/80:2239; NewStates '55/50:336–7; PastorPsy D'55/6:66; TimesLitSup '55:513; BrJPsy '56/47:71; Person '56/37:402–3; JPastorCare '58/12:195–6; SatNight 24My'58/72:27)

Individuation: A Study of the Depth Psychology of Carl Gustav Jung, by Josef Goldbrunner. (Ger.: *Individuation: Die Tiefenpsychologie von Carl Gustav Jung.* Munich: Erich Wesel Verlag, 1955.) London: Hollis & Carter, 1955; New York: Pantheon Books, 1956; Notre Dame, Ind.: U. of Notre Dame Press, 1964p* (204 + xii, incl. 4-p. ref. notes).

Citing Jung as the leader of the new depth psychology that "was extended and disengaged from neurology," Goldbrunner examines Jung's work, stating that "the life of the healthy soul and no longer merely the diseased soul is being investigated." He discusses the reality of the psyche;

the personal unconscious; neurosis; analysis; dreams; the problem of types; psychic energy; the collective unconscious and its analysis; archetypes; individuation; and religious experience. In the second part of the book he deals with social subjects such as religion, anthropology, ethics, education, and the cure of souls.

(Bk.revs.: AveM 12My'56/83:24; Blackf '56/51:501; BrJPsy '56/47:235–6; DownR '56/74:282–3; InwLight Spr-Sum'56/n53:44–5; IrEcclRec '56/86:265; IrTheolQ '56/23:288; JRelThought '56/14:87–8; Month '56/15:362–3; Tabl '56/12:360; PastorPsy Mr'57/8:59–60; TimesLitSup 23My'58:xii; JPastorCare '59/13:115–16; PsysomMed '65/27:295–6)

The Death and Rebirth of Psychology: Freud, Adler, Jung, and Rank and the Impact of Their Culminating Insights on Modern Man, by Ira Progoff. New York: Julian Press, 1956; New York: Delta Books/Dell, 1964p; New York: McGraw-Hill, 1973p* (275 + xii, incl. 9-p. bibl.).

Approaching historically his examination of the major authors of depth psychology, Progoff focuses on psychological concepts and tools in order to "provide a new basis for studies in the social sciences and humanities." His book includes sections on Jung on the road away from Freud; the deepening of Jung's personal perspective; dialogue of Freud and Jung on the magnitude of man (from Oedipus to the collective unconscious); and Jung at the outposts of psychology (the unconscious as part of nature, and the self as symbol and reality).

(Bk.revs.: LibJ '56/81:2680; NYTimesBkR 16D'56:6; Time 24D'56/68:51–2; AmJPsyth '57/11:433–4; BkRDig '57:746; BulMennClin '57/21:269; DrewGate '57/28:66–8; JBibRel '57/25:248–9; PastorPsy Mr'57/8:58–9; SatRLit 9F'57/40:19; TheolStud '57/18:304–7; ContemPsy '58/3:61; JPastorCare '58/12:122; InwLight Spr'58/n55:43–4; PerkSchTh Fall '58/12:26–7; JIndivPsy '60/16:216–17)

New Developments in Analytical Psychology, by Michael Fordham. London: Routledge & Kegan Paul, 1957*; New York: Humanities Press, 1957 (214, incl. 16-p. index, 7 illus., 4-p. foreword by Jung).

From a background in neurology and psychiatry, Fordham first defines the relation of these to the concept of unconscious archetypes and then reflects on archetypes and synchronicity and on image and symbol, with additional notes on the transference. He deals, in the remainder of the book, with his own specialty within analytical psychology, child psychology. There are essays on origins of the ego in childhood; the self and ego in childhood; child analysis; significance of archetypes for the transference in childhood; and a child guidance approach to marriage. Jung, in the foreword, "salutes the author's collaboration in the field of psychotherapy and analytical psychology" and draws attention to Fordham's discussion of the problem of synchronicity, dealt with "in a masterly manner."

(Bk.revs.: Blackf '58/39:344; BrJMedPsy '58/31:262; JAnPsy '58/3:167–71)

Theories of Personality, by Calvin S. Hall and Gardner Lindzey. London: Chapman & Hall, 1957; New York: Wiley & Sons, 1957; ed.2 1970; ed.3 1978* (725 + xvi, incl. 17-p. index, end-chap. bibl. refs., 18 illus.).

Among the eighteen theories of personality presented by Hall and Lindzey is a lengthy survey of Jung's analytic theory (chapter 4: pp. 113–54, including a five-page bibliography), which is discussed under the subjects of structure of the personality, the dynamics of the personality, and development of personal characteristics.

(Bk.revs. AmAnth '57/59:936–7; AmJSoc '57/63:243–4; AmSocR '57/22:471; BkRDig '57:306–7; ContemPsy '57/2:201–2; JNervMent '57/125:343–4; LibJ '57/82:546; Soc-SocRes '57/42:77–8; AmJPsychi '58/115:90; AmJPsy '58/71:186–7; AmJPsyth '58/12:586–8; BrJMedPsy '58/31:267–8; BulMennClin '58/22:41; JPastorCare '58/71:253–4; JPsysomRes '58/3:180; PsysomMed '58/20:253–4; PsychiQ '59/33:377–8; IntJGroup '61/11:350–2; Adoles '66/1:98; JCounsPsy '66/13:125; JSciStudRel '70/9:328; ContemPsy '71/16:490; JPersAssess '71/35:494–5; JBioPsy '77/19:423; ContemPsy '78/23:699; '79/24:752–3; BrJPsy '80/71:180; AmJPsychi '83/14:121)

Current Trends in Analytical Psychology: The Proceedings of the First International Congress for Analytical Psychology, Zurich, 1958, edited by Gerhard Adler. London: Tavistock Publications for International Association for Analytical Psychology (IAAP), 1961; New York: Humanities Press, 1961 (326 + ix, incl. 12-p. index, 21 illus.).

Consisting of eighteen papers delivered at the first congress of the IAAP (founded in 1956), this book represents a wide variety of themes. Contributions by authors included in this annotated bibliography are "Healing in Depth" (Barker); "The Emergence of a Symbol in a Five-year-old Child" (Fordham); "What Makes the Symbol Effective as a Healing Agent?" (Harding); "An Approach to Group Analysis" (Hobson); "An Analyst's Dilemma" (H. Kirsch); "The Problem of Dictatorship as Represented in *Moby-Dick*" (J. Kirsch); "Homoeroticism in Primitive Society as a Function of the Self" (Layard); "The Significance of the Genetic Aspect for Analytical Psychology" (Neumann); "From Schizophrenia to Art" (Westman); and "The Magical Dimension in Transference and Countertransference" (Whitmont). Papers by others deal with the topics of pairs of opposites; extraversion and introversion; the mother figure; the mother-child relationship; ego integration and *coniunctio;* Christian symbolism; homosexual transference; and self-realization.

(Bk.revs.: Blackf '62/43:193; BrJPsy '62/53:94–5; HibbJ '62/60:346–8; JChildPsy '62/3:209–10; JMentSci '62/108:115; JPsysomRes '62/6:146; Spring '62:161–2; JAnPsy '63/18:181–5)

The Psychology of Jung: A Critical Interpretation, by Avis M. Dry. London: Methuen, 1961; New York: John Wiley, 1961 (329 + xiv, incl. 9-p. indexes, 9-p. bibl.).

The subtitle indicates Dry's aim "to render the psychology of Jung more understandable" to general readers who are interested though uncommitted, trying to avoid both "enthusiastic supporters" and "uniformly hostile" orthodox psychiatrists. After discussing Jung's early, intermediate, and later concepts of the mind, she examines Jungian therapy and related insights; Jung's critique of Freud and psychotherapy; religion in the work of Jung; some cognitive and emotional factors of changes in Jung's work and its appeal; and the social background of Jungian psychology and its appeal.

(Bk.revs.: ArchGenPsy '62/7:227–9; BrJPsy '62/53:352; BrJPsychi '63/109:160; Bul-MennClin '63/17:114; ContemPsy '63/8:468–9; PsyanR '63–64/50:693; Spring '63:150; JAnPsy '64/9:96–7)

How the Mind Works: An Introduction to the Psychology of C. G. Jung, by David Cox. (Orig. subtitle: *A Simple Account of Analytical Psychology.* London: Darton, Longman & Todd, 1963; subsequently: *Teach Yourself Analytical Psychology.* London: English Universities Press, 1965; then: *Modern Psychology: The Teaching of Carl Gustav Jung.* New York: Barnes & Noble Everyday Handbook, 1968p.) London: Hodder & Stoughton, 1978p (Teach Yourself Books) (207 pp.).

Intending to popularize Jung's teachings, as indicated in the titles, Cox expresses more concern with human need for self-knowledge than for "clinical conditions of sickness and health." He deals with analytical psychology in relation to psychoanalysis and then with the subjects of consciousness; the unconscious and the psyche; how the psyche functions; the collective unconscious; psychological types; psychic development; archetypes; the self; and analysis; ending with an impression of "Jungianism."

(Bk.rev.: Choice '69/6:708–9)

Jung on Elementary Psychology: A Discussion between C. G. Jung and Richard Evans, by Richard Evans. (Orig. title: *Conversations with Carl Jung and Reactions from Ernest Jones.* Princeton, N.J.: D. Van Nostrand, 1964p.) New York: E. P. Dutton, rev. 1976p; London: Routledge & Kegan Paul, 1979p* (Reprinted as *Dialogue with C. G. Jung.* New York: Praeger, 1981*.) (242 + xi, incl. 5-p. index, 3-p. bibl., 65-p. transcription of four one-hour film interviews in 1957).

In an attempt to introduce Jung's ideas through the spontaneity of their conversation, Evans probes Jung's reactions to Freud and to various psychoanalytic concepts, such as psychosexual development, "ego," and "super-ego." He then questions Jung about his conception of psychological types and functions, motivation and psychic individuation, archetypes, dreams and the personal unconscious, and diagnostic and therapeutic practices.

(Bk.revs.: Choice '64/1:343; SatR 18Jy'64/47:36; Spring '65:144–5; JAnPsy '66/11:79–80; JChildPsy '66/7:89–90; LibJ '70/95:2787; Bklist '71/67:572; WilsonLibB '71/85:883; NYTimesBkR 12S'75/70:53; NYRevBks 15Ap'76/23:26–30; NYTimesBkR 27Jn'76:7; BkRDig '77:694; ContemPsy '77/22:532; SciBksFilm '77/13:31; JAnPsy '80/25:381–2)

What Jung Really Said, by E. A. Bennet. London: MacDonald, 1966; New York: Schocken, 1967 + p; ed.2 1983p* (180 + xiii, incl. 6-p. index, 6-p. ref. notes, 7-p. intro. by Anthony Storr).

Because Jung's views often are misunderstood, Bennet aims to present what Jung "really said" about key subjects in modern psychological thought, which he outlines as they developed in Jung's work. He begins with the stages in Jung's career and then discusses the topics of psychological types; unconscious mental activity; dreams; inner world; widening circle of Jung's thought; confrontation with the unconscious; the undiscovered self; and personality as a whole (conscious and the unconscious); ending with individuation as process (the self).

(Bk.revs.: Bklist '67/64:84; BrJPsychi '67/114:453; IntJPsy-An '67/48:472; LibJ '67/82:3049; LibJBkR '67:467; PsyToday S'67/1:13 + ; BkRDig '68:100; Choice '68/4:1446)

From the Life and Work of C. G. Jung, by Aniela Jaffé. (Ger.: *Aus Leben und Werkstatt von C. G. Jung.* Zurich: Rascher Verlag, 1968.) New York: Colophon Books/Harper & Row, 1971 + p; London: Hodder & Stoughton, 1972p; Zurich: Daimon Verlag, new edn. 1989p* (139 + ix).

These four essays by Jaffé, Jung's long-time secretary and an analyst herself, are presented at the request of various people who wanted clarification of certain problems in Jung's life and work. The essays deal with parapsychology (experience and theory of occultism and spiritualism, and synchronistic phenomena); the influence of alchemy in the work of Jung; Jung's attitude toward National Socialism (an account of favorable and unfavorable evidence as seen in historical perspective, together with a psychological interpretation); and an essay on Jung's last years that examines Jung's personality in human relationships. The new edition includes a 12-page commentary by van der Post on Jaffé's essay on Jung and Nazism entitled "Some Reflections on a Shadow that Refuses to Go Away." It also contains a fifth chapter on the creative phases in Jung's life which appeared earlier in *Jung's Last Years* (1984) (annotated in chapter 1).

(Bk.revs.: PubW 28Jn'71/99:65; JAmSocPsy '72/66:339; LibJ '72/97:76; LibJBkR '72:437; JPastorCare '73/27:141–2; BloomR S'89/9:8)

The Symbolic Quest: Basic Concepts of Analytical Psychology, by Edward Whitmont. New York: G. P. Putnam's Sons / the C. G. Jung Foundation for Analytical Psychology, 1969*; London: Barrie & Rockliff, 1969; New York: Colophon Books/Harper & Row, 1973p; Princeton, N.J.: Princeton U. Press, 1978 +p* (336, incl. 14-p. index, 4-p. bibl., 8-p. ref. notes).

Believing that the quest for symbolic experience has urgency and meaning for our time and that the most comprehensive and useful expression is in the discipline of analytical psychology, Whitmont presents a systematic survey of Jung's psychology. Beginning with an explanation of the symbolic approach and the use of nonrational and intuitive realms of functioning in the approach to the unconscious, he then covers the topics of the objective psyche; the complex; archetypes and myths; archetypes and the individual myth; and archetypes and personal psychology. He continues with discussions of psychological types; the persona; the shadow; male-female polarity; the anima and animus; the self; the ego; ego-self estrangement; ego development and the phases of life; concluding with the subject of therapy.

(Bk.revs.: IntJPsy-An '70/51:561; LibJ '70/95:76; LibJBkR '70:542–3; JAnPsy '71/ 16:110–12; InwLight '72/n81:42–5)

The Discovery of the Unconscious: The History and Evolution of Dynamic Psychiatry, by Henri F. Ellenberger. London: Allen Lane, 1970; New York: Basic Books, 1970; 1981p* (932 + xvi, incl. 21-p. name index, 11-p. subject index, 38 illus.).

In an extensive study of the history and evolution of dynamic psychiatry, Ellenberger discusses the systems of Janet, Freud, Adler, and Jung, closing with an interpretation of the dawn and rise of the new dynamic psychotherapy. He surveys Jung's psychology in chapter 9 (92 pp., including 264 reference notes), remarking that he interviewed Jung and later received annotations from Jung on the draft of his theories. His survey is comprised of family background and events, Jung's personality, and his work. It is arranged in eight sections, namely: the notion of psychological reality; Burghölzli; psychoanalysis (1909–13); psychological types; analytic psychology (psychic energetics; collective unconscious and archetypes; structure of the human psyche; individuation); psychotherapy; Eastern and Western wisdom; and the psychology of religion. He concludes with an analysis of Jung's sources and of the influence Jung has had.

(Bk.revs.: BehResTh '70/8:395–6; CanPsychiJ '70/15:507–9; LibJ '70/95:76; LibJBkR '70:528; NewSoc '70/16:296; PsychiQ '70/44:556–7; PsysomMed '70/32:657–60; AmJPsychi '71/127:980–1; AmJPsyth '71/25:474; ArchGenPsychi '71/44:191–2; BkRDig '71:385; BulMennClin '71/35:213; Choice '71/7:1740; IntJGroup '71/21:386–90; Isis '71/ 62:527–9; JHistBehSci '71/7:194–6; JIndivPsy '71/27:216–20; JNervMent '71/153:63– 4; PsyanR '71/58:126–34; TimesLitSup '71:639; BulHistMed '72/46:605–7; ContemPsy

'72/17:56–9; JAmPsyan '72/20:711–12; Psychi '72/35:209–12; PsyMed '72/2:438–9; JPersAssess '73/37:389–91; ContemPsyan '74/10:143; Mosaic Wint'74/7:157–61; PsyanQ '74/43:303–6; PsychiForum '75/5:39; BrJPsychi '82/141:544–5; NYRevBks '85/32:7; PsychiJOtt '86/11:174)

Understanding Jung, by Norman Winski. Los Angeles: Sherbourne Press, 1971 (133 pp.).

Asserting that his book "cuts through the labyrinth of Jung's scholarship to the diamond-hard essentials of his thinking," Winski aims to provide the "ABC's of Jungianism" for those who cannot afford a thorough reading of Jung. His short survey deals with the psyche, consciousness, the Jungian unconscious, the four functions, psychological types, dreams, and individuation and the self, concluding with a chapter on "What Is He Really Saying?" The dedication is addressed to "my black anima and my white anima."

Analytical Psychology: A Modern Science, edited by Michael Fordham et al. London: William Heinemann Medical Books for the Society of Analytical Psychology, 1973; London: Academic Press, new edn. 1980* (Library of Analytical Psychology, vol. 1) (209 + x, incl. 5-p. index, bibl. at end of each essay).

The first volume of The Library of Analytical Psychology consists of ten essays published originally in the *Journal of Analytical Psychology* between 1958 and 1969. The first half deals with such basic concepts as the self in Jung's work, symbols, archetypes of the collective unconscious, indivisibility of the personal and collective unconscious, ego and self in infancy, analyzing childhood for assimilation of the shadow, and individuation. Among the clinical studies, discussed in the second half, are reflections on not being able to use imagination, the problem of identity related to the image of a damaged mother, and invasion and separation.
(Bk.revs.: BrBkN '73:431; BrJPsychi '73/123:599; JAnPsy '74/19:122–4; '75/20:81–2; PsyPersp '75/6:197–203)

A Primer of Jungian Psychology, by Calvin S. Hall and Vernon J. Nordby. New York: J. P. Tarcher, 1973; London: Croom Helm, 1973; New York: Mentor Books/New American Library, 1973p* (142 + xi, incl. 4-p. index, 1-p. bibl., 4-p. guide for reading Jung, 16-p. biography of Jung).

Intending that this pocket book be purely expository, Hall and Nordby introduce basic concepts of Jungian psychology such as the structure, dynamics, and development of the normal personality. They do not make evaluations, criticisms, or comparisons with other approaches, and they omit Jung's views on abnormal behavior and psychotherapy. They present Jung's approach to the structure of personality (psyche; consciousness; personal unconscious; collective unconscious; interactions among the structures of personality), the dynamics of personality (psychic energy; psychic values; principle of equivalence; principle of entropy; progression and regression), the development of personality (individuation; transcendence and integration; stages of life), psychological types, and symbols and dreams, and end with an evaluation of Jung's place in the field of psychology.

(Bk.revs.: PsyToday S'73/7:100; BkRDig '74:491; Bklist '74/70:459; Choice '74/11:1218; ContemPsy '74/19:208–9; JPastorPsy '74/28:213; LibJ '74/99:143; LibJBkR '74:407; Tabl '74/228:132–3)

C. G. *Jung and the Scientific Attitude*, by Edmund D. Cohen. New York: Philosophical Library, 1975*; Totowa, N.J.: Littlefield, Adams, 1976p (167 + xii, incl. 6-p. index, 2-p. bibl.).

Given Western culture's emphasis on scientific materialism and positivism, Cohen aims to correct misconceptions that Jung is inconsistent or self-contradictory. His theories are "full of paradoxes and conjunctions of opposites, but what appear to be contradictory turn out, under close scrutiny, not to be so." Cohen analyzes the following topics: the complex, the structure of the psyche and psychological types, and the collective unconscious and universal forms. The latter part is devoted to an interpretation of Jung and the scientific attitude, Jung's social relevance, Jung and academic psychology, and the dangers of analytical psychology.

(Bk.revs.: Choice '75/12:451–2; ContemPsy '75/20:954–5; JAssnPerc '75/10:44; PsychiForum '75/5:39–40; CanPsychiJ '76/21:130–1; IsrAnPsychi '76/14:300–1; JNervMent '76/162:72–3; ContemPsy '77/22:677–8; JPersAssess '77/41:655–6; Leon '77/ 10:161–2)

Re-Visioning Psychology, by James Hillman. New York: Harper & Row, 1975; Don Mills, Ontario: Fitzhenry & Whiteside, 1975; New York: Colophon Books/Harper & Row, 1977p* (266 + xvii, incl. 6-p. indexes of names and subjects, 30-p. ref. notes).

In his attempt to "re-vision" psychology from the point of view of the soul, Hillman describes his thesis as "old-fashioned and radically novel because it harks back to the classical notions of soul and yet advances ideas that current psychology has not even begun to consider." He draws upon the accumulated insights of Western tradition from the Greeks to the Renaissance and beyond, to the Romantics and Freud and Jung, moving toward a new kind of psychological thinking and feeling. His re-visioning poses questions about personifying or imagining things, pathologizing or falling apart, psychologizing or seeing through, and dehumanizing or soul-making.

(Bk.revs.: CrossCurr '75/25:289–94; JAmAcadRel '75/43:586–90; KirkR '75/43:297; LibJ '75/100:301; LibJBkR '75:403–4; RBksRel(W) My'75/4:10; AmJPsychi '76/133:597; BkRDig '76:543; ChrCen '76/93:290; ContemPsy '76/21:175–7; JAnPsy '76/21:227–9; JSciStudRel '76/14:106–9; Parab '76/1:104–5; PastorPsy '76/25:145–8; RelStudR Ap'76/ 2:35; JIndivPsy '77/33:261–3; JRel '77/57:107; StudRel '78/7:81–2; PsyPersp '79/10:87– 9; RelStudR '80/6:278–85)

C. G. Jung and Analytical Psychology: A Comprehensive Bibliography, by Joseph F. Vincie and Margareta Rathbauer-Vincie. New York and London: Garland, 1977 (Garland Reference Library of Social Science, 38) (297 + xiv, incl. 18-p. author index, 15-p. subject index).

Containing 3,680 titles of works on Jung and analytical psychology and 344 titles of book reviews, this bibliography of books, articles in journals, and a section on book reviews of works by Jung is arranged chronologically (and alphabetically within each year) through 1975. Its international nature (it includes all major European languages) covers a wide range of subjects from psychology to philosophy, religion, mythology, literary criticism, and aesthetics. A work is defined as Jungian "if the author concerned himself with Jung, his work, or Analytical Psychology, if his article was published in a journal sponsored by a Jungian organization, or if he claimed to have been working within the Analytical Psychology tradition." Works by Jung are not included. Items are not annotated.

(Bk.revs.: LibJ '77/102:2335; LibJBkR '77:45 AmRefBksAn '78/9:696; ContemPsy '78/ 73:974; Harvest '78/24:181–2; ChrScholR '80/9:281; JAmAcadRel '80/48:149)

Catalog of the Kristine Mann Library of the Analytical Psychology Club of New York, Inc. Boston: J. K. Hall, 1978 (1412 + v, 2 vols.).

In 1978, the Analytical Psychology Club of New York published, in an oversize format, a catalog of its library, which contains more than 5,000 volumes, by photocopying cards from the library card file. Volume 1 consists of the author-title cards with approximately 19,000 entries. Volume 2, the subject catalog, includes works in analytical psychology and in related fields of religion, philosophy, art, anthropology, mythology, fairy tales, and alchemy.

The Wisdom of Jung, by Chester P. Szemborski. New Rochelle, N.Y.: Self-published, 1978p (120 + 5-p. bibl.).

The tone of this self-published book on Jungian thought, insights, and "just plain wisdom" is reflected in the author's statement that Jung's "psychology can reveal to us the ambiguities of our lives, no matter how religious or self-righteous we may be." Szemborski discusses the body; the uncon-

scious; dreams; complexes; neurosis; irrational functions; rational functions; instinct; psychotherapy; religion; education; personality; society; and consciousness.
(Bk.rev.: BestSell '78/38:156)

Jung and Freud Return, by Robert R. Leichtman. Columbus, Ohio: Ariel Press/ The Publishing House of Light, 1979p* (98, incl. 12-p. gloss., 1 illus.) (From Heaven to Earth Series, 4).

This book consists of interviews conducted mostly in 1973 with the spirits of Jung and Freud through the mediumship of D. Kendrick Johnson. Leichtman presents his conversation with Jung (34 pp.) and then a three-way conversation with Jung and Freud (23 pp.) dealing with their evaluation of current practices of psychiatry and psychology and potential extensions of their work, as well as their disagreements with each other during their physical lives. He provides a 9-page summary of their contributions to psychology in this small-format book.

Jung in Context: Modernity and the Making of Psychology, by Peter Homans. Chicago and London: U. of Chicago Press, 1978*; 1982p (234 + xi, incl. 14-p. index, 9-p. bibl., 10-p. guide to reading Jung.)

As the title suggests, Homans examines the formation of Jung's psychological ideas in the context of the psycho-biographical, religious, and sociological factors that intertwined to influence Jung's thought, especially in his early formative period. He characterizes Jung's central concept as a shift of meaning and order from the social sphere to the personal, psychological sphere.
(Bk.revs.: LibJ '79/104:2576; LibJBkR '79:369; Amer '80/142:326–8; AmJPsychi '80/ 137:757–8; BestSell '80/39:420–1; BkRDig '80:571–2; Choice '80/17:286; ChrCen '80/ 97:296; Commow '80/107:411–13; ContemPsy '80/25:732–3; Critic 1Ap'80/38:2–4; Horiz '80/7:387–9; JSciStudRel '80/19:233–4; NewRBksRel Ap'80/4:23; PerkSchTh Spr'80/33:44–5; Quad '80/13n1:106–7; SFJInstLib '80/1n3:24–5; SciBksFilm '80/16:61; SocThought Fall'80/6:53–8; Psychi '81/44:86–7; SocAn '81/42:80–1; Spring '81:228–9; JRel '82/62:72–4; AmJSoc '83/88:824–6; ChrScholR '83/12:173–4)

Discovering the Mind. Vol. 3, *Freud versus Adler and Jung,* by Walter A. Kaufmann. New York: McGraw-Hill Book Co., 1980* (494 + xviii, incl. 8-p. index, 12-p. bibl., 25 illus.).

Kaufmann's thesis is that "Adler and Jung tried to go beyond Freud while he was still living, but slowly and reluctantly, I have arrived at the conclusion that they obstructed rather than advanced our understanding of ourselves and others." Claiming to be no Freudian, he declares that his main objective is to present the real Freud, defending him as "patient, tranquil, tolerant, and nondogmatic," whereas he describes Jung as an "archetypal counter-revolutionary."

(Bk.revs.: Choice '81/19:310; ChrCen '81/98:947; KirkR '81/49:549; LibJ '81/106:886; NYorker 14S'81/57:201; PsyRec '81/31:608; AmJPsy '82/95:171–2; BkRDig '82:708; ContemPsy '82/27:112–14; IliffR Wint'82/39:31–7; Ethics '83/94:171; GerQ '83/56:532; JIndivPsy '83/39:208–12; ModSchman '83/60:132–3; PsyanR '83/70: 451–5)

The Rhizome and the Flower: The Perennial Philosophy—Yeats and Jung, by James Olney. Berkeley and Los Angeles: U. of California Press, 1980* (379 + xvi, incl. 9-p. index).

Olney takes a long time (two-thirds of the book—from ancient Greece through the intellectual history of the West) to get to Yeats and Jung, illustrating that his main subject is actually the perennial philosophy. Although Yeats and Jung did not meet, Olney observes that there is an astonishing agreement between them on many concepts. One spoke the language of poetry, the other of psychology. Olney characterizes the Yeatsian and Jungian flowers as having their roots (rhizomes) in classical Greece and in the depths of the collective unconscious. In chapter 8, he describes Jung's psychology as the psychology of the pleroma (fullness) and demonstrates that the psyche is a natural system, wherein truths are revealed by the unconscious.

(Bk.revs.: BkRDig '80:912; Choice '80/17:229; Criticism '80/22:394–6; LibJ '80/105:206; LibJBkR '80:286; TimesHighEd 170c'80:17; AUMLA '81/n55:111–13; PhilosLit '81/ 5:243–4; SewaneeR '81/89:472–3; SAtlQ '81/80:233–4; VaQR '81/57:554–7; JAnPsy '82/27:391–2; QueensQ '82/89:471–6; SHumR '82/16:86–7; Notes&Q '83/20:90–2; ProseStud '84/7:196–8; RelStudR '85/11:383)

Jungian Psychology in Perspective, by Mary Ann Mattoon. New York: Free Press/ Macmillan, 1981; 1985p*; Toronto: Collier Macmillan Canada, 1981; London: Collier Macmillan, 1982; 1986p* (334 + xvi, incl. 14-p. index, 36-p. bibl.).

Based on university lectures, Mattoon's book provides the first comprehensive introductory text on Jungian psychology for academic use, combining the approach of academic psychology with her Jungian clinical experience and giving attention to contemporary issues. She covers the topics of components of the psyche; the collective unconscious; attitude and function types; female and male psychology; psychic energy and self-regulation; complexes; projection; symbol; and synchronicity. This is followed by discussions of psychopathology; human development from birth to old age; the way of individuation; religion; relationships and sexuality; psychotherapy; dreams; social and political issues; and research in analytical psychology. Appended is a comprehensive, annotated bibliography.

(Bk.revs.: LibJ '81/106:1933; BkRDig '82:895; BrJPsychi '82/144:106–7; Choice '82/ 19:1328; Harvest '82/28:172–3; JAnPsy '83/28:77–9; PsyPersp '83/14:104–10; Quad '83/ 16n1:100–4; SocWork '83/28:167; PsyanQ '84/53:137–9; SFJInstLib '84/5n3:30–1; ContemPsy '87/32:194–5)

Freud and Jung: Conflicts of Interpretation, by Robert S. Steele. London and Boston: Routledge & Kegan Paul, 1982* (390 + x, incl. 16-p. index, 9-p. bibl., 3-p. ref. notes).

Steele's thesis is that Freud's and Jung's antithetical positions on many issues are due to one philosophical disagreement, namely, "that they did not agree on what reality was." Given their divergent views of reality, he states that Freud's case studies are better than Jung's and Jung's textual analyses are superior to Freud's. He considers that each one's life shaped his theories and then explores how each used his psychological insights to manage his life as well as his view of his own past.

(Bk.revs.: TimesLitSup '82:1080; BehResTh '83/21:196; BkRep '83/28:853; BkRDig '83:1375; ContemPsy '83/28:853; Choice '83/20:890; Harvest '83/29:146–51; IntRPsy-An '83/10:248; JAnPsy '83/28:82–3; SciBksFilm '83/18:244; AmJPsychi '84/141:132–4; HeythJ '84/25:509; NewIdeas '85/5:163–72)

Jungian Theory and Therapy, by Tom Laughlin. Los Angeles: Panarion, 1982p (vol. 2 of *Jungian Psychology;* vol. 1 not published) (358 + xiii, incl. 16-p. index, 4-p. bibl.).

Stating that his main objective is to reawaken interest in Jung's most fundamental concept, "his psychology of instincts," Laughlin aims to clearly establish Jung's authentic discoveries about humans and the "instinctual unconscious," which he contends have been muddied over with mythological nonsense. He examines a variety of subjects in order to point out the need for authentic Jungian guidelines, always maintaining that instincts are the foundations for all behavior.

C. G. Jung: The Fundamentals of Theory and Practice, by Elie G. Humbert. (Fr.: *C. G. Jung.* Paris: Editions Universitaires, 1983p) Wilmette, Ill.: Chiron Publications, 1988* +p* (147 + xix, incl. 5-p. index, 2-p. Humbert bibl., 3-p. chron. of Jung's life).

In showing the interrelationship between Jung's psychotherapeutic practice and his personal reflections, French Jungian analyst Humbert discusses the interaction of theory and practice and recognizes from his own experience the internal logic of Jung's own work, namely, that "analytic writing flows from analysts' own self-analysis, which is conducted in counterpoint to the analysis that they do with patients." He examines the fundamentals of

confrontation with the unconscious (conscious activity; dreams and active imagination; compensatory dynamics; symbol and feelings; images of the Other; and transference) and relations between consciousness and the unconscious (archetypes; consciousness and the unconscious; the individuation process; and analysis).
(Bk.revs.: JAnPsy '84/29:303–4; SFJInstLib '89/8n3:49–51)

In the Wake of Jung: A Selection from Harvest, edited by Molly Tuby. London: Conventure, 1983p* (207, incl. 2 illus., 1-p. editor's preface, 13-p. intro. by Gerhard Adler).

Covering a wide range of Jungian ideas that have appeared "in the wake of Jung," this collection consists of thirteen articles from *Harvest,* the journal of the Analytical Psychology Club of London. It includes articles on healing the child within (Barker); Gnosis and the single vision (Begg); psychics and psyche (Claude Curling); woman as mediator (de Castillejo); the Medusa archetype today (Andrea Dykes); reflections on Jung's concept of synchronicity (Gordon); death and renewal in East and West (Hannah); Jung and Marx: alchemy, Christianity, and the work against nature (David Holt); transformations of the persona (Faye Pye); the inner journey of the poet (Raine); opposites and the healing power of symbols (Tuby); a session with Jung (von der Heydt); and Jung and society (von Franz). Gerhard Adler provides an introduction on Jung's theories and significance.
(Bk.revs.: Resurg S-Oc'84/n106:44; JAnPsy '87/32:297–8)

Jung's Struggle with Freud, by George B. Hogenson. Notre Dame, Ind. and London: U. of Notre Dame Press, 1983p* (180 + xi, incl. 3-p. index, 3-p. bibl., 8-p. ref. notes).

By trying to consider Freud and Jung together rather than separately, Hogenson's philosophical critique of psychoanalysis is an attempt to "redress previous philosophical oversight" in the encounter of Freud and Jung. He interprets the confrontation as being a "conflict of mythologies," whereby Jung's Gnostic mythology projected an imagery that would allow him to overcome Freud's projected mythology of the primal killing of the father. He characterizes Jung's struggle as focusing on Freud's refusal to risk his authority as possessor of the only means of interpreting the unconscious.
(Bk.revs.: BestSell '83/43:267; Amer '84/150:19–20; Chiron '84/21:200–3; Choice '84/21:738; ContemPsy '84/29:590; Ethics '84/94:731; JAnPsy '84/29:203–5; RelStudR '84/10:47; BkRDig '85:741; PhilosSocSc '86/16:404–6; Harvest '88–'89/34:172–3; NewIdeas '88/6:385–90)

Jung in Modern Perspective, edited by Renos K. Papadopoulos and Graham S. Saayman. Hounslow: Wildwood House, 1984* (316 + ix, incl. 8-p. index, 22-p. ref. notes, 4 illus.).

This volume, the result of a symposium held at the University of Cape Town that commemorated the centenary of Jung's birth, offers the opportunity for a contemporary perspective on Jung's contributions to psychology and culture. The eighteen papers represent a variety of views. Included are articles on Jung's conceptions concerning the Other (Papadopoulos); rebirth (Alfred Plaut); active imagination (Elie Humbert); yoga (Phillip Faber and Graham Saayman); religion (John de Gruchy); history (Joseph Henderson); and musical art (Gunter Pulvermacher).

(Bk.revs.: BrJSocWork '85/15:535–6; JAnPsy '85/30:105–7)

Reading Jung: Science, Psychology, and Religion, by Volney P. Gay. Chico, Calif.: Scholars Press, 1984p* (American Academy of Religion Studies, 34) (149 + xvi, incl. 7-p. index, 20-p. bibl.).

In order to furnish serious students with a systematic way of reading the major works of Jung in a critical manner, Gay provides "a handbook or guide [designed] as if all its readers were intelligent generalists who have come upon Jung for the first time." He emphasizes Jung's earlier, more technical works rather than the more popular works of his later years. Major subjects are psychiatric studies of Jung's early period; symbols of transformation (the break with Freud); advent of analytical psychology (basic theories); psychology and religion; and individuation and the self. Gay provides a question sheet to allow readers to respond to arguments.

(Bk.revs.: ChingFeng '85/28:175; Ethics '85/95:982; JSciStudRel '85/24:234–5; RelStudR '85/11:180; JRel '86/66:231; RelStud '86/22:162–3)

Jung and the Post-Jungians, by Andrew Samuels. London and Boston: Routledge & Kegan Paul, 1985*; 1986p* (293 + x, incl. 9-p. index, 11-p. bibl.).

In discussing the current status of the field of analytical psychology, Samuels argues for its place within the wider field of psychotherapy. He compares three major contemporary Jungian schools of thought, which he defines as classical, developmental, and archetypal. His comprehensive attempt to describe and interpret the extraordinary developments in Jungian psychology since Jung's death in 1961 provides a basis for its increased recognition in the helping professions and in the wider culture. He critiques Jung's own views and "post-Jungian" points of view as well as other psychological theories in his chapters on archetype and complex; the ego; the self and individuation; development of personality; analytical process; gender, sex, and marriage; and dreams. He devotes a chapter to archetypal psychology and concludes with a comparison and evaluation of post-Jungian trends.

(Bk.revs.: Harvest '84/n30:130–3; BrJPsychi '85/146:678; BrJMedPsy '85/58:392; Br-JSocWork '85/15:535–6; Choice '85/22:1412; Econ 18My'85/296: SprBks17; JAnPsy '85/30:327–9; LATimesBkR 5My'85:12; NewSoc '85/71:183; PsyPersp '85/16:226–9; Quad '85/18n1:111–13; TimesLitSup 22F'85:190; BkRDig '86:1410; Chiron '86:213–16; IntRPsy-An '86/13:115–20; Resurg D'86/n119:49; SFJInstLib '86/6n4:12; CurrPsy '88/7:175–6)

Understanding Jung, Understanding Yourself, by Peter O'Connor. Melbourne: Methuen Haynes, 1985; New York and Mahwah, N.J.: Paulist Press, 1986p* (148 + xi, incl. 2-p. index, 3-p. bibl., 2 illus.).

Drawing on a series of introductory lectures on Jung for the layperson, O'Connor intends that the book, as the lectures, serve as "an 'introduction' to 'introductory' books on Jung." He intends that it should not be just about Jung's psychology but that it should also help in facilitating the process of understanding life. He discusses the nature of the psyche; archetypes and the collective unconscious; the personal unconscious; psychological types; the self and the individuation process; alchemy; anima and animus; marriage; and dreams and symbols.

(Bk.rev.: RelStudR '87/13:48)

International Abstracts in Analytical Psychology, edited by Peter Mudd. Wilmette, Ill.: Chiron Publications, 1989+ (annual publication).

The first issue (for 1986, published 1989) of international abstracts in analytical psychology, the idea for which was approved at the Berlin Congress of the International Association for Analytical Psychology, contains 144 abstracts of books and articles by eighty-three authors published during 1986 in English, German, French, Portuguese, Italian, Japanese, Korean, and Hebrew. In addition, 122 books and articles published during 1986 are listed without abstracts. Included is a 20-page subject index. The second issue (for 1987, published 1990) contains abstracts for 123 books and articles by 79 authors. There are thirty-nine listings without abstracts.

Soul and Body: Essays on the Theories of Jung, by C. A. Meier. Santa Monica and San Francisco: Lapis Press, 1986* +p* (351, incl. 17-p. index, 2-p. index of Greek words and phrases, 17-p. bibl., 7 illus., 3-p. intro. by Joseph L. Henderson).

Arranged chronologically, Meier's book presents seventeen papers and essays, most of which were delivered at congresses and conferences and later published in journals between 1937 and 1983. Swiss analyst Meier, who has tried to closely parallel his life with that of Jung's, though thirty years later, provides a wide range of subjects in analytical psychology, including the collective unconscious, psychotherapy, the transference, dreams, psychosomatic medicine, religion, psychological types and individuation, consciousness, and altered states of consciousness.

(Bk.revs.: Choice '87/24:1627; Harvest '87/33:221–3; LibJ 1Mr'87/112:80; Quad '87/20n2:90–1; BkRDig '88:1158; ContemPsy '88/33:260; JAnPsy '88/33:195–6)

A Jungian Psychology Resource Guide, compiled by James Arraj and Tyra Arraj. Chiloquin, Ore.: Tools for Inner Growth, 1987p* (136, incl. 6-p. index.).

In response to their view that "Jung's work . . . is spreading all over the world," the Arrajes provide information on approximately one hundred lay and professional Jungian groups (societies, clubs, centers, associations, institutes, and foundations), mainly in the United States. They also furnish information on psychological type organizations and Jungian conferences, periodicals, book publishers, sources for ordering books, and libraries and bibliographic tools of particular interest to students of analytical psychology. Also included is an 8-p. list of readings, along with information on Jungian analysis and training programs.

(Bk.revs.: SFJInstLib '88/8n1:67–9; AmRefBksAn '88/19:305)

Freud and Jung: Years of Friendship, Years of Loss, by Linda Donn. New York: Charles Scribner's Sons/Macmillan Publishing Co., 1988* (238 + xvi, incl. 11-p. index, 6-p. bibl., 32-p. ref. notes, 30 illus.).

Attracted to the idea of friendship between men of genius, a joining of intellect and passion, Donn grew to cherish the company of Freud and Jung in her imagination during four years of research about their lives, highlighted by many interviews with those who knew them. She provides descriptive accounts of images and scenarios that came to her from events selected from their childhoods and careers with particular attention given to their warm exchanges of ideas that developed into shared friendship with personal meetings and active correspondence. She reconstructs in detail the events of 1912–13 that strained the relationship to the breaking point, concluding that the long ordeal of Freud and Jung was a reminder that some piece of the psyche was "beyond comprehension."

(Bk.revs.: Bklist '88/85:516; KirkR '88/56:1577–8; LibJ D'88/113:118; PubW 280c'88/234:68; BkRDig D'89:34–5; Choice '89/26:1602; ContemPsy '89/34:876; Econ 15Ap'89/311:100; LATimesBkR 8Ja'89:4; SciBksFilm S'89/25:6)

A Guided Tour of the Collected Works of C. G. Jung, by Robert H. Hopcke. Boston and Shaftesbury: Shambhala Publications, 1989* (191 + xii, incl. 9-p. bibl. of the CW, 2-p. foreword by Aryeh Maidenbaum).

Aiming to help interested people gain entrance into Jung's writings and to "glimpse the heart and soul of Jung's thought," Hopcke provides a planned course of reading, a guided tour. This topically organized introduction to the wide variety of Jung's concepts is based on the belief that most of Jung's writing is accessible to a general readership. He divides the plan into four parts, the first and longest being "The Ways and Means of the Psyche" (62 pp.) followed by "Archetypal Figures," "Topics of Special Interest," and "Esoterica." He begins each of the forty topics with a short (2- to 4-page) discussion of each concept, following which are suggested readings under four categories ("to begin"—one or more of Jung's essays or works that are easiest to read first and that treat the topic at some length; "to go deeper"— more difficult than the first; "related works" of Jung; and "secondary sources" by Jungians and others). He arranges the topics so as to build on the material covered in the previous topic.

(Bk.rev.: Choice '89/27:561–2; Quad '90/23n1:129–31, 133–4)

Intimate Friends, Dangerous Rivals: The Turbulent Relationship between Freud and Jung, by Duane Schultz. Los Angeles: Jeremy P. Tarcher, 1990 +p (247 + xvi, incl. 7-p. index, 6-p. bibl., 8-p. notes).

Psychologist-historian Schultz examines the influences that shaped Freud's and Jung's natures and the needs that bound them to each other, followed by description and analysis of events of their six-year association— an "uneasy alliance," which he characterizes as more emotional than intellectual.

On Jung, by Anthony Stevens. London & New York: Routledge, 1990 (292 + x, incl. 11-p. index, 5-p. bibl., 13 illus.).

Following introductory chapters on Jung's psychology, Stevens examines Jung's life and work from birth to maturity and from midlife to death.

4 The Psyche

This subject category contains works that deal specifically with the structure and dynamics of the psyche, rather than those that cover analytical psychology more broadly, as in chapter 3. Jung defines *psyche* as the totality of all psychic processes—conscious as well as unconscious; and he defines *soul* as a clearly demarcated functional complex that can be described best as a "personality."

Following the five works by Jung, the material of the twenty-two works written by others is presented chronologically. Half of these were published after 1975.

Jung: *The Archetypes and the Collective Unconscious* [p. 55]
_____: *Four Archetypes* [p. 56]
_____: *On the Nature of the Psyche* [p. 56]
_____: *The Psychology of the Unconscious (See chapter 7, "Symbolic Life and Dreams")* [p. 127]
_____: *The Structure and Dynamics of the Psyche* [p. 56]
Adler: *Dynamics of the Self* [p. 62]
Ellenberger: *The Discovery of the Unconscious* (See chapter 3, "Jung's Psychology") [p. 42]
Fordham: *The Objective Psyche* [p. 58]
Frey-Rohn: *From Freud to Jung* [p. 60]
Guggenbühl-Craig (ed.): *The Archetype* [p. 59]
Harding: *Psychic Energy* [p. 57]
Hillman: *Archetypal Psychology* [p. 62]
_____: *Loose Ends: Primary Papers on Archetypal Psychology* [p. 61]
Jacobi: *Complex/Archetype/Symbol* [p. 59]
Lauter & Rupprecht (eds.): *Feminist Archetypal Theory* (See chapter 8, "Feminine and Masculine Psychology") [p. 182]
Meier: *The Unconscious in Its Empirical Manifestations* [p. 60]

Poncé: *The Archetype of the Unconscious* [p. 65]
Radin: *The Trickster* [p. 58]
Ribi: *Demons of the Inner World* [p. 65]
Roberts: *Tales for Jung Folk* (See chapter 10, "Creativity and Jung's Psychology") [p. 274]
Robertson: *C. G. Jung and the Archetypes of the Collective Unconscious* [p. 64]
Samuels: *The Plural Psyche* (See chapter 11, "Jungian Analysis") [p. 349]
Shapiro & Alexander: *Experience of Introversion* [p. 61]
Shelburne: *Mythos and Logos in the Thought of Carl Jung* [p. 64]
Stevens: *Archetypes* [p. 63]
Taub-Bynum: *The Family Unconscious* [p. 63]
van der Hoop: *Character and the Unconscious* [p. 57]
von Franz: *Number and Time* [p. 61]
von Franz: *Time: Rhythm and Repose* [p. 62]
Wheelwright (ed.): *The Reality of the Psyche* [p. 59]
Wickes: *The Inner World of Man* (See chapter 6, "Human Development and Individuation") [p. 81]
Woloy: *The Symbol of the Dog in the Human Psyche* [p. 65]
Young-Eisendrath & Hall (eds.): *The Book of the Self* [p. 64]

The Archetypes and the Collective Unconscious, by C. G. Jung. New York: Pantheon Books (Bollingen Foundation), 1959; London: Routledge & Kegan Paul, 1959*; Princeton, N.J.: Princeton U. Press/Bollingen, ed.2 1968*; 1980p* (CW 9, pt. 1) (451 + xi, incl. 31-p. index, 25-p. bibl., 84 illus.).

One of Jung's best known theories is the correlation of his concept of archetypes and that of the collective unconscious. Following the introduction of three essays to establish the basis of the concepts ("Archetypes of the Collective Unconscious"; "The Concept of the Collective Unconscious"; "Concerning the Archetypes"; originally published 1934–36), this volume of the *Collected Works* also contains six other essays dealing with psychological aspects (on the mother archetype; child archetype; rebirth; kore [maiden]; the phenomenology of the spirit in fairy tales; the trickster figure; 1939–54), along with two essays on individuation (on the process of individuation; and on the conscious, unconscious, and individuation; 1934–39) and one on mandala symbolism (1950) with interpretations of fifty-four mandala drawings and paintings. Appended is a 4-page article on mandalas (orig. 1955).

(Bk.revs.: CathEdR '60/58:421–3; Person '60/41:588–9; Spring '60:150; TimesLitSup '60:57; AmJPsychi '61/117:958–9; JAnPsy '61/6:161–8; BkWorld 9Ag'81/22:10)

The Structure and Dynamics of the Psyche, by C. G. Jung. New York: Pantheon Books (Bollingen Foundation), 1960; Toronto; McClelland & Stewart, 1960; London: Routledge & Kegan Paul, 1960; ed.2 1970*; Princeton, N.J.: Princeton U. Press/Bollingen, ed.2 1969* (*CW* 8) (588 + x, incl. 34-p. index, 18-p. bibl.).

These nineteen essays cover Jung's theories on the main structural and dynamic aspects of the psyche, formulated when he was developing his own concepts as distinct from those of Freud. Originally published between 1916 and 1947, most are lectures and articles from journals or collections, some of which are enlarged from the originals and revised. The longest is on synchronicity (101 pp.) which is accompanied by an earlier and more popular version. The most comprehensive is "On the Nature of the Psyche" (76 pp.), originally entitled "The Spirit of Psychology" in *Eranos Jahrbuch,* 1946. "On Psychic Energy" (64 pp.) and "General Aspects of Dream Psychology" (44 pp.) are other long essays. Others deal with the transcendent function; complex theory; constitution and heredity; human behavior; instinct and the unconscious; the nature of dreams; belief in spirits; spirit and life; basic postulates of analytical psychology; analytical psychology and *Weltanschauung* (philosophy of life); the real and the surreal; stages of life; and soul and death.

(Bk.revs.: NMexQ '60/30:3224-6; PsychiQ '60/34:579; Blackf '61/42:230; CrossCurr '61/ 11:389; RMeta '61/14:569; Spring '61:153; TimesLitSup '61:45; JRelThought '61/ 18:186–8; JAnPsy '62/7:157–62; JMentSci '62/108:114–15; LumenVitae '69/24:171)

On the Nature of the Psyche, by C. G. Jung. Princeton, N.J.: Princeton U. Press/ Bollingen, 1969p*; London: Routledge & Kegan Paul, 1982p; London: Ark Publications, 1988p* (166 + viii, incl. 10-p. index, 9-p. bibl.).

Extracted from volume 8 of the *Collected Works* (listed immediately above), this paperback consists of two essays, one being "On Psychic Energy," first published in 1928 and also translated and published the same year in *Contributions to Analytical Psychology;* the other being "On the Nature of the Psyche," which was published in 1954 in the *Psychologische Abhandlungen* journal. The latter essay considers the topics of the unconscious in historical perspective; significance of the unconscious in psychology; dissociability of the psyche; instinct and will; conscious and unconscious; the unconscious as a multiple consciousness; patterns of behavior and archetypes; and general considerations and prospects.

Four Archetypes: Mother, Rebirth, Spirit, Trickster, by C. G. Jung. Princeton, N.J.: Princeton U. Press/Bollingen, 1970p*; London: Routledge & Kegan Paul, 1971p*; London: Ark Publications, 1986p* (173 + viii, incl. 13-p. index, 8-p. bibl.).

Extracted from volume 9, part 1 of the *Collected Works (The Archetypes of the Collective Unconscious)*, this paperback brings together four essays on specific archetypes, following a brief introduction on theoretical aspects of the concept of archetypes. Presented are discussions on psychological aspects of the mother archetype (37 pp.), rebirth (35 pp.), phenomenology of the spirit in fairy tales (48 pp.), and psychology of the trickster figure (18 pp.), published originally in 1938, 1939, 1945, and 1954, respectively.
(Bk.rev.: BrJPsychi '73/122:361)

* * * * *

Character and the Unconscious: A Critical Exposition of the Psychology of Freud and Jung, by Johannes Hermanus van der Hoop. London: Kegan Paul, Trench, Trubner, 1923 (International Library of Psychology, Philosophy and Scientific Method); New York: Harcourt Brace, 1923; Washington, D.C.: McGrath, 1923) (223 + viii, incl. 3-p. index, 2-p. bibl.).

Writing at a time when psychology as a science was still in a state of early growth, van der Hoop discusses psychological types on the heels of the publication of Jung's treatise on the subject. However, his main focus is on the unconscious, particularly the unconscious in the normal mind and the relation between the conscious and the unconscious. This follows a discussion of the origins of psychoanalysis. He contrasts the analytic and the synthetic points of view and then considers the development of emotions.
(Bk.revs.: BrJMedPsy '23/3:253–4; TimesLitSup '23:343; Mind '24/ns33:103–5; AmJSoc '25/30:747; Person '25/6:147–8)

Psychic Energy: Its Source and Its Transformation, by M. Esther Harding. (Orig. subtitle: *Its Source and Goal.* London: Vision, 1942; New York: Pantheon Books (Bollingen Series X), 1948; ed.2 1963*.) Princeton, N.J.: Princeton U. Press/Bollingen, 1973p* (497 + xx, incl. 17-p. index, 7-p. bibl., 35 illus., 2-p. foreword by Jung).

From an idea conceived during World War II, Harding aims to throw light on the contents and processes of the unconscious "as discovered by Jung," in order "to tame more effectively or even to transform the primitive nature and barbaric repression of human behavior." She discusses sources of psychic energy within the concept of transformation of instinctive drives (sloth and restlessness; want and greed; enmity and friendship; will to dominate and self-respect; and sexuality). She emphasizes that the transformation of energy involves inner conflict, illustrated by the dragon and the hero. This conflict leads to the quest for wholeness that can in turn lead to a reconciliation of opposites as represented by the mandala pattern, contributing to the integration of the personality.

(Bk.revs.: BulAnPsyNY F'48/10:10–15; Mr'48/10:8–14; PsychiQ '48/22:757; SWRev '48/22:314–15; JPastorCare Sum'49/3:19–20; Isis '50/41:137–8; RofRel '50/14:416–20; JRelHealth '63/3:97–8; AmJPsychi '64/120:830; JRelThought '64/21:156–8; PsychiQ '65/39:586; PubW 5F'73/203:91)

The Trickster: A Study in American Indian Mythology, by Paul Radin. (Ger.: *Der göttliche Schelm.* Zurich: Rascher Verlag, 1955.) London: Routledge & Kegan Paul, 1956; New York: Philosophical Library, 1956; New York: Schocken Books, ed.2 1972p* (211 + xxv, incl. 17-p. comm. by Jung, 19-p. comm. by Kerényi).

As a symbol of the unconscious, Radin states, the trickster is one of the oldest mythic expressions of mankind and depicts "man's struggle with himself and with a world into which he has been thrust without his volition and consent." Knowing neither good nor evil yet responsible for both, duping others and always being duped himself, his problem is basically a psychological one. In the psychological commentary by Jung, the archetype of the trickster is characterized as "a collective shadow figure, an epitome of all the inferior traits of character in individuals . . . the figure nearest consciousness." Kerényi's commentary deals with the trickster in relation to Greek mythology.

(Bk.revs.: Blackf '56/37:499; BkRDig '56:762; ChrCen '56/73:1054; NMexQ '56–57/26:408–9; TimesLitSup '56:452; AnnAmAcad '57/309:180–1; IntJPsy-An '57/38:429–30; JAmFolk '57/70:280–1; JAnPsy '57/2:106–11; NEnglQ '57/30:542–4; OregHistQ '57/58:71–2; Person '57/38:443; RofRel '57/21:167–70; SFolkQ '58/22:156–7; WFolk '58/17:135–7; BulMennClin '69/33:257–8; SocSocRes '74/58:455–6)

The Objective Psyche, by Michael Fordham. London: Routledge & Kegan Paul, 1958; New York: Humanities Press, 1958 (214 + vii, incl. 18-p. index).

Fordham's aim in presenting these essays, which are less specialized than those in his 1957 book, *New Developments in Analytical Psychology,* is to compensate for the trend that has neglected studies of theory in personal, ego, and child psychology and has overlooked the importance of the transference in analytical practice. Following his outline of the development and status of Jung's researches, he discusses the concept of the objective psyche; individuation and ego development; problems of the active imagination; Jung's contribution to social psychiatry; individual and collective psychology; analytical psychology and religious experience; and analytical psychology and psychotherapy.

(Bk.revs.: BrJMedPsy '59/32:152; TimesLitSup '59:181; IntJPsy-An '60/41:84–5; JAnPsy '60/5:65–72; BulHistMed '65/39:590)

Complex/Archetype/Symbol in the Psychology of C. G. Jung, by Jolande Jacobi. (Ger.: *Komplex/Archetypus/Symbol in der Psychologie C. G. Jungs*. Zurich: Rascher Verlag, 1957.) London: Routledge & Kegan Paul, 1959; Toronto: McClelland & Stewart, 1959; New York: Pantheon Books (Bollingen Series LVII), 1959; Princeton, N.J.: Princeton U. Press/Bollingen, ed.2 1965; 1971p* (230 + xii, incl. 16-p. index, 11-p. bibl., 3-p. foreword by Jung).

Jacobi's objective is to clarify three basic concepts of Jung's that have given rise to many misunderstandings of his theories. She explains the central, interrelated concepts of complexes (feeling-toned groups of representations in the unconscious that are disturbing the normal course of the psychic association process); archetypes (profound riddles hidden in the depths of the psyche which arrange psychic elements into certain images); and symbols (manifested by archetypes and perceived in some form by the conscious mind). She devotes the second half of the book to a dream of an eight-year-old girl (taken from Jung's collection), given as an illustration of archetypal themes and their psychological interpretation.

(Bk.revs.: JNervMent '58/126:103–4; BrJMedPsy '59/32:303; Domin '59/44:420–2; AmJPsyth '60/14:242–3; CathEdR '60/58:421–3; InwLight Spr'60/n59:37–8; JAnPsy '60/5:73–4; PerkSchTh Wint'60/13:47; Person '60/41:421–2; PsychiQ '60/34:377; Spring '60:151; TimesLitSup '60:850; YaleR '60/ns49:436–7; BkRDig '61:690; PhilosQ '62/12:192; Psychi '62/25:88–92)

Der Archetyp/The Archetype: The Proceedings of the Second International Congress for Analytical Psychology, Zurich, 1962, edited by Adolf Guggen-bühl-Craig. Basel and New York: S. Karger Verlag, 1964 (234 pp.).

The nineteen papers delivered at the second congress of the IAAP, including fourteen in English, bring new aspects and delve more deeply into "the mystery of the human psyche" through analytical psychology. Contributions of authors whose books are in this annotated bibliography are on trinity and quaternity (Edinger); theory of archetypes as applied to child development with particular reference to the self (Fordham); and archetypes of culture (Henderson). Other papers are on the archetype and natural law (Aylward); angels as archetype and symbol (Allenby), archetype as a prognostic factor (Kluger); archetype of separation (Strauss); and adoration of the complex (van Leight-Frank).

(Bk.rev.: JAnPsy '65/10:196–7)

The Reality of the Psyche: The Proceedings of the Third International Congress for Analytical Psychology, Montreux, 1965, edited by Joseph B. Wheelwright. New York: G. P. Putnam's Sons for the C. G. Jung Foundation for Analytical Psychology, 1968*; London: Barrie & Rockliff, 1969 (316 pp.).

The third congress of the IAAP heard eighteen papers on a variety of topics within analytical psychology under the theme of reality of the psyche. Contributions by authors whose books are in this annotated bibliography are on individuation in childhood (Fordham); symbols: content and process (Gordon); reality of the psyche (Harding); fantasy of the "white child" (Hillman); flood dreams (Kluger); and symbols of the *unus mundus* (von Franz).

(Bk.revs.: Quad '68/n2:24–5; InwLight '69/n75:47–8; Spring '69:142; CanPsychiJ '70/15:233; ContemPsy '70/15:348 + 350; JAnPsy '70/15:190–2; UnionSemQR '70/25:251–4)

The Unconscious in Its Empirical Manifestations: With Special Reference to the Association Experiment of C. G. Jung, by C. A. Meier. (Ger.: *Die Empirie des Unbewussten.* Zurich, 1968.) Boston: Sigo Press, 1984*; 1990p* (*The Psychology of C. G. Jung,* vol. 1) (236 + xiv, incl. 10-p. index, 26-p. bibl., 13 illus., 4-p. intro. by Laurens van der Post).

Using a historical approach, Meier's aim is to provide a "conscientious account" of the empirical elements of Jung's psychology as they apply not only to the disturbing effects of the unconscious but to the creative effects as well. His "textbook" aims to follow Jung's original course of development and to leave open those questions which are still really open. He devotes nearly half of the text to the word-association experiment as developed by Jung between 1903 and 1907; he then examines the problem of interrelationships between psychic and physical phenomena ("soul and body"), ending with Jung's theory of complexes.

(Bk.revs.: LibJ '85/109:1678; Choice '85/23:206; BkRDig '86:1092; Chiron '86:211–13; ContemPsy '86/31:356–7; Harvest '86/32:151–2; JAnPsy '86/31:95–6; Quad '86/19n1:79–81; PsyPersp '87/18:138–40)

From Freud to Jung: A Comparative Study of the Psychology of the Unconscious, by Liliane Frey-Rohn. (Ger.: *Von Freud zu Jung: Eine vergleichende Studie zur Psychologie des Unbewussten.* Zurich: Rascher Verlag, 1969/Studien aus dem C. G. Jung-Institut, 19.) New York: G. P. Putnam's Sons for the C. G. Jung Foundation for Analytical Psychology, 1974; New York: Delta Books/Dell, 1976; Boston: Shambhala Publications (A C. G. Jung Foundation/Daimon Book), 1990p (345 + xiii, incl. 23-p. index, 11-p. bibl.).

In this continuation of her paper on "The Beginnings of Depth Psychology" in 1955, Frey-Rohn outlines the basic concepts of Freud and Jung, concentrating on the psychology of the unconscious, in order to gain a more comprehensive understanding of Jung's work. She traces Jung's development "from his initial fascination with Freud's ideas to his gradual liberation from these powerful concepts, leading to a final breakthrough into his own unique

being." Her historical-developmental approach follows Jung from trauma to the feeling-toned complex, from psychic "mechanism" to the total personality, from the personal to the collective contents of the psyche, from the unconscious drive to the collective unconscious, from libido to psychic energy, from the causal to the hermeneutic method, and from sign to symbol.
(Bk.revs.: IsrAnPsychi '71/9:181–2; JAnPsy '71/16:115; Quad '74/n17:53–4; BkRDig '75:439–40; Choice '75/12:292; LibJ '75/100:769–70; LibJBkR '75:400; InwLight '75–76/n86–87:68–71; JAnPsy '76/21:226–7; '79/24:82)

Number and Time: Reflections Toward a Unification of Depth Psychology and Physics, by Marie-Louise von Franz. (Ger.: *Zahl und Zeit.* Stuttgart: Ernst Klett Verlag, 1970.) Evanston, Ill.: Northwestern U. Press, 1974* +p*(Studies in Jungian Thought) (332 + xi, incl. 12-p. index, 15-p. bibl.).

Stimulated by a conjecture of Jung's, von Franz explores the archetypes of the natural numbers as a step into the realization of the unity of psyche and matter. She defines her work in principle as "an attempt to observe the phenomena of number from a new angle, one based on a consideration of the unconscious"; it is not intended to be a study of number symbolism. She concludes that number appears to be the structural key common to matter and psyche, the common ordering factor of both.
(Bk.revs.: LibJ '75/100:134; LibJBkR '75:346; Quad '75/8n1:62–5; Tabl '75/229:505; JAnPsy '76/21:100–1)

The Experience of Introversion: An Integration of Phenomenological, Empirical, and Jungian Approaches, by Kenneth Joel Shapiro and Irving E. Alexander. Durham, N.C.: Duke U. Press, 1975* (180 + xi, incl. 3-p. index, 6-p. bibl.).

In an effort to elucidate Jung's concepts of introversion by reexamining his writings on the subject, Shapiro and Alexander present an experiential formulation of introversion based on a union of newly developing phenomenological approaches and traditional empirical approaches to personality. Data on introversion were obtained by the use of a projective method, the Thematic Apperception Test (TAT).
(Bk.revs.: BkRDig '75:1152; Choice '75/12:918; LibJ '75/100:1332; LibJBkR '75:414; AmJPsychi '76/133:723–4; ContemPsy '76/21:354–5; JPersAssess '76/40:656–7; Psychi '76/39:97–8; JAnPsy '77/22:78–9)

Loose Ends: Primary Papers on Archetypal Psychology, by James Hillman. New York: Spring Publications for the Analytical Psychology Club of New York, 1975p; Dallas: Spring Publications, 1978p; 1986p* (212, incl. end-chap. ref. notes, 3-p. list of works by Hillman).

This miscellany, which Hillman groups under the general topic of archetypal psychology, contains twelve pieces (from lectures, articles, and

essays) published between 1963 and 1974. His themes include study; abandoning the child; nostalgia of the puer aeternus; betrayal; schism; three ways
of failure and analysis; an archetypal model of the masturbation inhibition;
and the psychology of parapsychology. He also discusses theories of archetypal psychology; Plotino, Ficino, and Vico as precursors of archetypal
psychology; Jung on archetypal theory; and methodological problems in
dream research.

(Bk.revs.: LumenVitae '75/30:455; Harvest '76/22:142–4; ContemPsy '89/34:506)

Time: Rhythm and Repose, by Marie-Louise von Franz. London: Thames &
Hudson (Art and Imagination Series), 1978; 1979p*; Magnolia, Mass.:
Peter Smith, 1983 (96, incl. 1-p. bibl., 143 illus.).

Composed of two-thirds pictures and one-third text, this large-format
book presents time as one of the great archetypal experiences of human
beings, which "has eluded all our attempts toward a completely rational
explanation, . . . [and was] originally looked upon as a Deity." Themes,
accompanied by many illustrations, are the stream of events; measuring the
flow of time; time as an aspect or emanation of God; the sun god as the
measure of time; measuring time by the sun; cyclical time; time as a
procession of the gods; linear historical time; evolution; time as rhythm;
measuring time by rhythm; necessity and change; divination; and transcending time.

(Bk.revs.: Parab My'79/4:102 + 104–6; JAnPsy '80/25:295; Quad '80/13n1:107–8)

Dynamics of the Self, by Gerhard Adler. London: Coventure, 1979p; London
and Boston: Coventure, repr. 1990* +p* (177 + xi, incl. 7-p. index, 6-p. ref.
notes).

These eight papers, given as lectures between 1955 and 1976, have the
creative power of the psyche as the common subject underlying all. Following
an introductory essay on basic concepts of analytical psychology, Adler
discusses the dynamics of the self; the logos of the unconscious; ego integration and patterns of the *coniunctio;* the question of meaning in psychotherapy; and depth psychology and the principle of complementarity. He includes
an essay on his personal encounter with Jung and his works.

(Bk.revs.: Harvest '80/26:208–9; BrJPsychi '81/138:445; JAnPsy '81/26:365–7; PsyPersp
'82/13:200–4; Quad '82/15n1:76–8)

Archetypal Psychology: A Brief Account, by James Hillman. (It.: "Psicologia
archetypica" in *Enciclopedia del Novecento,* 1981.) Dallas: Spring Publications, 1983p; 1985p* (92, incl. 18-p. list of works by Hillman).

First named as such by Hillman (1970 issue of *Spring*), archetypal psychology, as distinguished from "analytical" (Jung's) psychology, reflects "the deepened theory of Jung's later work which attempts to solve psychological problems beyond scientific models" and is preferred by Hillman because archetypal psychology "belongs to all cultures, all forms of activity." He explores the topics of image and soul; soul and myth; soul, metaphor and fantasy; soul and spirit; soul-making; polytheistic psychology and religion; psychopathology; the practice of psychotherapy; Eros; and personality theory.

Archetypes: A Natural History of the Self, by Anthony Stevens. (Orig. title: *Archetype*. London: Routledge & Kegan Paul, 1982*.) New York: W. W. Morrow, 1982; New York: Quill Paperback/Morrow, 1983p* (324, incl. 15-p. index, 8-p. bibl., 6-p. gloss.).

Stevens sees "no incongruity between Jung's archetypal hypothesis and the ethological approach to human psychology" and he supports "Jung's assertion that the archetype does not denote an inherited idea, but rather an inherited mode of functioning, [and is] biologically unimpeachable." After his discussion of archetypes in theory, he examines archetypes in practice (the family; the mother; the father; on the frustration of archetypal intent; personal identity and stages of life; archetypal masculine and feminine; and the archetypal energy of the shadow), concluding with a synthesis of his ideas.

(Bk.revs.: BestSell S'82/42:239; BkRDig '82:1291–2; Bklist '82/79:6; BrBkN '82:535; BrJPsychi '82/121:328; Harvest '82/28:171; KirkR '82/50:669–70; LibJ '82/107:1333; LondRBks 16S'82/4:18; NewSoc '82/60:309–10; PubW 4Jn'82/221:62; Resurg S'82/ 94:40–1; Tabl '82/236:961–2; JAdol '83/6:101; JAnPsy '83/28:80–2; PubW 17My'83/ 223:66; TimesLitSup '83:101; BioSci '84/34:587; Chiron '84:191–4; HeythJ '84/25:509– 10; JChildPsy '84/25:499; Quad '84/17:61–4; LuthForum '85/19n3:38–40; SFJInstLib '85/5n4:61–4)

The Family Unconscious: An "Invisible Bond", by E. Bruce Taub-Bynum. Wheaton, Ill., Madras, and London: Quest Books/Theosophical Publishing House, 1984p* (230 + xvi, incl. 4-p. index, 15-p. ref. notes, 2-p. gloss., 2 illus.).

The family unconscious refers to Jung's concept of the collective unconscious as the inherited thought patterns which appear in dreams in the form of archetypes or symbols. Taub-Bynum presents this family network of feeling, images, and energy as a powerful system in a shared field of related phenomena. Drawing on research and practice in biofeedback, his central theme is to reveal the interconnectedness of shared feelings or dreams in the family unconscious as he discusses personally shared affect, energy, and "dreamscape," as well as clinical phenomena of psi material.

(Bk.revs.: JAmSocPsy '86/80:451–4; JMarFamTh '86/12:205–6)

The Book of the Self: Person, Pretext, and Process, edited by Polly Young-Eisendrath and James A. Hall. New York and London: New York U. Press, 1987*; 1988p* (468 + xvi, incl. 6-p. index, 4 illus.).

Delivered at a conference on "Self" in 1983, these twenty-one papers by twenty-three authors represent a variety of disciplines in the humanities and provide various vantage points on the concept of the self. Major themes, as indicated in the subtitle, are self as person (self and necessity; self and consistency); self as pretext (self and meaning; self and death; self and gender); and self in process (self and experience; self and unity; self and terminology; self and transcendence). There are essays by Jungian analysts on the actions of the self (Fordham); Jacques Lacan, postmodern depth psychology and the birth of the self-reflexive subject (Paul Kugler); and the terminology of ego and self from Freud(ians) to Jung(ians) (Joseph Redfearn). The editors provide an introduction (on the study of self) and conclusion (on ways of speaking of self), stating that "The self is experienced as having and being certain kinds of states and images that are claimed as one's own in waking and dreaming."

(Bk.revs.: PsyPersp '88/19:348–50; ContemPsy '89/34:410; JAnPsy '89/34:199–200; SFJ InstLib '90/9n2:5–17)

C. G. Jung and the Archetypes of the Collective Unconscious, by Robin Robertson. New York: Peter Lang Publ., 1987* (American University Studies VIII—Psy., 7) (250 + xxi, incl. 10-p. index, 10-p. bibl., 9-p. foreword by Win Sternlicht).

Aiming to show that Jung's psychology is an expression of a "new paradigm, which believes that the world of matter and the world of the psyche are ultimately manifestations of a unitary cosmos," Robertson traces the development of ideas in the birth and death of the Renaissance ideal (discussing scientific method; Kant's legacy; experimental psychology; hypnosis; clinical psychology; and Freud). He then describes the psychology which Jung developed from its background to the model of the psyche and the shadow, anima/animus, Self, alchemy as a model of psychological development, and the mysterious unconscious. He concludes with a discussion of Gödel's proof, the roots of modern math, and self-referential systems, stating that Gödel's ideas support Jung's position.

(Bk.rev.: Gnosis '88/n6:51)

Mythos and Logos in the Thought of Carl Jung: The Theory of the Collective Unconscious in Scientific Perspective, by Walter A. Shelburne. Albany: State

U. of New York Press, 1988* +p* (180 + xi, incl. 8-p. index, 10-p. bibl., 21-p. ref. notes).

Shelburne attempts to answer the question of how the scientific elements of Jung's writings can be reconciled with the extrascientific aspects. He begins with a reconstruction of Jung's views of the collective unconscious and then critiques the psychoanalytic as well as theological criticisms of the theory of archetypes and of Hillman's archetypal psychology. He discusses scientific evidence for the existence of archetypes and how theories fit in with modern evolutionary biology.

(Bk.revs.: SciTechBkN Jn'88/12:1; Choice '89/26:879; UPrBkN Mr'89/1:4; ContemPsy '90/35:282–3)

The Archetype of the Unconscious and the Transfiguration of Therapy, by Charles Poncé. Berkeley, Calif.: North Atlantic Books, 1990 (120 pp.).

Demons of the Inner World: Understanding Our Hidden Complexes, by Alfred Ribi. Boston & London: Shambhala Publications, 1990p (231 + xi, incl. 7-p. index, 9-p. bibl., 7 illus.).

This book serves as both a survey of the principles of Jungian psychology and a practical introduction to the complexes, which Ribi describes as contemporary counterparts of the demons and spirits that plagued the lives of ancient and medieval peoples.

The Symbol of the Dog in the Human Psyche: A Study of the Human-Dog Bond, by Eleanora M. Woloy. Wilmette, Ill.: Chiron Publications, 1990p (Chiron Monograph Series; vol. 4) (88 + xiv, incl. 2-p. index, 5-p. bibl., 13 illus., 3-p. foreword by James Hall).

Woloy examines the symbol of the dog from her own personal experience with her pets, including one who was in her office while she saw analysands, and from her study of the association of the dog with the Earth Goddess. She concludes with her understanding of a Jungian view of the archetypal nature of the human-dog bond, particularly of the feminine aspect of the connection, suggesting the human's instinctive religious need for kinship to nature.

5 Psychological Types

Jung is well known for his early development of a theory of psychological types, which was stimulated by his contact and final confrontation with Freud. His terminology is widely accepted, and his system of classification of psychological and personality types has been adopted, modified, and used extensively, especially in the Myers-Briggs Type Indicator.

This chapter consists of comprehensive and detailed work by Jung on psychological types and the dictionary of analytical psychology (which is extracted from *Psychological Types*), followed by nineteen books by other authors (including three cross-referenced works), arranged chronologically.

Provost: *A Casebook: Applications of the Myers-Briggs Type Indicator* (See chapter 11, "Jungian Analysis") [p. 330]
Quenk: *Psychological Types and Psychotherapy* (See chapter 11, "Jungian Analysis") [p. 331]
Sharp: *Personality Types* [p. 72]
Spoto: *Jung's Typology in Perspective* [p. 73]
Stolorow & Atwood: *Faces in a Cloud* [p. 70]
von Franz & Hillman: *Lectures on Jung's Typology* [p. 68]

Psychological Types; or, The Psychology of Individuation, by C. G. Jung. (Ger.: *Psychologische Typen*. Zurich: Rascher Verlag, 1921.) London: Kegan Paul, Trench, Trubner, 1923 (International Library of Psychological, Philosophical and Scientific Method); New York: Harcourt Brace, 1923; London: Routledge & Kegan Paul, rev. 1971*; Princeton, N.J.: Princeton U. Press/ Bollingen, 1971*; 1976p* (CW 6) (608 + xv, incl. 22-p. index, 15-p. bibl.).

Based upon his many years of practical experience as a doctor and practicing psychotherapist, Jung's psychological typology is a "critical psychology dealing with the organization and delimitation of psychic processes that can be shown to be typical." Before arriving at the general description of the types (chapter 10), he devotes 323 pages to the problem of types in the history of classical and medieval thought, Schiller's ideas on the type problem, Apollonian and Dionysian opposites, and the type problem in human character, poetry (107 pp.) psychopathology, aesthetics, modern philosophy, and biography. The description of types and definitions of terms occupy 147 pages. He distinguishes eight basic types: extraverted thinking, extraverted feeling, extraverted sensation, extraverted intuitive, introverted thinking, introverted feeling, introverted sensation, and introverted intuitive. Appended are four short papers on psychological typology (published 1913–36).

(Bk.revs.: BkRDig '23:273–4; Bkman My'23/57:27; BrJMedPsy '23/3:122–8; EnglR '23/ 36:436–9; JAbnPsy '23/18:167–80; JPhilos '23/20:636–40; Mind '23/ns32:493–5; Nation '23/117:440; Nature '23/111:88; NewRep '23/36:287–8; NewStates 14Ap'23/ 21:22+; NYTimesBkR 10Jn'23:9+; Spec '23/131:54; TimesLitSup '23/117:448; HibbJ '24/22:399–401; JNervMent '24/60:221–4; Monist Ja'24/34:96–111; PsyanR '24/ 11:184–90; CanForum '25/5:371–2; AmJPsy '27/38:651–4; TimesLitSup '71:1489; AmJPsychi '72/129:244; BrJPsychi '72/120:462; Choice '72/9:438; JAnPsy '72/17:212– 14; BrJMedPsy '73/46:201; BehInfTec '86/5:291)

Dictionary of Analytical Psychology, by C. G. Jung. London and New York: Ark Paperbacks/Routledge & Kegan Paul, 1987p* (179, incl. 5-p. index, 5-p. bibl.).

Extracted from volume 6 *(Psychological Types)*, annotated immediately above, this paperback consists of chapters 10 ("Psychological Types") and 11 ("Definitions") and the epilogue. Consequently, it is not a dictionary in the ordinary sense of the word because the first seventy-eight pages consist of descriptions of the eight psychological types. This "dictionary" contains definitions of fifty-seven Jungian concepts, arranged alphabetically, from *abstraction* to *will,* the longest being *symbol* (7 pp.) and *soul/psyche.*
(Bk.rev.: BrJPsychi '88/152:157)

*   *   *   *   *

Manual: A Guide to the Development and Use of the Myers-Briggs Type Indicator, by Isabel Briggs Myers and Mary H. McCaulley. (Orig. *Myers-Briggs Type Indicator Manual.* Princeton, N.J.: Educational Testing Service, 1962; Palo Alto, Calif.: Consulting Psychologists Press, 1975p) Palo Alto, Calif.: Consulting Psychologists Press, ed.2 1985p* (309 + x, incl. 14-p. bibl.).

Implementing Jung's theory of psychological types by ascertaining certain basic differences in the way individuals prefer to use perception and judgment, Myers and McCaulley provide in this extensive manual information on Jung's theory that is essential for understanding the Myers-Briggs Type Indicator (MBTI). Following an introductory overview of Jung's theory and a discussion of the nature and uses of the indicator, they offer a guide for administering and scoring the MBTI, understanding the theory behind it and the sixteen types, and initial interpretation and verification of the results. They discuss practical applications for the use of type in counseling, career development, and education. Reliability and validity of the indicator are examined, and a data-filled appendix provides scores from widespread sources.
(Bk.revs.: BehInfTec '86/5:291; ContemPsy '86/31:819)

Lectures on Jung's Typology, by Marie-Louise von Franz and James Hillman. New York: Spring Publications for the Analytical Psychology Club of New York, 1971p; Dallas: Spring Publications, rev. printing 1979p* (Seminar Series, 4) (150, incl. 2-p. bibl., 5 illus.).

The first half of the book contains von Franz's analysis of the inferior function; the second half consists of Hillman's analysis of the feeling function. Following a general characterization of the inferior function of the personality, von Franz deals with the four irrational psychological types identified by Jung (extraverted sensation, extraverted intuitive, introverted sensation, introverted intuitive) and with the four rational types (extraverted thinking, extraverted feeling, introverted thinking, introverted feeling) in terms of each one's inferior counterpart, thereby revealing the role of the inferior function in psychic development. Hillman deals with one of the four functions, namely, feeling, defining it primarily as involving the use of evaluation rather than emotion. He discusses inferior feeling and negative feelings, feeling and the mother-complex, feeling and the anima, and education of the feeling function.

Personality Typing: Uses and Misuses, by Doris Webster Havice. Washington, D.C.: University Press of America, 1977p (171 + iv, incl. 17-p. bibl.).

Studying three recent theories of personality types (of Jung, William Sheldon, and Erich Fromm), Havice weighs their usefulness for moral philosophy. She shows in each of the three cases "how the type concept was elaborated, what problems this elaboration involves, and what further conclusions it leads to, especially for practical or moral philosophy." She concludes that no thoroughly satisfactory formulation of personality types is yet available, but is impressed most by Fromm's typology. She feels that Jung's typology "can be understood only in relation to various metaphysical and epistemological premises which have not been made sufficiently clear," and she doubts the applicability of the types to the classification of normal people.

Psychetypes: A New Way of Exploring Personality, by Michael Malone. New York: E. P. Dutton, 1977; New York: Simon & Schuster, 1980p (260 + xii).

Malone explains that his study of personality types is based on a theory of experiential typology developed by Harriet Mann and others at Princeton, which in turn had as its immediate source Jung's classification of psychological types. He recognizes eight basic psychetypes, namely, four "continuous" (thinking territorial, thinking aethereal, feeling volcanic, feeling oceanic) and four "discontinuous" (sensation volcanic, sensation territorial, intuitive oceanic, intuitive aethereal). He describes the book as a "how-are" rather than a "how-to" book, aimed at understanding "how we are alike, and how we are different."
(Bk.revs.: KirkR '76/44:1333; LibJ '77/102:1284; LibJBkR '77:448; PsyToday Mr'77/ 10:102; PubW 13D'77/210:57; Quad '78/11n1:94–6)

Please Understand Me: Character and Temperament Types, by David Keirsey and Marilyn Bates. Del Mar, Calif.: Prometheus Nemesis Books, ed.3 1978p*; 1984p* (210, incl. 2-p. bibl.).

Drawing on Jung's "invention of psychological types" and Isabel Myers's modification that pioneered a method of measuring type which is "personally significant" to any individual, Keirsey and Bates group the sixteen Myers-Briggs types into four temperaments. Temperament, in turn, is discussed in relation to mating, children, and leaders (including teachers). As they state it, "the point of this book is that people are different from each other" and there is a profound need to understand different temperaments and to value them. Included is a type test that the reader can take. A 41-page appendix consists of "portraits" of the sixteen Myers-Briggs types.

Faces in a Cloud: Subjectivity in Personality Theory, by Robert D. Stolorow and George E. Atwood. New York and London: Jason Aronson, 1979* (217, incl. 9-p. index, 5-p. bibl., end-chapter ref. notes).

Examining the personality theories of Freud, Jung, Wilhelm Reich, and Otto Rank, researchers Stolorow and Atwood analyze the topic of subjectivity. The 37 pages (chapter 3) devoted to Jung consist of an analysis of the psychological origin of Jung's personality theory in terms of secret, critical, and formative experiences, which is preceded by an examination of Jung's theory in terms of the collective unconscious and archetypes, self-dissolution, the disunited man, and individuation. They believe that Jung's contributions to understanding human experience are important and best understood when stripped of metaphysical mental constructs.

(Bk.revs.: Choice '79/16:727; ContemPsy '79/24:905–6; LibJ '79/104:1466; LibJBkR '79:381–2; BulMennClin '80/44:395; JAnPsy '80/25:296–8; JNervMent '80/168:190; Psychi '80/43:1788–81; PsyanR '80/67:147)

People Types and Tiger Stripes: A Practical Guide to Learning Styles, by Gordon Lawrence. Gainesville, Fla.: Center for Applications of Psychological Type, 1979p; ed.2 1982p* (119 + viii).

Following a long search for practical and effective ways of matching instruction to basic psychological differences in students, Lawrence adopts an approach based on Jung's ideas about psychological types with practical modifications by Myers. He considers the patterns of mental habits (patterns of "people types") as fundamentally important in the planning and execution of teaching styles and presents techniques through exercises and case studies that teachers can use to help students learn, as well as a model for introducing type theory into a school system. Included is a 19-p. reprint of Myers's *Introduction to Type.*

Gifts Differing, by Isabel Briggs Myers with Peter B. Myers. Palo Alto, Calif.: Consulting Psychologists Press, 1980* +p* (217 + xiii, incl. 3-p. bibl.).

The theme of this book is "the belief that many problems might be dealt with more successfully if approached in the light of C. G. Jung's theory of psychological types." Myers's aim is to devise a system that would reflect not only one's preference for extraversion or introversion but also one's preferred kind of perception and decision making. She extends Jung's theory by adding an auxiliary process to the dominant process, and she examines the effects of preferences on personality, providing detailed descriptions of the sixteen types resulting from various combinations of the preferences. Her practical implications of type include the use of opposites in understanding conflicts and the relation of type to marriage, early learning and learning styles, occupation, and the task of growing.

(Bk.rev.: SFJInstLib '81/3n1:37–54)

Dichotomies of the Mind: A Systems Science Model of the Mind and Personality, by Walter Lowen. London and New York: Wiley Interscience Publication/ John Wiley & Sons, 1982* (314 + xii, incl. 5-p. index, 3-p. bibl., nearly 400 illus.).

Lowen's efforts to understand the diversity of personalities led him to a combination of various theories about the mind, Jung's concepts, and the principles of information theory and systems engineering. Written in the language of mathematics, computers, and psychology, he presents static as well as dynamic models to understand the functioning of both the brain (processor of information) and the mind ("programmer"). The overall conceptual model has value for research in artificial intelligence and linguistic simulation, personality development, testing and career counseling, management, and creativity. He says that those interested in the psychology of personalities and the theories of Jung may want to concentrate mainly on the chapters dealing with profile interpretation, interpersonal relations, and creativity.

(Bk.revs.: HumSysManag '83/4:52–4; JMindBeh '83/4:431–2)

Insights: Understanding Yourself and Others, by Carolyn Marie Mamchur. Toronto: Ontario Institute for Studies in Education, 1984p* (232 + viii, incl. 2-p. bibl., 67 illus.) (OISE Occasional Papers, 23).

Drawing from experiences of directing workshops that always "centre around the concepts of personality functioning described by . . . Jung as his theory of psychological types," Mamchur weaves together stories, vignettes, photographs, cartoons, and paintings in order to illustrate the values of typology for individuals. She explores the significance of typology as a guide to personal identity and self-development, communication skills, career choice, and usefulness in business, marriage, and school, using the Myers-Briggs Type Indicator to characterize individuals. Chapters dealing with the four functions are entitled "Seeing Is Believing" for sensing, "In Other

Words" for intuition, "A Rose Is a Rose Is a Rose" for feeling, and "So What?" for thinking.
(Bk.revs.: Choice '85/23:165; EdLeader '85/43:93)

A Tool for Understanding Human Differences: How to Discover and Develop Your Type According to Dr. C. G. Jung and Dr. William Sheldon, by Tyra Arraj and Jim Arraj. Chiloquin, Ore.: Tools for Inner Growth, 1985p* (178, incl. 4-p. index, 10-p. bibl., 14 illus.).

In their attempt to understand what makes people different and to develop a tool that will identify significant differences, the Arrajes combine the typologies of William Sheldon's body and temperament types with Jung's psychological types, using the familiar Jungian terminology of eight types. In discussing the future of typology, they examine some of the literature on relationships between physical and psychological types, which suggest relations between physical illnesses and body types and between psychological illness and physical types.
(Bk.rev.: JMindBeh '85/6:447–8)

It Takes All Types!, by Alan W. Brownsword. San Anselmo, Calif.: Baytree Pub. Co. for Human Resources Management Group, 1987p* (118, incl. 15 illus.).

Brownsword introduces readers to both Jung's theories of psychological type as interpreted by Briggs Myers and to Keirsey's idea about temperament. Their relationship provides different and useful insights into human personality as "the continual ebb and flow of a personality between type and temperament." After outlining the preferences (attitudes of extraversion and introversion and the four functions of perceiving and judging), he provides detailed descriptions of the sixteen MBTI types that are grouped in Keirsey's four temperament types. The combinations are then related to each other and to the world of work as well as to the process of human development.

Personality Types: Jung's Model of Typology, by Daryl Sharp. Toronto: Inner City Books, 1987p* (Studies in Jungian Psychology by Jungian Analysts, 31) (123, incl. 4-p. bibl.).

Intending to illustrate the complexity of the model of psychological types and some of its practical implications, Sharp explains Jung's method ("not a critique nor a defence"). He views Jung's typology as a tool for psychological orientation, a way of understanding oneself as well as problems that arise between individuals. In his "close adherence to Jung's expressed views" he presents the theory and model of functions and attitudes and the role of the unconscious, as well as descriptions of the eight types. He concludes by

discussing the reasons for a typology and the topics of type testing and typology and the shadow. Appended are an article on "the clinical significance of extroversion and introversion" by H. K. Fierz and a thoughtful essay on how Jung's model of typology might look in everyday life as "a dinner party with the types."
(Bk.rev.: Harvest '88–89/34:175–7)

Type Talk: Or, How to Determine Your Personality Type and Change Your Life, by Otto Kroeger and Janet M. Thuesen. New York: Tilden Press Book/ Delacorte Press, 1988p* (293 + xv, incl. 3-p. bibl.).

The background of the book is the work of Katherine Briggs and Isabel Briggs Myers and beyond that, the work of Jung. As principal users and adaptors of the Myers-Briggs Type Indicator in consultations with individuals, families, corporations, and governments, Kroeger and Thuesen aim to "help people understand their differences and deal with them in a constructive way." They describe the functional preferences and temperaments and relate their "typewatching" to business, friends and lovers, and parent-child relationships.

A Practical Guide to C. G. Jung's Psychological Types, W. H. Sheldon's Body and Temperament Types, and Their Integration, by Tyra Arraj and James Arraj. Chiloquin, Ore.: Inner Growth Books, 1988p* (*Tracking the Elusive Human,* vol. 1 (176, incl. 2-p. index, 2-p. bibl., 40 illus.).

This is a complete revision of *A Tool for Understanding Human Differences* (Arraj and Arraj, 1985), which combined the typologies of Jung and Sheldon. Here the authors cover the basics of recognition and development of Jung's psychological types, following with discussions of types in marriage and of the challenge of the fourth function (inferior, or least-developed). They then present Sheldon's basic components of physique and temperament types, suggesting definite connections between body types and psychological types. Part Two is devoted to answering thirty typical questions about types, and an appendix offers notes on types from the point of view of development, along with hints about situations one might encounter on the journey into the inner psyche.

Jung's Typology in Perspective, by Angelo Spoto. Boston: Sigo Press, 1990 +p (200 pp.).

6 Human Development and Individuation

The concept of individuation, a process of differentiation having as its goal the development of the unique individual personality, plays a large role in Jung's psychology. It entails the recognition of both one's psychological strengths and limitations and is practically the same as the development of consciousness out of the original identity with the primordial unconscious state.

The process of individuation involves raising consciousness through the recognition of the operation of archetypes, including the archetype of the Self in its guiding function, as well as the conflict of opposites. It may encompass such methods or modes as synchronicity, astrology, *I Ching*, tarot, or yoga.

Nearly 120 books are listed in this subject category, plus twenty-five others cross-referenced from other subjects. As distinguished from the preceding chapter on the psyche, this topic deals primarily with consciousness, though dynamics of the unconscious are involved.

Following the six works by Jung, books by other authors are arranged chronologically in order to provide historical perspective. Nearly half of these were published after 1980.

Jung: *The Development of Personality* [p. 79]
———: *The Integration of the Personality* [p. 78]
———: *Psychology and Education* [p. 80]
———: *Synchronicity* [p. 79]
———: *The Undiscovered Self* [p. 80]
———: *The Undiscovered Self with "Symbols and the Interpretation of Dreams"* [p. 80]
Jung & Pauli: *The Interpretation of Nature and the Psyche* [p. 79]
Abrams (ed.): *Reclaiming the Inner Child* [p. 122]

Adler: *The Living Symbol* [p. 87]
Armstrong: *The Radiant Child* [p. 110]
Begg: *Myth and Today's Consciousness* [p. 108]
Bertine: *Human Relationships* [p. 86]
Bianchi: *Aging as a Spiritual Journey* [p. 103]
Bly: *A Little Book on the Human Shadow* [p. 118]
Bolen: *The Tao of Psychology* [p. 98]
Breaux: *Journey into Consciousness* [p. 120]
Brennan & Brewi: *Mid-Life Directions* (See chapter 9, "Religion and Jung's Psychology") [p. 235]
Brewi & Brennan: *Celebrate Mid-Life* (See chapter 9, "Religion and Jung's Psychology") [p. 242]
_____: *Mid-Life* (See chapter 9, "Religion and Jung's Psychology") [p. 228]
Bryant: *Jung and the Christian Way* (See chapter 9, "Religion and Jung's Psychology") [p. 230]
_____: *The River Within* [p. 97]
Burt: *Archetypes of the Zodiac* [p. 116]
Campbell: *The Hero with a Thousand Faces* [p. 84]
Campbell & Roberts: *Tarot Revelations* [p. 100]
Carotenuto: *Eros and Pathos* [p. 113]
_____: *The Vertical Labyrinth* [p. 103]
Clift & Clift: *The Hero Journey in Dreams* [p. 117]
Colegrave: *By Way of Pain* [p. 116]
Cox: *History and Myth* [p. 86]
_____: *Jung and St. Paul* (See chapter 9, "Religion and Jung's Psychology") [p. 209]
Dione: *Jungian Birth Charts* [p. 118]
Edinger: *The Bible and the Psyche* [p. 111]
_____: *The Christian Archetype* [p. 112]
_____: *The Creation of Consciousness* [p. 107]
_____: *Ego and Archetype* [p. 92]
_____: *Encounter with the Self* (See chapter 10, "Creativity and Jung's Psychology") [p. 278]
Fordham: *Children as Individuals* [p. 82]
_____: *Explorations into the Self* [p. 108]
Frey-Rohn: *Friedrich Nietzsche* [p. 107]
Gardner: *The Rainbow Serpent* [p. 122]
Goldbrunner: *Individuation* (See chapter 3, "Jung's Psychology") [p. 37]
Grant, Thompson & Clark: *From Image to Likeness* [p. 106]
Greene: *The Astrology of Fate* [p. 107]
_____: *The Outer Planets and Their Cycles* (See chapter 12, "Civilization in Transition") [p. 361]

McGann: *The Journeying Self* [p. 109]
_____: *Journeying Within Transcendence* [p. 117]
Meier: *Consciousness* [p. 94]
Miller, W.: *Make Friends with Your Shadow* [p. 102]
Moon: *Dreams of a Woman* [p. 105]
Mooney: *Storming Eastern Temples* [p. 95]
Moore: *The Planets Within* [p. 104]
Moreno: *Jung, Gods, and Modern Man* (See chapter 9, "Religion and Jung's Psychology") [p. 214]
Neumann: *The Child* [p. 87]
_____: *The Origins and History of Consciousness* [p. 84]
Newman: *The Tarot: A Myth of Male Initiation* [p. 106]
Nichols: *Jung and Tarot* [p. 99]
Oakes: *The Stone Speaks* [p. 115]
O'Connor: *Understanding the Mid-Life Crisis* [p. 102]
Olds: *Fully Human* (See chaper 8, "Feminine and Masculine Psychology") [p. 173]
Olney: *Metaphors of Self* (See chapter 1, "Life of C. G. Jung") [p. 11]
O'Neill: *The Individuated Hobbit* [p. 98]
Parker: *Return: Beyond the Self* [p. 98]
Pauson: *Jung the Philosopher* [p. 120]
Pearson: *The Hero Within* [p. 111]
Peat: *Synchronicity* [p. 115]
Phillips et al. (eds.): *The Choice is Always Ours* [p. 83]
Progoff: *Depth Psychology and Modern Man* [p. 86]
_____: *Jung, Synchronicity, and Human Destiny* [p. 93]
_____: *The Symbolic and the Real* [p. 88]
Redfearn: *My Self, My Many Selves* [p. 110]
Reed: *Emergence* [p. 99]
Richards: *The Hero's Quest for the Self* (See chapter 10, "Creativity and Jung's Psychology") [p. 278]
Roberts: *The Original Tarot and You* [p. 91]
Robertson: *After the End of Time* [p. 122]
Rudhyar: *Astrology and the Modern Psyche* [p. 94]
Ryce-Menuhin: *The Self in Early Childhood* [p. 118]
Sanford: *King Saul, the Tragic Hero* [p. 110]
_____: *The Kingdom Within* (See chapter 9) [p. 214]
_____: *The Man Who Wrestled with God* [p. 93]
Sharp: *Dear Gladys* [p. 120]
_____: *The Secret Raven* [p. 100]
_____: *The Survival Papers* [p. 119]
Sibbald: *The Footprints of God* [p. 117]
Sidoli: *The Unfolding Self* [p. 121]
Sidoli & Davies (eds.): *Jungian Child Psychotherapy* (See chapter 11, "Jungian Analysis") [p. 344]

Singer: *Energies of Love* (See chapter 8, "Feminine and Masculine Psychology") [p. 177]

Slusser: *From Jung to Jesus* [p. 111]

Smith: *Jung's Quest for Wholeness* (See chapter 9, "Religion and Jung's Psychology") [p. 248]

Stein: *In MidLife* [p. 106]

Storr: *Solitude: A Return to the Self* [p. 119]

Thompson: *Journey toward Wholeness* [p. 104]

van Waveren: *Pilgrimage to the Rebirth* [p. 96]

von Franz: *Individuation in Fairy Tales* [p. 95]

_____: *On Divination and Synchronicity* [p. 99]

_____: *Projection and Re-Collection* [p. 96]

Westman: *The Structure of Biblical Myths* (See chapter 9, "Religion and Jung's Psychology") [p. 231]

Wheelwright: *The Death of a Woman* [p. 102]

Wickes: *The Inner World of Childhood* [p. 81]

_____: *The Inner World of Choice* [p. 88]

_____: *The Inner World of Man* [p. 81]

Wilhelm: *The I Ching, or Book of Changes* [p. 85]

Willeford: *Feeling, Imagination, and the Self* [p. 113]

Williams: *Border Crossings* [p. 101]

Wing: *The I Ching Workbook* [p. 97]

Wolff-Salin: *No Other Light* (See chapter 9) [p. 237]

_____: *The Shadow Side of Community* [p. 119]

Wood: *Men Against Time* [p. 104]

Woolger: *Other Lives, Other Selves* [p. 114]

Young-Eisendrath & Hall: *The Book of the Self* (See chapter 4, "The Psyche") [p. 64]

_____: *Jung's Self Psychology* [p. 122]

The Integration of the Personality, by C. G. Jung. New York and Toronto: Farrar & Rinehart, 1939; London: Kegan Paul, 1940 (313, incl. 7-p. index, 1-p. bibl.).

Except for the initial essay on the meaning of individuation, which was written in English for this volume, the other five are lectures delivered by Jung at Eranos Meetings in Ascona, Switzerland, from 1932 to 1936. The introductory essay was rewritten and appears under the title of "Conscious, Unconscious, and Individuation" in the *Collected Works* (vol. 9, pt. 1). The longest essays are the ones on dream symbols of the process of individuation (109 pp.) and on the idea of redemption in alchemy (76 pp.). Others deal with archetypes of the collective unconscious, development of the personality, and a case study in the process of individuation.

(Bk.revs.: BkRDig '39:524; Bks 3D'39:18; SciBkClubR '39/10:4; BulAnPsyNY F'40/2:sup8; JAbnSocPsy '40/35:579–82; Listen '40/24:245–6; NYTimesBkR 21Ja'40:6; JEdSoc '40/13:568; TimesLitSup '40:341; AmSocR '41/6:289; BrJPsy '41/31:272; IntJPsy-An '41/22:172–4; PsyanQ '41/10:652–6; RofRel '41/5:232–4)

The Interpretation of Nature and the Psyche, by C. G. Jung and W. Pauli. (Ger.: *Naturerklarung und Psyche.* Zurich: Rascher Verlag, 1952/ Studien aus dem C. G. Jung-Institut, IV.) New York: Pantheon Books (Bollingen Series LI), 1955; London: Routledge & Kegan Paul, 1955 (247 + vii, incl. 5-p. index, 6 ill.).

Jung's long essay on "Synchronicity: An Acausal Connecting Principle" occupies two-thirds of this collaborative work, with Nobel Prize physicist Wolfgang Pauli's "The Influence of Archetypal Ideas on the Scientific Theories of Kepler" occupying the remaining third. In considering ideas and experiences that had puzzled him for more than twenty years in regard to the applicability of the causal principle in psychology, Jung presents the concept of synchronicity to mean "the simultaneous occurrence of a certain psychic state with one or more external events which appear as meaningful parallels."

(Bk.revs.: JAmSocPsy '54/48:27–38; Blackf '56/37:93; JRelThought '56/13:159–60; RofRel '56/21:84; Tabl '56/207:134; BrJPhilSci '57/8:73–6; BulMennClin '57/21:223; JPastorCare '58/12:56–8; TimeLitSup '58:515; Philos '59/34:259–62)

Synchronicity: An Acausal Connecting Principle, by C. G. Jung. London: Routledge & Kegan Paul, 1972 + p; Princeton, N.J.: Princeton U. Press/Bollingen, 1973p*; London: Ark Paperbacks, 1985p* (135 + vii, incl. 9-p. index, 6-p. bibl., 3 illus.).

Extracted from volume 8 of the *Collected Works,* this paperback includes the title essay, which originally appeared in *The Interpretation of Nature and the Psyche* (annotated above), along with an earlier essay, "On Synchronicity," that Jung gave as a lecture at the 1951 Eranos conference. Jung attributes the original stimulus for his idea of psychic synchronicity to his acquaintanceship with Einstein in Zurich between 1909 and 1913.

(Bk.revs.: JPsyTheol '74/2:324–5; Tabl '85/129:1288–9; PsyMed '86/16:481)

The Development of Personality, by C. G. Jung. New York: Pantheon Books (Bollingen Foundation), 1954*; London: Routledge & Kegan Paul, 1954; 1984p*; Toronto: McClelland & Stewart, 1954; Princeton, N.J.: Princeton U. Press/Bollingen, 1981p* (CW 17) (223 + viii, incl. 19-p. index).

The title of this collection of eight essays comes from an essay that appears here and in *The Integration of the Personality,* and that originated as a 1932 lecture. Other contributions deal with the psychology of childhood and education (psychic conflicts in a child; the gifted child; child development and education; analytical psychology and education; and the significance of the unconscious in individual education). He regards the psychology of parents and of educators to be of great importance in a child's growth to consciousness. The final chapter is an analysis of marriage as a pyschological relationship.

(Bk.revs.: Blackf '55/36:31; BrJEdStud '55/3:180–4; BrJPsy '55/46:149; Person '55/ 36:409; QueensQ '55/62:133–4; RofRel '55/19:155–7; SocSocRes '55/39:278; Thought '55/30:149; PsyanR '56/43:252–3)

The Undiscovered Self, by C. G. Jung (Ger.: "Gegenwart und Zukunft," in *Schweizer Monatshefte,* supp. XXXVI:12, 1957.) London: Routledge & Kegan Paul, 1958; 1974p*; Boston and Toronto: Atlantic Monthly/Little, Brown, 1958; 1971p; New York: Mentor Books/New American Library, 1959p; 1974p* (115 + viii).

Prompted by conversations with Carleton Smith, the National Arts Foundation director, Jung wrote this book at the age of eighty. He analyzes the topics of the plight of the individual in modern society; religion as the counterbalance to mass-mindedness; the position of the West on the question of religion; the individual's understanding of himself; the philosophical and the psychological approach to life; self-knowledge; and the meaning of self-knowledge. His concern for the survival of our civilization focuses on the quality of the individual, which requires understanding of the true nature of the individual human being and the gap between the conscious and unconscious aspects of the psyche.

(Bk.revs.: AmJPsychi '57/113:669–70; AmJPsyth '58/12:890–1; AmSchol '58/27:512+; BkRDig '58:587–8; BksAbroad '58/32:25; Bkmark '58/17:195; BulMennClin '58/22:199: CathWorld '58/187:468–9; Critic Jy'58/16:43; LibJ '58/83:1926; Month '58/20:219–24; NewStates '58/55:538–9; NYTimesBkR 20Ap58:18; PastorPsy Jn'58/9:61–2; SatNight 24My'58/73:26–8; SatR 7Jn'58/41:20–1; TimesLitSup '58:241; Frontier '59/2:64–5; JAnPsy '59/4:63–7; QueensQ '59/66:336)

The Undiscovered Self with "Symbols and the Interpretation of Dreams," by C. G. Jung. Princeton, N.J.: Princeton U. Press/Bollingen, 1990 +p (166, incl. intro. by William McGuire).

Psychology and Education, by C. G. Jung. Princeton, N.J.: Princeton U. Press/ Bollingen, 1969p (151 + vii, incl. 13-p. index).

Extracted from volume 17 (*The Development of Personality*) of the *Collected Works,* this paperback contains four essays on psychic conflicts in a child (1909 lecture, revised 1946), child development and education (1923 lecture, 1928 publication), analytical psychology and education (1924 lectures, 1936 publication), and the gifted child (1942 lectures, 1943 publication). More than half of the volume consists of Jung's three lectures on analytical psychology and education, in which he gives case studies of childhood disturbances and emphasizes that such psychogenic disorders of childhood often are caused by an unsatisfactory psychological relationship between the parents.

* * * * *

The Inner World of Childhood: Study in Analytical Psychology, by Frances Wickes. New York and London: D. Appleton, 1927; New York: Appleton-Century-Crofts, rev. 1930; 1955; rev. 1966; New York: Signet Books/New American Library, 1968p; London: Coventure, 1977p*; Englewood Cliffs, N.J.: Spectrum Books/Prentice-Hall, 1978p; Boston: Sigo Press, ed.3 1988* +p* (304 + xxiii, incl. 9-p. index, 7-p. intro. by Jung).

From many years of experience in child psychology, Wickes gives, as Jung says in the introduction, a "true picture of the difficulties that actually occur in the upbringing of children." Within a framework of analytical psychology, she discusses the topics of the influence of parental difficulties upon the unconscious of the child; three illustrations of the power of the image projected by a parent; early relationships; adolescence; the acceptance of consciousness; psychological types as a key to problems; imaginary companions; fear; sex; dreams; and a correlation of dreams and fantasy.

(Bk.revs.: BkRDig '27:806–7; Bklist '27/24:99–100; NewRep 7S'27/52:78; NYTimesBkR 4S'27:14; Surv '27/59:396; WilsonLibBul Oc'27/23:221; JAbnSocPsy '28/23:255–6; SatRLit '28/5:146; SocServR '28/2:663–8; AmJPsy '29/41:680; PsyanR '29/16:117–18; ReligEd '29/24:796–7; BkRDig '66:1295; CanMentH Jy-Ag'66/14:42–3; Choice '66/3:722; Nation '67/204:91–2; Parents Ag'66/41:71)

The Inner World of Man, by Frances G. Wickes. New York: Farrar & Rinehart, 1938; New York: Henry Holt, repr. 1948; Toronto: Oxford U. Press, 1948; London: Methuen, 1950; New York: Frederick Unger, 1959; Boston: Sigo Press, ed.2 1988* +p* (313, incl. 32 pp. of 79 drawings and paintings).

Drawing upon some twenty years of analytic practice, Wickes illustrates the concepts of Jung's analytical psychology through the workings of the unconscious in the apparently ordinary human life. She discusses the inner world and the appearance of images; parental images; ego; persona; shadow; anima; animus; the self; dreams of mother and anima; dream analysis in later life; fantasy; and visions. She illustrates her ideas by means of numerous drawings and paintings that she feels reflect the inner world.

(Bk.revs.: BkRDig '38:1036; NYTimesBkR 4D'38:42; SatRLit 17D'38/19:10; PsyanQ '39/ 8:266–9; ReligEd '39/34:128; Surv '39/75:60; JAbnSocPsy '43/38:299; AmJPsy '48/ 61:461; PsychiQ '48/22:378; SocSocRes '48/33:68; AmJPsychi '49/105:944; InwLight Spr'49/n34:27–8; JPastorCare Spr'49/3:38–9; AmJPsyth '50/4:345–7; BulMennClin '50/ 14:115–16; BrJMedPsy '51/24:146; BrJPsy '51/42:202; HibbJ '51/49:412–13)

Paracelsus: Selected Writings, edited by Jolande Jacobi. (Ger.: *Theophrastus Paracelsus: Lebendiges Erbe.* Zurich: Rascher Verlag, 1942.) London: Routledge & Kegan Paul, 1951; Toronto: McClelland & Stewart, 1951; ed.2 1958; New York: Pantheon Books (Bollingen Series XXVIII), 1951; ed.2 1958*; Princeton, N.J.: Princeton U. Press/Bollingen, ed.2 1988p* (347, incl. 9-p. bibl., 10-p. key to sources, 21-p. gloss., 148 illus., 2-p. foreword by Jung).

Paracelsus (c. 1494–1541), a Swiss physician and alchemist about whom Jung was invited to deliver two addresses at the 1941 Paracelsus Festival in Einsiedeln, is presented in this book by Jacobi as a solitary genius of "luminous inner unity." After presenting a brief description of his life and work, she selects essential and permanently relevant features of his contributions under the headings of man and the related world; man and his body; man and works; man and ethics; man and spirit; and man and fate; and ends with God as the eternal light.

(Bk.revs.: NYTimesBkR 29Ap'51:14; PsychiQ '51/25:350; TimesLitSup '51:664; BrJMedPsy '52/25:159–60; BrJPsy '52/43:316–17; Isis '52/43:64; NMexQ '52/22:235–9; PsysomMed '53/15:269–70; RofRel '53/17:170–2)

Children as Individuals, by Michael Fordham. (Orig. title: *The Life of Childhood: A Contribution to Analytical Psychology.* London: Kegan Paul, Trench, Trubner, 1944.) London: Hodder & Stoughton, 1969; New York: G. P. Putnam's Sons for C. G. Jung Foundation for Analytical Psychology, 1970 (233, incl. 9-p. index, 9-p. bibl., 11 illus.).

During the quarter-century between his introduction of child psychology to analytical psychologists and the new edition of this book, Fordham noted a change in the acceptance of analytical psychotherapy with children. Based on Jung's work but drawn largely from Fordham's own experience, this work analyzes children's play, dreams, and pictures, along with the family and the social setting, and sees them as basic factors in the application of the theory of archetypes and the ego to the processes of growth during childhood.

(Bk.revs.: BrBkNews '44:97; BrJPsy '44/34:100–1; TimesLitSup '44:596; BulAnPsyNY N'45/7:2–3; BrJPsychi '70/117:456–7; Choice '71/8:1092; JAnPsy '71/16:211, 212; JChildPsy '71/12:319–20; AmJArtTh '76/16:43)

Creation Continues: A Psychological Interpretation of the Gospel of Matthew, by Fritz Kunkel. New York: Charles Scribner's, 1947; Waco, Tex.: Word Books, rev. by Elizabeth Kunkel and Ruth Spafford Morris, 1973p; New York and Mahwah, N.J.: Paulist Press, 1987p* (286, incl. 3-p. bibl., 5-p. life of Kunkel, 3-p. intro. by John Sanford for 1987 ed.).

Kunkel, attempting to integrate the psychologies of Alfred Adler and Jung, presents Matthew's gospel from a psychological point of view, trying to understand the effect the image of Jesus' personality had on his disciples and "through Matthew on ourselves." He aims to stimulate individual, genuine religious discoveries, and he urges "dynamic reading" as the "mobilization of all the conflicting forces in the reader's soul." After the prelude (Matthew and the evolution of consciousness), he analyzes the story under the headings of the gate; the chart of initiation (sermon on the mount); the way; the crossroads; the new way; the new chart; and the new gate (inner gate, outer gate, and beyond the gate).

(Bk.revs.: BkRDig '47:511; ChrCen '47/64:433–4; Chman 1Ap '47/161:16; CrozerQ '47/24:357–8; IliffR '47/4:95–6; JBibRel '47/15:253; KirkR 1F'47/15:65; LibJ '47/72:159; UnionSemQR My'47/2:43–5; AnglTheolR '48/30:73–4; JRelThought '48/5:102–3; Person '48/29:325; DrewGate '49/20:40–1; ReligEd '74/69:512–13; JPastorPsy '89/43:99)

The Choice Is Always Ours: The Classical Anthology on the Spiritual Way, edited by Dorothy Berkley Phillips, Elizabeth Boyden Howes, and Lucille M. Nixon. (Orig. subtitle: *An Anthology on the Religious Way.* New York: Richard Smith, 1948; New York and Evanston, Ill.: Harper & Row, rev. and enlarged edn. 1960.) Wheaton Ill.: Re-Quest Books/Pyramid Publications for Theosophical Publishing House by arrangement with Harper & Row, rev. and abridged, 1975p; San Francisco: Harper & Row, 1989p* (493, incl. 4-p. index of authors, 15-p. subject index, 5-p. bibl.).

With its central theme of "the Way to ultimate meaning," this anthology of writings chosen from psychological, religious, philosophical, poetical, and biographical sources is comprised of short contributions by more than 180 authors. It is dedicated to Jung, Kunkel, Henry Sharman, and Sheila Moon. The largest number of excerpts are from Jung (21), Kunkel (15), and Jesus (15). Other authors include thirteen whose books are in this annotated bibliography. As a mosaic of human insight, the anthology moves from the Way (searching and finding, implications, and progression) to techniques (prayer and meditation, psychotherapy, fellowship, and action) and outcomes (inward renewal and outward creativity).

(Bk.revs.: BkRDig '48:661; BulAnPsyNY D'48/10:10–11; ChrCen '48/65:481; Chman 15N'48/162:16; JBibRel '48/16:246; JRelThought '48/6:96–8; NYTimesBkR 23My'48:20; PsychiQ '48/22:375–6; CrozerQ '49/26:90–1; ReligEd '49/44:124–5;

PastorPsy S'51/2:62–3; PsyanR '52/39:109; '53/40:387; JPastorCare '53/7:184; InwLight Spr'61/n61:51–2; ChrCen '90/107:162)

The Hero with a Thousand Faces, by Joseph Campbell. New York: Pantheon Books (Bollingen Series XVII), 1949; London: George Allen & Unwin, 1950; Cleveland: World, 1956; New York: Meridian Books, 1956p; Princeton, N.J.: Princeton U. Press/Bollingen, ed.2 1968*; 1972p*; 1990p; London: Sphere Books, 1975p; London: Paladin Books/Grafton Books, 1988p* (416 + xxiii, incl. 24-p. index, 45 illus.).

As reflected in the title, Campbell's concern is with a composite hero, who may be considered an archetypal figure in folklore and religion as well as a symbol of one's own eternal struggle for identity. He focuses more on the similarities than the differences among numerous mythologies and religions. He talks first about the "monomyth" in relation to myth and dream, tragedy and comedy, the hero and the god, and the world navel. Then he interprets the adventure of the hero in terms of departure, initiation, and return, and he analyzes the cosmogonic cycle which involves emanations, virgin birth, transformations of the hero, and dissolutions. He also discusses the relation of myth to society and the hero today.

(Bk.revs.: BkRDig '49:135; BulAnPsyNY '49/11n5:7; Commonw '49/50:321; Nation '49/ 169:17–18; NYHerTrib 24Jy'49:7; NYTimesBkR 26Ja'49:23; NYorker '49/25:113; PartisR '49/16:952; SFChron 11S'49:20; JAmFolk '50/63:121; SWRev '50/35:14; ExposTimes '69/80:305–6; Folk '69/80:156–7; PsyPersp '90/22:185–6)

The Origins and History of Consciousness, by Erich Neumann. (Ger.: *Ursprungs-geschichte des Bewusstseins.* Zurich: Rascher Verlag, 1949.) London: Routledge & Kegan Paul, 1954, 1982p*; Toronto: McClelland & Stewart, 1954; New York: Pantheon Books (Bollingen Series XLII), 1954; New York: Torchbook/Harper & Row, 1962p; Princeton, N.J.: Princeton U. Press/ Bollingen, 1970 +p* (493 + xxiv, incl. 31-p. index, 14-p. bibl., 31 illus., 2-p. foreword by Jung).

Applying the analytical psychology of Jung to his study of the origin and development of personality, Neumann focuses primarily on internal, psychic, and archetypal factors rather than external factors. He approaches the subject first by a study of the mythological stages in the evolution of consciousness, utilizing the creation myth and the hero myth. Then he outlines the psychological states in the development of personality from original unity to the separation of the systems and to the balance and crisis of consciousness. He also examines centroversion and the stages of life.

(Bk.revs.: AmJPsyth '53/7:180; JPastorCare '53/7:181–2; CrossCurr '54/4:378; NYTimesBkR 8Ag'54:17; Blackf '55/36:591; JPastorCare '55/9:172–3; QueensQ '55/ 62:283; RRelRes '55/20:90–2; TimesLitSup '55:353; IntJPsy-An '56/37:499; InwLight

Spr '56/n50:40–2; JRelThought '56/14:85–7; Person '56/37:331–2; JNervMent '61/
133:180–1; BulMennClin '62/26:265–6; ChrCen '70/87:392; JOttoRank '70/5:52; PubW
16Mr'70/197:58)

The I Ching, or *Book of Changes,* translated by Richard Wilhelm. New York:
Pantheon Books (Bollingen Series XIX:2), 1950; ed.2 1961; Toronto: Mc-
Clelland & Stewart, 1950; London: Kegan Paul, Trench, Trubner, 1951;
London: Routledge & Kegan Paul, ed.2 1965; ed.3 1968*; 1983p*; Princeton, N.J.: Princeton U. Press/Bollingen, ed.3 1967*; Toronto: Saunders,
ed.3 1968; London: Arkana/Penguin Books, 1988p* (740 + lxii, incl. 9-p.
gen. index, 2-p. hexagram index, 19-p. foreword by Jung).

· Considering the influence that the Book of Changes has had in China for
3,000 years and the interest that it is evoking in Western civilization,
Sinologist Wilhelm put the technique of the oracle into practice and interested
Jung in this singular book. Jung used it for more than thirty years because it
seemed to him to be of "uncommon significance as a method of exploring
the unconscious." Among his remarks in the long foreword, Jung states that
the *I Ching* insists on self-knowledge throughout; it is appropriate only for
thoughtful, reflective persons. He notes that what Westerners call coincidence
seems to be the chief concern of the Chinese mind rather than causality; and
Jung relates this to his synchronicity principle, which considers some coincidences of events as meaning something more than mere chance.

(Bk.revs.: BulAnPsyNY D'50/12:9–14; JRelThought '51/17:99; Listen '51/46:653;
TimesLitSup '51:563; HibbJ '52/50:191–3; RRelRes '52/17:99; PacAff '68/41:429–30;
TimesLitSup '68:381; NYTimesBkR 18My'69:7)

Journey into Self: An Interpretation of Bunyan's Pilgrim's Progress, by M. Esther
Harding. London and New York: Longmans, Green, 1956; London: Vision,
1958; New York: David McKay, 1963 (301 pp.).

Harding offers this psychological interpretation of Bunyan's classic as
an expression of the search for wholeness that confronts every individual
through archetypal patterns. She focuses on the inner region of subjective
experience and uses the allegory of the Pilgrim's quest to demonstrate that it
is not only the psychically sick who need to be reunited with the realm of the
inner life but that all of us have this need. Her chapters of the journey are
entitled "After the Slough of Despond," "From the House of the Interpreter
to the Cross," "The Valley of Humiliation," "Christian Finds a Friend,"
"The Adventures of Christian and Hopeful," and "The Journey Nears Its
End," followed by an interpretation of the pilgrimage in modern psychological terms.

(Bk.revs.: BkRDig '56:408; Bklist '56/53:170; LibJ '56/81:2319; Time 5N'56/68:116+;
Encoun '58/19:230–3; InwLight Spr'58/n21:45–7; JAnPsy '58/3:79–80; JRelThought '58/

15:176–7; LitPsy '58/8:25–6; Person '59/40:108; WallStJ 17F'65/145:14; LibJ 15Ap'85/ 110:77)

Human Relationships: In the Family, in Friendship, in Love, by Eleanor Bertine. (Ger.: *Menschliche Beziehungen: Eine psychologische Studie.* Zurich: Rhein Verlag, 1957.) New York and London: Longmans, Green, 1958; New York: David McKay, 1963 (237 + vii, incl. 2-p. foreword by Jung).

Drawing on thirty-five years of working in the analytic consulting room, Bertine uses her training with Jung to analyze relationships between the individual and members of the family, friends, the group, the opposite sex, and the marriage partner. Her years of experience provided "the opportunity to follow the events over a long period of time to see how the stories end." (Bk.revs.: KirkR '57/25:675; LibJ '57/82:2526; BkRDig '58:98; Bklist '58/54:432; Inw-Light Fall-Wint'58–59/n56:41–4; WilsonLibB '58/54:306)

Depth Psychology and Modern Man: A New View of the Magnitude of Human Personality, Its Dimensions and Resources, by Ira Progoff. New York: Julian Press, 1959; ed.2 1969; New York: McGraw-Hill, 1973p* (277 + xii).

Progoff aims to develop techniques and disciplines "for *evoking* the potentials of personality" through programs for inner growth as formulated in his *Intensive Journal,* a specially structured psychological workbook. His "new view of the magnitude of human personality" traces the history of depth psychology in the context of the transformation of the unconscious toward the wholeness of the individual. As models of modern men he presents Jan Smuts (natural evolution), Edmund Sinnott (biology), Wolfgang Pauli (physics), Herbert Read (art and civilization), Jacob Bronowski (science and art), and Friedrich Kekulé (chemistry), emphasizing their creative work and drawing upon Jung's depth psychology that provides an affirmatively and scientifically grounded conception of human life that can be used constructively. (Bk.revs.: JHumRel '59/8:151–3; LibJ '59/84:2068; NYTimesBkR 16Ag'59:12; BkRDig '60:1091; PerkSchTh Wint'60/13:47; AmJPsyth '61/15:490–1; ContemPsy '74/19:678)

History and Myth: The World Around Us and the World Within, by David Cox. London: Darton, Longman & Todd, 1961 (166 + xv).

Discussing the individual's "need for assurance about the connection between the inner and outer worlds," Cox states that the Christian mythos includes all the great themes of all myths and thereby expresses the deepest facts about the psyche; therefore, the confluence of myth and history in the life of Jesus can provide the individual with the assurance needed for an effective life. He analyzes the individual's inner world from the points of view of myth and ritual, myth and the mind, and Jung's model of the psyche.

The Living Symbol: A Case Study in the Process of Individuation, by Gerhard Adler. London: Routledge & Kegan Paul, 1961; Toronto: McClelland & Stewart, 1961; New York: Pantheon Books (Bollingen Series LXIII), 1961* (473 + xii, incl. 21-p. index, 16-p. bibl., 32 illus.).

In presenting a detailed study of a case of claustrophobia, Adler aims to show clearly the stages of the individuation process which Jung has described. Considered to be a typical case of neurosis and its analytical treatment, the basic pattern of the integrative process is revealed to show the inner logic and meaningfulness with which unconscious imagery unfolds. Adler analyzes the creative function of the unconscious as revealing the wealth and vitality of symbols from which gradually emerges a pattern of inner order. The material comprises more than one hundred fifty dreams, along with thirty-two paintings and drawings by the patient to illustrate the symbolism of dreams associated with the process of integration.

(Bk.revs.: LibJ '61/86:2952; AmJPsyth '62/16:529–30; BkRDig '62:8; BrJPsy '62/53:209–11; BulMennClin '62/26:271–2; Harvest '62/8:99–100; JAnPsy '62/7:162–7; RMeta '62/15:522; Spring '62:160–1; TimesLitSup '62:76)

The Child: Structure and Dynamics of the Nascent Personality, by Erich Neumann. (Ger.: *Das Kind: Struktur und Dynamik der werdenden Persönlichkeit.* Zurich: Rhein Verlag, 1963.) London: Hodder & Stoughton, 1973; New York: G. P. Putnam's Sons for the C. G. Jung Foundation for Analytical Psychology, 1973; New York: Colophon Book/Harper & Row, 1976p; London: Maresfield Lib./H. Karnac, 1988p*; Boston: Shambhala, 1990p (221, incl. 5-p. index, 7-p. ref. notes).

In describing and analyzing the structure and dynamics of the emerging personality of the child, Neumann begins with a discussion of the primal relationship of child to mother in terms of psychic nourishment and the need for formation of a positive-integral ego that is able to assimilate and integrate even negative or unpleasant qualities of both outer and inner worlds. The development of the child's ego-Self relationship results in disturbances of the primal relationship, whose nature and consequences Neumann presents in a context of transition from the psychological matriarchate to the psychological patriarchate. Neumann did not live to complete the work. If he had, it would have included a discussion of the stage of development at which the female child requires separate treatment.

(Bk.revs.: LibJ '73/98:3009; LibJBkR '73:444; BkRDig '74:885; Bklist '74/70:459; Choice '74/10:1938–9; JAnPsy '74/19:218–19; JPastorCare '74/28:211)

The Inner World of Choice, by Frances G. Wickes. New York: Harper & Row, 1963; Englewood Cliffs, N.J.: Prentice-Hall by arrangement with the C. G. Jung Institute of San Francisco, 1976p; London: Coventure, 1977p*; Boston: Sigo Press, ed.3 1988* +p* (318+ xxii, incl. 6-p. bibl.).

Basing this work on seminars given during 1954–55 at the C. G. Jung Institute in Zurich, Wickes enlarged the material at Jung's request and presents the thesis that "modern man is unaware of the myth that lives itself within him, of the image, often invisible, that dynamically impels him toward choice." She studies the mysterious relationship of consciousness to the unconscious as it reveals a dynamic power which acts to enlarge and enrich the growing ego consciousness through integration of the non-ego unconscious forces. She discusses the gift of choice of consciousness; early choices of good and evil; enemies of choice; opposition and interplay; the masculine and feminine principles; woman in man and man in woman; interplay and relatedness; journey toward wholeness; and faith beyond fear.
(Bk.revs.: AmJPsyth '63/17:324–5; InwLight Fall-Wint'63/n65:57; JRelHealth '63/3:103–4; ContemPsy '64/9:282–3; TheolLife '64/7:163–4; AmSchol '65/34:502–8; JAnPsy '65/10:200)

The Symbolic and the Real: A New Psychological Approach to the Fuller Experience of Personal Existence, by Ira Progoff. New York: Julian Press, 1963; New York: McGraw-Hill, 1973p*; London: Coventure, 1977* +p*; Magnolia, Mass.: Peter Smith, 1983 (234 + xv, incl. 8-p. bibl.).

In his aim to expand and stimulate from deep psychic levels the process of growth that is inherent in everyone, Progoff presents the principle and methodology of psyche-*evoking* in contrast to psycho*analysis*. Psyche-evoking is directed toward "drawing forth the potentials of personality," something that Progoff points out is the essence of the Socratic method. His non-analytic approach to the depth dimension seeks to elicit energy and guidance from symbols by using such procedures as his "Twilight Imagining."
(Bk.revs.: BulMennClin '64/28:228; InwLight Sum-Fall'64/n66:55–6; LibJ '64/89:273; PastorPsy S'64/15:61–2; JSciStudRel '66/5:322–3; JPastorPsy '66/20:118; JLegalEd '86/36:274)

The Wisdom of the Serpent: The Myths of Death, Rebirth and Resurrection, by Joseph L. Henderson and Maud Oakes. New York: George Braziller, 1963; Toronto: Ambassador, 1963; New York: Collier, 1963p; New York: Collier/Macmillan, 1971p; Princeton, N.J.: Princeton U. Press, 1990p (262 + xxiv, incl. 8-p. index, 7-p. bibl., 50 illus.).

Two-thirds of the text of this joint work is comprised of Oakes's treatment of the myths of death, rebirth, and resurrection, with death and rebirth being viewed as cosmic patterns and cycles of nature, along with an analysis of initiation as a spiritual education and psychic liberation. Jungian analyst Henderson, following his introductory comments on the fear of death, also deals with death and rebirth (the dance of Shiva) and cycles of nature (the descent of Innana), as well as with initiation (the magic flight). He then concludes with the topic of resurrection as rebirth in the process of individuation, presenting this perennial problem in terms of observation and analysis of patients' dreams and fantasies.

(Bk.revs.: AmAnth '64/66:961; BkRDig '64:551; JAnPsy '64/9:188–9; VaQR '64/40:xlii; Etc '65/22:519–20; JAmFolk '65/78:353–4)

The "I" and the "Not-I": A Study in the Development of Consciousness, by M. Esther Harding. New York: Pantheon Books (Bollingen Series LXXIX), 1965*; Princeton, N.J.: Princeton U. Press/Bollingen, 1970; 1973p* (244 + x, incl. 14-p. index, 6-p. bibl., 6 illus.).

This work is based on lectures given in St. Louis, San Francisco, and New York in 1963. In it, Harding introduces Jung's concept of ego ("I") development and his theory of personality structure, which includes both the personal part of the unconscious as well as the collective unconscious. She explores the stages by which consciousness develops, including identification with family, projections onto persons of the same sex, and projections onto persons of the opposite sex, along with an analysis of anima and animus and of the "Not-I" of the inner world that includes archetypal figures that stimulate both instinctual and spiritual experiences.

(Bk.revs.: Bklist '65/62:8; Choice '65/2:434; LibJ '65/90:2863; PhilosPhen '65/26:458–9; CrossCurr '66/16:363–5; JAnPsy '67/12:78–9; JNervMent '67/145:342–4)

The Way of Individuation, by Jolande Jacobi. (Ger.: *Der Weg zur Individuation*. Zurich: Rascher Verlag, 1965.) London: Hodder & Stoughton, 1967; New York: Harcourt, Brace & World, 1967; New York: Meridian Books/New American Library, 1983p* (177 + ix, incl. 7-p. index, 7-p. bibl.).

Jacobi signalizes the way of individuation as the keystone which distinguishes Jung's psychology from other schools. Understanding it as the growing self-awareness of the individual and society, she contrasts the difference between the natural growing process and that which is deepened by analytical insights that are experienced consciously. She defines the two main phases of the individuation process (first and second halves of life) and their stages and discusses the relations of ego to Self and the "central, archetypal, structural elements of the psyche." Her analysis of conscious realization and integration of potentialities in the individual leads to a discussion of the religious

function of the psyche and the conscience as related to the dual nature of human beings.
(Bk.revs.: BkRDig '67:665; JAnPsy '67/12:177–8; KirkR '67/35:243; LibJ '67/92:1169; LibJBkR '67:474; NYTimesBkR 20Ag'67/72:16; PastorPsy Oc'67/18:62–4; PubW 6F'67/191:73)

Masks of the Soul, by Jolande Jacobi. (Ger.: *Die Seelenmaske: Einblicke in die Psychologie des Alltags.* Olten and Freiburg im Breisgau, Switzerland: Walter Verlag, 1967.) Grand Rapids, Mich.: William Eerdmans, 1976p; London: Darton, Longman & Todd, 1976; 1977p* (94 pp.).

Jacobi intends the four essays as "only spotlights to illumine some of the dark corners of the soul" and thereby to be used as a guide to everyday life. In her essays on "What is Psychology For?," "Man in His Mask" (persona mediating inner and outer worlds), "People without Love," and "Man between Good and Evil," she hopes, as a result of her long experience as a Jungian analyst, to stimulate reflection and self-understanding by many who feel lost in life and fail to understand themselves and others.
(Bk.revs.: JAnPsy '77/22:367–9; ChrScholR '78/8:191–2)

The Myth of Meaning in the Work of C. G. Jung, by Aniela Jaffé. (Ger.: *Der Mythus vom Sinn im Werk von C. G. Jung.* Zurich: Rascher Verlag, 1967.) London: Hodder and Stoughton, 1970; New York: G. P. Putnam's Sons for the C. G. Jung Foundation for Analytical Psychology, 1971; New York and Baltimore: Penguin Books, 1975p; Zurich: Daimon Verlag, 1984p* (186, incl. 8-p. bibl., 20-p. ref. notes).

Jaffé's aim is to show what kind of "meaning" Jung contrasted with the "meaninglessness of life" that he noted in about one-third of his cases who were not suffering from any clinically definable neurosis and that in most instances went hand in hand with a sense of religious emptiness. Jaffé presents and interprets Jung's theories of the unconscious and the archetypes; the hidden reality (the unconscious below consciousness); inner experience; individuation; good and evil; *Answer to Job*; individuation of mankind; man in the work of redemption; the one reality (inner unity); and the individual. She ends with a discussion of Jung's myth of meaning as the myth of consciousness that values the unconscious and its creative power.
(Bk.revs.: JAnPsy '68/13:80; IsrAnPsy '69/7:119–20; BkRDig '71:683–4; Choice '71/8:1094; LibJ '71/96:3145; LibJBkR '71:428; Theol '71/74:333–4; BrJMedPsy '72/45:94; JAnPsy '72/17:98–9; RBksRel(W) 15F'72/1:1–2; ContemPsy '75/20:954–5)

Thresholds of Initiation, by Joseph L. Henderson. Middletown, Conn.: Wesleyan U. Press, 1967; 1979p* (260 + ix, incl. 8-p. index, 8-p. bibl., 11-p. ref. notes).

Basing his study on Jung's theory of archetypes, and in particular on the archetype of initiation, Henderson presents this work after thirty years of testing the theory in his analytical practice. Considering archetypes as predictable patterns of conditioning from within that bring about certain basic changes, he traces parallels between individual psychological self-searching and rites which marked initiation in times past. His topics include the uninitiated; return of the mother; remaking a man; the trial by strength; the rite of vision; thresholds of initiation; initiation and the principle of ego-development in adolescence; and initiation in the process of individuation. (Bk.revs.: AmAnth '68/70:1193–4; AmJPsychi '68/125:858–9; Choice '68/5:1048; JAnPsy '68/13:161–4; Spring '68:139; ContemPsy '71/16:86, 88)

The Original Tarot and You, by Richard Roberts. (Orig. title: *Tarot and You.* Hastings-on-Hudson, N.Y.: Morgan & Morgan, 1971.) San Anselmo, Calif.: Vernal Equinox Press, 1987p* (296 + xiv, incl. 20 illus.).

Aiming to demonstrate that tarot cards can be a valuable psychological tool for self-knowledge and self-transformation, Roberts has created a "Jungian spread," a layout of cards whose reading reveals past patterns and future probabilities as well as present-moment realities that demonstrate conscious-unconscious relationships. He interprets the Self as the central and organizing entity of the psyche that, during the process of shuffling the cards, may be organizing them from the unconscious. He uses the free-association method of psychology, in which the meaning is created by the individual. Four case examples of readings using the Jungian spread cover seventy-two pages, by far the longest treatment of the seven methods presented. (The other methods are the ancient Celtic method, the magic seven spread, the wish spread, the pyramid spread, the three sevens, and the yes-no spread.)

Striving towards Wholeness, by Barbara Hannah. New York: G. P. Putnam's Sons for the C. G. Jung Foundation for Analytical Psychology, 1971; Toronto: Longmans, Green Canada, 1971; London: Allen & Unwin, 1973; Boston: Sigo Press, 1987* +p* (316 + xiv, incl. 4-p. bibl., 5-p. foreword by Vernon Brooks in 1987 edn.).

Stimulated by the interest shown in her first lecture in 1931 on the writings of the Brontë sisters and many lectures and seminars given subsequently on the Brontës and several other writers, Hannah eventually wrote this book to illustrate the importance of the individuation process. She points out that the process is unusually clear in the Brontës' writings and was visible in their lives as well. Following two introductory chapters in which she uses Jungian theory to set up the psychological terms of her theme, Hannah then illustrates the unconscious attempt of individuals to regain the wholeness of human nature, using as examples the work of Stevenson (*Jekyll and Hyde*), Mary Webb (*Precious Bane*), and the Brontë children (*Jane Eyre, Villette, Agnes Grey, Wildfell Hall, Wuthering Heights*). Her study of individuation in literature characterizes the urge toward wholeness as an attempt to integrate both negative and positive elements of the individual psyche.

(Bk.revs.: Harvest '72/18:75–7; JAnPsy '72/17:224–5; RBksRel(W) 15F'72/1:1–2; Engl '73/22:118–19; TimesLitSup 11My'73:638; InwLight Fall'74/n85:43–6)

Ego and Archetype: Individuation and the Religious Function of the Psyche, by Edward F. Edinger. New York: G. P. Putnam's Sons for the C. G. Jung Foundation for Analytical Psychology, 1972; Harmondsworth and New York: Pelican/Penguin Books, 1973p* (304 + xv, incl. 8-p. index, 69 illus.).

Edinger's theme is the conscious encounter between the ego and archetypal symbols of the collective unconscious in which the ego becomes increasingly aware of its dependence upon and its origin from the archetypal psyche. He presents this as Jung's process of individuation and views it in the context of the religious function of the psyche with the goal being the reconciliation of science and religion. In analyzing the process of individuation, Edinger defines the stages of development as the inflated ego, the alienated ego, and the encounter with the Self; and he interprets individuation as being the search for meaning as a way of life. In this way he sees Christ as a paradigm of the individuating ego. He concludes with a discussion of the way the blood of Christ and the philosopher's stone are symbols of the goal of individuation.

(Bk.revs.: PubW 13M'72/202:43; BkRDig '73:343; BkWorld 8Ap'73/7:13; Choice '73/ 10:536; JAnPsy '73/18:173–5; LibJ '73/98:552; LibJBkR '73:434; Quad '73/n13:18–21; TheolStud '73/34:343–4; AmJPsychi '74/131:1425–6; Commonw '74/99:513; JPastorPsy '74/28:211; PsyPersp '74/5:74–7; ReligEd '74/69:95–6; Intell '75/103:529–31; Psychi-Forum '75/5:39–40)

The Choicemaker, by Elizabeth Boyden Howes and Sheila Moon. (Orig. title: *Man, the Choicemaker.* Philadelphia: Westminster Press, 1973.) Wheaton, Ill.: Quest Books/Theosophical Publishing House, 1977p* (221, incl. 3-p. index, 8-p. ref. notes).

From each one's experience of more than twenty-five years as analytical psychotherapists in the Jungian tradition and as seminar leaders in the combined fields of religion, analytical psychology, art, and mythology, Howes and Moon evolved a new integration of religion and depth psychology. In considering the eternal question "Man, where art thou? Where are you going?," they examine the (sometimes difficult) need to confront the inner world and search for wholeness, as well as the need to see egocentricities in concrete ways. They also describe techniques for self-discovery in the process of making choices, such as hearing the body's truth, dialoguing between the inner self and the outer self, withdrawing projections, analyzing dreams, meditation, and prayer.

(Bk.revs.: KirkR '73/41:895; ChrCen '74/91:106; JPastorPsy '74/28:212; LuthQ '74/26:360–1; InwLight Fall-Wint '75–76/n86–87:71–4; Encoun '76/37:108–9; JBibLit '76/95:661–2)

Jung, Synchronicity, and Human Destiny: C. G. Jung's Theory of Meaningful Coincidence, by Ira Progoff. (Orig. subtitle: *Noncausal Dimensions of Human Experience,* New York: Julian Press, 1973; New York: Dialogue House, 1973p; New York: Delta/Dell Publ. Co., 1975p.) New York: Julian Press, 1987p* (176, incl. 4-p. bibl., 3 illus.).

The starting point of Progoff's inquiry is that, if one considers the complexity of an infinite universe, basic levels of understanding can be achieved by a number of interpretive principles. He examines in a large, philosophical perspective Jung's hypothesis of the principle of synchronicity as an acausal relationship that complements the laws of causality by including nonphysical as well as physical phenomena that have noncausal but meaningful relationships. He associates Jung's work with that of Teilhard de Chardin, Leibniz, and Einstein.

(Bk.revs.: BkRDig '74:984; Choice '74/11:1028; ContemPsy '74/19:617–18; JPastorPsy '74/28:211–12; LibJ '74/99:340; LibJBkR '74:416; Quad '74/n17:54; ClinSocWkJ '75/3:316; InwLight '75–76/n86–87:71–4)

The Man Who Wrestled with God: Light from the Old Testament on the Psychology of Individuation, by John A. Sanford. King of Prussia, Penn.: Religious Publishing Co., 1974; New York and Ramsey, N.J.: Paulist Press, 1981p; rev. 1987p* (140 + iii, incl. 5-p. secular index, 3-p. biblical index).

By presenting and analyzing four ancient, archetypal stories from the Old Testament, Sanford illustrates the unfolding of psychological development and spiritual awareness as examples of Jung's principle of individuation, the process of personal growth toward wholeness. The first, which lends itself to the title of the book, is the story of Jacob's cunning, and his suffering, transformation, and reconciliation; the second is of Joseph's arrogance, and his suffering, transformation, and reconciliation; the third is of Moses' killing of the Egyptian, and his exile and transformation to reluctant hero; and the fourth is an interpretation of Adam and Eve in their painful process of psychological development. Appended is a summary of the psychologies of Jung and of Fritz Kunkel, in which Sanford elaborates Jung's concept of individuation and fills in gaps from Kunkel's thinking.

(Bk.revs.: LibJ '74/99:2859; LibJBkR '74:441; RBksRel(W) Oc'74/4:3; PsyPersp '75/6:100–2; ReligEd '75/70:462; InwLight Fall '77/n90:50–1; BestSell '81/41:270–1; Commonw '81/108:573; LibJ '81/106:670; JPsyTheol '83/22:55–8)

Consciousness, by C. A. Meier. (Ger.: *Bewusstsein,* 1975?.) Boston: Sigo Press, 1989*; 1990p *(The Psychology of C. G. Jung,* vol. 3) (128 + x, incl. 6-p. index, 4-p. bibl., 4-p. ref. notes, 15 illus.).

Observing that there is no publication that compiles Jung's views on consciousness, Meier here undertakes the task. He begins with a discussion of the paradox that one's ego observes one's own consciousness as subject *and* object and then proceeds in the first part to present the phenomenology of consciousness (as a system; interaction with both external world and internal world; limitation of time; tension of attentiveness; narrowness; memory), the structure and dynamics of consciousness, and the localization of the actual seat of the conscious. In the second part he deals with adaptive mechanisms and basic functions of consciousness, using Jung's major work on psychological types as a "compass" orientating the four functions and two attitudes and at the same time bringing in the role of the compensatory function and the attitude of the unconscious.

Astrology and the Modern Psyche: An Astrologer Looks at Depth Psychology, by Dane Rudhyar. Davis, Calif.: CRCS Publications, 1976p (182, 6 illus., incl. birth charts of Freud, Adler, Jung, and Kunkel).

Rudhyar's interest in "astro-psychology" began in 1932 with a reading of Wilhelm's *The Secret of the Golden Flower* (containing Jung's commentary). His aim in this book is to bring deeper psychological insights to people attracted to the field of astrology, devoting the first part to depth psychology's pioneers (Freud, Adler, and Jung), for whom he provides birth charts. His emphasis on Jung involves Jung's positive approach to the unconscious, his approach to personality and the astrological way to self-realization, and the use of anima and animus in Jungian analysis with reference to the moon symbol in astrology. He also discusses Kunkel and "we-psychology," Moreno and psychodrama, Assagioli and psychosynthesis, the Self, the astro-psychological approach to self-education and self-realization, astrology psychoanalyzed, mysteries of sleep and dreams, the great turning points in human life, and meeting crises successfully.

Saturn: A New Look at an Old Devil, by Liz Greene. York Beach, Maine: Samuel Weiser, 1976p*; London: Aquarian Publications, 1977p (196, incl. 1 illus.).

Jungian analyst and astrologer Greene analyzes the planet Saturn as a symbol of the psychic process, in which the experiences of pain, restriction, discipline, self-control, tact, thrift, and caution may lead to greater consciousness and fulfillment. She believes that Saturn symbolizes an initiator of the psychic process that brings about an inner experience of completeness within the individual.

Storming Eastern Temples: A Psychological Exploration of Yoga, by Lucindi Frances Mooney. Wheaton, Ill.: Quest Books/Theosophical Publishing House, 1976* + p (212, incl. 4-p. index, 3-p. bibl., 14-p. ref. notes).

Drawing upon Jung's interest in Eastern psychology, Mooney is "storming Eastern temples" to get beyond our Western shadow and heritage and to fathom the nature of self beyond ego-consciousness; and she characterizes the circumambulating, instinctive movement of the individual to self as "exodus" to the "inner East," which symbolizes renewal, rebirth, and new beginning. She discusses the topics of dimensions of self (a fantastic invasion) and ego (island of consciousness and breakdown of values); shadow (departure and gateway to the abyss); identification; projection; human relationships; collective shadow; collective unconscious and archetypes; syzygy; chthonic mother/wise old man; the movement to the East (yoga as an inner happening externalized); individuation (returning to the Self); and reordering a new direction (synchronicity and parapsychology).

Individuation in Fairy Tales, by Marie-Louise von Franz. Zurich: Spring Publications for the Analytical Psychology Club of New York, 1977; Dallas: Spring Publications, 1982p* (Seminar Series, 12); Boston & London: Shambhala Publications, rev. edn. 1990 p (A C. G. Jung Foundation Book) (230 + vii, incl. 8-p. index, 3-p. ref. notes).

Jung's theory of the process of individuation is illustrated by von Franz in a series of seminars given at the Jung Institute of Zurich, in which she uses six fairy tales to interpret the symbolization of the bird motif. Two-thirds of the book is devoted to two tales, namely, "The White Parrot," a Spanish tale whose central motif is borrowed from the Orient, and "The Secret of the Bath Bâdgerd" (castle of nothingness), a Persian fairytale also with parrot symbolization. Von Franz also analyzes four short tales with bird motifs that, as in the longer tales, mirror typical phases in the individuation process.

Relating: An Astrological Guide to Living with Others on a Small Planet, by Liz Greene. Wellingborough: Aquarian/Thorsons, 1977; 1986p*; Wellington, N.Z.: Reed, 1978; York Beach, Maine: Samuel Weiser, 1978p; ed.2 1978p* (294, incl. 5-p. index, 4-p. bibl.).

Citing Jung's courage to learn astrology and use it in his research on the psyche, Greene examines the ways in which people relate to one another in her analysis of the joint explorations of the ancient wisdom of astrology and the modern insights of depth psychology. She discusses the topics of the language of the unconscious; the planetary map of individual potential; psychological types related to the elements of air, water, earth, and fire; Beauty and the Beast (the shadow); the inner partner (animus and anima); the sex life of the psyche; the inner experience of archetypal parents; the infallible inner clock (progressions and transits); and relating in the Aquarian Age.

Astro-Psychology: Astrological Symbolism and the Human Psyche, by Karen Hamaker-Zontag. (Dutch: Amsterdam: W. N. Schors, 1978.) Wellingborough: Aquarian Press, 1980p*; New York. Samuel Weiser, 1980p*; York Beach, Maine: Samuel Weiser, 1990p as *Astrological Psychology.* (224, incl. 2-p. bibl., 25 illus.).

Recognizing the similarity of many of Jung's concepts to the more symbolic idiom of astrology, Hamaker-Zontag's aim is to place Jungian psychology within an astrological framework. She examines the traditional wisdom of astrology in relation to Jung's psychology by analyzing quadruplicities as forms of psychic energy, the four elements as psychological types, the zodiac as a path of life, the structure of the houses as the psychic structure of the individual, and planets as symbols of archetypal psychic drives. She views psychic growth from a Jungian perspective as it relates to astrological symbolism.

Pilgrimage to the Rebirth, by Erlo van Waveren. New York: Samuel Weiser, 1978p* (126, incl. 1-p. ref. notes, 3-p. foreword by the author's wife, Ann van Waveren).

In this tribute to Jung, van Waveren shares entries from his journal of his travels on the road to self-awareness in which he becomes acquainted with the Self. Affirming that the inner journey is an ancient road, he experiences his dreams as intimate encounters that lead to transformation and a new consciousness. As van Waveren draws upon his inner signposts, he asserts that his awareness of the ancestral psychic components compels him to write "a song of opposites" in balance.

Projection and Re-Collection in Jungian Psychology: Reflections of the Soul, by Marie-Louise von Franz. (Ger.: *Spiegelungen der Seele: Projektion und innere Sammlung.* Stuttgart: Kreuz Verlag, 1978.) LaSalle, Ill. and London: Open Court Publishing Co., 1980, 1985p* (253 + ix, incl. 13-p. index, 8-p. bibl., 7 illus.) (Reality of the Psyche Series).

Starting with Jung's concept of projection as an unconscious transfer of one's own subjective psychic elements onto an external object or person, von

Franz discusses the five stages involved in the withdrawal of projections. This is followed by a discussion of the withdrawal of projections in ancient religious hermeneutics and of the expression of projection in modern science. She examines the resistance inherent in the withdrawal of a projection involving evil demons (in antiquity and Christianity), the great mediating daimons (good-evil spirits), and the inner companion (guardian spirit). She states that consciousness and inner wholeness, which clear away clouds of unconscious projections, are the result of common sense, reflection, and self-knowledge.

(Bk.revs.: Choice '81/18:1022; JAnPsy '81/26:277; SFJInstLib '81/2n4:34–9; Spring '81:226–7; JAmAcadRel '82/50:170; Quad '82/15n2:72–3; PsyPersp '83/14:217–25)

The River Within: The Search for God in Depth, by Christopher Bryant. London: Darton, Longman & Todd, 1978p*; Nashville: The Upper Room, 1983p (152 + viii).

Bryant's aim is to illuminate the Christian spiritual tradition and life using modern, mainly Jungian, psychology. He describes the course of the river "within" through the stages of life from infancy and childhood (needs and problems of infancy; infant roots of some personality disorders; tasks of childhood; growth of conscience), on to the age of uncertainty (crises of adolescence; the personality ideal; the religion of adolescents) and years of responsibility (tasks of adulthood; stages in adult life; resources of the gospel), to the journey's end when one achieves an integrated personality and growth in spiritual maturity by realizing God's presence through prayer, contemplation, and worship.

(Bk.revs.: Harvest '78/24:174–5; Month '78/11:210–11; Theol '78/81:466–7; HeythJ '79/20:442–4; NewBlackf '79/60:187–8; JAnPsy '80/25:115; SpirToday '80/32:371)

Elements and Crosses as the Basis of a Horoscope, by Karen Hamaker-Zontag. (Dutch: Amsterdam: W. N. Schors, 1979.) Wellingborough: Aquarian Press, 1984p*; York Beach, Maine: Samuel Weiser, 1984p* (Jungian Symbolism and Astrology Series, vol. 1) (116, incl. 32 illus.).

In this handbook for astro-psychology based on comparisons between astrology and Jung's psychology, Hamaker-Zontag provides a basis for interpretation of horoscopes that derives from the symbolism, background, and function of both elements and crosses in terms of activity and direction of psychic energy. Together the elements and crosses provide the foundation for the structure of personality. She also discusses personal planets within the divisions of element and cross, along with sample horoscopes.

The I Ching Workbook, by R. L. Wing. Garden City, N.Y.: Doubleday, 1979p*; London: Aquarian Press, 1983* (180, incl. 11 illus.).

The author comments on the excitement with which Jung came across Richard Wilhelm's translation of the *I Ching* (or *Book of Changes*) whose images, arranged into sixty-four hexagrams, represent what Jung called archetypes. Wing relates this tapestry of symbols to the union of human nature and cosmic order in the collective unconscious, characterizing the ritual of stopping time (change) by consulting the *I Ching* as an aligning of one's Self and one's consciousness with the universe. The workbook contains a brief explanation of the *Book of Changes* itself and how the oracle works in making an inquiry. Descriptions of the hexagrams comprise most of the book.

The Individuated Hobbit: Jung, Tolkien, and the Archetypes of Middle-Earth, by
   Timothy R. O'Neill. Boston: Houghton Mifflin, 1979; London: Thames &
   Hudson, 1980 (200 + xv, incl. 16-p. index, 2-p. bibl., 14-p. gloss., 13 illus.).

In relating Tolkien's writings to Jung's personality theories, O'Neill discusses the themes of Self-realization through transforming archetypes and of personifying archetypes in the psyche. Following a brief description of the theory and construct of analytical psychology, he analyzes Tolkien's inventive ideas and the topics of Numenor lost (neurosis of Middle-earth); the individuated hobbit; "Frodos Dreme" (Frodo's dream); white lady, dark lord, and grey pilgrim; trickster, tree, and terminal man; Numenor regained (individuation of the West); and the relationship of archetype to allegory.
(Bk.revs.: Bklist '79/76:86; KirkR '79/47:920; Mythlore Fall'79/n22:25; PubW 13Ag'79/ 216:56; Chry&Lit '80/29n4:78–9; VaQR Sum'80/56:92; SewaneeR '81/89:286–9)

Return: Beyond the Self, by Thomas E. Parker. Saratoga, Calif.: Polestar Publications, 1979p (141 + iii).

From an early interest in the nature of the world and reality, through the study of physics and cosmology and, later, Jung's psychology, Parker has come to believe that the physical world and the psyche are intermeshed. His study and practice of the techniques of raja yoga and self-realization affirm this belief. Combining these experiences, he discusses the topics of developing a world view; the dilemma of life; the ego and the will (experiencing and overcoming duality); the illusion of separateness; the problem of evil; the purpose of pain; meaning (expansion of consciousness); the hidden body; the ladder of consciousness; the problem of balance; non-attachment; the process of becoming; and return (the path to joy).
(Bk.rev.: SFJInstLib '80/2n1:32–40)

The Tao of Psychology: Synchronicity and the Self, by Jean Shinoda Bolen. San
   Francisco: Harper & Row, 1979; 1982p*; Hounslow: Wildwood, 1980p
   (111 + xiii, incl. 3-p. index, 5-p. bibl.).

The connection between the human psyche and external events, between inner and outer worlds, is a basic concept of Eastern thought. Because interconnectedness and totality are Bolen's subjects, she makes a circular journey around the theme by first describing what the Tao is ("what the dance is") and then discusses Jung, synchronicity ("meaningful coincidence") and the Self, followed by the topics of "the Agatha Christie approach to synchronicity"; "like a waking dream"; significant meetings and the synchronistic matchmaker; synchronistic wisdom of the *I Ching;* parapsychological pieces of the synchronicity puzzle; Tao as path with heart; and the message of the Tao experience ("we are not alone").

(Bk.revs.: Choice '80/17:143; JAnPsy '80/25:383–4; SFJInstLib '80/1n2:10–11; AntiochR '81/39:393; Quad '81/14n2:107–8; JChinPhilos '83/10:91–2)

Emergence: Essays on the Process of Individuation Through Sand Tray Therapy, Art Forms, and Dreams, by Jeannette Pruyn Reed. Albuquerque, N.M.: J.P.R. Publishers, 1980p* (89 + x, incl. 3-p. bibl., 14 illus.).

The process of individuation is examined by Reed, who illustrates the power of the unconscious and potential transformation of individual lives through sand tray therapy, a method applicable to children and adults, which she describes as the experience in miniature of the quest for wholeness. She analyzes dreams in the sand, the sand tray as active imagination, myth and fairy tales in the sand tray, and symbols and archetypes in the sand. She illustrates the process with case studies and illustrations; and she also presents the process of emergence through art forms.

(Bk.rev.: Spring '81:230)

Jung and Tarot: An Archetypal Journey, by Sallie Nichols. New York: Samuel Weiser, 1980; York Beach, Maine: Samuel Weiser, 1984p* (392 + xv, incl. 7-p. ref. notes, 87 illus., 3-p intro. by Laurens van der Post).

Jung's archetypal approach, as understood by Nichols, is used to interpret the tarot, whose Major Arcana (trumps) are related to personal growth and Jung's concept of the individuation process. She relates the symbolism of the cards to a journey into one's own depths toward self-realization. Following brief introductory material on the origins and history of tarot and of Jung's archetypal approach to symbolism, she presents detailed essays on each of the twenty-two cards, whose wisdom can help solve personal problems and find creative answers to the universal questions that confront us all.

(Bk.revs.: LibJ '81/106:1638; Harvest '82/28:173–7; Quad '82/15n1:80–1; PsyPersp '82/ 12:86–94; Gnosis '85/n1:47)

On Divination and Synchronicity: The Psychology of Meaningful Chance, by Marie-Louise von Franz. Toronto: Inner City Books, 1980p* (Studies in Jungian Psychology by Jungian Analysts, 3) (123, incl. 5-p. index, 17 illus.).

Based on a series of lectures delivered at the Jung Institute of Zurich in 1969, this work by von Franz elucidates Jung's principle of synchronicity with a focus on divination, a technique practiced in all primitive civilizations and in sanctuaries and churches. She examines, in terms of the psychological background of number and time, the mysterious dimensions of meaningful coincidences that have no apparent relation to cause and effect. She also explores the meaning of irrational methods of divining fate, such as *I Ching*, astrology, tarot cards, and palmistry.

(Bk.revs.: Harvest '81/27:185–6; JAnPsy '81/26:170–1; Quad '82/15n1:79–80)

Planetary Symbolism in the Horoscope, by Karen Hamaker-Zontag. (Dutch: Amsterdam: W. N. Schors, 1980) York Beach, Maine: Samuel Weiser, 1985p* (Jungian Symbolism and Astrology Series, 2) (196, incl. 3 illus.).

Continuing with the series on Jungian symbolism and astrology, Hamaker-Zontag considers the symbolism of the planets from a Jungian point of view. She introduces the planets in relation to stages in the history of human development and then presents the modes of planetary expression as well as the planets in relation to the elements of fire, earth, air, and water. Avoiding a collection of ready-made interpretations of the planets in the signs, she discusses the planets as symbols of the psyche and human motivation and as types of personal conduct and interpersonal relationships.

The Secret Raven: Conflict and Transformation in the Life of Franz Kafka, by Daryl L. Sharp. Toronto: Inner City Books, 1980p* (Studies in Jungian Psychology by Jungian Analysts, 1) (128, incl. 4-p. index, 3-p. bibl., 8-p. ref. notes, 9 illus.).

Using fundamental concepts of Jung's psychology, analyst Sharp examines conflict and transformation in Kafka's life first from a biographical point of view (work; women and marriage; family; two worlds) and then from a psychological view (conflict; chthonic or earthy shadow; provisional life and the feminine; transformation). In illuminating some of the psychological factors, he pays special attention to the compensatory significance of Kafka's dreams in analyzing Kafka the man, with few references to his writings. He gives special attention to the psychology of the puer aeternus, the mother complex, the repressed shadow, and the provisional-life neurosis (the neurosis of the modern age).

(Bk.revs.: Choice '81/18:666; JAnPsy '81/26:283–4; Quad '81/14n1:85–7; SFJungInstLibJ '82/3n3:41–54)

Tarot Revelations, by Joseph Campbell and Richard Roberts. San Francisco: Alchemy Books, 1980p; San Anselmo, Calif.: Vernal Equinox Press, ed.2

1982; ed.3 1987p* (294 + xiv, incl. 9-p. ref. notes, 37 illus., 8-p. intro. by Colin Wilson).

Campbell's participation involves a 5-page foreword in which he explains his interest in the tarot and an 18-page interpretation of the symbolism of the Marseilles Deck (pictorial cards allegorically representative of material forces, natural elements, virtues, and vices). Other than Wilson's introduction, the remainder of the book consists of Roberts's analysis of the symbolism of the deck, which draws not only on its background in esoteric, astrological, Gnostic, and alchemical traditions but also from Jung's archetypology. He characterizes the tarot as a kind of Western *Book of the Dead*, an alchemical revelation of the spiral descent and ascent of Hermes/Mercurius following the traditional ladder of souls or stairway of planets.

Border Crossings: Carlos Castaneda's Path to Knowledge, by Donald Lee Williams. Toronto: Inner City Books, 1981p* (Studies in Jungian Psychology by Jungian Analysts, 8) (153, incl. 5-p. index, 3-p. bibl., 8-p. ref. notes, 9 illus.).

Interpreting the imagery of Castaneda's experience as apprentice to the shaman don Juan by means of Jung's understanding of the unconscious, Williams analyzes the pursuit of experience and authentic knowledge as a natural process of psychological evolution. He examines in psychological detail the images and motifs of the five novels as having parallels in mythology and fairy tales; and he illustrates the process of becoming conscious with examples from his analytical practice and from life, viewed as unfolding images that lead toward integration.
(Bk.revs.: CanBkRAn '81:359; ContemPsy '82/27:658; Quad '83/16:78–81)

Caring: How Can We Love One Another?, by Morton T. Kelsey. New York and Ramsey, N.J.: Paulist Press, 1981p* (198 + ix, incl. 6-p. ref. notes).

Based on fourteen lectures given at the New Mexico Benedictine monastery retreat in 1974, this book by Kelsey aims to present an integration of both classical, orthodox Christianity and secular psychology—specifically the psychology of Jung, whom Kelsey considers, along with some of Jung's followers, to have seen the "spiritual, divine implications of love." He discusses the topics of centrality of love; love and story; the theology of love; the fine art of loving ourselves; love and listening; loving the family and those who love us; love, sex, and Christianity; learning about people and how to love them; loving the acquaintance; loving the enemy; loving the stranger; love and social action; and creativity of love.
(Bk.revs.: Amer '81/145:166; BestSell Ja'81/41:112; Jy'81/41:41; BkRDig '81:769; LibJ '81/106:670; NatCathRep 160c'81/17:23; SisToday Oc'81/53:125; SpirLife '81/27:255; Tabl '81/235:915; Commonw '82/109:122; StAnth Mr'82/n89:49; SpirToday '82/34:276)

The Death of a Woman, by Jane Wheelwright. New York: St. Martin's Press, 1981; Venice, Calif.: Lapis Press, 1981* (287, incl. 11-p. gloss., 2 illus., 2-p. intro. by von Franz).

Trained in Jung's depth psychology, Wheelwright records the analysis of a dying cancer patient during the last months of the woman's life, revealing the slow transformation which the psyche experiences when death is imminent. She interprets a series of the patient's life-enhancing dreams to illustrate how the unconscious prepares one for death and assists in making suffering bearable.

(Bk.revs.: JAnPsy '81/26:376–8; LibJ '81/106:1230; PubW 23Ja'81/210:108; SFJInstLib '81/2n4:25–33; PsyPersp '82/13:95–7; Quad '83/16n2:83–4; DeathEd '84/8:186–8)

The Houses and Personality Development, by Karen Hamaker-Zontag. (Dutch: *Aard en Achtergrond van de Huizen.* Amsterdam: W. N. Schors, 1981.) York Beach, Maine: Samuel Weiser, 1988p* (Jungian Symbolism and Astrology Series, 3) (189 + x, incl. 3-p. bibl.).

Hamaker-Zontag, in the third of the series on Jungian symbolism and astrology, deals with the relationship of personality development to the twelve houses of the horoscope. She presents numerous relationships and interpretations not generally mentioned in books of astrological meanings; and she analyzes the distinctive psychological meanings that the houses have in their influence on human development and character. She covers the topics of the relationships of the houses and analytical psychology; symbolism of the houses; house interrelationships; planets in the houses; and five interpreted combinations.

Make Friends with Your Shadow: How to Accept and Use Positively the Negative Side of Your Personality, by William A. Miller. Minneapolis: Augsburg Publishing House, 1981p* (142 pp.).

Crediting Jung and his writings with providing valuable assistance in dealing with the dark and shadowy side of one's self, Miller provides from his own professional experiences of psychological counseling and his personal experiences with his shadow suggestions of how to accept and use in a positive way the negative side of one's personality. In addition to an introductory chapter on the shadow and personality development, he examines the relationship of shadow to myth, Jesus, innocence, St. Paul, projection, control, discovery, and wholeness.

Understanding the Mid-Life Crisis, by Peter O'Connor. Melbourne, Australia: Sun Books, 1981; New York and Mahwah, N.J.: Paulist Press, 1988p* (144 + viii, incl. 2-p. index, 5-p. ref. notes).

Recognizing as major sources of stimulus and reinforcement the writings of Jung and the poetry of Eliot, O'Connor writes about the midlife crisis from his own personal experience and from his experience in counseling. Starting with the observation that "others have been there before," he discusses the crisis in terms of the social context, the individual, the family, the occupational context, and marriage, concluding with an analysis of the Self and the anima and of ways of approaching the inner world.

The Vertical Labyrinth: Individuation in Jungian Psychology, by Aldo Carotenuto. (It.: Rome: Casa Editrice Astrolabio, 1981.) Toronto: Inner City Books, 1985p* (Studies in Jungian Psychology by Jungian Analysts, 20) (140, incl. 6-p. index, 7-p. ref. notes, 2-p. gloss. of Jungian terms).

The context of Carotenuto's study is that the psychological development of an individual parallels the historical evolution of consciousness along a labyrinthine path as one searches for meaning and inner strength. He illustrates the process with a case that concerns the sufferings of a successful painter, augmented by the background of many other experiences from his analytical practice. Carotenuto discusses the profound inner discord one experiences if there is a discrepancy between outer existence and the inner dimension of being. Other topics include mythical unconscious; solitude and psychology; development of consciousness; psychic reality; destiny of great souls; creative relationships; death and rebirth; immense light; conscious discrimination; and human dignity.
(Bk.revs.: CanBkRAn '85:399–400; JAnPsy '85/30:394; Chiron '86:208–11; ContemPsy '86/31:715; Quad '86/19n2:80–2)

Aging as a Spiritual Journey, by Eugene C. Bianchi. New York: Crossroad Publishing Co., 1982; 1984p* (285, incl. 7-p. index, 14-p. ref. notes).

By noting close interplay between spiritual and Jungian perspectives, Bianchi establishes a general framework for the spirituality of aging, his basis being broadly Christian with occasional "excursions" into Judaism and oriental religions. His basic theme is the need for persons in midlife to become more contemplative within the context of active, worldly endeavors. The first part of the book is devoted to the challenges of midlife (identity; world and work; intimacy) and potentials in midlife (developing self; world and work; friendship and intimacy) as well as reflections on earlier years and midlife (childhood and family influences; crisis, conversion, and life direction; midlife transitions). He devotes the latter part of the book to "elderhood" with its challenges (to self; from the world; from immediate others) and with its potentials, along with reflections on elderhood and on confronting death and life after death.

(Bk.revs.: Amer '83/148:242–4; BestSell Ap'83/43:26; Commonw '83/110:573; Nat-CathRep 11N'83/20:17; NewCathWorld '83/226:236–7; SisToday '83/54:640; SpirLife '83/29:183–4; SpirToday '83/35:373; StudForm '83/4:425–6; TheolStud '83/44:530–1; Chman Oc'84/198:17; Horiz '84/11:197; JRelAging '84/1:83–4; RforRel '84/43:466–7; StLukeJTh '84/27:227–9; ConsJud Fall'85/38:101; JPsyth '85/13:68; JPastorCare S'86/40:281–5)

Journey toward Wholeness: A Jungian Model of Adult Spiritual Growth, by Helen Thompson. New York and Ramsey, N.J.: Paulist Press, 1982p* (108 + ix, incl. 2-p. bibl., 5-p. ref. notes, 11 illus.).

Crediting Teilhard de Chardin, Jung, Evelyn Underhill, William Johnston, Erich Neumann, and Robert Ornstein as major resources, Thompson examines her five-year quest toward understanding human spirituality that grew out of her own midlife crisis. Beginning with the method of symbol (intuitive mode of consciousness) which precedes the method of science (rational analytical mode of consciousness), she suggests that this process reflects the basic pattern of the search for meaning in human life.

(Bk.revs.: SpirToday '82/24:364; RelStudR My'83/8:104–6)

The Planets Within: Marsilio Ficino's Astrological Psychology, by Thomas Moore. Lewistown, Penn.: Bucknell U. Press, 1982*; London and Toronto: Associated Universities Press, 1982 (Studies in Jungian Thought) (227, incl. 5-p. index, 5-p. bibl., 9-p. ref. notes).

Treating Renaissance philosopher Ficino as if he were a living psychologist with something to say about the modern psyche, Moore characterizes Ficino's psychology as an expression in images rather than in logical, linear statements; and he credits Jung and Hillman as exemplars of such imaginative playing with psychological and symbolic matters. He uses Ficino's writings on astrology to provide a look at the "planets" within, not the planets of the night, focusing on the recovery of the soul and the well-tempered life.

(Bk.revs.: JAnPsy '83/28:391–2; Parab My'83/3:104–6)

Men Against Time: Nicolas Berdyaev, T. S. Eliot, Aldous Huxley, and C. G. Jung, by Douglas K. Wood. Lawrence, Kans.: U. Press of Kansas, 1982* (245 + x, incl. 3-p. index, 12-p. bibl., 27-p. ref. notes).

In tracing the early development of the twentieth-century revolt against time, Wood exemplifies the vigorous efforts of four remarkable antitemporalists (Berdyaev, Eliot, Huxley, Jung) to move beyond history, time-philosophy, and progress by "re-creating" the concept of eternity from symbolic language. In the chapter (35 pp.) on "C. G. Jung and the Masks of God," he characterizes Jung's retreat-house at Bollingen as a protest against time by exploring the timeless dimension of the psyche. He also discusses the dualistic tendencies in Jung's concept of the structure of the unconscious (which Wood labels "unconscious Platonism"), the mandala (as a unifying symbol), and *Aion* and synchronicity (circular historical process), citing Jung's idea that the human psyche actually does touch on a form of existence outside time and space.

(Bk.revs.: AmHistR '83/88:1245–6; Choice '83/20:1582; Hist '83/12:30–1; TheolToday '83/40:107–8; BkRDig '84:1685; SAtlR '86/51:115–17)

A Time to Mourn: Growing Through the Grief Process, by Verena Kast. (Ger.: *Trauern: Phasen und Chancen des psychischen Prozesses.* Stuttgart: Kreuz Verlag, 1982.) Einsiedeln, Switzerland: Daimon Verlag, 1988p* (156, incl. 5-p. bibl., 5-p. footnotes).

Confronted with the pressing importance of mourning in the therapeutic process, Kast spent ten years in her Jungian analytic practice gathering material (particularly dreams) on the subject. She observes that in the treatment of many depressive illnesses the experience of loss has been mourned too little. She illustrates the way in which the unconscious prompts one to deal with mourning, moving from a discussion of the experience of a loved one dying to death and mourning as mirrored in a series of dreams. She examines dreams as guides during the four phases (denial; emotional chaos; search and separation; new relationship) of the process of mourning and then analyzes problems that develop when mourning is prolonged or repressed during each of the phases—especially unexpressed anger and guilt feelings in the phase of chaos. She concludes with discussions of symbiosis and individuation and of how to make a commitment to life while living with leave-taking.

(Bk.rev.: Quad '90/23n1:134–5, 137)

Dreams of a Woman: An Analyst's Inner Journey, by Sheila Moon. Boston: Sigo Press, 1983* +p* (207 + xiii, incl. 13 illus., 2-p. foreword by Liliane Frey-Rohn).

In her quest for self-discovery and understanding of her own individuation process, Jungian analyst Moon traces the journeying of her inner life, the vast reaches of inner space, in an effort to encourage others that it is worthwhile to try to know one's Self. She reveals her inner psychological and religious journey of nearly fifty years and discusses 235 personal dreams (including dreams about Jung and Jungians), which she interprets in the context of her struggle to reconcile opposites (negative masculinity and timid femininity) in her psyche.

(Bk.rev.: PsyPersp '85/16:107–10)

From Image to Likeness: A Jungian Path in the Gospel Journey, by W. Harold
Grant, Magdala Thompson, and Thomas E. Clarke. New York and Ramsey,
N.J.: Paulist Press, 1983p* (249 + v).

In viewing human development as a journey from the image of God
toward the likeness of God, the authors credit Jung with emphasizing the
importance of the God-image and the Christ-image (the latter being considered a symbol of the Self). They define the goal of the individuation process
as the disclosure and liberation of the Self and the fulfillment of human
destiny. Based on their experiences of conducting retreats and workshops on
"the gospel journey," they correlate Jungian psychological types (using the
Myers-Briggs Type Indicator) with the ways in which different types pursue
the journey toward wholeness. Appended is a classification of the development patterns of the different types for four periods between the ages of six
and fifty.

(Bk.revs.: Amer '83/150:119; CrossCurr '84/34:125–6; StAnth Jy'84/92:50; SisToday
Ag'84/56:41; SpirLife '84/30:177–8; SpirToday '84/36:275; TheolStud '84/45:782;
Church '85/1:59; RelStudR '85/11:171–2)

In MidLife: A Jungian Perspective, by Murray Stein. Dallas: Spring Publications,
1983p* (Seminar Series, 15) (149, incl. 3-p. bibl.).

Based on an eight-week seminar given at the Jung Center of Chicago in
1980, this work by Stein reflects on midlife (*transition,* if relatively calm;
crisis, if dramatic) in which formerly held ego-consciousness begins to
experience stress or loss of meaning and neglected or repressed parts of the
personality emerge—in some ways as a kind of second adolescence. Hermes,
as the guide of souls through liminality (threshold situations), is evoked in
chapters on the stages of burying the dead (loss of energy and desire); entry
into transition; liminality and the soul; return of the repressed; the lure to
soul-mating; steep descent (through the region of Hades); and the road to
life after midlife.

(Bk.rev.: Quad '84/17n1:71–2)

The Tarot: A Myth of Male Initiation, by Kenneth D. Newman. New York: C.
G. Jung Foundation for Analytical Psychology, 1983p* (152 + vii, incl. 4-p.
index, 4-p. bibl., 26-p. ref. notes, 25 illus.).

Viewing the tarot as a living symbol and ultimately a mirror wherein
each of us sees ourself as an expression of the psyche, like a myth, legend, or
fairy tale, Newman relates the twenty-two Major Arcana (trumps) to psychic
development. His psychological commentary, based on Jungian concepts,
uses actual case histories to illustrate possible interpretations. In his analysis,

Newman focuses on a man's psychology, though the tarot, like a fairy tale, can be interpreted from either a masculine or feminine point of view. (Bk.rev.: Quad '84/17n2:91–3)

The Astrology of Fate, by Liz Greene. York Beach, Maine: Samuel Weiser, 1984p*; London: Allen & Unwin, 1984; London: Mandala Books/Unwin, rev. 1985p* (370, incl. 10-p. index, 5-p. ref. notes, 13-p. gloss. of mythological names, 23 diagrams, incl. 21 birth charts).

Recognizing that it is difficult to distinguish the concept of fate from Providence, karma, or natural law, Greene considers the terminology provided by psychology (hereditary disposition, patterns of conditioning, complexes, and archetypes) to be more attractive. Her examination of the concept of fate includes the study of myths, fairy tales, and zodiacal signs, as well as the idea of the daimon (guardian spirit) that guides an individual's pattern of development. Using case material from her Jungian practice, she demonstrates the workings of fate in actual people's lives, demonstrating that it appears to be both psychic and physical, as well as personal and collective. (Bk.revs.: LondRBks 21Mr'85/7:17–18; Quad '85/18n2:94–6)

The Creation of Consciousness: Jung's Myth for Modern Man, by Edward F. Edinger. Toronto: Inner City Books, 1984p* (Studies in Jungian Psychology by Jungian Analysts, 14) (120, incl. 6-p. index, 9 illus.).

Considering the creation of consciousness to be the purpose of human life, Edinger presents this new central myth discovered by Jung as giving meaning to the deepest questions of life. He uses the concepts of analytical psychology, mythology, alchemical texts, dreams, and religion to emphasize the need not only of becoming more conscious of each one's creative potential but of one's dark and destructive side as well. His psychological and theological interpretations of Jung's *Answer to Job* point toward a new psychological dispensation centered in experience rather than in law or faith, wherein the individual's relation to God is to the incarnated God-image, the Self, the transpersonal center of the psyche. (Bk.revs.: CanBkRAn '84:466–7; PsyPersp '84/15:222–7; JAnPsy '85/30:213–15; Quad '85/18n1:113–16; Zygon '85/20:230–2; CanJPsychi '89/34:161)

Friedrich Nietzsche: A Psychological Approach to His Life and Work, by Liliane Frey-Rohn, edited by Robert Hinshaw and Lele Fischli. (Ger.: *Friedrich Nietzsche im Spiegel seiner Werke.* Zurich: Daimon Verlag, 1984.) Einsiedeln, Switzerland: Daimon Verlag, 1988p* (305 +xx, incl. 7-p. indexes, 4-p. bibl., 1 illus., 2-p. pref. by Helmut Barz).

Believing that the tragedy of Nietzsche's life began when he started regarding himself as the archetype of the man-god, Frey-Rohn analyzes the effects of his revolutionary discoveries on his own life. She analyzes, from a Jungian point of view, the psychological factors that influenced his alternating conditions of intense loneliness and loss with self-glorification and hero-worship.
(Bk.rev.: PsyPersp '89/20:182–3)

Jesus' Answer to God, by Elizabeth Boyden Howes. San Francisco: Guild for Psychological Studies Publishing House, 1984* +p* (257 + xxii, incl. 23-p. indexes, 9 illus.).

Basing her approach on the idea that Jesus of Nazareth lived his own inner myth with an enthusiasm grounded in his relation to God and the inner world of the soul, Howes views this book as an interpretation of how a religiously committed ego can live the way of individuation. She incorporates Jung's understanding of the human psyche in her analysis of how Jesus articulated eternal archetypal patterns in his life and teachings. The title posits Jesus' involvement and interaction with God and the Self.
(Bk.revs.: TheolToday '85/42:411–12; InwLight '87–88/n102:49–50)

Myth and Today's Consciousness, by Ean Begg. London: Coventure, 1984p* (112 + xi).

Begg's theme is that there is a new recognition of the importance of striving for consciousness, whereby individuals work with inner psychic potentialities and choose their own paths toward self-realization. He views the newly emerging polytheism as an inner pantheon of gods that represents archetypal modes leading to new ways of experiencing the world and one's self. His topics include the metamorphosis of the gods; the astrological pantheon; the world as proving ground of the soul; the many faces of consciousness; Herakles (champion of the self); a Gnostic alternative to orthodox belief; the fall of Sophia (a neo-Gnostic meditation); sex and individuation; Lilith; and Wotan.
(Bk.rev.: Harvest '85/31:149–51)

Explorations into the Self, by Michael Fordham. London: Academic Press for the Society of Analytical Psychology, 1985* (The Library of Analytical Psychology, vol. 7) (235 + xiii, incl. 9-p. index, 7-p. bibl., 3-p. foreword by Kenneth Lambert).

Jung believed that more or less mature persons in the second half of life use the philosophical and religious concepts of the self as an inner guiding principle. Fordham contends that the same self can be recognized in child-hood through integrative (primary state) and deintegrative (environmental interaction) processes. He analyzes ambiguities in Jung's definition of the Self and discusses the relationships of ego and Self by using clinical studies, consideration of countertransference in psychoanalytic work, defenses of the Self, and Jung's thesis about synchronicity, as well as Jungian views of body-mind relations. He concludes with reflections on religion ("Is God Supernat-ural?"), the mysticism of St. John of the Cross, and alchemy.

(Bk.rev.: JAnPsy '87/32:59–62)

Individuation and Narcissism: The Psychology of the Self in Jung and Kohut, by Mario Jacoby. (Ger.: *Individuation und Narzissmus: Psychologie des Selbst bei C. G. Jung und H. Kohut.* Munich: J. Pfeiffer Verlag, 1985.) London and New York: Routledge, 1990 (267 + xi, incl. 5-p. index, 9-p. bibl., 4-p. ref. notes).

Aiming to question certain postulates of psychoanalysis and of Jung's analytical psychology on the subject of narcissism, Jacoby examines their empirical basis and their experiential reality. Following his introduction to the myth of Narcissus from a Jungian perspective, he examines in detail Freud's essay on narcissism (1914) and then discusses the ego and self in analytical psychology (Jung, Neumann, Fordham) and in psychoanalysis (mainly Kohut) by comparing various concepts. He discusses the individua-tion process and maturation of the narcissistic libido, examining not only Jung's concepts (as postulated by Kohut) but also positions taken by Winni-cott. He concludes with a discussion of the forms of narcissistic disturbances in the psyche and psychotherapeutic treatment of narcissistic personality disorders.

The Journeying Self: The Gospel of Mark through a Jungian Perspective, by Diarmuid McGann. New York and Ramsey, N.J.: Paulist Press, 1985p* (224 + vi, incl. 25-p. ref. notes).

In using the analytical psychology of Jung to relate his own inner journey to the structure and movement of the gospel of Mark, McGann views life's journey as a story of self in the process of individuation. From McGann's point of view, Mark's story depicts Jesus moving through "stages" such as the good news, the desert, the call through conflict, the shadow, the feminine, blindness and sight, transfiguration, the temple, Gethsemani, the passion, and "beyond the empty tomb." He relates the story of self to his own experiences, drawing on the inspiration of four main "teachers"—his family of origin, a seminary professor, Teilhard de Chardin, and college professors and fellow psychology students.

(Bk.revs.: LibJ '85/110:77; Horiz '86/13:193–4; StAnth 8N'86/93:50; Tabl '86/240:206)

King Saul, the Tragic Hero: A Study in Individuation, by John A. Sanford. New York and Mahwah, N.J.: Paulist Press, 1985p* (144 + vi, incl. 7-p. index).

In his psychological study of Saul as the potential hero who failed, Sanford points out that one may learn more from failures and the mistakes of others than from successes. Sanford applies a broad background of both biblical scholarship and Jungian depth psychology in analyzing the first king of Israel with his fears and self-deception, his plots and strivings. The author describes Saul's rise and decline and ultimate transformation through dream interpretation in which he faces his egocentricity at his death. Appended is a fourteen-page analysis of depth psychology with emphasis on individuation, using both Jung's and Kunkel's ideas.
(Bk.revs.: BestSell My'83/45:74; RelStudR '85/11:283–4; JPsyTheol '86/14:360)

My Self, My Many Selves, by J. W. T. Redfearn. London: Academic Press for the Society of Analytical Psychology, 1985* (The Library of Analytical Psychology, vol. 6) (142 + xiv, incl. 6-p. index, 3-p. bibl., 2-p. foreword by Rosemary Gordon).

As reflected in the title, one of the main aims of Redfearn's book is to point out the numerous sub-personalities within one's total personality that represent an attempt to balance possible roles, a kind of migratory nature of the sense of "I." He discusses the various terminologies of ego and self in psychoanalysis and devotes a chapter to the Jungian Self, as well as a chapter on personal religious experiences at different ages (God and myself; God as myself). He also examines the topics of the omnipotent "I" and the realistic "I"; the body and body-image and the Self; the location of the feeling of "I"; sub-personalities (archetypes and complexes); the winning of conscious choice (the emergence of symbolic activity); and boundaries and mandalas.
(Bk.revs.: Harvest '86/32:157–8; JAnPsy '87/32:63–4)

The Radiant Child, by Thomas Armstrong. Wheaton, Ill.: Quest Books/Theosophical Publishing House, 1985p* (203 + viii, incl. 9-p. index, 10-p. ref. notes, 4 illus.).

In addition to well-known characteristics of childhood, such as emotional expressiveness, spontaneity, and imagination, Armstrong suggests that childhood represents a storehouse of extraordinary experiences, a hidden side that needs to be acknowledged in the ways that children may be raised and educated. He calls this hidden line of development the growth of the child *from the spirit down,* and he recognizes in its potential the child's initial connection with the collective unconscious and the Self which gives direction and coherence to psychic growth. He presents many different instances of non-ordinary childhood experiences, drawing upon child psychology, mythology, metaphysics, comparative religion, anthropology, philosophy, and literature.

(Bk.revs.: JTranspPsy '85/17:217–18; WCoastRBks '86/12n2:45)

The Bible and the Psyche: Individuation Symbolism in the Old Testament, by Edwad F. Edinger. Toronto: Inner City Books, 1986p* (Studies in Jungian Psychology by Jungian Analysts, 24) (172, incl. 7-p. index, 4-p. bibl., 6 illus.).

In presenting the theme that the Old Testament is a treasury of the symbols of individuation, Edinger relates the dialogue between human beings and God to Jung's psychological concept of the encounter between the ego and the Self. He employs the new insights of depth psychology to understand Old Testament images of numinous, or divinely awesome, encounters in terms of the process of self-realization or progressive relation to the Self, the central archetype in the psyche. He interprets and amplifies these interrelationships from the creation through the patriarchs, the exodus and theophany in the wilderness, the prophets and kings and exile to the emergence of the feminine (divine wisdom) and the messiah (the Self realized).

(Bk.revs.: CanBkAn '86:52–3; Harvest '87/33:212–13; JAnPsy '87/32:389–91; PsyPersp '87/18:141–4; Quad '87/20n1:98–9)

From Jung to Jesus: Myth and Consciousness in the New Testament, by Gerald H. Slusser. Atlanta: John Knox Press, 1986p* (170 + viii, incl. 8-p. index, 7-p. ref. notes).

Within the context of understanding human nature in a religious perspective and within the framework of viewing the nature of human understanding as essentially mythic as well as rational, Slusser believes that Jung's basic ideas are meaningful for the present. In his fundamental thesis, he focuses on the archetype of the hero (emphasizing that the hero's journey is applicable to both men and women) and he considers the story of Jesus to be of central importance. He analyzes the hero's birth story, the meaning of the birth of the hero, departure and initiation, battle with the dragon, and the sacred marriage of the hero.

(Bk.revs.: CrossCurr '86–87/36:485–6; Amer '87/156:139–40; BkRDig '87:1740; Choice '87/24:1236; ReligEd '87/82:656–7)

The Hero Within: Six Archetypes to Live By, by Carol S. Pearson. San Francisco: Harper & Row, 1986p* (176 + xxiv, incl. 4-p. ref. notes).

Utilizing insights of "post-Jungians" James Hillman and Joseph Campbell and sources other than archetypal psychology such as developmental psychology (Perry, Kohlberg, Gilligan), feminist theory, process therapy, and the New Age movement, Pearson explores both female and male life-journey patterns, emphasizing basic similarities as well as differences. She presents six archetypes that are important to the hero's "journey" of individuation. These "fundamentally friendly" archetypes are the Innocent (complete trust), the Orphan (longing for safety), the Martyr (self-sacrifice), the Wanderer (exploring), the Warrior (competing), and the Magician (authenticity and wholeness), all of which evolve through phases and stages that are more circular and spiral than linear.

Inner Work: Using Dreams and Active Imagination for Personal Growth, by Robert A. Johnson. San Francisco: Harper & Row, 1986*; 1989p* (222, incl. 1-p. bibl.).

Johnson discusses dreams in relation to Jung's model of the unconscious, the evolution of consciousness, the ego in the midst of the unconscious, the inner life, the process of individuation, seeking the unconscious, alternative realities of the world of dreaming, the realm of imagination, archetypes and the unconscious, conflict and unification, inner work through dreams, and active imagination techniques. He provides four-step approaches to dream work (association, dynamics, interpretation, rituals) and to active imagination (invitation, dialogue, values, rituals) that can help in the effort to integrate one's ego and the unconscious and work toward wholeness.
(Bk.revs.: LibJ Jy'86/111:92; CommBound '87/5:6–7; ContemPsy '87/32:284; InwLight Sum'89/n105:45–7)

The Christian Archetype: A Jungian Commentary on the Life of Christ, by Edward F. Edinger. Toronto: Inner City Books, 1987p* (Studies in Jungian Psychology by Jungian Analysts, 28) (143, incl. 4-p. index, 2-p. bibl., 34 illus.).

Aiming to present Jung's interpretation of the Christian myth, Edinger analyzes the incarnation myth of the life of Christ as the process of individuation. He summarizes the drama of the archetypal life of Christ that describes in symbolic images the events of the conscious life, representing the vicissitudes of the Self as it undergoes incarnation in an individual ego. His psychological commentary includes an examination of thirty images that cover the incarnation cycle in thirteen essential stages from the Annunciation to Pentecost (involving the same image of descent of the Holy Ghost at the beginning and at the end), as well as a discussion of the Virgin Mary's assumption and coronation.
(Bk.rev.: Mission Fall'88)

The Development of the Personality, by Liz Greene and Howard Sasportas. London: Routledge & Kegan Paul, 1987p*; York Beach, Maine: Samuel Weiser, 1987p* (Seminars in Psychological Astrology, vol. 1) (319 + xiv, incl. 2-p. bibl., 8 birth chart illus.).

Combining astrology and analytical psychology, Greene and Sasportas discuss the problem of the meaning of life which is often at the root of the myriad problems that drive people to see a psychotherapist or an astrologer. In dealing with the mystery of the human psyche and the overall meaning of an individual's life journey, they present the topics of the stages of childhood; parental marriage in the horoscope; subpersonalities and psychological conflicts; and *puer* (youth) and *senex* (old age) complexes.
(Bk.rev.: Quad '88/21n2:109)

Ecstasy: Understanding the Psychology of Joy, by Robert A. Johnson. San Francisco: Harper & Row, 1987; 1989p* (100 + xii, incl. 2-p. ref. notes).

Using Jung's concept of archetypes and drawing on the worlds of psychology and mythology, Johnson explores the meaning of the Dionysian archetype of ecstasy. He offers ways of reclaiming and expressing true joy that, unlike the ephemeral state of "happiness," has a lasting value which nourishes and sustains spirit as well as body. He emphasizes that repression of the archetype has led to the emergence of that psychic energy in negative forms, including drug and alcohol abuse, sexual repression, violence, racial hatred, and terrorism, which are antithetical to original Dionysian principles.
(Bk.rev.: Gnosis '88/n7:62)

Eros and Pathos: Shades of Love and Suffering, by Aldo Carotenuto. (It.: *Eros e pathos: margini dell'amore e della sofferenza*. Milan, 1987.) Toronto: Inner City Books, 1989p* (Studies in Jungian Psychology by Jungian Analysts, 50) (141, incl. 4-p. index).

Having become familiar with love and suffering ("life's two most overwhelming emotional experiences") during many years of Jungian analytic practice, Carotenuto discusses love and hate, pain, creativity, power, and the need to balance one's outer life with knowledge of one's inner world. His topics include the evocation of images; the basis of emptiness; the secret of seduction; the sacredness of the body; suffering for the other; self-knowledge and eroticism; fear of loss and jealousy; betrayal and abandonment; solitude and creativity; suffering and humiliation; the desire for power; staying aware; and hidden truth.

Feeling, Imagination, and the Self: Transformations of the Mother-Infant Relationship, by William Willeford. Evanston, Ill.: Northwestern U. Press, 1987* +p* (467 + xi, incl. 19-p. index, 21-p. ref. notes, 9 illus.).

The title of this work derives from Shakespeare's drama *The Winter's Tale,* in which Queen Hermione's waiting-woman takes the queen's baby from prison to King Leontes, whose insane jealousy has caused him to accuse the queen of adultery, in order to appeal to his "feeling, imagination and self." Although the king is unwilling to free the queen, it is the action of the appeal that provides the theme for Willeford's book in which he explores the implications of the waiting-woman's sound psychological understanding. He deals with feeling and the self and their effect on the ego by drawing on his experience in the fields of analytical and archetypal psychology. (Bk.revs.: Choice '88/26:528; JAnPsy '89/34:306–7)

Jungian Symbolism in Astrology: Letters from an Astrologer, by Alice O. Howell. Wheaton, Ill.: Quest Books/Theosophical Publishing House, 1987p* (219 + xxvi, incl. 5-p. bibl., 3-p. foreword by Sylvia Brinton Perera).

Using the format of writing letters to a dear friend, who also is a Jungian psychotherapist, Howell shows the deep connection between Jung's archetypal processes in the psyche and the planetary processes in a person's birth chart. Her underlying theme is the connection of astrology to the spiritual dimension and the value of symbolic language as a key to leading a symbolic life. In this context she examines the meaning of the birth chart and its use in the process of Jungian analysis. (Bk.rev.: Quad '88/21n2:109)

Old Age, by Helen M. Luke. New York: Parabola Books, 1987* +p* (Society for the Study of Myth and Tradition) (112 + x, incl. intro. by Barbara Mowat, Folger Shakespeare Library).

Reflecting upon the insights of Jung and using images from familiar literary texts, Luke reveals psychological meanings in the works of Homer (the *Odyssey*), Shakespeare (*King Lear; The Tempest*) and Eliot ("Little Gidding"). She analyzes the inner journey of the phase of life leading into old age, drawing upon her own experiences of the transition. She points out that individuals choose how they enter into their last years and how they approach death. (Bk.rev.: KirkR '87/55:1386)

Other Lives, Other Selves: A Jungian Psychotherapist Discovers Past Lives, by Roger J. Woolger. New York: Dolphin Books/Doubleday, 1987*; Toronto and New York: Bantam Books, 1988p* (386 + xx, incl. 14-p. index, 6-p. bibl., 10-p. ref. notes, 6-p. gloss., 3-p. foreword by Ronald Wong Jae, Association of Transpersonal Psychology).

Maintaining as his foundation Jung's concepts of the complex and archetype, Woolger proposes a third term, "past life complex," to describe the ancient doctrines of karma and reincarnation in a psychological way for modern individuals. He cites his own experience of personal and professional evolution from Jungian analyst to Jungian past life therapist, and he states that his goal is to put past life work in the broader perspective of spiritual development and Jung's concept of individuation.

(Bk.revs.: Gnosis '88/n7:58–9; KirkR '88/55:1384; PsyPersp '89/20:190–1; Quad '89/ 22n1:68–71; SFJInstLib '89/8n3:21–7)

The Stone Speaks: The Memoir of a Personal Transformation, by Maud Oakes. Wilmette, Ill.: Chiron Publications, 1987* +p* (148 + xxv, incl. 4-p. index, 3-p. bibl., 4-p. ref. notes, 28 illus., 3-p. foreword by William McGuire, 10-p. intro. by Joseph L. Henderson).

In the story of individuation and of her personal transformation, anthropologist-artist Oakes focuses on the large stone that Jung had just finished carving when she visited his retreat house at Bollingen in 1951. Her search for inner meaning has included meditations on the symbolism of the richly and mysteriously carved stone, the interpretation of dreams through Jungian analysis, and active imagination with Hermes as guide to the unconscious where she learned to experience the archetypes. She amplifies the symbolism of Jung's stone in order to illustrate the principle that health is the product of inner change.

Synchronicity: The Bridge Between Matter and Mind, by F. David Peat. New York: New Age Books/Bantam Books, 1987p* (245 + ix, incl. 4-p. index, end-chapter notes, 14 illus.).

Peat developed an interest in Jung and the idea of the collective unconscious while working with physicist David Bohm. Receiving encouragement from Arthur Koestler, Arnold Mindell, and Marie-Louise von Franz, he began to pursue the notion of synchronicity, positing the thesis that synchronicity provides a starting point for building a bridge between interior and exterior worlds of reality. Such a bridge spans the worlds of mind and matter, of physics and psyche, whose patterns he examines; and he pursues the notion that synchronicities provide a glimpse beyond connotations of time and causality into the immense patterns of nature.

(Bk.revs.: Bklist '87/83:1155; VillVoice Jy'87/32:3; Quad '88/21n1:87–9)

Archetypes of the Zodiac, by Kathleen Burt. St. Paul: Llewellyn Publications, 1988p* (Llewellyn Modern Astrology Library) (544 + xx, incl. 21-p. bibl., 8-p. gloss., 27 illus.).

Presented first as a workshop series during 1982–85, this work by Burt explores the archetypal energies in the horoscope ("the most personal tool we have for individual growth") in order to integrate them. She experiments with the "higher" energy of the esoteric ruler (subjective reality) of each of the twelve signs of the zodiac as well as the energy of the mundane ruler (objective reality) which most people express instinctively (unconsciously) every day in their striving for inner equilibrium. She presents the zodiacal signs as representing searches for a separate identity (Aries), value and meaning (Taurus), variety (Gemini), the mother goddess (Cancer), being and wholeness (Leo), meaningful service (Virgo), one's soul mate (Libra), transformation (Scorpio), wisdom (Sagittarius), dharma (Capricorn), the Holy Grail (Aquarius), and the castle of peace (Pisces).

By Way of Pain: A Passage into Self, by Sukie Colegrave. Rochester, Vt.: Park Street Press/Inner Tradition, 1988p* (160 + xv).

Told through the interweaving of fiction and psychological discussion drawn from her own life and the lives of people she has known and worked with in her therapeutic practice, Colegrave's book examines the passages of change which characterize the healing journey that leads from suffering to a place of serenity that does not deny body and earth but instead includes and celebrates them. She views the task of psychotherapy as exchanging neurotic suffering for real suffering, which is explored for its possibilities of psychological acceptance, integration, and transformation. Expressing indebtedness to the ideas and practice of Jungian analysis, she discusses the journey ("passage") under the topics of images of the soul; the marriage of heaven and earth; the birth of the Self; dying; a longer life; and growing out of pain.

Dynamics of the Unconscious, by Liz Greene and Howard Sasportas. York Beach, Maine: Samuel Weiser, 1988p* (Seminars in Psychological Astrology, vol. 2) (363 + xi, incl. 3-p. bibl., 9 birth charts).

Unconscious dynamics of the adult personality are discussed in four seminars that deal particularly with its darker dimensions, the areas that remain hidden in the unconscious and are generally unacceptable to consciousness, even though they may embody much of an individual's best potential. Sasportas presents the astrology and psychology of aggression, both destructively blind aggression and affirmative autonomy and individuality; and he examines the quest for the sublime as the experience of meaning and of finding the Higher Self. Greene analyzes depression as the other side of aggression and as part of a process that can lead to fuller expression of life, showing how depression reveals itself astrologically; and she interprets alchemical symbolism in the horoscope through stages of psychological and spiritual development.

The Footprints of God: The Relationship of Astrology, C. G. Jung, and the Gospels by Luella Sibbald. San Francisco: Guild for Psychological Studies Publishing House, 1988p* (167 + viii).

Based on her experience of Jungian analysis and her interest in astrology and training with Jung's daughter, astrologer Gret Baumann, Sibbald interconnects the factors of astrology, Jung, and the Gospels. Starting with an overall view of astrology (cosmic evolution in the meaning of the new age), she then analyzes the significance of the Great Year of the Zodiac (approximately 25,800 terrestrial years), followed by discussions of the first month of the Great Year (Piscean Age) and the second month (Aquarian Age), into which the earth is now moving. She examines Jesus as Aquarian man, though he was born at the beginning of the Piscean Age, and reflects that so many things Jung talked about carry the same essence of truth as did many of Jesus' statements. She ends with the value of the astrological chart and how she uses it in therapy.

The Hero Journey in Dreams, by Jean Dalby Clift and Wallace B. Clift. New York: Crossroad Publishing Co., 1988* (214 + xi, incl. 8-p. index, 8-p. ref. notes).

Integrating their studies of Jung's psychology and seminary studies of spiritual growth, the Clifts interpret life's journey for both men and women as a complex drama of the hero story. Dreams are used to illustrate various motifs of the journey such as the call to adventure, crossing the threshold, rites of passage, and return. The authors also discuss dreams and suicide, a monk's dream, a nun's dream, and prayer and active imagination. (Bk.revs.: Commow '88/115:659; PsyPersp '90/22:198–9)

Journeying Within Transcendence: A Jungian Perspective on the Gospel of John, by Diarmuid McGann. New York and Mahwah, N.J.: Paulist Press, 1988p* (217 + iv, incl. 18-p. ref. notes).

Drawing heavily on Jung's work, as he did in his earlier (1985) Jungian perspective on the Gospel of Mark, McGann reads his own story "in and through the story of Jesus" as presented in the Gospel of John. He examines metaphors and symbols in the gospel story by interpreting such opposites as secular and sacred, bondage and freedom, blindness and sight, death and life, humiliation and exaltation. These, he states, summon him to prayer,

meditation, and "living within the transcendent" in relating his own life to that of Jesus.
(Bk.revs.: LibJ 1My'88/113:83; ExposTimes '89/100:232)

Jungian Birth Charts: How to Interpret the Horoscope Using Jungian Psychology, by Arthur Dione. Wellingborough: Aquarian Press/Thorsons, 1988p* (Aquarian Astrology Handbook) (144, incl. 4-p. index, 2-p. bibl., 5 illus.).

With joint goals of teaching astrology students how to use Jungian symbols in horoscope interpretation and of helping others to explore the deeper realms of the individual birth chart, Dione aims to demonstrate that depth psychology and astrology complement one another and ought to be used together in analyzing charts. He discusses the topics of the elements in astrology as related to psychological type; the zodiac; planetary archetypes; the aspects; dynamics of psychic energy; and Jungian chart interpretation. Appended are a summary of basic astrology, a glossary of astrological terms, and a glossary of Jungian terminology.

A Little Book on the Human Shadow, by Robert Bly, edited by William Booth. San Francisco: Harper & Row, 1988p* (81 pp.).

The poet Robert Bly recounts his own relationship to the shadow, the dark side of one's personality, as well as those of writers Stevenson, Conrad, and Jung, adding some of his own ideas through poetry, storytelling, and psychological commentary. He describes the shadow as "the long bag we drag behind us" which contains parts of oneself of which parent or society does not approve; he then presents five stages in the process of exiling, hunting, and retrieving the shadow, a quest undertaken in order to change one's life.

The Self in Early Childhood, by Joel Ryce-Menuhin. London: Free Association Books, 1988* +p*; New York: Columbia U. Press, 1988* (273 + xii, incl. 5-p. index, 17-p. bibl., 11 illus.).

Using Jung's work to define self psychology and his own experience as Jungian analyst and sandplay therapist, Ryce-Menuhin develops a new model of the self-ego in infancy. He examines at length the contributions of Jung and the neo-Jungians to self psychology, analyzing the Jungian background, Jung's theories of the self, and Fordham's deintegration concept. He also explores the contributions of Freud and neo-Freudians and contributions by Winnicott and Kohut toward the self concept. He discusses autism in terms of the childhood self in disorder and in the relationship of self and physiology, using sandplay clinical material as illustrations.

(Bk.revs.: Harvest '88–89/34:170–2; TimesEdSup 9S'88:33; Choice '89/26:1411; JAnPsy '89/34:307–8)

The Shadow Side of Community and the Growth of the Self, by Mary Wolff-Salin. New York: Crossroad Publishing Co., 1988* (188 + xvi, incl. 8-p. ref. notes).

Drawing on her own and other people's experiences rather than on reading and research, Wolff-Salin reflects on community living (including marriages and families), particularly in terms of their problems. She presents first a study of the religious community, looking specifically at the shadow side as evidenced in the pain, conflict, and brokenness that arise from the effects of power, anger, fear, and withdrawal. In her study of other forms of community she considers marriage, tribal structures, and a therapeutic community. Using a Jungian approach to explore the meaning of individuation and the shadow, Wolff-Salin's goal is to promote greater integration and growth of the self and of the community.

(Bk.revs.: LibJ 1S'88/113:175; SpirLife '89/35:56–7)

Solitude: A Return to the Self, by Anthony Storr. (U.K.: *The School of Genius*. London: Andre Deutsch, 1988*.) New York: Free Press/Macmillan, 1988*; New York: Ballantine/Random House, 1989p* (216 + xv, incl. 15-p. index, 8-p. ref. notes).

Storr discusses how diverse factors such as childhood, inherited gifts and capacities, and temperament influence whether individuals predominantly turn toward others or toward solitude to find meaning in their lives. He focuses upon the significance of human relationships, the capacity to be alone, the uses of solitude, the effects of enforced solitude, solitude and temperament, separation, isolation and the growth of imagination, bereavement, and depression.

(Bk.revs.: AmSpec D'88/21:21; BkRDig '88:1671–2; BkWorld 17Jy'88/18:4; Bklist '88/84:1692; Choice '88/26:575; Encoun 2'88/71:59; GuardW 10Jy'88/139:27; KirkR '88/56:683; Listen 7Jy'88/120:24; LATimesBkR 28Ag'88:2; LondRBks 4Ag'88/10:14; NewStatSoc 1Jy'88/1:43–4; NYTimesBkR 2Oct'88:12; Observ 26Jn'88:42; PubW 3Jn'88/233:75; Spec 25Jn'88/260:39; TimesEdSup 15My'88:22; TimesLitSup '88:852; BkWorld 25Jn'89/19:12; Commonw '89/116:123; Observ 13Ag'89:41; TimesEdSup 15Ag'89:17)

The Survival Papers: Anatomy of a Midlife Crisis, by Daryl Sharp. Toronto: Inner City Books, 1988p* (Studies in Jungian Psychology by Jungian Analysts, 35) (159, incl. 6-p. index, 6 illus.).

The author takes Jung's view that symptoms such as conflict and depression associated with psychological problems in midlife are really attempts at self-cure. Sharp sees such manifestations as evidence of a basically healthy psyche trying to find a proper balance. He presents, as an example, the case of a man's midlife breakdown and his first year in Jungian analysis. In viewing the crisis as an opportunity for his patient to consider a new level of awareness that could lead to a conscious individuation process, he discusses such topics as neurosis; midlife crisis and individuation; purpose of a midlife crisis; adaptation and breakdown; self-regulation of the psyche; the hero's journey; reality as we know it; and the transcendent function.

(Bk.rev.: QuillQuire S'88/54:73)

Dear Gladys: The Survival Papers, Book 2, by Daryl Sharp. Toronto: Inner City Books, 1989p* (Studies in Jungian Psychology by Jungian Analysts, 37) (141, incl. 3-p. index, 2 illus.).

In this sequel to the anatomy of a midlife crisis in *The Survival Papers,* Sharp continues with the case study of a man in his second year of Jungian analysis, during which "he found his feet and lived to writhe again." His lively account of the analysis is interspersed with psychological commentary about the ongoing struggle between consciousness and the unconscious, projections, complexes, and archetypal motifs. Sharp also reflects on experiences from his own life.

(Bk.rev.: SmallPr Jn'89/7:45–6)

Journey into Consciousness: The Chakras, Tantra, and Jungian Psychology, by Charles Breaux. York Beach, Maine: Nicolas-Hays, 1989p* (254 + xviii, incl. 6-p. index, 4-p. bibl., 6-p. gloss., 37 illus.).

Wanting to lay a foundation for a practical psychological understanding of the chakras, Breaux elaborates on the historical and philosophical context of Tantra and shows how complementary it and Jungian psychology are. In both systems, human consciousness is transformed by the progressive awakening of various dimensions of the psyche. After an introduction to Tantric roots and relevance to Jungian psychology (12 pp.), he interprets the path of the physical-psychological-spiritual continuum from the root chakra (unconscious grounding with the life force in the body) up through the six other chakras, seen as progressive stages in the evolution of the psyche. He suggests a way that the Tantric method may be integrated with Western approaches for the development and healing of body-mind.

Jung the Philosopher: Essays in Jungian Thought, by Marian Pauson. New York and Bern: Peter Lang Publishers, 1989* (New Studies in Aesthetics, vol. 3) (235 + xiii, incl. 8-p. index, 19-p. bibl., end-chapter ref. notes, 10 illus.).

Noting that Jung the psychotherapist is well known but that Jung the philosopher is not, and stating that all psychologies are rooted in philosophical presuppositions as all philosophies likewise are grounded in psychological orientations, Pauson presents Jung's point of view with regard to the enduring philosophical questions. She begins with Jung's philosophic mentors and then examines his views on the basis of knowledge, the impact of human consciousness on the dynamics of the world (including synchronicity), human creation in art and life, the problem of evil, the roots of symbolic forms, Jung's typology and its educational implications, and education for the second half of life. She ends with a discussion of going beyond the rational (Jung and mystics) and an analysis of the stages in the creative process ("The Seven Days of Creation").

The Unfolding Self: Separation and Individuation, by Mara Sidoli. Boston: Sigo Press, 1989* +p* (203 + xiii, incl. 9-p. index, 5-p. bibl., end-chapter bibl. ref., 2 illus., 2-p. preface by Michael Fordham).

Combining her more traditional Jungian training in child analysis with her exposure to Kleinian and Freudian theory and praxis, Sidoli offers a means of empirically validating Jung's theories about the self and the archetypes. She presents a picture of the unfolding self in various patients at various ages. Following an introduction to the self in infancy, she illustrates by clinical examples the topics of separation (the growing child moving away from mother, both physically and intrapsychically); the unconscious negative mother-baby relationship (developing into the child's magic archetypal world); jealousy and sibling rivalry, and their roots; the shame of being a baby (feelings of inadequacy); the value of regression in child analysis; disorders of the self; the "abandoned child" theme; and separation in adolescence (how the deintegrative-reintegrative process unfolds).

Was C. G. Jung a Mystic? and Other Essays, by Aniela Jaffé. Einsiedeln, Switzerland: Daimon Verlag, 1989p* (119 + viii, incl. 2-p. foreword by Robert Hinshaw).

Spanning a period of about forty years, these four essays provide varied insights from Jaffé's long years of association with Jung. Appearing for the first time is the title essay of the book, in which she states that an analogy between mysticism and Jungian psychology in no way denies its scientific basis since numinous experiences of images do enter into consciousness from unconscious reality. Her 1950 essay on the romantic period in Germany is translated from her book on images and symbols in Hoffmann's fairy tale "The Golden Pot." Her 1974 Eranos Conference paper on the individuation of mankind interprets Jung's ideas of the collective consciousness as a gradual religious-psychological transformation and unfolding of the image of God. The 1985 essay on transcendence deals with conversations with Jung about post-mortal existence.

After the End of Time: Revelation and the Growth of Consciousness, by Robin Robertson. Virginia Beach, Va.: Inner Vision, 1990p (254, incl. 3-p. bibl.).

Robertson's reading of the Book of Revelation as a symbolic description of the transition to a higher level of consciousness leads to an analysis of the symbolic language of dreams and visions, as well as myths and fairy tales. Among the topics examined are the nature of oracles, Jung's *Answer to Job,* man and God, creation myths, Armageddon and the millennium, the nature of evil, and the new Jerusalem.

(Bk.revs.: PsyPersp '90/22:180–1)

The Gilgamesh Epic, by Rivkah Kluger. Einsiedeln, Switzerland: Daimon Verlag, forthcoming in 1990.

Jungian Synchronicity in Astrological Signs and Ages, by Alice O. Howell. Wheaton, Ill.: Theosophical Publishing House, forthcoming in 1990p.

Jung's Self Psychology, by Polly Young-Eisendrath and James A. Hall. New York: Guilford Press, 1990 (250 pp.).

The Rainbow Serpent: Bridge to Consciousness, by Robert L. Gardner. Toronto: Inner City Books, 1990p (Studies in Jungian Psychology by Jungian Analysts, 45) (127, incl. 4-p. index, 4-p. bibl., 13 illus.).

Drawing on aboriginal myth, Gardner explores the basis for a neurotic split in which the Australian white and black communities each represent the unknown or shadow side that is repressed by the other. In addition to investigating the myth of the Wawilak women, he discusses the making of a Wuradjeri medicine man as an example of the integration by one person of opposing psychological principles of the two cultures, which he interprets as a process of individuation.

Reclaiming the Inner Child, edited by Jeremiah Abrams. Los Angeles: Jeremy P. Tarcher, 1990p* (323 + xi, incl. 4-p. bibl., 9-p. ref. notes).

Intending to give "the best, most readable, inspiring material available" on the compelling and timely subject of the inner child, Abrams presents thirty-seven selections ranging widely from psychology to other disciplines. He divides the collection of articles or excerpts from books into six parts, namely, the promise of the inner child; the abandoned child; eternal youth and narcissism; the wounded child within; recovering the child; and the future of parenting. Contributions by Jungian analysts or therapists are Joel Covitz, "Narcissism: The Disturbance of Our Time"; Gilda Frantz, "Birth's Cruel Secret," on abandonment; James Hillman, "Abandoning the Child"; Helen Luke, "The Little Prince"; Rose-Emily Rothenberg, "The Orphan Archetype"; Jeffery Satinover, "The Childhood Self and Origins of Puer Psychology"; Susanne Short, "The Whispering of the Walls"; June Singer, "The Motif of the Divine Child"; Robert M. Stein, "On Incest and Child Abuse" and "Redeeming the Inner Child in Marriage and in Therapy"; Marie-Louise von Franz, "Puer Aeternus"; and Marion Woodman, "The Soul Child." Also included is an excerpt from Jung's essay on "The Psychology of the Child Archetype." Editor Abrams provides an introduction on the inner child and introductions for each article.

(Bk.revs.: PsyPersp '90/22:207–9; Quad '90/23n2: 108–9)

7 Symbolic Life and Dreams

According to Jung, to be able to express the need of the soul to participate in the ritual of life and to be able to create a life that is meaningful, we need to be connected to the symbolic side of life. In contrast to a life that is too rational, a symbolic life expresses the facts of the unconscious and works to fulfill the desire of one's soul. Since dreams are the most frequent and universally accessible sources for investigating one's unconscious and inner functioning, the psychic life-process of an individual's total personality may be understood by the interpretation of dreams and their symbolic images.

More than seventy books comprise this subject category, plus sixteen that are cross-referenced from other subjects. They have been arranged chronologically, with Jung's works listed first, followed by the works of others. Of the latter, half have been published since 1978.

Jung: *Alchemical Studies* [p. 131]
———: *The Archetypes and the Collective Unconscious* (See chapter 4, "The Psyche") [p. 55]
———: *Dream Analysis* (See chapter 11, "Jungian Analysis") [p. 292]
———: *Dreams* [p. 132]
———: *Man and His Symbols* [p. 130]
———: *Mandala Symbolism* [p. 132]
———: *Nietzsche's Zarathustra* [p. 128]
———: *Psychology and Alchemy* [p. 129]
———: *Psychology and the Occult* [p. 132]
———: *The Symbolic Life* (See chapter 2, "Collections of Jung's Writings") [p. 26]
———: *Symbols of Transformation* [p. 127]
———: *Mysterium Coniunctionis* [p. 130]

_____: *The Undiscovered Self* (See chapter 6, "Human Development and Individuation") [p. 80]

_____: *C. G. Jung: The Visions Seminars* [p. 128]

Wilhelm & Jung: *The Secret of the Golden Flower* [p. 127]

Argüelles & Argüelles: *Mandala* [p. 142]

Becker: *The Understanding of Dreams* [p. 139]

Bell: *The Dictionary of Classical Mythology* [p. 148]

Bosnak: *A Little Course in Dreams* [p. 153]

Broadribb: *The Dream Story* [p. 154]

Campbell: *The Inner Reaches of Outer Space* [p. 153]

_____: *The Mythic Image* [p. 143]

_____: *Myths To Live By* (See chapter 9, "Religion and Jung's Psychology") [p. 216]

Champernowne: *A Memoir of Toni Wolff* [p. 147]

Chetwynd: *Dictionary of Symbols* [p. 148]

Cirlot: *A Dictionary of Symbols* [p. 136]

Clift & Clift: *The Hero Journey in Dreams* (See chapter 6, "Human Development and Individuation") [p. 117]

_____: *Symbols of Transformation in Dreams* [p. 151]

Cooper: *An Illustrated Encyclopedia of Traditional Symbols* [p. 145]

Coudert: *Alchemy* [p. 147]

Covitz: *Visions of the Night* [p. 156]

Dale-Green: *The Archetypal Cat* [p. 138]

de Vries: *Dictionary of Symbols and Imagery* [p. 143]

Eliade: *The Forge and the Crucible* [p. 135]

Fierz-David: *The Dream of Poliphilo* [p. 134]

Fodor: *Freud, Jung, and Occultism* [p. 141]

Foster: *The World Was Flooded with Light* [p. 152]

Globus: *Dream Life, Wake Life* [p. 154]

Hall: *Clinical Uses of Dreams* (See chapter 11, "Jungian Analysis") [p. 313]

_____: *Hypnosis* (See chapter 11, "Jungian Analysis") [p. 348]

_____: *Jungian Dream Interpretation* [p. 150]

Hannah: *Encounters with the Soul* [p. 148]

The Herder Symbol Dictionary [p. 144]

Herzog: *Psyche and Death* [p. 137]

Hillman: *The Dream and the Underworld* [p. 146]

Howell: *Jungian Symbolism in Astrology* (See chapter 6, "Human Development and Individuation") [p. 114]

Jacobsohn, von Franz & Hurwitz: *Timeless Documents of the Soul* [p. 135]

Jaffé: *Apparitions* [p. 135]

Jobes: *Dictionary of Mythology, Folklore, and Symbols* [p. 138]

Johnson: *Inner Work* (See chapter 6, "Human Development and Individuation") [p. 112]

Kaplan-Williams: *Jungian-Senoi Dreamwork Manual* [p. 147]

Kelsey: *God, Dreams, and Revelation* [p. 140]

Kirsch: *The Reluctant Prophet* [p. 142]

Knapp: *Dream and Image* (See chapter 10, "Creativity and Jung's Psychology") [p. 263]

Kugelmann: *The Windows of the Soul* (See chapter 11, "Jungian Analysis") [p. 329]

Layard: *The Lady of the Hare* (See chapter 11, "Jungian Analysis") [p. 298]

Leach & Fried (eds.): *Funk & Wagnalls Dictionary of Folklore, Mythology, and Legend* [p. 134]

Lockhart: *Psyche Speaks* [p. 155]

Mahoney: *The Meaning in Dreams* [p. 140]

Mattoon: *Understanding Dreams* [p. 145]

McDonald: *Dreams* [p. 151]

Meier: *The Meaning and Significance of Dreams* [p. 142]

Mindell: *Dreambody* [p. 149]

———: *River's Way* [p. 152]

Moon: *Dreams of a Woman* (See chapter 6) [p. 105]

Nicoll: *Dream Psychology* [p. 133]

O'Connor: *Dreams and the Search for Meaning* [p. 155]

Olderr: *Symbolism: A Comprehensive Dictionary* [p. 154]

Parsifal-Charles: *The Dream: Four Thousand Years of Theory and Practice* [p. 152]

Poncé: *Working the Soul* [p. 150]

Reid: *Dreams* [p. 149]

Rossi: *Dreams and the Growth of Personality* (See chapter 11, "Jungian Analysis") [p. 307]

Sanford: *Dreams* [p. 140]

Savary, Berne & Kaplan-Williams: *Dreams and Spiritual Growth* (See chapter 9, "Religion and Jung's Psychology") [p. 232]

Serrano: *The Visits of the Queen of Sheba* [p. 138]

Signell: *Wisdom of the Heart* [p. 156]

Spiegelman: *The Knight: The Potentials of Active Imagination* [p. 149]

Spier: *The Hands of Children* [p. 133]

Streatfeild: *Persephone* [p. 137]

von Franz: *Alchemical Active Imagination* [p. 146]

———: *Alchemy* [p. 146]

———: *Aurora Consurgens* [p. 136]

———: *On Dreams and Death* [p. 150]

von Franz & Boa: *The Way of the Dream* [p. 155]

Watkins: *Invisible Guests* [p. 153]

———: *Waking Dreams* [p. 144]

Weaver: *The Old Wise Woman* [p. 139]

Whitmont & Perera: *Dreams* (See chapter 11) [p. 347]
Wickes: *The Inner World of Man* (See chapter 6, "Human Development and Individuation") [p. 81]
Willeford: *The Fool and His Scepter* [p. 141]
Zeller & Dallett: *The Dream* [p. 144]

Symbols of Transformation: An Analysis of the Prelude to a Case of Schizophrenia, by C. G. Jung. (Ger.: *Wandlungen und Symbole der Libido*. Leipzig and Vienna: Deuticke Verlag, 1912.) (Orig. Engl. title: *Psychology of the Unconscious: A Study of the Transformation and Symbolism of the Libido*. New York: Moffat, Yard, 1916; ed.2 1919; London: Kegan Paul, Trench, Trubner, 1917–51; New York: Dodd Mead, 1925–71.) London: Routledge & Kegan Paul, 1951; 1956*; New York: Bollingen Foundation, 1956; New York: Harper & Row, 1962p; Princeton, N.J.: Princeton U. Press/Bollingen, ed. 2 1967*; 1976p* (*CW* 5) (557 + xxix, incl. 59-p. index, 30-p. bibl., 131 illus.).

Written in his thirty-sixth year and rewritten at the age of seventy-five, this book is a landmark of where Jung's way diverged from the psychoanalytical school of Freud, whose framework of ideas about psychic phenomena was too narrow for Jung. The work is a very extensive commentary, with numerous symbolic illustrations, on Jung's practical analysis of the precursory stages of schizophrenia of a patient. The symptoms of the case provide the thread by which Jung is guided into the labyrinth of symbols from dreams, for which he interprets parallels by amplification from a great variety of sources. Jung deals primarily with two major dreams from the patient's complicated fantasy system. He then discusses at length the topics of the concept of libido; transformation of the libido; origin of the hero; symbols of the mother and of rebirth; the battle of deliverance from the mother; the dual mother; and sacrifice. His intricate study of symbolic parallels is drawn from mythology, religion, ethnology, art, and literature, as well as psychiatry.

(Bk.revs.: BkRDig '16:302–3; Dial '16/60:555–6; JAbnPsy '16/11:177–9; JNervMent '16/44:382–4; Nation '16/103:127–9; NewRep '16/7:21–2; NYTimesBkR 21My'16:217; PsyanR'16/3:352–4; Surv '17/37:497; AmSchol '57/26:378+; Blackf '57/38:442; BulMennClin '57/21:224; HarvDivBul '57/23:180–2; JRelThought '57/14:179–80; PerkSchTh Spr'57/10:35; RMeta '57/10:271; TimesLitSup '57:659; JPastorCare '58/12:197; Person '58/39:178–9; PsychiQ '58/32:193; RofRel '58/22:203–7; PastorPsy '60/11:63–4; PsychiQ '62/36:769–70; ContemPsy '86/31:715; PsyMed '86/16:481)

The Secret of the Golden Flower: A Chinese Book of Life, translated and explained by Richard Wilhelm, with a foreword and commentary by C. G. Jung. (Ger.: *Das Geheimnis der goldenen Blüte*. Munich: Dorn, 1929.)

London: Kegan Paul, Trench, Trubner, 1931; New York: Harcourt, Brace, 1931; New York: Harcourt Brace & World, rev. 1962p; New York: Harvest Books/Harcourt Brace Jovanovich, 1970p*; New York: Causeway Books, 1975; London: Arkana, 1984p* (149 + xvi, incl. 19 illus.).

Jung emphasizes that this text of a Taoist alchemical treatise, which was sent to him by Wilhelm in 1928, helped confirm his findings concerning the processes of the collective unconscious. Aiming to build a bridge of psychological understanding between East and West by emphasizing the similarities between psychic states and Taoist symbolism, Jung brings his developing theories of depth psychology to bear on Eastern philosophy, characterizing both the fundamental concepts of the Tao (or conscious way) and the circular movement of psychic development as being activated by the light and dark forces of the human desire for self-knowledge. He discusses the disintegration of consciousness by the unconscious; animus and anima; detachment of consciousness from entanglements of the world so that the unconscious is recognized as a codetermining factor along with consciousness; and fulfillment by evolution of a higher consciousness. Jung presents ten examples of European mandalas drawn by patients (and by himself) to illustrate the parallel between Eastern philosophy and the unconscious mental processes of the West.

(Bk.revs.: TimesLitSup '31:832; Criterion '32/11:517–19; Nature '32/129:332; NYTimesBkR 10Ja'32:13; JNervMent '33/78:665–6; PsyanR '34/21:117–19; TimesLitSup '63:46; StudComRel '73/7:189; StudComRel '84/16:251)

C. G. Jung: The Visions Seminars, from the complete notes of Mary Foote. (Orig. title: *Interpretation of Visions: Notes on the Seminar in Analytical Psychology given by Dr. C. G. Jung, Zurich, 1930–1934.* 11 vols., mimeog.) Zurich: Spring Publications, 1976p in 2 vols.; Dallas: Spring Publications, 1983p (548 + iv, incl. 12-p. index, 28 illus.).

Drawing upon the visionary experiences of a woman client in her thirties to whom Jung introduced visioning (active imagination) as a therapeutic measure, Jung conducted an extended seminar in English following the 1928–30 seminar on dream analysis. His theme is the development of the transcendent function, which operates through dreams and visions to bring images from the unconscious to help in the reconciliation of opposites and in the ultimate synthesis of the individual's psychic processes. Among the topics which emerge are the independence of the unconscious; the shadow; projections; animus; yang and yin; tao and individuation; levels of consciousness; mandalas; astrological symbolism; enantiodromia (emergence of the unconscious opposite); the power of suffering; dismemberment; and the positive role of the Self.

(Bk.rev.: JAnPsy '78/23:367–8)

Nietzsche's Zarathustra: Notes of the Seminar Given in 1934–1939 by C. G. Jung, edited by James L. Jarrett. Princeton, N.J.: Princeton U. Press (Bollingen Series XCIX:2), 1988* in 2 vols.; London: Routledge & Kegan Paul, 1989* in 2 vols. (C. G. Jung Seminars, vol. 2) (v.1 = 764 + xxvii, incl. 13-p. editor's intro.; v.2 = pp. 765–1578 + vi, incl. 32-p. index).

Characterizing *Thus Spake Zarathustra* as a sort of collection of sermons in verse that depict the evolutionary incidents in Nietszche's life, Jung follows the same analytical technique in this seminar that he applied to the visions seminars. He interprets the events and inner experiences of Nietzsche's life as a series of manifestations of the unconscious (often of a visionary character). Nietzsche's eccentricity, brilliance, and decline into psychosis both fascinated and disturbed Jung in his youth when he lived in Basel (where Nietzsche had been a professor at the University of Basel during the 1870s) from 1879 to his graduation from medical training in 1900. Jung's initial curiosity about both Nietzsche's genius and his neurotic tendencies influenced his thought throughout his life.
(Bk.revs.: Choice '89/26:1603; Quad '89/22n2:101–2; PsyPersp '89/20:173–6, 179–81; Spring '89:49:157–8; WilsonQ Spr'89/13:109; ContemPsy '90/35:288–9)

Psychology and Alchemy, by C. G. Jung. (Ger.: *Psychologie und Alchemie.* Zurich: Rascher Verlag, 1944.) New York: Pantheon Books (Bollingen Foundation), 1953; Toronto: McClelland & Stewart, 1953; London: Routledge & Kegan Paul, 1954*; Princeton, N.J.: Princeton U. Press/Bollingen, ed.2 1968*; 1980p*; London and Henley-on-Hudson: Routledge & Kegan Paul, ed.2 1968; 1980p; 1989p*; London: Ark, 1987p* (CW 12) (571 + xxxiv, incl. 46-p. index, 38-p. bibl., 270 illus.).

Published first, though not as volume 1 of the *Collected Works* of Jung, this volume on psychology and alchemy represents a major portion of the material upon which Jung's later work is based. As a study of analogies between alchemy, psychological symbolism, and religious dogma, Jung relates the concepts of alchemy from its symbol formation, extending over some seventeen centuries, to the individuation process. Following an introduction to the religious and psychological problems of alchemy, he uses a large number of examples from more than seventy dreams of a young male patient to illustrate the connection between individual dream symbolism and medieval alchemy. He particularly emphasizes the symbolism of the mandala. The remaining half of the book deals with religious ideas in alchemy and includes discussions on the basic concepts of alchemy, the psychic nature of alchemical work, the work itself, the prima materia, the parallel between

Christ and the philosopher's stone, and alchemical symbolism in the history of religion.

(Bk.revs.: Ambix '48/3:64–7; Isis '48/39:44–8; AmMerc S'53/77:139–40; CrossCurr '53/ 4:78; Listen '53/50:312–13; NewRep 18My'53/128:17–18; NYTimesBkR 2Ag'53:6; PastorPsy S'53/4:81; PsychiQ '53/27:530; Tabl '53/202:230; AmJPsychi '54/111:395; Blackf '54/35:125; HudsonR '54/6:611–19; InwLight Wint'54/n45:33–4; JPastorCare '54/ 8:119–20; JRelThought '54/11:82–3; Person '54/35:312–13; PsysomMed '54/16:530–2; QueensQ '54/61:134; Thought '54/29:317–20; TimesLitSup '54:808; BrJMedPsy '55/ 28:82; RMeta '55/9:71–89; RofRel '55/10:150–5; UTorQ '55/24:202–4; PastorPsy S'56/ 7:64; AmJPsyth '57/11:438–40; JAnPsy '69/14:189–92; TimesLitSup '69:251; ContemPsy '71/16:162–4; Isis '71/62:236–8; Month '81/14:392; PsyMed '81/11:864)

Mysterium Coniunctionis: An Inquiry into the Separation and Synthesis of Psychic Opposites in Alchemy, by C. G. Jung. (Ger.: *Mysterium Coniunctionis: Untersuchung über die Trennung und Zusammensetzung der seelischen Gegensatze in der Alchemie*, with the collaboration of Marie-Louise von Franz. Zurich: Rascher Verlag, 1955.) New York: Pantheon Books (Bollingen Series XX), 1963; London: Routledge & Kegan Paul, 1963; ed.2 1970*; Toronto: McClelland & Stewart, 1963; Princeton, N.J.: Princeton U. Press/Bollingen, ed.2 1970*; 1977p* (CW 14) (702 + xix, incl. 45-p. index, 45-p. bibl., 26 illus.).

Completed in his eighty-first year, Jung's last major work provides a final account of his lengthy and extensive researches on alchemy, synthesizing the symbolical significance of alchemy in terms of modern depth psychology. His comparative study of the problems of philosophical alchemy and the synthesis of opposites in the human psyche provides a way of viewing neurotic and psychotic processes. The symbolism of alchemy provides the psychology of the unconscious with a meaningful historical basis which can be rediscovered in dreams, wherein the entire alchemical procedure for uniting the opposites can represent the patient's individuation process. The two stages of the conjunction are, first, a dissociation of the personality caused by the ego coming to terms with its own shadow (in other words, knowledge of one's self) and then a reunion of spirit with the body, making real the knowledge of one's paradoxical wholeness and discovering the existence of a sense of inner security.

(Bk.revs.: AmJPsychi '56/112:949; AmJPsy '56/69:696–7; BrJPsy '56/47:154–5; AmJPsyth '57/11:953; BkRDig '64/636–7; CathEdR '64/62:273–5; ContemPsy '64/ 9:375–6; IntJParapsy '64/6:380; RMeta '64/17:628; TimesLitSup '64:30; VaQR '64/ 40:xliv; JAnPsy '65/10:189–93; PsychiQ '65/39:590; AnnAmAcad '66/366:199–201)

Man and His Symbols, by Carl G. Jung, M.-L. von Franz, Joseph L. Henderson, Jolande Jacobi, and Aniela Jaffé. Garden City, N.Y.: Windfall Books/ Doubleday, 1964*; London: Aldus Books in connection with W. H. Allen/ Doubleday, 1964; New York: Dell, 1968p*; London: Aldus Books/Jupiter

Books, 1975p; London: Picador/Pan Books, 1978p* (320, incl. 3-p. index, 5-p. ref. notes, 500+ illus.).

Containing Jung's last work, completed when he was nearly eighty-six, these collective writings by himself and four of his close associates represents a richly illustrated, large-format book addressed to the general reader. Jung's essay, "Approaching the Unconscious" (which is the longest in the book), discusses the importance, function, and analysis of dreams; the problem of personality types; the archetype in dream symbolism; the soul; the role of symbols; and healing the split between the conscious mind and the unconscious. Von Franz describes the process of individuation (pattern of psychic growth; first approach of the unconscious; realization of the shadow; anima; animus; and Self). Henderson relates ancient myths and modern man (eternal symbols; heroes and hero makers; the archetype of initiation; Beauty and the Beast; Orpheus and the son of man; symbols of transcendence). Jaffé interprets symbolism in the visual arts (sacred symbols; stone and animal; symbol of the circle; modern painting as symbol; the secret soul of things; retreat from reality; union of opposites). Jacobi analyzes the symbols that evolved in an interesting and successful individual analysis.

(Bk.revs.: LibJ '64/89:4812+; NatR '64/16:1113; NewStates '64/68:478–9; SatR 30c'64/47:38; BkRDig '65:658; Bklist '65/61:446; Frontier '65/8:235; NewRep 16Ja'65/152:22–4; NYRevBks 25F'65/4:5–6; Playboy '65/12:34; SciBks '65/1:4–5; Spring '65:144; Tabl '65/219:40; TimesLitSup '65:11; JAnPsy '66/11:78–9; PastorPsy My'66/17:59–61; AmArtist Mr'74/38:13; BksBkmen Ap'76/21:14–15; TimesEdSup 21Ap'78:20)

Alchemical Studies, by C. G. Jung. New York: Bollingen Foundation, 1967*; London: Routledge & Kegan Paul, 1968*; 1983p*; Princeton, N.J.: Princeton U. Press/Bollingen, 1983p* (CW 13) (444 + xiv, incl. 62-p. index, 28-p. bibl., 54 illus.).

Five essays, composed by Jung between 1929 and 1945 and revised later, are arranged chronologically in this collection in order to illustrate the researches in alchemy that preoccupied him during the last thirty years of his life. First is Jung's commentary on the ancient Taoist alchemical text *The Secret of the Golden Flower,* described above. His psychological interpretation (1937) of the visions of Zosimos, an alchemist and Gnostic of the third century A.D., reveals the alchemist as unconsciously projecting onto chemical substances an inner, psychic experience whose symbolism reflects the individuation process. In "Paracelsus as a Spiritual Phenomenon" (1941), Jung interprets Paracelsus as not only a medieval physician and Christian but also as an alchemical philosopher, a pioneer of chemical medicine and empirical psychology. In "The Spirit Mercurius" (1942), he surveys the Mercurius concept in alchemy, drawing on Grimm's fairy tale of the spirit in the bottle.

In "The Philosophical Tree" (1945), he analyzes many representations of the tree symbol (illustrated by thirty-two paintings and drawings by patients) as a central symbol in alchemy.
(Bk.revs.: LibJ '68/93:2250; LibJBkR '68:514; Spring '68:133; AmJPsychi '69/126:279–80; BrJPsychi '69/115:499–500; Isis '71/62:236–8)

Mandala Symbolism, by C. G. Jung. Princeton, N.J.: Princeton U. Press/Bollingen, 1972p* (121 + ix, incl. 11-p. index, 10-p. bibl., 85 illus.).

Consisting of three excerpts from the *Collected Works* (vol. 9, pt. 1), this collection opens with a concise summary of mandalas published in a popular Swiss magazine in 1955. In a long essay, "A Study in the Process of Individuation," which was revised and expanded from a 1933 lecture, Jung illustrates the process with a case study of a young woman, in which twenty-four mandala paintings are interpreted in detail as representations of material from her unconscious in the initial stages of individuation. His 1950 essay, "Concerning Mandala Symbolism," offers a selection of fifty-four mandala pictures, most of which were produced spontaneously by patients in the course of analysis.
(Bk.revs.: SatR 2D'72/55:72; JAnPsy '75/20:90)

Dreams, by C. G. Jung. Princeton, N.J.: Princeton U. Press/Bollingen, 1974p*; London: Routledge & Kegan Paul, 1982p*; London: Ark Paperbacks, 1985p* (337 + xix, incl. 2-p. index, 13-p. bibl., 107 illus.).

Reportedly having carefully analyzed about 2,000 dreams per year, Jung's devotion to and experience with dream material is reflected in all of his writings. Six excerpts from the *Collected Works* (vols. 4, 8, 12, and 16) are arranged under the headings of dreams and psychoanalysis (a 1909 essay on the analysis of dreams and a 1910 article on the significance of number dreams); dreams and psychic energy (a 1916 essay and a 1948 expansion of general aspects of dream psychology; and a 1945 article and a 1948 revision on the nature of dreams); the practical use of dream analysis (a 1931 lecture); and individual dream symbolism in relation to alchemy.
(Bk.revs.: PsychiQ '74/48:590–1; AmJPsychi '75/132:882–3; Tabl '85/239:1288–9; PsyMed '86/16:481; Resurg Mr–Ap'86/n115:48–9)

Psychology and the Occult, by C. G. Jung. Princeton, N.J.: Princeton U. Press/Bollingen, 1977p*; London: Routledge & Kegan Paul, 1982p; London: Ark Paperbacks, 1987p* (167 + x, incl. 9-p. bibl.).

Among the eight excerpts from the *Collected Works* (vols. 1, 8, and 18) on the subject of psychology and the occult, the longest (86 pp.) is Jung's

1902 doctoral dissertation, "On the Psychology and Pathology of So-called Occult Phenomena," which contains a detailed analysis of cases of severe hysteria, focusing particularly on a somnambulistic adolescent girl who professed to be a spiritualistic medium. Also included are a 1905 lecture on spiritualistic phenomena, a 1919 paper on the psychological foundations of belief in spirits, a 1934 article on soul and death, a 1948 article on psychology and spiritualism, and forewords to Moser's book on spooks (1956) and Jaffé's book on apparitions and precognition (1958), as well as a two-page article on the future of parapsychology (1960).

(Bk.revs.: Quad '78/11n1:99–102; BrBkN '87:210–11)

* * * * *

Dream Psychology, by Maurice Nicoll. London: Oxford U. Press, 1917; London: Oxford Medical Publications/Oxford U. Press and Hodder & Stoughton, ed.2 1920; York Beach, Maine: Samuel Weiser, 1979p* (194 + xv, incl. 4-p. index, 2-p. bibl.).

Expressing his debt to Jung, Nicoll aims to present a view of dreams that is not purely deterministic. Following his discussions of the psyche, the problem of the neurotic, and mental background, he focuses on compensation, overcompensation, undercompensation, fantasy, and rumor. He also examines the topics of the unconscious, complexes, extraversion and introversion, balance, regression, and responsibility.

(Bk.revs.: Bkman '17/52:147; PsyanR '19/6:353–4)

The Hands of Children: An Introduction to Psycho-Chirology, by Julius Spier. London: Kegan Paul, Trench, Trubner, 1944; London: Routledge & Kegan Paul, ed.2 1955; New Delhi: Sagar Publications, 1983p* (179 + xvi, incl. 11-p. index, 87 figures, 23 handprints, 2-p. intro. by Jung).

In his introduction, Jung expresses his impression of Spier's work of chirology as a valuable contribution to psychology. After presenting the theoretical foundation and some general remarks about psycho-chirology, Spier examines in detail characteristics of the outer hand, the fingers, the position of the hand, the relationship of the fingers toward each other, the peculiarities of each finger, the significance of the right and left hands, the mounts, the main lines in the palm of the hand, and subsidiary lines and various other features of the inner hand. In this book he applies chirology to the hands of children, appending specimen prints with analyses. The second edition contains an appendix, by Herta Levi, on the mentally ill.

(Bk.revs.: Listen '44/31:586; BrJPsy '55/46:240)

The Dream of Poliphilo: The Soul in Love, related and interpreted by Linda Fierz-David. (Ger.: *Der Liebestraum des Poliphilo.* Zurich: Rhein Verlag, 1947.) New York: Pantheon Books (Bollingen Series XXV), 1950; Toronto: McClelland & Stewart, 1950; Princeton, N.J.: Princeton U. Press/Bollingen, rev. 1969; Dallas: Spring Publications, ed.2 1987p* (Jungian Classics Series, 8) (133 + xv, incl. 34 illus., 3-p. foreword by Jung).

Applying methods of Jungian interpretation to the literary monument of Renaissance psychology, *The Dream of Poliphilo* (also known as *The Strife of the Love Dream*), which was ascribed to a Venetian monk, Fierz-David analyzes the story in terms of three superimposed strata: namely, the tradition of the courtly love of women, the humanistic conception of the revival of classical culture, and the alchemical conception of transmutation of matter. All three represent the religious principle of transformation or rebirth. Jung, in the foreword, opines that her undertaking is entirely successful and performed with intelligence and intuition; he credits his own labored research on the *Dream* many years before as aiding him greatly in putting him "on the track of the royal art," namely, alchemy.

(Bk.revs.: Poetry '50/77:168–73; BulAnPsyNY Ja'51/13:1–5; PsyanR '52/39:205–6; Quad '88/21n2:96–9; SmallPrBkR Mr–Ap'88/3:24)

Funk & Wagnalls Dictionary of Folklore, Mythology, and Legend, edited by Maria Leach and Jerome Fried. New York: Funk & Wagnalls, 1949–50, in 2 vols.; 1972, in 1 vol.; London: Mayflower, 1951; Toronto: Ryerson Press, 1951; London: New English Library, 1975; New York: Harper & Row, 1984p* (1236 + xvii, incl. 40-p. supp. providing cross-ref. for 2405 countries, regions, culture areas, peoples, tribes, and ethnic groups).

This comprehensive dictionary is written by forty-two contributors and includes fifty-five survey articles, mostly on regional folklore. It contains information on folk heroes, culture heroes, tricksters, the folklore of animals, birds, plants, insects, stones, gems, stars, dances, folk songs, ballads, festivals and rituals, food customs, games and children's rhymes, riddles, divination, witches, omens, magic charms and spells, demons, ogres, werewolves, vampires, and fairies, along with folk tales and motifs out of story, ballad, and song.

(Bk.revs.: BkRDig '49:326; KirkR '49/17:643; LibJ '49/74:1463–4; PsychiQ '49/23:791; Bkmark '50/78:9; KenyonR '50/12:721–2; NYTimesBkR 31D'50:15; SatR 21Ja'50/ 23:41–2; SFolkQ '50/14:123–8; TimesLitSup '50:90; Folk '51/62:107–9, 470–2; Int-JAmLing '51/17:186–8; JAmFolk '51/64:325–8; MidwFolk '51/1:267–72; PsychiQ '51/ 25:519–20; SFolkQ '51/15:171–2; TimesLitSup '51:320; JAmOrSoc '52/72:127; Specul '52/72:228–34; SocSocRes '54/39:134; Bklist '73/70:253; JAmFolk '73/86:411; LibJ '73/

98:858; LibJBkR '73:716; RQ '73/12:318; RefServR Ap'73/1:22; ClassWorld '74/66:142–3; BksBkmen S'76/21:64; RefServR '84/12:13; RelStudR '85/11:184)

Timeless Documents of the Soul, by Helmuth Jacobsohn, Marie-Louise von Franz, and Siegmund Hurwitz. (Ger. *Zeitlose Dokumente der Seele.* Zurich: Rascher Verlag, 1952/Studien aus dem C. G. Jung-Institut, III.) Evanston, Ill.: Northwestern U. Press, 1968 (Studies in Jungian Thought) (263 + xii, incl. 23-p. index, 9-p. bibl.).

Psychological interpretations of three "timeless documents of the soul" reveal examples of the contribution of depth psychology toward understanding the attempts of the conscious personality to struggle with revelations from within the unconscious. Egyptologist Jacobsohn's interpretation of the dialogue of a world-weary man of four thousand years ago dealing with his *Ba* (soul), center of his individuality and inner power, is that he feels the tragedy of helplessness and wrestles with the problem of suicide. Von Franz's analysis of the so-called "great dream" of young Descartes (c. 1620), an archetypal dream still of interest today in that it reveals the inadequacy of a purely rational view of the world, is that the archetype of Self was seeking to become integrated into his new thinking. Hurwitz's study of the psychological aspects of early Hasidic literature and in particular the Great Maggid (early 1700s) deals with the relating of consciousness and the unconscious, Sefiroth symbolism, symbolism of numbers and names, *coniunctio* mysticism, and the unconscious dream-prophecy.

(Bk.revs.: Spring '69:143–6; JAnPsy '70/15:195–6; UnionSemQR '70/25:255–6)

The Forge and the Crucible: The Origins and Structure of Alchemy, by Mircea Eliade. (Fr.: *Forgerons et Alchimistes.* Paris: Ernest Flammarion, 1956.) London: Rider, 1962; New York: Harper & Row, 1962; New York: Torchbook/Harper & Row, 1971p; Chicago and London: Phoenix Book/U. of Chicago Press, ed.2 1978p* (238, incl. 4-p. index, 34-p. appendixes on sources).

As a historian of religions, Eliade aims in this study to gain "an understanding of the behavior of primitive societies in relation to Matter and to following the spiritual adventures in which they become involved when they found themselves aware of their power to change the mode of being of substances." He examines the ideology and techniques of alchemy (dwelling at some length on the less well-known Chinese and Indian alchemy) in terms of both the experimental and mystical character of alchemical technique. He characterizes the alchemist as collaborating in the perfecting of matter while at the same time securing perfection for himself; and he credits at length Jung's contributions in making alchemy significant for modern culture.

(Bk.revs.: Isis '58/49:451–3; Folk '62/73:140; RforRel '63/22:706; RRelRes '63/5:55–6; JRelThought '64–65/21:162–3)

Apparitions: An Archetypal Approach to Death Dreams and Ghosts, by Aniela Jaffé. (Ger.: *Geistererscheinungen und Vorzeichen.* Zurich: Rascher Verlag, 1957.) (Orig. title: *Apparitions and Precognition: A Study from the Point of View of C. G. Jung's Analytical Psychology.* New Hyde Park, N.Y.: University Books, 1963.) Dallas: Spring Publications, 1979p (Jungian Classics Series, 1) (214, incl. 8-p. index, 4-p. foreword by Jung).

Drawing from more than 1,200 letters containing about 5,000 accounts of apparitions, premonitions, and prophetic dreams that were received in response to an inquiry by the editor of a popular Swiss fortnightly, Jaffé applies Jung's psychological findings in order to interpret such astonishing "wonder tales" from the unconscious, including synchronistic phenomena, ghosts, and the "nearness" of departed spirits.

(Bk.revs.: CanJTheol '64/10:144–6; IntJParapsy '64/6:227–37; Jubilee Mr'64/11:48–50; LibJ '64/89:120; PsychiQ '64/38:560)

Aurora Consurgens: A Document Attributed to Thomas Aquinas on the Problem of Opposites in Alchemy, edited, with a commentary, by Marie-Louise von Franz. (Ger.: *Aurora Consurgens: Ein dem Thomas von Aquin zugeschriebenes Dokument der alchemistischen Gegensatzproblematik* (Part III of *Mysterium Coniunctionis,* by C. G. Jung). Zurich and Stuttgart: Rascher Verlag, 1957.) London: Routledge & Kegan Paul, 1966; New York: Pantheon Books (Bollingen Series LXXVII), 1966 (555 + xv, 25-p. general index, 6-p. index of Biblical references and parallels, 44-p. bibl.).

At Jung's request, von Franz prepared a psychological interpretation of this document as a companion work to Jung's *Mysterium Coniunctionis* as it fit into the history of alchemy. Not concerned with the hypothesis that the text might represent the last words of St. Thomas Aquinas, she concludes that the author was not a practising alchemist but that, while undergoing unmistakably numinous experiences within himself, he intuitively articulated the inexpressible by using existing alchemical symbols. She examines the "flight of ideas" as methodically as though it were a dream, attempting to discover its meaning by the use of amplification and symbolic allusions.

(Bk.revs.: Choice '67/4:30; Spring '67:150–1; Tabl '67/221:236; TimesLitSup '67:50; JAnPsy '68/13:77–9)

A Dictionary of Symbols, by J. E. Cirlot. (Sp.: *Diccionario de Símbolos Tradicionales.* Barcelona: L. Miracle, 1958.) London: Routledge & Kegan Paul, 1962; ed.2 1972; 1983p*; New York: Philosophical Library, 1962; ed.2

1971* (419 + 1v, incl. 19-p. index, 13-p. bibl., 119 illus., 2-p. foreword by Herbert Read).

Expressing his debt to the works of Jung, Emma Jung, von Franz, Hillman, Liz Greene, Streatfeild, and others, Cirlot presents more than 800 entries in his dictionary of "traditional symbols," arranging them alphabetically and specifying the precise sources for each item. He draws from various fields of knowledge, using his background as an artist to clarify symbolism in all of its aspects. Many entries may be read as independent essays, as well as for use in dream analysis or for other purposes.

(Bk.revs.: Americas '62/19:113–14; ArtActiv My'62/51:130; BkRDig '62:223–4; ClassBul '62/38:62; JAesthArt '62:234; SchArts Jn'62/61:49; Tabl '62/216:380; Archaeol Mr'63/ 16:80; CathBibQ '63/25:231–2; HispAmHistR '63/43:148; Spring '63:151; TimesLitSup '63:69; CathLib '72/44:311; LibJBkR '72:719; WilsonLibB S'72/17:89; Choice '73/ 9:1429; SpecLib '81/72:256; PsyMed '84/14:479)

Persephone: A Study of Two Worlds, by D. Streatfeild. London: Routledge & Kegan Paul, 1959; New York: Julian Press, 1959 (360 + v, incl. 11-p. indexes).

Expressing his "obvious dependence on the system of Jung," which makes human behavior intelligible, Streatfeild shows that the inner world is real and no less objective than the outer world; and he accepts the existence of entities of an unfamiliar nature, such as the collective unconscious and the archetypes. His study of "two worlds" was occasioned by reading an episode in Hadley Chases's *No Orchids for Miss Blandish* that was extraordinarily close to a passage in a work of fiction that he had written but never published. In the course of analyzing that book, he examines the problem of reality and likens it to Persephone's experience in the underworld.

Psyche and Death: Death-Demons in Folklore, Myths, and Modern Dreams, by Edgar Herzog. (Ger.: *Psyche und Tod: Wandlungen des Todesbildes im Mythos in den träumenheutiger Menschen.* Zurich: Rascher Verlag, 1960/ Studien aus dem C. G. Jung-Institut, vol. II.) London: Hodder & Stoughton, 1966; New York: G. P. Putnam's Sons for the C. G. Jung Foundation for Analytical Psychology, 1967; Dallas: Spring Publications, 1983p* (Jungian Classics Series, 5) (224, incl. 10-p. indexes, 3-p. bibl.).

Crediting Jung's psychology with providing a new method of working in ethnology, ethnic psychology, and mythology, Herzog presents the subject of death as an aspect of becoming, of transformation, by which the human condition transcends itself. He discusses first how humankind has always attempted to come to terms with death by means of images, drawing upon symbols from a wide range of animal and human forms. He then discusses dreams in relation to the repression and acceptance of death; killing; archaic forms of the death-demon; the kingdom of the dead, death, procreation, and rebirth; and dreams of death as an expression of the process of development. (Bk.revs.: KirkR '66/34:1315; ChrCen'67/84:238; Spring '67:151–2; Folk '68/70:313; JAnPsy '83/28:387–8)

The Visits of the Queen of Sheba, by Miguel Serrano. Bombay: Asia Publishing House, 1960; London: Routledge & Kegan Paul, ed.2 1972; New York: Harper & Row, 1973p; New York: Methuen, 1974 (61 + xi, incl. 8 illus., 1-p. foreword/letter by Jung).

Considering Jung's comment that the unconscious presents itself to Serrano in its poetic aspect, resulting in an ongoing dream and in dreams within dreams, Serrano recounts this proliferating dream. The aesthetic nature of the work is reflected in the titles of the chapters: "The Great Mother"; "The River"; "The Story of the Moonstone"; "Parvati"; "The Visits of the Queen of Sheba"; "The Brother of Silence"; "Footsteps in the Sand"; "The Return of the Queen of Sheba"; "The Quest"; "The Servants"; "Melchizedek"; "The Lamb"; "The Bird of Paradise"; "The Mass"; "The White Horse"; and "The Last Flower."
(Bk.revs.: LibJ '61/86:2666; LitEW '62/6:105–8; StudComRel '74/8:64)

Dictionary of Mythology, Folklore, and Symbols, by Gertrude Jobes. New York: Scarecrow Press, 1961* (2,241 in 3 vols., incl. 24-p. bibl., 482-p. index as vol. 3).

Collecting from a wide variety of sources, Jobes has compiled an extensive dictionary of mythology, folklore, and symbols, arranging the descriptions and the explanations for general items, such as animals and plants, in the following categories: universal and popular symbolism, dream significance, heraldic significance, occult significance, mythological and religious significance, word explanation, and cognates or comparisons.
(Bk.revs.: Bklist '61/58:207–8, 210–12; BkRDig '62:617)

The Archetypal Cat, by Patricia Dale-Green. (Orig. title: *Cult of the Cat.* London: William Heinemann, 1963; Boston: Houghton Mifflin, 1963; London: Heinemann, 1970p; New York: Tower, repr. 1970p) Dallas: Spring Publications, ed.2 1983p* (189 + v, incl. 7-p. index, 4-p. bibl., 31 illus.).

Stating her thesis that people need to adopt a realistic attitude toward the cat's paradoxical nature and "allow it to communicate its wisdom," Dale-Green contrasts images of the white cat (including deity, sun, moon, immortal, seer, healer, hunter, mother, seed, virgin, talisman, charm, musician, servant, sacrifice) and of the black cat (including devourer, witch, familiar, devil, demon, vampire, bewitcher, traitor, trickster, fighter, victim). She also discusses the cat as bridge between light and darkness and as psychopomp. Employing the traditional Jungian methodology of amplification, she uses a wide range of sources from folklore, fairy tales, legends, myths, religions, and dreams.

(Bk.revs.: Harvest '63/9:77; Folk '64/75:131–2; Quad '84/17n2:95–9)

The Old Wise Woman: A Study in Active Imagination, by Rix Weaver. London: Vincent Stuart, 1964; New York: Putnam's/C. G. Jung Foundation, 1973 (174, incl. 4-p. bibl., 2-p. ref. notes, 4-p. gloss., 6 illus., 1-p. intro. by C. A. Meier). Boston: Shambhala, repr. 1991p.

Weaver presents an example of the use of the method of active imagination, providing a psychological commentary on a long myth that came to one of her analysands. She analyzes the successive stages of the woman's inner journey that were represented by small clay models of the central figures. Following discussions of some aspects of the technique of active imagination and of the individual nature of such, she interprets the myth, using clay modeling, through the stages of the old man, the old woman, the journey, tribulation, the attainment, and the jewel. She also includes an example of active imagination as used following a recurring dream.

(Bk.revs.: Spring '65:146:AmJArtTh '74/13:331; JAnPsy '75/20:82–3)

The Understanding of Dreams; or, The Machinations of the Night, by Raymond de Becker. (Fr.: *Les Machinations de la nuit.* Paris: Edition Planete, 1965.) London: George Allen & Unwin, 1968; New York: Hawthorn Books, 1968 (432, incl. 12-p index, 8-p bibl.).

Drawing on his own five-year self-analysis of dreams and on two years with a Jungian analyst during a period of vital, pressing personal problems, Becker acknowledges his debt to Freud and Jung and offers an examination of dreams as a kind of energy at work in the depths of individuals that motivates action. Beginning with the historical influence of dreams (religious, political, cultural, and in art and literature) and the analysis of dream incubation and induced dreams, he then discusses interpretation and theories (dream books; theories of dreams in pre- and para-Christian civilizations; the Christian attitude toward dreams; the physiological approach to dreams since the nineteenth century; the psychical structure of dreams; Freud versus Jung; self-analysis and the character of the interpreter), concluding with the subject of transcendence in dreams (dreams and the individuation process; dreams, space, and time; and dreams and degrees of reality).

(Bk.revs.: NewStates '68/76:550; TimesLitSup '68:964; Bklist '69/65:460; GaR '69/23:267–8; PsyToday Ap'69/2:6+; RforRel Mr'69/28:315; Theol '69/72:377; IntJPsy-An '70/51:558)

Dreams: God's Forgotten Language, by John A. Sanford. (Ger.: *Gottes vergessens Sprache.* Zurich: Rascher Verlag, 1966/Studien aus dem C. G. Jung-Institut, vol. 13.) New York: J. B. Lippincott, 1968; New York: Crossroad Publications, 1982p; 1986p; San Francisco: Harper & Row, 1989p* (194 + xiv, incl. 4-p. index, 6-p. ref. notes).

Sanford's aim is to show the "extraordinary at work in the ordinary" by examining the relationship of dreams to religious experience, taking the point of view that the ego is purposively directed by dreams from a central authority in the psyche. He discusses dreams and visions in the Bible, the nature and structure of dreams, and the Christian view of the relationship between dreams and God, in which dreams represent the image of God within (the Self or psychic center) as well as transcendental reality. He interprets fifteen dreams to illustrate problems of the shadow and self-confrontation, guilt and forgiveness, literal, shortsighted collective attitudes, and wholeness (as opposed to perfection).

(Bk.revs.: LumenVitae '67/22:568; ChrCen '68/85:1220; KirkR '68/36:805; LibJ '68/93:3565; LibJBkR '68:420; PubW 8Jy'68/194:164; BkRDig '69:1158; ChryToday '69/13:18–19; PsyToday Ap'69/2:6+10; JforRel Ja'69/28:155; InwLight '70–71/n78:47–8; FriendsJ Jy'90/36:42)

The Meaning in Dreams and Dreaming: The Jungian Viewpoint, by Maria F. Mahoney. Secaucus, N.J.: Citadel Press/Lyle Stuart, 1966p (256, incl. 13-p. index).

In presenting information about dreams and their interpretation according to Jung's principles, Mahoney provides an analytical treatment of the subject and offers advice on how to recognize and interpret dream images using amplification and integration. She devotes nearly half the book to a summary of Jung's psychology, discussing the semantics of the psyche, archetypes and symbols, the four functions, persona and shadow, projection, and anima and animus. Using more than fifty dreams as examples, she comments on the meanings of compensatory or complementary dreams, reductive dreams, reactive dreams, prospective dreams, somatic dreams, telepathic dreams, and archetypal dreams.

(Bk.rev.: Harvest '67/13:82)

God, Dreams, and Revelation, by Morton T. Kelsey. (Orig. title: *Dreams: The Dark Speech of the Spirit.* New York: Doubleday, 1968.) Minneapolis: Augsburg Publishing House, rev. 1974p* (264 + x, incl. 8-p. bibl.).

Thanking Jungian analysts for first opening his mind and heart to the significance of dreams, Kelsey aims to show that the main strand of Christian tradition up to modern times views the dream as one way of God's speaking. He traces historical attitudes toward dreams, looking at the Hebrews, Greeks, and other ancient peoples and examines the dreams and visions of the first Christians and the dreams of the "victorious" Christian church. He also discusses how psychologists explore the dream and ends with the modern Christian interpretation of dreams.

(Bk.revs.: KirkR '68/36:588; LibJ '68/93:2879; LibJBkR '68:403; PubW 3Jn'68/193:123; StLukeJTh Oc'68/12:66–7; JSciStudRel '69/8:366; PsyToday '69/2:6+10; Spring '69:150–1; JPastorPsy '74/28:211; LuthQ '74/26:470–1; ReligEd '74/69:746–7; R&Expos '74/71:410–11; SWJTheol '74/17:118–19; SpirLife '74/20:224; LumenVitae '82/37:468)

The Fool and His Scepter: A Study of Clowns and Jesters and Their Audiences, by William Willeford. Evanston, Ill.: Northwestern U. Press, 1969* +p* (265 + xxii, incl. 7-p. index, 21-p. ref. notes, 35 illus.).

Jungian analyst Willeford characterizes the symbol of the fool as a pervasive archetypal figure found throughout history in a variety of places, such as records of folk festivals and court jesters, the literature of the late Middle Ages and early Renaissance, plays by Shakespeare and others, vaudeville and circus clown skits, and magazine cartoons. He examines the contexts of the settings in which fools appear and the psychological sources of individuals' responses to fools, such as hopes and fears and patterns of decorum, including the interactions between the fool-actor and the audience. Among the examples of this powerful imaginative form are Hamlet (the tragic dimension of folly), King Lear (the sovereign fool), and Buster Keaton (the cosmic dimension of folly).

(Bk.revs.: BkRDig '69:1412; BkWorld 31Ag'69:6–7; Bklist '69/66:374; LibJ '69/94:4007; LibJBkR '69:377; AmAnth '70/72:1194–5; Choice '70/7:531–2; JEGP '70/69:552–3; ModLangQ '70/31:245–8; Quad '70/7:20–1; JAmFolk '71/84:356–7; JAnPsy '71/16:115–16; ModPhilol '71/68:409; PsyRec '71/21:572; ShakStud '71/7:456–66; ShakesQ '73/24:228–9)

Freud, Jung, and Occultism, by Nandor Fodor. New Hyde Park, N.Y.: University Books, 1971; New York: Lyle Stuart, 1972 (272 pp.).

In this work, Fodor focuses on Freud's and Jung's relationship to God and the devil, psychic participation, poltergeists, telepathy, the trauma of birth, religious conversion, audio clairvoyance, déjà vu, and the double. Other topics include chance, omens and synchronicity, premonitions of disaster, telling fortune and fate, the fatal influence of numbers, mystic participation, Jung and the archetypes, Freud and the archaic, the archetype in dreams, and the first time Jung died. Appended is a 1960 journal article on the psychic world of Jung (by Aniela Jaffé) and a 1963 book review of Jung's autobiography (by Martin Ebon).

(Bk.revs.: AmJPsychi '72/129:773–4; ContemPsy '72/17:664–5; LibJ '72/97:3322–3; LibJBkR '72:453; Choice '73/9:1662; PsyanR '73/60:636–8; PsyPersp '74/5:74–7)

Mandala, by José Argüelles and Miriam Argüelles. Berkeley, Calif. and London: Shambhala Publications, 1972; Boston and London: Shambhala Publications, 1985p* (140, incl. 5-p. index, 5-p. bibl., 150+ illus., foreword by Chögyam Trungpa).

The Argüelleses credit the popular reintroduction of the mandala concept to Jung's rediscovery of it. The mandala, a depiction of symbols usually in the form of a circle, can be used as a therapeutic integrative art form that is created naturally by patients in their search for individuation. The authors' detailed study, illustrated by numerous mandala paintings, traces the mandala through numerous traditions and relates the technique to the life process. Topics are the universality of the mandala, the ritual of the mandala, and the mandala as a visual process, an art form, a key to symbolic systems, and a point of departure.

(Bk.revs.: AmArtist D'72/36:28; JTranspPsy '72/4:211–12; LibJ '72/97:3697; LibJBkR '72:33; SatR 2D'72/55:72; BkRDig '73:33; Choice '73/10:476; StudComRel '73/7:187; Syst '73/11:64–7; Bklist '75/72:558)

The Meaning and Significance of Dreams, by C. A. Meier. (Ger.: *Die Empirie des Unbewussten*. 1972.) Boston: Sigo Press, 1987*; 1990p (*The Psychology of C. G. Jung*, vol. 2) (163 + xi, incl. 5-p. index, 11-p. bibl., 8-p. ref. notes, 6 illus.).

Regretting that Jung did not provide an extensive and comprehensive treatment of the dream, Meier aims to do so, citing his own good fortune at receiving the notes used by Jung when he taught the subject at Zurich's Higher Technical University. Meier discusses basic aspects of Jung's methodology and approach to the structure, function, and symbolism of dreams; and he provides a history of dream research and ancient dream theories. He also interprets the meaning of the dream in the context of Jung's theory of the complex and, using a series of six dreams, he describes the technique of analyzing dreams.

(Bk.revs.: PsyPersp '88/19:341–3; Harvest '89–90/35:223–5; JAnPsy '89/34:399–400)

The Reluctant Prophet, by James Kirsch. Los Angeles: Sherbourne Press, 1973; distributed by Daimon Verlag, Einsiedeln, Switzerland (214, incl. 6-p. index).

Comparing nineteenth-century Orthodox Rabbi Wechsler of Bavaria to Melville and Nietzsche, Jungian analyst Kirsch relates how the reluctant prophet was so stirred by the numinous dreams that came to him between ages twenty-nine and thirty-seven that he published in 1881 a brochure warning of the holocaust to come. Starting with a discussion of European anti-Semitism of the time, Wechsler's personality, and a diagnosis of the contemporary culture's sickness, Kirsch describes the twelve dreams, along with Wechsler's theory of dreams and its Jewish sources, and then interprets the dreams, including a "Christ" dream and two "Elijah" dreams. He analyzes the personal message of the dreams as a call for the rabbi to reevaluate his orthodox religious beliefs as a part of the process of individuation.

(Bk.revs.: Harvest '74/20:26–7; JAnPsy '74/19:208–9; PsyPersp '74/5:185–8; Quad '74/n17:52–3)

Dictionary of Symbols and Imagery, by Ad de Vries. Amsterdam and London: North-Holland Publishing Co., 1974; ed.2 1976; Amsterdam: Elsevier Science Publishers, 3rd printing, 1984* (515 + xiv).

Although the material chosen is restricted to Western symbols and imagery, de Vries has compiled an extensive selection with no fine distinction being made between symbols, in the limited sense, and allegories, metaphors, signs, types, and images. More than 2,500 items comprise the volume, including numerous symbolic names and places; and many symbols exhibit a great range of meanings. He supplies background information from a number of fields, showing the ambiguity of many symbols and preventing a too-limited approach to imagery. Often, several given meanings may apply simultaneously. There are some general entries, such as archetype, calendar, dream, elements, inversion, multiplicity, mystery, and riddle.

(Bk.revs.: CollResLib '75/36:313; BibSocAm '76/70:448; EnglStud '76/57:285–6; Int-JSymb '76/7:82; AmRefBksAn '77/8:548)

The Mythic Image, by Joseph Campbell. Princeton, N.J.: Princeton U. Press (Bollingen Series C), 1974; 1981p* (552 + xiii, incl. 12-p. index, 10-p. ref. notes, 442 illus., incl. 7 maps).

Drawing upon the mythology ("the mysteries of being beyond thought") of the world's cultures during five millenia, Campbell brings an impressive wealth of visual forms to illustrate mythic themes. He argues that a door to mythology is opened through dreams and that myths, and dreams, arise from an inner world unknown to waking consciousness. He analyzes myth as an expression in symbolic form of the world as a dream and discusses the idea of a cosmic order in both folk traditions and the great world religions of Buddhism, Christianity, and Islam.

(Bk.revs.: BkRDig '75:201–2; BkWorld 9Mr'75/9:4; BksAbroad '75/49:861–2; Choice '75/12:824; KirkR '75/43:271; LibJ '75/100:870; LibJBkR '75:277; NewRep 8Mr'75/ 172:33; NYTimesBkR 28D'75:15–16; NYorker 21Jy'75/51:86–8; Newswk 31Mr'75/ 85:75–6; PubW 24F'75/207:112; Quad '75/8n1:69–70; RforRel '75/34:634; RBksRel Jn'75/4:11; Time 22D'75/106:62; VaQR '75/51:646; WallStJ 12My'75/185:12; Wilson-LibB '75/49:620; AmBkColl Jy'76/26:2+; AmJPsychi '76/133:1098; Commonw '76/ 103:155; Parab Wint'76/1:99–103; SewaneeR '76/84:lvi–lix; StudRel '76–77/6:568–71; Thought '76/51:450–1; WFolk '76/35:80–2; JAnPsy '77/22:279–81; SHumR '77/11:321– 2; Chr&Lit '78/27n3:45–7; PsyanQ '78/47:134–6; RelStudR '80/6:261–71; Kliatt Wint'82/16:24)

The Dream—The Vision of the Night, by Max Zeller, edited by Janet O. Dallett. Los Angeles: Analytical Psychology Club of Los Angeles and the C. G. Jung Institute of Los Angeles, 1975; Boston: Sigo Press, ed.2, 1990 +p (183 + xvi, incl. 2-p. biography of Max Zeller, 1-p. foreword by James Kirsch).

For the occasion of Zeller's seventieth birthday in 1974, a collection of eighteen essays was assembled in his honor. Included are eight lectures and four articles from journals and books, as well as a remembrance of a Christmas Eve in Nazi Germany, Zeller's comments (from a meeting commemorating the tenth anniversary of Jung's death) on the symbol of the well as the source where Jung and others started on the search, and two other previously unpublished essays (one on Jung's psychology and the religious quest; one on the case of a successful man, illustrated by seven dreams).

Waking Dreams, by Mary M. Watkins. New York: Interface Book/Gordon & Breach, 1976 (Psychic Studies Series); New York: Colophon Book/Harper & Row, 1977p; Dallas: Spring Publications, 1984p; 1986p* (174 + xii, incl. 6-p. index, 13-p. bibl.).

Recognizing Jung as "the bridge between the past and the present," Watkins directs the reader's attention to the continual aliveness of the imaginal, her focus being the waking dream as the conscious experiencing of the imaginal. She deals with the topics of the half-dream state, the mythopoetic function in the early history of psychology, waking dreams in European psychotherapy, and imagery and imagination in American psychology. She also discusses the interpretation of movements in imaginal space, movements from and towards the imaginal in daily life, and imagining about imagining. She appends information on autogenic relaxation and media for waking dreams.

(Bk.revs.: Choice '76/13:726; ContemPsy '77/22:475; JCommun '77/27n2:221–2; AmJArtTh '86/24:104–5)

The Herder Symbol Dictionary, translated by Boris Matthews. (Ger.: *Herder Lexikon: Symbol.* Freiberg: Herder Verlag, 1978.) Wilmette, Ill.: Chiron Publications, 1986p* (222 + vi, incl. 450 illus., pocket-size).

Containing more than a thousand entries with 450 illustrations of symbols from many cultures, particularly those familiar or close to Western European consciousness, this dictionary defines the concept of symbol quite broadly but does not include allegories or signs. Mythological figures, such as gods and heroes are not included, except for various monsters or animal-human hybrids of antiquity. Although every symbolic meaning has psychological significance, mention of psychoanalytic interpretations of symbols appears only occasionally.

(Bk.rev.: AmRefBksAn '88/19:309)

An Illustrated Encyclopaedia of Traditional Symbols, by J. C. Cooper. London: Thames & Hudson, 1978; 1979p*; New York: Thames & Hudson, 1979; 1987p* (208, incl. 5-p. bibl., 2-p. gloss. of foreign phrases, 210 illus.).

In presenting nearly 1,500 entries representing a great variety of symbols, Cooper provides not only the generalized or universally accepted interpretation of a symbol but also its various geographic and cultural applications. She demonstrates that symbolism is basic to the human mind and serves intellectual, emotional, and spiritual needs. Symbols from the Far East are especially well represented. The glossary contains fifty-nine terms, including most of the Latin phrases often used by Jung.

(Bk.revs.: Choice '79/16:363–4; RQ '79/19:85–6; RelStudR '79/5:313; WilsonLibB '79/ 53:651; AmRefBksAn '80/11:521; BkRDig '80:251–2; Bklist '80/76:1384 + ; RelStudR '81/7:154; SpecLib '81/72:156)

Understanding Dreams, by Mary Ann Mattoon. (Orig. title: *Applied Dream Analysis: A Jungian Approach.* Washington, D.C.: V. H. Winston/Scripta Technica Publishers, 1978.) Dallas: Spring Publications, rev. 1984p* (248 + xv, incl. 8-p. index, 6-p. bibl., 2-p. foreword by Joseph Wheelwright).

Considering Jung's approach to dream interpretation to be the most comprehensive and generally applicable, Mattoon systematizes Jung's theory, gives examples of every major point, and suggests supplementation and modification from material drawn from her own clinical work or that of other Jungian analysts. She discusses the nature of dreams; the dream context; individual amplifications; archetypal amplifications; the conscious situation of the dreamer; dream series; approaching the interpretation of dreams; objective and subjective characterization of dream images; the compensatory function of dreams; non-compensatory dreams; dreams and the therapeutic process; childhood dreams; the dream interpretation; and verifying the dream interpretation.

(Bk.revs.: LibJ '78/103:2432; LibJBkR '78:387; ContemPsy '79/24:405; JIndivPsy '79/ 35:251–2; JPersAssess '79/43:551–3; AmJPsychi '80/137:139–40; CanJPsychi '80/

25:604–5; JAnPsy '80/25:207–8; PsychiAn Ja'80/10:54–5; Quad '80/13n1:125–6; SFJInstLib '80/1n4:55–6; Harvest '81/27:187–8; InwLight '81–82/n97:50–1)

Alchemical Active Imagination, by Marie-Louise von Franz. Irving, Tex.: Spring Publications, 1979p* (Seminar Series, 14) (116 pp.).

In this transcript of a series of five lectures given at the Jung Institute of Zurich in 1969, von Franz first presents a short history of alchemy as viewed from the psychological standpoint and then interprets a specific text by Gerhard Dorn, one of the few introverted alchemists at the end of the sixteenth century who realized that alchemical symbolism and tradition implied a religious problem. She emphasizes that the introverted approach in alchemy shows that it is just as much an investigation of the collective unconscious as of matter and that many of the alchemists practised active imagination. Her topics include God-power in matter; the body as problem (redeeming the Christian shadow); mind and body; and medieval magic and modern synchronicity.
(Bk.revs.: Harvest '80/26:110–11; Quad '80/13n2:131–3)

The Dream and the Underworld, by James Hillman. New York: Harper & Row, 1979; New York: Colophon Books/Harper & Row, 1979p*; Magnolia, Mass.: Peter Smith, 1983 (243 + vi, incl. 9-p.index, 4-p. bibl., 27-p. ref. notes).

Aiming to explore a view of the dream different from the usual viewpoints, Hillman "re-visions" the dream in the light of myth, imagining dreams in relation to the soul and death. His psychology of dreams contains a sense of the underworld: he discusses death; Hades; the underground and the underworld; images and shadows; dream persons; and the death metaphor. He presents the barriers to grasping the underworld as the psychic realm as being materialism, oppositionalism, and Christianism. He deals in the final section with dream romantics, the dream-ego, dreamwork, and dream material.
(Bk.revs.: BkRDig '79:578; Bklist '79/76:70; KirkR '79/47:920; LibJ '79/104:1573; LibJBkR '79:369; NYTimesBkR 6Ag'79/84:7; Newswk 3S'79/94:63; Parab Ag'79/4:112–14; PsyPersp '79/10:97–100; SFJInstLib '79/1n1:11–13; SFRBks S'79/5:31; Choice '80/17:286; ContemPsy '80/25:502–3; Quad '80/13n1:112–14; RelStudR '80/6:278–85; Harvest '81/27:176–8)

Alchemy: An Introduction to the Symbolism and the Psychology, by Marie-Louise von Franz. Toronto: Inner City Books, 1980p* (Studies in Jungian Psychology by Jungian Analysts, 5) (280, incl. 8-p. index, 83 illus.).

Designed in 1959 for trainees at the Jung Institute in Zurich, this series of nine lectures introduces the subject of alchemy so that Jung's own writings on alchemy can be better understood. Von Franz furnishes deep insights into what alchemists were searching for, and her own long experience of study of alchemy and grasp of Jung's theories provides an interpretive history of the psychological significance of alchemy from the Greek, Arabic, and European eras. She analyzes a great amount of material drawn from the alchemists' projection of unconscious images into matter, abundantly illustrated by old drawings and engravings and by a few modern paintings and drawings.

(Bk.revs.: Harvest '81/27:170–2; Quad '82/15n1:78–9; NewIdeas '86/4:253–6)

Alchemy: The Philosopher's Stone, by Allison Coudert. London: Wildwood House, 1980p; Boulder, Colo.: Shambhala Publications, 1980p; Sydney: Bookwise Australia, 1980 (239, incl. 9-p. index, 9-p. bibl., 56 illus.).

Announcing that alchemy shares a vocabulary of symbols common to all myths and religions, Coudert envisions alchemists questing for wealth, spirituality, and eternal life, willing to go beyond science and religion in their search for perfection. She points out that their endeavors resulted in the beginnings of chemistry, and their visions became the source of psychological insights and surrealist art. Jung believed that the philosopher's stone as the goal of alchemy is a fitting image for the "Self," a unity formed from opposites. In chapter 6, Coudert goes into detail about Jung's discovery of the psychic nature of alchemy. Elsewhere she discusses the alchemists' credo, alchemical riddles, the elixir of the soul, and the secret art of alchemy.

(Bk.revs.: NewSci '80/88:822; Choice '81/18:974; Isis '81/72:511—12; AnnSci '82/39:524)

Jungian-Senoi Dreamwork Manual, by Strephon Kaplan-Williams. Berkeley, Calif.: Journey Press, 1980p; ed.2 1980p*; smaller format 1985p*; 1989p* (319, incl. 1-p. index, 80+ illus.).

Bringing together Jung's approach to symbolism and the Malayan Senoi people's ritual of daily work with dreams, therapist Kaplan-Williams presents a manual in which he describes thirty-five dreamwork methods. He credits the sources for the book as the real dreams and dreamwork of everyday people struggling with their lives as well as his own personal dreamwork experience. His topics include reflections on types of dreams; the functions of dreams; seven basic archetypes (Self, Feminine, Masculine, Heroic, Adversary, Death-Rebirth, and Journey); and the relationship of consciousness to healing.

A Memoir of Toni Wolff, by Irene Champernowne. San Francisco: C. G. Jung Institute of San Francisco, 1980p* (56, incl. 15 illus., 4-p. foreword by Joseph L. Henderson).

In remembrance of her experience as an analysand of Toni Wolff in Zurich, Champernowne shares an account of deep visionary experiences which she has represented in paintings. She states that Jung quietly accepted her experience with sparse comment, "allowing it its inherent validity," and that Mrs. Jung felt the material to be important for women in general. Champernowne comments that she was even nearer Jung's inner wisdom when she was in analysis with Toni Wolff than when she was with Jung himself and that Wolff was Jung's inner companion-guide in his journey through the unconscious.

Encounters with the Soul: Active Imagination as Developed by C. G. Jung, by Barbara Hannah. Santa Monica: Sigo Press, 1981* +p* (254 + vii, incl. 3-p. bibl., 2-p. introduction by Marie-Louise von Franz).

Drawing on her many years of contact with Jung and particularly on his concept of active imagination, Hannah promotes its understanding as a powerful method of encountering the unconscious by illustrating, through historical and contemporary case studies, the steps, pitfalls, and successes of this therapeutic method. She comments on Jung's experiences and views and discusses the use of active imagination in confronting the unconscious, using as examples Jacob and Rachel in the Old Testament and Odysseus and Menelaus in the *Odyssey*. She describes and interprets three cases of contemporary active imagination, two dealing with midlife and the other with imminent death, as well as an ancient example, the "world-weary man," a medieval example, Hugh de St. Victor's conversation with his anima, and finally a recent example of the healing influence of active imagination in a case of neurosis. She concludes that all of these describe the eternal search for the inner Great Spirit.
(Bk.revs.: Choice '81/19:446; ContemPsy '82/27:66; PsyPersp '83/14:102–4)

The Dictionary of Classical Mythology: Symbols, Attributes, and Associations, by Robert E. Bell. Oxford and Santa Barbara: ABC-Clio, 1982* (390 + xi, incl. 16 illus.).

Limiting his scope to Greek and Roman mythology, with occasional references to Assyrian, Phoenician, Etruscan, and Egyptian mythology, Bell selects approximately a thousand subject headings under which the number of entries range from one to one hundred. He intends this as a topical dictionary to be used by historians, novelists, and poets.
(Bk.revs.: Choice '82/20:552; RQ Wint'82/22:199; WilsonLibB N'82/57:250; BkRDig '83:110; Bklist '83/80:342–3; CollResLib '83/44:48–9)

Dictionary of Symbols, by Tom Chetwynd. London, Toronto, Sydney, and N.Y.: Paladin Book/Granada Books, 1982p* (459 + xv, incl. 21-p. index, 75 illus.).

Most indebted to Jung and his followers (especially von Franz and Hillman) for explaining convincingly why symbols are of vital everyday concern, Chetwynd presents a reference work on psychology, myth, and folklore designed to complement others already in existence. His dictionary is for people who want to use symbols to explore and develop the resources of their own psyche. He follows a brief introduction on symbolism (the symbolic way; symbolic language; dreams; deprived or overwhelmed symbols; and comparative symbolism) with 265 subject entries.

Dreambody: The Body's Role in Revealing the Self, by Arnold Mindell. Santa Monica: Sigo Press, 1982* + p*; London: Routledge & Kegan Paul, 1984p* (219 + xii, incl. 11-p. index, 7-p. bibl., 52 illus., 2-p. intro. by Marie-Louise von Franz).

Combining his background in theoretical physics and his training in Jungian psychology, Mindell relates his interest in the interaction of psyche and matter to a personal illness that stimulated him to study the mystery of psycho-physical reality. He presents the concept of the dreambody first by surveying the relationships of the real body to the dreambody and discusses the image of the body in Western religion, medicine, and physics. He then looks at the dreambody in relation to vibrations and fields, dance, shamanism, clairvoyant vision, and the chakra system. Other topics include the dreambody in fairy tales, the dreambody and individuation, and working with the dreambody (working with fingers; inner pain; amplification; working on skin; dance; visionary surgery; the existential unconscious; acupressure; meditation; and dream interpretation).
(Bk.revs.: Choice '82/20:650; BkRDig '83:1011; LibJ '83/108:56; Resurg N-D'85/n113:39; SFJInstLib '85/5n4:22-7)

The Knight: The Potentials of Active Imagination, by J. Marvin Spiegelman. Phoenix: Falcon Press, 1982p (87, incl. 1-p. bibl., 11 illus.).

Taking a tale from his book on psycho-mythology (*The Tree*), Spiegelman combines the tale "The Adventures of the Knight" (56 pp.) with essays on Jung's method of active imagination and its development into Spiegelman's own "psycho-mythology" technique. He relates the active imagination method to potentially increased creativity, to development of the personality, and to the art of self-healing.
(Bk.rev.: JAnPsy '83/28:286-7)

Dreams: Discovering Your Inner Teacher, by Clyde H. Reid. Minneapolis: Winston-Seabury Press, 1983p* (108 + xi, incl. 2-p. bibl., 2-p. journal form, 2-p. foreword by Edith Wallace).

Reid provides an introduction to the art of interpreting dreams, the "inner teacher," and learning to listen to one's own inner wisdom. He discusses how to "unlock" one's dreams, turn dreams upside down, and pursue dreams, and he comments on dreams and the inner teacher, dream-sharing groups, and the relationship between symbols and archetypes. He also provides a form for keeping a dream journal.

(Bk.revs.: Quad '84/17:70; RelStudR '84/10:150)

Jungian Dream Interpretation: A Handbook of Theory and Practice, by James A. Hall. Toronto: Inner City Books, 1983p* (Studies in Jungian Psychology by Jungian Analysts, 13) (127, incl. 6-p. index, 2-p. ref. notes, 2-p. gloss. of Jungian terms).

Using basic principles of Jungian psychology, Hall presents practical advice on dream interpretation illustrated by many clinical examples. In addition to discussing Jung's model of the psyche, the nature of dreaming, and the Jungian approach to dreams, he analyzes dreams as diagnostic tools and explores the question of technique. Other topics include ego-images and complexes in dreams, common dream motifs, the dream framework (such as synchronicity), symbolism in alchemy, and dreams related to the individuation process of the dreamer.

(Bk.revs.: CanBkRAn '83:449–50; Harvest '84/n30:140; JAnPsy '84/29:388–90: Quad '84/17n2:84–8; ContemPsy '85/30:42)

Working the Soul: Reflections on Jungian Psychology, by Charles Poncé. (Orig. title: *Papers Toward a Radical Metaphysics: Alchemy.* Berkeley, Calif.: North Atlantic Books, 1983 +p.) Berkeley, Calif.: North Atlantic Books, 1988p* (130, incl. 6-p. index, 7 illus.).

Gathering six of his essays on alchemy written over a period of ten years, Poncé writes sometimes from a psychological perspective, other times from a mythological or metaphysical perspective, hoping that alchemy might be the key to the "new metaphysic." His essays deal with "praise of Bombast" (the early 16th-century Swiss physician and alchemist Theophrastus Bombastus von Hohenheim, known as Paracelsus); Paracelsus and the wound as means of transformation; Saturn and the art of seeing the nature of limitation and frustration; Genesis as an alchemical allegory; woman, the feminine, and alchemy; and the androgyne as the uniting of opposites.

(Bk.revs.: SFJInstLib '88/n1:59–64)

On Dreams and Death: A Jungian Interpretation, by Marie-Louise von Franz. (Ger.: *Traum und Tod.* Munich: Kösel Verlag, 1984.) Boston and London:

Shambhala Publications, 1986*; 1987p* (193 + xvi, incl. 11-p. index, 8-p. bibl., 15-p. ref. notes, 13 illus.).

Dealing primarily with what the unconscious, as perceived through one's instincts and dreams, says about the fact of impending death, von Franz examines the manner in which nature, through dreams, prepares one for death. She discusses present-day death experiences and death dreams, as well as the symbolism of death and resurrection in Western tradition, using basic concepts of Jung's psychology as they apply to the second half of life and to death. Her analysis draws upon a wide range of material from mythology, alchemical traditions, religious and cultural precepts related to death, modern physics, and some aspects of parapsychology.

(Bk.revs.: LibJ Jy'86/111:93; Parab N'86/11:99–100; PsyPersp '86/17:245–9; PubW 11Ap'86/220:75; ContemPsy '87/32:753–4; JAnPsy '87/32:306–7; Quad '87/20n1:95–6; AgeingSoc '88/8:353–4; Commonw '88/115:150; JAmSocPsy '88/82:305–7)

Symbols of Transformation in Dreams, by Jean Dalby Clift and Wallace B. Clift. New York: Crossroad Publishing Co., 1984; 1986p* (155 + xi, incl. 3-p. index, 1-p. bibl., 3-p. ref. notes).

Working with Jung's insights into the meaning of life and of dreams, the authors use them as a basis for understanding their own spiritual journey within the Christian tradition. Following brief examinations of the nature of dreams, the unconscious, and symbolic language, they make more detailed analyses of such motifs of transformation as the persona, the shadow, the anima and animus, snakes, the trickster, and death and rebirth. They use many examples of dreams, including a number of their own.

(Bk.revs.: JPsyTheol '85/13:217; RelStudR '85/11:172; BksRel My'86/14:9)

Dreams: Night Language of the Soul, by Phoebe McDonald. Baton Rouge, La.: Mosaic Books, 1985; New York: Continuum, 1987p* (233 + viii, incl. 5-p. index, 2-p. bibl.).

Based on McDonald's thirty years of counseling experience, as well as her study of Freud and Jung, this book focuses on the symbolic language of dream messages from the psyche, emphasizing Jung's attention to the dream's purpose of indicating psychic growth potential. Following a summary of the interpretation of dreams, with examples, she discusses the mechanisms of the unconscious; aspects of the inner self; people in dreams; the body in dreams; sexual symbols; birth and death symbols; dreams for emotional growth; animals in dreams; structure, places, and natural elements in dreams; children's dreams; archetypal and guidance dreams; and reincarnation.

(Bk.revs.: Bklist '85/81:1600; ContemPsy '86/31:1007)

River's Way: The Process Science of the Dreambody, by Arnold Mindell. London and Boston: Routledge & Kegan Paul, 1985* +p* (167 + viii, incl. 12-p. index, 5-p. bibl., 8-p. ref. notes, 10 illus.).

Taking Jung's empiricism and his attitude toward dreamwork as a model, Mindell explains his own many-channeled process science that rests on Jung's teleological view of the collective unconscious as well as gestalt-oriented process work, Buddhist meditation, electronic communication theory, and the phenomenological attitude of theoretical physics. Starting with an elaboration of process science and channels (body; relationship; world), he then discusses the origins of some of his concepts, such as channels in Taoism, patterns in the I Ching, and the alchemical opus.
(Bk.revs.: JRelPsyRes '86/9:183–4)

The World Was Flooded with Light: A Mystical Experience Remembered, by Genevieve W. Foster. Pittsburgh: U. of Pittsburgh Press, 1985* (202 + xiii, incl. 6-p. index, 10-p. bibl.).

Foster's account of a mystical vision from almost forty years ago and her interpretations of the continuing place of that experience in her life reveal her Jungian outlook and interest in depth psychology. She provides an intimate description of the effects of the vision on her life and of the peculiar attitude placed on visionary experiences by modern culture. Her essay is accompanied by a 97-page commentary on mystical experience in the modern world, contributed by anthropologist David Hufford, who examines the present state of knowledge about mystical experience in general and discusses Foster's experience in particular, illustrated by examples of the mystical experiences of others.
(Bk.revs.: LibJ 15My'85/110:69–70; JAmFolk '86/99:487–8; JPsyTheol '86/14:170–1; RelStudR '87/13:232)

The Dream: Four Thousand Years of Theory and Practice; A Critical, Descriptive, and Encyclopedic Bibliography, by Nancy Parsifal-Charles. West Cornwall, Conn.: Locust Hill Press, 1986* in 2 vols. (576 + vi, incl. 39-p. indexes of names and subjects).

Containing more than seven hundred books and monographs in English and other European languages, Parsifal-Charles's detailed, critical, and descriptive bibliography provides a comprehensive body of knowledge relating the many approaches to dreams and dream interpretation. She includes ancient and classical dream-work, as well as significant contributions from the Middle East and Asia, along with dream interpretation practiced by tribal peoples. Also included are theories of dream interpretation in Freudian and Jungian psychology and sources of recent experimental research on dreaming.

(Bk.revs.: Choice '87/24:1679; ContemPsy '87/32:579; JMindBeh '87/8:357–8; PsyPersp '87/18:440–2; AnRefBksAn '88/19:301; PsychiJOtt '88/13:111)

The Inner Reaches of Outer Space: Metaphor as Myth and Religion, by Joseph Campbell. New York: Alfred van der Marck Editions, 1986; San Francisco: Harper & Row, 1988 + p* (155, incl. 5-p. ref. notes, 17 illus.).

Consisting of lectures given at the San Francisco Jung Institute between 1981 and 1984, Campbell's book discusses metaphor as fact and fact as metaphor; metaphors of psychological transformation; threshold figures; the metaphorical journey; and metaphorical identification. Citing Jung's analyses of universal ideas as the most insightful and illuminating, Campbell states that the imagery of a mythology is metaphorical of the psychological posture of the people to whom it pertains, as that of a dream is metaphorical of the psychology of its dreamer.

(Bk.revs.: Quad '86/19n2:84–6; Parab F'87/12:101–4; SFJInstLib '87/7n4:5–12)

Invisible Guests: The Development of Imaginal Dialogues, by Mary M. Watkins. Hillsdale, N.J.: Analytic Press, 1986*; Boston: Sigo Press, 1990 + p (207 + x, incl. 8-p. index, 16-p. bibl., 9-p. ref. notes).

"Invisible guests" are those involved in "imaginal dialogues." Their function and lines of development form the theme of Watkins' contribution. Following her discussion and critical analysis of various theorists' points of view on the nature, functions, and development of imaginal dialogues, she employs the help of depth psychology, anthropology, religion, and the accounts of novelists and dramatists to reconceive a developmental theory of imaginal dialogues. She ends by presenting some of the therapeutic implications of the approach presented, including a case history told from the points of view of each of the characters.

(Bk.revs.: Choice '87/24:946; IntRPsy-An '87/14:427–8; Quad '87/20n1:108–10; ContemPsy '88/33:249–50; JPhenPsy '90/21)

A Little Course in Dreams, by Robert Bosnak. (Dutch: *Kleine droomcursus.* Rotterdam: Lemniscaat, 1986.) Boston and Shaftesbury: Shambhala Publications, 1988p* (121 + ix, incl. 1-p. bibl., 1-p. foreword by Denise Levertov).

Using his own personal journey in the world of dreaming as well as dreams of patients and students, Bosnak illustrates strategies and exercises for studying dreams. He provides advice on memory exercises for remembering and recording dreams, how to listen to dreams and discover underlying themes by studying a series of dreams, and how to work on dreams alone or in pairs or groups. He analyzes a dream text and concludes with advice on using the techniques of amplification and active imagination.

(Bk.revs.: Quad '89/22n2:106–7; PsyPersp '90/22:195–6)

Symbolism: A Comprehensive Dictionary, compiled by Steven Olderr. Jefferson, N.C. and London: McFarland Publishers, 1986* (153 + vi).

Stating that the purpose of the dictionary is to make the artist's or the author's meaning clear, compiler Olderr presents 6,115 ancient to modern terms of general symbolism and of specialized meaning categorized as allusion, association, attribute, emblem, or symbol. Terms are selected from literature, art, religion, the Bible, mythology, folklore, flower language, astrology, numerology, alchemy, and heraldry.

(Bk.revs.: RefResBkN '86/1:4; SmallPrBkR Jy–Ag'86/2:14)

Dream Life, Wake Life: The Human Condition through Dreams, by Gordon G. Globus. Albany: State U. of New York Press, 1987* +p* (SUNY Series in Transpersonal Psychology) (203 + x, incl. 7-p. indexes, 8-p. bibl., 7-p. ref. notes).

Expressing his main concern with dreaming and the dream as "opening a window on the waking human condition," Globus first examines Freud's psychoanalytic interpretation of dreams, followed by discussions on dream phenomenology, the cognitive approach to dreaming, transpersonal psychology, and existentialism. He devotes chapter 5 ("The Dream as Oracle") to a discussion of dreaming from a Jungian transpersonal viewpoint, in which he characterizes the dream as potentially an oracle, expressing wisdom, rather than raw wish.

(Bk.revs.: BrJPsychi '87/151:569; JMindBeh '87/8:469–72; JTranspPsy '87/19:88–9; Philos '87/17:551–2)

The Dream Story, by Donald Broadribb. Nedlands, Australia: Cygnet Books, 1987p*; Toronto: Inner City Books, 1990p (Studies in Jungian Psychology by Jungian Analysts, 44) (238 + xiv, incl. 2-p. index of dreams).

Stressing the point that dreams mean something valuable for self-knowledge, analyst Broadribb bases his goal of learning to understand the language of dreams on first-hand research, from which eighty-five dreams are given verbatim as related to him by the dreamer. He begins with the story each dream-drama tells, and follows by examining the people in the dreams, the nature and use of symbolism, and the purpose of the dream. He also discusses nightmares, sex in dreams, and a series of ten dreams that illustrate

the cumulative effect of the discussion. He concludes with an evaluation of the dream discussion group and an account of a discussion between a dreamer and an analyst working on a dream. Appended are eleven dreams (along with explanatory material) for the reader to interpret.
(Bk.revs.: AusNZJPsy Mr'89/23:134–5; AusJPsy '89/41:225)

Dreams and the Search for Meaning, by Peter O'Connor. New York and Mahwah, N.J.: Paulist Press, 1987p* (247 + xiii, incl. 6-p. index, 10-p. bibl. notes).

Influenced by the writings of Jung and, in particular, Hillman, O'Connor is basically concerned with how to use a dream to approach the unconscious, rather than how to interpret the dream. His interest is in the restoration of this realm of imagination, and he seeks to interpret dreams using active imagination rather than rationality. Topics discussed include a history of dreams; Freud and Jung on dreams; the persona, shadow, animus, and anima in dreams; and archetypal dreams. He offers practical suggestions for keeping a dream diary.
(Bk.revs.: LumenVitae '87/42:464; RelStudTh My'87/7:75)

Psyche Speaks: A Jungian Approach to Self and World, by Russell A. Lockhart. Wilmette, Ill.: Chiron Publications, 1987* +p* (Chiron Monograph Series, vol. I) (130 + xi, incl. 8-p. index, 4-p. bibl., 8-p. ref. notes, 2 illus.).

This book consists of three lectures given in 1982 to inaugurate the C. G. Jung Lectures at New York's C. G. Jung Foundation for Analytical Psychology. Lockhart expresses concern about nurturing psychic development and learning to listen to the psyche in our overlooked and undervalued daily life; and he emphasizes that the psyche can be heard through dreams, visions, synchronicities, and psychopathologies of everyday life. He comments on wandering in the labyrinth of "inner and outer as threads of one weaving" and says that one needs to be cautious of the tendency to listen so quickly with the mind that we forget to hear with the ear when psyche speaks.
(Bk.revs.: PsyPersp '88/19:158–9; Quad '88/21n2:91–3; Harvest '89–90/35:229–31; SmallPr Jn'89/7:56)

The Way of the Dream, by Marie-Louise von Franz in conversation with Fraser Boa. Toronto: Windrose Films, 1987* (361 + xix, incl. 9-p. index).

In this work drawn from the documentary series *The Way of the Dream* (twenty half-hour films), producer-director and Jungian analyst Boa presents an easily accessible, in-depth guide to analytical psychology and Jungian dream analysis by von Franz, "Jung's foremost living successor," based on her own study of more than 65,000 dreams. Boa has grouped the twenty chapters into seven parts: an introduction, the basic psychology of Jung, the dreams of our culture, the psychology of men, the psychology of women, relationship, and the self. Texts of more than seventy-five dreams are quoted, of which twenty-seven are interpreted by von Franz.

(Bk.revs.: Parab '87/12:86–91; ChrCen '88/105:995)

Visions of the Night: A Study of Jewish Dream Interpretation, by Joel Covitz. Boston & London: Shambhala Publications, 1990p (149 + xii).

Covitz, a Jungian analyst and rabbi, examines the Jewish literature for insights into the nature of dreams that can illuminate the practice of dream-work in psychotherapy. The book includes a translation of a sixteenth-century Hebrew text, "The Interpretation of Dreams," by Rabbi Solomon Almoli.

Wisdom of the Heart: Working with Women's Dreams, by Karen A. Signell. New York: Bantam Books, 1990p (325 + xxv, incl. 11-p. index, 7-p. bibl., 4-p. ref. notes, 4-p. foreword by Riane Eisler).

Jungian analyst Signell uses eighty-four dreams to illustrate her view of dreams as a source of feminine knowledge and a way to cultivate imagination and gain confidence in one's own intuition. She discusses finding the inner guide (the Self), dealing with aggression, recognizing negative and positive qualities of the shadow, relationships, and sexual issues.

8 Feminine and Masculine Psychology

Although attempts are made in psychology to assign the concept of relatedness to the feminine principle and the concept of discrimination and detachment to the masculine principle, it is difficult to categorize the psychic structure and dynamics of an individual in terms of clear-cut feminine or masculine characteristics. However one may define feminine and masculine principles, Jung stressed that both are equally essential in each person's life. His own writings on the subject deal mostly with archetypal aspects, particularly his conceptions of anima and animus as unconscious contrasexual personifications of human qualities that are complementary to the character of the persona and inevitably projected upon a real person or object.

This subject category consists of more than eighty books, plus eighteen more that are cross-referenced from other subjects. More than half of the writings have been published since 1982.

Jung: *Aspects of the Feminine* [p. 160]
_____: *Aspects of the Masculine* [p. 160]
_____: *Essays on a Science of Mythology* [p. 161]
Bauer: *Alcoholism and Women* (See chapter 11, "Jungian Analysis") [p. 323]
Begg: *The Cult of the Black Virgin* [p. 181]
Berry (ed.): *Fathers and Mothers* [p. 168]
Birkhäuser-Oeri: *The Mother* (See chapter 10, "Creativity and Jung's Psychology") [p. 264]
Bolen: *Goddesses in Everywoman* [p. 177]
_____: *Gods in Everyman* [p. 189]
Brunner: *Anima as Fate* [p. 165]

Caprio: *The Woman Sealed in the Tower* [p. 176]
Carlson: *In Her Image* [p. 189]
Colegrave: *The Spirit of the Valley* [p. 170]
Colman & Colman: *The Father* [p. 172]
de Castillejo: *Knowing Woman* [p. 168]
Desteian: *Coming Together/Coming Apart* [p. 189]
Douglas: *Woman in the Mirror* [p. 193]
Downing: *The Goddess* [p. 173]
_____: *Journey Through Menopause* [p. 185]
_____: *Myths and Mysteries of Same-Sex Love* [p. 191]
_____: *Psyche's Sisters* [p. 187]
Engelsman: *The Feminine Dimension of the Divine* (See chapter 9, "Religion and Jung's Psychology") [p. 222]
Fierz-David: *Women's Dionysian Initiation* [p. 164]
Grant, T.: *Being a Woman* [p. 184]
Grinnell: *Alchemy in a Modern Woman* [p. 167]
Guggenbühl-Craig: *Marriage: Dead or Alive* (See chapter 11, "Jungian Analysis") [p. 314]
Gustafson: *The Black Madonna* [p. 192]
Guzie & Guzie: *About Men and Women* [p. 182]
Hall: *The Moon and the Virgin* [p. 171]
_____: *Those Women* [p. 188]
Harding: *The Way of All Women* [p. 161]
_____: *Woman's Mysteries* [p. 162]
Haule: *Divine Madness* [p. 192]
Hillman: *Anima* [p. 180]
Hillman (ed.): *Puer Papers* [p. 170]
Hopcke: *Jung, Jungians, and Homosexuality* [p. 190]
_____: *Men's Dreams, Men's Healing* [p. 192]
Hurwitz: *Lilith—First Eve* [p. 192]
Johnson: *Femininity Lost and Regained* [p. 192]
_____: *He: Understanding Masculine Psychology* [p. 168]
_____: *She: Understanding Feminine Psychology* [p. 170]
_____: *We: Understanding the Psychology of Romantic Love* [p. 178]
Jung, E.: *Animus and Anima* [p. 163]
Kast: *The Nature of Loving* [p. 180]
Kerényi: *Athene* (See chapter 9, "Religion and Jung's Psychology") [p. 203]
_____: *Eleusis* (See chapter 9, "Religion and Jung's Psychology") [p. 210]
_____: *Hermes, Guide of Souls* (See chapter 9, "Religion and Jung's Psychology") [p. 203]
_____: *Zeus and Hera* (See chapter 9, "Religion and Jung's Psychology") [p. 216]

Koltuv: *The Book of Lilith* [p. 183]
_____: *Weaving Woman* [p. 193]
Lauter & Rupprecht (eds.): *Feminist Archetypal Theory* [p. 182]
Leonard: *On the Way to the Wedding* [p. 183]
_____: *The Wounded Woman* [p. 176]
Luke: *Woman, Earth, and Spirit* [p. 174]
Mahdi, Foster & Little (eds.): *Betwixt and Between* [p. 184]
Mankowitz: *Change of Life* [p. 178]
Monick: *Phallos* [p. 186]
Moon: *Changing Woman and Her Sisters* [p. 180]
_____: *Dreams of a Woman* (See chapter 6, "Human Development and Individuation") [p. 105]
Moore & Gillette: *King, Warrior, Magician, Lover* [p. 192]
Neumann: *Amor and Psyche* [p. 162]
_____: *The Great Mother* [p. 163]
Olds: *Fully Human* [p. 173]
Paris: *Pagan Meditations* [p. 184]
Perera: *Descent to the Goddess* [p. 172]
Perry: *Lord of the Four Quarters* [p. 165]
Pratt et al.: *Archetypal Patterns in Women's Fiction* (See chapter 10, "Creativity and Jung's Psychology") [p. 270]
Qualls-Corbett: *The Sacred Prostitute* [p. 187]
Roberts: *From Eden to Eros* [p. 182]
Samuels (ed.): *The Father* [p. 181]
Sanford: *The Invisible Partners* [p. 171]
Sanford & Lough: *What Men Are Like* [p. 188]
Schapira: *The Cassandra Complex* (See chapter 11) [p. 342]
Schectman: *The Step-Mother in Fairy Tales* [p. 193]
Schellenbaum: *How to Say No to the One You Love* [p. 179]
Scott-Maxwell: *Women and Sometimes Men* [p. 164]
Shorter: *An Image Darkly Forming* [p. 185]
Singer: *Androgyny* [p. 169]
_____: *Energies of Love* [p. 177]
Spignesi: *Starving Women* (See chapter 11) [p. 328]
Stroud & Thomas (eds.): *Images of the Untouched* [p. 175]
Toor: *The Road by the River* [p. 186]
Ulanov: *The Feminine in Jungian Psychology and in Christian Theology* [p. 166]
_____: *Receiving Woman* [p. 173]
Ulanov & Ulanov: *Cinderella and Her Sisters* [p. 176]
_____: *The Witch and the Clown* [p. 187]
von Franz: *The Golden Ass of Apuleius* (See chapter 10, "Creativity and Jung's Psychology") [p. 259]
_____: *Problems of the Feminine in Fairy Tales* [p. 167]

_____: *Puer Aeternus* [p. 166]
Washbourn: *Becoming Woman* [p. 169]
Weber: *WomanChrist* (See chapter 9, "Religion and Jung's Psychology") [p. 241]
Wehr: *Jung and Feminism* [p. 185]
Wheelwright: *The Death of a Woman* (See chapter 6, "Human Development and Individuation") [p. 102]
_____: *For Women Growing Older* [p. 179]
Whitmont: *Return of the Goddess* [p. 175]
Wilmer (ed.): *Mother/Father* [p. 190]
Woodman: *Addiction to Perfection* (See chapter 11) [p. 323]
_____: *The Owl Was a Baker's Daughter* (See chapter 11, "Jungian Analysis") [p. 321]
_____: *The Pregnant Virgin* (See chapter 11, "Jungian Analysis") [p. 334]
_____: *The Ravaged Bridegroom* (See chapter 11, "Jungian Analysis") [p. 352]
Woolger & Woolger: *The Goddess Within* [p. 192]
Wyly: *The Phallic Quest* [p. 191]
Young-Eisendrath: *Hags and Heroes* [p. 331]
Young-Eisendrath & Wiedemann (eds.): *Female Authority* [p. 340]
Zweig (ed.): *To Be a Woman* [p. 193]

Aspects of the Masculine, by C. G. Jung. Princeton, N.J.: Princeton U. Press/ Bollingen, 1989p*; London: Ark/Routledge, 1989p* (183 + xvii, 7 illus., 11-p. introduction and headnotes by John Beebe).

Considering that there is no single work in which Jung presented either the psychology of men or the wider unconscious psychology of the masculine, this collection of nineteen excerpts from eight volumes of the *Collected Works* and from other writings of Jung (ranging from 1909 to 1957) reveals some of what Jung himself understood about the contribution that gender made to his "personal equation." The writings are organized under the headings of the hero; initiation and the development of masculinity; the father; Logos and Eros (personification of opposites); the masculine in women; the anima; and the spirit.
(Bk.revs.: BloomR S'89/9:8; ResRefBkN Oc'89/4:1; UPrBkN S'89/1:4)

Aspects of the Feminine, by C. G. Jung. Princeton, N.J.: Princeton U. Press/ Bollingen, 1982p*; London: Routledge & Kegan Paul, 1983p*; London: Ark Paperbacks, 1986p* (179 + v).

Consisting of a small range of Jung's writings on aspects of feminine psychology, eight excerpts from nearly as many volumes of the *Collected Works* make up this paperback. Arranged chronologically, the essays include "The Worship of Woman and the Worship of Soul" (1921); "The Love Problem of a Student" (1924); "Marriage as a Psychological Relationship" (1925); "Woman in Europe" (1927), "Anima and Animus" (1928); "Psychological Aspects of the Mother Archetype" (1938); "Psychological Aspects of the Kore" (1951); and "The Shadow and the Syzygy" (1951).

(Bk.revs.: RelStudR '84/10:47; BrJPsychi '87/121:138)

Essays on a Science of Mythology: The Myth of the Divine Child and the Mysteries of Eleusis, by C. G. Jung and C. Kerényi. (Ger.: *Einfuhrung in das Wesen der Mythologie*. Amsterdam: Pantheon Akademische Verlagsanstalt; Zurich: Rascher Verlag, 1941.) New York: Pantheon Books (Bollingen Series XXII), 1949; New York: Torchbook/Harper & Row, rev. 1963p; Princeton, N.J.: Princeton U. Press/Bollingen, ed.2 1969 + p* (U.K.: *Introduction to a Science of Mythology*. London: Routledge & Kegan Paul, 1951; 1985p*) (200 + viii, incl. 4-p. index, 13-p. bibl., 5 illus.).

Collaborating with mythologist Kerényi on mythological motifs of the child and the kore [maiden], Jung provides detailed amplifications of their psychological aspects. Considering the archetype as a symbol belonging to the unconscious of the entire human race and not merely to the individual, Jung presents the child motif as the preconscious, childhood aspect of the collective unconscious, a divine child not yet integrated into the human being. Moreover, he characterizes the child as a hero signifying the potential synthesis of the "divine" unconscious and human consciousness, evolving toward independence. His psychological evaluation of the kore presents that archetype as generally a double one in a woman (mother *and* maiden, as in the Demeter and Persephone myth).

(Bk.revs.: AmSocR '50/15:833; JPastorCare Fall '50/4:54; Poetry '50/77:168–73; PsychiQ '50/24:207–8; PsyanQ '51/20:464–6; TimesLitSup '51:457; BrJMedPsy '52/25:63–4; RofRel '52/16:169–73; TimesLitSup '61:457; ContemPsy '64/9:456; TimesLitSup '85:651)

*   *   *   *   *

The Way of All Women: A Psychological Interpretation, by M. Esther Harding. London and New York: Longman's Green, 1933; New York: G. P. Putnam's Sons for the C. G. Jung Foundation for Analytical Psychology, rev. 1970; London: Rider 1971p; rev. 1983p*; New York: Colophon Books/Perennial Library/Harper & Row, 1975p*; Boston & London: Shambhala Publications, 1990p (314 + xviii, incl. 10-p. index, 1-p. bibl., 4-p. intro. by Jung).

162 FEMININE AND MASCULINE PSYCHOLOGY

Analyst M. Esther Harding was one of Jung's first "trainees." In this book on the psychology of women, Harding strives for a middle way between the experiences of materialism and of other-worldliness in an effort to clarify the confusion that exists in the relationship between the sexes, analyzing woman in the contexts of lover, co-worker, friend, marriage partner, mother, and mistress.

(Bk.revs.: BkRDig '33:404; Bklist '33/29:258–9; Bks 19Mr'33:2; JHomeEc '33/25:516; JNervMent '33/78:689–90; NewRep 13S'33/76:137; NYTimesBkR 19Mr'33:19; TimesLitSup '33:532; BrJMedPsy '34/14:301; Criterion '34/13:480–1; JEdSoc '34/7:529; PsychiQ '34/8:609–10; Tabl '34/163:39; BrJPsy '35/25:410; PsyanR '35/22:106–7; Marriage F'71/53:38–44; JAnPsy '72/17:89–92)

Woman's Mysteries, Ancient and Modern: A Psychological Interpretation of the Feminine Principle as Portrayed in Myth, Story, and Dream, by M. Esther Harding. London, Toronto, and New York: Longman's Green, 1935; New York: Pantheon Books, 1935; ed.2 1955; London: Rider, 1971 + p; 1982p*; New York: G. P. Putnam's Sons for the C. G. Jung Foundation for Analytical Psychology, 1972; New York: Bantam Books, 1975p; New York: Colophon Books/Perennial Library/Harper & Row, 1976p*; Boston & London: Shambhala Publications, 1990p (A C. G. Jung Foundation Book) (256 + xvi, incl. 15-p. index, 44 illus., 4-p. intro. by Jung).

Harding sketches a picture of the feminine psyche, utilizing Jung's methods of exploring the unconscious and her own psychotherapeutic experience. She depicts the psychic facts and conditions of feminine psychology as portrayed in story, myth, and dreams, focusing in particular on the theme of the ancient moon initiations in the name of Eros. Her topics include the moon as giver of fertility; the moon in modern life; early representations of the moon deity; the moon cycle in women and its inner meaning; the man in the moon; the moon mother; the virgin goddess; and priests and priestesses of the moon. She concludes with interpretations of the sacred marriage; Ishtar; Isis and Osiris; the sacrifice of the son; rebirth and immortality; the changing moon; and inspiration and the self.

(Bk.revs.: BkRDig '35:435–6; Bks 12My'35:13; NYTimesBkR 5My'35:23; TimesLitSup '35:634; AmJPsy '36/48:552; Folk '36/47:226; JNervMent '36/83:358–60; PsychiQ '36/10:178–80; AmJSoc '37/42:763; PsyanQ '37/6:265–6; PsyanR '37/24:206–7; BulMennClin '56/20:97–8; ContemPsy '56/1:198–9; JAnPsy '56/1:210–11; PsychiQ '56/30:355; Bkman '72/49:421; InwLight '72/82:42–7; RBksRel S'72/2:4; SatRev 6My'72/55:85–6; TheolStud '72/33:782–4; Harper F'74/248:97; AmPoetR Jy-Ag'76/5:34–5; SWRev '77/62:429–30; RelStudR '79/5:147)

Amor and Psyche: The Psychic Development of the Feminine, by Erich Neumann. (Ger.: *Apuleius: Amor und Psyche*. Zurich: Rascher Verlag, 1952.) London: Routledge & Kegan Paul, 1956; Toronto: McClelland & Stewart, 1956; New York: Pantheon Books (Bollingen Foundation), 1956; New York:

Torchbook/Harper & Row, 1962p; Princeton, N.J.: Princeton U. Press/ Bollingen, 1971p*; 1990p (181 + vii, incl. 11-p. index, 4-p. bibl.) (Bollingen Series LIV)

Using the classic tale of Amor and Psyche from the *Metamorphoses* or *The Golden Ass* of Lucius Apuleius, Neumann illustrates an unusual study of feminine psychology within the framework of Jung's depth psychology. He offers insights into the psychic life of women through the mythical tale of the mortal maid Psyche, the great goddess Aphrodite, and the god Amor (Aphrodite's son and Psyche's husband). His presentation of the tale is followed by a 105-page commentary on the psychic development of the feminine in which he comments on the unity of the feminine psychology which flows from a "matriarchal psychology" discernible in any number of myths, rites, and mysteries.

(Bk.revs.: PsychiQ '57/31:180; JAnPsy '58/3:83–4; JPastorCare '58/12:121–2)

The Great Mother: An Analysis of the Archetype, by Erich Neumann. (Ger.: *Die Grosse Mutter: Archetyp des grossen Weiblichen.* Zurich: Rhein Verlag, 1956.) London: Routledge & Kegan Paul, 1955; 1982p*; Toronto: Mc-Clelland & Stewart, 1955; New York: Pantheon Books (Bollingen Series 47, 1955; Princeton, N.J.: Princeton U. Press/Bollingen, ed.2 1963*; 1972p* (379 + xliii + 185 pp. of plates, incl. 24-p. index, 14-p. bibl., 323 illus.).

Supported by an abundance of illustrations of the archetype of the Great Mother, Neumann employs Jung's analytical psychology in his structural analysis of the archetype's inner growth and dynamic, as well as its manifestation in myths and symbols. He discusses the topics of the archetypal feminine and the Great Mother, central symbolism of the feminine, transformation mysteries, functional spheres of the feminine, and the dynamic of the archetype. He interprets the elementary character of the archetype under the topics of the primordial goddess, the positive elementary character, and the negative elementary character; and he interprets the archetype's transformative character as symbolized by the lady of the plants and the lady of the beasts.

(Bk.revs.: CathWorld '55/182:156+; LibJ '55/80:2518; AmSchol '56/25:248–9; BkRDig '56:671; BrJPsy '56/47:235; ContemPsy '56/1:198–200; PastorPsy '56/10:120; JRelThought '56/13:157–9; PerkSchTh Wint'56/9:36–7; PsychiQ '56/30:355; RMeta '56/9:522; AmJPsyth '57/11:163–4; BulMennClin '57/21:76; JAnPsy '57/2:97–101; Person '57/38:199; RofRel '57/21:173–5; JAesthArt '58/17:128–9; TimesLitSup 23My'58:xii; PubW 3Ap'72/201:73; Resurg My–Jn'81/n86:37–8; StudMyst '84/7:71)

Animus and Anima, by Emma Jung. New York: Spring Publications for Analytical Psychology Club of New York, 1957; Zurich and New York: Spring

Publications, 1969p; Dallas: Spring Publications, 1981p; 1985p* (94, incl. 8 pp. of end-chapter notes).

Jung's wife Emma, an analyst herself, presents essays on the basic relational archetypes (animus in the woman and anima in the man) in this publication of her 1931 lecture on the nature of the animus delivered at the Psychological Club of Zurich (published in German in 1934 and in English in 1941) and her contribution to the Jung Institute of Zurich's studies series on the anima as an elemental being (published in 1955). She depicts the animus and anima as a connecting link or bridge between consciousness and collective unconscious, functioning in ways compensatory to the outer personality, and conditioned jointly by outer experiences with persons of the other sex and by the collective image of the other sex carried by the psyche. The animus and anima are described as both conscious and outward manifestations and as images and figures within the psyche that appear in dreams and fantasies.

Women and Sometimes Men, by Florida Scott-Maxwell. London: Routledge & Kegan Paul, 1957; New York: Borzoi Book/Alfred A. Knopf, 1957; New York: Harper & Row, 1957p; 1971p (207 pp.).

Acknowledging her use of Jung's concepts, Scott-Maxwell presents a study of the relationship of feminine and masculine elements in present-day women and the ways in which women are searching for a new balance between these elements. Writing at age seventy-four, with a perspective gained by twenty years as an analytical psychologist, she reflects on problems created by women's new independence, especially in professions, that can bring about painful conflicts in which the masculine side of their dual nature may get "out of control." She analyzes woman's latent masculinity, her long-repressed "inner man" that confronts her with the problem of living out both sides of her nature and proposes a new morality based on women learning to experience and express their own individuality.

(Bk.revs.: BestSell '57/17:233; BkRDig '57:832; ChiSunTrib 10N'57:MagBks 12; Critic '57/15:14; KirkR '57/75:515; LibJ '57/82:2030–1; NYHerTrib 60c'57:4; NYTimesBkR 22S'57:20; SFChron 10N'57:26; SatR 260c'57/40:18; TimesLitSup '57:180; JAnPsy '58/3:85–7)

Women's Dionysian Initiation: The Villa of Mysteries in Pompeii, by Linda Fierz-David. (Ger.: *Psychologische Betrachtungen zu der Freskenfolge der Villa der Misteri in Pompeii: Ein Versuch.* Zurich: Psychology Club of Zurich, mimeo., 1957.) Dallas: Spring Publications, 1988p* (Jungian Classics Series, 11) (149 + xvii, incl. 3-p. ref. notes, 2 illus., 1-p. preface by Heinrich Karl Fierz, 7-p. intro. by M. Esther Harding).

At Jung's request, Fierz-David prepared a psychological study of the ancient fresco art of Pompeii as represented by a series of ten scenes in the Villa of Mysteries which depict a woman's initiation ceremony with figures of initiates, priestesses, and mythic figures related to the worship of Dionysos. She provides a history and description of the Villa, including its initiation chamber and discusses a mythological hypothesis concerning the mystery cult of Dionysos and Ariadne. She interprets the scenes as sacred dreams that seem, from the depths of the unconscious, to represent the way of feminine individuation; and she distinguishes Ariadne's point of view from the psychologies of her mother, Pasiphaë (wife of Minos, king of Crete), of her tragic sister Phaedra, and of Medea.

(Bk.revs.: Gnosis '88/n9:62; SmallPress F'89/7:60)

Anima as Fate, by Cornelia Brunner. (Ger.: *Die Anima als Schicksalsproblem des Mannes.* Zurich: Rascher Verlag, 1963/Studien aus dem C. G. Jung-Institut, vol. XIV) Dallas: Spring Publications, 1986p* (Jungian Classics Series, 9) (277 + xxvi, incl. 13-p. ref. notes, 5-p. preface by Jung).

Written at Jung's suggestion, Brunner's book presents two examples of the anima as fate. She regards the anima as the powerful personal complex of the countersexual soul-component ("unconscious feminine soul") of a man. The first half of the book is devoted to Rider Haggard and his bestseller, *She* (1866), seen as the classic example of a writer dealing with the significant motif of the anima as it unfolds. Brunner provides not only a psychological interpretation of the spontaneous fantasy and an explanatory summary of the symbolism but also a discussion of Haggard's own adventurous life. The second half of the book describes a series of sixty-nine dreams of a young physician over an eight-year period as an example of the dreams of a contemporary man that are strikingly similar to the motifs in the novel. Brunner interprets the series to show how the anima can develop and change as a result of conscious discussion, using her clinical experience and extensive mythological and literary material.

(Bk.revs.: SmallPr Mr–Ap'87/4:98–9; ContemPsy '88/33:542)

Lord of the Four Quarters: Myths of the Royal Father, by John Weir Perry. New York: George Braziller, 1966; New York: Collier, 1970p (272 + xvi, incl. 8-p. index, 13-p. bibl., 32 illus.).

Interested in his repeated encounter with symbolic figures of kingship in the unconscious products of patients, Perry studies the mythology and ceremonies of archaic times whose complex rituals of renewal in seasonal festivals illustrate the reconstitutive process of the psyche. He interprets the king as Royal Father who concentrates in his person the properties of the masculine principle and becomes a constellation of attributes such as virility, authority, and integrity. Following discussions of myth and ritual, the cosmological order, and the development, function, and archetypal nature of kingship, he surveys the myths of the Royal Father archetype from cults of the Nile (Egypt and the Shilluk) to the Near Eastern sequence (Mesopotomia, Canaan, Israel), Indo-European diffusion (India, Iran, Hittites), Greece, Rome, Norse lands, the New World, and China.

(Bk.revs.: KirkR '65/33:1008; LibJ '65/90:5406; Adoles '66/1:289; Choice '66/3:796; BkRDig '66:945–6; JAnPsy '67/12:178–9)

Puer Aeternus: A Psychological Study of the Adult Struggle with the Paradise of Childhood, by Marie-Louise von Franz. (Orig. title: *The Problem of the Puer Aeternus.* New York: Spring Publications for the Analytical Psychology Club of New York, 1970p) (Seminar Series, 2) Santa Monica: Sigo Press, ed.2 1981* +p* (293, incl. 1-p. bibl., 11 illus.).

Consisting of twelve lectures given at the Jung Institute of Zurich during 1959–60, this work by von Franz shows how the adolescent psychology of the *puer aeternus* (literally, "eternal boy") persists into adulthood. Analyzing Bruno Goetz's novel *The Kingdom Without Space (1919) and* Antoine de Saint-Exupéry's *The Little Prince* (1942), a child's fable for adults, she also deals with the psychological and cultural issue of the contemporary man who is identified with the archetype of the *puer aeternus* and remains too long in adolescent psychology. This disturbance typically is coupled with too great a dependence on the mother, often leading to the neurosis of the "provisional life."

(Bk.revs.: Choice '81/19:556; Quad '82/15n1:84–5; PsyPersp '83/14:214–17)

The Feminine in Jungian Psychology and in Christian Theology, by Ann Belford Ulanov. Evanston, Ill.: Northwestern U. Press, 1971; 1980p (Studies in Jungian Thought) (347 + xi, incl. 5-p. index).

Asserting Jung's view of the existence of the feminine as a leading element, "not only in women but in men as well," Ulanov explores the Jungian approach as well as the place of the feminine in Christian theology. She analyzes the neglected feminine's need to recover its role in human consciousness, the development of the human spirit, and its relation to religious life. Following a summary of Jung's approach to the psyche, she discusses religion and the psyche (the religious function of the psyche; symbol and theology; analytical psychology and religion; and remythologizing life) and the psychology of the feminine (descriptions of the feminine; feminine consciousness and feminine spirit; archetypes of the feminine; and stages of anima and animus development), concluding with an analysis of the feminine and Christian theology as related to the doctrines of man, God and Christ, and spirit. She appends a short discussion on Eros and Logos (7 pp.).

(Bk.revs.: BkRDig '72:1320; Choice '72/9:581; CrossCurr '72/22:346–7; LibJ '72/ 97:2106; LibJBkR '72:449; UnionSemQR '72/28:134–6; PsyPersp '73/4:200–5; AmJPsychi '74/131:945–6; Signs '76/2:434; InwLight '82/n98:40–2; TeachColRec '86/ 88:300)

Problems of the Feminine in Fairy Tales, by Marie-Louise von Franz. New York: Spring Publications for the Analytical Psychology Club of New York, 1972p; Irving, Tex.: Spring Publications, rev. repr. 1976p; Dallas: Spring Publications, repr. 1986p* (Seminar Series, 5) (200, incl. 6-p. index).

Consisting of twelve lectures presented at a seminar at the Zurich Jung Institute during 1958–59, this work by von Franz poses the paradox that some fairy tales illustrate real women and others the man's anima (or inner feminine counterpart). She presents seven principal fairy tales from the Brothers Grimm and interprets them psychologically from the feminine viewpoint with numerous amplifications. The tales are "The Sleeping Beauty" or "Briar Rose," "Snow White and Rose Red," "The Handless Maiden," "The Woman Who Became a Spider," "The Six Swans," "The Seven Ravens," and "The Beautiful Wassilissa" (the Russian version of "Cinderella"). These fairy tales illustrate such subjects as ignored femininity, the mother-daughter paradise, the father complex, animus possession, the negative feminine, and the Self and the process of individuation.

Alchemy in a Modern Woman: A Study in the Contrasexual Archetype, by Robert Grinnell. Zurich: Spring Publications for the Analytical Psychology Club of New York, 1973p; Dallas: Spring Publications, repr. 1989p* (Seminar Series, 8) (181, incl. 14-p. index, 2-p. ref. notes).

Assuming the reader's acquaintance with Jung's alchemical studies (in particular, *Mysterium Coniunctionis*), Grinnell explores the problem of the woman who enters as a rival into the masculine world and experiences the strains to which her feminine nature is subjected. He emphasizes the deeper meaning of the phenomena illustrated by the "modern woman" at the archetypal level, wherein the masculine archetype and her archetypal femininity are conjuncted and the processes cannot be integrated but must be borne. He considers the problem within the context of the Sol-Luna (sun-moon) symbolism of the alchemists, Sol symbolizing masculine consciousness and the unconscious in a feminine personality, and Luna symbolizing feminine consciousness and the unconscious in a masculine personality. He analyzes the stages of the individuation process of the "modern woman," whose development he illustrates with a series of dreams.

(Bk.rev.: BloomR S'89/9:8)

Fathers and Mothers, edited by Patricia Berry. (Orig. subtitle: *Five Papers on the Archetypal Background of Feminine Psychology*) Dallas: Spring Publications, 1977p; ed.2 1990p (259 + xii)

Archetypal aspects of the father and mother are discussed in essays by Robert Bly, James Hillman, Augusto Vitale, Marion Woodman, Patricia Berry, Mary Watkins, Jackie Schectman, Ursula Le Guin, Erich Neumann, and C. G. Jung. (The first edition contained the essays "The Devouring Father" by Murray Stein and "On the Father in Psychotherapy" by Vera von der Heydt.)

Knowing Woman: A Feminine Psychology, by Irene Claremont de Castillejo. London: Hodder & Stoughton, 1973; New York: G. P. Putnam's Sons for the C. G. Jung Foundation for Analytical Psychology, 1973*; New York: Colophon Books/Harper & Row, 1974p*; Boston & London: Shambhala Publications, 1990p (A C. G. Jung Foundation Book) (188, incl. 4-p. index, 2 illus.).

Drawing on twenty years of experience as a Jungian analyst, de Castillejo discusses her concern about women who are today "face to face with some unforeseen consequences of their new equality with men" as reflected in marital conflicts and misunderstandings between men and women. She analyzes psychological aspects of various kinds of women and their effects on men. Her topics include responsibility and the shadow; man the hero; the role of woman as mediator; the animus; the meaning of love; the older woman; and soul images of woman.

(Bk.revs.: Choice '73/10:1283; Harvest '73/19:74–5; InwLight Wint'73–74/n84:45–6; JContemPsy '73/6:94; PsyPersp '73/4:195–9; PubW 5F'73/203:86; Quad '73/14:16–19; RBksRel(W) Oc'73/3:1+; TimesLitSup '73:333; VillVoice 8Jn'73/18:27; PastorPsy '74/28:212)

He: Understanding Masculine Psychology, by Robert A. Johnson. King of Prussia, Penn.: Religious Publishing Co., 1974; New York: Perennial Library/Harper & Row, 1977p; reissue in larger format 1986p; rev. 1989* + p* (83 + xi, incl. 1-p. bibl.; early edns.: 6-p. intro. by John A. Sanford).

Using Jungian psychological concepts, Johnson interprets the legend of Parsifal and his search for the Grail as a story of developmental masculine psychology that illustrates the struggle involved in the change from boyhood to mature manhood. He portrays Parsifal as torn between his masculine, sword-wielding quality and his feminine "Grail" hunger which constantly interact and need to be brought into balance. This represents the integration of the man's assertive quality and his soul (anima) which searches for love and union. He interprets Parsifal's glimpse of the Grail as the epitome of the feminine, increasing his consciousness of the soul's longing that comes from the unconscious and expresses the anima's warmth and strength. The individuation process includes freeing himself from his mother-complex and from identification with the father or brother. Sanford's introduction (in earlier editions) discusses mythology and the knowledge of God as they relate to Jung's concept of individuation.

(Bk.revs.: LibJ '74/99:2972–3; LibJBkR '74:409)

Androgyny: The Opposites Within, by June Singer. (Orig. subtitle: *Toward a New Theory of Sexuality.*) Garden City, N.Y.: Anchor Press/Doubleday, 1976; 1977p; London: Routledge & Kegan Paul, 1976; 1977p; Boston: Sigo Press, ed.2 1989* +p* (273 + xiv, incl. 11-p. index, 8-p. bibl., 8-p. ref. notes, 12 illus.).

Growing out of her struggle in an earlier book (1972) over a chapter about inner images of men that are experienced by women and inner images of women that are experienced by men, Singer offers a new theory of sexuality based on androgyny that provides a corrective for old theories founded on the dominance of one sex and the compliance of the other. She is concerned with the interaction of masculine and feminine within each individual, rather than hermaphroditism or bisexuality, and with the potential for each person to consciously accept the interplay of masculine and feminine energies and values. She discusses androgyny in a historical context (matriarchy, patriarchal monotheism, zodiacal man, Plato's androgyne, the Gnostic vision, alchemy, Kabbalah, the Tao and other manifestations in the East) and she ends with an analysis of experiences of androgyny "today and tomorrow."

(Bk.revs.: DenverQ '76/11:145–7; InwLight '76–77/n88–89:57–60; JTranspPsy '76/8:144–5; KirkR '76/44:895; LibJ '76/101:2498; LibJBkR '76:416; Ms 5N'76/5:38; PubW 2Ag'76/210:107; BestSell '77/36:354; BkRDig '77:1230; ContemPsy '77/22:908–9; JAnPsy '77/22:194–5; PsyToday Mr'77/10:96+; Quad '77/10n1:44–5; RelStudR '77/3:260; SciBksFilm '77/13:64; SWRev '77/62:429–30; JApplBehSci '78/14n2:250–4; TimesLitSup '78:372; Resurg Mr–Ap'79/n73:32; Signs '79/4:783–4; ContemSoc '80/9:293–4)

Becoming Woman: The Quest for Wholeness in Female Experience, by Penelope Washbourn. New York: Harper & Row, 1976; 1979p*; Toronto: Fitzhenry & Whiteside, 1976 (174 + xvi, incl. 6-p. index, 13-p. ref. notes).

Drawing upon her own life's experiences and Jungian analysis, Washbourn interprets the stages of her life as a continuing search for wholeness and integrity from the point of view of the uniqueness of her female identity and of the spiritual value of her own self. She examines the spiritual dimensions of her life through ten stages (menstruation; leaving home and the crisis of identity; sexual maturity; love; failure and loss; marriage; pregnancy and birth; parenthood; the change of life; and anticipated death), identifying herself as woman, theologian, wife, and parent.

(Bk.revs.: KirkR '76/44:1163; BkRDig '77:1389; BksCan My'77/6:31; CanAuthBk '77/53n1:26; ChrCen '77/94:434; Dialog '77/16:305–6; JAmAcadRel '77/45:538–9; LibJ '77/102:394–5; LibJBkR '77:486–7; NewRBksRel My'77/1:10; PastorPsy '77/26:137–8; QuillQuire '77/49n3:11; RelStudR '77/3:186; Encoun '78/39:212–13; JPastorCare '78/32:65–6; RforRel '78/37:156–7; ReformR '79/33:35; StudRel '81/10:133)

She: Understanding Feminine Psychology, by Robert A. Johnson. King of Prussia, Penn.: Religious Publishing Co., 1976; New York: Perennial Library/Harper & Row, 1977p; reissue 1986p* in larger format; rev. 1989* + p* (81 + xiii, incl. 1-p. bibl.).

Johnson examines the Greek myth of Amor and Psyche and its powerful collective meaning for feminine psychology that speaks not only about women, but also about man's anima, his feminine side. He interprets the story in terms of the psychic conditions of Psyche's life, from her almost unapproachable, lonely, princess-like childhood to her patriarchal marriage to Eros (Amor) and subsequent trials that ultimately lead to increasing levels of self-understanding as she deals with her largely unconscious, masculine component in terms of her own feminine personality.

Puer Papers, edited by James Hillman. Dallas: Spring Publications, 1979p* (246, incl. 8-p. index, end-chapter ref. notes).

Citing it as an evocation, rather than an explanation of the *puer* (youth), Hillman characterizes this collection of nine essays as a psychological book, not a "psychology" book, meant for artist, analyst, and scholar alike. Divided into three parts (archetypal phenomenology; puer pathologies; puer in myths and literature), the two essays in the first part (on senex and puer, and the soul/spirit distinction as the basis for the differences between psychotherapy and spiritual discipline) and two in the second part (puer wounds and the scar of Ulysses, and notes on opportunism) are contributed by Hillman. The other two, on puer pathologies, are written by Henry A. Murray (on the American Icarus) and by Randolph Severson (reflections on the psychology of skin disease). Under myths and literature are essays on Artemis and the puer (by Tom Moore); the puer figure in Melville (by James Baird); and on *Finnegans Wake* (by Thomas Cowan).

(Bk.revs.: Harvest '80/26:104–8; PsyPersp '80/11:91–4; Quad '80/13n2:127–9)

The Spirit of the Valley: Androgyny and Chinese Thought, by Sukie Colegrave. (1981 subtitle: *Harmonizing the Masculine and Feminine in the Human*

Spirit.) (1989 reprint title: *Uniting Heaven and Earth*; 5-p. foreword by Robert Bly). London: Virago Pub. Co., 1979 +p; Los Angeles: J. P. Tarcher, 1981; 1989p* (244 + xii, incl. 7-p. index, 12-p. bibl., 18-p. notes, 8-p. gloss., 11 illus.).

Using insights gained from Jungian therapy, the work of Rudolf Steiner, and the study of Chinese culture, Colegrave explores the hypothesis that the true nature of the human being is androgyny—a synthesis of the masculine and feminine principles in the psyche. She chooses to study it through Chinese culture because of its recognition of yin and yang (feminine and masculine principles) as the central polarity in the individual and in the cosmos. She discusses the history and theory of yin and yang and then analyzes masculine consciousness and feminine consciousness and the expression of yin and yang in the individual person.

(Bk.revs.: Harvest '79/25:90–1; LibJ '81/106:2142; Choice '82/19:1258; BkRDig '83:307)

The Invisible Partners: How the Male and Female in Each of Us Affects Our Relationships, by John A. Sanford. New York and Ramsey, N.J.: Paulist Press, 1980p* (139, incl. 7-p. index, 4-p. bibl., 2 illus.).

Aiming to bring together Jung's most important ideas on the psychology of the sexes, Sanford examines the sexual duality of human nature from the point of view of "invisible partners" in every man or woman. These invisible partners are the projected images, charged with psychic energy, that arise in every romantic relationship, expressing the androgynous natures of the people involved. He interprets the yang-yin concept of Chinese philosophy and the anima-animus archetypes of Jungian psychology as the eternal tension of opposites with an urge toward wholeness. He discusses the positive and negative effects of anima or animus projections and behavior, using a number of examples from mythology, literature, and life; and he concludes with an analysis of a religious understanding of marriage and sexuality. Appended is a ten-page description of how to use the method of active imagination.

(Bk.revs.: BestSell Ag'80/40:179–80; Quad '81/14n2:117–18; StAnth '81/88:51; JPsy-Theol '83/11:55–8)

The Moon and the Virgin: Reflections on the Archetypal Feminine, by Nor Hall. New York: Harper & Row, 1980 +p*; London: Women's Press, 1980p* (284 + xvii, incl. 10-p. index, 9-p. bibl., 30 illus.).

Although more aligned with Jung, Hall's attempt to locate the feminine "begins and continues where Freud left off" in her re-formation of feminine values. In her quest for origins she begins with the Mother, the preconscious matriarchal phase of human existence, using ancient Greek mythology and literature as well as modern poetry to illustrate her points. The topics she discusses include Psyche's search; mothers and daughters; spiritual pregnancy; Artemis; the Hetaira; the Sibyl; the Old Wise Woman; and reflection and fabrication.

(Bk.revs.: Critic Oc-2'80/39:7; KirkR '80/48:415–16; LibJ '80/105:1089; LibJBkR '80:385; PubW 11Ap'80/217:67; Anima '81/8:77–9; AntiochR '81/39:390–1; Choice '81/ 10:446; Epiph '81/2:72–9; Harvest '81/27:178–80; JAnPsy '81/26:278–9; Quad '81/ 14n2:108–11; Resurg My–Jn'81/n86:36)

Descent to the Goddess: A Way of Initiation for Women, by Sylvia Brinton Perera. Toronto: Inner City Books, 1981p* (Studies in Jungian Psychology by Jungian Analysts, 6) (111, incl. 4-p. index, 3-p. bibl., 8-p. notes, Jungian gloss., 2 illus.).

Modern woman's quest for wholeness is examined by Perera in the context of the myth of the Sumerian goddess Inanna (Ishtar), using as illustrations some of her patients' relevant dreams. She sees the myth as a pattern of psychological health for the feminine in both women and men. She analyzes in detail the symbols of Inanna's "initiation," the descent to the underworld, and her destruction and transformation. The descent into the unconscious with its full range of feminine instincts and energy patterns, and the return to an individuating, balanced ego is seen as part of the developmental pattern in women reconnecting to the Self (the archetype of wholeness) in a masculine-oriented society.

(Bk.revs.: CanBkRAn '81:358–9; Choice '81/19:313; Harvest '82/28:166–8; Parab Ja'82/ 7:118–21; Quad '82/15n2:65–7; SFJInstLib '82/3n3:18–21; InwLight '82–83/n99:47–8; Resurg My–Jn'85/n110:41; PsyPersp '90/23:202–3)

The Father: Mythology and Changing Roles, by Arthur Colman and Libby Colman. (Orig. title: *Earth Father/Sky Father: The Changing Concept of Fathering*. Englewood Cliffs, N.J.: Spectrum Book/Prentice Hall, 1981* +p*.) Wilmette, Ill.: Chiron Publications, 1988* +p* (206 + xix, incl. 6-p. index, 23 illus.).

Utilizing Jung's theories concerning archetypes and the unconscious, the Colmans examine the changing conception of fathering, emphasizing that fathers and families need new images of what a father can be, especially an acknowledgement of the father as a potent nurturant force. In addition to presenting the images of earth father and sky father as two sides of the basic paternal archetype (the earth father in the center of the family as nurturant, and the sky father as integrating outside and family involvement) they add images of the father as creator, as royal (total) father, and as dyadic father (sharing of earth and sky roles by both partners). They discuss the images of the sky father through the life cycle as well as describing images of the nontraditional father.

(Bk.revs.: BkWorld 24Ja'82/12:11–12; PsyPersp '89/21:205–7; SFJInstLib '90/9n2:19–29)

Fully Human: How Everyone Can Integrate the Benefits of Masculine and Feminine Sex Roles, by Linda Olds. Englewood Cliffs, N.J.: Spectrum Books/Prentice-Hall, 1981 +p (274 + xiv, incl. 6-p. index, 13-p. bibl.).

Using insights of social and clinical psychology, Olds aims to go "beyond the stereotypic traits narrowly defined for each sex" by developing a full range of personality characteristics and bringing about a dynamic balance between them. She discusses dichotomous approaches to sex role polarity and integrative approaches to sex roles in terms of fears, concerns, and possibilities; and she examines patterns of development and changes in attitude that would be involved in people becoming more androgynous. She urges the recovery of a living sense of myth and presents an introduction to Jungian thought in her discussion on the integration of the anima and animus. Her analysis of how to strengthen the inner man includes the basic hero myth (Parsifal) and variations on that theme, and the feminine hero journey (Psyche); her focus on nourishing the inner woman includes recovering the Great Goddess, depatriarchizing myth, and nourishing the feminine in daily life.

(Bk.rev.: Choice '82/19:1328)

The Goddess: Mythological Images of the Feminine, by Christine Downing. New York: Crossroad Publishing Co., 1981; 1984p* (250 + xii, incl. 4-p. index, 10 illus.).

From her own life experience, Downing, "like Jung," has needed to learn what myth was living her, discovering that her own dreams and fantasies as well as events in waking life and her study of myths about the goddesses were mutually illuminated. Thereby she has "re-visioned" her life in order to gain an understanding of the sacredness of the feminine and the "complexity, richness, and nurturing power of female energy." After telling her dream-vision experience and instructing the reader on how to imagine the goddess (very much like that of interpreting a dream), she interprets her experiences with Persephone (innocent goddess of spring in the underworld realm of the soul and the imaginal), Ariadne (anima and mistress in center of the labyrinth), Hera (wifeliness), Pallas Athene (prototype of artistically creative woman), Gaia (the "great" mother from before time), Artemis (fearless self-sufficiency beckoning from afar), and Aphrodite (with her intimately entangled relationships). She ends with the Child (unrealized potentials of the self).

(Bk.revs.: KirkR '81/49:1124+; InwLight Spr'82/n98:45–7; LibJ '82/107:182; Parab '82/7:118–21; PsyPersp '82/13:210–14; Signs '83/9:299–302; SHumR '83/17:179–81; CrossCurr '84/34:109–11; JAmAcadRel '84/52:787–8; NewDirWom N'84/13:13; RelStudR '85/11:40)

Receiving Woman: Studies in the Psychology and Theology of the Feminine, by Ann Belford Ulanov. Philadelphia: Westminster Press, 1981p* (187, incl. 9-p. ref. notes).

Bringing insights from her classes and conferences with women students and patients in her analytical practice, as well as women who are friends, Ulanov interprets the feminine aspects of personality and their bearing on belief in God. She describes "receiving woman" as receiving all of herself (including nurture, compassion, power, intellect, and ambition), as being received (seen in her own light, including masculine and feminine elements), and as receiving others in full reciprocity. Her theme leads from discrimination, old stereotypes, and androgyny to relocating the issue of projection of stereotypes, and receiving and assimilating instead of disowning these aspects of being. She discusses what the feminine elements of being really are, the birth of otherness (relating insights of conception, pregnancy, and birth to the nascent stages of spiritual life), the authority of women attendant on integrating the animus (masculine side), and woman receiving her distinct potentialities.

(Bk.revs.: BestSell '81/41:152; Choice '81/19:449; ChrCen '81/98:1168–9; CrossCurr '81/31:221–3; Found '81/24:283–6; LibJ '81/106:1430; LivLight '81/18:287; TheolStud '81/42:723; BkRDig '82:1374; JAmAcadRel '82/50:329–30; JSciStudReg '82/21:186–7; RelStudR '82/8:54; CovenantQ '83/41:47–9; EAsPastorR '83/20:96; JPastorCare '83/37:70–1; PastorPsy '83/32:148–50; PsyPersp '83/14:225–34; StudForm '83/4:284–5; TheolToday '83/39:479; UnionSemQR '83/37:351–3; Quad '84/17n2:88–91)

Woman, Earth, and Spirit: The Feminine in Symbol and Myth, by Helen M. Luke. New York: Crossroad Publishing Co., 1981; 1986p* (102 + vi, incl. 2-p. ref. notes).

Luke's theme is that modern woman must maintain her roots in her basic feminine nature ("earth"), while at the same time discriminating and relating to the spirit. She believes that only the well of symbols and images within can bring about transformation. She draws upon Jungian training, *I Ching,* poetry (Dickinson, Eliot, and Charles Williams), and Greek mythology and drama to illustrate her interpretation of new levels of consciousness based on feminine values, including the goddess of dawn, goddess of the hearth, and mother and daughter mysteries. She also discusses consciousness and the mature woman, money and the feminine principle of relatedness, and revenge of the repressive feminine.

(Bk.revs.: BestSell '81/41:183; ChrCen '82/99:276+278; Chr&Lit '82/31n3:73; Quad '82/15n2:65–7; SpirToday '82/34:182; InwLight '82–83/n99:48–51; RelStudR '83/9:250; SHumR '83/17:179–81; NewDirWom N'84/13:13; PsyPersp '84/15:232–5)

Images of the Untouched: Virginity in Psyche, Myth and Community, edited by Joanne Stroud and Gail Thomas. Dallas: Spring Publications for The Dallas Institute of Humanities and Culture, 1982p* (The Pegasus Foundation Series, I) (201, incl. 17-p. index, 2-p. ref. notes, 4 illus.).

Consisting mainly of papers delivered at a 1979 conference in Dallas, these nine essays offer various views of the complex image of virginity, particularly psychic virginity. Essays by Jungian analysts are on the virginities of image (Patricia Berry), alchemical psychology (James Hillman), the meeting of pathology and poetry (Rafael López-Pedraza), and the incest taboo and the virgin archetype (John Layard). Other contributors whose books also appear in the present bibliography are David Miller (reflections on Christian imagery of the virgin and the moon) and Tom Moore (the virgin and the unicorn). Other essays are on the landscape of virginity (Robert Sardello), Faulkner's image of virginity (Louise Cowan), and the church as virgin and mother (Thomas Carroll).

(Bk.rev.: CaudaPav Spr'83/ns2:2)

Return of the Goddess, by Edward C. Whitmont. New York: Crossroad Publishing Co., 1982; 1986p*; London: Routledge & Kegan Paul, 1983p; Blauveldt, N.Y.: Freedleds/Garber, 1984p; London: Arkana, 1987p* (272 + xv, incl. 5-p. index, 9-p. ref. notes, 6 illus.).

Incorporating new experiential methods (body, imaginal, group, Gestalt) into his Jungian frame of reference, Whitmont urges revalidation of the basic instinctual energies in the depths of the unconscious psyche and recognition of the return of the ancient Goddess as a guide toward transformation. He begins his interpretation of the modern dilemma as the polarization of basic instinctual urges that may impair psychological functioning; and he summarizes the evolution of consciousness from the magical phase to the mythological or imaginal phase (Dionysus and Apollo) and to the mental (ego) phase, after which he analyzes the patriarchal myths of divine kingship (rationalizing, abstracting, controlling), of human exile (paradise lost), of the scapegoat (sin and atonement of guilt), and of the feminine and its repression. He proposes the Grail legend as the myth of our time that illustrates the discovery of the self in terms of inner and outer relatedness, and the learning process of awareness and acceptance of one's self.

(Bk.revs.: BkRDig '83:1536; Choice '83/20:1307; ChrCen '83/100:555–6; JPsyChry Spr '83/2:95; LibJ '83/108:214; Quad '83/16n1:109–13; SFJInstLib '83/4n3:1–18; TheolToday '83/40:255; Harvest '84/n30:134–5; JAmAcadRel '84/52:424; JAnPsy '84/29:85–

7; RelStudR '84/10:370; RelStudBul '84/4:48–9; Resurg Ja-F'84/n102:37–8; Horiz '85/
12:216–17; Resurg My-Jn'85/n110:41–2; PsyanR '86/73:393–7; HeythJ '87/28:108–9;
Resurg Ja-F'88/n126:45)

*The Woman Sealed in the Tower; Being a View of Feminine Spirituality as
Revealed by the Legend of Saint Barbara,* by Betsy Caprio. New York and
Ramsey, N.J.: Paulist Press, 1982p* (105, incl. 18 illus.).

Attracted to the legend of early martyr St. Barbara (c. A.D. 250) because
of her concern with the spiritual growth of women, Caprio applies Jung's
psychology to Christian tradition in her interpretation of the maiden who
was kept in a tower by her pagan father and beheaded when she refused to
recant her belief. Caprio analyzes the legend in terms of ancient symbols of
the four elements as they are lived out in all women as earth (sealed in the
tower), air (uplifting view from the top of the tower), water (third window at
which relationship and baptism occurred), and fire (story completed by spark
of transformation within), which represent the feminine development of the
four psychological functions of sensation, thinking, feeling, and intuition.
She provides some background on the spirituality of women, the feminine
principle, the masculine principle, and the God dwelling within. Appended
are some exercises, meditations, and prayers based on symbols in the story.
(Bk.revs.: LibJ '83/108:138; JPsyTheol '84/12:143–4; StAnth Ap'84/91:50; TheolToday
'84/40:472 +)

Wounded Woman: Healing the Father-Daughter Relationship, by Linda Schierse
Leonard. Athens, Ohio and Chicago: Swallow Press Books/Ohio U. Press,
1982*; Boulder and London: Shambhala Publications, 1983p* (179 + xix,
incl. 6-p. ref. notes).

From her own personal story and from analytical work with many
women clients who suffer from a wounded relationship with their fathers,
Leonard presents the story of her alcoholic father (himself wounded both in
relation to his feminine side and his masculinity), her own resulting distrust
of men, as well as problems of shame, guilt, and lack of confidence. Her
belief is that the injury must be understood and accepted so that healing and
compassion may come. Using her Jungian training and many examples from
dreams, myths, literature, and films, she analyzes the processes of wounding
(the father-daughter wound, the sacrifice of the daughter, and rage and tears)
and healing (redeeming the father and finding the feminine spirit).
(Bk.revs.: LibJ '82/107:1665–6; PubW 13Ag'82/222:65–6; SFJInstLib '82/4n1:1–15;
PsyPersp '83/14:207–10; PubW 16S'83/224:124; Bklist '84/80:772; LATimesBkR
15Ja'84:5; JAnPsy '87/392–3)

Cinderella and Her Sisters: The Envied and the Envying, by Ann Ulanov and
Barry Ulanov. Philadelphia: Westminster Press, 1983p* (186, incl. 6-p. index,
3-p. bibl., 8-p. ref. notes, 4-p. gloss.).

Examining envy from the viewpoint of both the envied and the envious, the Ulanovs use the tale of Cinderella and her sisters to discuss this "wounded space in human relationship," including the central role of envy in the very nature of society. They explore the psychological aspects (being envied; envying; envying the mother; envying the masculine; and envying the good) and the theological aspects (envy as sin; the envier's spiritual plight; the envier's sexual plight; the plight of the good; repentance; consent; grace; and goodness). They emphasize the fact that, if suffered consciously, envy can be a means of recovering one's being through insight and emotional struggle.

Energies of Love: Sexuality Re-visioned, by June Singer. Garden City, N.Y.: Anchor Books/Doubleday Publishing Co., 1983; Boston: Sigo Press, 1990p as *Love's Energies* (314, incl. 6-p. index, 7-p bibl.).

Sensing a great void in the study of human psychosexual developments, Singer aims at a more comprehensive perspective on sexuality. She "re-visions" the energies of love partly from training with her spiritual mentor Jung and more recently from transpersonal psychology, viewing the stages of development from pre-personal (emergence) to personal (rise of conscious-ness), to transition (from personal to transpersonal), and transpersonal (uniting). She presents an extensive background analysis of psychohistorical and religious traditions from the Middle Ages onward, including "four men in search of enlightenment" (Jung, Abraham Maslow, Alan Watts, and Huston Smith). She emphasizes unity as the individual experience of integrat-ing psychic opposites and she sees it as an integral part of a dynamic universe, in which sexuality belongs to both aspects, being a matter of personal intimacy and a key to how the individual participates in life in response to patterns in nature.

(Bk.revs.: Bklist '83/80:315; JTranspPsy '83/15:231–3; KirkR '83/51:951; LibJ '83/108:1801; PsyPersp '84/15:227–32; Quad '84/17n1:59–61; Chiron '85:228–31; SFJInstLib '85/5n3:32–4)

Goddesses in Everywoman: A New Psychology of Woman, by Jean Shinoda Bolen. Los Angeles: J. P. Tarcher, 1983; San Francisco: Harper & Row, 1984; Toronto: Fitzhenry & Whiteside, 1984; San Francisco: Colophon Books/Harper & Row, 1985p* (334 + xiv, incl. 14-p. index, 8-p. bibl., 10-p. ref. notes, 4-p. foreword by Gloria Steinem).

Acknowledging that her descriptions of "goddesses" are composites of many women—patients, friends, colleagues—Bolen posits a new psychologi-cal delineation of women and the feminine based on images of the Greek goddesses. These "powerful inner patterns" (archetypes) provide women with a basis for understanding themselves and their relationships with others.

Starting with a discussion of her conception of goddesses in every woman as inner images and the idea of activating the different goddesses, she interprets in turn the archetypal patterns of the virgin goddesses (Artemis, Athena, and Hestia), personifying the independent, active nonrelational aspects of women's psychology; the archetypal patterns of the vulnerable goddesses (Hera, Demeter, and Persephone), personifying relationship-oriented aspects of women's psychology; and the archetypal patterns of the alchemical goddess (Aphrodite), personifying transformation. She ends with a discussion of how the powerful archetypal patterns compete for expression and describes the potential for the heroic journey that resides in every woman.

(Bk.revs.: NewAge Oc'83/9:63; BestSell '84/44:142; Bklist '84/80:1414; KirkR '84/52:434; LibJ '84/109:1334; PsyToday S'84/18:12–13; PubW 27Ap'84/225:76–7; Anima '85/12:75–8; BkRDig '85:162; JTranspersPsy '85/17:87–8; WomRBks My'85/2:7–8; SFJInstLib '86/6n4:13–24; JPsyChry Sum'87/6:85–6; RelStudR '87/13:48; JEmplCouns '89/26:42)

We: Understanding the Psychology of Romantic Love, by Robert A. Johnson. San Francisco: Harper & Row, 1983; 1985p*; London: Routledge & Kegan Paul, 1984p; London: Arkana, 1987p* (204 + xv, incl. 3-p. bibl.).

Characterizing romantic love as the single greatest energy system as well as the great wound in the Western psyche, Johnson applies the principles of Jung's psychology to interpret the myth of Tristan and Iseult as the first story in Western literature that dealt with romantic love. Analyzing the myth in detail, Johnson believes that it gives specific psychological information and teaches deep truths about the psyche, particularly that the man "falling in love" goes beyond love itself to worship his soul-in-woman (anima) that becomes a cycle of illusion as he projects his idealized feminine. The outcome for Tristan was death. In contrast, his marriage to Iseult of the White Hands held the potential for human love, in which one sees the other as an individual rather than as anima-fantasy—"loving" rather than "being in love."

(Bk.revs.: BestSell '84/44:265; Bklist '84/80:830; Horiz '84/11:211–12; InwLight '84/n100:83–6; LibJ '84/109:186; VaQR Spr'84/60:64; Sojour Jy'85/14:44; JPsyChry Spr'88/7:92–3)

Change of Life: A Psychological Study of Dreams and the Menopause, by Ann Mankowitz. Toronto: Inner City Books, 1984p* (Studies in Jungian Psychology by Jungian Analysts, 16) (123, incl. 3-p. index, 4-p. bibl., 3-p. notes, 2-p. gloss., 2 illus.).

Mankowitz's book is a study of a woman client in Jungian analysis at a transitional time of both body and mind. It involves extraordinary dreams and the special significance of menopause ("the change of life") for the analysand, the analyst, and other women, which the author believes can provide an opportunity for psychological integration and rebirth. Following preliminary discussions on what menopause is, and the use of dreamwork in analysis, she describes dreams and the role of menopause in her analytic work with "Rachel," including the topics of the fear of knowing; narcissistic mortification; sex and menopause; the death of the womb; anger and jealousy; rebirth; creativity and individuation; the archetypal masculine in women; integration of the feminine; and separation and individuation. (Bk.revs.: CanBkRAn '84:467–8; ContemPsy '85/30:740; PsyPersp '85/16:229–32; SFJInstLib '86/6n3:1–20)

For Women Growing Older: The Animus, by Jane Hollister Wheelwright. Houston: C. G. Jung Educational Center, 1984p (59 + vii, incl. 2-p. gloss. of Jungian terms).

Considering the subtitle as the main subject of the essay, Wheelwright shows that a meaningful later life for women is a by-product of "the conscious or unconscious experience of the animus." She discusses, after defining animus in Jung's terms, how to live one's animus without being caught by it and how the animus works in everyday life and in dreams. She describes and interprets the topics of the animus in the past and the animus today; dynamics of the animus; how to disidentify from the animus; tragedies of animus identification in older women; old women as models for the future; and the animus in the service of the ego. She ends with a brief account of Naomi James, author of Alone Around the World, as her example of the ideal modern woman who has integrated her animus. (Bk.revs.: JAnPsy '86/31:400; SFJInstLib '86/6n3:1–20)

How to Say No to the One You Love, by Peter Schellenbaum. (Ger.: Das Nein in der Liebe. Stuttgart: Kreuz Verlag, 1984.) Wilmette, Ill.: Chiron Publications, 1987* (136 + v, incl. 3-p. bibl.).

Affirming that it is impossible to fundamentally transform one's personality from within unless one's life is shared with another person whom one loves, Schellenbaum explores the problem of boundaries within intimacy in both successful and unsuccessful relationships, using many clinical and personal examples. He presents insights from a Jungian point of view on the meaning of love not only in the completion of two persons living together but also in each of those two separate individuals becoming whole. Beginning with the topic of "Does Saying No Belong in Love?", he discusses the tragedy of the happy couple; merging and resisting; the self-destruction of the stronger partner; and pursuit and flight without love. He deals with the topics of heterosexuals' homosexual fantasies; hate and love; love relationships without sexual intimacy; becoming more feminine—even as a man; the "no"

of separation and divorce; interpretations of surrender and discovery of Self in sexuality; and the attitude of Eros.
(Bk.rev.: Harvest '89–90/35:236–7)

The Nature of Loving: Patterns of Human Relationships, by Verena Kast. (Ger.: *Paare.* Zurich: Dieter Breitsohl, 1984.) Wilmette, Ill.: Chiron Publications, 1986p* (107 + v, incl. 4-p. index, 2-p. bibl., 9 illus.).

Hoping to stimulate an awareness of the significance of fantasies, within a relationship as well as intrapsychically, that awaken archetypal feminine and masculine elements and create feelings of vitality and wholeness, Kast presents myths of divine couples to show how they are embodied in literature, in dreams, and in the daily life of the individual. Her models include Shiva and Shakti (the ideal of complete union with possibilities and problems), Pygmalion (longing to form a partner in one's own image), Merlin and Viviane (the wise old man and the young girl), and brotherman-sisterwife (Solomon and Shulamite in the Song of Songs). Her interpretations involve dreams, active imagination, and clinical material, and she concludes with a critical appraisal of Jung's anima-animus concept.
(Bk.rev.: JAnPsy '89/34:93–4)

Anima: An Anatomy of a Personified Notion, by James Hillman. Dallas: Spring Publications, 1985p* (188 + x, incl. 5-p. ref. notes, 42 illus.).

Recognizing that experience and notion are interrelated, Hillman looks more closely at the rather neglected phenomenology of the *notion* of the anima, the root metaphor upon which his work "has always been based." He discusses the topics of anima and contrasexuality; anima and Eros; anima and feeling; anima and the feminine; anima and psyche; anima and depersonalization; integration of the anima; the anima as mediatrix of the unknown; anima as unipersonality; and anima in syzygy (union with animus). He arranges the text of the book so that his commentary on the right-hand page is accompanied by relevant quotations from Jung appearing on the left-hand page.
(Bk.revs.: Choice '86/23:1463; Quad '86/19n2:82–3; JAnPsy '87/32:391–2; ContemPsy '89/34:607; Harvest '89–90/35:231–2)

Changing Woman and Her Sisters: Feminine Aspects of Selves and Deities, by Sheila Moon. San Francisco: Guild for Psychological Studies Publishing House, 1985* +p* (232, incl. 11-p. bibl.).

Using Native American (mostly Navajo) myths of the feminine goddesses, Moon takes feminine mythic characteristics from stories still told in

ceremonies and rituals with their complexity of interrelationships. She places them in three stages: "from the first" (first woman, salt woman), incompleteness (changing-bear-maiden, shaping vagina, wolf chief's wife), and towards wholeness (spider woman, changing woman, snake woman). She interprets each stage both mythically and psychologically for symbolic meanings that ground one's understanding of the feminine, which she believes to be the more neglected, rejected, and misunderstood of the masculine/feminine opposites operative in all individuals. To illustrate the process, she uses examples from her Jungian practice of more than twenty-five years.
(Bk.rev.: Choice '85/23:165–6)

The Cult of the Black Virgin, by Ean C. M. Begg. London and Boston: Arkana/ Routledge & Kegan Paul, 1985p* (289, incl. 15-p. index, 10-p. bibl., 10 illus., 115-p. gazetteer/maps).

Marveling at the survival of scores of Black Virgin statues in great basilicas, tiny village churches, museums, and private collections, Begg explores the extent and nature of these Madonnas from a viewpoint of archetypal psychology. He interprets the return of the Black Virgin, whose blackness tends to be ignored, to the forefront of collective consciousness as coincident with the "profound psychological need to reconcile sexuality and religion," to circumvent patriarchal rigidities, and to facilitate healing. He discusses the influence of the East, classical tradition, natural religion (Celtic and Teutonic sources), and the whore wisdom in the Christian era as background to interpret the symbolic meaning of the Black Virgin.
(Bk.revs.: Harvest '86/32:161–2; Tabl '86/240:345)

The Father: Contemporary Jungian Perspectives, edited by Andrew Samuels. London: Free Association Books, 1985* +p*; New York: New York U. Press, 1986; 1988p* (266 + v, incl. 10-p. index, 8-p. gloss., 4 illus.).

Trying to redress the imbalance in Jungian analysts' professional interest in the mother and mother-child relations, Samuels collects ten essays on the role of the father in psychological maturing. Not a sociological analysis of patriarchal society nor an "oblique integration of feminist ideas," the collection represents the psychological perspective with a Jungian orientation. In addition to the long introduction, Samuels adds an essay on the image of the parents in bed. Other selections (mostly by London analysts) are on the father archetype in feminine psychology (Amy Allenby); the father's anima (John Beebe); aspects of the development of authority (Hans Dieckmann); the archetypal masculine (Barbara Greenfield); paternal psychopathology and the emerging ego (David Kay); the search for a loving father (Ralph Layland); the absent father (Eva Seligman); and the concealed body language of anorexia nervosa (Bani Shorter). Also included is Jung's article on the significance of the father in the destiny of the individual.

(Bk.revs.: BrJPsychi '86/149:394; Harvest '86/32:152–3; JAnPsy '86/31:396–9; Econ 4Ap'87/303:92; RefResBkN Wint'87/2:2; SciBksFilm '87/23:7; BkRDig '88:538; SFJInstLib '90/9n2:30–40)

Feminist Archetypal Theory: Interdisciplinary Re-Visions of Jungian Psychology, edited by Estella Lauter and Carol Schreier Rupprecht. Knoxville: U. of Tennessee Press, 1985* (281 + xx, incl. 11-p. index, 5-p. bibl., 9 illus.).

Aiming to "reflect women's experiences more accurately" by reformulating key Jungian concepts in a "re-vision" of Jungian thought and its "successor discipline" (archetypal psychology), Lauter and Rupprecht present five essays in an interdisciplinary approach. Lauter presents a study of visual images of women (a test case for the theory of archetypes), and Rupprecht discusses the common language of women's dreams. Other essays deal with a feminist perspective on the religious and social dimensions of Jung's concept of the archetype (Demaris Wehr); Jung, Frye, Lévi-Strauss, and feminist archetypal theory (Janis Pratt); and the descent of Inanna: myth and therapy (Sylvia Brinton Perera).

(Bk.revs.: AppalJ '86/13:311–13; Quad '86/19n1:71–6; SFJInstLib '86/6n3:1–20 + 21–32; SAtlR '86/51:113–15; CommBound '87/5:6; RelStudR '88/14:49)

From Eden to Eros: Origins of the Put Down of Women, by Richard Roberts. San Anselmo, Calif.: Vernal Equinox, 1985p* (166, incl. 9 illus.).

Examining the "war between the sexes" from ancient history to the present, Roberts analyzes patriarchy's basis for the put down of women, the root cause of a great psychic split. In the first part of the book he discusses Eden, patriarchy, matriarchy, and witches. He then explores the subject of our attitudes toward nature, the body, and sex, which are conditioned by our attitudes toward the goddess Gaia, or Great Mother. He describes the way in which Eros operates as a facilitator that makes the marriage of warring opposites possible. He proposes that resolution can take place only through our recognition of the role that archetypes play in our individual lives.

(Bk.rev.: SFJInstLib '86/6n4:41–5)

About Men and Women: How Your "Great Story" Shapes Your Destiny, by Ted W. Guzie and Noreen Monroe Guzie. New York and Mahwah, N.J.: Paulist Press, 1986p* (161 + iv, incl. 13 illus.).

The authors present "Great Stories" that illustrate archetypes that men and women have been living in every era and culture, including feminine stories (mother, companion, amazon, mediatrix) and masculine stories (father, seeker, warrior, sage); and they examine "quirks and qualities" of mother and father, amazon and warrior, seeker and companion, and mediatrix and sage. In addition, they discuss the gender opposites, marriage, midlife, and maturity. They append an analysis of archetypes as they relate to the Myers-Briggs Type Indicator.

(Bk.revs.: LibJ 1S'86/111:207; BkRDig '87:760; JPsyChry Fall '87/6:75–6; SchLibr '87/33:122)

The Book of Lilith, by Barbara Black Koltuv. York Beach, Maine: Nicolas-Hays, 1986p* (127 + xii, incl. 5-p. bibl.).

Characterizing this book as a psychological anthology of Lilith's story, Jungian analyst Koltuv explores the myths of the "she-demon of the night" from Sumerian, Babylonian, Assyrian, Canaanite, Persian, Hebrew, Arabic, and Teutonic mythology. She examines the meaning of Lilith in the modern psyche, seeing her as representing the personification of the rejected and neglected aspects of the Great Mother archetype, whose powerful psychic energy holds the potential for transformation. Following a discussion of Lilith's origins, life, and deeds, the author describes her relationship to the daughters of Eve and her role as a seductress "cast out and redeemed."

(Bk.rev.: JAnPsy '88/33:198–9)

On the Way to the Wedding: Transforming the Love Relationship, by Linda Schierse Leonard. Boston and London: Shambhala Publications, 1986* +p* (261 + ix, incl. 8-p. ref. notes).

Having always longed for a soulmate, that "other half" which would make one whole, Leonard interprets the ascent that followed her psychological descent (as described in *The Wounded Woman*, 1982) as a transformation from despair into affirmation. In this transformation, she discovers her "inner man of heart" as well as her own inner feminine spirit, and she describes it using the metaphor of the wedding, drawing on her personal experiences, dreams, Jungian analytic work, myths and fairy tales, films, and literature. Her story, described almost like a fairy tale itself, is divided into three sections: the wandering (through the woods; prince charming and the special princess; the ghostly lover; bewitchment; the demon lover; the ring of power), the loving (into the clearing; the bridegroom and the woman in black; beauty and the beast), and the wondering (the divine wedding; the veil; the vow; the ring of love).

(Bk.revs.: LibJ '86/111:71; Harvest '87–'88/33:219–21; PsyToday Ap '87/21:76; Quad '87/20n2:82–4; JAnPsy '88/33:200–1; InwLight '89/n104:53)

Pagan Meditations: The Worlds of Aphrodite, Hestia, Artemis, by Ginette Paris. Dallas: Spring Publications, 1986p; repr. 1989p* (204, incl. 5-p. ref. notes).

Drawing from the field of social psychology and theories of Jung, Paris focuses upon integrating the fields of ecology, psychology, and human relations. She meditates on the goddesses Aphrodite (seven short chapters), Artemis (six), and Hestia (three), describing her approach as an "imaginative feminism" that seeks to nourish a new feminine identity and a renewed set of values that can confront the roots of the patriarchal age and directly address pressing social issues such as ecology, overpopulation, abortion, and defense spending.

(Bk.revs.: Choice '86/24:344; LATimesBkR 24Ag'86:5; Quad '87/20n1:102–4; BkRDig '88:1319; JAmAcadRel Spr'88/56:16)

Being a Woman: Fulfilling Your Femininity and Finding Love, by Toni Grant. New York: Random House, 1988*; 1989p*; New York: Avon Books, 1989p* (233 + xviii, incl. 6-p. bibl.).

Drawing on her experience with patients in her therapeutic practice and her daily radio program devoted to women's questions, Grant offers a theory of feminine psychology that would speak to "the mother, the career woman, the wife, and the mistress." Having discovered the "compelling work" of Jung and his associates, and in particular the idea of the need for both men and women to integrate the male and the female within, she presents the challenge that Bette Davis expressed in *All About Eve*: "being a woman," no matter how many other careers one has. She follows the theme of the new Amazon Woman who must learn to integrate her newfound identity as a person of accomplishment with her needs for love and feminine fulfillment. Her topics cover "the big lies of liberation"; the four aspects of woman; the Madonna; embracing femininity; finding your hero; managing men; sweet surrender; and fulfilling femininity.

Betwixt and Between: Patterns of Masculine and Feminine Initiation, edited by Louise Mahdi, Steven Foster, and Meredith Little. LaSalle, Ill.: Open Court Publishing Co., 1987* +p* (Reality of the Psyche) (498 + xv, incl. 15-p. index, end-chapter ref. notes).

Mahdi and associate editors Foster and Little use a practical approach to examine patterns of initiation, those "betwixt and between" times that signal potential transformation and initiation to another level of consciousness. Consisting of thirty-one essays by thirty-five authors (including seventeen Jungian analysts), this interdisciplinary compendium provides a variety of approaches that are organized under six groupings (initiation of youth;

initiation of men; initiation of women; personal initiation; initiation into old age and dying; ancient and modern initiations). Contributors whose books appear in this bibliography are Bernstein, Bly, Gustafson, Sandner, Luke, Woodman, J. Hall, Odajnyk, M. Stein, Wheelwright, Meier, Buehrmann, Monick, and von Franz.

(Bk.revs.: Choice '87/25:351; PsyPersp '87/18:443–7; CommBound Jy-Ag'88/6:23–4; Quad '88/21n1:83–5; RelStudR '88/14:46; Harvest '89–90/35:219–21; JAnPsy '89/34:309–10)

An Image Darkly Forming: Women and Initiation, by Bani Shorter. London and New York: Routledge & Kegan Paul, 1987p* (154 + xii, incl. 8-p. index, 3-p. bibl., 6-p. ref. notes).

In therapeutic practice as a Jungian analyst, Shorter weaves her own experiences with those of five women who were challenged and changed during crucial periods of transition in their lives. She interprets their journeys as they are initiated into being themselves, instinctively creating rituals in times of crises and transition. She presents and amplifies the Greek myth of Persephone and the Christian myth of Mary as archetypal images for women's internal journeys, in which the body is the container for divine transformation. Symbolic exposure through rituals (including Jungian analytic "ritual") gives initiation experiences their meaning, though validation and confirmation is left to the individual, as in the interpretation of dreams.

(Bk.revs.: BrJDevPsy '88/6:301; Choice '88/25:1438; Harvest '88–89/34:168–70)

Journey Through Menopause: A Personal Rite of Passage, by Christine Downing. New York: Crossroad Publishing Co., 1987; New York: Continuum, 1989p* (164 + xii, incl. 8-p. ref. notes, 13 illus.).

By examining her own journey through menopause, Downing emphasizes the need to remythologize the experience by viewing it developmentally rather than pathologically, not only as a physiological event but as a psychological one with a spiritual significance. Interpreting her own three-year period of transition as a typical pattern of the rite of passage, her preparatory phase was initiated by a dream that led her to examine psychology, mythology, and dreams, followed by a journey around the world which became her literal passage through menopause, ending with the acceptance of physical weakness and vulnerability on her return "home" to Hestia, ready for the beginning of another life-stage.

(Bk.revs.: Bklist 1S'87/84:15; LibJ '87/112:131; Commonw '88/115:637–8; RelStudR '88/14:359; BkRDig Ag '89:80)

Jung and Feminism: Liberating Archetypes, by Demaris S. Wehr. Boston: Beacon Press, 1987; 1989p*; London: Routledge & Kegan Paul, 1988p* (148 + xii, incl. 6-p. index, 16-p. ref. notes).

Aiming to build a bridge between feminism and Jung, Wehr brings feminist theory to bear on analytical psychology in order to liberate the archetypes from their "static and eternal associations." Her thesis is that Jung's psychology, if divested of sexism, is invaluable for understanding one's self and the world. She discusses the topics of Jung and feminism; feminist theory in psychology and religion; Jung's model of the psyche; individuation and our "inner cast of characters"; experience as something sacred (Jung's psychology as religion); and analytical psychology through a feminist lens.

(Bk.revs.: LibJ Jy'87/112:84; PubW 19Jn'87/231:107; RefResBkN Fall '87/2:18; AmJPsyth '88/42:492–3; AntiochR '88/46:121; HudsonR '88/41:580; PubW 18N'88/234:75; Quad '88/21n2:93–6; SFJInstLib '88/8n2:23–5; SexRoles '88/19:119–22; WqmRBks My'88/ 5:20; ContemPsy '89/34:273; Horiz '89/16:196–7; RelStudR '89/15:134; Signs '89/ 15:191–4)

Phallos: Sacred Image of the Masculine, by Eugene Monick. Toronto: Inner City Books, 1987p* (Studies in Jungian Psychology by Jungian Analysts, 27) (141, incl. 6-p. index, 3-p. bibl., 5-p. ref. notes, 31 illus.).

Citing a lack of contemporary Jungian writings about masculine issues in general and the need for men to understand the psychological underpinnings of their gender and their sexuality, Monick affirms that archetypal masculinity means phallos (erect penis), the image of instinctual will and power. He begins with discussions of phallos and religious experience and of the archetypal phallos (phallic worship; a transpersonal phallic dream; the Cerne Giant; and Epstein's St. Michael and the devil), followed by interpretations of phallos and psychoanalysis (Freud's "final" statement; Jung's "first" dream; the power of the mother) and the psychoid nature of phallos (Neumann's double-phallos concept; psychoid aura; proto-phallos and the psychoid unconscious). He concludes with analyses of archetypal images of phallos (Hermes; Mercurius; Dionysus; and Zeus and Ganymede), the shadow side of phallos, and phallos out of the ordinary (two men's dreams; homosexuality; and animus, phallic energy in women).

(Bk.revs.: BksCan My'87/16:21; CanBkRAn '87:327; PsyPersp '87/18:438–40; ContemPsy '88/33:623; JAnPsy '88/33:199–200; Quad '88/21n1:86–7; SFJInstLib '89/ 8n3:53–66; PsyPersp '90/23:191–2)

The Road by the River: A Healing Journey for Women, by Djohariah Toor. San Francisco: Harper & Row, 1987*; 1990p (227 + x, incl. 3-p. bibl. notes).

Acknowledging her indebtedness to many women who generously allowed her to use their dreams, stories, and growth experiences to illustrate the material, Toor deals with the healing process and the detours and summits of the journey to the feminine self. She examines the struggle of women to move past their wounds and unearth the human spirit within themselves; and

she analyzes how one gets wounded and how one can grow from that. Following an introductory view of the road by the river, she discusses the beginning of the journey (a time for change); awakening consciousness (deeper waters of the Self); roads to the inner woman; images of the mother; fathers as heroes and adversaries; the woman beyond the mask; awakening relationships; and soul-making.
(Bk.rev.: NewDirWom N'87/16:18)

The Witch and the Clown: Two Archetypes of Human Sexuality, by Ann Ulanov and Barry Ulanov. Wilmette, Ill.: Chiron Publications, 1987p* (337 + ix, incl. 3-p. name-index, 5-p. subject-index, 21-p. notes, 19 illus.).

Recognizing the archaic energies of sexuality and spirit as archetypal images in the collective unconscious, the Ulanovs explore the archetypes of the witch and the clown as points of entry for the outlawed opposites within the person, the witch personifying what the stereotyped image of woman omits (primordial intellectual capacities; drive; inordinate power) and the clown personifying what the stereotyped view of man omits (bumbler; vulnerable fool; feeling-centered man). After describing aspects of the archetypal witch and clown in general, they analyze the witch archetype (voracious, distant, sexual, aggressive) as well as bewitchment, the hag complex, redemption of the hag, and the witch in men, which is followed by an analysis of the clown archetype (the clown complex, the clown rescued, the clown redeemed, and the clown in women).
(Bk.revs.: Choice '87/25:392; Quad '88/21n2:104–7; JAnPsy '88/33:314–16)

Psyche's Sisters: Re-Imagining the Meaning of Sisterhood, by Christine Downing. San Francisco: Harper & Row, 1988* (188 + xi, incl. 4-p. index, 9-p. ref. notes, 5 illus.).

Realizing that the bond between sisters had been neglected in her study of the relevance of Greek goddess traditions to contemporary women, Downing draws upon myths and folktales, her own sisterly experience, and Jungian depth psychology to examine the mysteries of sisterhood. She interprets fairy tale sisters, Psyche and her sisters, mythic siblings, tragic sisters, divine sisters and biblical brothers, inner sisters, Oedipus's sisters, and feminism's sisters, focusing on the struggles that arise between sisters and showing how they may result in individual differentiation and growth.
(Bk.revs.: KirkR '87/55:1709; Bklist '88/84:957; Commonw '88/115:637; LibJ 1F'88/113:69; PubW 15Ja'88/233:84–5; BloomR S'89/9:8; BkRDig S'89:49; PsyPersp '89/20:203–5; RelStudR '89/15:341)

The Sacred Prostitute: Eternal Aspect of the Feminine, by Nancy Qualls-Corbett. Toronto: Inner City Books, 1988p* (Studies in Jungian Psychology by

Jungian Analysts, 32) (171, incl. 5-p. index, 4-p. bibl., 23 illus., foreword by Marion Woodman).

With a Jungian orientation, Qualls-Corbett examines the potentially life-enhancing interrelationships of sexuality and of spirituality as seen through the archetypal image of the sacred prostitute. She first presents the historical background of the goddess of love and her virgin priestesses and then the psychological significance of sacred prostitution, followed by inter-pretations of the sacred prostitute in masculine psychology (anima as man's image of woman; anima in dreams; Lawrence's *The Man Who Died;* stages of the anima; anima development in middle life) and in feminine psychology as illustrated by dreams of three sexually uninitiated middle-aged women and a married woman, as well as by Lawrence's story *The Virgin and the Gipsy.* She concludes with a discussion on the restoration of the soul (the split feminine; Mary Magdalene; the Virgin Mary and the Black Madonna; the goddess through time; and the search for integration).
(Bk.revs.: Gnosis '88/n8:58; Harvest '88–89/34:182–3; QuillQuire My'88/54:27)

Those Women, by Nor Hall. Dallas: Spring Publications, 1988p* (84 + ix, incl. 2-p. bibl., 5 illus.).

In this book, which was originally conceived as an introduction to Jungian analyst Fierz-David's larger book *Women's Dionysian Initiation,* and then became a separate "tribute to a tremor in the subtle history of the women's movement," Hall shares her fascination with the contemporary look of the women in the frescoes at the Villa of Mysteries in ancient Pompeii. Integrating psychological analysis with her perspective as a poet and classicist, Hall sees reality in myth. In this case, the woman in the fresco follows the course of initiation in Orphic tradition in the same way that the patient undertakes the long journey of analysis through the unconscious.
(Bk.revs.: Gnosis '88/n9:62; SmallPress F'89/7:60)

What Men Are Like, by John A. Sanford and George Lough. New York and Mahwah, N.J.: Paulist Press, 1988p* (315, incl. 11-p. index, end-chapter bibl.).

Sanford and Lough describe psychological masculine development from the basic points of view of Jung and Kunkel, blending case histories and historical, cultural, and literary references. They examine masculine psychol-ogy from boyhood through adolescence, the tyranny of the ego, a man and his work, and the midlife crisis; and then they discuss a man and his feminine side (anima), masculine relationships (men as friends and lovers; men as fathers and sons), masculine sexual fantasies, individuation and old age, and

the anima and masculine development in dreams, fairy tales, myths. They append a 4-page summary of Jungian psychological typology and a 12-page analysis of adolescent development as illustrated by *Alice in Wonderland.*
(Bk.revs.: CathNewTimes 14My'89/13:1; NewAge Mr'89/6:74)

Coming Together/Coming Apart: The Union of Opposites in Love Relationships, by John A. Desteian. Boston: Sigo Press, 1989* +p* (184 + xv, incl. 2-p. index, 2-p. bibl., 12 illus.).

Drawing from his prior experience as a divorce lawyer, as well as his current experience as Jungian analyst and relationship counselor, Desteian examines the question of why initial infatuation often leads to an unsatisfactory marriage and a painful and prolonged separation in which the same kind of heat and passion is occurring for opposite reasons. He discusses animation (physical, emotional, psychological, and spiritual states that happen in the process of infatuation); some of the structures and components of the personality (including the process of the unconscious); a theoretical analysis of the psychic source of feelings and behaviors (the why of infatuation); the interpretation of dreams during infatuation (illumination of unconscious processes); the dynamics of marriage and separation; and the process of reunion. He concludes by emphasizing that the symbolic life is the goal of the work of individuation.

Gods in Everyman: A New Psychology of Men's Lives and Loves, by Jean Shinoda Bolen. San Francisco: Harper & Row, 1989*; 1990p (338 + xiv, incl. 7-p. index, 5-p. bibl., 11-p. ref. notes).

Bolen uses depth psychology, taking both powerful inner archetypes and demanding outer stereotypes into consideration, in order to understand men and their thoughts, feelings, and dreams. She points out that gods and goddesses represent different qualities, whose contrasexuality appears in both men and women. Recognizing that there are gods (innate patterns or archetypes) in every man, she first relates a myth about patriarchy, then interprets the pantheon of archetypes of fathers (Zeus: realm of will and power; Poseidon: emotion and instinct; Hades: souls and the unconscious), and the archetypes of sons (Apollo: lawgiver, favorite son; Hermes: communicator, trickster, traveler; Ares: warrior, dancer, lover; Hephaestus: craftsman, inventor, loner; Dionysus: mystic, lover, wanderer). She concludes with a discussion about "re-membering ourselves," reconnecting what has been psychologically "dismembered," through finding one's own myth.
(Bk.revs.: PubW 3Mr'89/235:90; SciTechBkN Jn'89/13:1; SFJInstLib '90/9n2:41–9)

In Her Image: The Unhealed Daughter's Search for Her Mother, by Kathie Carlson. Boston and Shaftesbury: Shambhala Publications, 1989*; 1990p

(A C. G. Jung Foundation Book) (152 + xiii, incl. 5-p. index, 3-p. bibl., 9-p. ref. notes, 17 illus.).

From her experiences as a therapist, teacher, mother, and daughter, Carlson writes about the daughter's relationship with her mother, which she describes as the birthplace of the daughter's ego identity, sense of security in the world, and feelings about herself, her body, and other women. She begins with the child's view of preserving her centrality and her need for mother, the feminist view of assessing the effects of the collective environment on the relationship, and the transpersonal view that puts human mothering within its archetypal background of the Great Mother. She discusses positive bonds between mother and daughter; negative relationships ("binding" or "banishing"); the significance of touch in the mother-daughter relationship; matrophobia (fear of becoming just like mother) and its transformation; the unhealed child-daughter (with partial solutions and healing possibilities); and the archetypal dynamic of the Great Mother in personal experience.

Jung, Jungians, and Homosexuality, by Robert H. Hopcke. Boston and Shaftesbury: Shambhala Publications, 1989*; 1991p (210 + x, incl. 6-p. index, 8-p. ref. notes).

Drawing upon his master's thesis, Hopcke examines what Jung and Jungian writers have had to say about homosexuality. Following a brief introduction, he surveys Jung's statements concerning homosexuality and then discusses Jung's attitudes and theories, after which he examines the writings of Jungians and "tentatively" considers a theory of sexual orientation that brings together many strands of Jungian thought. He aims to discern archetypal themes in the collective and personal lives of gay men in contemporary American culture and analyzes the archetypal feminine in gay men, the imagery of the archetypal masculine in gay male culture, and the androgyne. He concludes with "looking forward by looking back" and proposes a theory of sexual orientation that represents both Jungian insights and the empirical reality of contemporary gay people.

Mother/Father, edited by Harry A. Wilmer. Wilmette, Ill.: Chiron Publications, 1989p* (182 + xx).

Consisting mostly of lectures given at the Institute for the Humanities at Salado, Texas, during 1984–85, Wilmer's essays are divided into sections on "My Mother, My Father" and "The Mother, The Father," the former being about famous parents or by famous children now parents themselves, the latter being about transpersonal and archetypal mothers and fathers. Jungian contributions appear in part two, namely, mother and daughter relationships

(Mary Briner), the significance of Jung's father in Jung's destiny as a therapist of Christianity (Murray Stein), and Jung as father and son (Harry Wilmer). Other selections are on father and son (Robert Bly); on being born, on daring, and on dying (Elisabeth Kübler-Ross); my mother and my father (Mary Catherine Bateson); powerful women: mother and great-grandmother (Betty Sue Flowers); power and limitations of parents (Jerome Kagan); the eternal woman: the worship of Mary in art (Elizabeth Silverthorne); and myth of the hero (John Silber).

Myths and Mysteries of Same-Sex Love, by Christine Downing. New York: Continuum Publishing Co., 1989* (317 + xxx, incl. 11-p. index, 18-p. ref. notes, 4 illus.).

Downing relates how she moved away from a taken-for-granted hetero-sexuality through important relationships with gay men to a deep commit-ment to her woman lover. She reflects on how depth psychology (particularly Freud) and classical mythology illuminate what same-sex love means to the psyche. She devotes the first half of the book to "psychology's myths," in which she examines Freud and Jung in terms of the personal dimension, theory, and cases they had with an emphasis on female homosexuality. In the second part she discusses demythologizing Greek homosexuality and inter-preting same-sex love among the gods, in the age of heroes, and among the goddesses, as well as what Greek writers Sappho and Plato had to say about the homoerotic. In the epilogue she discusses sexuality and AIDS.

The Phallic Quest: Priapus and Masculine Inflation, by James Wyly. Toronto: Inner City Books, 1989p* (Studies in Jungian Psychology by Jungian Ana-lysts, 38) (124, incl. 3-p. index, 3-p. bibl., 29 illus.).

Using the phallus, the physiological instrument of male creativity, as a metaphor for masculinity, Wyly examines the causes of destructive masculine inflation and the potential for transcending it and discovering a healthy sense of creative masculine energy. He explores physiology and imagination, fact and metaphor, and psychology and mythology to interpret the archetypal background of the phallus, represented on the collective level by myths and cultural phenomena and on the individual level by dreams of contemporary men. He starts with the archetypal figure of Priapus, the god with enormous genitals, by describing him in mythology, classical literature, and twentieth-century literature. He interprets the phallic quest, which involves exposition (splitting off; inflation), development (pruning; the quest; abandonment of the quest), and resolution (divine intervention; transformation), concluding with the implications of an unbridled priapic drive.

(Bk.revs.: JAnPsy '90/35:90; PsyPersp '90/23:192)

The Black Madonna, by Fred Gusafson. Boston: Sigo Press, 1990 +p (176 pp.).

Divine Madness: Archetypes of Romantic Love, by John R. Haule. Boston & Shaftesbury: Shambhala Publications, 1990 (301 + ix, incl. 11-p. index, 9-p. bibl.).

Taking the perspective that human love is a species of divine love and that our experience of romantic love both reveals and conceals the "ultimate Lover and Beloved," Haule focuses on the psychological and spiritual meaning of the experiences, drawing widely from the world's literature and from mythology.

Femininity Lost and Regained, by Robert A. Johnson. New York: Harper & Row, 1990 (101 + vi).

Johnson believes that the loss of feminine qualities and energy is an urgent psychological issue in modern society that affects not only a woman's central feminine identity but also affects a man's capacity for feeling and valuing. He interprets the feminine in Western culture (Greek heritage; Sophocles; the story of Oedipus; the inner meaning of incest; the fate of Antigone; the Oedipal legacy) as well as the feminine in Hindu mythology, using as an example the myth of Nala and Damayantī (from the *Mahabharata*) that conveys the East Indian attitude toward feminine wisdom and power. He concludes with a discussion of the problems and challenges involved in the realization of femininity lost and in the task of working toward femininity regained.

The Goddess Within: A Guide to the Eternal Myths That Shape Women's Lives, by Jennifer Barker Woolger and Roger J. Woolger. New York: Fawcett/ Columbine, 1990p.

King, Warrior, Magician, Lover: Rediscovering the Archetypes of the Mature Masculine, by Robert Moore and Douglas Gillette. San Francisco: Harper & Row, 1990.

Lilith—The First Eve, by Siegmund Hurwitz. Einsiedeln, Switzerland: Daimon Verlag, 1990p.

Men's Dreams, Men's Healing, by Robert H. Hopcke. Boston & London: Shambhala Publications, 1990p (220 + viii, incl. 4-p. bibl., 7-p. index).

In discussing his dreamwork with two men in psychotherapy—one heterosexual and one homosexual—Hopcke spotlights aspects of masculine psychology such as lack of feeling awareness, fear of intimacy, authority issues, the anima, and fatherhood, drawing on Jungian psychology as well as Greek myths and Christian symbolism.

The Step-Mother in Fairy Tales, by Jacqueline M. Schectman. Boston: Sigo Press, 1990p.

Weaving Woman: Essays in Feminine Psychology from the Notebooks of a Jungian Analyst, by Barbara Koltuv. York Beach, Maine: Nicolas-Hays, 1990p (122 + x).

The Woman in the Mirror: Analytical Psychology and the Feminine, by Claire Douglas. Boston: Sigo Press, 1990 +p (345 + xviii).

To Be a Woman: The Birth of the Conscious Feminine, edited by Connie Zweig. Los Angeles: Jeremy P. Tarcher, 1990p (279, incl. 5-p. ref. notes).

Of these twenty-three essays, thirteen are by Jungian analysts, including essays on Athena, Artemis, Aphrodite, and initiation into the conscious feminine (Jean Shinoda Bolen); redeeming the father and finding feminine spirit (Linda Leonard); thesomorphia: women's fertility ritual and desires (Betty DeShong Meador); descent to the dark goddess Inanna (Sylvia Perera); developing the animus as a step toward the new feminine consciousness (Manisha Roy); how the father's daughter found her mother (Lynda Schmidt); finding the lost feminine in the Judeo-Christian tradition (June Singer); from the liberation of women to the liberation of the feminine (Robert Stein); beyond blood (Elizabeth Strahan); breakdown of animus identification in finding the feminine (Jane Wheelwright); future of the feminine (Edward Whitmont); conscious femininity (Marion Woodman); and rethinking feminism, the animus, and the feminine (Polly Young-Eisendrath).

9 Religion and Jung's Psychology

One of the most provocative aspects of Jung's psychology is its relationship to the religious dimension of life. Many of his most important works, particularly the last ones, deal with psychological aspects of the religious problems of a Christian. While declaring his allegiance to Christianity, he differs in many respects from traditional, institutional Christianity. From the standpoint of psychology, he is aware that the psyche spontaneously produces images that have a religious content; and he sets a boundary between his empirical understanding and Christian demands for metaphysical faith. He speaks of God and of his personal experiences of the numinous.

More than one hundred forty books comprise this subject category, including more than twenty cross-referenced from other subjects. Recent expansion of interest is indicated by the fact that half of the works have been published since 1980.

Moore (ed.): *Carl Jung and Christian Spirituality* [p. 241]
Moore & Meckel (eds.): *Jung and Christianity in Dialogue* [p. 248]
Moorish: *The Dark Twin: A Study of Evil—and Good* [p. 223]
Moreno: *Jung, Gods, and Modern Man* [p. 214]
Paris: *Pagan Meditations* (See chapter 8, "Feminine and Masculine Psychology") [p. 184]
Parker: *Return: Beyond the Self* (See chapter 6, "Human Development and Individuation") [p. 98]
Phillips et al. (eds.): *The Choice Is Always Ours* (See chapter 6, "Human Development and Individuation") [p. 83]
Philp: *Jung and the Problem of Evil* [p. 209]
Raine: *The Human Face of God* [p. 227]
Reid: *The Return to Faith* [p. 218]
Rollins: *Jung and the Bible* [p. 230]
Rudin: *Psychotherapy and Religion* [p. 210]
Sandner: *Navaho Symbols of Healing* (See chapter 11, "Jungian Analysis") [p. 318]
Sanford: *Evil: The Shadow Side of Reality* [p. 224]
_____: *Fritz Kunkel: Selected Writings* [p. 232]
_____: *The Kingdom Within* [p. 214]
_____: *The Strange Trial of Mr. Hyde* [p. 240]
Santa Maria: *Growth Through Meditation and Journal Writing* [p. 230]
Savary, Berne & Kaplan-Williams: *Dreams and Spiritual Growth* [p. 232]
Schaer: *Religion and the Cure of Souls in Jung's Psychology* [p. 204]
Singer: *Seeing Through the Visible World* [p. 249]
_____: *The Unholy Bible* (See chapter 10, "Creativity and Jung's Psychology") [p. 260]
Slusser: *From Jung to Jesus* (See chapter 6, "Human Development and Individuation") [p. 111]
Smith: *Jung's Quest for Wholeness* [p. 248]
Spiegelman (ed.): *Catholicism and Jungian Psychology* [p. 242]
Spiegelman & Khan: *Sufism and Jungian Psychology* [p. 249]
Spiegelman & Miyuki: *Buddhism and Jungian Psychology* [p. 231]
Spiegelman & Vasavada: *Hinduism and Jungian Psychology* [p. 239]
Stein, M.: *Jung's Treatment of Christianity* [p. 235]
Stein & Moore: *Jung's Challenge to Contemporary Religion* [p. 239]
Suzuki: *Introduction to Zen Buddhism* [p. 202]
Thompson: *Journey Toward Wholeness* (See chapter 6, "Human Development and Individuation") [p. 104]
Thornton: *The Diary of a Mystic* [p. 213]
Ulanov, A.: *The Feminine in Jungian Psychology and Christian Theology* (See chapter 8, "Feminine and Masculine Psychology") [p. 166]

Psychology and Religion, by C. G. Jung. New Haven: Yale U. Press and London: Oxford U. Press, 1938*; Toronto: Ryerson Press, 1938; New Haven: Yale Paperbound, 1960p* (131, incl. 15-p. ref. notes).

Written in English and delivered at Yale University as the fifteenth series of Terry Lectures on Religion in the Light of Science and Philosophy (1937), these three lectures Jung gave come "from a purely empirical point of view" that deals with the autonomy of the unconscious mind, dogma, and natural symbols, and with the history and psychology of a natural symbol. In the first lecture he gives a few glimpses of the way practical psychology relates to religion, using illustrations from his medical practice, including interpretation of dreams from the unconscious. In the second lecture he is concerned with facts that demonstrate an authentic religious function in the unconscious, in which dogma and symbols are involved, such as the central Christian symbol of a Trinity as contrasted with the formula of a quaternity as presented by the unconscious. The third lecture deals with religious symbolism of the unconscious processes, particularly the mandala symbol of wholeness which is experienced in dreams.

(Bk.revs.: AmJPsychi '38/95:504–6; AmSocR '38/3:907; BkRDig '38:513; Bklist '38/34:297; Bks 90c'38:16; BrJPsy '38/29:200; ChurchQR '38/n126:332–6; Chman '38/152:172; JBibRel '38/6:162; JRel '38/18:458; Nation '38/146:510–11; NewStates '38/15:660+; NYTimesBkR 20Mr'38:14; RofRel '38/3:224–6; SatR 26Mr'38/17:18; SciBkClubR Mr'38/9:3; Tabl '38/171:406; TimesLitSup '38:323; AmJSoc '39/44:612–13; Person '39/20:206–7; Philos '39/14:248–9; PsyanQ '39/8:392–3; PsyBul '39/36:131–2; Thought '39/14:335–6; PsyanR '40/27:114–15; JNervMent '43/97:615–17; PastorPsy Jn'57/8:63–4)

Aion: Researches into the Phenomenology of the Self, by C. G. Jung. (Ger: *Aion: Untersuchungen zur Symbolgeschichte*. Zurich: Rascher Verlag, 1951, with a contribution by Marie-Louise von Franz.) New York: Pantheon Books (Bollingen Foundation), 1959; Toronto: McClelland & Stewart, 1959; London: Routledge & Kegan Paul, 1959*; Princeton, N.J.: Princeton U. Press/Bollingen, ed.2 1968; 1979p* (CW 9, pt.2) (333 + xi, incl. 31-p. index, 28-p. bibl., 16 illus.).

With the help of Christian, Gnostic, and alchemical symbols of the self, Jung interprets the changes of the psychical situation within the "Christian aeon" (in Greek, *aion*) in terms of the archetypal image of wholeness, which has its forerunners in history (for instance, in the Christ figure) and appears frequently as a product of the unconscious in the form of dream images. He starts with a summary of the key concepts of his system of psychology (ego, shadow, anima and animus, the self) and then discusses the topics of Christ as a symbol of the self; the sign of the fishes; the prophecies of Nostradamus; the historical significance of the fish; the ambivalence of the fish symbol; and alchemical interpretation of the fish. This leads to his interpretation of the psychology of Christian alchemical symbolism as well as the Gnostic symbols of the self, ending with an overall picture of the structure and dynamics of the self.

(Bk.revs.: BulAnPsyNY My'52/14:sup6; TimesLitSup '58:744; BrJMedPsy '59/32:302; LibJ '59/84:2194; PsychiQ '59/33:395–6; CathEdR '60/58:421–3; JAnPsy '60/5:159–66; JNervMent '60/130:178–81; Person '60/41:266–7; PsysomMed '60/22:243–4; Spring '60:150; TimesLitSup '60:57)

Answer to Job, by C. G. Jung. (Ger.: *Antwort auf Hiob*. Zurich: Rascher Verlag, 1952.) London: Routledge & Kegan Paul, 1954; 1979p; Great Neck, N.Y.: Pastoral Psychology Book Club, 1956; Cleveland: Meridian Books/World Pub. Co., 1960p; London: Hodder & Stoughton, 1965p; Princeton, N.J.: Princeton U. Press/Bollingen, 1973p*; London: Ark Paperbacks, 1984p* (121 + xv, incl. 11-p. index, 1-p. bibl.).

Having been occupied for years with the central problem of Job, who expected help from God against God, Jung approaches this major religious problem through its historical evolution from the time of Job to the most recent symbolic phenomena, such as the Assumption of Mary. His thesis is that if Christianity claims to be a monotheism, it becomes unavoidable to assume that opposites are contained in God. By using Jungian theory, mythology, and alchemical theory, he analyzes the narrative of Job within the framework of an evolutionary view of consciousness, with Yahweh at that time being relatively unconscious in comparison with human consciousness. Jung asserts the awesome power of the opposites in Yahweh, interpreting the treatment of Job as the projection of Yahweh's uncertainty about his own goodness and justice, concluding with a view of Yahweh's need for incarnation to gain consciousness.

(Bk.revs.: BrJPsy '55/46:242; DublR '55/229:337; Encoun(L) Ap'55/4:85–7; JRelThought '55/12:127–8; Tabl '55/205:135; TimesLitSup '55:693; AmJPsychi '56/112:952; JPastorCare '56/10:188; PastorPsy Ja'56/6:82–3; Philos '56/31:259–60; DrewGate '60/31:53–4; ScotJTheol '67/20:120–1; PsyMed '85/15:443; TeachColRec '86/88:300)

Psychology and Religion: West and East, by C. G. Jung. New York: Pantheon Books (Bollingen Foundation), 1958; London: Routledge & Kegan Paul, 1958; ed.2 1970*; Toronto: McClelland & Stewart, 1958; Princeton, N.J.: Princeton U. Press/Bollingen, ed.2 1969* (CW 11) (690 + xii, incl. 48-p. index, 30-p. bibl., 5 illus.).

Although not a complete collection of Jung's writings on psychology and religion, since such books as *Aion* and *Psychology and Alchemy* also deal with "religion," this volume of the *Collected Works* consists of sixteen studies grouped under the headings of Western and Eastern religions. The longest are his 1952 book, *Answer to Job* (114 pp.), and his 1937 lectures, *Psychology and Religion* (101 pp.), followed by 1940 and 1941 Eranos Conference lectures (later expanded) on a psychological approach to the dogma of the Trinity (92 pp.) and transformation symbolism in the mass (94 pp.). Also on Western religion are a 1928 article on psychoanalysis and the cure of souls, a 1933 review of a book on Brother Klaus (patron saint of Switzerland), and forewords to Werblowsky's *Lucifer and Prometheus* and to White's *God and the Unconscious.* Articles on Eastern religion include psychological commentaries on *The Tibetan Book of the Dead* and *The Tibetan Book of the Great Liberation,* a lecture on the psychology of Eastern meditation, essays on yoga and the West and on holy men of India, and forewords to Suzuki's *Introduction to Zen Buddhism* and to Wilhelm's translation of *The I Ching,* or *Book of Changes.*

(Bk.revs.: AmSocR '58/23:741; CathEdR '58/56:499–502; BulMennClin '58/22:237; Domin '58/43:333–6; LibJ '58/283:1926; Month '58/20:219–24; NYTimesBkR 20Ap'58:1+; RMeta '58/12:146; JAnPsy '59/4:68–83; Person '59/40:309–10; QueensQ '59/66:334–6; AmJPsychi '60/117:92; ConcordiaTh '60/31:461)

Psychology and the East, by C. G. Jung. Princeton, N.J.: Princeton U. Press/ Bollingen, 1978p*; London: Routledge & Kegan Paul, 1982p; London: Ark Paperbacks, 1986p* (211 + vi).

In addition to Jung's writings on Eastern religion in *Psychology and Religion: West and East,* excerpts on the philosophy and culture of the East from other volumes of the *Collected Works* also are collected in this paperback edition, all of which are arranged chronologically (1929–1956). The longest is his psychological commentary on the Taoist text *The Secret of the Golden Flower,* an alchemical treatise also concerned with Chinese yoga. The other writings on Eastern subjects from other sources of Jung's work are the very brief articles on the dream-like world of India (1939), what India can teach us (1939), and the discourses of Buddha (1956), which come from observations made during his trip to India in 1937–38, and his 1949 foreword to Lily Abegg's *Ostasien denkt anders* (East Asia thinks otherwise).

Psychology and Western Religion, by C. G. Jung. Princeton, N.J.: Princeton U. Press/Bollingen, 1984p*; London: Ark Paperbacks/Routledge & Kegan Paul, 1988p* (307 + vii).

Most of this paperback edition consists of excerpts from volume 11 of the *Collected Works* (*Psychology and Religion: West and East*), omitting the books *Answer to Job* and the Terry Lectures (*Psychology and Religion*), which have been published separately. Included are Jung's writings on the Trinity, symbolism in the mass, the clergy, the cure of souls, and Brother Klaus. The remaining quarter contains excerpts from volume 18 (*The Symbolic Life*), the longest being extensive abstracts (entitled "Jung and Religious Belief") from H. L. Philp's book, *Jung and the Problem of Evil,* which contains Jung's answers to questions from Philp and David Cox. Also included are a 1954 letter to Père Lachat on the Holy Spirit and a 1954 letter to the Los Angeles Jung Institute seminar members in answer to questions on resurrection.

(Bk.revs.: RelStudR '85/11:171; TimesLitSup '89:203)

*   *   *   *   *

The Tibetan Book of the Dead; Or, The After-Death Experiences on the Bardo Plane, according to Lāma Kazi Dawa-Samdup's English Reading, compiled and edited by W. Y. Evans-Wentz. (Ger.: *Das tibetanische Totenbuch.* Zurich: Rascher Verlag, 1935.) London: Oxford U. Press, 1927; ed.1 1949; ed.3 1957; New York: Galaxy Book/Oxford U. Press, ed.3 1960p; 1980p*; New York:

Causeway, 1973 (249 + lxxxiv, incl. 7-p. index, 9 illus., 20-p. foreword by Sir John Woodroffe; ed.3 contains 18-p. psychol. comm. by Jung based on Ger. edn.).

Jung's analysis of the Tibetan treatise on the after-death experiences of everyman provides a psychological interpretation of the set of instructions for the dead, a guide through the Bardo realm of existence for forty-nine days between death and rebirth (reincarnation). He discusses the process of the psychic happenings at the moment of death (all consciousness surrendered at that spiritual climax), followed by the terrifying dream-state immediately after death ("karmic illusions" resulting from psychic residue of previous existences) and the descent which eventually ends in a womb, after which the person is born into the earthly world again with its accompanying "birth trauma." Jung suggests that the Western mind should read this Bardo process backwards.

(Bk.revs.: TimesLitSup '27:770; LondMerc '28/17:493; Person '51/32:209; FarEQ '53/12:452–4; JAmOrSoc '57/77:237–8; Person '58/39:409–10; AmJPsy '59/72:323–4)

Jungian Psychology and Modern Spiritual Thought, by D. C. Daking. London and Oxford: Anglo-Eastern Publishing Co., 1933 (133, incl. 1-p. bibl., 4 illus.).

Concerned with relating "psychology" and "religion" for the people who do go to church as well as those who don't, Daking brings Jung to the attention of spiritually minded people and explains to his psychological friends an article written by the English Benedictine Abbot of Pershore. His intention is to catch a glimpse of God and to understand a bit about human nature. His topics include prayer; "the necessary instincts"; our depths and our consciousness; earth and the spirit; men and women; sin and the law; and understanding of human nature.

(Bk.rev.: TimesLitSup '34:515)

An Introduction to Zen Buddhism, by Daisetz Suzuki. Kyoto: Eastern Buddhist Society, 1934; New York: Philosophical Library, 1949; London: Rider, 1949; rev. 1969p; ed.3 1983p*; 1986p*; Toronto: George J. McLeod, 1949; London: Arrow Books, 1959p; New York: Evergreen Black Cat Book/ Grove Press, 1964p; 1987p*; Causeway Books, 1974 (136, incl. 4-p. index, 21-p. foreword by Jung).

Drawing on both Oriental and Western knowledge and emphasizing that Zen Buddhism is "primarily and ultimately a discipline" aimed at self-understanding, Suzuki presents the practical aspects of the discipline with illustrations of each aspect. Jung's long foreword emphasizes how very different Oriental religious conceptions usually are from Western ones, especially the transformation process of *satori* (enlightenment); and he views a direct transplantation of Zen to Western conditions as neither commendable nor even possible. As a psychotherapist he is moved when he sees the end ("making whole") toward which the Eastern method of psychic "healing" is striving, a process that requires intelligence and will power.

(Bk.revs.: BkRDig '49:895; ChrCen '49/66:1543; CrozerQ '49/26:366–8; EastWorld D'49/3:22–3; IntAff '49/55:548; ReligEd '49/44:373; AmJPsy '50/63:464–7; Ethics '50/ 60:151; JBibRel '50/18:80–1; JPhilos '50/47:477–8; Person '50/31:412; PhilosPhen '50/ 11:279–80; JAsianStud '65/24:516–17)

Catholic Thought and Modern Psychology, by William P. Witcutt. London: Burnes, Oates & Washbourne, 1943 (57 pp.).

Given his point of view that the theories of Freud and Adler were incompatible with Catholic teaching, while those of Jung may be studied and "in part" absorbed by Catholic philosophy, Witcutt aims to discern how much of Jung may be accepted. He deems Jungian psychology to be a potent instrument for good, considering Jung's research into the "most hidden parts of the hidden mechanism" as a practical as well as theoretical science; but it must be evaluated in the hand of "someone who knows what he is about" (a Catholic philosopher or theologian), with "due respect to Jung." He discusses Freud, Adler, libido, the unconscious, the types, the purpose of life, dream and myth, and the archetypes.

(Bk.rev.: IrEcclRec '44/64:70 +)

Hermes, Guide of Souls: The Mythologem of the Masculine Source of Life, by Karl Kerényi. (Ger.: *Hermes der Seelenführer.* Zurich: Rhein Verlag, 1944.) Zurich: Spring Publications for the Analytical Psychology Club of New York, 1976p; Dallas: Spring Publications, reissue 1986p* (Dunquin Series, 7) (104 + vi, incl. 13-p. ref. notes, 2-p. prefatory note by Magda Kerényi).

Kerényi's favorite Greek god, Hermes, is characterized as the archetypal figure of the "speech-gifted mediator and psychogogue" (literally, life-soul leader), the common guide for those to whom life is an adventure of love or spirit. He examines the complex role of Hermes in classical tradition (the "Hermes idea"; Hermes of the *Iliad* and the *Odyssey*; Hermes of the hymn; Hermes and the night) and then discusses the Hermes of life and death (Hermes and Eros; Hermes as the companion of goddesses; the mystery of the Herm, the ithyphallic symbol of masculine life-source; Hermes and the ram; and Silenos, "teacher of Dionysos and Hermes").

Athene, Virgin and Mother: A Study of Pallas Athene, by Karl Kerényi. (Ger.: *Die Jungfrau und Mutter der griechischen Religion: Eine Studie über Pallas*

Athene. Zurich: Rhein Verlag, 1946.) Zurich: Spring Publications, 1978p; Dallas: Spring Publications, 1988p* (Dunquin Series, 9) (106, incl. 6-p. index, 20-p. notes, 9-p. comments by Murray Stein).

Describing his research method as fundamentally psychological, Kerényi characterizes the archetypal image of Athene as polarized, containing an inner tension between wounder and healer, the "mighty, high-minded, gracious daughter of the Lord of Heaven," whose bondedness to the Father defends his interests and spirit in achievement. His is a study in the history of the Greek religion and is also an interpretive analysis of an archetypal image. Stein's "afterthoughts" contribute an archetypal view of Athene as a power in the life of the psyche that motivates fantasy, feelings, and behavior that keep one grounded in "real projects" and works to convert analysis into therapeutic improvement. The image of Athene, which also protects against the dark aggressiveness of the Father, provides insight into the complexities of defense by strategic reflection.

(Bk.revs.: RofRel '53/18:117; BksAbroad '54/28:333)

Prometheus: Archetypal Image of Human Existence, by C. Kerényi. (Ger.: *Prometheus: Das griechische Mythologem von der Menschlichen Existenz.* Zurich: Rhein Verlag, 1946.) London: Thames & Hudson, 1963; Philadelphia: R. West, 1963; New York: Pantheon Books (Bollingen Series LXV:1), 1963* (Archetypal Images in Greek Religion, vol. 1) (152 + xxvi, incl. 6-p. index, 10-p. bibl., 18 illus.).

Emphasizing the mythological aspect of Greek religion and defining "archetypal images" not on the basis of any explanatory theory (though recognizing Jung's psychological explanation of the phenomenon as a factor) but *"phenomenologically,* describing mythology and tracing it back to its foundation in Greek existence," Kerényi deals with Prometheus as archetypal image of human existence. He approaches the mythologem (writing preserving a myth) through the work of Goethe, with some discussion of archaic Prometheus mythology, stating that Prometheus stands in the most remarkable relation to humankind, presenting a striking resemblance and a striking contrast to the Christian savior. Kerényi interprets Prometheus as interceding for humanity by suffering the "hallmarks of human existence," wounded by injustice, torment, and humiliation for stealing the fire that is denied the animals, the possession of which made human existence *human.*

(Bk.revs.: RofRel '47/11:159–64; LibJ '63/88:2015; VaQR '63/39:clv; BkRDig '64:654; Criticism '64/6:89–92; TimesLitSup '64:57; ClassBul '65/41:47–8; ClassR '66/ns16:122–3; CompLit '69/21:76–80)

Religion and the Cure of Souls in Jung's Psychology, by Hans Schaer. (Ger.: *Religion und Seele in der Psychologie C. G. Jungs.* Zurich: Rascher Verlag,

1946.) New York: Pantheon Books (Bollingen Series XXI), 1950; London: Routledge & Kegan Paul, 1951; New York: Schocken Books, 1966 (266, incl. 4-p. index).

Asserting that everything Jung has published has to do with religion to a greater or lesser degree and is not confined to Christianity, Schaer states that one must first come to terms with Jung's whole structure of psychic reality in order to gain understanding of religion in Jung's psychology. He first discusses the elements in Jungian psychology (especially the unconscious, but also shadow, persona, anima/animus, psychological attitudes and types), then the psychic bases of religion and religion as a psychic function, particularly in the process of individuation through increasing consciousness. The long chapter on "man and religion" deals with examination of Jung's ideas on the God-image (with special attention to Meister Eckhart's concepts) and his distinction between Church and religion. He concludes with an evaluation of Jung's significance in the religious situation of today, particularly from the Protestant standpoint. It may be noted that this was written before Jung's *Aion* and *Answer to Job*.

(Bk.revs.: BkRDig '50:796; BulAnPsyNY D'50/12:4–8; ChrCen '50/67:923–4; JPastor-Care Fall'50/4:54–5; PastorPsy S'50/1:60–1; PhilosQ '50/1:185–6; Poetry '50/77:168–73; SchSoc '50/71:302; BrJPsy '51/42:381–2; RelThought '51/8:80–1; PsychiQ '51/25:174; InwLight '52/n41:132–4; TimesLitSup 23My'58:xii)

Asklepios: Archetypal Image of the Physician's Existence, by C. Kerényi. (Ger.: *Der göttliche Arzt: Studien über Asklepios und seine Kultstätten*. Basel: Ciba, 1947.) New York: Pantheon Books (Bollingen Series LXV:3), 1959* (Archetypal Images in Greek Religion, vol. 3); Aldershot: Thames & Hudson, 1960; London: Routledge & Kegan Paul, 1967 (151 + xxvii, incl. 9-p. index, 13-p. bibl., 58 illus.).

Kerényi presents the Greek god Asklepios as the prototype of the healer, the wounded healer as primordial physician. He studies the origins in Greek medicine in Epidauros with its temple and sanctuary, as well as the topics of Asklepios in Rome; the sons of Asklepios on the island of Kos as ancient center of medical science; and the physician of the gods in Homer.

(Bk.revs.: BkRDig '60:736; GuardW 24Jn'60:6; LibJ '60/85:296; Person '60/41:563–4; Spec 1Jn'60:34; VaQR '60/36:xci; ClassR '61/75:175–6; TimesLitSup '61:27; ClassBul '63/39:44–5)

Satan in the Old Testament, by Rivkah Schärf Kluger. (Ger.: *Die Gestalt des Satans im Alten Testament*. Zurich: Rascher Verlag, 1948.) Evanston, Ill.: Northwestern U. Press, 1967 (Studies in Jungian Thought) (173 + xvii, incl. 11-p. index, 3-p. foreword by James Hillman).

Eschewing metaphysical speculation about God and the devil, Kluger assembles statements concerning the mythological figure of Satan and examines the psychological content of which it is the symbolic expression. Based upon Jung's fundamental views concerning the problem of God and the devil as primal images and archetypes of the human psyche, she traces the concept of "Satan," both in the profane realm and in the metaphysical realm, looking at its development in the Old Testament, as in the story of Balaam and in the Book of Job, and discussing Babylonian traits in the image of Satan in Job, as well as Satan as an independent demon.

(Bk.revs.: LibJ '67/92:4506; LibJBkR '67:371; BkRDig '68:743; Choice '68/5:360; JAnPsy '68/13:173–4; Spring '68:138; JSciStudRel '69/8:169–72; Judaism '69/18:492–5)

The Passion of Perpetua, by Marie-Louise von Franz. (Orig. title: "The Passio Perpetuae" in *Spring,* 1949.) Dallas: Spring Publications, 1980p (Jungian Classics Series, 3) (81, incl. 6-p. ref. notes).

Impressed by the visions of St. Perpetua (martyred A.D. 203) and the fact that she had interpreted her own visions, von Franz provides a modern interpretation based on Jung's psychology, using more or less contemporary material to show how the same images appeared in the conscious minds of other people of the time and appeared even more often in spontaneous manifestations of the unconscious, regardless of the consciously held creed. In addition to presenting the life of St. Perpetua, the four visions, and interpretation of the visions, von Franz examines the problem of the orthodoxy of the martyrs, analyzing it from a psychological point of view.

(Bk.rev.: Quad '80/13n2:137)

God and the Unconscious, by Victor White. London: Harvill Press, 1952; Cleveland: World Publishing Co., 1952; Chicago: Henry Regnery, 1953; London: Fontana/Collins, 1960p; New York: Meridian Books/World Pub. Co., 1961p; London: Collins, 1967p; Dallas: Spring Publications, 1982p* (Jungian Classics Series, 4) (245 + xxxiii, incl. 3-p. index of authors quoted and other persons mentioned, 5-p. index of books and periodicals quoted from or referred to, 7-p. intro. by William Everson, 13-p. foreword by Jung).

Expressing indebtedness and gratitude to Jung's personal friendship and frank discussions, Dominican priest White presents disagreement or misgivings about some of Jung's views on the relationship of depth psychology and religion, chief of which is the dispute regarding the doctrine of *privatio boni* (evil as privation of good). Following two brief chapters that were to have been the introduction to an abandoned treatise, he offers ten essays and addresses from 1942 to 1952 that form a reasonably consecutive unity. These are the topics of the frontiers of theology and psychology; Freud, Jung, and

God; the unconscious and God; Aristotle, Aquinas, and man; revelation and the unconscious; psychotherapy and ethics; the analyst and the confessor; devils and complexes; gnosis, Gnosticism, and faith; and the dying God.

(Bk.revs.: Amer '53/89:251; AmCathSoc '53/14:268–9; AmMerc S'53/77:138–9; BestSell 1Ag'53/13:89; Blackf '53/34:104–5; BkTrial '53/11:342; BrJMedPsy '53/26:319–22; CathWorker My'53/19:3 +; CrossCurr '53/3:287; Domin '53/28:261–3; DownR '53/71:95–7; DublR '53/227:79–83; HibbJ '53/51:314 +; Integ 4Jy'53/7:20–4; JTheolStud '53/ns4:158; LifeSpir '53/7:360; Month '53/9:186–8; QueensQ '53/60:142; Tabl '53/201:8–9; TheolStud '53/14:499–505; TimesLitSup '53:273; 20Cen '53/153:393–4; JPastorCare '54/8:101–3; NewScholas '54/28:240–3; Thought '54/29:126; JAmPsyan '58/6:548; JAnPsy '83/28:396–7)

Religion and the Psychology of Jung, by Raymond Hostie. (Dutch: *Analytische Psychologie en Goddienst.* Utrecht and Antwerp: Universitaires bibliotheek voor psychologie, 1954.) London and New York: Sheed & Ward, 1957 (249 +vi, incl. 5-p. index, 21-p. bibl.).

While valuing repeated personal contact with Jung and his close associates, Jesuit Hostie has based this critical study primarily on Jung's publications. In the first part he examines the empirical method in analytical psychology, fundamental views of analytical psychology (energetic conception of the libido; imago and symbol; archetypes; individuation), and synthesis or compromise by the complementarity of opposites. He then interprets Jung's view of the psychology of religion as being that the religious instinct is the "chief cornerstone" of the imposing psychic structure, after which he discusses the relationships between psychotherapy and spiritual direction and between psychology and dogma (the self as a mandala's center; the problem of evil; trinity and quaternity). His critique ends with an analysis of religion and analytical psychology, concluding that the religious function is rooted in the psyche, but revealed truths have their source in God, whose realities should not be confused.

(Bk.revs.: AmCathSoc '57/18:246–7; ClergyR '57/42:307; Domin '57/42:241–2; DownR '57/75:393–5; IrEcclRec '57/87:475–6; IrTheolQ '57/24:278; JTheolStud '57/ns8:380–1; LifeSpir S'57/12:141; Signs N'57/37:73; Thought '57/32:465–6; TimesLitSup '57:659; ConcordiaTh M'58/29:72; Interp '58/12:77–8; JAnPsy '58/3:59–71; JPastorCare '58/12:109–10; ModSchman '58/35:151–4; SocOrder F'58/8:86; ReligEd '59/54:72 +; PastorPsy F'59/10:52–4)

The Tibetan Book of Great Liberation; Or, The Method of Realizing Nirvana Through Knowing the Mind, edited by W. Y. Evans-Wentz. London and New York: Oxford U. Press, 1954; London, New York, and Toronto: Galaxy Book/Oxford U. Press, 1968p; 1978p* (261 + lxiv, incl. 7-p. index, 9 illus., 36-p. psychological commentary by Jung).

Jung's psychological commentary on *The Tibetan Book of Great Liberation* comes after the text that consists of the life and teachings of Tibet's great guru Padma Sambhava and the last testamentary teachings of guru Phadampa Sangay. Jung first discusses the difference between Eastern and Western thinking (including the self-liberating power of the introverted mind in contrast to the Western extraverted religious attitude) and then interprets the text, including commentary on the results of desires, the great self-liberation, the nature of mind, the names given to the mind, the timelessness of the mind, mind in its true state, the yoga of introspection, the dharma within, and the yoga of the nirvanic path.

(Bk.revs.: TimesLitSup '54:215; JAsianStud '55/14:429; RofRel '55/19:170–4; HeythJ '69/10:453)

Mysticism: Sacred and Profane, by Robert Charles Zaehner. Oxford: Clarendon Press, 1957*; New York: Galaxy Books/Oxford U. Press, 1961p; 1969p* (256 + xvi, incl. 22-p. index).

Profound disagreement with Aldous Huxley's conclusions in *The Doors of Perception* stimulated Zaehner to make this study of comparative mysticism in which he distinguishes between what seem to be radically different types of mystical experience and relates them to one another. He brings together a cross-section of mystical writing from European and Asiatic sources, including mystic experiences of Proust, Rimbaud, Baudelaire, Huxley, Richard Jefferies, and himself, drawing widely on Jung's ideas with regard to Oriental religion. His topics include mescaline, nature mystics, madness, integration and isolation, and monism versus theism and theism versus monism. In an appendix the author writes of his own experience with mescaline.

(Bk.revs.: Blackf '57/38:301–10; BkRDig '57:1023; ChurchQR '57/158:524–5; Month '57/18:274–81; SatR 10Ag'57/40:34–5; Tabl '57/210:390; TimesLitSup '57:368; BrJPsy '58/49:83)

Conscience, edited by the Curatorium of the C. G. Jung Institute, Zurich. (Ger.: *Das Gewissen.* Zurich: Rascher Verlag, 1958/Studien aus dem C. G. Jung-Institut, vol. VII.) Evanston, Ill.: Northwestern U. Press, 1970* (Studies in Jungian Thought) (211 + xi, incl. 9-p. index, 4-p. preface by James Hillman).

Consisting of a series of seven lectures given at the Jung Institute in Zurich during 1957–58 on the subject of conscience, this book covers a significant range of perspectives starting with an essay on conscience in our time (Hans Zbinden) and followed by conscience in economic life (Eugen Bohler), the concept of conscience in Jewish perspective (R. J. Zwi Werblowsky), a Protestant view of conscience (Hans Schaer), a Catholic view of conscience (Josef Rudin), and Freud and conscience (Ernst Blum). The book concludes with a psychological view of conscience by Jung (reprinted in volume 10 of the *Collected Works*).

(Bk.rev.: JAnPsy '71/16:218–20)

Jung and the Problem of Evil, by Howard L. Philp. London: Rockliff, 1958; New York: Robert M. McBride, 1959 (271 + xiii, incl. 7-p. index, end-chapter ref. notes, 6-p. gloss.).

From a background of long and intense interest in Jung's work, including two long talks and an ongoing correspondence between Jung and the author concerning religion and psychology with particular attention to the significance of evil, Philp developed his own commentary as he became "increasingly critical of some of his [Jung's] writings on evil." He includes the texts of the first five and "final" fifteen questions and answers contained in their correspondence, along with somewhat lengthy answers by Jung to questions from David Cox. His own remarks are concerned with the topics of *privatio boni* (evil as privation of good) and a definition of evil; Satan; the quaternity; sin and the shadow; sin and the sinner; Jung's approach in *Answer to Job* and Philp's criticism; individuation; and "Christification of many." He concludes with admiration for Jung's "purely psychological contribution, but for writings on religion I personally find the theologians and many of the philosophers more objective and exact."

(Bk.revs.: AmJPsy '59/2:654–5; ChurchQR '59/160:401; Theol '59/62:163–5; JAnPsy '60/5:170–6)

Jung and St. Paul: A Study of the Doctrine of Justification by Faith and Its Relation to the Concept of Individuation, by David Cox. London and New York: Longmans Green, 1959; New York: Association Press, 1959 (358 + xiv, incl. 6-p. index, 2-p. bibl.).

Cox believes that psychotherapy and Christianity are "not incompatible" but that much that is said by psychotherapists is incompatible with the true Christian faith because it reduces religion to a would-be psychological system. His aim in this book is to show how "explanations" of theology and psychology differ and how they may be related. Largely concerned with Jung's complex psychological "system," he discusses the doctrine of justification by faith in relation to Jung's concept of the individuation process. He also discusses the topics of the bondage of sin, penitence, projection, faith, the Self, and Christ.

(Bk.revs.: Frontier '59/2:2224–6; LibJ '59/84:3138; NYTimesBkR 20S'59:40; PastorPsy Ap'59/10:61–4; PerkSchTh Fall'59/13:35–6; ReformThR Oc'59/18:89–90; ReligEd '59/54:545; StudIrQR '59/48:123–5; JAnPsy '60/5:166–70; JBibRel '60/28:452+; Month '60/23:114–15; Person '60/41:390–1; ScotJTheol '60/13:192–4; Theol '60/63:247–9; TimesLitSup 15Ap'60:xvi; CrossCurr '61/71:389)

Jung's Analytical Psychology and Religion, by C. A. Meier. (Orig. title: *Jung and Analytical Psychology*. Newton Centre, Mass.: Andover Newton Theological

Seminary, 1959p.) Carbondale and Edwardsville, Ill.: Arcturus Paperbacks/ Southern Illinois U. Press, 1977p; London and Amsterdam: Feiffer & Simons, 1977p (88pp.).

Originally given as four lectures to theological students and rearranged in the 1977 edition to deal with what Jung called the "religious factor," Meier's book follows the evolution of Jung's ideas on analytical psychology in the first three chapters, stressing the word association test that led to his theory of the complexes. He uses numerous examples in his discussion of the interpretation of dreams, using his knowledge of mythology, symbolism, and ancient rituals, particularly the healing practice of incubation in Greece about which he has written at length. He recognizes his limitation in covering such a complex subject as psychology and religion; and he emphasizes Jung's view that the acquisition or restoration of a religious disposition is essential for therapy.

(Bk.revs.: Spring '60:151–2; JAnPsy '77/22:367)

Eleusis: Archetypal Image of Mother and Daughter, C. Kerényi. (Dutch: *Eleusis: de heiligste mysterien van Griekenland.* The Hague: Servire, 1960.) London: Routledge & Kegan Paul, 1967; New York: Pantheon Books (Bollingen Series LXV: 4), 1967* (Archetypal Images in Greek Religion, 4); New York: Schocken Books, 1977p (257 + xxxvii, incl. 21-p. index, 17-p. bibl., 26-p. ref. notes, 89 illus.).

In his series of studies on Greek existence, Kerényi examines the Eleusinian gods as "archetypal images," defining archetype as a "primordial figure" that is not only typical of a particular cult but of human nature in general. He reconstructs the geographical, chronological, and mythological settings of the goddesses Demeter and Persephone, describing the lesser mysteries and preparations for the great mysteries, and the secret of Eleusis with its procession and birth in fire accompanied by a beatific vision. He also provides a hermeneutical essay on the meaning of the mysteries of the grain, the pomegranate seed, and the vine, as well as the duality of the mother-daughter vision of the feminine source of life, which is the common source of life for men and women alike.

(Bk.revs.: BkRDig '67:715; Choice '67/4:855; LibJ '67/92:2416–17; LibJBkR '67:371; Spring '67:152; JAnPsy '68/13:171–2; VaQR '68/44:cxxxii; EngHistR '69/84:373; ReprBulBkR '77/22n4:37)

Psychotherapy and Religion, by Josef Rudin. (Ger.: *Psychotherapie und Religion: Seele, Person, Gott.* Olten, Switzerland: Walter Verlag, 1960.) Notre Dame, Ind. and London: U. of Notre Dame Press, 1968 (244 + xiii, incl. 2-p. index, 3-p. letter by Jung to the author).

Recognizing the real or apparent opposition between the new insights of depth psychology and the basic convictions of theology, especially of moral theology, Jesuit Rudin addresses the concern that the energy-stream rising out of the unconscious from the "nature-given life-dynamic" may not only illuminate but may damage consciousness. He values the contribution of Jung's depth psychology as a bridge between the upper and lower layers of the psyche in reawakening understanding of great primordial symbolism of the soul and in giving impetus toward a more integrated, authentic, and psychically productive life. He discusses the topics of the "normal man"; soul anxiety; aspects of personal development, depth psychology and freedom; personal life; religious experience in the conscious and the unconscious; *Answer to Job;* the neuroticized God-image; psychotherapy and spiritual guidance; neurosis, perfectionism, and piety; and reflections on prayer life.

(Bk.revs.: LibJ '68/93:562; LibJBkR '68:524; BkRDig '69:1140; Choice '69/6:440; Month '69/41:58–9; Spring '69:149–50; Thom '69/33:395–7; PastorPsy Ja'70/21:54–5; JSci-StudRel '70/9:328–9; JPastorCare '71/25:201–2)

Soul and Psyche: An Enquiry into the Relationship of Psychotherapy and Religion, by Victor White. London: Collins & Harvill Press, 1960; New York: Harper & Bros., 1960 (312, incl. 4-p. index of proper names, 47-p. ref. notes).

Asserting a common ground between soul and psyche whether approached from theological or psychological standpoints, White explores the connections in lectures given at the University of Birmingham during 1958–59, drawing upon his long personal friendship and correspondence with Jung. He discusses the common ground of religion and psychology and interprets the Jungian approach to religion before examining the topics of symbol and dogma in psychology and in Christianity, the trinity and quaternity, the missing feminine, the feminine in Christianity, the interpretation of evil, the predicament of the psychotherapist, health and holiness, and religion and mental health. His points of disagreement with Jung, especially Jung's *Answer to Job,* are dealt with more specifically in the appendixes.

(Bk.revs.: Blackf '60/41:183–5; ChryToday 5D'60/5:33; ChurchQR '60/161:505–6; Chman D'60/174:13; Harvest '60/2:76–7; Month '60/23:370–2; Tabl '60/214:276; TimesLitSup '60:469; 20Cen '60/167:484+; CrossCurr '61/11:389; DownR '61/79:61–3; HomPastorR '61/61:504; JAnPsy '61/6:171–5; LuthQ Jy'61/13:186–7; Spring '61:157–8; TheolStud '61/22:326; Thought '61/336:144–5; InwLight '62/n63:43–6; JRelHealth '62/2:85–6)

Evil, edited by the Curatorium of the C. G. Jung Institute, Zurich. (Ger.: *Das Böse.* Zurich: Rascher Verlag, 1961/Studien aus dem C. G. Jung-Institut, vol. XIII.) Evanston, Ill.: Northwestern University Press, 1967 (Studies in Jungian Thought) (211 + xii, incl. 15-p. index, 2-p. foreword by Jung).

This book consists of a series of seven lectures given at the Jung Institute in Zurich during 1959–60 on the subject of evil. The essays deal with the problem of evil in mythology (Carl Kerényi), the problem of evil in fairy tales (Marie-Louise von Franz), the principle of evil in Eastern religions (Geo Widengren), evil in the cinema (Martin Schlappner), aspects of evil in the creative (Karl Schmid), evil from the psychological point of view (Liliane Frey-Rohn), and the philosophical concepts of good and evil (Karl Löwith). (Bk.revs.: JAnPsy '68/13:173–5; Spring '68:137–8)

The Springs of Creativity: The Bible and the Creative Process in the Psyche, by Heinz Westman. New York: Atheneum Publications, 1961; Toronto: Longmans Green Canada, 1961; London: Routledge & Kegan Paul, 1961; Wilmette, Ill.: Chiron Publications, ed. 2 1986p* (271, incl. 5-p. ref. notes, 75 illus., 3-p. intro. by Sir Herbert Read).

Using the case of "Joan," which was presented in 1958 to the International Congress of Analytical Psychology, as the basis for this book on creativity from a religious perspective, Westman first discusses personal identification and anxiety, masks (persona) and shadow, archetypes and the archetypal Self, and the nature of dreams. This is followed by portions taken from his 1936 Eranos Lecture which deal with psychological interpretations of Old Testament symbolism which shifts from images of wholeness to images of opposites in Genesis, Cain and Abel, Noah, Ham, Lot, Abraham and the "sacrifice" of Isaac, Jacob and Esau, and the Book of Job. Finally, through fifty-two black-and-white and four color drawings, he illustrates Joan's quest for self-expression, self-knowledge, and individuality. (Bk.revs.: LibJ '61/86:2325; BrJPsy '62/53:209–11; JAnPsy '62/6:175–6; JRelHealth '62/1:187–8; PsyanQ '62/31:272–6; UnionSemQR '62/17:285–6; BrJPsychi '63/109:160; BulMennClin '63/27:52; ArtJ '64–65/24:212 + ; SFJInstLib '87/7n2:23–50)

Intersection and Beyond, by Elizabeth Boyden Howes. San Francisco: Guild for Psychological Studies Publishing House, 1963; rev. and enlarged 1971p* as vol. 1; vol. 2 1986p* (vol. 1: 218, incl. 24-p. index; vol. 2: 139, incl. 9-p. index).

The Guild for Psychological Studies runs a program to train therapists and group leaders using a combination of Jung's and Kunkel's approaches to analytical psychology. In volume 1, Howes commingles religious values and analytical psychology in her discussions of the religious function of the ego; the ethics of personal freedom; forgiveness as wound and healing; the significance of physical death in the death-rebirth mystery cycle; the forgotten feminine in the gospels; and the Son of Man as expression of the Self. In volume 2 she continues to weave together religion and depth psychology by

discussions of the kingdom of God and the Self; mythic truth, historical truth, and religious consciousness; descent-ascent as the journey of the Holy Spirit; transformation in the life of Jung; religious imagery and Jung; new symbolic meanings in liturgy, creed, and prayer; the darkness of God; and the division and reconciliation of opposites.
(Bk.revs.: InwLight '73/n83:46; PastorPsy '74/28:211)

The Diary of a Mystic, by Edward Thornton. London: Allen & Unwin, 1967; New York: Hillary House Publishers, 1967 (180, incl. 3-p. index, 2-p. foreword by C. A. Meier).

Associated with the New Delhi Institute of Psychic and Spiritual Research, Thornton here shares his "divine" experience of mystical promptings which he believes is ultimately available to every person. He presents some of his personal background out of which his inner life emerged, citing Jung's great work in the realm of psychology as particularly important in throwing light on the nature and significance of the unconscious psyche.
(Bk.revs.: TimesLitSup '68:326; JRel '69/49:68; RforRel '69/28:151)

The Face of the Deep: The Religious Ideas of C. G. Jung, by Charles B. Hanna. Philadelphia: Westminster Press, 1967 (203, incl. 7-p. ref. notes, 2-p. gloss.).

Offering this work in the spirit of concern about a certain kind of sterility that comes over the Christian outlook on life and willing to face a challenge that is directed toward it by Jung, Hanna listens to Jung's testimonies to the value and importance of the deepest aspects of Christian faith while disagreeing with some of Jung's critique. He discusses God and the unconscious; God and God-image; God and the dawn of consciousness; sin, guilt and the shadow; symbolic thinking; psychology of the soul; and synchronicity.
(Bk.revs.: KirkR '67/35:188; LibJ '67/92:1163; LibJBkR '67:364; TheolStud '67/28:891; BkRDig '68:560; Choice '68/5:38; InwLight '68/n73:50–1; JAnPsy '68/13:172; Spring '68:136–7)

Insearch: Psychology and Religion, by James Hillman. London: Hodder & Stoughton, 1967p; New York: Charles Scribner's Sons, 1967p; 1970p; Dallas: Spring Publications, 1979p; reissue 1984p* (Jungian Classics Series, 2) (126 pp.).

Drawing on lectures given to ministers concerned with analytical psychology and pastoral counseling, Hillman aims to "re-mythologize" human experiences with religious implications, his emphasis being on the inner search ("insearch"). He examines human encounters and the inner connection in analysis and counseling, following with discussions of the unconscious as experience (inner life, dealing with the concept of "soul," soul and the unconscious, complexes, moods, dreams, religious concerns of the soul, and rediscovery of inner myth and religion). He then comments on the unconscious as a moral problem (inner darkness, including the morality of analysis, images of the shadow, moral struggles, conscience, self-regulation, the Devil and archetypal evil), concluding with an analysis of anima reality and religion (inner femininity, including anima figures and their effects, emotions and moods, the feminine side of comparative religion, problems of sexual love, marriage, psychosomatics, and the feminine ground of the religious movement).

(Bk.revs.: Frontier '67/10:143–5; LondQHolb '67/192:351–2; Month '67/37:375–6; PerkSchTh Wint–Spr'67–68/21:80–1; PubW 25D'67/192:55; TimesLitSup '67:514; Bk-RDig '68:610; Bklist '68/64:1010; CathLib '68/39:612; ChrCen '68/85:234; Colloq '68/3:90–2; CrossCurr '68/18:368–70; HeythJ '68/9:85–7; JAnPsy '68/13:164–6; JPastorCare S'68/22:180–1; LibJ '68/93:556; LibJBkR '68:400; PastorPsy Ja'68/19:57–61; ReligEd '68/63:252; RforRel '68/27:759; SWJTheol '68/11:144; Spring '68:135–6; Theol '68/71:331–2; UnionSemQR '68/23:415–16; Encoun '69/30:177–8; LuthWorld '69/16:101–2; Person '69/50:405–6; StLukeJTh F'69/12:196–7; JSciStudRel '70/9:328–9; JAmAcadRel '73/14:292–3; RelStudR '80/6:278–85; JRelPsyRes Oc'86/9:237–40)

Jung, Gods, and Modern Man, by Antonio Moreno. Notre Dame, Ind.: U. of Notre Dame Press, 1970; London: Sheldon Press Book/S.P.C.K., 1974 +p (274 + xiii, incl. 5-p. index, 5-p. bibl.).

Moreno's aim is to examine Jung's main ideas about religious factors and the elements related to them and to make a critical analysis of Jung's controversial views about the Trinity, Christ, the Holy Ghost, mythology, and God as a quaternity that includes evil. He first discusses Jung's ideas on the collective unconscious, which he interprets as the source of religious factors and revelation, and on individuation, which he interprets as being intimately associated with the development of the archetype of the Self (identified with Christ). He then makes a critical analysis of Jung's ideas on religion and individuation. He concludes with discussions of Jung's ideas on evil, religion and myth, neurosis, and Nietzsche, appending an analysis of the relationship between dreams and the Christian life.

(Bk.revs.: AmJPsychi '71/128:246–7; CrossCrown '71/23:486; JPastorCare '71/25:199–201; PastorPsy '71/22:64; TheolStud '71/32:554–5; TheolToday '71/28:259–61; Thom '71/35:549–50; AmJPsyth '72/26:139–40; HeythJ '72/13:237; JTheolStud '72/ns23:569–70; ChrScholR '73/3:65–7; ExposTimes '74/85:340; Theol '74/77:608–9; TimesLitSup '74:374; IntJPhRel '75/6:258–9)

The Kingdom Within: A Study of the Inner Meaning of Jesus' Sayings, by John A. Sanford. Philadelphia and New York: J. B. Lippincott, 1970p; New York and Ramsey, N.J.: Paulist Press, 1980p; San Francisco: Harper & Row, rev. 1987p* (188, incl. 7-p. index, 2-p. scripture index, 1-p. bibl.).

Relating Jesus' sayings to the insights of Jungian depth psychology, Sanford emphasizes the need for the unfolding of the whole personality from within as a balance to the outwardly oriented emphasis of the Church's institutional life and social situation. He first presents the concept of the kingdom of God within by analyzing the personality of Jesus, applying Jung's description of what comprises a person's totality and interpreting the images of the treasure of the kingdom. The remainder of the book consists of psychological-spiritual interpretations of the inner meaning of Jesus' sayings, including entering into the kingdom (recognizing the reality of the inner world and responding); the price of discipleship (following the call to the individual rather than collective way); the pharisee in each of us (mask of false outer personality); the inner adversary (shadow of the outer "front"); the role of evil and sin; the faith of the soul (connection to inner depths); the lost coin (unredeemed humanity within); and the coming of the kingdom.

(Bk.revs.: KirkR '70/38:266; LibJ '70/95:2266; LibJBkR '70:430; StLukeJTh Ja'71/14:62–3; JPastorCare '73/27:67; Tabl '81/235:502; JPsyTheol '83/11:55–8)

A Magic Dwells: A Poetic and Psychological Study of the Navaho Emergence Myth, by Sheila Moon. Middletown, Conn.: Wesleyan U. Press, 1970; San Francisco: Guild for Psychological Studies Publishing House, 1985p* (206 + ix, incl. 12-p. ref. notes).

Trained in analytical psychology, Moon sets forth a sample of the content and symbolism of a great religious tradition by describing and interpreting the Navaho Indian creation myth. She presents its symbols as being meaningful to the psychological and religious growth of the individual personality. She begins her poetic-psychological study with the topic of forms and images (creators and created, maternal substance, emerging directions, darkness and danger). She then discusses conflicting forces; witchcraft and holiness (use and misuse of evil); man and woman (place of crossing waters, the separation, sacrifice and relationship); and the consummation (form and flood, making the world breathe), concluding with a chapter of end and beginning, along with a synopsis of the emergence myth.

(Bk.revs.: AmAnth '71/73:1359–60; Choice '71/7:1585; ContemPsy '71/16:101+104; BkRDig '72:917)

Depth Psychology and Religious Belief, by Christopher Bryant. Mirfield, Yorkshire: Mirfield Publications, 1972p; London: Darton, Longman & Todd, rev. 1987p* (75 + v, incl. 1-p. foreword by R. F. Hobson).

From his standpoint as a Christian whose faith has been deepened by his study of psychology, and Jung's ideas in particular, Bryant aims to show

how depth psychology can shed light on the experience of believing, citing Jung's statement that patients in middle life who came to him for psychological treatment never would really get well unless they acquired or recovered a religious attitude to life. He deals with depth psychology's view of human behavior as it relates to inner motives and unconscious fears and wishes, as well as the experience of God that is common to all, whether acknowledged or not. He also discusses the relationship of belief to maturity and self-realization, concluding with an outline of the kind of Christian belief which can stand up to the criticisms of psychologists.

(Bk.revs.: Month '73/6:127; NewBlackf '74/55:96; Theol '74/77:160–1; BrBkN '87:758)

Myths to Live By, by Joseph Campbell. New York: Viking Press, 1972; London: Condor Books/Souvenir Press, 1973; New York: Bantam Books, 1973p; 1978p; 1984p*; London: Paladin/Grafton Books, 1985p* (276 + x, incl. 6-p. index, 4-p. ref. notes, 2-p. intro. by Johnson Fairchild).

Comprised of twelve essays selected from a series of talks he gave at Cooper Union Forum during 1958–71, this work by Campbell describes and interprets the impact of science on myth; the emergence of mankind; the importance of rites; the separation of East and West and the confrontation of East and West in religion; the inspiration of oriental art; Zen; the mythology of love and mythologies of war and peace; and schizophrenia as the inward journey and the moon walk as the outward journey. He discusses individuation and his own belief (echoing Jung's) that the imageries of mythology and religion serve positive, life-furthering ends.

(Bk.revs.: BestSell '72/32:164; BkRDig '72:203–4; Choice '72/9:1118; Commonw '72/96:528–30; KirkR '72/40:167; LibJ '72/97:2420; LibJBkR '72:519; NYorker 3Jn'72/48:111; PubW 14F'72/201:63; SatR 24Jn'72/55:68; JRelThought '73/30:648; PsyanQ '75/44:157–63; PsyPersp '90/22:187)

Zeus and Hera: Archetypal Image of Father, Husband, and Wife, by C. Kerényi. (Ger.: *Zeus und Hera: Urbild des Vaters, des Gatten, und der Frau*. Leiden: E. J. Brill, 1972.) London: Routledge & Kegan Paul, 1975*; Princeton, N.J.: Princeton U. Press (Bollingen Series LXV:5) (Archetypal Images in Greek Religion, 5), 1975* (211 + xvii, incl. 12-p. index, 14-p. bibl.).

Tracing the history of Greek religion from an archetypal point of view, Kerényi reconstructs the beginnings of the Zeus tradition and its early history. He considers the emergence of the Olympian divine family to be the expression of a humane religion with the father image of Zeus as supreme god and the image of Hera as wife in the archetypal form of marriage. He also discusses Poseidon as a father and husband archetype, as well as interpreting the relationship of Zeus and Hera, brother and sister joined in "sacred marriage," as the restoration of a bisexual totality. He ends with a description of Hera cults in the Peloponnese, Euboea, and Boeotia along with the significance of the Great Goddess Hera's temples on the island of Samos and in Paestum.

(Bk.revs.: Choice '76/13:539; Spec 29My'76/236:32; VaQR Sum'76/52:91; ClassR '78/ ns28:287–9; ClassWorld '78/72:246–7)

The New Polytheism: Rebirth of the Gods and Goddesses, by David L. Miller. New York: Harper & Row, 1974; Dallas: Spring Publications, ed.2 1981p* (148, incl. 6-p. index, 8-p. ref. notes, 6-p. prefatory letter by Henry Corbin, 34-p. appendix by James Hillman, incl. 5-p. ref. notes).

From his experience of "imaginal theologizing," in which polytheistic theology is grounded in stories of gods and goddesses, Miller proposes that such stories, like dreams and angels, are images. He explores the theological and philosophical relationships between monotheism and polytheism in order to determine whether they are mutually exclusive modes of consciousness. He examines the possibility of remythologizing Western thought, not to give up logic and reason but to enable ancient stories of gods and goddesses to put life and feeling back into Western thinking. He also discusses the task of "re-relating" religious explanations to life experiences by way of a polytheistic psychology, citing Hillman's arguments on archetypal psychology. A lengthy appendix by Hillman entitled "Psychology: Monotheistic or Polytheistic" is included.

(Bk.revs.: PubW 3D'73/204:39; AnglTheolR '74/56:500–1; BkRDig '74:832; Choice '74/ 11:1331; ChrCen '74/91:323; Chman Jn–Jy'74/188:16; Critic My'74/32:77–8; Horiz '74/ 1:120–1; JAmAcadRel '74/42:344–9; JSciStudRel S'74/13:376–8; LibJ '74/99:370; Lib-JBkR '74:413; LuthQ '74/26:464–6; ReligEd '74/69:755–6; ReligHum '74/8:142–3; ReligLife '74/43:513–14; RBksRel(W) My'74/3:5; SWJTheol '74/17:119–20; DrewGate '75/46:147–51; CrossCurr '76/26:110–11; Dialog '76/15:90–1; JAmAcadRel '76/44:745–6; Parab Oc'81/6:109–11; JAnPsy '83/27:388–90; RelStudR '83/9:242; BksRel S'86/14:9–10)

Psyche and the Bible: Three Old Testament Themes, by Rivkah Schärf Kluger. New York and Zurich: Spring Publications for the Analytical Psychology Club of New York, 1974p (144 pp.).

Consisting of lectures given in Zurich and London during 1946–56, this book by Kluger presents three themes from the Old Testament, the first dealing with the idea of the chosen people (42 pp.), which she approaches from the point of view of the symbolism of the individuation process. She also interprets psychological aspects of the relation of King Saul to the spirit of God (36 pp.) and of the Queen of Sheba in the Bible and in legends (60 pp.).

The Return to Faith: Finding God in the Unconscious, by Clyde H. Reid. New York: Harper & Row, 1974 (106 + xii, incl. 14 illus.).

Reflecting on the state of religion while studying at the C. G. Institute of Zurich, Reid developed the theme of an emerging religion of consciousness which would allow a person to integrate mind and body, and consciousness and the unconscious, rather than simply maintaining the carefully monitored, rational, conscious self favored by many religious persons. Here he examines the meaning of full consciousness from the point of view of analytical psychology, and discusses some myths that must die (Christian exclusiveness; original sin; the nice guy; morality; the masculine God). He affirms that religion is not something one joins, but is something one is.

(Bk.revs.: BkRDig '74:1006; ChrCen '74/91:708; JPsyTheol '74/2:325–6; LibJ '74/99:1966; LibJBkR '74:440; Critic '75/33n3:67–8+)

Religion and the Unconscious, by Ann Ulanov and Barry Ulanov. Philadelphia: Westminster Press, 1975; ed.2 1985p* (287, incl. 8-p. index, 28-p. ref. notes).

The Ulanovs identify the pains and pleasures that accompany efforts to define one's own identity or the identities of others. In relation to that struggle, they emphasize the extraordinary need and use that religion and depth psychology have for each other, neither usurping the other. They urge a knowing acceptance of a certain imbalance or turmoil that one's understanding of the nature of consciousness and the unconscious brings and the pains which are associated with sin and moral transgression in religion and with neurosis and psychosis in depth psychology. Following an interpretation of the convergences and divergences of conscious and unconscious, as well as the function of religion for the human psyche and the function of psychology for religion, they discuss the topics of soul and psyche; Jesus as figure and person; symbol and sacrament; history and ethics after the discovery of the unconscious; healing; moral masochism and religious submission; suffering and salvation; and reality.

(Bk.revs.: KirkR '75/43:1172; LibJ '75/100:1639; LibJBkR '75:416; AnglTheolR '76/58:516–17; BkRDig '76:1226; Choice '76/13:540; CrossCurr '76/26:377–81; Horiz '76/3:298+; JPastorCare '76/30:208–9; JRelHealth '76/15:302–3; LivLight '76/13:624; ReligLife '76/45:510–11; RelStudR Oc'76/2:57; SocAn '76/37:368–9; ChrCen '77/94:204–5; ChrScholR '77/7:215–16; JPsyTheol '77/5:265–6; PastorPsy '77/26:481; ReligEd '77/72:240; UnionSemQR '77/32:122–5; JAmAcadRel '78/46:107)

Dionysos: Archetypal Image of Indestructible Life, by C. Kerényi. London: Routledge & Kegan Paul, 1976; Princeton, N.J.: Princeton U. Press (Bollingen Series LXV:2) (Archetypal Images in Greek Religion), 1976* (474 + xxxvii, incl. 22-p. index, 30-p. bibl., 28-p. Kerényi bibl., 2-p. biography of Kerényi, 146 illus.).

Writing from a dual viewpoint as a historian of religion (with close attention to traditional myths, cultural actions, and festivals of the ancient world) and as a historian of Greek and Minoan culture, Kerényi presents a historical account of the religion of Dionysos from its beginnings in the Minoan culture down to its transition to a cosmic and cosmopolitan religion of late antiquity under the Roman Empire. He deals with Dionysos as the archetypal image of indestructible life in terms of the "quiet, powerful, vegetative element" of the life force.

(Bk.revs.: BkRDig '77:718; Choice '77/14:880; LibJ '77/102:819; LibJBkR '77:476; VaQR Sum'77/53:110; ClassWorld '78/72:246; Quad '78/11n1:96–9)

The Other Side of Silence: A Guide to Christian Meditation, by Morton T. Kelsey. New York and Paramus, N.J.: Paulist Press, 1976 +p*; London: S.P.C.K., 1977p* (314 + viii, incl. 6-p. ref. notes, 8 illus.).

Acknowledging that Jungian psychology has helped his understanding of the spiritual world, Kelsey presents a "practical manual" for encountering God that utilizes a unique Christian method of meditation. Starting with the problem of intimacy (with God) that is involved in meditation, as well as the relation of psychological types to the inner life and how art is related to meditation, he lays out the elements of the atmosphere or environment in which meditation can grow; he then considers preparations for the inward journey, the uses of images in meditation, and adventures on the other side of silence.

(Bk.revs.: NatCathRep 5N'76/13:12; USCath Oc'76/41:50–1; Amer '77/136:133–4; BkRDig '77:714; ChrCen '77/94:513–14; Chman F'77/191:17; LibJ '77/102:394; Lib-JBkR '77:475–6; LivLight '77/14:479; LumenVitae '77/32:365; NewRBksRel F'77/1:24; Parab '77/2n3:104–5; StAnth My'77/84:47; SisToday '77/48:411; SpirLife '77/23:120; Tabl '77/231:769; TheolStud '77/38:207; AnglTheolR '78/60:373–4; JPastorCare '78/32:69–70; ReligEd '78/73:110–11; Theol '78/81:224–6; HeythJ '79/20:358; ModChman '79/ns22:129–30; CistStud '80/15:291–5)

Prospects for the Soul: Soundings in Jungian Psychology and Religion, by Vera von der Heydt. London: Darton, Longman & Todd, 1976 (110, incl. 2-p. bibl.).

Expressing gratitude to Jung, von der Heydt presents essays based on her analytical experiences. Following interpretations of aspects of the parent archetype, the animus, psychic energy, personal enthusiasm, and loneliness, she examines the relationship of analytical psychology and religion with chapters on Jung and religion, alchemy, psychological implications of the dogma of the Assumption, the treatment of Catholic patients, and fear, guilt, and confession.

(Bk.revs.: Econ 3Ap'76/259:133–4; Harvest '76/22:138–9; Month '76/9:283–4; JAnPsy '77/22:77–8)

Subject and Psyche: Ricoeur, Jung, and the Search for Foundations, by Robert M. Doran. Washington, D.C.: University Press of America, 1977 (313 + vi, incl. 4-p. bibl.).

Asserting that he is using neither depth psychology nor systematic theology, but theological method, Doran searches for foundations for theology. He focuses on basic notions of Jungian analytical psychology, clarifying some ambiguities in Jung's thought with the aid of Paul Ricoeur's philosophy of the symbol and Bernard Lonergan's analysis of human intentionality. He begins with a long treatment of Lonergan's thought and then discusses immediacy, symbols, sublations, and psyche and intentionality. He reviews Ricoeur's reading of and debate with Freud and describes his own reading and debate with Jung. Topics include mystery and myth; individuation; psychic energy; intentionality and psyche; psychic conversion; and the psychic and the psychoid. He concludes with a chapter on psyche and theology, emphasizing Lonergan's thought on the function of psychic self-appropriation in relation to the foundations of theology.
(Bk.rev.: TheolStud '79/40:780–2)

Imago Dei: A Study of C. G. Jung's Psychology of Religion, by James W. Heisig. Lewisburg, Penn.: Bucknell U. Press, 1978*; London: Assoc. University Presses, 1979* (253, incl. 13-p. index, 30-p. bibl.) (Studies in Jungian Thought).

In consideration of Jung's struggle with God, which Heisig evaluates as the typical turning point of sympathy for or alienation from Jung's life work, Heisig examines the entire body of Jung's writings with a focus on the notion of the *imago Dei* (God-image) in order to critique Jung's "strange and powerful genius." He traces the life story of the theme from Jung's early years (writings on the psychology of the unconscious and psychological types) through the middle years (writings on psychology and religion) to the later years (writings on *Answer to Job* and Jung's *Memories, Dreams, Reflections*). Following critical comments on Jung's methodology, he presents his own "factual material" about the *imago Dei* and discusses his interpretation of psychological theory, science, and therapy.
(Bk.revs.: BkRDig '79:360; Choice '79/16:1038; LibJ '70/104:2219; LibJBkR '79:304; JAmAcadRel '80/48:639; JSciStudRel '80/19:79; Harvest '81/27:168–70; JRel '81/61:119–20)

Occult Psychology: A Comparison of Jungian Psychology and the Modern Qabalah, by Alta J. LaDage. St. Paul, Minn.: Llewellyn, 1978 (193 + x, incl. 9-p. index, 2-p. bibl., 5 illus.).

Speaking to the intuitive mind and the unconscious rather than to the thinking mind, LaDage examines the inner correspondences between the Qabalah (Jewish occult philosophy and mystical interpretation of Scripture) and Jung's psychology. She places Jung in the mainstream of the Western occult tradition in consideration of his use of alchemy, much of whose cosmology and philosophical writings were derived from the Qabalah. Her topics include the eternal quest; the roots of the Qabalah; the universal force; the collective unconscious; the archetypes as psychological factors; the four functions; and the process of individuation.
(Bk.rev.: JPhenPsy '79/10:236–7)

Changing of the Gods: Feminism and the End of Traditional Religions, by Naomi R. Goldenberg. Boston: Beacon Press, 1979 + p* (152 + viii, incl. 4-p. index, 8-p. ref. notes).

The women's movement has brought about religious changes on a massive scale with a re-evaluation of the roles that men and women have been taught to consider as God-given. In light of this, Goldenberg examines the need of Christianity and Judaism to adapt to nonsexist culture in order to survive. A significant part of the book is devoted to Jungian psychology and religion. Topics include the search for a living religion; how to build a community; archetypes; Jung's discovery of the religious process within; feminism and God; oedipal prisons; Lilith and Mary; androgynes; feminist witchcraft; mysticism; and excursions into dream and fantasy.
(Bk.revs.: Anima '79/6:76–7; BkRDig '79:479; Bklist '79/15:1262; Choice '79/16:857; ChrCen '79/96:826; KirkR '79/47:235–6; LibJ '79/104:1468; LibJBkR '79:399; New-RBksRel Jn'79/3:22; NYTimesBkR 29Jy'79:10–11 + ; PubW 5Mr'79/215:94; CrossCurr '80/30:340–2; JAmAcadRel '80/48:141–2; JEcumStud '80/17:525–6; Kliatt Fall'80/14:37; Parab N'80/5:118–20; Signs '80/6:328–33; SpirToday '80/32:376; UTorQ '80/49:506–12; ChrScholR '81/10:179–80; RelStudR '81/7:45; StudRel '81/10:136–7; WomStudIntQ '81/4:284; InwLight '82/n98:42–4; JRel '82/62:74–5)

Discovering God Within, by John R. Yungblut. Philadelphia: Westminster Press, 1979p (197, incl. 3-p. ref. notes).

Addressing himself to some "unknown seeker" who may discover in those hidden places of the heart and mind what Wordsworth called "obstinate questionings," Yungblut speaks directly to the interior being of those who may be persuaded to cultivate the mystical or contemplative faculty in themselves. He builds on insights from depth psychology, particularly from Jung, in presenting the mystical way in Christianity, in which he discusses the meaning of religion, the meaning of mysticism, the cultivation of the mystical faculty, and the vagaries and aberrations of the mystical way. He describes some varieties of Christian mysticism, in which he interprets Jesus as the

Jewish mystic, the Christ-mysticism of Paul, the God-mysticism of the fourth Gospel (John), the aesthetic mysticism of Augustine, the philosophical mysticism of Meister Eckhart, and the material mysticism of Teilhard de Chardin.

(Bk.revs.: Choice '79/16:1041; LibJ '79/104:1149; LibJBkR '79:413; NewRBksRel Oc'79/ 4:18; ReformR '79/33:42; JAmAcadRel '80/48:628–9; ReligLife '80/49:247–9; SpirToday '80/32:73; PersRelStud '82/9:92–3)

The Feminine Dimension of the Divine, by Joan Chamberlain Engelsman. Philadelphia: Westminster Press, 1979p; Wilmette, Ill.: Chiron Publications, 1987p* (203, incl. 3-p. index, 22-p. bibl., 21-p. ref. notes).

Engelsman focuses on mythological and theological speculation about feminine symbols for God, particularly from a Jungian point of view. She recognizes the view of feminists who consider the nature of Jungian archetypes to be stereotypical and urges common sense and a raised consciousness to minimize some of the more obvious problems of criticism. She begins with a description of Jung's concept of archetypes, particularly feminine archetypes, and Freud's understanding of the phenomena of repression and then traces the feminine dimension of the divine in the Hellenistic world (Demeter and Isis), in the expression and repression of Sophia, and in the patristic doctrines of Mariology, ecclesiology, and Christology.

(Bk.revs.: LibJ '79/104:2106–7; LibJBkR '79:397; BkRDig '80:357; Choice '80/17:233– 4; CrossCurr '80/30:342–3; Dialog '80/19:239–40; ReformR '80/33:170; ReligLife '80/ 49:242–3; RelStudR '80/6:310; RforRel '80/39:477–8; StLukeJTh '80/24:56–8; Spir-Today '80:32:71; TrinSemR '80/2:43–4; TSF '80/4:13; AnglTheolR '81/63:212–14; Horiz '81/8:142–4; Interp '81/35:87–8; JAmAcadRel '81/49:159–60; PersRelStud '81/8:163–4; InwLight '82/n98:48–51; Anima '83/9:153–5; JEcumStud '84/21:330–1)

Imagination Is Reality: Western Nirvana in Jung, Hillman, Barfield, and Cassirer, by Roberts Avens. (Orig. title: *Imagination: A Way Toward Western Nirvana.* Washington, D.C.: University Press of America, 1979.) Dallas: Spring Publications, 1980* (127, incl. 5-p. bibl., 19-p. ref. notes).

Aiming to synthesize, by circumambulation, the imaginal "inscape" of the psyche, Avens examines the work of a quaternity of Western thinkers (Jung and Hillman at the psychological end of the spectrum and Ernst Cassirer and Owen Barfield at the literary-philosophical end), who regard imagination (imagemaking) as the characteristically human faculty which works toward self-transcendence and reconciliation of spirit and world. He first explores the phenomenon of imagination as the common ground of both Western and Eastern spirituality and then envisions imagining as a potential Western alternative to Eastern nirvana, satori, or Brahman-Atman.

(Bk.revs.: CrossCurr '79/29:367–9; Choice '80/18:165; Harvest '81/27:180–2)

The Dark Twin: A Study of Evil—and Good, by Ivor Moorish. Romford: L. N. Fowler, 1980p* (144, incl. 3-p. bibl., ref. notes, 3 illus.).

Attracted by Jung's writings on the problems of good and evil, and basing his study to a very large extent upon Jung's concepts of symbolism and archetypes, Moorish suggests that the eternal mystery of the problem of evil exists within one's own innermost nature rather than on some external and intangible cosmic level. He first examines the background of the concept of the good and evil twins in mythology and then discusses the shadow, the divided self, the lamed or blemished self, the freedom of the self, the integrated self, and the existential reality of the self.

Facing the Gods, edited by James Hillman. Dallas: Spring Publications, 1980p* (172 + iv, incl. 5-p. index, 19-p. ref. notes).

Proposing that one must know the gods and goddesses of myth in order to face the archetypal backgrounds that affect personal experience, the authors of nine papers present the psychological possibilities of workings of those archetypes. Editor Hillman provides two essays, on Dionysos in Jung's writings and the necessity of abnormal psychology, while others deal with Artemis as a mythological image of girlhood (Kerényi); the Amazon problem (René Malamud); Hephaistos as a pattern of introversion (Murray Stein); Red Riding Hood and Grand Mother Rhea as images in a psychology of inflation (David Miller); Hestia as a background of psychological focusing (Barbara Kirksey); Hermes' heteronymous appellations (William Doty); and Ariadne as mistress of the labyrinth (Christine Downing).
(Bk.revs.: Choice '81/18:723; Harvest '81/26:186)

The Psyche as Sacrament: C. G. Jung and Paul Tillich, by John P. Dourley. Toronto: Inner City Books, 1981p* (Studies in Jungian Psychology by Jungian Analysts, 7) (121, incl. 5-p. index, 2-p. gloss. of Jungian terms).

Aiming at a systematic analysis and correlation of Jung's and Tillich's views, Dourley compares the positions they take on the nature of religious consciousness and its symbolic expression for the psychological meanings of God, Christ, the Church, and the future. His topics are the apologetic problem; psyche as sacrament; God, the union of opposites, and the Trinity; the search for the nonhistorical Jesus; aspects of the Spirit; and the Church, morality, and eschatology. He perceives that the psychological task and the religious task are one in the depths of the soul (psyche).
(Bk.revs.: CanBkRAn '81:93–4; Choice '82/19:777; Harvest '82/28:157–8; PsyPersp '82/13:100–2; Quad '82/15n2:73–5; RelStudR '85/11:40; StudRel '85/14:510–12; TorJTheol '86/2:142–4)

Christs: Meditations on Archetypal Images in Christian Theology, by David Miller. New York: Seabury Press, 1981* (200 + xxiv, incl. 6-p. index, 36-p. ref. notes).

In "re-visioning" Christianity's traditional forms of thought in doctrines, teachings and beliefs whose luster and lively images lie dormant and well hidden in the unconscious, Miller presents the idea of a polytheistic, archetypal theology with a focus on the doctrine of Christ. He examines the images of the theology of Christ (Good Shepherd, Clown, Great Teacher) as archetypal ideas that impress most profoundly on the life of the self or psyche ("soul"). He explores the archetypal images of not only the gods of Greece but also contemporary imaginal versions, such as the "shepherd" in Shakespeare and in Eliot, the "fool" in Joyce and in Gogol, and the "teacher" in Hopkins and in Baudelaire, showing how fundamental christological images impinge on human experience today.

(Bk.revs.: ChrCen '81/98:1234; NatCathRep 11S'81/17:19; TheolStud '81/42:709–10; AnglTheolR '82/64:267–9; Commonw '82/109:542–3; ReligHum '83/17:197–8)

Evil: The Shadow Side of Reality, by John A. Sanford. New York: Crossroad Publishing Co., 1981*; 1987p* (161, incl. 5-p. index).

Sanford examines the nature and reasons for evil from the standpoint of the unconscious in order that he may learn more about the nature of God. His approach to the problem of evil and the relationship of evil to God begins with an analysis of ego-centered and divine perspectives on evil, followed by analyses of the problem of evil in mythology, the Old Testament, and the New Testament. He also discusses the shadow side of reality; Jesus and Paul and the shadow; the problem of shadow and evil in Dr. Jekyll and Mr. Hyde; and the devil in post-Biblical mythology and folklore. He concludes with an interpretation of the ontology of evil.

(Bk.revs.: BestSell Ag'81/41:193; Choice '81/19:393; LibJ '81/106:1086; SpirLife '81/27:254; TheolStud '81/42:712–13; AnglTheolR '82/64:421–2; BestSell D'82/42:360; BkRDig '82:1178; PastorPsy '82/31:67–9; PsyPersp '82/13:196–200; RelStudBul '82/2:36; TheolToday '82/39:112–13; JAmAcadRel '83/51:703–4; JPsyTheol '83/11:55–8; RBksRel(C) F'84/12:5; RforRel '85/44:470–1; Zygon '85/20:83–9; InwLight '86/n101–102:64–7)

Jung's Hermeneutic of Doctrine: Its Theological Significance, by Clifford A. Brown. Chico, Calif.: Scholars Press, 1981p (American Acad. of Religion Dissertation Ser.) (226 + vii, incl. 23-p. appendixes, 9-p. bibl.).

The author believes that theological interpreters of Jung have been most prone to misconstrue him because they do not understand the nature of the method underlying his interpretive work and in particular his doctrinal studies. In this book, Brown calls attention to the hermeneutical nature of Jung's method and its respect for the inherently symbolic nature of Christian doctrine. He proposes to make the doctrine and its interpretation the common meeting-ground between Jungian psychology and Christian theology. After discussing Jung's theological interpreters, he analyzes symbol and psyche in Jung's psychology, Jung's symbolics of fantasy, and Jung's psychology of doctrine, concluding with the consideration of a theological appropriation of Jung.

(Bk.revs.: AnglTheolR '82/64:595–6; RelStudR '82/8:53; TheolStud '82/43:343–4; Horiz '83/10:408–10; JAmAcadRel '83/51:326)

Christo-Psychology, by Morton T. Kelsey. New York: Crossroad Pub. Co., 1982; 1984p*; London: Darton, Longman & Todd, 1983p* (143 + xii, incl. 6 diagrams).

Intended as a practical guide for people who wish to combine the insights of depth psychology with those of vital Christianity, this work by Kelsey interprets Jung's theories as offering no obstacles to the realization that salvation comes only through divine grace which alone brings about transformation within one's self. His topics include a personal journey into faith; the importance of Freud; Jung and Christianity; psychology and theology (the importance of experience); the soul and its capacities; psychological types and the religious way; counseling, individuation, and confession; love and transference; moving toward integration; dreams and the spiritual way; archetypes; and relating to the unconscious through active imagination and meditation.

(Bk.revs.: LibJ '82/107:2262; Amer '83/148:365; BestSell '83/42:475; BkRDig '83:796–7; ExposTimes '83/94:380–1; JPsyChry Spr'83/2:88; JPsyTheol '83/11:258; NewCath '83/226:235–6; RelStudR '83/9:243; StMarkThR '83/n116:34–6; SisToday Ag'83/55:54; SpirToday '83/35:367; TheolToday '83/40:386; AnglTheolR '84/66:113–18; CrossCurr '84/34:125; HumDev '84/4:44; JAmAcadRel '84/52:628–9; LivLight '84/20:368; Month '84/17:71; DoctLife '85/35:179; Furrow '85/36:389; IrTheolQ '85/51:251; R&Expos '85/82:472–3; HeythJ '86/27:349; RforRel '86/45:311–12)

The Darkness of God: Theology After Hiroshima, by Jim Garrison. London: S.C.M. Publications, 1982p*; Grand Rapids, Mich.: William B. Eerdmans Publishing Co., 1983p (238 + x, incl. 3-p. bibl., 20-p. ref. notes).

Garrison focuses on the salvific potential of the bombing of Hiroshima and its implications for the death of the species in the nuclear age. He perceives God at work in the atom bomb, working divine wrath through man's arrogance but always creatively integrating the strands of evil and good together. He examines the question of evil in the context of the inherited Christian tradition and the "mighty acts of God," then looks at Hiroshima as symbolizing the possibility of the cataclysmic termination of history. He discusses Hiroshima in dynamic tension with the confessional Christian heritage of the classical apocalypse and the wrath of God. His synthesis of Hiroshima and the apocalypse utilizes Jung's description of the psyche as composed of both light and dark dimensions. He discusses as well the topics of Jung's *Answer to Job;* Wotan; the theology of the cross; the revelation of John; modern thought on the antinomy (contradiction) of God; and the paradox of apocalypse. He concludes by characterizing Hiroshima as the gateway to Christ crucified.

(Bk.revs.: ExposTimes '83/94:153; ModChman '83/ns26:61; SpirLife '83/29:249; Theol '83/86:48–50; RBksRel(C) '84/12:8; Sojour Ag'84/13:36–8; WordWorld '84/4:203+; HeythJ '85/28:202; RelStudR '85/11:387; Colloq Oc'86/19:67–9; ConradG '86/4:284– 90)

The End of God: Important Directions for a Feminist Critique of Religion in the Works of Sigmund Freud and Carl Jung, by Naomi Ruth Goldenberg. Ottawa: Ottawa U. Press, 1982p* (128 + xiv, incl. 6-p. bibl.).

Drawing on the theories of depth psychology of both Freud and Jung, Goldenberg examines the concerns of women who are estranged from Jewish and Christian traditions but who nonetheless struggle to retain a "religious" view of life. She believes that both Freudian and Jungian theory are surprisingly useful in understanding the iconographic impoverishment feminists are working to resolve and offer direction for the development of new images and symbols. She discusses the oppressiveness of the Jewish and Christian religions as described by Freud; alternatives to contemporary religions as envisioned by Jung and Jung's interest in adding feminine imagery to religion and to psychology; and the need for the perspective of depth psychology in a feminist critique of religion.

(Bk.rev.: CanBkRAn '82:97)

The Gnostic Jung and the Seven Sermons to the Dead, by Stephen A. Hoeller. Wheaton, Ill., Madras, and London: Quest Books/Theosophical Publishing House, 1982*; 1989p* (239 + xxviii, incl. 11-p. index, 2-p. Gnostic gloss.).

Consisting of lectures given at UCLA's Institute for the Study of Religion in 1977, this work by Hoeller views Jung as a healer of souls and the culture, whose greatness he relates to the Gnostic belief concerning humanity's need for wholeness through gnosis (knowledge of spiritual truth). His interpretation of Jung's *Seven Sermons to the Dead* draws parallels between ancient Gnostic systems and Jung's psychology. He compares Jung's insights into the structure of the psyche and the nature of the collective unconscious, in terms of the dynamic of the individuation process, to the Gnostics' expression of their inner experience, given in mythological and poetic language. He considers moral fervor, faith in God or in political ideologies, advocacy of harsh law and rigid order, and apocalyptic, messianic enthusiasm as imperfect solutions to spiritual problems.

(Bk.revs.: Choice '83/20:1372; JAnPsy '83/28:388–9; WCoastRBks N–D'83/9:50; Quad '84/17n1:70–1; '87/20n2:77–9)

The Human Face of God: William Blake and the Book of Job, by Kathleen Raine. London: Thames & Hudson, 1982* (320, incl. 4-p. index, 2-p. bibl., 13-p. ref. notes, 130 illus.).

Although this book consists mainly of her description and interpretation of the twenty-one plates from Blake's illustrations to the Book of Job, along with many others of Blake's drawings, in the last section (32 pp.) Raine presents a discussion of Blake's Job and Jung's Job. Explaining that both Blake and Jung devoted their lives to their inner worlds and both had read and followed the same ancient Gnostic texts and other sources of knowledge, she examines the many resemblances and differences in their interpretation of the story of Job. Seeing it as the enactment of the individuation process, she considers Blake's view paradoxically more "Jungian" than that of Jung himself. She interprets the issue for Jung between God and Job as the confrontation between a righteous man and the evil in God and, for Blake, the breaking down of the moral self-righteousness of the human Selfhood (ego). Raine concludes that there is much in Blake's writings that supports Jung's view that opposites mutually exist in God.

(Bk.revs.: BkRDig '82:1100; BurlMag '82/124:772–3; Choice '82/20:64; ExposTimes '82/ 94:30–1; Harvest '82/28:162–4; JRoySoc '82/130:595–6; NewStates 2Ap'82/103:23; Resurg N–D'82/n95:40; Tabl '82/236:517–18; TimesLitSup '82:432; BrJ18Cen '83:76; Commonw '83/110:91–3; LATimesBkR 6F'83:4; Blake '86/19:151–5)

Imaginal Body: Para-Jungian Reflections on Soul, Imagination, and Death, by Roberts Avens. Washington, D.C.: University Press of America, 1982 +p (252 + ix, incl. 3-p. bibl.).

Adopting a viewpoint of Jungian thought as "re-visioned" by Hillman's archetypal psychology, Avens reflects on the idea that one's presumed spirituality is a sham which must be discarded in favor of a "realistic" view of life, and he presents the idea of an "imaginal body" that stands between the two extremes of spiritualism and materialism. He explores the subjects of the ghost of imagination; mind and matter; reality of the psyche; death; the psyche and parapsychology; and the subtle body in traditional thought.

Jung and Christianity: The Challenge of Reconciliation, by Wallace B. Clift. New York: Crossroad Publishing Co., 1982; 1986p; Blackburn, Australia: Dove, 1983 (169 + xiii, incl. 11-p. ref. notes).

Recognizing Jung's contributions to psychology and to the psychology of religion, Clift concurs with Jung's belief that the spiritual life of the individual is basic to human life in its search for meaning and in affirmation of the existence of God. He discusses the basic concepts in Jung's psychology (pastor of souls; psychic reality and psychic energy; structure of the psyche; stages of life; the process of psychotherapy) and Jung's contributions to the psychology of religion (individuation and the problem of opposites; the uniting quality of symbols; myth as meaning-giver; religious experience as the union of opposites). He follows with his interpretation of Jung's challenge to Christianity by analyzing the language of religion; the problem with dogma; the voice of God; evil as the "dark side" of God; evil and the resurrection symbol; and the Holy Spirit and the new age of consciousness.

(Bk.revs.: BestSell '82/42:158; BkRDig '82:242; Choice '82/19:1573; ChrCen '82/99:1290-1; LibJ '82/107:1228; NICM Fall'82/7:81-5; AnglTheolR '83/65:242-3; Commonw '83/110-124; Horiz '83/10:408-10; HumDev '83/4:46; JAmAcadRel '83/51:523; JPsyChry Sum'83/2:66; JPsyTheol '83/11:260-1; Quad '83/16n2:87-8; RelStudBul '83/3:51-4; RelStudR '83/9:49; RforRel '83/42:788; SpirToday '83/35:375; Chry&Lit '84/34n1:47-8; PastorPsy '84/32:291-2; RBksRel(C) Ja'84/12:8; JPsyTheol '85/13:217-18; JRel '86/66:355-6)

Mid-life: Psychological and Spiritual Perspectives, by Janice Brewi and Anne Brennan. New York: Crossroad Publishing Co., 1982; ed.2 1987p* (146 + x, incl. 7-p. bibl.).

Jung believed that one cannot live the second half of life (the "afternoon") according to the program of the first half ("life's morning"). In the spirit of this statement, the authors, who conduct seminars and workshops, examine the life cycle and the midlife crisis from both psychological and theological perspectives, interpreting the midlife transition through the doctrines of creation and incarnation; and they offer insights for midlife tasks and spirituality in terms of Jungian personality theory. They also discuss the midlife task of clarifying and owning one's values; and they analyze storytelling and prayer as ways of dealing with midlife crisis and transition.

(Bk.revs.: ChrCen '82/99:1260; LibJ '82/107:643; LivLight '82/19:372; SisToday '82/54:178; SpirLife '82/281:125; BkRDig '83:185; HumDev Spr'86/8:46; StAnth '86/93:50)

Primary Speech: A Psychology of Prayer, by Ann Ulanov and Barry Ulanov. Atlanta: John Knox Press, 1982p*; London: S.C.M. Press, 1985p* (178 + ix, incl. 42-p. ref. notes).

The Ulanovs examine the idea of the language of prayer as primary speech and as that primordial discourse in which one asserts one's own being. They focus on the relationships between prayer and desire, projection, fantasy, fear, aggression, and sexuality from a Jungian point of view. They

also discuss praying for others, answers to prayer, and transfiguration. Appended is an 8-page list of composers, poets, painters, and sculptors whose works of art have proved to be useful for the "art of prayer."
(Bk.revs.: LibJ '82:1886; Quad '83/16n2:75–6; JPsyTheol'84/12:69; RelStudR '84/10:48; SpirLife '84/30:183; AnglTheolR '85/67:110–11; ExposTimes '85/97:62; RforRel '85/44:942–3; TSF My–Jn'85/8:30 + ; BksRel '86/14:18; Theol '86/89:68–70)

Prophetic Ministry: The Psychology and Spirituality of Pastoral Care, by Morton Kelsey. New York: Crossroad Publishing Co., 1982* (210 + xii, incl. 7-p. bibl., 4 illus.).

Consisting of papers written for various religious and psychological journals and lectures given at Notre Dame University, Kelsey's book asserts that Jung's view of the universe gives a new way of believing that the traditional view of the Church has a real validity. Two essays deal with Jung as philosopher and theologian and with Jung and the theological dilemma. He presents Jung's suggestions for finding a way out of meaninglessness and for the importance of religion and meaning for both psychological and physical health. Most of the book is concerned with the healing ministry, pastoral counseling, and ministry to the lonely, the homosexual, the violent, and the dying.
(Bk.revs.: Commonw '82/109:477; SisToday Ag–S'82/54:56; SpirLife '82/28:190; Amer '83/148:174–5; HumDev Wint'83/4:44; JPsyChry Fall'83/2:87; NewCath '83/226:46–7; PastorPsy '83/31:287–8; NatCathRep 16N'84/21:23; SWJTheol '84/26:112)

Spiritual Pilgrims: Carl Jung and Teresa of Ávila, by John Welch. New York and Ramsey, N.J.: Paulist Press, 1982p* (228 + x, incl. 4-p. index, 3-p. bibl., 2-p. foreword by Morton Kelsey).

Studying Jung and Teresa of Ávila together, Welch proposes that each illuminates the individual's interiority but from a different perspective—Jung from the relationship of the person to his or her own psychic depths, St. Teresa from the relationship of the person's soul to God. His theme is Christian individuation, the movement of one's personality toward wholeness as union with God deepens, and the potential for living a fully human yet spiritual life. He describes the process of individuation through a series of images: the castle (the image of wholeness), deep waters (the inner world), a map (life's journey), serpents and devils (the shadows), butterfly (the image of healing), marriage (of the inner masculine and feminine), and Christ (the symbol of the Self).
(Bk.revs.: LibJ '82/107:1470; Columbia Ag'83/63:29; Commonw '83/110:124; CrossCurr '83/33:82–3; RBksRel(C) Ap'83/11:3; Horiz '84/11:195–7; TheolStud '84/45:598–9; JAnPsy '85/30:397–8)

Growth Through Meditation and Journal Writing: A Jungian Perspective on Christian Spirituality, by Maria L. Santa Maria. New York and Ramsey, N.J.: Paulist Press, 1983p* (147 + vi, incl. 9-p. bibl.).

Believing that Jung's psychology provides a unique perspective for dealing with the psychological problems of adulthood and the search for meaning, Santa Maria discusses the concept of the receptive mode as the feminine aspect of personality that is essential in the development of a mature adult spirituality. She explores the use of guided imagery, keeping a journal, and meditation in her discussions of the topics of inner life and the feminine mode; elements of contemporary Christian spirituality; classical approaches to the spiritual life; the covenant life; and seven dimensions of Christian spirituality, stressing that a search for meaning is a search for God.
(Bk.rev.: SisToday Ag-S'84/56:43; RelStudR '85/11:172)

Jung and the Bible, by Wayne Gilbert Rollins. Atlanta: John Knox Press, 1983p* (153 + x, incl. 4-p. index of names and subjects, 3-p. index of Biblical ref., 2-p. bibl., 13-p. ref. notes, 2-p. chron. of Jung's life, 17 illus.).

Exploring Scripture as a treasury of soul, Rollins states his belief that the study of the soul was Jung's main goal. He first analyzes the relationship between Jung and the Bible and presents a lengthy description of Jung's psychology from a biographical point of view. Then he discusses the Bible and the life of the soul, Biblical symbols as vocabulary of the soul, and Biblical archetypes (particularly the Self in Scripture). He also examines a Jungian approach to "letting the Bible speak" and a Jungian perspective of God, the Bible, and the Self, concluding with an analysis of psychological criticism and scriptural studies.
(Bk.revs.: LibJ '82/107:2262; Commonw '83/110:665; JPsyChry Fall'83/2:86; JPsyTheol '83/11:259–61; TheolStud '83/44:722–4; JAnPsy '84/29:207–8; RelStudR '84/10:47–8; JBibLit '85/104:503–4)

Jung and the Christian Way, by Christopher Bryant. London: Darton, Longman & Todd, 1983p*; Minneapolis: Seabury Press, 1984p* (127 + x, incl. 1-p. bibl.).

Basing his book on lectures given at a London church in 1980, Bryant expresses his debt to Jung for the spiritual relevance of Jung's exploration of the human psyche and the light shed on the Christian faith and way of life. He discusses various aspects of Jung's views on religion, finding Jung's understanding of dogma to be partial and inadequate, though believing that Jung can provide Christians with a deeper understanding of their faith. His topics include dreams and their interpretation; God's providence and the

Self; God's providence and the stages of life; the shadow and the Redeemer; individuation and the archetypes; and individuation and the spiritual life.

(Bk.revs.: ExposTimes '83/94:348; Harvest '83/29:155; Tabl '83/237:354–5; CanCathR My'84/2:32; Theol '84/87:72–4; BksRel Ap'85/13:7; JPsyTheol '85/13:217; SpirToday '85/37:363; TheolStud '85/46:756; Horiz '86/13:109–10; JPsyChry Sum'87/6:86–8)

Jung, Hesse, Harold: The Contributions of C. G. Jung, Hermann Hesse, and Preston Harold (Author of The Shining Stranger*) to a Spiritual Psychology,* by Winifred Babcock. New York, Harold Institute Book/Dodd, Mead & Co., 1983 (185 + xiii, incl. 7-p. index, 2-p. bibl., 10-p. ref. notes).

Developing her own synthesis, following the "creative synthesis" by Harold of Jung's findings and Hesse's influences, Babcock attempts to bring into closer focus religion-based psychology and psychology-based religion, whose theme is the search for Self and meaning in life. Her topics include, among others, the self (the authority-ego); the shadow (mystery of good and evil); the rebirth of consciousness in this life; the paradoxical necessity both to accept and reject life in this world; becoming an artist of life (the Ten Commandments as psychic guidelines to achieve psychic health); and transcending theology and psychology.

The Structure of Biblical Myths: The Ontogenesis of the Psyche, by Heinz Westman. Dallas: Spring Publications, 1983p*; Shaftesbury: Element Books, 1984 (447 + xxii, incl. 23-p. ref. notes, 40 illus., 5-p. preface by David Miller).

Based on nearly fifty years of analytical practice, this work by Westman presents a psyche-centered interpretation of the Bible as a source of themes which reveal the ontogenesis (life history) of the psyche, the essence of the individual experience of life. In discussing this unique development of each individual, he cites religious writing from the most ancient to the contemporary, as well as manifestations in political life and modern science, with frequent reference made to the Hebraic-Christian Bible. He declares that Biblical stories not only reveal the working of the human mind, but that they provide one with the satisfaction of one's essential need to experience "consciously" a meaning for one's own life.

(Bk.revs.: Chman Oc'84/198:18; Commonw '85/112:508; ExposTimes '85/96:253; JAmAcadRel '85/53:318–19; JAnPsy '85/30:105; Quad '85/18n2:93–4; UnionSemQR '85/40n1–2:106–7; HeythJ '86/27:71; JRelPsyRes '87/10:178–80; SFJInstLib '87/7n2:23–50)

Buddhism and Jungian Psychology, by J. Marvin Spiegelman and Mokusen Miyuki. Phoenix: Falcon Press, 1984; 1985p* (190, incl. 20 illus.).

Stimulated by Jung's appreciation of Eastern religion and thought, analysts Spiegelman and Miyuki (who is also a Zen priest) aim to integrate

Jungian psychology with Buddhism, providing insights that may integrate the "Other," and realizing the essential difficulty in the concept of the ego in Western and Eastern philosophies. They discuss East and West from the personal point of view; the Zen oxherding pictures; self-realization; and aspects of Buddhism and Jungian psychology.

(Bk.revs.: PsyPersp '86/17:259–61; JAnPsy '87/32:393–4; Harvest '88–89/34:183–4; PsyPersp '90/22:171–3)

Dreams and Spiritual Growth: A Christian Approach to Dreamwork, by Louis M. Savary, Patricia H. Berne, and Strephon Kaplan-Williams. New York and Ramsey, N.J.: Paulist Press, 1984p* (241, incl. 3-p. bibl.).

Applying the insights and research of depth psychology to the Judaeo-Christian dreamwork tradition, Savary, Berne, and Kaplan-Williams present a method for using dreams to connect a person to God, one's self, and the believing community. They offer more than thirty-five dreamwork tools and techniques, as well as a selected list of important Biblical dreams and visions. The section entitled "Relating to God" includes the topics of God's guidance through dreams; the continuing revelation; the disrepute of dreamwork in the Church; the rediscovery of dreamwork among contemporary Christians; and dreamwork and prayer. The section on relating to one's self includes the topics of welcoming the dream's perspective as a personal journey; dreamwork as destiny; dreamwork and the personality; and dreamwork as healing. In the section on the Christian community, they discuss dreams and the Holy Spirit; the spiritual director's perspective; the therapist's perspective; dreams and prophecy; and a theology of dreams and dreamwork.

(Bk.revs.: SisToday '84/56:246; CalvTheolJ '85/20:157–9; SpirToday '85/37:175; Chr-ScholR '86/15:77–8; TrinSemR '86/8:107; AsbSem '87/42:91–2)

Fritz Kunkel: Selected Writings, edited, with an introduction and commentary, by John A. Sanford. New York and Ramsey, N.J.: Paulist Press, 1984p* (410 + x, incl. 7-p. index, 5-p. bibl., 11 diagrams).

Concerned with illustrating the relevance of Kunkel's thought for today, Sanford bases his presentation on two of Kunkel's twenty books and compares Jung's theories to those of Kunkel, who perceived God's power working in his patients, himself, and the world situation. Sanford presents Kunkel's main thesis (from *In Search of Maturity*) that one lives either a creative life from the Self or a constricted life from the egocentric ego. He follows this with Kunkel's idea on the origin and nature of egocentricity (from *How Character Develops*). He then describes from parts of both books Kunkel's analysis of how one can find one's way creatively through the crisis when egocentric life patterns no longer work (including the shadow and negative life, self-education, idolatry, conscious growth, and practical aids). Sanford concludes with his own essay on Kunkel's work and on contemporary issues in psychology and religion (88 pp.).

(Bk.revs.: JPsyTheol '84/12:326–7; LibJ '84/109:497; CalvTheolJ '85/20:170–1; JAnPsy '85/30:217–19; JPastorCare '85/39:186–8; PsyPersp '85/16:233–5; RelStudR '85/11:383; TheolToday '85/42:150; LumenVitae '86/41:464; JPsyTheol '87/15:360)

The Illness That We Are: A Jungian Critique of Christianity, by John P. Dourley. Toronto: Inner City Books, 1984p* (Studies in Jungian Psychology by Jungian Analysts, 17) (121, incl. 5-p. index, 16-p. ref. notes, 5 illus.).

Dourley focuses on the need for the recovery of a revitalized Christian spirituality and theology. He cites Jung's appreciation of the psychospiritual potentialities inherent in the Christian myth, qualified by a perception of its shortcomings, and proceeds to examine that qualified perception in Jung's ambivalence toward Christianity. He explores "how the West was lost," surveying Jung's analysis of Western spiritual development from church fathers to the Middle Ages; scholasticism, mysticism and the alchemical tradition; Kant, Hegel and modern theology; and theopathology and Christopathology. He also discusses the topic of mandalic ("image of radical divine immanence in the individual psyche") versus holocaustic faith, ending with interpretations of pastoral psychology and the psychology of pastors, and of the Gnostic Christian and "Jung's call for a return to the Gnostic sense of God as an inner, directing presence."

(Bk.revs.: CanBkRAn '84:122; Choice '85/22:831; JAnPsy '85/30:329–31; JPsyTheol '85/13:217; RelStudR '85/11:40–1; StudRel '85/14:510–12; Epiph '86/6:82–90; TorJTheol '86/2:142–4; SFJInstLib '87/7n3:35–7)

Prayer and Temperament: Different Prayer Forms for Different Personality Types, by Chester P. Michael and Marie C. Norissey. Charlottesville, Va.: The Open Door, 1984p* (190, incl. 3-p. bibl., 6-p. gloss.).

Following a survey of the development of the theory of temperament, Michael and Norissey analyze how temperament has affected Christian spirituality and then proceed to interpret the relationships of prayer and spirituality with different personality types. They describe prayer forms as Benedictine, Ignatian, Augustinian, Franciscan, and Thomistic; and they explore the subject of using one's personal shadow and one's inferior function in prayer and consider the relationship of temperament to liturgical prayer. Included are prayer suggestions for each of the sixteen psychological types developed by Isabel Briggs Myers from Jung's original system.

The Voice Within: Love and Virtue in the Age of the Spirit, by Helen M. Luke. New York: Crossroad Publishing Co., 1984p (118 + x, incl. 3-p. bibl. notes).

Consisting of essays and reflections written over twenty years or more, Luke's book expresses some of the thoughts and images that have come from within (or from the unconscious, in Jung's terminology) and relates them to the outer voices in the world. She urges careful discrimination among the voices from within in order to distinguish the voice that comes from the ground of one's being. She first discusses the subjects of vow and doctrine in the New Age (the Spirit and the law; the marriage vow; religious vows of poverty, chastity, and obedience; and the mystery within). She then focuses on the subject of the subtitle, discussing courtesy and an interior hierarchy of values; the king and the principles of the heart; the joy of the fool; exchange as the way of conscious love; inner relationship and community in the *I Ching*; pride; suffering; and the Lord's prayer.

(Bk.revs.: Amer '85/152:417; Parab My'85/10:100–104)

Essays on Jung and the Study of Religion, edited by Luther H. Martin and James Goss. Lanham, Md., New York, and London: University Press of America, 1985 +p (205 pp.).

Consisting of papers delivered between 1979 and 1981 at the annual meetings of the American Academy of Religion's consultation on Jungian psychology and the study of religion, this collection edited by Martin and Goss contains twelve essays, including two by Martin (on Jung as a Gnostic and Jung and the history of religion) and one by Goss (on eschatology, autonomy, and individuation). Essays by Jungian analysts include a study on differences between Jung and Hillman (James Hall); a Jungian approach to the Jodoshinshu concept of the "wicked" (Mokusen Miyuki), and an essay on Jung and the study of religion (Ann Belford Ulanov). Other essays are on Ireland, land of eternal youth (Mary Brenneman and Walter Brenneman); Jung as a Christian or post-Christian psychologist (Peter Homans); the descent to the underworld in Jung and Hillman (David Miller); the anima in religious studies (Thomas Moore); Jung and the phenomenology of religion (William Paden); and Jung on scripture and hermeneutics (Wayne Rollins).

(Bk.revs.: JSciStudRel '86/25:525–6; RelStudR '86/12:134; JAnPsy '87/32:298–300; JRel '88/68:184–5)

Jung and Eastern Thought, by Harold G. Coward. Albany: State U. of New York Press, 1985* +p* (SUNY Series in Transpersonal and Humanistic Psychology) (218 + xv, incl. 4-p. index, 22-p. annotated bibl., 5-p. intro. by Joseph L. Henderson).

Seeking to assess the overall impact of Eastern thought on Jung's life and ideas, Coward examines the influences that Jung found useful and those he drew back from. He discusses Jung's encounter with yoga and the point at which Jung drew the line in his acceptance of yoga; and he includes an analysis of Jung's criticism of yoga spirituality by John Borelli. The second half of the book deals with conceptual comparisons of Jung and Indian thought, which consists of essays by Coward on Jung and karma and kundalini, and on mysticism in the psychology of Jung and the yoga of Patanjali. This is followed by essays by J. F. T. Jordens on a comparison of Jung's concepts of the collective unconscious and spirit (Self) with key concepts of prakriti (potential matter) and purusha (spirit) of Patanjali, and on a comparison of the concepts of libido and consciousness with prana (life breath) and prajna (supreme knowledge, or wisdom). Also included is an annotated bibliography by Borelli on C. G. Jung and Eastern religious traditions.

(Bk.revs.: Choice '85/23:589; JAmAcadRel '86/54:573–4; JTranspPsy '86/18:84–5; Rel-StudR '86/12:43; StudRel '86/15:251–3; BkRDig '87:396; JAnPsy '87/32:300–1; JPsy-Chry Sum'87/6:86–8)

Jung's Treatment of Christianity: The Psychotherapy of a Religious Tradition, by Murray Stein. Wilmette, Ill.: Chiron Publications, 1985*; 1986p* (208 + vii, incl. 8-p. index, 5-p. bibl.).

Stein examines Jung's writings on Christianity from the point of view of a psychotherapeutic relationship. He looks at Jung's personal life and psychological thought, particularly in the last twenty years of Jung's active intellectual life, and his strong urge to heal Christianity. Beginning with an interpretation of Jung as an empirical scientist, hermeneutical revitalist, doctor of souls, and modern man, Stein presents Jung's method of psychotherapeutic treatment (including anamnesis and reconstruction, the role of interpretation, and transference/countertransference process). He analyzes Jung's interpretation of Christianity's God symbol, the mass, Christian history and its repressions and central symbols, and the countertransference of *Answer to Job.* He concludes with the therapist's vision of Christianity's future wholeness.

(Bk.revs.: RelHum '85/19:500; ChrCen '86/103:148–9; JAnPsy '86/31:183–4; TheolStud '86/47:355–6; JRel '87/67:597–8; PsyanQ '87/86:697–9; JPsyChry Spr'88/7:92–3; Zygon Jn'88/23:209; ContemPsy '89/34:99)

Mid-Life Directions: Praying and Playing, Sources of New Dynamism, by Anne Brennan and Janice Brewi. New York and Ramsey, N.J.: Paulist Press, 1985p* (186 + vi, incl. 16-p. bibl.).

In their midlife workshops, seminars, and retreats, Brennan and Brewi combine Jung's psychological perspective with the meaning of Christian spiritual tradition. Citing the Christian spiritual concept of "change and

become like little children," they relate play to the individuation process and to personal spirituality. They present individuation as a life goal and discuss the unconscious and the shadow in Jung's theory of the personality and then relate the unconscious and the shadow to prayer in the second half of life.
(Bk.revs.: SisToday N'85/57:178; Amer '86/155:126–7; HumDev Spr'86/7:46; LivLight '86/22:183; StAnth '86/93:50; SpirLife '86/32:52–3)

Chaos or Creation: Spirituality in Mid-life, by L. Patrick Carroll and Katherine Marie Dyckman. New York and Mahwah, N.J.: Paulist Press, 1986p* (169 + iv, incl. 8-p. bibl.).

Directing their book to religious people searching in the middle of their lives for meaning, Carroll and Dyckman see the religious and psychological journeys as a single path. Using Jung's point of view as the overarching model of the midlife challenge, they discuss Erik Erikson's developmental theory, cautions by Carol Gilligan, Sanford's and Kunkel's analyses of egocentricity, and Daniel Levinson's adaptations for men and women. They describe the midlife crisis as a religious experience, referring especially to James Fowler's stages of faith, and the "pieces of brokenness" (burnout, depression, loneliness, intimacy, and sexuality) one can feel in a heightened way at that time. They conclude with a discussion of prayer at midlife and sharing one's brokenness with a meditation on Jesus and the cross.
(Bk.revs.: LibJ 10c'86/111:1026; Church '87/3:56; JPsyChry Fall'87/6:74–5; Marriage Oc'87/69:24; SisToday '87/58:621; SpirLife '87/33:119; RforRel '88/47:150–1)

Christianity as Psychology: The Healing Power of the Christian Message, by Morton T. Kelsey. Minneapolis: Augsburg Publishing House, 1986p* (143, incl. 5-p. index, 5-p. bibl., 6-p. ref. notes, 4 illus.).

Believing that a fully lived Christian "drama" is a profound psychological as well as religious experience, Kelsey argues that Christian psychology can deal with emotional problems such as feelings of meaninglessness and low-grade depression. He believes there is a place for God in psychology and examines the healing emphasis in the Christian tradition, looking at the major schools of psychological thought (and giving special attention to Jung) to see how different they are in their ideas about human beings and the ways to treat them. He concludes by pointing out the implications of Christian life, practice, and belief for psychologists.
(Bk.revs.: JPsyTheol '87/15:82; LumenVitae '87/42:457; LuthTheolJ '87/21:101–2; Rel-StudR '87/13:148; StLukeJTh '87/30:287–8; JPastorCare '88/42:65–6; ReformR '88/42:65–6)

Jung's Psychology and Tibetan Buddhism: Western and Eastern Paths to the Heart, by Radmila Moacanin. London: Wisdom Publications, 1986p* (128

+ xi, incl. 7-p. index, 11-p. ref. notes, 3 illus., 3-p. gloss. of Buddhist and Jungian terms).

Gently urged by the Tibetan Buddhist master Lama Thubten Yeshe to give a talk on Jung's psychology and its relation to Tibetan Buddhism, Moacanin pursued her interest to learn and experience more of the two traditions, and this book is the result. With the purpose of making a bridge between some aspects of Eastern and Western thought, particularly their philosophical and spiritual traditions and their psychological and ethical systems, she presents similarities and differences between Jung's psychology and Tantric Buddhism that are most directly concerned with the process of growth of consciousness and spiritual transformation, issues that preoccupied Jung throughout his life. Among other topics she examines the union of opposites; the middle way and the Madhanamika philosophy; ego and non-ego; suffering and methods of healing; the redemption of God; Jung's views of Eastern traditions; and ethical issues.
(Bk.rev.: Harvest '88–89/34:183–4)

The Mind of the Bible-Believer, by Edmund D. Cohen. Buffalo: Prometheus Books, 1986*; 1988p* (423 + v, incl. 15-p. indexes).

Drawing upon his experience of teaching advanced courses in social psychology, theories of personality, and the history of psychology, Cohen presents his major thesis that the Bible is a psychological document whose claimed didactic content (so long and so bitterly debated) is incidental to the document's psychological purpose. His contention that the Bible is a most successful manipulation leads to a sorting out of the psychological understanding that went into its making, revealing his concern about Evangelical mind-control. He explores the topics of psychological premises and brainwashing; Freud; Jung; the Bible view of human nature; the Evangelical mind-control system; mental-health implications; religion in politics; scapegoating; and the end of the world.
(Bk.revs.: Choice '87/24:1085; JPsyChr Sum'87/6:93; JPsyTheol '88/16:388–9)

No Other Light: Points of Convergence in Psychology and Spirituality, by Mary Wolff-Salin. New York: Crossroad Publishing Co., 1986; 1989p* (234 + xi, incl. 16-p. ref. notes, 3-p. foreword by Sebastian Moore, O.S.B.).

In reflecting on the convergence of the disciplines of depth psychology and spirituality, Wolff-Salin speaks much more, though not exclusively, of the West than of the East, more of Christianity than of other faiths, and more of Jung than of Freud. She states that perhaps psychology (notably, though not exclusively, that of Jung) can reveal to the Judeo-Christian world the

other half of its psyche or soul. She discusses the beginning of spiritual life and psychological growth; the structure of the human psyche; shadow; conflict; persona, ego, and self; faces of the animus and anima; solitude, discretion, and virtue; projection; the objectivity of the psyche; listening, silence, and obedience; spiritual guides and therapists; memory; peace; and the sacred marriage. Appended is an article on Benedictine humility in the light of Jungian thought and an essay on reflections on Jung's *Answer to Job*.
(Bk.revs.: Choice '86/24:644; LibJ '86/111:124; BkRDig '87:2021; TheolStud '87/48:796–7)

Picturing God, by Ann Belford Ulanov. Cambridge, Mass.: Cowley Publications, 1986p* (198, incl. 14-p. ref. notes).

Convinced that the worlds of depth psychology and religion lie close together and "must endlessly seek to learn from each other," Ulanov presents these essays that reflect a bridge between the unknown territories of the self and the unknowable provinces of God. She emphasizes that one's inability to cross over the gap between one's images of God and God's reality is met by the miracle of God crossing over to one's self. The twelve essays, written between 1974 and 1985, deal with the topics of the Christian fear of the psyche; ministry of the mentally ill; the two strangers (outer and inner life); need, wishes, and transcendence; aging; dreams and the paradoxes of the spirit; prayer; religious experience in pastoral counseling; the disguises of the good; the psychological reality of the demonic; heaven and hell; and picturing God.
(Bk.revs.: AnglTheolR '87/69:311–13; Quad '88/21n1:89–91; CrossCurr '89/39:114)

St. John of the Cross and Dr. C. G. Jung: Christian Mysticism in the Light of Jungian Psychology, by James Arraj. Chiloquin, Ore.: Tools for Inner Growth, 1986p* (199, incl. 3-p. index, 10-p. bibl., 9-p. ref. notes).

Arraj explores the challenges of theological misgivings about the compatibility of Jung's psychology with Christian belief, the misinterpretation of St. John's doctrine of contemplation, and the need to clarify the relationship between contemplation and Jung's process of individuation. Following an analysis of the relationship between Jung's psychology and Christian faith, he discusses the dawn of contemplation (St. John's sixteenth-century revolution of mystical consciousness as the transition from meditation to infused contemplation) and then throws a "psychological light" on John of the Cross and the life of prayer (a typological portrait of St. John; psychic energy and contemplation; and beginners and contemplatives).
(Bk.rev.: Choice '87/24:156)

Three Faces of God: Traces of the Trinity in Literature and Life, by David Miller. Philadelphia: Fortress Press, 1986p* (164 + x, incl. 6-p. index, 24-p. ref. notes, 13 illus.).

In his concern to recover the peculiar power of traditional religious images, Miller presents a "re-visioning" of a trinitarian theology of today that requires religion to relearn its own sacred truths from secular culture. He first explores the recovery of images which lie dormant in the theological ideas of the Trinity and the discovery of the likenesses of such images to psychological, everyday life, discussing the Trinity in terms of modern depth psychology (Freud and Jung). He then "presses" the trinitarian image backward and downward into the depths of mythic imagination, "contemplating" the trinity in ancient myth; neoplatonic, Gnostic, and alchemical theologies; and in contemporary philosophy and letters. He concludes by examining "loving by triangulation," noting the existence of images of the trinitarian idea in modern secular literature.

(Bk.revs.: BksRel S'86/14:9–10; ChrCen '86/103:817–18; AnglTheolR '87/69:197–8; JAmAcadRel '87/55:407–8; RelStudR '87/13:159; JRel '88/68:124–5; RelStudR '88/14:543; BkRDig '88:1179–80)

Hinduism and Jungian Psychology, by J. Marvin Spiegelman and Arwind U. Vasavada. Phoenix: Falcon Press, 1987p* (207 + vii, incl. 13 illus.).

In this collection, each author provides a perspective on India and Jungian psychology from a personal point of view. Spiegelman's contributions consist of a 40-page commentary on kundalini yoga (using his own views as well as Jung's) and a fictional tale of kundalini ("Maya, the Yogini," taken from his book *The Tree*). Contributions by Vasavada consist of nine short essays (the yogic basis of psychoanalysis; a comparison of the process of individuation and of self-realization; alchemy and catatonic depression; a reflection on Jung's autobiography; the philosophical roots of the psychotherapies of the West; the unconscious and the myth of the Divine Mother; Dr. Jung: a psychologist or a guru?; fee-less practice and "soul work"; and meeting Jung) followed by a two-page letter from Jung to Vasavada.

Jung's Challenge to Contemporary Religion, edited by Murray Stein and Robert Moore. Wilmette, Ill.: Chiron Publications, 1987p* (190 + vi, incl. endchapter ref. notes).

Stein and Moore present eleven papers from a 1985 conference sponsored by the Jung Institute of Chicago. Papers by Jungian analysts are on Jung's green Christ vision as a healing symbol for Christianity (Stein); ritual process, initiation, and contemporary religion (Moore); patriarchy in transformation from Judaic, Christian, and clinical perspectives (Nathan Schwartz-Salant); Jung's Gnosticism and contemporary gnosis (June Singer); and Jung and the archetype of death and rebirth (David Dalrymple). Other contributions are on the church as crucible for transformation (William Dols); Jung's critique of the Christian notions of good and evil (Carrin Dunne); the female self in the image of God (Joan Engelsman); womansoul as a feminine correction to Christian imagery (Julia Jewett); the anti-Christianism of depth psychology (David Miller); and Jung's challenge to Biblical hermenutics (Wayne Rollins).

Love, Celibacy and the Inner Marriage, by John P. Dourley. Toronto: Inner City Books, 1987p* (Studies in Jungian Psychology by Jungian Analysts, 29) (122, incl. 4-p. index, 13-p. ref. notes, 2 illus.).

Dourley takes the title of this book from the second essay on Jung and Mechthilde of Magdeburg, a medieval mystic who exemplifies the inner marriage of the ego and the inner contrasexual element. Preceding that essay he examines Jung and the coincidence of opposites in God, the universe, and the individual. His other topics include an examination of Jung's understanding of mysticism from psychological, theological, and philosophical perspectives; Jung and Tillich reconsidered and the correlation of psychic with religious experience; Jung's impact on theology and religious studies; and Jung's thoughts on the religious nature of the psyche.

(Bk.revs.: Harvest '88–89/34:180–2; PsyPersp '88/19:350–3)

The Strange Trial of Mr. Hyde: A New Look at the Nature of Human Evil, by John A. Sanford. San Francisco: Harper & Row, 1987* (182, incl. 4-p. subject index, 1-p. Scripture index).

In presenting a new look at the nature of human evil, Sanford employs a fantasy of a court trial, with fictional characters of his own invention, to see that justice is done to Edward Hyde, who is charged with being evil. The scenario involves the testimony of a panel of experts in human affairs and behavior from the viewpoints of Jungian psychology, Christianity, the average person, and feminism. This is followed by Sanford's commentary on the trial, in which he goes into the psychological and philosophical background on the origin of evil and Jung's views of the problem of evil, with contrasting views by Kunkel and others, including "why the shadow isn't the devil." Sanford's definition of evil as whatever opposes the creative goals and energies of the Self places it as a part of the archetype of choice. Appended is a 16-page synopsis of Stevenson's story, *The Strange Case of Dr. Jekyll and Mr. Hyde*, taken from Sanford's 1981 book on evil.

(Bk.revs.:-JPsyTheol '87/15:360–3; KirkR '87/55:361; PsyPesp '88/19:161–4; Quad '88/ 21n1:91–3; RefResBkN Ap'88/3:2)

WomanChrist: A New Vision of Feminist Spirituality, by Christin Lore Weber. San Francisco: Perennial Library/Harper & Row, 1987p* (178 + xi, incl. 3- p. ref. notes).

In attemtping to "re-vision" and reconstruct a Christian spirituality of women's mysteries and to wed Christian archetypes with other natural energies constellated in her psychic depths, Weber records her own spiritual searching for connections which she characterizes as "Christ in woman and woman in Christ." Her journey involves an idyllic and contemplative childhood with love for the mystery of nature, the intricacies of a theological education, the intimacy of marriage, encounters as a spiritual director and pastoral counselor, and the "sacred metamorphosis" of widowhood. She characterizes her experience as womanbody, womansoul, womanpower, and womanwisdom.

(Bk.revs.: Bklist '87/84:348; Horiz '88/15:419–20)

Body Metaphors: Releasing God-Feminine in Us All, by Genia Pauli Haddon. N.Y.: Crossroad Publishing Co., 1988* (250 + xvii, incl. 10-p. index, 19-p. ref. notes, 49 illus.).

Taking the theme of a new image of God-Feminine (differentiating it from the term "Goddess" in order to emphasize its immediate roots within the God-religion of the Christian or Jewish faith), Haddon proposes a new paradigm of masculinity and femininity that discredits stereotypical role definitions by regrounding in body differences. She agrees with Jung's sensitive respect for the spiritual dimension of human experience and attitude toward the psyche, but she differs from his definitions of masculinity and femininity in the places where the message from the body differs. She designates God-masculine and God-feminine as naming the single God from different perspectives, considering the absolute Deity as mysterious and unknowable.

(Bk.revs.: Bklist '88/84:1204; LibJ 1Mr '88/113:71)

Carl Jung and Christian Spirituality, edited by Robert L. Moore. New York and Mahwah, N.J.: Paulist Press, 1988p* (Jungian Psychoanalysis and Contemporary Spirituality, vol. 1) (252 + xii, incl. end-chapter ref. notes).

Moore offers a collection of twelve essays by various authors to support the growing interest in the implications of Jungian psychology for the theory and practice of spirituality and spiritual direction. Consisting mainly of articles published originally in journals, they include four by Jungian analysts: the cross as an archetypal symbol (M. Esther Harding); the Self as other (Ann Ulanov); problem of evil in Christianity and analytical psychology (John Sanford); and persona and shadow: a Jungian view of human duality (Thayer Greene). Other selections are on Jungian psychology and religious experience (Eugene Bianchi); Jungian types and forms of prayer (Thomas Clarke); Jungian psychology and Christian spirituality (Robert Doran); rediscovering the priesthood through the unconscious (Morton Kelsey); Jung and scripture (Diarmuid McGann); Jungian typology and Christian spirituality (Robert Repicky); psychologically living symbolism and liturgy (Ernest Skublics); and the archetypes as a new way of holiness (Patrick Vandermeersch).

(Bk.revs.: Choice '88/26:662; LibJ 1Ap'88/113:91; BkRDig S'89:32)

Catholicism and Jungian Psychology, edited by J. Marvin Spiegelman. Phoenix: Falcon Press, 1988p* (270, incl. end-chapter ref. notes).

Of the twenty-one essays collected here, nine are written by Jungian analysts. These include essays on Jungian psychology and Catholicism in our nuclear age (Gerd Max Cryns); Jung and Catholicism (John Dourley); the treatment of Catholic patients (Vera von der Heydt); on being Catholic and being Jungian (Russell Holmes); Hermes: a guide to the role of priest (Thomas Lavin); Catholicism and Jungian psychology (Terence McBride); Jung and Catholicism (Roger Radloff); a new constellation of the feminine (Mokusen Miyuki); and psychotherapists and the clergy (Spiegelman).

(Bk.rev.: Harvest '89–90/35:234–6)

Celebrate Mid-Life: Jungian Archetypes and Mid-Life Spirituality, by Janice Brewi and Anne Brennan. New York: Crossroad Publishing Co., 1988*; 1989p* (296 + xii, incl. 30-p. bibl.).

Taking as a major thesis Jung's archetypal perspective on human development and focusing on midlife experiences taken from their numerous workshops and retreats, Brewi and Brennan celebrate midlife experience as an essential gift of the human journey. They discuss four archetypal experiences, namely, midlife itself (unconscious elements of the human psyche; Jesus and the archetypes; midlife spirituality; reflective exercises); the shadow (as archetypal friend or foe; owning one's shadow; integrating shadow manifestations; Jesus and the shadow and new life); the inner child (dreams and transformation; healing the inner child; child and persona); and emerging wisdom.

(Bk.revs.: LibJ 1Ap'88/113:90; SpirLife '88/34:186; StAnth Jy'88/96:50; SisToday Ag-S'88/60:50)

The Dove in the Stone: Finding the Sacred in the Commonplace, by Alice O. Howell. Wheaton, Ill., Madras, and London: Quest Books/Theosophical Publishing House, 1988p* (199 + xiv, incl. 5-p. bibl., 25 illus., 4-p. intro. by Christopher Bamford).

Returning to the "tiny, precious" island of Iona in the Hebrides for the eleventh time, Howell savors the sacred Celtic isle with reminiscences of her past and the joys of the present. She believes that there is an "inner beauty in each of us hungering to be matched in outer experience." She integrates her account of exploring the rocky island with symbolic musings of life's meanings in which she interprets symbology of stones, trees, crosses, wands, serpents, and flowers. Among her symbolic meanings are the Philosopher's Stone (represented in the small, black, pyramidal stone which she found and retained from the first visit), the Tree of Life, Celtic crosses, a magic wand to awaken, the wise serpent, the lotus in the East and the rose in the West as feminine symbols, and the dove as the connection between Holy Wisdom (Sophia) and the Holy Ghost. Illustrated throughout with legends, mythology, poetry, and Howell's own insights as a Jungian astrologer and teacher, the book focuses on divine, universal Sophia ("hidden in symbols of stone, representing manifest earth, and the serpents of the spinal energy, and the dove pointing to the wings of higher consciousness, a consciousness uniting opposites").

The Gentle Art of Spiritual Guidance, by John R. Yungblut. Amity, N.Y.: Amity House, 1988p* (148 + xi, incl. 2-p. ref. notes).

Addressing himself primarily to the individual with an interest in the vocation of spiritual guidance as well as to the seeker on the inward journey to the self, Yungblut interprets spiritual guidance as the art of discerning "that of God" in another and helping that person be true to the divine spark. He takes into account Jung's ideas of the psyche, and the vision of continuing creation through evolution as discerned by Teilhard de Chardin. Within the context of Christ-consciousness, individuation, and wholeness, he discusses the relationship between sexuality and spirituality, distinctions between contemporary psychotherapy and spiritual guidance, cultivating the gift for spiritual guidance, disciplines of devotion for the spiritual guide, the dynamics of the counseling session, and John the Apostle as spiritual guide par excellence.

Jung and the Quaker Way, by Jack H. Wallis. London: Quaker Home Service, 1988p* (216, incl. 4-p. general index, 3-p. index to Jung quotations, 4-p. bibl., 9-p. ref. notes).

Concerned with aspects of Jung's work and teaching that are most relevant to Quaker faith and practice as well as the relevance of Quaker faith and practice for depth psychology, Wallis expresses the conviction that they can illuminate and enrich each other by their similarities and their differences. He begins by saying that Quaker thought and worship and Jung's teachings converge at a time of religious uncertainty, spiritual exploration, and mistrust of authority; and he follows with discussions on such topics as faith and doubt; perfection and growth toward wholeness; balance and stability; images of God and Jesus; personality and persona; and maleness and femaleness. He ends with an analysis of the Quaker response to Jung's ideas on harmonizing pairs of opposites, the tension between personal vocation and the collective unconscious, and symbols of transcendence.
(Bk.rev.: FriendsJ N'88/34:42–3)

Jung's Three Theories of Religious Experience, by J. Harley Chapman. Lewiston, N.Y. and Queenstown, Ontario: Edwin Mellen Press, 1988* (Studies in the Psychology of Religion, vol. 3) (178 + ix, incl. 11-p. index, 7-p. bibl., end-chapter ref. notes).

In explaining rather than interpreting the pervasive and important human phenomenon of religious experience, Chapman explores Jung's ideas and claims that Jung has not one but three different but related theories, none of which he ever explicitly or completely spelled out. Jointly taking into consideration varying explanatory intent, shifts in the meaning of key terms, and the employment of different models, he presents the three theories as scientific-psychological, phenomenological-mythological, and metaphysical-theological. He characterizes the models of the human psyche as a "stream" of vital energy (libido), a "quest" for wholeness, and a "creature" or "splinter" of the infinite deity.
(Bk.rev.: Choice '89/26:1534 +)

Lady of the Beasts: Ancient Images of the Goddess and Her Sacred Animals, by Buffie Johnson. San Francisco: Harper & Row, 1988*; 1990p (386 + xii, incl. 7-p. index, 6-p. bibl., 12-p. ref. notes, 385 illus.).

Johnson's aim is to recapture a nonverbal manner of comprehending the world through the imagery of the Great Goddess, abundantly illustrated in this volume. Although archetypal images may be "translated" into words, they are understood only in the deep recesses of the psyche. She associates the Great Mother with animal archetypes, symbols of fertility and death from prehistory, which define her nature and exemplify her power, acting in myths as they do in fairy tales and dreams as guides and soul carriers. Relying on symbolism and the connections drawn between one idea or object

and another, she presents thirteen sacred animals (symbolizing death and rebirth in matrifocal cultures), namely, bird, lion, dog, serpent, butterfly, ewe and ram, spider, deer, fish, pig, cow and bull, scorpion, and bear.
(Bk.revs.: NewDirWom Jy'89/18:21; NYTimesBkR 5F'89/94:22)

The Wisdom of the Psyche, by Ann Belford Ulanov. Cambridge, Mass.: Cowley Publications, 1988p* (144, incl. 36-p. end-chapter ref. notes).

Consisting of four lectures given in 1985 at the Protestant Episcopal Seminary in Alexandria, Virginia, Ulanov's book addresses the ministry of the ego, the "Devil's trick," women's wiles, and the wisdom of the psyche. She interprets the ministry of the ego as the responsibility to house what one has been given to be and to give it back to the giver, to be the portal for the larger self coming into the world. She pictures the Devil's trick as capturing one in the gap between what one yearns toward as the ideal (image of God) and what actually confronts one as reality, admitting the evil that belongs to one's self and claiming the good that is given. She presents the wiliness of women as prudent, practical wisdom that builds up the good and seeks connections, and she concludes with an examination of how and where the psyche establishes its place in the religious scheme of things.
(Bk.revs.: Bklist '88/85:103; LibJ 1S'88/113:175; Amer '89/160:403–4; ExposTimes '89/ 100:397–8; Quad '89/22n2:118–19 + 121; '90/23n1:119–121; RelIntell '89/6:243–5)

Behold Woman: A Jungian Approach to Feminist Theology, by Carrin Dunne. Wilmette, Ill.: Chiron Publications, 1989p* (Chiron Monograph Series, vol. II) (97 + xv, incl. 7-p. index, 5-p. ref. notes, 6 illus.).

Beginning with her own image of "woman," which came in a dream while she was pondering a response to Jung's critique of the Christian notions of good and evil for a Jungian conference, Dunne amplifies the archetypal dream image in her effort to distinguish between woman as idea and real women, between woman's soul and woman as soul, and between the heavenly woman (the feminine aspect of God) and the earthly woman (her fallenness). The first, and longest, chapter is on whether women have souls, in which she discusses five approaches to an image of wounding ("original sin"). Chapter 2 deals with Jung's theory of the contrasexual character of the psyche, while the following chapter focuses on the struggle between male and female religion from the point of view of the soul. Her interpretations involve the legends of Innana and Gilgamesh, Lilith and Adam, Semele and Zeus, Psyche and Eros, and Beauty and Beast, among others.

A Blue Fire: Selected Writings, by James Hillman; introduced and edited by Thomas Moore in collaboration with James Hillman. New York: Harper &

Row, 1989* (323 + x, incl. 9-p. index, 8-p. bibl., 11-p. prologue by Thomas Moore).

Consisting of excerpts from fifteen books and pamphlets and forty-one articles by Hillman, this collection is arranged in three parts: Soul, World, and Eros. The topics include the poetic basis of mind; many gods, many persons; imaginal practice: greeting the angel; therapy: fictions and epiphanies; anima mundi; the salt of soul, the sulfur of spirit; pathologizing: the wound and the eye; psychoanalysis in the street; mythology as family; dreams and the blood soul; love's torturous enchantments; and the divine face of things. Moore introduces each of the chapters with brief commentary. He discusses in the prologue Hillman's significance as an "artist of psychology" who challenges one all along the way to rethink, to "re-vision," and to reimagine. The largest number of excerpts are from Hillman's *Re-Visioning Psychology* (1975).

(Bk.revs.: Bklist '89/86:118; LibJ 1Oc'89/114:109; PubW 28Jy'89/236:213)

God Is a Trauma: Vicarious Religion and Soul-Making, by Greg Mogenson. Dallas: Spring Publications, 1989p* (167 + vii, incl. 9-p. ref. notes).

Focusing on the religious dimension of the psychology of traumatic events, Mogenson, like Jung, refers to God as the God-image or God-complex that stirs within the soul, rather than to theology's soul-transcending God. He distinguishes between the traumatized soul which seeks solace through conversion, giving itself over to spirit and ceasing to be psychological, and the traumatized soul that mediates itself by making differences between itself and everything that happens. He defines therapy of the psyche as the doctoring of the soul's capacity to make differences between itself and matter and between itself and spirit, since soul is the realm between matter and spirit. In pursuing the theme of the impact on the soul of monotheistic theology's "no-name God," he states that psychotherapy heals the soul by insisting that it experience its afflictions within the dimensions of the images in which the afflictions reside.

Hells and Holy Ghosts: A Theopoetics of Christian Belief, by David L. Miller. Nashville, Tenn.: Abingdon Press, 1989p* (224, incl. 4-p. index of historical and mythological names, 26-p. ref. notes).

Miller reflects on Christian beliefs in the descent of Christ into Hell and resurrection of the dead, and particularly on the use of the term "ghost" to refer both to divinity (Holy Ghost) and to the motif of life after death. He makes his own "descent" into the underworld of Christianity's creedal beliefs and observes "modern resurrections of the dead" in literature and life.

Following an introduction on "not giving up the ghost," he discusses descents into history and imagination; laughter; archetypal sadomasochism; the hells of modern literature; holy ghosts; the death of ghosts; ghosts in language; ghosts of folklore; ghosts of Scripture; ghosts of depth psychology; and ghosts of modern literature.

Jung and the Lost Gospels: Insights into the Dead Sea Scrolls and the Nag Hammadi Library, by Stephan A. Hoeller. Wheaton, Ill.: Quest Books/ Theosophical Publishing House, 1989* +p* (268 + xix, incl. 14-p. index, 8-p. ref. notes, 10 illus., 7-p. foreword by June Singer).

Calling Jung the greatest of modern Gnostics, Hoeller endeavors to elucidate the Lost Gospels in psychological terms, remarking that they are books about Gnosis, that is, about the true individuation of the human psyche. His evaluation of certain aspects of the Dead Sea Scrolls of Qumran has led to the view that Jewish Essenes and Christian Gnostics were exponents of the same stream of spirituality and that the discovery of their long-lost scriptures portends well for the revival of a similar spirituality today. Following a prologue on the loss and recovery of Western psychological spirituality, he discusses the "other tradition," including the people of the scrolls, the Essene Messiah and the Gnostic Christ, feminine wisdom, and the odyssey of Gnosis; after which he interprets the myths of Gnosticism and analyzes the "other gospels": the Gospel of Thomas, the Gospel of Philip, the Gospel of Truth, and the Gospel of the Egyptians).

(Bk.rev.: WCoastRBks '89/15:30)

Archetypal Process: Self and Divine in Whitehead, Jung, and Hillman, edited by David Ray Griffin. Evanston, Ill.: Northwestern U. Press, 1989* +p* (290 + x, incl. 6-p. index, 16-p. ref. notes).

These essays, from a conference held at Claremont University in 1983, focus on bringing process theology into dialogue with the work of Jung and James Hillman, who has introduced modifications into Jung's thought. Following Griffin's introduction on archetypal psychology and process philosophy as complementary "postmodern" movements are five essays with accompanying responses, replies to responses, and Hillman's post-conference responses to the papers. Other than Hillman's own essay entitled "Back to Beyond: On Cosmology," the only other Jungian contribution is Robert Moore's response to "Psychocosmetics and the Underworld Connection" by Catherine Keller. Two other authors, whose work appears in this annotated bibliography, are James Heisig (who writes on the mystique of the nonrational) and Gerald Slusser (on Jung and Whitehead and the necessity of symbol and myth). Griffin concludes with an essay on a metaphysical psychology to "un-Locke" our ailing world.

C. G. *Jung's Psychology of Religion and Synchronicity*, by Robert Aziz. Albany: State U. of New York Press, 1990 +p (Transpersonal and Humanistic Psychology Series) (269 + ix, incl. 7-p. index, 10-p. bibl., 29-p. ref. notes).

In exploring the significant role that synchronistic phenomena played in the life and work of Jung, Aziz presents considerable case material in terms of Jung's psychology of religion and his concept of individuation. He first discusses Jung's psychology of religion in relation to his intrapsychic model. This is followed by a systematic study of synchronistic experiences and an analysis of the psyche as microcosm, in which he examines the development of Freud's thinking on telepathy and points of conflict and agreement between Freud and Jung. He also discusses the type of synchronistic experience found in traditional Chinese philosophy and offers a synchronistic model of Jung's psychology of religion as a synthesis of both the intrapsychic and synchronistic models.

The Goddess Mother of the Trinity, by John P. Dourley. Lewiston, N.Y.: Edwin Mellen Press, 1990.

Jung's Quest for Wholeness: A Religious and Historical Perspective, by Curtis D. Smith. Albany: State U. of New York Press, 1990 +p (192pp.).

Jung and Christianity in Dialogue: Faith, Feminism, and Hermeneutics, edited by Robert L. Moore and Daniel Meckel. New York and Mahwah, N.J.: Paulist Press, 1990p (265 + ix).

Liberating the Heart: Spirituality and Jungian Psychology, by Lawrence W. Jaffe. Toronto: Inner City Books, 1990p (Studies in Jungian Psychology by Jungian Analysts, 42) (175, incl. 5-p. index, 5-p. bibl.).

Jaffe seeks to convey Jung's healing message to those who have lost their sense of meaning in life. He pursues the central theme of individuation as an expression of the psychological dispensation in which each person is bound to God who is incarnating in each individual. This is in contrast to the Jewish dispensation (bound to a covenant) and to the Christian dispensation (bound as His child in God-man Christ). He illustrates his thoughts with material drawn from Jung's psychology, religion, literature, and his own experiences as a Jungian analyst. He discusses individuation; the reality of the psyche; the union of science and religion in Jung's psychology; Christ as model for individuation; the psychological law of compensation; the need for meaning in life; Jung and mechanistic science; Jewishness and individuation; the Sabbath; the feminine in the Godhead; and women and men in the psychological dispensation.

Seeing Through the Visible World: Jung, Gnosis, and Chaos, by June Singer. San Francisco: Harper & Row, 1990 (230 + xxv, incl. 5-p. index, 4-p. bibl.).

Singer "touches the mysteries" of the invisible world and its apparent chaos by examining the frontiers of science, questions posed by images of the apocalypse and messianism, and the psychology of the unconscious. She also deals with the means of bringing knowledge of the invisible world to the world of contemporary problems from the perspective of individual experience.

Sufism and Jungian Psychology, by J. Marvin Spiegelman and Pir Vilayat Inayat Khan. Las Vegas: Falcon Press, 1990p.

10 Creativity and Jung's Psychology

The subject of creativity and Jung's psychology relates mainly to the creative power of the unconscious as the very source of the creative impulse, whose forms or patterns reflect a tremendous, wordless kind of intuition striving for expression in art or literature that may range from the ineffably sublime to the perversely grotesque. Jung distinguishes between literary or artistic works that spring wholly from the author's or artist's intention to produce a particular result, which he labels the psychological mode of artistic creation, and those works that positively force themselves upon the creator who is overwhelmed by a flood of thoughts and images which he or she never intended to create, which he labels the visionary mode of artistic creation. He observes that the secret of creativeness is a transcendent problem that the psychologist cannot answer but can only describe and that the creative urge which finds its clearest expression is irrational, rooted in the immensity of the unconscious.

More than ninety books are in this subject category, including eighteen that are cross-referenced from other subjects. More than one-half of these have been published since 1980.

Jung: *The Spirit in Man, Art, and Literature* [p. 253]
Allan: *Inscapes of the Child's World* (See chapter 11, "Jungian Analysis") [p. 343]
Aronson: *Psyche and Symbol in Shakespeare* [p. 261]
Barnaby & D'Acierno (eds.): *C. G. Jung and the Humanities* [p. 282]
Bickman: *American Romantic Psychology* [p. 267]
Birkhäuser: *Light from the Darkness* [p. 268]
Birkhäuser-Oeri: *The Mother: Archetypal Image in Fairy Tales* [p. 264]
Blackmer: *Acrobats of the Gods* [p. 282]
Bolander: *Assessing Personality through Tree Drawings* [p. 263]

———: An Introduction to the Interpretation of Fairy Tales [p. 259]
———: Patterns of Creativity Mirrored in Creation Myths [p. 260]
———: Problems of the Feminine in Fairy Tales (See chapter 8, "Feminine and Masculine Psychology") [p. 167]
———: The Psychological Meaning of Redemption Motifs in Fairy Tales [p. 269]
———: The Golden Ass of Apuleius [p. 259]
———: Shadow and Evil in Fairy Tales [p. 262]
Werblowsky: Lucifer and Prometheus [p. 254]
Westman: The Springs of Creativity (See chapter 9, "Religion and Jung's Psychology") [p. 212]
Whitman: Fairy Tales and the Kingdom of God [p. 274]
Willeford: The Fool and His Scepter (See chapter 7, "Symbolic Life and Dreams") [p. 141]
Wilson: The Nightingale and the Hawk [p. 258]
Witcutt: Blake: A Psychological Study [p. 253]

The Spirit in Man, Art, and Literature, by C. G. Jung. Princeton, N.J.: Princeton U. Press/Bollingen, 1966*; 1971p*; London: Routledge & Kegan Paul, 1967; London: Ark, 1984p* (CW 15) (160 + viii, incl. 8-p. index, 6-p. bibl.).

The theme underlying this collection of nine essays is the archetype of Spirit, the source of scientific and artistic creativity in those persons with qualities of personality who pioneered in realms as diverse as medicine, psychoanalysis, Oriental studies, the visual arts, and literature. All appeared as articles in journals, with some also presented as lectures or addresses, the longest being a lecture (1922) and article on the relation of analytical psychology to poetry and an article (1930) on psychology and literature. Others include memorial addresses on the life and work of physician-alchemist Paracelsus, noted Sinologist Richard Wilhelm, and Freud, along with a critical analysis of James Joyce's Ulysses and a psychological interpretation of Picasso.

(Bk.revs.: BkRDig '67:695; LibJ '67/92:1020; LibJBkR '67:494; Spring '67:148; VaQR '67/43:xcii; TimesLitSup '68:17; JAnPsy '72/17:93–5)

*   *   *   *   *

Blake: A Psychological Study, by W. P. Witcutt. London: Hollis & Carter, 1946; Toronto: McClelland & Stuart, 1946; New York: Kennikat Press, reissue 1966; Folcroft, Penn.: Folcroft Library Editions, repr. 1974; Philadelphia: Richard West, repr. 1977 (127 pp.).

Using the "instrument of Jungian psychology" to provide a key for understanding the work of William Blake, Witcutt indicates a path through the Blakean jungle, a plan of the maze to interpret the problems of mythology and symbolism of the strangely named characters which make up "Prophetic Books." He points out that similar psychic patterns are to be found in the psyche of everyone, altered by the circumstances of each one's individuality and revealed in dreams. His topics include the nature of imagination; the supreme introvert; the four Zoas (daimons, or spirits); the birth of the functions; the anatomy of disintegration; conflict of the Zoas; reintegration; Blake's map of the psyche; and "an introvert looks at the world." The appendix contains an examination of the use of symbols in the Romantic poets, in which he describes Blake as an intuitive introvert and symbolist par excellence, living in a continual waking dream and experiencing, as did Shelley, archetypes appearing as visions.

(Bk.revs.: Blackf '47/28:188–9; Tabl '47/189:286; TimesLitSup '47:93; BulAnPsy Oc'50/ 12:1–4)

Lucifer and Prometheus: A Study of Milton's Satan, by R. J. Zwi Werblowsky. London: Routledge & Kegan Paul, 1952; New York: AMS Press, 1952; repr. 1977* (120 + xix, incl. 4-p. index, 2-p. bibl., 4-p. intro. by Jung).

Stating that Jung's analytical psychology insists on bringing the devil and the problem of shadow to the fore, Werblowsky studies one of the greatest and most towering Satans of literature, along with a study of Milton himself. He claims that Milton's Satan in fact contains Promethean elements and he contends that the archetypal similarities between the mythology of Satan and of Prometheus led to contaminations of which the strange Satan of *Paradise Lost* is the result. Werblowsky discusses the topics of the hero and the fool; pride and ambition; Satan as the antagonist of heaven's almighty king; sin; and obedience. Jung comments in the foreword that the Satan-Prometheus parallel shows that Milton's devil stands for the essence of the individuation process.

(Bk.rev.: TimesLitSup '52:410)

Art and the Creative Unconscious: Four Essays, by Erich Neumann. (Ger.: *Kunst und schöpferisches Unbewusste.* Zurich: Rascher Verlag, 1954.) London: Routledge & Kegan Paul, 1959*; Toronto: McClelland & Stewart, 1959; New York: Pantheon Books (Bollingen Series LXI:1), 1959*; New York: Torchbooks/Harper & Row, 1961; Princeton, N.J.: Princeton U. Press/ Bollingen, 1971 + p* (232, incl. 14-p. index, 7-p. bibl., 10 illus.).

Neumann holds the point of view that a part of the creative person's consciousness is always receptive to the unconscious, and he observes that the creative principle in art has achieved prominence in contemporary times because the symbol-creating collective forces of mythology and religious rites and festivals have lost most of their power. His four essays on this subject are on Leonardo da Vinci and the mother archetype (78 pp., including four illustrations of paintings by da Vinci), art and time (54 pp.), Marc Chagall (14 pp.), and creative man and transformation of consciousness (57 pp.).

(Bk.revs.: LibJ '59/84:1901; YaleR '59/49:137; ArtJ '60/20:120+; BkRDig '60:991; JAesthArt '60/19:237; JAnPsy '60/5:177; Person '60/41:221; BksAbroad '61/35:189–90; TimesLitSup '61:180; AmJArtTh '71/11:68; Leonardo '83/16:251)

Icon and Idea: The Function of Love in the Development of Human Consciousness, by Herbert Read. London: Faber & Faber, 1955; Cambridge, Mass.: Harvard U. Press, 1955; New York: Schocken Books, 1965p (with new intro.) (161, incl. 9-p. index, 12-p. ref. notes, 103 illus.).

Consisting of seven lectures given in 1953–54 at Harvard University, this book explores the theme that the symbols of art have a priority claim in that the image always precedes the idea in the development of human consciousness. Read states that ideas are manipulated by logic or scientific method but are come upon in the contemplation of images. He discusses the vital image; the discovery of beauty; symbols for the unknown; the human as the ideal; the illusion of the real; the frontiers of the self; and the constructive image. Read is a coeditor of Jung's *Collected Works*.

(Bk.revs.: Listen '55/54:903; SatR 26N'55/38:18–19; Tabl '55/206:584; BkRDig '56:768; BksAbroad '56/30:226; JAesArt '56/15:258–60; KenyonR '56/18:157–62; LibJ '56/81:528+; NYTimesBkR 4Mr'56:28; RMeta '56/9:522; '57/10:474–81; TimesLitSup '56:277–8; AmSchol '56–57/26:92+; CompLit '57/9:91–3)

The Archetypal World of Henry Moore, by Erich Neumann. London: Routledge & Kegan Paul, 1959; Toronto: McClelland & Stewart, 1959; New York: Pantheon Books (Bollingen Ser. LXVIII), 1959*; New York: Torchbooks/Harper & Row, 1965p; Princeton, N.J.: Princeton U. Press/Bollingen, 1984p* (216, incl. 2-p. bibl., 3-p. ref. notes, 107 illus.).

Neumann uses depth psychology to analyze the art of English sculptor Henry Moore (one of the greatest artists of the twentieth century), seeing Moore and his work not only as molded by his milieu and childhood but also as part of a collective psychic situation. He interprets the connection between Moore's artistic creation and the archetypal reality of the unconscious as evidence of a creative individual whose work revolves around the centrality of the definitive "Primordial Feminine," the reclining figure of mother and child.

(Bk.revs.: BkRDig '59:747; CanArt '59/16:287; Commonw '59/70:502–3; LibJ '59/64:1881; NYTimesBkR 10My'59:7; ArtJ '60/20:120; JAnPsy '60/5:177–8 Spring '60:152; TimesLitSup '60:124; BurlMag '61/103:31; PsychiQ '65/39:751; SatR 26Jn'65/48:43)

The Forms of Things Unknown: Essays Towards an Aesthetic Philosophy, by Herbert Read. London: Faber & Faber, 1960; New York: Horizon Press, 1960; New York: Meridian Books/World Publishing Co., 1965p (248, incl. 10-p. index, 11 illus.).

In this book, Read discusses the controlling influence of such factors as image, symbol, myth, and icon in the development of human culture and the part played by the creative mind in the maintenance of aesthetic values. Contrasting this with the technological revolution of our time, Read emphasizes the need not to ignore the "subtle springs of creation." Among the fourteen essays (three of which are lectures and articles published elsewhere), three are specifically Jungian. They are on the creative process, the created form (illustrated by three of Henry Moore's sculptures), and the reclining image (Jung's concept of the archetypal Self in the individuation process). Others include a discussion of the limitation of a scientific philosophy; art as a symbolic language; psychoanalysis and the problem of aesthetic value from a Freudian viewpoint; art and the development of the personality; creative experience in poetry; the contemporary revolution in the visual arts; and the creative nature of humanism.

(Bk.revs.: BrJAesth '60/1:26–7; Econ '60/196:637; HibbJ 60/59:101–2; Listen '60/64:479; SatR 3D'60/43:22–3; Spec '60/205:188; Tabl '60/214:276; 20Cen '60/168:578–81; ArtActiv 1F'61/49:30; BkRDig '61:1168; BurlMag '61/103:75; Encoun S'61/17:83–5; LibJ '61/86:101; MexLife Jn'61:35; Month '61/25:55–6; SFChron 12F'61:ThisWorld 24 + 31)

The Grail Legend, by Emma Jung and Marie-Louise von Franz. (Ger.: *Die Graalslegend in psychologischer Sicht.* Zurich: Rascher Verlag, 1960.) New York: G. P. Putnam's Sons for C. G. Jung Foundation for Analytical Psychology, 1970; London: Hodder & Stoughton, 1971; Boston: Sigo Press and London: Coventure, ed.2 1986* +p* (452, incl. 34-p. index, 17-p. bibl., 23 illus.).

Emma Jung and von Franz explore the remarkable blend of fairy tale and Christian legend that gives the Grail stories a peculiar character, reflecting not only fundamental human problems but also the dramatic psychic events which form the background of Christian culture. Among the symbols interpreted within the presentation of the story are the Grail as vessel, the sword and the lance, the Grail as stone, the table, the carving platter, and the two knives. Following the interpretation of the story, they discuss the topics of the Trinity, the figure of Adam, the figure of Merlin, and the solution of the Grail problem.

(Bk.revs.: Frontier My'71/14:111–14; Harvest '71/17:63–6; BkRDig '72:684; Choice '72/ 9:640; LibJ '72/97:1811; LibJBkR '72:311; PsyToday Ag'72/6:8; InwLight '73/n83:41–2; LATimesBkR 31Ag'86:3 + ; ContemPsy '87/32:982–3)

Outline of a Jungian Aesthetics, by Morris H. Philipson. Evanston, Ill.: Northwestern U. Press, 1963 (214 + ix, incl. 2-p. index of proper names, 5-p. bibl.).

In his application of psychoanalytic thought to problems of art, Philipson suggests that Jung's reflections on the nature of symbols are based on his "image of man." He discusses the concept of symbol in Jung's psychology (the distinction between signs and symbols; symbols and psychic energy in the service of "wholeness"; the transcendent function of symbols; the collective unconscious; and the conditions of symbolic interpretation) and then presents an outline of a Jungian aesthetics (Jung's criticism of Freud's aesthetics; the work of art; creative energy; psychic significance of artworks and the creative process; and the literary artist). He ends with a critical analysis of Jungian psychology and aesthetics, symbolism, and epistemology. (Bk.revs.: BkRDig '64:928; BrJAesth '64/4:274–5; JAesthArt '64/22:475–6; LibJ '64/89:94; LitPsy '65/15:57–64; NYRevBks 25F'65:5)

Rosegarden and Labyrinth: A Study of Art Education, by Seonaid M. Robertson. London: Routledge & Kegan Paul, 1963; New York: Barnes & Noble, 1963; Lewes: Gryphon, 1982p*; Dallas: Spring Publications, ed.2 1982p* (216 + xxx, incl. 6-p. index, 6-p. bibl., 106 illus., 2-p. foreword by Herbert Read in ed.1, 1-p. foreword by Peter Abbs in ed.2).

Convinced that the arts play an absolutely vital role in life, especially among young people who are seeking a new and more deeply rooted life in the context of an increasingly more vulnerable planet Earth, Robertson tells of her exploratory approach to teaching the visual arts. She describes her intuitive response to Jung's ideas, particularly his theories of symbols and archetypes, which she gained during years of study of psychology, and her study of Maud Bodkin's research on archetypal images in poetry. Following her account (amply illustrated) of experiences in the classroom and a commentary on gardens and labyrinths, she appends a brief summary of the arts of early history relevant to her study. (Bk.revs.: BrJEdStud '63/12:100; TimesLitSup '63:29; ContLearn '64/3:240; NewStates '64/68:969; Choice '65/2:390; BrJAesth '83/23:268–70; Harvest '83/29:164; JArtDesEd '84/3:125; AmJArtTh '85/24:26–7; ArtsPsyth '85/12:45–6)

Wagner's Ring and its Symbols: The Music and the Myth, by Robert Donington. London: Faber & Faber, 1963; ed.2 1969 +p; ed.3 1974* +p*; Toronto: British Book Service, 1963; New York: St. Martins Press, 1963; ed.2 1969; ed.3 1974p* (342, incl. 13-p. index, 13-p. bibl.).

Indebted both to the fundamental discoveries of Freud's depth psychology and to the crucial amplification of them by Jung, music critic Donington offers fresh insights into certain aspects of Wagner's meaning in *Der Ring des Nibelungen* by analyzing the poetical and musical symbols that Wagner brought into artistic consciousness. Following an introductory discussion of the relations of myth and music, he interprets the prelude to *Das Rheingold* and then the tetralogy of human dramas (*Das Rheingold, Die Walküre, Siegfried,* and *Götterdämmerung*). Appended are some musical examples and a chart of selected leading motives.

(Bk.revs.: BkRDig '63:275; Harvest '63/9:78–9; LibJ '63/88:2911; MusJ S'63:97; Mus-Opin N'63:90; MusR '63/24:354–7; MusTimes My'63:336; NewStates '63/66:366; NYTimesBkR 21Jn'63:6; Tempo Sum'63:27; TimesLitSup '63:228; ContLearn '64/3:240; GerQ '64/37:541–2; JAesthArt '64/22:477–8; JAnPsy '64/9:187–8; QueensQ '64/70:598–606; VaQR '64/40:clxxii; BksBkmen My'74/19:54–6; Choice '74/11:1485; ClassWorld '75/46:451; MusicEdJ Mr'75/61:96; Studies '75/64:74–9; Composer '77:36)

The Nightingale and the Hawk: A Psychological Study of Keats' Ode. by Katherine M. Wilson. London: George Allen & Unwin, 1964; New York: Barnes & Noble, 1965 (157, incl. 2-p. index).

Starting with the premise that Keats's "Ode to a Nightingale" acts like a personality test, Wilson sees a "fantastic correspondence" between Keats and aspects of Jung's psychology. Although her interest is primarily literary, she uses Keats to illustrate what is relevant in Jung's psychology, explaining the deep layer of unconsciousness; archetypes, among which the archetype of the Self has a special place; archetypal imagery in poetry; the individuation process; anima and ego; and what of God the individual finds within one's self. She interprets an actual nightingale's song in Keats's experience as constellating the archetypal Self by lowering the threshold of consciousness into the deepest unconscious; and she interprets the hawk as an animal eagerness related to his loss of ego-interest in ambition, in other words, a time when the Self took the place of the ego. This led to a new attitude toward his vocation as a poet.

(Bk.revs.: TimesLitSup '64:940; Choice '65/2:390; English '65/15:145–6; Listen '65/73:26; Spring '65:146; InwLight '66/n70:46–7; ModLangR '66/61:114–15)

Shakespeare's Royal Self, by James Kirsch. New York: G. P. Putnam's Sons for the C. G. Jung Foundation for Analytical Psychology, 1966; Toronto: Longmans Canada, 1966 (422 + xix, incl. 3-p. foreword by Gerhard Adler).

Kirsch aims to demonstrate that all great art springs from the collective unconscious. He focuses particularly on the work of Shakespeare, which Kirsch feels represents his "royal self." He employs three plays (*Hamlet,* a drama of haunted men; *King Lear,* a play of redemption; and *Macbeth,* a descent into hell and damnation) to study significant steps in Shakespeare's own inner development. In each of them the unconscious appears as a separate factor, sometimes as a dramatic figure or because the consciousness of the hero is for a time concentrated on the unconscious and characteristically changed by it. He analyzes each with great detail in order to show the whole process of individuation, treating each play in the same way that a dream is to be analyzed by giving full attention to each detail of its structure, sequence, and content.

(Bk.revs.: KirkR '65/33:1249; BkRDig '66:652–3; Bklist '66/2:1026; Choice '66/3:770; Harvest '66/12:84; LibJ '66/91:1911; NYTimesBkR 15My'66/71:4+; QJSpeech '66/52:402; ContemPsy '67/12:136+; InwLight '67/n71:42–4; JHighEd '67/38:117–18; Poetry 67:312; Spring '67:152–3)

An Introduction to the Interpretation of Fairy Tales, by Marie-Louise von Franz. New York: Spring Publications for the Analytical Psychology Club of New York, 1970p; Irving, Tex.: Spring Publications, repr. 1972p* (Seminar Series, 1) (160 + iv, incl. 5-p. index, 4-p. bibl., 3 illus.).

Based on seven lectures given in 1963 at the Jung Institute of Zurich, this work by von Franz presents fairy tales as the purest and simplest expression of the collective unconscious psychic processes, representing the archetypes in their most basic form. Before explaining the specific Jungian form of interpretation, she gives the history of the science of fairy tales and theories of different schools and distinguishes between fairy tales and myths and other archetypal stories. She then discusses the steps involved in a psychological interpretation of fairy tales and gives an example of a tale interpreted (a very simple Grimm's tale, "The Three Feathers"). She continues by analyzing motifs of stories related to Jung's concepts of the shadow ("Prince Ring," a Norwegian story); the challenge of the anima ("The Bewitched Princess" and parallel tales); the female shadow ("Shaggy-Top"); the powers of the animus ("Thrushbeard," "The Woman Who Became a Spider," "The Woman Who Married the Moon and the Kele"); and the motif of relationship ("The White Bride and the Black Bride").

The Golden Ass of Apuleius: The Liberation of the Feminine in Man, by Marie-Louise von Franz. (Orig. title: *A Psychological Interpretation of* The Golden Ass *of Apuleius.*) New York: Spring Publications for the Analytical Psychology Club of New York, 1970p; Dallas: Spring Publications, repr. 1980p. (Seminar Series, 3) (188 pp.).

Von Franz is convinced that Lucius Apuleius' novel, which was written in the second century A.D. and is the earliest Latin novel extant in its entirety, still has a message to bring and should be placed among such inspired works as *Faust* or *The Divine Comedy.* Her psychological interpretation of *The Golden Ass,* whose metamorphoses involve the hero's restoration to human

shape with the aid of the goddess Isis, is concerned in particular with the problem of the incarnation of the feminine principle and of its "reconnection" in a patriarchal Christian universe.
(Bk.revs.: ClassPhilol '81/76:244; Harvest '82/28:158–61)

The Unholy Bible: Blake, Jung and the Collective Unconscious, by June Singer. (Orig. subtitle: *A Psychological Interpretation of William Blake).* New York: G. P. Putnam's Sons for the C. G. Jung Foundation for Analytical Psychology, 1970; New York: Harper & Row, 1972p; Boston: Sigo Press, 1986* +p* (272 + xx, incl. 4-p. index, 6-p. bibl., 13-p. ref. notes, 24 illus., 6-p. intro. by M. Esther Harding).

Drawing on her diploma thesis at the Jung Institute of Zurich, Singer uses Jungian ideas to interpret Blake and his writings. She translates Blake's intuitive grasp of the unconscious background of life into contemporary terms that reflect the struggle with the dual aspect of God in one's own contradictory experience. She interprets Blake's imagery of a marriage in *The Marriage of Heaven and Hell* as a reconciliation of body and spirit. She also examines his later prophetic writings and minor prophecies (*The Book of Urizen, The Book of Ahania, The Book of Los, The Song of Los,* and *Europe*), as well as *The Four Zoas,* which are elaborations of mystical and metaphysical systems with complicated symbolism. She concludes with a look at Blake's poems on Milton and Jerusalem, revealing the depth and energy of his active imagination.
(Bk.revs.: PubW 9N'70/198:53; Amer '71/124:640; BkRDig '71:1260-1; Choice '71/ 8:678; Quad '71/n10:27–8; InwLight '72/n81:146–7; JAnPsy '72/17:99–101; Blake '73/ 6:100; JAmAcadRel '73/41:460–1; Gnosis '86–87/n3:43–4; Harvest '87–88/33:211–12; ContemPsy '88/33:548)

Patterns of Creativity Mirrored in Creation Myths, by Marie-Louise von Franz. New York: Spring Publications for the Analytical Psychology Club of New York, 1972p; Dallas: Spring Publications, 5th printing, 1986p* (Seminar Series, 6) (250, incl. 8-p. index, 11 illus.).

This book consists of twelve lectures given at the Jung Institute of Zurich during 1961–62. In it von Franz interprets psychological motifs that occur frequently in creation myths, which are different from other myths (for example, hero myths or fairy tales) in that they deal with the ultimate meaning of the origin of nature and human existence. Following a discussion of the nature of the creation myth, she examines the subjects of creation as awakening and creation by accident; creation from above and creation from below; the two-creator motif; *Deus faber* (God as the artisan); chaos and unconsciousness; subjective moods of the creator; the motif of germs and eggs; the two-fold and four-fold division of the universe; abortive attempts at creation; long chains of creation (generations, particles, and numbers); and creation renewed and reversed.

Psyche and Symbol in Shakespeare, by Alex Aronson. Bloomington, Ind.: Indiana U. Press, 1972. (343 + vi, incl. 9-p. index, 6-p. bibl., 20-p. ref. notes).

Aronson believes that some of Jung's basic psychological concepts establish a close and meaningful connection between the act of dreaming and the act of literary creation. In relation to this, he sets out to reinforce the claim made by Dryden and Dr. Johnson that Shakespeare had "the largest and most comprehensive soul" and that his characters are "the genuine progeny of common humanity." Aronson illustrates the way in which the objective psyche (the collective unconscious) operates through Shakespeare, assuming the existence of a dualism in the human personality that is expressed frequently by symbols derived from light and darkness. He states that all drama originates in psychic polarity, in the conflicting natures of ego and Self, the conscious and the unconscious, and mask and face. He first examines the ego, defining the Shakespearean hero in terms of his conscious mind only, then the anima, which he sees as the shift from the prevalence of the conscious mind to the gradual domination by unconscious forces, and finally the Self that leads from conflict to resolution by the process of individuation, whose full integration no Shakespearean hero ever accomplishes.

(Bk.revs.: LibJ '72/97:2601; LibJBkR '72:289; AmJPsyth '73/27:628; BkRDig '73:29; Choice '73/10:771; Encoun Jy'73/41:69; Quad '73/14:19–21; TimesLitSup 2F'73:126; Criticism '74/16:172–6; JAnPsy '74/19:215–16)

Inward Journey: Art as Therapy, by Margaret Frings Keyes. (Orig. subtitle: *Art and Psychotherapy for You.* Millbrae, Calif.: Celestial Arts, 1974.) La Salle, Ill.: Open Court, rev. 1983p; 1985p* (Reality of the Psyche Series, vol. III) (133 + viii, incl. 5-p. bibl., 40 illus.).

Keyes explores how psychological work can be enhanced by including the arts. She believes that artistic expression promotes healing through touching an integrative life principle that brings together the scattered and opposing parts of one's self. In her "maps and charts" of the creative process she develops graphic and plastic art techniques using painting, mandalas, sculpture, music, and myths as therapeutic strategies to understand hidden talents and desires. She discusses the uses of transactional analysis, the Gestalt approach, and Jungian depth psychology. Appended is a 9-page essay on active imagination by Marie-Louise von Franz.

(Bk.revs.: PubW 23S'74/296:157; AmJArtTh '75/15:29; LibJ '75/100:488–9; LibJBkR '75:406; AmJArtTh '83/22:144; PsyPersp '84/15:116–18)

Shadow and Evil in Fairy Tales, by Marie-Louise von Franz. Zurich: Spring Publications for the Analytical Psychology Club of New York, 1974p; Dallas: Spring Publications, 6th printing 1987p* (Seminar Series, 9) (284, incl. 13-p. index, 2 diagrams).

In this work based on fourteen lectures given at the Jung Institute of Zurich in 1957 and 1964, von Franz examines the problem of the shadow in fairy tales, the shadow being all that is within one's psyche which one does not know about, including partly personal and partly collective elements of the unconscious. Consideration of the shadow in fairy tales focuses on the collective or group shadow. The shadow of the collective can be particularly destructive because people, as the collective, support each other in their blindness. Von Franz interprets tales under the topics of the shadow (including "The Two Wanderers," "The Loyal and the Disloyal Friend," "Faithful John," "The Two Brothers," and "The Golden Children"); evil ("The Horse Mountain Ghost," "The Spear Legs"); possession by evil and meeting the powers of evil ("The Beautiful Wassilissa"); hot and cold evil (including "Getting Angry" and "Snow White and Rose Red"); and magical contests (including "The Black Magician Czar" and "The King's Son and the Devil's Daughter").

The Tree: A Jungian Journey—Tales in Psycho-Mythology, by J. Marvin Spiegelman. Los Angeles: Phoenix House, 1974; Phoenix: Falcon Press, repr. 1982 + p* (464 + ix, incl. 1-p. bibl.).

In this first book of a trilogy on "psycho-mythology" (a literature in which an individual's fantasy reaches the collective unconscious, transcending the personal level, and straddles both Jung's "active imagination" method and art), Spiegelman presents a series of ten stories in which each narrator tells his or her individuation experiences. As told at The Tree of Life in Paradise, the ten people represent different religions or beliefs, namely, Gnosticism, Islam, Buddhism, atheism, paganism, kundalini yoga, Taoism, Christianity, Judaism, and alchemy.
(Bk.revs.: ContemPsy '75/20:985; PsyPersp '86/17:254–8)

Dark Wood to White Rose: A Study of Meanings in Dante's Divine Comedy, by Helen M. Luke. Pecos, N.M.: Dove Publications, 1975p* (162 + iv, incl. 2-p. ref. notes, 2-p. gloss.).

Drawing her basic approach to the symbolism of Dante from Jung's psychology, Luke emphasizes that the *Divine Comedy* is both divine and human. She believes that it echoes the double nature of reality: that without divinity there can be no conscious humanity, and without humanity the divine remains an abstraction. Reflecting on Dante's own life journey within the framework of the medieval theories of life and death, she interprets his story from the "dark wood" of lost innocence wandering in blindness and near despair to a vision of the heavenly white rose—from the *Inferno,* through the *Purgatorio,* to the *Paradiso.* She characterizes the journey as a tremendous symbolic account of the way of individuation.

(Bk.revs.: RforRel '75/34:492; SisToday '75/46:617; TheolStud '75/36:386; Choice '76/ 13:670; ChrScholR '76/5:419–20; Mythlore Jn'76/n12:21–2; InwLight '80/n94:48–50)

Assessing Personality through Tree Drawings, by Karen Bolander. New York: Basic Books, 1977 (421 + xix, incl. 9-p. index, 10-p. bibl., 105 illus., 3-p. foreword by Joseph Di Leo).

Although characterizing her own clinical orientation as being fairly eclectic, Bolander states that she has been influenced by studies in Jungian analytical psychology. This is reflected both in certain underlying concepts and in her choice of language, particularly in the treatment of nonrational symbolism. Following her presentation of the origins of her study, she explains her methodology and approach to the interpretation of tree drawings as they reflect personality. She then makes sample analyses of three case histories and concludes with a discussion of the influences that are brought to bear on the drawings and the elements that are involved in the rendering of style.

(Bk.revs.: AmJPsychi '78/135:1581; AmJPsyth '78/32:477–8; Choice '78/14:1567; ContemPsy '78/23:586–7; JPersAssess '78/42:648–50)

Dream and Image, by Bettina L. Knapp. Troy, N.Y.: Whitson Publishing Co., 1977* (426 + xi, incl. 10-p. index, 14-p. bibl., 3-p. preface by Andrée Chedid).

Drawing on Jung's concepts of the collective unconscious and archetypal imagery, Knapp evaluates the mythical, psychological, and philosophical factors in key dreams as narrated by French writers. She analyzes Descartes's "The Dreams Came from Above," Racine's dream and prophetic vision in *Athaliah* (from the seventeenth century), Diderot's *D'Alembert's Dream,* and Cazotte's dream initiation in *The Devil in Love* (from the eighteenth century). Nineteenth-century selections include Nodier's sacred marriage of sun and moon in *The Crumb Fairy;* Balzac's legend of the thinking man in *Louis Lambert;* Baudelaire's drama of the poetic process in "Parisian Dream"; Hugo's dark night of the soul in "What the Mouth of Darkness Says"; Huysmans's satanism and the male psyche in *Down There;* Rimbaud's dream of chaos in "After the Flood"; and Mallarmé's depersonalization process and the creative encounter in *Igitur, or Elbehnon's Folly.*

(Bk.revs.: FrR '78/51:891; ModLangJ '78/62:362–3; 19CenFrStud '78/6:279; StudRom '78/17:512–14; SubStance '78/n21:165–6; Sympos '78/32:363–5; WorldLit '78/52:525; GaR '79/33:210–11; Notes&Q '79/26:474–5; RockyMtR '79/33:213–14; AntiochR '82/ 40:372; FrStud '84/38:362–3)

The Ego King: An Archetypal Approach to Elizabethan Political Thought and Shakespeare's Henry VI *Plays,* by James T. Henke. Salzburg: Institut für Englische Sprache und Literatur, 1977p* (Jacobean Drama Studies, University of Salzburg) (100 + iv, incl. footnote refs.).

Henke applies the Jungian theory of a collective unconscious and collective archetypes to Shakespeare's *Henry VI* trilogy to reveal the basic psychic vision it contains. He examines how the same vision informs both the plays and the popular attitude toward kingship prevalent in that era, his goal being to reveal how the "collective unconscious" of Shakespeare's age blends with the material from his own unconscious to produce the plays. Following a discussion of archetypal criticism and Jung's theories, he explores archetypal theory and Elizabethan political thought. He looks at the relationship of archetype to *Henry VI,* in which he interprets a basic vision as projected on two complementary dramas (one describing political chaos, superimposed upon another describing a form of human insanity "with almost clinical accuracy").

The Mother: Archetypal Image in Fairy Tales, by Sibylle Birkhäuser-Oeri. (Ger.: *Die Mutter im Märchen.* Stuttgart: Adolf Bonz Verlag, 1977.) Toronto: Inner City Books, 1988p* (Studies in Jungian Psychology by Jungian Analysts, 34) (172, incl. 5-p. index, 8-p. notes, 1-p. foreword by Marie-Louise von Franz).

Birkhäuser-Oeri investigates the psychological meaning of mother figures in fairy tales, recognizing an almost endless variety of positive and negative images of the archetypal Earth Mother, which she classifies and interprets as typical recurring motifs. These include the terrible mother; the jealous stepmother; mothers that metamorphose into animals; the fire mother; the imprisoning sorceress; the indifferent mother; the terrible mother; mother as fate; the life-giving nature mother; the healing nature mother; the self-renewing mother; and the transforming mother. Beginning with an analysis of the mother archetype, she ends with an analysis of the Great Mother in our time.

(Bk.rev.: JAnPsy '89/34:191–2)

Robertson Davies, by Patricia Morley. Agincourt, Ontario: Gage Educational Pubs., 1977 +p (Profiles in Canadian Drama Series) (74 + vii, incl. 3-p. index, 3-p. bibl., end-chap. ref. notes, 2-p. preface by Geraldine Anthony).

Characterizing Canadian writer Robertson Davies as "the entertainer" in his seventeen plays, Morley surveys the work of the romantic idealist and satirist who is equally preoccupied with middle-class Canadian pretensions and Jung's analytical psychology. Following brief chapters on Davies' works and his life, she discusses the recurring theme of his early drama as a state of cultural malnutrition that prevails in the land. She also analyzes the early plays. In the chapter "The Comedy Company of the Psyche" (as Davies labels Jung's theory of personality structure in his novel *The Manticore*), she analyzes the most Jungian of his plays, namely *General Confession* (an ingenious dramatization of Jung's psychology climaxed by the Jungian goal of personal integration), *Question Time* (which has the same theme of self-knowledge and integration and uses four major archetypes of the collective unconscious to serve as principal actors), and *Hunting Stuart* (a "romance of heredity" pervaded by Jungian ideas of the collective unconscious and the psychic baggage of ancestry).
(Bk.revs.: BksCan Ap'77/16:22; CanTheatR Spr'77/14:101–3; QueensQ '77/84:686; BkFor '78/4:56–63)

Blake and the Assimilation of Chaos, by Christine Gallant. Princeton, N.J.: Princeton U. Press, 1978 (198 + xi, incl. 2-p. index, 9-p. bibl.).

Gallant considers Jungian psychology to be particularly apt for understanding the Romantic poet William Blake, since she considers Jung himself in many ways a Neo-Romantic. She examines how Blake struggles with the question of how chaos can be assimilated into imaginative order in all of his works, recognizing chaos as a mythic principle of existence, and using art to understand what is happening to him psychologically as his consciousness tries to comprehend the unconscious without being overwhelmed by it. She analyzes *The Four Zoas* as a study of the experience of "divided existence," in which the exploration of the nature of the unconscious involves the cycle of generation, death, and regeneration to "unity." She interprets the poem *Milton* as an exploration of the personal and collective unconscious of Blake and *Jerusalem* as the "humanizing" of chaotic contents of the unconscious into consciousness by the impulse of the unifying archetype of the Self, concluding that the ultimate goal of a work of art is the balance of polarities in the psyche as it strives for individuation, evoking archetypal symbols.
(Bk.revs.: Blake '80/13:200–2; JAnPsy '80/25:300)

Melville's Moby-Dick: *A Jungian Commentary; An American Nekyia,* by Edward F. Edinger. New York: New Directions Books, 1978 +p* (150, incl. 3-p. bibl., 4-p. gloss.).

Seeking not so much to understand Melville the man as to understand the psyche (especially the collective psyche) as exemplified by the genius of

Melville's imagination, Edinger elucidates the psychological significance of the novel *Moby-Dick* and thereby demonstrates analytical psychology's methods of dealing with symbolic forms and the basic orientation underlying its therapeutic approach. He interprets the classic adventure story of the wild pursuit of the white whale as a kind of negative dialogue with the Self, describing symbolically the stormy process of Melville's own experience of spiritual transition that led to the underworld of the unconscious and the corrective experience of the "defeat of the ego" by the redeeming encounter with the Self. He analyzes in detail the symbolism involved in Ishmael, Queequeg, Captain Ahab, the whale, and Fedallah.

(Bk.revs.: Bklist '78/75:270; LibJ '78/103:2521; LibJBkR '78:258; BkRDig '79:359; Choice '79/16:220; JAnPsy '79/24:353–4; ModFictStud '79–80/25:726–8; PsyPersp '79/10n2:83–6; Quad '79/12n1:80–4; StudNovel '79/11:242–4; 19CenFict '80/34:479–82; WCoastR 14Ap'80/14:13–17; ArizQ '81/37:371; RelStudR '82/8:277)

Twice-Told Tales: The Psychological Use of Fairy Tales, by Hans Dieckmann. (Ger.: *Gelebte Märchen.* Berlin: Gerstenberg Verlag, 1978.) Wilmette, Ill.: Chiron Publications, 1986p* (139 + xiv, incl. 3-p. index, 1-p. index of fairy tales retold, 5-p. bibl., 6-p. foreword by Bruno Bettelheim).

Presenting this work as both a source of information for the layperson interested in the psychology of fairy tales and as a brief introduction for the physician and psychologist working analytically, Dieckmann analyzes the symbolic language of fairy tales for meaning in relation to personal development and self-understanding. He discusses the relationship of fairy tale and dream; the symbolic language of fairy tales; whether fairy tales are only for children; fairy tale motifs in dreams; one's favorite fairy tale from childhood; cruelty in fairy tales; and the fairy tale as a source of structure in the process of emotional development. His focus on fairy tale material arising from the analytic process is predominantly on adult patients and on processes in the unconscious that have not only negative-irrational effects but also creative effects on consciousness.

(Bk.revs.: PsyPersp '87/18:148–50; ContemPsy '88/33:522–3)

Creative Man: Five Essays, by Erich Neumann. Princeton, N.J.: Princeton U. Press/Bollingen, 1979*; 1982p* (Bollingen Series LXI:2) (Essays of Erich Neumann, vol. 2) (264 + xviii, incl. 6-p. index, 4 illus. by Marc Chagall, biographic note on Erich Neumann by Gerhard Adler).

Presented as a sequel to his book *Art and the Creative Unconscious,* this collection of five essays deals with the creative life and work of Franz Kafka, Marc Chagall, Georg Trakl, Freud, and Jung. The longest (110 pp.) is a depth psychology interpretation of Kafka's "The Trial" (written in 1933), which reflects all the basic ideas of analytical psychology (shadow, complex, archetype, anima, and Self). In the article on Chagall and the Bible, Neumann analyzes an extensive number of illustrations (105 etchings and 25 lithographs) that Chagall created during the decades of the European Holocaust, revealing the depth of inner feeling that Chagall maintained. The long essay on the poet Trakl examines his heroic struggle in "wringing" from his severely disturbed personality an output of poetic work that possesses universal validity. Neumann's short essay on Freud and the father image includes comments on Freud's genius and his "magnificent battle" with his unconscious Jewish problem of the Father archetype and the Father-God. His short eulogy on the eightieth birthday of Jung is highly laudatory, characterizing him as "the greatest psychologist of our time."

(Bk.revs.: BkRDig '80/885–6; Choice '80/17:598; ContemPsy '80/25:695–6; LibJ '80/ 105:104; LibJBkR '80:285; Quad '80/13n2:129–31; SFJInstLib '80/1n3:33–5; HeythJ '81/22:218–19; JAnPsy '81/26:277–8; QueensQ '82/89:476–7)

Jungian Psychology in Literary Analysis: A Demonstration Using T. S. Eliot's Poetry, by Joyce Meeks Jones. Washington, D.C.: University Press of America, 1979p (52, incl. 4-p. bibl., 3-p. gloss.).

Writing primarily for college students, Jones illustrates the techniques involved in the psychological evaluation of a literary work, using what she calls the "individuational approach." In it she summarizes development stages rather than performing the "average Jungian analysis" of a literary work as a study of archetypal imagery. Following a brief presentation of the basic features of Jungian psychology, she describes what is involved in a typological approach to T. S. Eliot's poetry and she concludes with an interpretation of her theme of individuation as literary analysis, outlining the basic procedure as a tool for general analysis.

(Bk.rev.: Choice '80/17:214+)

American Romantic Psychology: Emerson, Poe, Whitman, Dickinson, Melville, by Martin Bickman. (Orig. title: *The Unsounded Centre: Jungian Studies in American Romanticism.* Chapel Hill, N.C.: U. of North Carolina Press, 1980.) Dallas: Spring Publications, ed.2 1988p* (209 + xviii, incl. 5-p. index, 12-p. bibl., 14-p. ref. notes, new intro.).

Viewing American Romanticism as part of the progressive self-discovery of the psyche, Bickman perceives that such literature serves not only as illustrative material for this psychology but also illuminates the nature and origins of Jung's psychology. He uses Jung's theory of individuation as a basic form of Romantic thought in the process of unity from division to reintegration. Following a "methodological" discussion of the symbol in

Jungian thought, he interprets Poe's *Eureka,* Emerson's "Plato," and Whitman's "Passage to India" as "voyages of the mind's return" and then devotes separate chapters to Poe ("To Helen" and four tales illustrating positive aspects of the anima); Emerson (an essay on "Experience" illustrating confrontation with the problem of alienation); Whitman ("Out of the Cradle Endlessly Rocking," "The Sleepers," "Chanting the Square Deific"); and Dickinson (a cluster of poems containing images of psychic transformation). Appended is a 19-page essay on "Melville and the Mind."

(Bk.revs.: LibJ '80/105:1735; LibJBkR '80:260; AmLit '81/53:339–40; BkRDig '81/125–6; Choice '81/18:656; DickStud '84/n41:43–5; 19CenFict '81/36:212–13; PoeStud Jn'81/14:14–16; SHumR '81/15:364–6; WaltWhitR '81/27:45; CanRAmStud '82/13:349–62; JAmStud '82/16:457–9; JAnPsy '82/27:392–4; Review '83/5:31–4; StudAmFict '83/11:125–6)

Joyce between Freud and Jung, by Sheldon R. Brivic. Port Washington, N.Y. and London: Kennikat Press, 1980* (National University Publications/Literary Criticism Series) (226, incl. 4-p. index, 6-p. ref. notes).

Brivic believes that Joyce and Jung had much in common as thinkers: both admired religious values without subscribing to a particular religion, and both were preoccupied by mythology and self-realization and the unconscious. Using depth psychology to trace Joyce's career as a "relentless spiral of transformation," Brivic begins by showing the origins of Joyce's obsessions from a Freudian perspective. He then attempts to connect the unconscious aspects of Joyce's personality to the meanings and values in consciousness, devoting a chapter to Joyce's system and Jung's psychological types. He concludes with an exploration of the value that Joyce found in life through his mythology.

(Bk.revs.: Choice '81/18:656; JAnPsy '81/26:374–5; ModFictStud '81/27:310–16; Spring '81:230; SHumR '82/16:369–70; REnglStud '83/ns34:96–9)

Light from the Darkness: The Paintings of Peter Birkhäuser, by Peter Birkhäuser. (Bilingual German/English ed.: *Licht aus dem Dunkel: Die Malerei von Peter Birkhäuser.*) Basel, Boston, and Stuttgart: Birkhäuser Verlag, 1980 (139, incl. 38 plates/28 in color, 8-p. biography of Peter Birkhäuser).

Believing that Jung may have shown the way leading out of the chaos in which art has lost itself, Swiss artist Birkhäuser presents pictures that are pure products of his unconscious mind. He painted many of his more than 3,400 recorded dreams, visions of his inner world that shaped his life. Jungian analyst Marie-Louise von Franz provides short commentaries as hints to possible interpretations of 28 full-page oils and nine crayon/lithography reproductions. Also included is a chalk portrait of Jung. Contents of the pictures are reflected in the titles, among which are The World's Wound; Depression; The Inward Gaze; The Fourth Dimension; Imprisoned Power; The Hidden Power; Fire Gives Birth; The Outcast; Puer; The Magic Fish; At the Door; With Child; Anima with Crown of Light; The Observer; Bear at the Tree of Light; Window on Eternity; Lighting the Torch; The Fourfold Face; Duel; Constellation; and Birth from the Chrysalis. Also included is a 15-page essay on analytical psychology and the problems of art.

(Bk.revs.: AmJArtTh '81/21:35–6; InwLight '81–82/n97:43–5; Quad '83/16n1:105–8)

Perspectives on Creativity and the Unconscious: Proceedings of Jungian Conference Hosted by Miami University, Oxford, Ohio, 2–4 June, 1979, edited by Donald W. Fritz. Oxford, Ohio: Miami U. Press, 1980 (116, incl. 19 illus., 5-p. intro. by editor/conference director Fritz).

These five papers on perspectives on creativity and the unconscious include an essay by Jungian analyst June Singer on creativity in the analytical psychology of Jung; an examination of Jung and modern art by Pulitzer Prize-winning poet Richard Howard; a personal view of creativity by architect Walter Netsch; a non-creative look at the creative process by painter and art critic Walter Darby Bannard; and an essay on new psychological approaches to creativity by psychiatrist Silvano Arieti.

The Psychological Meaning of Redemption Motifs in Fairy Tales, by Marie-Louise von Franz. Toronto: Inner City Books, 1980p* (Studies in Jungian Psychology by Jungian Analysts, 2) (124, incl. 5-p. index, 1 illus.).

In this book consisting of seven lectures delivered at the Jung Institute of Zurich in 1956, von Franz distinguishes between the Christian idea of redemption and the psychological meaning of redemption motifs in fairy tales in which one is cursed or bewitched and later redeemed through certain occurrences. She discusses motifs from various tales to show different types of curses that have important psychological meaning; a human being in a neurotic state might be compared to a bewitched person in which one particular structure of the psyche is damaged in its functioning and the whole is affected. She comments that such fairy tales do not dwell much on problems of the curse but on the method of redemption, which is relevant to therapeutic procedures and the healing process.

(Bk.rev.: Quad '81/14n1:87–8)

A Psychology of Fear: The Nightmare Formula of Edgar Allan Poe, by David Saliba. Lanham, Md.: University Press of America, 1980 +p (267 + ix, incl. 11-p. index, 12-p. bibl., 28-p. end-chapter notes).

Drawing a parallel between Jung's theory of a "collective unconscious" and Poe's idea of "soul," Saliba considers a study of the development of Poe's art as a study in Poe's developing understanding of the human psyche, which cannot be understood fully in rational terms but only experienced through its images and symbols. He examines Poe's formula of fear by analyzing the psychology and mechanics of fear, the elements of the nightmare, and the nightmare as literary form and illustrates Poe's early development of the formula in the tales "Metzengerstein," "MS Found in a Bottle," and "Berenice" and his later achievement in "Ligeia," "The Fall of the House of Usher," and "The Pit and the Pendulum." He concludes with an interpretation of the philosophical and psychological implications of Poe's art.
(Bk.revs.: PoeStud Jn'81/14:16–17; StudShFict '81/18:473–4)

Theatre and Alchemy, by Bettina L. Knapp. Detroit: Wayne State U. Press, 1980*
    (283 + xiii, incl. 9-p. index, 5-p. bibl., 3-p. foreword by Mircea Eliade).

Basing her approach on the relationship Jung suggested between psychology and alchemy, Knapp states that any play may be interpreted alchemically, that is to say, that it can be shown to pass through the alchemical phases of *nigredo* (blackening), *albedo* (whitening), and *rubedo* (reddening) that occur in the union of disparate parts into a harmony of opposites. As examples of the first stage (chaos, or experience of the collective unconscious), she interprets Strindberg's *A Dream Play* and de Ghelderode's *Escurial.* The second stage (washing, or consciousness) is represented by Claudel's *Break of Noon,* Yeats's *The Only Jealousy of Emer,* and Witkiericz's *The Water Hen,* and the third (union of opposites) by de l'Isle-Adam's *Axël* and Ansky's *The Dybbuk.* As examples of the world/spiritual/soul concept of alchemy, she analyzes a fourteenth-century Noh drama (*Matsukaze*) and a second-century B.C. Sanskrit play, *Shakuntala,* which is drawn from the *Mahabharata.* She concludes that the theatre may be viewed as operational alchemy in that the play allows one to reach beyond one's limited vision toward the Infinite, an instinctive activity within the psyche which cannot be explained rationally any more than can genius or talent.
(Bk.revs.: Choice '81/19:95; ModDrama '81/24:572–4; Quad '81/14n2:115–17; WorldLit '81/55:733–4; BkRDig '82:738; CanTheatR '82/36:132; 19CenFrStud '82/10:369–70; PerfArtsJ '82/6n2:114–15; TheatResInt '82/7:144–6; WHumR '82/36:75–6; CanRCompLit '84/11:111–14)

Archetypal Patterns in Women's Fiction, by Annis Pratt with Barbara White, Andrea Lowenstein, and Mary W. Hyer. Bloomington: Indiana U. Press, 1981 +p; Brighton: Harvester Press, 1981 +p (211 + x, incl. 5-p. index, 17-p. bibl. of women authors, 11-p. ref. notes).

Pratt approaches women's fiction from an archetypal and analytic viewpoint (differentiating it from that of Jung, Harding, and Campbell), perceiving patterns both from the world shared by men and women and from a feminine self-expression very often at odds with the world. She draws from a wide range (more than 300 books) by women writers, mainly minor authors, of the past 300 years. She categorizes them according to the following types: novels of development (the clash between concepts of individual liberty and personal fulfillment and contradictory norms of chastity and social submission); novels of marriage and novels of social protest (enclosure in the patriarchy); novels of love between men and women (the quest for sexuality); novels of love and friendship between women and novels of singleness and solitude (Eros as expression of the Self); and novels of rebirth and transformation (female heroes in middle and old age). She closes with a chapter that connects these patterns with the Demeter/Kore and Ishtar/Tammuz myths, the Grail legends, and archetypal and ritual materials constituting the Craft of the Wise, or witchcraft.

(Bk.revs.: LibJ '81/106:2141; BkRDig '81:1076; Choice '82/19:1234; CollLit '82/9:156–7; Ms S'82/11:88; StudNovel '82/14:297–8; TulsaStud '82/1:94–6; VillVoice S'82/27:19; ModFict '83/29:347–9; Quad '83/16n1:115; CanRCompLit '85/12:505–9; RelStudR '85/11:62–3; ModLangR '86/81:184–6)

A Jungian Psychoanalytic Interpretation of William Faulkner's As I Lay Dying, by Dixie M. Turner. Washington, D.C.: University Press of America, 1981 +p (99 + viii, incl. 8-p. bibl., 3-p. gloss. of Jungian terms).

Using her conception of Jungian archetypes as collective entities that exist both in Faulkner's mind and in the mind of "Everyman," Turner aims to present a composite portrait of the total human experience by interpreting the novel *As I Lay Dying* (1930). She analyzes each member of the Bundren family (Addie, Anse, Jewel, Darl, Dewey Dell, Cash, and Vardaman) in terms of the archetypal postulates of the Self, Persona, Shadow, Wise Man, Great Mother, Hero-Savior, and Child.

(Bk.rev.: ModFictStud '82/28:675–9)

The Alchemy of Discourse: An Archetypal Approach to Language, by Paul K. Kugler. Lewisburg, Penn.: Bucknell U. Press, with London and Toronto: Associated University Presses, 1982* (Studies in Jungian Thought) (141, incl. 7-p. index, 11-p. bibl.).

In proposing the concept of archetypal linguistics, Kugler aims to demonstrate that the individual is separated from the material world and initiated into a shared archetypal system of meaning-relations through the acquisition of language, which transfers matter into imagination. In his exploration of the archetypal approach to language he discusses Jung's psycholinguistic research at Burghölzli Hospital and the relationship of dreams and language. He examines the paradigm shift from substance to relations in archetypal structures as evidenced in physics (Maxwell, Planck, and Einstein), linguistics (Ferdinand de Saussure), depth psychology (Jung), and anthropology (Lévi-Strauss). He also discusses the topics of archetypal linguistics and French structuralism, the language of the unconscious, the phonetic imagination, and the alchemy of discourse.

(Bk.revs.: Quad '83/16n2:76–8; CaudaPav Fall'84/ns3:8; JAnPsy '84/29:91–3)

The Inner Story: Myth and Symbol in the Bible and Literature, by Helen M. Luke. New York: Crossroad Publishing Co., 1982* (118 + viii).

Citing Jung's discovery of the life-giving wonder of the inner myth (or the story) behind his life following his confrontation with the powers of the unconscious, Luke claims that each individual's story, originating in the experience of inner darkness, can begin to be found in response to the great stories of the world. She explores myth and symbol in the Bible through interpretations of the stories of Saul and Jacob and also looks at an African tale, Euripides's *The Bacchae* (405 B.C.), Antoine de Saint-Exupéry's *The Little Prince* (1943), Frodo's Mythril Coat in Tolkien's *The Lord of the Rings* (1966), and Shakespeare's *King Lear* (1608).

(Bk.rev.: BestSell Jy'82/42:159)

The Japanese Psyche: Major Motifs in the Fairy Tales of Japan, by Hayao Kawai. (Jap.: *Mikashibanashito Nihonjin no Kokoro.* Tokyo: Iwanami Shoten Publ., 1982.) Dallas: Spring Publications, 1988p* (234 + vi, incl. 1-p. bibl., 3-p. ref. notes, 9 illus.).

Jungian analyst Kawai compares Japanese consciousness with Western consciousness as illustrated by the tale "Faithful John" and concludes that the essence of Japanese fairy tales can be seen better through "female eyes" (looking at the world through eyes located in the unconscious depths, though qualified as "half-closed" eyes in order to avoid a contradiction with consciousness). He interprets tales that illustrate concepts of consciousness, the Great Mother, mother-daughter unity, the relationships of brother and sister and mother and son, nonhuman females, and happy marriages. The appendix (35 pp.) consists of translations of "The Bush Warbler's Home"; a synopsis of "Faithful John"; "The Woman Who Eats Nothing"; "The Laughter of Oni"; "Three-eyes"; "White Bird Sister"; "Urashina Taro"; "Crane Wife"; "The Handless Maiden"; "Hyotoku"; and "The Charcoal Maker of Chojya."

(Bk.revs.: JAsianStud '89/48:866–7; Quad '89/22n2:125 + 127; SmallPr Jn'89/7:56)

The Smaller Infinity: The Jungian Self in the Novels of Robertson Davies, by Patricia Monk. Toronto, Buffalo, and London: University of Toronto Press, 1982* (214 + ix, incl. 8-p. index, 21-p. ref. notes).

Stating that all of the work of novelist Robertson Davies manifests his interest in and admiration for Jung, Monk focuses on Davies' own concentrated interest on the "mystery of human personality." Her title, taken from Jung's reference (in *Seven Sermons to the Dead*) to "the smaller or innermost infinity" of the microcosm, denotes an inner universe of the personality just as infinite as the outer universe. Starting with the history of Davies' affinity to Jungian thought, involving folklore, magic, religion, archetypes, literature, and the individuation theory, she then interprets his writings as giving concrete, creative form to the workings of the human psyche. Her analysis takes her from Davies' first book (*Shakespeare's Boy Actors,* 1939) through the Salterton trilogy (the conflict between illusion and psychic identity) to the Deptford trilogy (*Fifth Business; The Manticore; World of Wonders,* 1970–75). In all of these she sees Davies dealing with transcendent psychic reality and mundane physical reality, the movement toward self-understanding under analysis, and the exploration of good and evil.

(Bk.revs.: CanForum Oc'82/62:30; Choice '82/20:583–4; WorldLitEngl '82/21:625–8; BkRDig '83:1018; BksCan Jn'83/12:29; CanBkRAn '83:276–7; CanLit '83/n99:69–72; UTorQ '83/52:498–500; DalhousieR '84–85/64:812–14; EnglStudCan '84/10:476–88; EssCanWrit Spr'84/n28:102–6)

Archetype, Dance, and the Writer, by Bettina L. Knapp. New York: Bethel, 1983p (176 + v, incl. 6-p. ref.notes, 1-p. preface by Werner H. Engel).

Knapp, employing a Jungian approach, explores the psychological, philosophical, and aesthetic implications of archetypal dance in literature. She examines the imagery and archetypes of dance episodes in the works of Melville (the sailors' dance on an archetypal sea journey in *Moby-Dick*); Baudelaire (the archetypal death dance in "Danse Macabre"); Flaubert (dance and the archetypal harlot, wife, and castrator from *Travel Notes; Correspondence; Hérodias;* and *Madame Bovary*); Wilde (the erotic dance archetype in *Salome*); Nietzsche (dance and the Dionysian archetype in *Thus Spake Zarathustra;* Strindberg (archetypal alienation and dance in *The Dance of Death*); Yeats (archetypal *vagina dentata* dances in *A Full Moon in March*); Valéry (the Socratic archetypal dancer in "The Soul of the Dance" and "The Philosophy of Dance"); Bharata Natyam (archetypal body language in the Indian temple dance drama); and Zeami Motokiyo (dance and archetypal wandering in the Noh play *Lady Han*).

(Bk.revs.: 19CenFrStud '84/12n4–13n1:218–19; WorldLit '84/58:482–3)

Fairy Tales and the Kingdom of God, by Allen Whitman. Pecos, N.M.: Dove Press, 1983p (132, incl. 2-p. ref. notes, foreword by Morton Kelsey).

Interested in the Jungian approach to fairy tales, Whitman examines them as illuminators of the inner and outer truth of the Gospel of the Kingdom of God. He believes that fairy tales not only convey truth in folk art form but illuminate and bring a fresh perspective to the teaching about the Kingdom. First, he interprets the familiar tales of "Three Feathers," "Jack and the Beanstalk," "The Emperor's Clothes," "Rumpelstilkskin," "Snow White," "The Frog King," "The Spirit in the Bottle," "Hansel and Gretel," and "The Cobbler and the Tailor." He then discusses Tolkien's *The Lord of the Rings* and *The Chronicles of Narnia* by C. S. Lewis, examining their use of imaginative language and symbol. He concludes with a section about writing one's own fairy tale out of one's own depths.

Snow White: Life Almost Lost, by Theodor Seifert. (Ger.: *Schneewittchen.* Zurich: Kreuz Verlag, 1983.) Wilmette, Ill.: Chiron Publications, 1986p* (131 + ix, incl. 1-p. ref. notes).

Seifert characterizes the tale of Snow White as a life that was almost lost and likens its theme to the experience of persons in psychotherapy in which life seems to stand still and the person feels "as if dead." He poses the central question to which Snow White seeks and finds an answer as: "How do I win back the life I thought I had lost?" He analyzes the tale in twenty stages, including small, scarcely perceptible feelings (snowflakes), great conflict (drops of blood in the snow), self-condemnation for better or worse (mirror, mirror), the secret life of the soul (in the wild forest), hidden growth (with the dwarfs), between life and death (in the glass coffin), encounter, sacrifice, and treasure (the king's son comes into the forest), being rooted in one's own earth, and collective cold and heat.

Tales for Jung Folk: Original Fairytales for Persons of All Ages Dramatizing C. G. Jung's Archetypes of the Collective Unconscious, by Richard Roberts. San Anselmo, Calif.: Vernal Equinox Press, 1983* +p* (101, incl. 12 illus.).

Drawing on the experience of dreams in the form of fairy tales, which he extended and completed by the process of active imagination, Roberts presents (in the order in which they came from the unconscious) six tales, whose inspiration occurs in what he calls the Dream Castle. He adds to each story an explanatory primer (with appropriate quotations from Jung), namely, archetypes and the unconscious for "The Dream Castle," the shadow for "Ruckus in the Well," the persona for "The Mask That Wore the Man," the Self for "The Seed's Secret," active imagination for "Travels with Mozart," and projection for "The Crystal People." Also included is a tale of "The Four Rings" (the four functions), which contains many conscious elements, such as riddles, in addition to active imagination.

A Jungian Approach to Literature, by Bettina L. Knapp. Carbondale and Edwardsville, Ill.: Southern Illinois U. Press, 1984* (402 + xvi, incl. 12-p. index, 5-p. bibl., 9-p. ref. notes).

Knapp explores the universal applicability of Jungian archetypal analysis and criticism by taking literary works out of their original and conventional contexts and relating them to "humankind in general." She studies the works of ten authors, probing "this eternally rich world" of the human psyche through the writings of creative geniuses of past centuries. She presents the life, times, literary structure, and archetypal analysis of each, starting with *The Bacchae* (405 B.C.) by Euripides and continuing with Wolfram von Eschenbach's *Parzival* (c. 1200), which involves the creation of the archetypal hero; three essays illustrating the individuation process by Montaigne; dramatic poems by Corneille; *Elective Affinities* (1809) by Goethe; *Hymns to the Night* (1800) by Novalis; *The Master of Prayer* (ego's exile from the Self and struggle to reintegrate) by Rabbi Nachman; *At the Hawk's Well* (1916) by Yeats; *The Kalevala* (the Finnish national epic); and *The Conference of the Birds,* the story of a Sufi religious quest.
(Bk.revs.: JMindBeh '84/5:517–20; Choice '85/22:809; Chry&Lit '85/34n4:79–80; Quad '85/18n1:109-11; WorldLit '85/59:324; BkRDig '86:900)

Prospero's Island: The Secret Alchemy at the Heart of The Tempest, by Noel Cobb. London: Coventure, 1984* (224, incl. 3-p. index, 3-p. bibl., 9-p. ref. notes, 37 illus.).

Characterizing Shakespeare as walking a path which sought harmony between that which is above and that which is below ("like some strange Western incarnation of a Taoist sage"), Cobb presents him as representing the complete individual and his drama *The Tempest* as the "impeccable culmination" of his life's work. Feeling that Shakespeare can help in revisioning the soul-spirit polarity (referring to the pioneering work of Jung, and, more recently, Hillman, in distinguishing spirit and soul and bringing the soul back into psychology), he states that alchemical images permeate the play, which was written at the time of the golden age of alchemy. He suggests that these images are still valid today and provide symbols of reconciliation for the often warring inner opposites. Prospero, as the image-quickening

Magus of Imagination, is viewed as living the contradiction of perceiving the absolute and yet living amidst the relative.
(Bk.revs.:BrBkN '84:310; Harvest '84/30:137–8; JAnPsy '84/29:390–1; Resurg My-Jn '84/n104:38)

The Quest: Further Adventures in the Unconscious, by J. Marvin Spiegelman. Phoenix: Falcon Press, 1984p* (175 + x, incl. 2 illus.).

In this second volume of his trilogy on psycho-myth, which he defines as a blend of fiction and psychological fact and describes in the introduction to the first work of the trilogy (*The Tree,* 1974), Spiegelman presents further adventures into the unconscious, the result of many years of using Jung's method of active imagination. He narrates three stories, entitled "The Son of the Knight," "Mother and Daughter," and "The Vessel," which deal symbolically with the process of self-discovery and individuation.
(Bk.rev.: PsyPersp '86/17:254–8)

Mental Forms Creating: William Blake Anticipates Freud, Jung, and Rank, by Jerry Caris Godard. Lanham, Md., New York, and London: University Press of America, 1985* +p* (173, incl. 5-p. index, 6-p. ref. notes, 6-p. gloss. of terms, 10 illus.).

Inspired by the spirit of William James and his sensitivity to the integrity of the ideas of others, Godard examines, in turn, the theories of Freud, Jung, and Otto Rank (designated "heirs apparent" by Freud) with an analysis of Blake's anticipation of each. He views Blake's insights as multifaceted and sharply-focused portrayals of human nature, and he characterizes Blake's anticipations as bringing into relief the human experiences of consciousness, rationality, love, individuality, and terror.

The Nymphomaniac: A Study in the Origins of a Passion of the Soul Along with Two Essays on the Jungian Techniques of Active Imagination, by J. Marvin Spiegelman. Phoenix: Falcon Press, 1985p* (78 + ii, incl. 1-p. bibl. notes, 12 illus.).

Preceding a 9-page commentary and his 32-page "psycho-mythological tale" of Sybilla, the Nymphomaniac, which is the second of five stories narrated by women in the tale *The Tree* (1974), Spiegelman presents an essay on the potential of active imagination (also published in *The Knight*) and another essay on the potentials and limitations of active imagination (presented in London in 1984), all of which provide amplification and explanation of the background and meaning of the tale. He emphasizes, however, that the story itself is relatively timeless and can stand alone as a story of "the feminine," whether in man or woman.

Word/Image/Psyche, by Bettina L. Knapp. University, Ala.: U. of Alabama Press, 1985* (247 + ix, incl. 9-p. index, 4-p. bibl., 7-p. ref. notes, 31 illus.).

Citing Jung's theories on creativity and the unconscious, Knapp presents reactions by nine writers, who are not primarily critics but rather poets, essayists, and novelists, to paintings and sculptures that have stimulated the depths of the collective unconscious in each. She discusses, chronologically, Gautier's confrontation with aestheticism versus asceticism in the paintings of Ribera and Zurbarán; Baudelaire's appraisals of Delacroix's paintings as "the celebration of a mystery"; the Goncourt brothers' distinctive style of *écriture-sensation* (an almost obsessive focus on the tactile aspect of graphic and plastic arts); Huysmans's "catalytic eye" (able to transform art into verbal pictures); Henry James's view of portraiture and anima in *The Ambassadors;* Rilke's writing inspired by Rodin's creative genius (the puer-senex dynamic); Kokoschka's apocalyptic experience illustrated by his own drawings for *Murderer, Hope of Womankind;* Virginia Woolf's examination of impressionism and Cézanne in *To the Lighthouse;* and Malraux's essay on the shadowy inner world as portrayed in Goya's stupendous "Saturn Devouring One of His Children."

(Bk.revs.: Choice '85/23:92; 19CenFrStud '85–86/14:181–3; LibJ '85/110:98–9; WorldLit '85/59:666; BkRDig '86:900; BrJAesth '86/26:182–4; FrR '87/60:385; SHumR '87/21:375)

Archetype, Architecture, and the Writer, by Bettina L. Knapp. Bloomington, Ind.: Indiana U. Press, 1986* (208 + xvi, incl. 6-p. index, 3-p. bibl., 5-p. ref. notes).

Viewing Jung's tower-building as an archetypal metaphor for an inner psychic climate, Knapp looks at architecture as a spatial creation that is the "outer garment of a secretive and vital system," a nonverbal manifestation of a preconscious condition. She presents archetypal interpretations of "metaphoric visions" in the writings of ten authors, starting with an architectural archetype of emptiness within in Ibsen's *The Master Builder;* introversion in Maeterlinck's *The Intruder* and *Interior;* the entrapped shadow in the archetypal house in James's "The Jolly Corner"; the self-made man in Ansky's "The Tower of Rome"; the archetypal land surveyor in Kafka's *The Castle;* house of a matriarchate in García Lorca's *The House of Bernarda Alba;* the hexagonal gallery in Borges's "The Library of Babel"; a parapsychological happening in an architectural construct in Fuentes' "In a Flemish Garden"; architectonic archetype in Wang Shih-Fu's *The Romance of the Western*

Chamber (thirteenth century); and an archetypal feminine sun and masculine moon in Hushima's *The Temple of the Golden Pavilion* (1956). (Bk.revs.: Choice '86/23:1536–7; Quad '86/19n2:86–8; BkRDig '87:1027; 19CenFrStud '87/15:331–3; WorldLit '87/61:169)

The Compensatory Psyche: A Jungian Approach to Shakespeare, by H. R. Coursen. Lanham, Md.: University Press of America, 1986* +p* (217 + xii, incl. 4-p. index, 5-p. bibl., 15-p. ref. notes).

By approaching Shakespeare through Jung's metaphor of the "self-compensatory psyche," the unconscious as a balance to consciousness, Coursen emphasizes the dynamic relationship of the unconscious to the "time zone known as ego." Following a brief look at Shakespeare's *Richard III* and Richard's nightmare, which the author feels demonstrates the universality and depth of the self-compensatory psyche, he discusses the topics of symbols of transformation, comedy and the problem play, and *Henry V* before interpreting *Hamlet, Othello, King Lear,* and *Macbeth,* ending with *The Tempest.* He analyzes Shakespeare's characterizations in terms of Jung's categories of psychological types in order to understand the psychological structures of individual characters and the interaction between characters.

Encounter with the Self: A Jungian Commentary on William Blake's Illustrations of the Book of Job, by Edward F. Edinger. Toronto: Inner City Books, 1986p* (Studies in Jungian Psychology by Jungian Analysts, 22) (75, incl. 26 illus.).

Believing Jung's *Answer to Job* to be correct in asserting that Job's story represents an individual ego's decisive encounter with the Self ("the Greater Personality"), Edinger characterizes Blake's illustrations of the Book of Job as reflecting the objective (collective) psyche. He presents descriptions and psychological interpretations of the twenty-one paintings as the wounded encounter which provokes a descent into the unconscious, a *nekiya* ("journey to Hades"), similar to Edinger's own interpretation of the night sea journey of Melville's *Moby-Dick,* or Goethe's *Faust.* His analysis of Blake's rendering of the Job story shows the effect of this archetypal image on the unconscious, wherein the encounter with the Self (transpersonal center of latent consciousness) is at first a defeat for the ego, but with perseverance results in a light that is born from the darkness. (Bk.revs.: PsyPersp '86/17:252–4; CanBkRAn '87:83; Harvest '87/33:209–11; JAnPsy '87/32:293–6; Quad '87/20n1:97–8)

The Hero's Quest for the Self: An Archetypal Approach to Hesse's Demian *and* Other Novels, by David G. Richards. Lanham, Md.: University Press of America, 1987* + p* (153 + iii, incl. 21-p. index, 5-p. bibl., 5 illus.).

Richards considers that Hesse's presentation of the process of individuation in *Demian* (1919) actually anticipates some of Jung's subsequent insights. He likens the general reprocity of influence between Hesse and Jung (between poet and psychologist) to the discovery by the youth of the 1960s of Hesse and Jung as guides for the inward journey. He analyzes *Demian* as a poeticized model of Jung's central concept, which proceeds from confrontation with the shadow (the fall) to retreat from individuation (return of the prodigal son), the hero's journey (departure), symbol of unity and the Self (the discovery of Abraxas), rebirth and the path to selfhood, arrival and fulfillment, and the signs of collective rebirth.

(Bk.revs.: Choice '88/25:911; GerStudQ '88/11:173)

Howard Hawks: A Jungian Study, by Clark Branson. Santa Barbara: Garland-Clarke Editions/Capra Press, 1987* + p* (332 + viii, incl. 4-p. bibl., 2-p. ref. notes, 3-p. gloss. of cinematic and dramatic terms, 43 illus., 2-p. foreword by Judith Harte).

Branson presents the motifs and patterns of Hawks's films as illustrations of the basic features of Jung's thought. His "comprehensive descriptive analysis" deals with thirty-nine films produced by Hawks between 1925 and 1970 (including, among others, *Scarface, His Girl Friday, Only Angels Have Wings,* and *Rio Bravo*), preceding which he discusses Hawks and Jung under the topics of Hawks and archetypal expression; Hawks as a Jungian subject; the quaternity and the extraverted sensation function; the shadow; the anima; the self and the transcendental function; the collective unconscious; rites of passage; Hawks as *auteur;* the mysticism of Hawks; and the fraternal return motif.

(Bk.revs.: Choice '87/25:137; UHartStud '87/19:79–85; FilmQ Sum'88/41:37; JPop-FilmTV '88/16:135; SmallPr F'88/5:40; SmallPrBkR Mr'88/3:10; WAmLit '88/23:147)

The Secret of the Black Chrysanthemum, by Charles Stein. Barrytown, N.Y.: Station Hill Press, 1987* (Clinamen Studies Series) (225 + xxvii, incl. 4-p. bibl., 5-p. ref. notes, 17 photos).

In this study of Charles Olson (1900–1970), originator of the theory of projective verse, Stein aims to remain close to Olson's reading of Jung by examining copies of Jungian texts that were in Olson's possession (fourteen volumes, mostly closely read and heavily marked). Stein deals primarily with the period of Olson's mature creative activity beginning with the planning of *The Maximus Poems.* He discusses the topics of projection; the archetypes; the libido; the projection of archetypal force onto persons, language, and place; and Jung's notion of the Self with a reading of *The Maximus Poems* as a manifestation of this archetype. The title of the book comes from

Olson's "culminating vision" of the world, with echoes of *The Secret of the Golden Flower.*
(Bk.rev.: SmallPr Jn'88/5:32)

Women in Twentieth-Century Literature: A Jungian View, by Bettina L. Knapp. University Park, Penn.: Pennsylvania State U. Press, 1987* (249, incl. 7-p. index, 4-p. bibl., 5-p. ref. notes).

Using Jung's basic analytical technique and vocabulary and "reevaluating and revising some of his concepts," Knapp explores various feminine types in her study of some of the feminine characters in various literary works. She describes and interprets a woman's mystery in García Lorca's *Yerma;* the teenage archetype of exile in Elizabeth Bowen's *Death of the Heart;* an alchemical transfiguration ritual in Dinesen's "Peter and Rosa"; two young girls growing up in Mussolini's Italy in Ginzburg's *All Our Yesterdays;* sacrifice in O'Connor's "Everything That Rises Must Converge"; mother/daughter identification and alienation in Rhys's *Wide Sargasso Sea;* androgyny and the creative process in Sarraute's *Between Life and Death;* the patriarchate dismembered in Pa Chin's *Family;* a sacred mystery in Fumiko Enchi's *Masks;* and a rite of the great-grandmother's exit in Anita Desai's *Fire on the Mountain.*
(Bk.revs.: Choice '88/25:1237; ModFictStud '88/34:329–30; Quad '89/22n1:71–3; WorldLit Wint'89/68:170)

Jungian Literary Criticism 1920–1980: An Annotated, Critical Bibliography of Works in English (with a selection of titles after 1980), by Jos van Meurs, with John Kidd. Metuchen, N.J. and London: The Scarecrow Press, 1988* (353, incl. 27-p. indexes).

As a comprehensive survey of all secondary works (books and articles, critical and scholarly) written in English that apply the psychology of Jung to the interpretation of literary texts (monographs, articles, dissertations), van Meurs presents 902 bibliographic entries, along with explanatory information on the aims and scope of the project, research and collaboration, the format of bibliographical entries, critical standards, bibliographical sources, comprehensiveness, and further research.
(Bk.revs.: AmLib '88/19:1022; ResRefBkN D'88/3:22; AmRefBksAn '89/20:278; Choice '89/26:785–6; PsyPersp '89/20:187 + 189–90; Spring '89/49:158–9)

Music, Archetype, and the Writer: A Jungian View, by Bettina L. Knapp. University Park, Penn. and London: Pennsylvania State U. Press, 1988* (234, incl. 6-p. index, 5-p. bibl., 6-p. ref. notes).

Quoting Jung's comment that "music should be an essential part of every analysis," Knapp examines the interaction of archetypal music (arising from the collective unconscious and expanding consciousness to reveal the psyche's potential) and the written word. She analyzes the work of twelve authors, drawn from ancient and contemporary Western and Eastern literatures and written under the influence of archetypal music. Her interpretations deal with archetypal music and active imagination in Hoffmann's "Kreisleriana"; archetypal music as science and art in Balzac's "Gambara"; Baudelaire on Wagner's archetypal operas; archetypal music as a demonic force in Tolstoy's "Kreutzer Sonata"; archetypal resonances in word, color, line, and rhythm in Kandinsky's *Sounds;* an archetypal auditory experience in Joyce's "Evangeline"; archetypal music as an exercise in transcendence in Proust's *Remembrance of Things Past;* jazz in Sartre's *Nausea;* archetypal violin music and the prophetic experience in Yizhar's "Habakuk"; a Sanskrit sacred ritual in Bhasa's *Dream of Vasavadatta* (c. first century B.C.); archetypal music as multiplicity of oneness in Hanquing's *Jade Mirror-Stand* (fourteenth century); and audible and inaudible archetypal soundings in Mishima's Noh drama *The Damask Drum* (1955).

(Bk.revs.: BkRDig N'89:89; Choice '89/26:928; JBlackSacM Spr'89/3:74; ModFictStud '89/35:383–4; Quad '89/22n2:116–17; TimesLitSup '89:274; WorldLit '89/63:372)

The Place of Creation: Six Essays, by Erich Neumann. Princeton, N.J.: Princeton U. Press/Bollingen, 1988* (Bollingen Series LXI:3) (Essays of Erich Neumann, vol. 3) (398 + xii, incl. 16-p. index).

In this book consisting of six lectures given at Eranos Conferences in Switzerland from 1952 to 1960 (ending four months before his death at age 55), Neumann addresses the theme of creation, focusing on the "inseparable link that unites the individual, the immediate background to which he himself belongs, and the world that surrounds him and that he creates." He aims to develop the concept of "unitary reality" by expanding the concepts of analytical psychology and by establishing a more comprehensive definition of the archetype than Jung used. The essays, expanded and revised from the lectures, include a metaphysical essay on the psyche and the transformation of the reality planes (1952); the experience of the unity reality (1955); creative man and the "great experience" (1956); man and meaning (1957); peace as the symbol of life (1958); and the psyche as the place of creation (1960).

Shakespeare's Antony and Cleopatra: *A Jungian Interpretation,* by Priscilla Murr. Berne, Frankfurt-am-Main, New York, and Paris: Peter Lang, 1988p* (European University Studies: Series XIV—Anglo-Saxon Lang. & Lit., vol. 187) (196 + xii, incl. 5-p. bibl., 16-p. ref. notes, 4-p. gloss. of Jungian terms).

Combining years of work in English literature with Jungian clinical practice, Murr presents her dissertation as a psychological interpretation of Shakespeare's *Antony and Cleopatra*. She proceeds from the setting of the tragedy ("If it be love indeed . . .") to the sealing of the tragedy ("What's brave, what's noble . . ."), followed by analytic interpretations of Antony and his anima, Cleopatra and her animus, the archetype of the trinity (in God, in government, and in the lack of acceptance of the feminine in the individuation process), and the archetype of the Great Mother. She concludes with discussions of Octavius Caesar as the single-minded persona, whose aims exhibit none of Antony's doubts and scruples; and of the individuation process, which posits Antony's dilemma as the inner urge to become his own self.

Acrobats of the Gods: Dance and Transformation, by Joan Dexter Blackmer. Toronto: Inner City Books, 1989p* (Studies in Jungian Psychology by Jungian Analysts, 39) (124, incl. 4-p. index, 5-p. bibl., 40 illus.).

Calling upon a reawakened feminine spirit which she believes lies beneath the energetic explosion of physical activity in our time, Blackmer suggests the need to make conscious an evolving feminine archetype that reflects the energy and instinctive wisdom of the body, to tame it rather than renounce it. Stating that dancers are indeed acrobats of God (taken from the title of a dance choreographed in 1960 by Martha Graham) or, speaking psychologically, of the Self, she draws on twenty years' experience as both victim and beneficiary of the physical compulsion to train her body as a dancer, with which she combines her training in the principles of Jungian psychology. She discusses first the vessel (the sacred in dance; ego-body identity; body as shadow) and then analyzes the preparation of the body (the process; the third eye; the sixth sense; the value of pain). Next, she interprets approaching the center (complex of opposites; image and meaning; image of the stone to center the front of the body; image of the tree to center the back) and concludes with the transformation of energy in dance.

C. G. Jung and the Humanities: Toward a Hermeneutics of Culture, edited by Karin Barnaby and Pellegrino D'Acierno. Princeton, N.J.: Princeton U. Press, 1989* (372, incl. 18-p. index, 8-p. list of the *Collected Works,* end-chap. ref. notes, 19 illus., 15-p. editors' preface, 5-p. intro. by Philip T. Zabriskie).

This book is comprised of thirty papers presented by thirty-five partici-pants at the 1986 international, interdisciplinary conference held at Hofstra University. They demonstrate Jung's far-reaching impact on our culture and represent a number of views from traditional Jungian to contemporary non-Jungian and anti-Jungian positions. Organized under the three general headings of the archetypal tradition, creativity, and post-Jungian contributions, topical subheadings are mythology, religion, anthropology, popular culture, architecture, imagination, art, dance and theater, literature, gender issues, and postmodernism. Contributions by Jungian analysts, in addition to Zabriskie's introduction on Jung and the humanities, are on Jung's impact on religious studies (John Dourley); William Blake (June Singer); meaning in art (Stephen Martin); the feminine, pre- and post-Jungian (Beverley Zabriskie); beyond the feminine principle (Andrew Samuels); the unconscious in a postmodern depth psychology (Paul Kugler); and creativity, Jung, and postmodernism (James Hillman).

Death and Rebirth in Virgil's Arcadia, by M. Owen Lee. Albany: State U. of New York Press, 1989* +p* (SUNY Series in Classical Studies) (140 + xi, incl. 4-p. index of names, 15-p. ref. notes).

Addressing himself to the reader who wants both an introduction to Virgil's *Eclogues* (pastoral poems written 41–39 B.C.) and an interpretation of them, Lee describes Arcadia as the land within the imagination where a young poet discovers himself by distancing himself from the present. Lee utilizes Jungian theory and terminology, characterizing Virgil as "an intensely intuitive artist." He discusses metaphorical Arcadia, in which everything has symbolic value, as a composite picture of past tradition (Sicily, the origin of Theocritus's pastorals), personal experience (Mantua, close to Virgil's birthplace on a farm), and a mythic memory of primeval innocence (Arcadia). He then interprets the *Eclogues* under the topics of music (*Eclogues* 3 and 7), love (2 and 8), the city (1 and 9), the Golden Age (4), death (5), and leaving Arcadia (10), concluding with chapters on reading and interpreting the *Eclogues* (6).

In the Ever After: Fairy Tales and the Second Half of Life, by Allen B. Chinen. Wilmette, Ill.: Chiron Publications, 1989p* (203, incl. 9-p. index, 18-p. bibl., 21-p. ref. notes).

Taking the thesis that fairy tales about "old" protagonists reveal the psychology of maturity and that elder tales symbolize the developmental tasks individuals must master in the second half of life, Chinen interprets fifteen tales, relying upon psychodynamic theories of human development—particularly those of Jung and Erickson. One-third of the tales are from Japan, the remainder from Korea, Tibet, Burma, India, Arabia, Asia Minor, Croatia, Italy, and Germany, with one Jewish tale as well. Following each tale are reflections on its psychological meaning, covering the topics of loss and return of magic; confrontation; mask and self; wisdom; wisdom and evil; self-transcendence; self-transcendence and God; self-transcendence and the inner self; emancipated innocence; ego-integrity and innocence; the return of wonder; mediation and transcendence; mediation and the emancipation of society; return and transfiguration; and the elder cycle completed. (Bk.rev.: PsyPersp '90/22:179)

Machine, Metaphor, and the Writer: A Jungian View, by Bettina L. Knapp. University Park, Penn. and London: Pennsylvania State U. Press, 1989* (244 + viii, incl. 14-p. index, 5-p. bibl., 6-p. ref. notes).

In considering the theme of the impact of the machine on the literary mind, Knapp presents writings by French, Irish, Japanese, Israeli, German, Polish, and American authors and interprets how the increasing domination by technology is affecting our lives.

The Water of Life: A Jungian Journey through Hawaiian Myth, by Rita Knipe. Honolulu: U. of Hawaii Press, 1989* (176 + xv, incl. 4-p. index, 4-p. bibl., 2-p. gloss. of Hawaiian words, 13 illus.).

Knipe comments that mythology flows like a subterranean stream throughout Hawaii and that the mythic material presented here has been determined by her own position beside this stream as shaped by personal and professional experiences. Interpreting myths that illustrate certain universal themes or Jungian concepts, she retells stories of characteristic myths and mythological figures from the pantheon of Hawaiian deities, amplifying the symbols with psychological commentary and a number of dreams. Following a brief introduction, in which she recounts her love affair with the Islands, she presents the myths of the life-giving water of the god Kane; the Kumulipo creation chant; love stories of Halemano and Kamaldlawalu and of Hiku and Kawelu; Maui, light-bringer of the Pacific; Hina, goddess of the moon; miraculous Menehune; volcanic fire goddess Pele; Kamapua'a, the pig god; and the helpful goddess Hi'iaka.

Goethe's Faust: *Notes for a Jungian Commentary,* by Edward F. Edinger. Toronto: Inner City Books, 1990p (Studies of Jungian Psychology by Jungian Analysts, 43) (111, incl. 4-p. index, 3-p. bibl., 3 illus.).

Asserting, as did Jung, that Goethe's *Faust* is profoundly significant as a "document of the soul" and for the psychological understanding of modern individuals, Edinger offers some notes as a "beginning" of a Jungian interpretation of the legend. He views Faust's encounter with Mephistopheles as having been paved by the process of enantiodromia (running counter to) in which the figure of Christ is replaced by Antichrist. The corollary to this is the God-image (a metaphysical projection) falling out of heaven in the sixteenth century and ultimately landing in the human psyche. He examines the Faust legend as being generated like a compensating dream from the unconscious, which demonstrates that the individuation process is accompanied by guilt. The danger here is that when guilt reaches consciousness the ego may be overwhelmed by a sense of its own evil. He believes that Faust's struggle for fulfillment originates in the Self, which shares the guilt incurred by the ego, and that "redemption" is the result of an unconscious process. He states that Faust is "perhaps the central 'collective dream' of the Western psyche during the final quarter of the Christian eon."

Lyrical-Analysis: The Unconscious through Jane Eyre, by Angelyn Spignesi. Wilmette: Ill.: Chiron Publications, 1990p (349 + x).

11 Jungian Analysis

Analytical psychology, as a body of thought, has numerous applications. As a practical discipline, Jungian analysis is committed to the goal of psychological healing. It has taken its place among accepted methods of psychological treatment, even though, in the popular view, it retains an esoteric aura. The Jungian approach puts primary emphasis on revealing the fundamental and often unconscious blocks in the personality. Jung's ideas are being used increasingly in routine and down-to-earth ways in the helping professions, particularly in analysis, psychotherapy, and counseling.

More than one hundred forty books comprise this subject category, plus more than twenty that are cross-referenced from other subjects. It is the largest subject among the twelve in this book. More than half of these books were published from 1981 onward.

_____: Hermes and His Children [p. 313]

Mankowitz: Change of Life (See chapter 8, "Feminine and Masculine Psychology") [p. 178]

Mattoon: Understanding Dreams (See chapter 7, "Symbolic Life and Dreams") [p. 145]

Mattoon (ed.): Personal and Archetypal Dynamics in the Analytical Relationship [p. 352]

McCully: Jung and Rorschach [p. 305]

McNeely: Touching: Body Therapy and Depth Psychology [p. 341]

Meier: Healing Dream and Ritual [p. 299]

Middelkoop: The Wise Old Man [p. 334]

Mindell: Coma [p. 346]

_____: Dreambody (See chapter 7, "Symbolic Life and Dreams") [p. 149]

_____: The Dreambody in Relationships [p. 339]

_____: River's Way (See chapter 7, "Symbolic Life and Dreams") [p. 152]

_____: Working with the Dreaming Body [p. 335]

Mogenson: God Is a Trauma (See chapter 9, "Religion and Jung's Psychology") [p. 246]

New England Society of Jungian Analysts: The Analytic Life [p. 346]

Perera: The Scapegoat Complex [p. 338]

Perry: The Far Side of Madness [p. 309]

_____: Roots of Renewal in Myth and Madness [p. 311]

_____: The Self in Psychotic Process [p. 300]

Provost: A Casebook: Applications of the Myers-Briggs Type Indicator in Counseling [p. 330]

Quenk: Psychological Types and Psychotherapy [p. 331]

Reed: Emergence (See chapter 6, "Human Development and Individuation") [p. 99]

Rossi: Dreams and the Growth of Personality [p. 307]

_____: The Psychobiology of Mind-Body Healing [p. 337]

Rudin: Psychotherapy and Religion (See chapter 9, "Religion and Jung's Psychology") [p. 210]

Samuels: The Plural Psyche [p. 349]

Samuels (ed.): Psychopathology [p. 350]

Samuels, Shorter & Plaut (eds.): A Critical Dictionary of Jungian Analysis [p. 336]

Sandner: Navaho Symbols of Healing [p. 318]

Sanford: Dreams and Healing [p. 315]

_____: Healing and Wholeness [p. 313]

Savage: Mourning Unlived Lives [p. 349]

Schapira: The Cassandra Complex [p. 342]

Schwartz-Salant: The Borderline Personality [p. 341]

_____: *Pregnant Virgin* [p. 334]
_____: *The Ravaged Bridegroom* [p. 352]
Young-Eisendrath: *Hags and Heroes* [p. 331]
Young-Eisendrath & Wiedemann: *Female Authority* [p. 340]
Ziegler: *Archetypal Medicine* [p. 317]
Zoja: *Drugs, Addiction, and Initiation* [p. 348]
Zoja & Hinshaw (eds.): *The Differing Uses of Symbolic and Clinical Approaches* [p. 327]

Studies in Word-Association: Experiments in the Diagnosis of Psychopathological Conditions Carried Out at the Psychiatric Clinic of the University of Zurich, under the Direction of C. G. Jung. (Ger.: *Diagnostische Assoziationsstudien: Beiträge zur experimentellen Psychologie.* Leipzig: Barth Verlag, 1906–09, in 2 vols.) New York: Moffat, Yard, 1918; London: Heinemann, 1919; New York: Russell & Russell, repr. 1969; London: Routledge & Kegan Paul, reissue 1969 (595 + ix, incl. 7-p. index, 7-p. bibl.).

During his early career as First Assistant and later (1905) Chief Physician at Burghölzli Hospital, Jung directed a research project involving a word-association test in order to gain an understanding of how to treat patients. The test, which had been used only on conscious lines of thought, was here applied to unconscious mental processes, drawing Jung's attention to complexes that he came to believe exist in everyone. The longest contribution (165 pp.) is a series of studies written jointly by Jung and Franz Riklin on associations of normal subjects. Jung alone contributed reports on the analysis of the associations of an epileptic; on reaction-time ratio in association experiments; on psychoanalysis and association experiments; association, dream, and hysterical symptoms; and on disturbances in reproduction in association experiments.

(Bk.revs.: PsyBul '05/2:242–50, '06/2:275–80; TimesLitSup '18:487, 507; BrJPsy '19/9:373–4; JMentSci '20/66:159–61; JNervMent '20/51:593–4; PsyanR '20/7:209; BrJPsy '70/61:277; Choice '70/6:1663; BrJMedPsy '71/44:190–1; BrJSocClin '72/11:90–1)

The Psychology of Dementia Praecox, by C. G. Jung. (Ger.: *Über die Psychologie der Dementia praecox.* Halle: Carl Marhold, 1907.) New York: Journal of Nervous and Mental Disease Publishing Co., 1909 (Monograph Series No. 3); 1936 (different translation); Princeton, N.J.: Princeton U. Press/Bollingen, 1974p (222 + ix, incl. 8-p. index).

Drawing upon three years' experimental researches and clinical observations in the word-association project and stimulated by the new approach to dementia praecox (schizophrenia) suggested by Burghölzli Director Eugen Bleuler, Jung proposed to answer the question of why the complexes are so resistant to treatment in dementia praecox. He presents first a critical survey of theoretical views on the psychology of dementia praecox and then interprets the feeling-toned complex (the affects of pleasure and displeasure) and its general effects on the psyche and its influence on the valency of associations. He also discusses the similarities between dementia praecox and hysteria in terms of disturbances of the emotions, abnormalities of character, intellectual disturbances, and stereotypy. The remaining one-third of the study is devoted to his analysis of a case of paranoid dementia as a paradigm in which he first interprets simple word associations and then continuous associations as reflected in wish fulfillment, the complex of injury, and the sexual complex.

(Bk.revs.: PsyBul '07/4:196–7; JMentSci '08/54:584–5; JNervMent '08/35:62–3; JMent Sci '10/56:327–8; JNervMent '10/37:206; JIndivPsy '75/31:98–9)

The Theory of Psychoanalysis, by C. G. Jung. (Ger.: *Versuch einer Darstellung der psychoanalytischen Theorie.* Leipzig and Vienna: Deuticke, 1913.) New York: Journal of Nervous and Mental Disease Publishing Co., 1915 (Monograph Series No. 19); New York: Johnson Reprint Corp., repr. 1971 (135 + iii).

In this work consisting of nine lectures written in German but given in English as a course at Fordham University, Jung's aim is to reconcile his practical experiences in psychoanalysis with the approaches of existing theory, especially his attitude to the guiding principles of his "honored teacher Sigmund Freud." He does put forth certain views that deviate from hypotheses of Freud, "not as contrary assertions but as illustrations of the organic development of the basic ideas Freud has introduced into science." After reviewing early hypotheses, he discusses the theory of infantile sexuality; the concept of libido; neurosis and causal factors in childhood; fantasies of the unconscious; the Oedipal complex; an investigation of the causes of neurosis; and therapeutic principles of psychoanalysis. He ends by describing a case of neurosis in a child, used to illustrate the actual process of treatment.

(Bk.rev.: JMentSci '16/62:607–9)

Dream Analysis: Notes of the Seminar Given in 1928–1930 by C. G. Jung, edited by William McGuire. Princeton, N.J.: Princeton U. Press/Bollingen Series XCIX:1, 1984*; London: Routledge & Kegan Paul, 1984* (757 + xxiii, incl. 39-p. index, 10-p. editor's preface).

This dream seminar, conducted by Jung in English at weekly meetings over a seven-month period, reveals Jung's lively and learned style of presentation. Along with the interpretations of the thirty dreams of a male patient, by which one sees the gradual unfolding of the unconscious in the dreams, Jung provides a wide range of experience and learning that serves to amplify the analyses. He comments broadly on analytical psychology, discussing such topics as projections, shadow, archetypes, anima, animus, mandalas, and astrology, as well as consciousness and the unconscious.

(Bk.revs.: JAnPsy '84/29:383; JPsyTheol '84/12:244; LibJ '84/109:1678; LATribBkR 9S'84:12; TimesLitSup '84:803; Chiron '85:223–7; Dial '85/24:155–8; Harvest '85/31:146–7; JAnPsy '85/30:97–9; PsyPersp '85/16:221–5; Quad '85/18n2:103–4)

The Practice of Psychotherapy, by C. G. Jung. New York: Pantheon Books (Bollingen Foundation), 1954; London: Routledge & Kegan Paul, 1954*; Toronto: McClelland & Stewart. 1954; Princeton, N.J.: Princeton U. Press/Bollingen, ed.2 1966*; 1985p* (CW 16) (384 + xiii, incl. 26-p. index, 15-p. bibl., 19 illus.).

Consisting of nine essays under the heading of general problems of psychotherapy and three works under specific problems of psychotherapy, this collection provides an idea of the empirical foundations of psychotherapy from Jung's experience as a practicing therapist. The first part contains generally short lectures (also published as articles) on the subjects of principles of practical psychotherapy; what is psychotherapy?; aspects of modern psythotherapy; aims of psychotherapy; psychotherapy and a philosophy of life; medicine and psychotherapy; and psychotherapy today (1941); as well as two articles on problems in modern psychotherapy (1929) and fundamental questions of psychotherapy (1951). The second part consists of articles on the therapeutic value of abreaction (removal of a complex) and on the practical use of dream analysis; and a book-length study (161 pp.) on the psychology of the transference, an account of transference phenomena based on the ten illustrations in "Rosarium Philosophorum." Appended is a lecture (previously unpublished) on the realities of practical psychotherapy.

(Bk.revs.: PastorPsy Jn'54/5:65; R&Expos '54/51:559–60; TimesLitSup '54:808; AmJPsychi '55/111:716; Blackf '55/36:591; CrossCurr '55/5:275; JPastorCare '55/9:57–8; JRelThought '55/12:57–8; PastorPsy F'55/6:61–3; Person '55/36:303–4; QueensQ '55/62:133–4; RMeta '55/9:71–89; RofRel '55/19:157–9; BulMennClin '56/20:280; IntJSocPsy '56/1:67–9; AnnAmAcad '56/366:199–201; UCLALawR '80/27:816; ContemPsy '86/31:912; WilsonQ '86/10n5:141)

Psychiatric Studies, by C. G. Jung. New York: Pantheon Books (Bollingen Foundation), 1957; London: Routledge & Kegan Paul, 1957*; Toronto: McClelland & Stewart, 1957; Princeton, N.J.: Princeton U. Press/Bollingen, ed.2 1970*; 1983p* (CW 1) (260 + xiii, incl. 22-p. index, 11-p. bibl.).

This collection, consisting of short studies on descriptive and experimental psychiatry, along with Jung's dissertation for his medical degree, comprises the first publications by Jung, appearing between 1902 and 1906. His dissertation, "On the Psychology and Pathology of So-called Occult Phenomena," (U. Zurich, 1902) is a detailed analysis of a case of somnambulism in a girl who professed to be a spiritualistic medium. The eight articles, published in professional journals, are a case of hysterical stupor in a prisoner in detention; manic mood disorder; simulated insanity; hysterical misreading; a medical opinion on a case of simulated insanity; cryptamnesia; the psychological diagnosis of facts; and a third and final opinion on two contradictory psychiatric diagnoses.

(Bk.revs.: Blackf '57/38:442; BrJMedPsy '57/30:280; PastorPsy My'57/8:60–1; AmJPsyth '58/12:856; JAnPsy '58/3:71–4; JPastorCare '58/12:196–7; Person '58/39:293; PsysomMed '58/20:168–9; Isis '71/62:1)

The Psychogenesis of Mental Disease, by C. G. Jung. New York: Pantheon Books (Bollingen Foundation), 1960*; London: Routledge & Kegan Paul, 1960*; Toronto: McClelland & Stewart, 1960; Princeton, N.J.: Princeton U. Press/ Bollingen, 1982p* (*CW* 3) (303 + viii, incl. 17-p. index, 12-p. bibl.).

More than half (151 pp.) of this collection of writings on the psychogenesis of mental disease is occupied by Jung's monograph on the psychology of dementia praecox (1907); in addition, three lectures/articles on schizophrenia are included (psychogenesis of schizophrenia (1939); recent thoughts on schizophrenia (1956); and schizophrenia (1958)). Other lectures or addresses, also previously published in journals, are on the content of the psychoses (1908); psychological understanding and the importance of the unconscious in psychopathology (1914); and the problem of psychogenesis in mental disease (1919). Also included are an article on a criticism of Bleuler's theory of schizophrenic negativism (1911) and a newspaper article on mental disease and the psyche.

(Bk.revs.: Blackf '61/42:279; BrJMedPsy '61/34:308; HarvDivBul Ap–Jy'61/25:24; JAnPsy '61/6:168–71; PsychiQ '61/35:400; Spring '61:152–3; TimesLitSup '61:45; BulMennClin '62/26:51; CathEdR '62/60:63–5; Person '62/43:149–50)

Freud and Psychoanalysis, by C. G. Jung. New York: Pantheon Books (Bollingen Foundation), 1961*; London: Routledge & Kegan Paul, 1961*; Toronto: McClelland & Stewart, 1961; Princeton, N.J.: Princeton U. Press/Bollingen, 1985p* (*CW* 4) (368 + xii, incl. 16-p. index, 8-p. bibl.).

The collection illustrates essential elements in Jung's changing views on the subject of Freud and psychoanalysis. The first part contains nine brief studies from the period of Jung's enthusiastic collaboration as one of the leading spokesmen for and practitioners of psychoanalysis. They deal with Freud's theory of hysteria; the analysis of dreams; the significance of number dreams; the psychology of rumor; and a criticism of psychoanalysis. Parts two and three contain the essentials of criticism that led to the formal rupture with Freud, part two being the book-length *The Theory of Psychoanalysis* (series of lectures given at Fordham University in 1912). Part three consists of lectures dealing with psychoanalysis and neurosis (1912), and general aspects of psychoanalysis (1913), as well as correspondence between Jung and Dr. Loy on some crucial points in psychoanalysis (1913), along with prefaces to *Collected Papers on Analytical Psychology* (1916, 1917). Also included is a newspaper article on Freud and Jung written in 1929.

(Bk.revs.: HarvDivBul Ap'61/25:22–3; RMeta '61/15:343; Blackf '62/43:193; Bul-MennClin '62/26:212; CathEdR '62/60:63–5; Spring '62:158–9; TimesLitSup '62:76; JAnPsy '63/8:175–81)

The Psychology of the Transference, by C. G. Jung. Princeton, N.J.: Princeton U. Press/Bollingen, 1969p*; London: Ark Paperbacks, 1983p* (198 + xiii, incl. 16-p. index, 15-p. bibl., 16 illus.).

As one of the first in the series of Princeton/Bollingen Paperbacks (which consist of extracts from the *Collected Works*), this volume deals with the phenomenon called "transference," which appears to be bound up in a very fundamental way with the success or failure of lengthy treatment. It is excerpted from volume 16 (*The Practice of Psychotherapy*). Jung states his aim to be to provide an orientation that is addressed "exclusively to those who have already gained sufficient experience from their own practice"; but it is not an account of the clinical phenomena of the transference. He analyzes the subject using the illustrations to the "Rosarium Philosophorum" (1550), a set of ten alchemical pictures that symbolize the alchemical opus which involves, in general, the refining of the materia prima, the unconscious contents, through the unification of conflicting polarities within the psyche in order to reach a higher plane in the individuation process toward integration of the personality. He takes for granted some knowledge of his *Psychology and Alchemy*.

Experimental Researches, by C. G. Jung. Princeton, N.J.: Princeton U. Press/ Bollingen, 1973*; 1981p*; London: Routledge & Kegan Paul, 1973* (CW 2) (640 + xii, incl. 10-p. index, 11-p. bibl.).

Jung's experimental researches, which evidenced a revolutionary advance in the use of experimental techniques during the first decade of the twentieth century, are collected in this volume, whose principal contents are his contributions to the famous *Studies in Word-Association* (published 1906–09 in German; 1918 in English). In addition to six contributions published in the studies, three additional ones (experimental observations on the faculty of memory; psychological diagnosis of evidence; psychopathological significance of the association experiment) are included in this collection. Also included are two lectures on the association method that Jung delivered at Clark University in 1909. Three articles on psychophysical researches comprise part two of the volume, including Jung's first publication in English (on the association experiment), which was published in 1907.

(Bk.revs.: Econ 19My'73/247:131–2; PsyToday S'73/7:100; Spec '73/230:817; Times-LitSup '73:1080; AmJPsychi '74/131:1057–8; AmJPsy '74/87:319–20; ContemPsy '74/19:206; JAnPsy '74/19:107–8; PsychiQ '74/48:150)

The Psychoanalytic Years, by C. G. Jung. Princeton, N.J.: Princeton U. Press/ Bollingen, 1974p* (168 + vii, incl. 8-p. index, 4-p. bibl.).

These excerpts from the *Collected Works* come from the period between 1906 and 1912, when Jung, who was then in his thirties, was Freud's leading follower and the leading psychoanalyst after Freud. With the exception of the 1906 article on psychoanalysis and the association experiments (from CW 2) and the 1909 lecture on psychic conflicts in a child, delivered at Clark University in his series on "The Association Method" (from CW 17), these excerpts come from CW 4. They include articles on Freud's theory of hysteria; the psychology of rumor; a critical review (1911) of Morton Prince's article on the mechanism and interpretation of dreams; an article on the criticism of psychoanalysis; an article concerning psychoanalysis; and an article on the significance of the father in the destiny of the individual (1909; rev. 1927 and 1949).

Critique of Psychoanalysis, by C. G. Jung. Princeton, N.J.: Princeton U. Press/ Bollingen, 1975p (259 + vi, incl. 13-p. index, 4-p. bibl.).

The chief content of this collection is the set of nine Fordham Lectures (1912) on the theory of psychoanalysis (144 pp.), which is described above, under *Freud and Psychoanalysis.* Also included are other extracts from volume 4 of the *Collected Works,* namely, general aspects of psychoanalysis; psychoanalysis and neurosis; some crucial points in psychoanalysis; prefaces to *Collected Papers on Analytical Psychology;* an introduction to Kranefeldt's *Die Psychoanalyse* (1930, translated and published as *Secret Ways of the Mind* in 1932); and contrasts between Freud and Jung. From volume 18 is the three-page "Answers to Questions on Freud" in which Jung responded to a questionnaire from a representative of the *New York Times* in Geneva in connection with a projected article on Freud in 1953. So far as it is known, the *Times* did not publish the answers; but they were published in the journal *Spring* in 1968.

* * * * *

The Problem of the Nervous Child, by Elida Evans. New York: Dodd, Mead, 1920; London: Kegan Paul, Trench, Trubner, 1921 (299 + viii, incl. 3-p. index, 1 diagram, 4-p. intro. by Jung).

In searching for practical results of the "newer psychology of the unconscious," Evans presents an introduction to the psychoanalytical treatment of nervous problems of the child from the special point of view of the relation between parent and child. Jung comments on how much stress Evans places on the parents' mental attitude and its importance for the child's psychology. Evans's discussions encompass the development of repression; symbolic thought; the child's reactions; the parent complex; buried emotions; child training; muscular erotism; the tyrant child; teaching of right and wrong; and self and character.

(Bk.revs.: AmJPsy '20/31:218; BkRDig '20:170; Bklist '20/16:303; JAbnPsy '20–21/ 15:422–3; JNervMent '20/51:597–8; PsyBul '20/17:312; ReligEd '20/15:298; Surv '20/ 44:494–5; AmJPsy '21/32:299; BrJPsy '21/11:359–60; JPhilos '21/18:249–50; PsyanR '21/8:111)

The Re-Creating of the Individual: A Study of Psychological Types and Their Relation to Psychoanalysis, by Beatrice M. Hinkle. London: George Allen & Unwin, 1923; New York: Harcourt, Brace, 1923; New York: Dodd, Mead, 1949 (465 + xiii, incl. 15-p. index, 11 illus.).

Drawing on more than twenty years of study and treatment of individuals suffering from neuroses and psychic disturbances, as well as "normal people," Hinkle identifies her work as closely related to Jung's and acknowledges the value of his conceptions. She relates the self-knowledge that can be obtained from psychoanalysis to a study of psychological types that offers the possibility of a new creative synthesis. Following a brief discussion of analytical psychology in the development of the individual, she examines the Freudian sexual interpretation of the child and the topics of dynamic manifestations of the unconscious in human life; symbolism in dream and fantasy and their present and prospective value for the dreamer; a study of psychological types; masculine and feminine psychology; the psychology of the artist and the significance of artistic creation; the process of reintegration of the individual; and the significance of psychoanalysis for the spiritual life.

(Bk.revs.: BkRDig '23:240; Surv '23/51:350; AmJSoc '24/30:238; Bklist '24/20:281; Bkman '24/66:181; JApplSoc '24/8:251; NYTimesBkR 13Ja'24:12; PsyanR '24/11:329– 36; IntJEth '25/35:209; BulAnPsyNY F–Mr'50/12:8–10; PastorPsy Ap'50/1:63–4; RofRel '50/14:411–16; AmJPsyth '53/7:760–2)

The Organism of the Mind: An Introduction to Analytical Psychology, by Gustav Richard Heyer. (Ger.: *Der Organismus der Seele, eine Einführung in die analytische Seelenheilkunde.* Munich: Lehman's Verlag, 1932.) London: Kegan Paul, Trench, Trubner, 1933; New York: Harcourt, Brace, 1934 (271 + xiii, incl. 5-p. index, 37 illus.).

Aiming to present the fundamentals of mental life (being, becoming, and transformation) and to show what psychotherapy is and why and how it is practiced, Heyer follows the developmental trend in analytical psychology as it is "beginning to evolve into a general doctrine of life." Nearly half of the book is devoted to a discussion of organ neuroses and vital cycles, in which the author examines psychological treatment by suggestion and other methods. In the other half he explores specific analytical methods of treatment, with a chapter each given to sexual analysis (Freud: 26 pp.), individual psychology (Adler: 17pp.), and Jung's analytical psychology (36 pp.).

(Bk.revs.: BkRDig '34:437; Nature '34/135:816; NewRep '34/80:345; TimesLitSup 25Ja'34:63)

Mythology of the Soul: A Research into the Unconscious from Schizophrenic Dreams and Drawings, by Helton Godwin Baynes. London: Balliere, Tindall & Cox, 1940; Baltimore: Wood/Williams & Wilkins, 1940; London: Methuen, 1949; New York: British Book Centre, 1949; London: Routledge & Kegan Paul, repr. 1955; New York: Humanities Press, 1955; London: Rider, ed.2 1969 (980 + xiii, incl. 27-p. index, 79 illus.).

Calling for an introverting psychological approach as the only suitable one for the investigation of schizophrenia, Baynes, an early assistant of Jung, employs Jung's analytical method in his own analysis of two individuals who manifest contrasts in attitude toward the irruption of primitive tendencies from the unconscious but who both have the same doubt about the validity of their own nature or the stability of their own mind. Following an introduction of psychiatric antecedents of the psychological conception of mental disorders, he analyzes dreams and interprets the patient's drawings in order to provide a wide amplification of the material reflecting the unconscious processes.

(Bk.revs.: BrJMedPsy '41–45/19:324–6; BulAnPsyNY My'41/3:sup8; JAbnSocPsy '41/36:129; PsyanQ '42/11:236–8; NYTimesBkR 5N'50:22; BulMennClin '51/15:30–1; PsyanR '53/40:375; BrJPsy '55/46:315–16; IntJPsy-An '56/37:295–6)

The Lady of the Hare: A Study in the Healing Power of Dreams, by John Layard. London: Faber & Faber, 1944; New York: AMS Press, repr. 1977; Boston & London: Shambhala Publications, repr. 1988p* (277, incl. 29-p. index, 22 illus., 1-p. foreword by Robert Johnson in 1988 ed.).

Layard presents the case history of a hard-working English country wife as an example of the practice of analytical psychology in which the analyst's part, as well as the patient's part, in the process is recorded. The dream analysis is comprised of twelve interviews involving twenty-five dreams and visions with direct use of Christian symbolism. He follows with a comprehensive interpretation of the mythology of the hare as an archetype, discussing its motif in India, China, ancient Egypt, North America, Africa, Europe, and in classical antiquity. He concludes with a section on more dreams about hares and rabbits, showing the mythological motives on which they are based and their relation to everyday life.

(Bk.revs.: DownR '45/63:55–6; Folk '45/56:321–2; LifeLtrsToday Jn'45/45:129–36; Psychi '45/8:507–13; TimesLitSup '45:21; BrJPsy '46/36:107; Mind '46/ns55:349–53)

Healing Dream and Ritual: Ancient Incubation and Modern Psychotherapy, by C. A. Meier. (Orig. title: *Ancient Incubation and Modern Psychotherapy.* Evanston, Ill.: Northwestern U. Press, 1967 (Studies in Jungian Thought).) (Ger.: *Antike Inkubation und Moderne Psychotherapie.* Zurich: Rascher Verlag, 1949/Studien aus dem C. G. Jung-Institut, vol. I.) Einsiedeln, Switzerland: Daimon Verlag, 1989p* (160 + v, incl. 10-p. subject index, 6-p. name index, 2-p. bibl., 11 illus., 2-p. foreword by Jung).

Recognizing Jung's concept of the self-healing tendency of the psyche and connecting it with his own work in a psychiatric clinic, Meier became convinced of the need to study incubation in the ancient world. Here he presents the results of his studies, describing the ancient incubation ritual in the sanctuaries of Asclepius and at the oracle of Trophonius at Lebadea as exemplary of the mystery of healing, which he interprets with the help of analytical psychology. He examines the implications of similarities between the ancient Greek healing rites and modern therapeutic practice in the sense that the curing of illness is bound up closely with understanding the meaning of illness and its connection to the total life of the sufferer. He illustrates this with 13 dreams by modern persons.

(Bk.revs.: ContemPsy '69/14:395–6; Spring '69:147–8; JAnPsy '70/15:192–5; Union-SemQR '70/25:254–5; Isis '71/62:99–102)

Wisdom, Madness, and Folly: The Philosophy of a Lunatic, by John Custance (pseud.). London: Gollancz, 1951; Toronto: Longmans Canada, 1951; New York: Pellegrini & Cudahy, 1952 (London edition lacks Jung's preface) (254, incl. 4-p. preface by Jung, 3-p. foreword by L. W. Grensted).

While in his middle thirties, the author suffered a bout of manic depression, accompanied by an interesting emotional religious experience. Custance (a pseudonym) claims that his experience bears out Jung's theories of the unconscious. During the manic or elated periods of the illness, he felt a sense of revelation of ultimate harmonies, which he describes as psychic reality rather than a "quality of 'revelation.' " He examines the topics of meaning and mania; universe of bliss; universe of horror; fantasia of opposites; delusion and reality; and the theory of actuality. Appended are comments on the management of mental homes and mental treatment, reactions to specific treatments, and results of Szondi and Rorschach tests.

(Bk.revs.: BrJMedPsy '51/24:309–10; Econ '51/161:450; Listen '51/45:967; TimesLitSup '51:514; AntiochR '52/12:503; BestSell '52/12:116; BkRDig '52:221; JMentSci '52/98:343; KirkR '52/10:394; LibJ '52/77:1300; Nation '52/175:179; NYTimesBkR 7S'52–7; SFChron 14S'52:This World 27; PastorPsy Oc'53/4:62–3; JPastorCare '55/9:112–13)

The Self in Psychotic Process: Its Symbolism in Schizophrenia, by John Weir Perry. Berkeley and Los Angeles: U. of California Press, 1953; London: Cambridge U. Press, 1954; Dallas: Spring Publ., repr. 1987p* (Jungian Classics Series, 10) (184 + xxiii, incl. 6-p. index, 2-p. bibl., 11-p. ref. notes, 38 illus., 4-p. foreword by Jung).

Expressing profound appreciation to the patient (a 27-year-old housewife) and her family for allowing her experience and fantasy productions to be used, Perry recounts her case history from the initial delusions onward. He discusses and analyzes the development of the problem; the resolution; the nature of the material; the amplification of the symbol; the psychological concept; the interpretation of the process; the symbolism of the quadrated circle and its meaning in the East and in the West; the symbolism of opposites; the symbolism of rebirth; and the psychology of the symbolism. Appended is a detailed account of the patient's history and material.

(Bk.revs.: PsyanR '54/41:295; RofRel '54/19:85–7; AmJPsyth '55/9:754–6; JNervMent '55/121:293; PsyanQ '55/24:138–40; JAnPsy '88/33:191–2)

Emotion: A Comprehensive Phenomenology of Theories and Their Meanings for Therapy, by James Hillman. London: Routledge & Kegan Paul, 1960; Evanston, Ill.: Northwestern U. Press, 1961 (318 + x, incl. 6-p. index, 21-p. bibl.).

In this slightly revised version of his doctoral dissertation written at the University of Zurich (1958), Hillman examines wide divergences in explanations of emotion, which he characterizes as a "total pattern of the soul." He differentiates the totality of emotion from partial psychological events such as feeling, sensation, and will. After discussing the phenomenology of the theories of emotion and the various denials, he explores the different forms emotion takes: a distinct entity; an accompaniment; an energy; a quantity; a totality; a signification; a conflict; a disorder; and a creative organization. He also discusses isomorphism; the unconscious; psychological location; situation; the subject-object relation; spirit; and integration.

(Bk.revs.: Blackf '61/42:280; BrJMedPsy '61/34:308; Spring '61:153–4; JPsysomRes '61/ 5:292; TimesLitSup '61:91; AmJSoc '62/67:720–1; JAnPsy '62/7:168–9; PsyRec '62/ 12:240; PsysomMed '62/24:615)

The Integrity of the Personality, by Anthony Storr. London: William Heinemann, 1960; New York: Atheneum Press, 1961; Harmondsworth and Baltimore: Pelican Books/Penguin, 1963p; 1970p (186, incl. 4-p. index, 4-p. bibl. notes).

Having been trained both as a general psychiatrist and as an analyst in the "school of Jung," Storr aims to define the basic hypotheses of his practice, emphasizing that the analytic attitude to the patient is far more important than the "school." Representing psychotherapy as being concerned with the basic themes of human life from the point of view of self-realization and integrity of personality, he discusses his ideas under the topics of the relativity of personality; the mature relationship; development of personality; emergent personality; identification and introjection; projection and dissociation; identification and projection; heterosexual love and relationship; the psychotherapeutic process; transference and countertransference; and psychotherapy and indoctrination.

(Bk.revs.: NewStates 13Ag'60/60:221; BkRDig '61:1366; Bklist '61/57:344; IntJSocPsy '61/8:73–4; JAnPsy '61/6:180–1; JMentSci '61/107:346–7; 986–7; JPsysomRes '61/ 5:151; LibJ '61/86:1149; NYTimesBkR 29Ja'61:26; PsyanQ '63/32:101–3; ContemPsy '64/9:460; PastorPsy Mr'64/15:54–6)

Western Psychotherapy and Hindu-Sadhana: A Contribution to Comparative Studies in Psychology and Metaphysics, by Hans Jacobs. London: Allen & Unwin, 1961; New York: International Universities Press, 1961 (232, incl. 3-p. index, 30 illus.).

Combining nine years of psychiatric practice in Australia, three years of study in analytical psychology at Zurich, and four years in India and Ceylon, Jacobs presents his quest for understanding the intrinsic connections between Western psychotherapy and Indian philosophy, particularly the question of the essential quality of mental acts and their crystallization into concrete ideas and mental images. He discusses the approaches of Freud and Jung and compares them to the Hindu approach, concluding that the deep insights of yoga commit him to the Hindu path of self-realization. He criticizes Jung's position on the applicability of yogic practices for Western individuals.

(Bk.revs.: TimesLitSup '61:439; BulMennClin '62/26:266–7; ChurchQR '62/163:109–10; JNervMent '62/135:278–9; AmJPsychi '63/119:698–9; JAsianStud '64/23:639–41; IntJSocPsy '65/11:235–6)

The Logos of the Soul, by Evangelos Christou. Vienna and Zurich: Dunquin Press, 1963; Dallas: Spring Publications, 1977p; reissue 1987p* (104 + iv, incl. 1-p. foreword by C. A. Meier, 4-p. intro. by James Hillman).

The author follows Jung in taking psychotherapy as the starting point for psychology and in developing his logos of the soul from the phenomenology of the soul itself. Christou presents the idea that psychology becomes more scientific when it works out its own premises within the context of its own kind of reality, the psyche being the first reality. Following a general clarification of philosophical-scientific concepts, in which he discusses reality in psychological experience, he moves toward a "science of the soul" with discussions of psychology and the body, mind, and soul, and meaning in psychological experience. Unfortunately, the final part of the work was not completed before his death in an auto accident at age 34. It was to contain illustrations from case material resulting from actual therapeutic situations in which he used his principle and method.

Suicide and the Soul, by James Hillman. London: Hodder & Stoughton, 1964; New York: Harper & Row, 1964; 1973p; Zurich: Spring Publications for the Analytical Psychology Club of New York, repr. 1976p*; Dallas: Spring, repr. 1978p; 1985p* (Dunquin Series, 8) (191, incl. 7-p. index, 5-p. bibl.).

By questioning suicide prevention and examining the death experience, Hillman approaches the suicide problem in relation to death and the soul and not from the viewpoint of life, society, and "mental health," regarding suicide as not only an exit from life but also as an entrance to death. Among the topics he discusses are medicine, analysis, and the soul; the healer as hero; diagnosis and the analytical dialectic; and hoping, growing, and the analytical process. He concludes with the subject of "medical secrecy and the analytic mystery."

(Bk.revs.: NewStates '64/68:999; BkRDig '65:575–6; Bklist '65/61:846; BrJPsychi '65/111:558–9; BulMennClin '65/29:53; Choice '65/2:267; Commonw '65/82:416–17; Harvest '65/n11:80–1; JAnPsy '65/10:198–9; Nation '65/200:344; PastorPsy N'65/16:60–1; Spring '65:145–6; TimesLitSup '65:167; ConcordiaTh '66/37:683–4; IntJParapsy '66/8:490–1; InwLight '66/n69:54–5; JPastorCare '66/20:172; ContemPsy '67/12:449–50; CrossCurr '75/25:294–7; RelStudR '80/6:278–85; Resurg N–D'85/n113:39)

The Parental Image: Its Injury and Reconstruction, by M. Esther Harding. New York: G. P. Putnam's Sons for the C. G. Jung Foundation for Analytical Psychology, 1965; Boston: Sigo Press, repr. 1990 +p (238, incl. 4-p. index, 25 illus., 4-p. foreword by Franz Riklin).

Drawing upon nearly forty years of practice as a Jungian analyst, Harding presents selected case material concerning the problem of the injured parental image and its transformation and restoration to an appropriate place in the inner life of the individual. She begins with a discussion of the Babylonian myth of the Beginnings of Creation and of the overcoming of the parents and their consequent injury. She analyzes actual case material to show how separation from the archetypal parents appeared in the dreams of clients and how experiences led them to become free from the effects of parental control that came from the unconscious rather than from the conscious control by the actual parent. Not until the unconscious itself participated in the movement toward release from the power of the parental archetype was the person enabled to become an individual in his or her own right.

(Bk.revs.: BkRDig '65:540; Bklist '65/62:8; CanForum '65/45:162–3; ChrCen '65/82:712; InwLight '65/n68:52–4; JCounsPsy '65/12:440; JRelHealth '65/4:466–9; KirkR '65/ 33:410; LibJ '65/90:1918; SatR 4S'65/48:35; Choice '66/2:911–12; JAnPsy '66/11:74–6; Harvest '67/n11:82–3; ContemPsy '68/13:152–3)

The Psychotherapy of C. G. Jung, by Wolfgang Hochheimer. (Ger.: *Die Psychologie von C. G. Jung.* Bern and Stuttgart: Hans Huber Verlag, 1966.) New York: G. P. Putnam's Sons for the C. G. Jung Foundation for Analytical Psychology, 1969; Toronto: Longmans Canada, 1969 (160 + viii, incl. 10-p. index, 3-p. bibl., 2-p. intro. by Edward C. Whitmont).

Selecting from the long list of Jung's publications those which show a special connection with psychotherapy, Hochheimer states that Jung's basic theory and his psychotherapy cannot be reduced to a single method. He characterizes Jung's theory as containing many details stemming from Freud, though there are divisive and permanent differences; he refers to Jung's method as "synthetic, even constructive," in contrast to Freud's "scientific" method of reductive and causal-genetic analysis. He discusses the special nature of Jung's theories and the problem of their presentation; Jung's basic concepts regarding human nature and psychology; some remarks on Jung's analytical psychology; Jung's theory of neuroses; contributions to psychotherapeutic methodology; transference and countertransference; and the dream and its treatment.

(Bk.revs.: JAnPsy '67/12:179–80; Bklist '69/66:91; LibJ '69/94:1642; LibJBkR '69:516–17; Quad '69/n4:5; Spring '69:142–3; BkRDig '70:661; Choice '70/7:1142)

Sandplay: A Psychotherapeutic Approach to the Psyche, by Dora M. Kalff. (Ger.: *Sandspiel: Seine therapeutische Wirkung auf die Psyche.* Zurich: Rascher Verlag, 1966.) (Orig. subtitle: *Mirror of a Child's Psyche.* San Francisco: Browser Press, 1971p.) Santa Monica: Sigo Press, rev. 1980p* (166, incl. 1-p. bibl., 75 illus.).

Kalff has observed in her psychotherapeutic practice with children and adolescents that the dynamics of the individuation process in adults as described by Jung are also present in childhood. She outlines these findings and analyzes separate stories of development of seven children and two adults as expressed through sandplay therapy, in which patients create three-dimensional "pictures" using numerous objects such as figurines and toys. She first presents the theory of sandplay as a pathway to the psyche, whereby the psychic situation of a problem is played out like a drama in the sandbox that may lead to a turning point and healing in the therapeutic process. The cases are characterized as "overcoming an anxiety neurosis," "cure of an inhibition to learn," "separation from an overpowering mother fixation," "healing of an enuresis," "loss of instinct due to an identification with an extraverted mother," "conquest of a speech-block," "the background of an adopted child's inability to read," "restoring a weak ego," and "religious background in a case of blushing."

(Bk.revs.: JAnPsy '67/12:179; Spring '67:155; Quad '81/14n2:119; PsyPersp '82/13:97–100; JPsyTheol '83/11:149)

The Analytic Process: Aims, Analysis, Training: The Proceedings of the Fourth International Congress for Analytical Psychology, Zurich, 1968, edited by Joseph B. Wheelwright. New York: G. P. Putnam's Sons for the C. G. Jung Foundation for Analytical Psychology, 1971; Toronto: Longmans Canada, 1971* (316 + xi, incl. 17 illus., 1-p. editor's preface).

Nine of these twenty-one essays are by authors whose books appear in this annotated bibliography, namely, "Favorite Fairytales from Childhood as a Therapeutic Factor in Analysis" (Dieckmann); "Reflections on Training Analysis" (Fordham); "The Artist's Relation to the Unconscious" (Henderson); "Pictures from the Unconscious in Four Cases of Obsessional Neurosis" (Jacoby); "Experiences with Far Eastern Philosophers" (Kalff); "Psychological Types and Individualism" (Meier); "Emotions and Object Relations" (Perry); and "The Destiny Concept in Psychotherapy" (Whitmont). Other papers deal with transformation symbols; schizophrenic patients; the transcendental function; the principle of complementarity; the analyst's own involvement; child psychotherapy; Hippocrates; the attempt to accelerate the analytical process; the analyst and a damaged victim of Nazi persecution; and the relation between individual and collective development.

(Bk.revs.: AmJArtTh '72/11:203; JAnPsy '72/17:220–1; RBksRel(W) 15F'72/1:1–2)

Neurosis and Crime, by Frances Smart, edited by B. Curtis Brown. London: Gerald Duckworth, 1970; New York: Barnes & Noble, 1970 (178 + xx, incl. 10-p. index, 2-p. bibl., 3-p. gloss. of Jungian terms, 4-p. ref. notes, 1-p. foreword by I. G. W. Pickering, 6-p. preface by Brown).

Drawing on ten years' experience as visiting psychotherapist at an English men's prison, Smart aims to show the possibilities that lie in the psychological treatment of offenders and to elucidate the psychopathology of men's and boys' antisocial behavior. Her approach, based primarily on the psychology of Jung, studies the personality of the offender with its unconscious motivations and seeks to find the origins of such behavior. Following a brief history of the study of crime and of psychotherapy in prison, she discusses the origin of crime in terms of social, biological, and psychological factors and then analyzes normal development, inner sources of control and conditions for normal development, and factors which interfere with normal development. She also discusses specific criminal manifestations and the question of whether criminal behavior is a neurosis or a crime. In conclusion, she discusses individual psychotherapy and its aims and application; principles of treatment; factors making for success or failure in treatment; and what lies behind the treatment. Close friend and writer Brown completed the final section after Smart's death.

(Bk.revs.: NewSoc '70/15:321–2; TimesLitSup '70:473; ContemPsy '71/16:725; Crim-LawR '71:609; JAnPsy '71/16:213–14)

Jung and Rorschach: A Study in the Archetype of Perception, by Robert S. McCully. (Orig. title: *Rorschach Theory and Symbolism: A Jungian Approach to Clinical Material.* Baltimore: Williams & Wilkins, 1971; Edinburgh: Churchill Livingstone, 1971.) Dallas: Spring Publications, ed.2 1987p* (281 + viii, incl. 20-p. index, end-chapter notes, 22 illus.; 4-p. foreword by Zygmunt A. Piotrowski).

Recognizing Jung's depth psychology as a general inspiration for his study, McCully aims to offer a fresh point of view in interpreting inkblot-mediated imagery and to call attention to the fact that the Rorschach experience reveals information about psychic structure. Following discussions of the interlacing of genius of Hermann Rorschach and Jung, Jung's concepts, and the nature of the Rorschach experience, he explores a kind of "paleopsychology," in which he traces archetypal sources and symbols back through time. He then outlines and illustrates a method for analyzing processes in the Rorschach experience and analyzes five sets of case materials that are selected to show the kinds of processes and qualities of psychic dynamics which demonstrate how ego consciousness reacts alongside influences from archetypal sources.

(Bk.revs.: Quad '72/n12:21–4; AmJPsychi '73/130:1304–5; AmJPsyth '73/27:462–3; JAnPsy '73/18:181–3; JPersAssess '73/37:93–5; AusPsyist '74/9:91; ContemPsy '74/19:454–5; JNervMent '74/158:470–3; PsyPersp '89/20:198 + 200 + 202)

Power in the Helping Professions, by Adolf Guggenbühl-Craig. (Ger.: *Macht als Gefahr beim Helfer.* Basel: S. Karger Verlag, 1971.) New York: Spring Publications for the Analytical Psychology Club of New York, 1971p; Dallas: Spring Publications, repr. 1979p; 1985p* (155 + iii).

Although workers in the helping, "ministering" professions make very specialized and deliberate attempts to help the unfortunate and the ill, analyst Guggenbühl-Craig recognizes that they can cause harm directly by their very desire to help. In concentrating chiefly on the power problems of the doctor and psychotherapist and admitting his own problems as an analyst, he discusses the subject under the topics of initial contact between analyst and analysand; relationship in fantasy; the analyst and the patient's extra-analytical life; sexuality and analysis; the destructive fear of homosexuality; the analyst as flatterer; abuse of the search for meaning; the powerful doctor and the childish patient; the "healer-patient" archetype and power; splitting of the archetype; closing of the split through power; physician, psychotherapist, social worker, and teacher; shadow, destructiveness, and evil; is analysis condemned to failure?; Eros; individuation; the helpless psychotherapist; and Eros again.

Success and Failure in Analysis: The Proceedings of the Fifth International Congress for Analytical Psychology, London, 1971, edited by Gerhard Adler. New York: G. P. Putnam's Sons for the C. G. Jung Foundation for Analytical Psychology, 1974 (229 + viii, incl. end-chapter ref. notes, 15 illus., 1-p. editor's preface).

Among the eighteen Congress papers in this volume, seven are essays by authors whose books appear in this annotated bibliography, namely, "The Constellation of the Countertransference in Relation to the Presentation of Archetypal Dreams" (Dieckmann); "Ending Phase as an Indicator of the Success or Failure of Psychotherapy" (Fordham); "Has Analysis Failed as a Therapeutic Instrument?" (Guggenbühl-Craig); "Three Ways of Failure and Analysis" (Hillman); "The Therapeutic Community Disease" (Hobson); "What We May Expect of Acute Schizophrenia" (Perry); and "Mandala Symbols and the Individuation Process" (Redfearn). Other essays include "Clinical Aspects of Dieckmann's Subject " (Rudolf Blomeyer); "The Group as Corrective for Failure in Analysis" (C. E. Brookes); "Can We Evaluate Analysis in Terms of Success and Failure?" (Gustav Dreifuss); "Family Therapy: When Analysis Fails" (George H. Hogle); "The Timing of Analysis" (David Holt); "Images of Success in the Analysis of Young Women Patients" (Faye Pye); "Analysis in Korea" (Bou-Yong Rhi); "Relativization of the Ego as a Criterion for Success in Jungian Analysis" (Georges Verne); "Psycho-therapeutic Success with 'Hippies' " (William Walcott); and "Success and Failure in Analysis: Primary Envy and the Fate of the Good" (Mary Williams).
(Bk.revs.: JAnPsy '75/20:230–1)

Boundaries of the Soul: The Practice of Jung's Psychology, by June Singer. Garden City, N.Y.: Doubleday, 1972; Anchor Books/Doubleday, 1973p*;

London: Gollancz, 1973; New York: Jason Aronson, 1975 (469 + xxxv, incl. 17-p. index, 5-p. bibl.).

In answering requests to write about the Jungian analytic process and how it works, and recognizing that Jung provides a bridge between the scientific-intellectual and the religious-nonrational aspects of life, Singer shares her experience as an analytical psychologist. She discusses first the topics of analyst and analysand; complexes by day and demons by night; from associations to archetypes; are archetypes necessary?; and analysis and counter-culture; following which she analyzes the subjects of individuation (the process of becoming whole); psychological types (the key to communications); persona and shadow; anima and animus (will one sex ever understand the other?); circumambulating the Self; understanding our dreams; dreaming the dream onward (active imagination); religion and other approaches to the unknowable; and "we are born dying."

(Bk.revs.: KirkR '72/40:288; PubW 230c'72/202:43; AmJOrthopsy '73/43:492; AmJPsychi '73/130:830; AmJPsyth '73/27:122–3; BkRDig '73:1206; BkWorld 8Ap'73/7:13; Bklist '73/69:657; ChrCen '73/90:707; LibJ '73/98:172; LibJBkR '73:449; PsyToday Oc'73/7:30, 134; PsythTheor '73/10:366; ContemPsy '74/19:206–7; IntJGroup '74/24:366–70; JAnPsy '74/19:107–9; PastorPsy '74/28:210; PsychiQ '74/48:150; Quad '74/n16:39–40)

Dreams and the Growth of Personality: Expanding Awareness in Psychotherapy, by Ernest Lawrence Rossi. New York: Pergamon Press, 1972; New York: Brunner/Mazel, ed.2 1985* (247 + xv, incl. 11-p. index, 7-p. bibl., 8 illus.).

In exploring the growth of personality through the expansion of awareness and the creation of new identity by modern depth psychology, Rossi places Jung in the larger context of humanistic psychology. Rossi provides a nontechnical introduction to the growth process in psychotherapy and to the expansion of awareness by way of dreams. For the professional psychotherapist, he explores the phenomenology of dreams in the process of self-reflection, synthesis, and change. His approach is an integration of laboratory research on the biology of sleep and dreams and of the place of dreams in the psychology of the individual. He also discusses psychosynthesis and recent advances in psychophysiological theories of dreaming.

(Bk.revs.: ChrCen '72/89:758; LibJ '72/97:2740; LibJBkR '72:446; AmJPsyan'73/33:224–5; ContemPsy '73/18:377–8; PsyToday Jy'73/7:22, 94; Quad '73/n14:24–7; RBksRel(W) F'73/2:1+; AmJClinHyp '75/18:138–9; JPersAssess '76/40:107–8; JContemPsy '77/9:119; AusNZJPsy '86/20:254; PsyPersp '86/17:262–5; ContemPsy '87/32:539)

Healing in Depth, by Culver M. Barker. London: Hodder & Stoughton, 1972; Mystic, Conn.: Lawrence Verry, 1972 (191, incl. preface by Laurens van der Post, foreword by Paul Seligman, and intro. by H. I. Bach).

This collection of posthumous papers reflects Barker's early study with Jung (beginning in 1927) and his continued appreciation of Jung's ideas as evidenced in his essay on "C. G. Jung, the Man and His Work." He discusses the field of psychiatry and problems in psychotherapy, including his development of a special method of treatment which he calls "feedback" and his interrelated theory of the "area of critical hurt," by which he illustrates with case histories the treatment of tracing the "original hurt" by interpretation of dreams. The final essay is entitled "The Religious Cord," in which he presents a general view of the meaning of life and the psyche.

(Bk.revs.: Frontier '72/15:253 +; Harvest '72/18:78–9; Quad '72/n12:24–7; TimesLitSup '72:613; JAnPsy '73/18:77–8; NewBlackf '74/55:96; Theol '74/77:212–13)

The Myth of Analysis: Three Essays in Archetypal Psychology, by James Hillman. Evanston, Ill.: Northwestern U. Press, 1972* (Studies in Jungian Thought); Toronto: Fitzhenry & Whiteside, 1972; New York: Torchbooks/Harper & Row, 1978p; 1983p (313 + ix, incl. 8-p. subject index, 7-p. index of proper and mythological names).

Originally given by Hillman as lectures at the Eranos Conferences in 1966, 1968, and 1969, with later enlargement and revision, these essays cover the topics of psychological creativity, psychological language, and psychological femininity. He distinguishes his perspective from a psychology based on analysis (analytical psychology), characterizing his view as the freeing of psychic phenomena from the "curse of the analytical mind" and the transformation of "psyche into life." He advocates moving the psyche by moving it, not from its sickness, but from its sick view of itself as being in need of professional care. He offers some archetypal patterns for understanding the psyche's syndromes and sufferings and suggests the approach of asking the psyche to move *with* its sickness into life.

(Bk.revs.: PsythTheor '73/10:288; RBksRel(W) My'73/2:7; AmJPsychi My'74/131:613–14; ContemPsy '74/19:207; Harvest '75/21:116–17; RelStudR '80/6:278–85)

Incest and Human Love: The Betrayal of the Soul in Psychotherapy, by Robert Stein. New York: Third Press, 1973; Baltimore: Penguin Books, 1974p; Dallas: Spring Publications, ed.2 1984p* (Jungian Classics Series, 7) (200 + xxi, incl. 8-p. index, 6-p. ref. notes).

Stein attributes the origin of this book to the failure of his own analysis to heal the original wounding split within his own nature. Through considerable soul searching and with further analytical help, Stein reevaluates the goals and limits of psychotherapy. He explores the incest mystery from an archetypal approach under the topics of incest and wholeness; the incest wound; infantile sexuality and narcissism; the archetypal family situation;

rejection and betrayal; rejection and resistance in analysis; the dual parent myth; and the Oedipus myth and the incest archetype. He also discusses phallos in relation to masculine and feminine psychology, Eros (Eros and Thanatos; transformation of Eros; Eros and the analytical ritual), and transference (archetypal view; beyond transference: a new analysis), ending with comments on a more soul-centered approach to the psychotherapeutic relationship. Appended are ten short essays on love, sex, and marriage.

(Bk.revs.: Quad '74/n16:40–2; JAnPsy '75/20:237–8)

The Far Side of Madness, by John Weir Perry. Englewood Cliffs, N.J.: Spectrum/ Prentice-Hall, 1974 +p; Dallas: Spring Publications, 1989p* (177 + viii, incl. 5-p. index, 7-p. bibl.).

By focusing on psychic experience in depth and exploring only inner reaches and potentials, Perry presents a distinctly interior approach to psychosis, drawing on the experience of a dozen selected cases of acute schizophrenic episodes of young adults in an ordinary hospital setting from 1949 to 1961. He begins by describing the contents of the psychotic episode within a discussion on madness and then examines historical and archetypal considerations under the topics of reorganization of the self; the nature of the kingship archetype; the ritual drama of renewal; the messianic hero; mysticism and its heroes; mysticism and madness; societal implications of the renewal process; and love and power in madness. He concludes with comments on the creative element in the renewal process and on a philosophy and method of therapy.

(Bk.revs.: LibJ '74/99:1719–20; LibJBkR '74:415; PubW 20My'74/205:65; PsyPersp '75/ 6:96–9; AusJPsy '76/28:127–8; JContemPsy '78/9:192)

Technique in Jungian Analysis, edited by Michael Fordham, Rosemary Gordon, Judith Hubback, Kenneth Lambert, and Mary Williams. London: William Heinemann Medical Books for the Society of Analytical Psychology, 1974*; New York: Academic Press, 1981; 1989p* (Library of Analytical Psychology, vol. 2) (335 + xii, incl. 7-p. index).

Demonstrating the results of some twenty years of work on the theme of technique in Jungian analysis, eleven members of the Society of Analytical Psychology of London present eighteen papers on the subject. They focus particularly on problems of transference and countertransference, interconnected themes that are constantly present in the psychotherapeutic process. Essays on technique include "The Symbolic Attitude in Psychotherapy" (Hubback); "The Personality of the Analyst in Interpretation and Therapy" (Lambert); "Flexibility in Analytic Technique" (L. Zinkin); "The Process of Reconstruction" (Lambert); "The Management of the Countertransference

Evoked by Violence in the Delusional Transference" (R. Campbell); and "Terminating Analysis" (Fordham). Essays on transference include "Notes on the Transference" (Fordham); "Transference in Analytical Psychology" (A. Plaut); "Transference as Creative Illusion" (A. Cannon); "Transference as the Fulcrum in Analysis" (Gordon); and "Transference as a Form of Active Imagination" (D. Davidson). Essays on countertransference include "The Changes of Unrecognized Countertransference" (Kraemer); "Counter-transference" (Fordham); "Countertransference" (R. Strauss); "Technique and Countertransference" (Fordham); and "Transference/Countertransference" (Lambert).

(Bk.revs.: BrBkN '74:657; JAnPsy '74/19:220–1, 222–3; CanMentHealth D'75/23:17: JAssnStudPerc '75/10:44; PsyPersp '75/6:197–203)

Three Worlds of Therapy: An Existential-Phenomenological Study of the Therapies of Freud, Jung, and Rogers, by Anthony Barton. Palo Alto, Calif.: National Press Books/Mayfield Publishing Co., 1974 +p (271 + x, incl. end-chapter refs.).

In exploring the orientation and understanding of psychotherapy as developed by Freud, Jung, and Rogers, the author uses an existential-phenomenological approach aimed at a comprehension and integration of the various schools. In sequence, he presents each of the three "worlds of therapy" in terms of the therapist's view of the patient, the approach to treatment, and how each therapist would treat "The Case of Mary." His section on Jung (78 pp.) consists of Jung's view of the patient (comprehensive individualizing; the patient's condition; projection and other systems of neurosis; the collective or universal unconscious; Self-unity as the goal of life; the theory of complexes; the ego-self and the real self); Jungian approach to psychotherapy (toward integration; symbolic soul meeting; recognition of the shadow; principle of compensation; amplification; the general activities of the therapist; development of the archetypal self); and the treatment of "Mary's case" according to the Jungian approach.

(Bk.revs.: Choice '74/11:1546; CanMentHealth Mr'75/23:19; ContemPsy '75/20:474–5; JBSP '76/7:212)

Astrology, Psychology, and the Four Elements: An Energy Approach to Astrology and Its Use in the Counseling Arts, by Stephen Arroyo. Reno: CRCS Publications, 1975 +p* (186 + xvi, incl. 2-p. bibl.).

Arroyo offers a new kind of astrology by relating it to the theories of depth psychology. Most of the first part (on astrology and psychology) is drawn from his master's thesis, in which he discusses limitations of the old framework of astrology, different approaches to knowledge and the question of proof, archetypes and universal principles, approaches to astrology, and humanistic psychology and humanistic astrology. He ends the first part with comments on the uses of astrology in the counseling arts and notes on the education and training of astrological counselors. In the second part, he presents an energy approach to interpreting birth charts in terms of the four elements.

(Bk.revs.: LibJ '76/101:1538; LibJBkR '76:419)

The Forbidden Love: The Normal and Abnormal Love of Children, edited by William Kraemer. London: Sheldon Press, 1976 (150 + x, incl. 5-p. gloss. of mostly Jungian terms).

Conceived by an informal group called "Freud-Jung," which produced the Centre for the Analytical Study of Student Problems, this study is about the child within ourselves and others, recognizing the complexity of paedophilia, and the need for more clinical investigation and more understanding on analytical lines. The collection of four studies, written by analytical psychologists of the Jungian school, consists of "A Paradise Lost" (William Kraemer); "Paedophilia: Normal and Abnormal" (Rosemary Gordon); "The Scope and Dimensions of Paedophilia" (Kenneth Lambert); and "A Struggle for Normality" (Mary Williams).

(Bk.revs.: BrBkN '76:652; JAnPsy '77/22:70–1; Theol '77/80:304–6; Harvest '78/24:174)

Guru, Psychotherapist, and Self: A Comparative Study of the Guru-Disciple Relationship and the Jungian Analytic Process, by Peter Coukoulis. Marina del Rey, Calif.: DeVorss, 1976* +p* (120 + iv, incl. 6-p. bibl., 5-p. gloss., 4-p. ref. notes).

Coukoulis examines the psychological aspects of the guru-disciple relationship in regard to self-realization and makes a comparative analysis of that relationship and the Jungian analyst-analysand relationship. He begins with a comparison of Eastern and Western concepts of the Self and its realization, drawing on conceptions in the Upanishads, Hindu schools of philosophy, and Buddhism, followed by a discussion of Tantric views regarding the qualifications and role of the human guru and disciple in comparison with those of the Jungian analyst and analysand, along with an explanation of the relationship of guru and disciple in the Bhagavad-Gita. He examines how Sri Aurobindo, Ramakrishna, and Tibet's great yogi Milarepa viewed the role of guru. He demonstrates the personal as well as archetypal significance of the transference relationship in Jungian analysis.

Roots of Renewal in Myth and Madness, by John Weir Perry. San Francisco: Jossey-Bass Publications, 1976 (256 + xii, incl. 4-p. index, 8-p. bibl., 22-p. ref. notes).

Reflecting on thirty years of work in psychotherapy with schizophrenic young adults, Perry explores the renewal process of the center in his search for the "roots of renewal," going deeply into matters of psychological theory and of archetypal myth and ritual forms. He examines the topics of healing factors in the psychotic episode, emotional development and the self-image, the chronically regressive personality, the acute psychotic regression, and the ritual drama of renewal, whose phases are characterized as the center, death, and the return to the beginnings, followed by the clash of opposites, apotheosis, the union of opposites, new birth, the renewal society, and the quadrated world. He likens the renewal of the center to the change "from monarch to messiah."

(Bk.rev.: ContemPsy '77/22:775–6)

The Self and Autism, by Michael Fordham. London: William Heinemann Medical Books for the Society of Analytical Psychology, 1976* (The Library of Analytical Psychology, vol. 3) (296, incl. 4p. index, 5-p. bibl.).

Considering this to be his culminating work on the self in childhood, Fordham presents his investigations on the importance of childhood when the ground plan of individuation is laid down. He puts forward the concept of the self as a defense system designed to establish and maintain a child's individuality. His theme moves from the theory of the archetypes and the self to the topics of symbolization; religious experiences; individuation; the primary self and primary narcissism; maturation in the first two years of life (Freudian and Jungian concepts compared); infantile autism (a disorder of the self); reflections on child analysis and therapy; family interviews; child analytical psychology therapy; and notes on the therapy of infantile autism. He concludes with case studies in autism.

(Bk.revs.: JAnPsy '77/22:67–8; JChildPsy '78/19:193)

The Symbolic Profile, by Ruth Thacker Fry and Joyce Hall. Houston: Gulf Publishing Co. for C. G. Jung Educational Center, 1976 (85, incl. illus.).

Following twenty years of use of the Symbolic Profile, Fry and Hall provide an instructive manual to guide in administering and analyzing the Profile. Designed to "unlock" blocked areas of the psyche in which the client is maladjusted to certain life situations, the Profile is aimed at identification and articulation of psychological problems. Following explanatory information (sample of the Profile, description, purpose, procedure, approach to analysis), the authors use thirty-one cases to illustrate the use of the Profile, which consists of two pages of personal information, a page of squares in which to draw "ego," "fantasy," "Self-determination," "religion," and "potential," and a page with forty statements to be completed on such topics as "I like . . . ," "I want . . . ," and "My family. . . ."

(Bk.revs.: JPastor Care '77/31:214–15; JNervMent '78/166:76; Quad '79/12n1:93–4)

Clinical Uses of Dreams: Jungian Interpretation and Enactments, by James A. Hall. New York: Grune & Stratton/Harcourt Brace Jovanovich, 1977; Boston & London: Shambhala, 1991p as *Patterns of Dreaming* (367 + xxix, incl. 17-p. index, 2-p. foreword by Edward C. Whitmont).

Hall utilizes Jung's conception of the psyche, particularly the central paradox of ego and Self, to see the dream not only as a reflection of problems in one's everyday world but as an indication of the archetypal foundations of one's experience. He first presents a history of dream interpretation (dreams from antiquity to Freud; other theories of dreams; laboratory studies of sleep and dreams) and then describes Jungian dream interpretation (clinical concepts; the dream in Jungian theory; technique of dream interpretation; the relationship between dream ego and waking ego; Polanyi's theories); the clinical uses of dreams; dreams as indicators; dream recall; phenomena related to dreaming; the actual dream; personal dreams; and types of dreams. He concludes with examples of ways of enacting dream images.

(Bk.revs.: AmJClinHyp '79/22:114–15; AmJPsychi '79/136:252–3; Quad '81/14n1:78–85; JAnPsy '82/27:191–2; SFJInstLib '82/3n4:18–24)

Healing and Wholeness, by John A. Sanford. New York, Ramsey, N.J., and Toronto: Paulist Press, 1977 +p (162 + vii, incl. 5-p. index).

Sanford examines where healing comes from, drawing upon ancient and modern lore and wisdom, his own experience with mentors and people seeking help from him, and his own personal search for healing. Beginning with an introduction on contemporary psychological distress and the process of individuation, he discusses the relation of body, soul, and wholeness in terms of illness and health, followed by interpretations of the topics of ancient Greek healing mysteries; the healing emphasis of early Christianity; shamanism; the wisdom of the American Indian; and the perspective on healing furnished by Jung. He concludes with an analysis of personal healing by such means as relating to others, keeping a journal, taking care of the body through diet and exercise, meditation, active imagination, and the healing power of dreams.

(Bk.revs.: BkRDig '78:1146; Choice '78/15:1090; ChrCen '78/95:801; LibJ '78/103:177; LibJBkR '78:392; NatCathRep 5Jy'78/14:16; SisToday Ag–S'78/40:52; InwLight '79/n92:47–8; CathCharis Jn–Jy'80/5:44)

Hermes and His Children, by Rafael López-Pedraza. Zurich: Spring Publications, 1977p (Seminar Series, 13); Einsiedeln, Switzerland: Daimon Verlag, expanded edn. 1989p* (205 + 18 plates of drawings and paintings; 1st edn.: 1-p. pref. by James Hillman, 1-p. foreword by Adolf Guggenbühl-Craig).

Affirming that Jung was a Hermetic man who had an understanding of Hermes' psychology that guided him along the road to creativity, López-Pedraza aims to "thieve Hermetically" from classical images and from the scholars in order to gain insights into archetypal images of Hermes and to carry them into psychotherapy. He examines mythology and scholarly works to provide the background for his study of the psychology of archetypes that constellate and appear in psychotherapy. He emphasizes the need to train one's self in the imagination basically needed for psychotherapy, and he provides insights into some of the most obscure phenomena of human character. He discusses Ovid's classic *Metamorphoses*, "The Homeric Hymn to Hermes," a tale of Homer (on the adultery of Aphrodite), engravings by Picasso, the Homeric "Hymn to Pan," and Priapus as son and father of Hermes.

Marriage: Dead or Alive, by Adolf Guggenbühl-Craig. Zurich: Spring Publications, 1977p; Dallas: Spring Publications, repr. 1981p; 1986p* (126 pp.).

Affirming that the central issue in marriage is not happiness nor well-being, but the "soul's salvation," Guggenbühl-Craig states that the objective of marriage involves two people who are trying to individuate. He discusses the topics of war and peace in marriage; marriage and family; the many faces of marriage and family life; well-being and salvation; individuation; marriage as one pathway of salvation; masculine and feminine; an individuation marriage; the nonsense of normal sexuality; sexuality and individuation; the demonic side of sexuality; divorce; and the relationship of salvation, well-being and individuation. He concludes with the slogan, "marriage is dead, long live marriage!"
(Bk.rev.: JAnPsy '78/23:370–1)

Methods of Treatment in Analytical Psychology: The Proceedings of the Seventh International Congress for Analytical Psychology, Rome, 1977, edited by Ian F. Baker. Fellbach, West Germany: Adolf Bonz Verlag, 1980 (247, incl. 4-p. intro. by Gerhard Adler).

Among the twenty-two Congress papers in this volume, ten are contributions by authors whose books appear in this annotated bibliography. These are on the relationship to the psychological type of the analyst (Katherine Bradway and Jane Wheelwright); the methodology of dream interpretation (Dieckmann); principles of analytical psychotherapy in childhood (Fordham); active imagination (von Franz); alchemy and analytical psychology (Henderson); the therapeutic value of alchemical language (Hillman); active imagination questioned and discussed (Humbert); use of the dream in contemporary analysis (Lambert); imaginative activity versus interpretation of the dream (Perry); and problems for the psychotic patient and the therapist in achieving the symbolic situation (Redfearn). Others include essays on ego and image; children's drawings; archetypal sphere of effect; alchemy, Marx, and clinical imagination; dreams and psychological types; motivation in child therapy; delusion in analytical psychology; active imagination and type; psychotherapy in depressive psychotic states; establishing connections between two worlds; depressive delusion; and treatment of chronic psychoses.

(Bk.revs.: Quad '81/14n1:90–1; JAnPsy '82/27:85–7)

Dreams and Healing, by John A. Sanford. New York, Ramsey, N.J., and Toronto: Paulist Press, 1978p* (164 + vi, incl. 10-p. index).

Feeling the need for a detailed and comprehensive book on dreams, especially as they relate to healing and soul, Sanford here combines a long section on understanding dreams with two sections dealing with dreams in the lives of a young man and of a forty-year-old woman. First, he discusses the topics of the spiritual heritage of dreams; King Nebuchadnezzar's dreams; the different levels of dreams; the healing power in dreams; the drama and structure of dreams; the use of dreams in therapy; and working with one's own dreams. In the second part, he interprets eight dreams of a young university student, whose clarity and impact in the setting of "ordinary life" resulted in guidance and eventual reawakening of his religious life. In the third part, he discusses five dreams (over a two-week span), whose unusual intensity is interpreted as an invitation to wholeness in the life of a middle-aged married woman seeking a career.

Dying and Creating: A Search for Meaning, by Rosemary Gordon. London: Academic Press for the Society of Analytical Psychology, 1978* (The Library of Analytical Psychology, vol. 4) (186, incl. 6-p. index, 4-p. bibl., 9-p. gloss.).

The theme of a search for meaning engages analytical psychologist Gordon in a wide search through myths, rituals, and clinical symptoms. She is looking for a parallelism in which dying as a process is similar to the process of creating, as both involve an acceptance of change and the ability to venture into the unknown. She begins with a background of social attitudes about death and then discusses Freud, Jung, and the death wish, followed by a pilot study of four dying patients who are on the threshold of death. Her explanation of the way in which individuals relate to the fact of death includes some African stories of birth and death, rites for the dead, and psychopathological ways of dealing with death. Her exposition of current psychological ideas on the nature of symbolization and the expression of creative processes by symbols and symbol formation leads to reflections on clinical technique. She deals with the nature of and hindrances to the creative process, concluding with an analysis of the intrapsychic interdependence of death, creation, and transformation.

(Bk.revs.: JAnPsy '79/24:75–8, 167–70; IntJPsy-An '82/63:91)

Jesus the Therapist, by Hanna Wolff. (Ger.: *Jesus als Psychotherapeut.* Stuttgart: Radius Verlag, 1978.) Oak Park, Ill.: Meyer-Stone Books, 1987* +p* (178 + xiii, incl. 2-p. index, 5-p. ref. notes, 7-p. foreword by John Sanford).

Impressed by the frequency with which some Biblical expression to designate a psychic phenomenon or to encapsulate an insight would emerge in the course of her psychotherapeutic practice, Wolff characterizes Jesus as a therapist and a model of modern psychotherapy due to the abundance of his therapeutic insights in the New Testament. She discusses the topics of the will to be well; the courage for self-encounter; getting into training; the human image of the human being; and who is a genuine psychotherapist?

(Bk.revs.: PubW 22Ap'88/233:58; CrossCurr '88/39:112–13)

Jungian Psychotherapy: A Study in Analytical Psychology, by Michael Fordham. Chichester and New York: John Wiley, 1978 +p; London: Maresfield Library/H. Karnac Books, 1986p* (185 + x, incl. 9-p. index, 4-p. bibl.).

Maintaining that many of Jung's psychotherapeutic practices were based more on analytical method than is usually believed, Fordham defines analysis as a starting point for investigations that lay more emphasis than is usual on personal development in its social and cultural setting. He asserts the need to evolve a unique treatment method for each case, considering that the personality of the therapist enters into the procedures adopted. His topics include Jung's conception of psychotherapy; dreams; amplification and active imagination; the setting of analysis; starting analysis; transference and countertransference; some less-organized behavior of therapists; interpretation; the analysis of childhood and its limits; the origins of active imagination; terminating analysis; training; and the application of the therapeutic method.

(Bk.revs.: AmJPsychi '79/136:737–8; BrJPsychi '79/135:375–61; Choice '79/16:596; JAnPsy '79/24:263–4; JPsysomRes '80/24:49; Quad '80/13n1:108–10; SFJInstLib '80/ 2n1:3–10; BrJPsychi '88/152:300)

The Shaman from Elko: Papers in Honor of Joseph L. Henderson on His Seventy-Fifth Birthday, edited by Gareth Hill. San Francisco: C. G. Jung Institute of San Francisco, 1978p; Boston: Sigo Press, repr. 1990 +p (272, incl. 5-p. list of Henderson's writings, 6 illus., 2-p. editor's foreword and chapter on the life and work of Henderson).

This book consists of twenty papers, contributed by professional colleagues and friends, honoring the life and work of Joseph Henderson. The first selections relate to his interest in Native American cultures and shamanism, including "The Navaho Prayer of Blessing" (Donald Sandner); "Shamanistic Principles of Initiation and Power" (William Reed); and "The Blessing Way Ceremony" (Maud Oakes). Clinically-oriented papers include "The Hidden Life of Mary Jo Spencer: Clinical Thoughts on Introversion and/or Schizoid Personality" (Thomas Kirsch); "Empathy in the Analytic Process" (Charles Klaif); "The Hierarchy of Symbols" (Julius Travis); "An Acute Schizophrenic Process Treated by Analytical Therapy" (Howard Levene); and "The Clinical Usefulness of an Initial Dream" (Renaldo Maduro). Other papers deal with culture, philosophy, and literary themes of psychological interest.
(Bk.rev.: JAnPsy '80/25:206–7)

Archetypal Medicine, by Alfred J. Ziegler. (Ger.: *Morbismo: von der Besten aller Gesundheiten.* Zurich: Schweizer Spiegel, 1979.) Dallas: Spring Publications, 1983p* (169 pp.).

Ziegler defines archetypal medicine as a type of psychosomatic medicine which tries to bring about change in disease symptoms through images which carry the symbolic essence of what is observed and are accompanied by a perceptible physical resonance. He draws upon Jungian concepts to seek causes for conditions of the psyche which appear as physical ailments full of symbolic meaning. He states that archetypal medicine's prerequisite does not lie so much in the capacity for registering sense perceptions as it does in subjective, introverted intuition and an understanding of symbols, commenting that "our shadows take on substance." Following a presentation of theory, he discusses the practice of archetypal medicine under the topics of asthmatic construction; itches and itching; cardiac dysrhythmia; anorexia nervosa; rheumatism; and pain and punishment. There are addenda on fever and on drinking and dryness.
(Bk.revs.: JAnPsy '84/29:392; Quad '84/n17:66–8; Resurg N–D'85/n113:38–9)

The Art of Psychotherapy, by Anthony Storr. London: Martin Secker & Warburg with Heinemann Medical Books, 1979 +p*; New York: Methuen, 1980* +p*; New York: Routledge, repr. 1989p* (191 + x, incl. 5-p. index, end-chapter ref. notes).

Recognizing a considerable debt to Jung's ideas and to his own general psychiatric training and reading, Storr provides a practical manual for the practice (and art) of psychotherapy, primarily for postgraduate doctors who are embarking upon specialist training. His view is that psychotherapy should be analytical and individual and that it is more concerned with understanding persons as whole beings and with changing attitudes than it is with abolishing symptoms directly. He proceeds systematically from the setting and the initial interview to establishing a pattern, making progress, interpretation, dreams, daydreams, paintings, writings, objectivity and intimate knowledge, and transference. He discusses the hysterical personality, the depressive personality, the obsessional personality, and the schizoid personality, concluding with comments on cure, termination, and results, and the factor of the personality of the psychotherapist.

(Bk.revs.: BrBkN '80:164; BrJPsychi '80/137:192; NYTimesBkR 5Oc'80/85:9+38–9; PsyMed '80/10:600; PsyToday D'80/14:119–20; Spec 12Ja'80/244:20–1; TimesLitSup '80:530; AmJPsychi '81/138:129–30; BkRDig '81:1392; BrJAddic '81/76:219–20; Bul-BrPsySoc '81/34:71; JAnPsy '81/26:169–70; NYTimesBkR 8N'81/86:51; ClinSocWkJ '82/ 10:137–9; ContemPsy '82/27:106–7)

Navaho Symbols of Healing, by Donald R. Sandner. New York and London: Harvest Book/Harcourt, Brace, Jovanovich, 1979p (290 + xii, incl. 16-p. bibl., 20 illus.).

In searching for the "ancient roots of our own healing disciplines," Jungian psychiatrist Sandner explores the general principles governing the process of symbolic healing as exemplified by the Navaho process of healing, which is the main substance of their religion. The healing process is not directed toward specific bodily symptoms, but it uses striking symbolic images to create harmony between the psyche and the forces around it in order to bring about change in the patients. Sandner's topics include symbolic healing; guardians of the symbols; the constituent parts of the Navaho religion and the whole of action; fear of possession; return to the origins; the ritual control of evil; the process of renewal through death and rebirth; mandalas of healing and the pollen path; the Navaho synthesis; and ancient and modern symbolic healing.

(Bk.revs.: Bklist '79/75:1328; InwLight '79/n93:47–8; LibJ '79/104:845; LibJBkR '79:526; JAnPsy '80/25:208–9, 384–5; SocSciMed '80/14A:256; JAmFolk '82/95:214–15)

The Spiral Way: A Woman's Healing Journey, by Aldo Carotenuto. (It.: *La scala che scende nell'acqua,* Rome: Editore Boringhieri, 1979.) Toronto: Inner City Books, 1986p* (Studies in Jungian Psychology by Jungian Analysts, 25) (139, incl. 6-p. index, 6-p. ref. notes, 2-p. Jungian gloss., 2 illus.).

In order to illustrate the analytic process, Carotenuto presents a woman's case that covers five years of formal Jungian analysis and five further years of observation. Although outwardly healthy, the middle-aged woman expressed serious inner conflicts and private suffering, while her dreams and their interpretation indicated the times of transition. Carotenuto analyzes the sequence of dreams as: a gift (dream 1); dependence on the mother (2); a healing journey (3–4); temple and cross (5–6); action and transformation (7); music of analysis (8); quality of existence (9–10); a slight manipulation (11–14); depression and revelation (15–16); the analyst is tempted to give an answer (17–20); a religious development (21–23); tables of the law (24–26); images of the psyche (27–28); stairs that go down to the water (29–30); false suffering (31–32); a vision of the world (33–34); and separation at end of analysis (35). He also discusses the question of the influence of the analyst and respect for patient's individuality.

Eros on Crutches: On the Nature of the Psychopath, by Adolf Guggenbühl-Craig. (Orig. subtitle: *Reflections on Psychopathy and Amorality.* Dallas: Spring Publications, 1980p) Dallas: Spring Publications, 1986p* (126 pp.).

Noting that a large portion of medical endeavors are concerned with psychosomatic and neurotic disorders, Swiss analyst Guggenbühl-Craig examines the nature of the psychopath in terms of the archetype of the invalid, describing psychopathy as the invalidism of Eros, wherein something in the psyche is missing or markedly underdeveloped. He discusses the archetype of the invalid as an inborn pattern of behavior, a typically human situation in which all human beings come into the world deficient, lacking something; and they become more deficient as lives progress through accidents, illnesses, aging processes, and invalid complexes. Following his analysis of invalidism and of Eros, he discusses psychopaths in literature and the historical development of the term psychopathy, after which he analyzes five primary symptoms of psychopathy, namely, inability to love anything, missing or deficient sense of morality, lack of psychic development, chronic background of depression, and background of fear. Also described are secondary symptoms of psychopathy, compensated psychopaths, and the treatment of psychopaths.

(Bk.revs.: AmJPsyth '82/36:283; Quad '82/15n1:83)

The Longing for Paradise: Psychological Perspectives on an Archetype, by Mario Jacoby. (Ger.: *Sehnsucht nach dem Paradies.* Fellbach, West Germany: Adolf Bonz Verlag, 1980.) Santa Monica: Sigo Press, 1985* + p* (229 + viii, incl. 7-p. index, 6-p. bibl., 8 illus.).

Considering that the "longing for paradise" (freedom from conflict, suffering, and deprivation) is frequently the more or less conscious motivation prompting people to begin an analysis, Jungian analyst Jacoby, initially intending to focus on the therapeutic process, circumambulates the archetypal image of paradise through the realms of social psychology, ethnology, religion, theology, and anthropology. In the first part ("paradise as an image of primal bliss"), he discusses the relationship between mother and child, the mother archetype, infant paradise and infant hell, the father archetype, and motherhood and career, among other topics. The second part concerns a psychological interpretation of the Biblical tale of Paradise and the Fall, including original sin, moral code, superego and conscience, the problem of the shadow, and consciousness and striving for "bliss." He concludes with an interpretation of paradise as hope for the future in early Judaism and the New Testament; ideas of happiness in ancient Greek philosophy; medieval concepts of earthly paradise; the Self in Jung's psychology; and paradise and the process of individuation.

(Bk.revs.: Quad '82/n15:75–7; WCoastRBks S–Oc'85/11:41; JAnPsy '86/31:395–6; SmallPr Ja–F'86/3:26)

Money, Food, Drink, Fashion, and Analytic Training: Depth Dimensions of Physical Existence; The Proceedings of the Eighth International Congress for Analytical Psychology, San Francisco, 1980, edited by John Beebe. Fellbach-Oeffingen, West Germany, Adolf Bonz Verlag, 1983; Dallas: Spring Publications, 1983* (512 pp.).

This volume consists of forty-two papers contributed on the subjects of money (six papers); food, drink, and feast (five); fashion (two); training (eight); clinical practice and research (fourteen); and theoretical explorations (seven). Nineteen are presented by authors whose other works appear in this annotated bibliography. They are "The Training of Shadow and the Shadow of Training" (Berry); "Training of Analytical Psychologists and Xhosa Medicine Men" (Buhrmann); "Myth and Money" (Covitz); "Projections: Soul and Money" (Guggenbühl-Craig); "Polanyi and Jungian Psychology: Dream-ego and Waking-ego" (James Hall); "Soul and Money" (Hillman); "Has Training Gone Too Far?" (Jacoby); "Coins and Psychological Change" (Lockhart); "Self-realization in the Ten Oxherding Pictures" (Miyuki); "The Psyche, Wealth, and Power" (Perry); "Fragmentary Vision: A Central Training Aim" (Samuels); "The Concealed Body Language of Anorexia Nervosa" (Shorter); "The Singer-Loomis Inventory of Personality" (Singer); "The Image of the Jungian Analyst and the Problem of Authority" (Spiegelman); "Coupling/Uncoupling: Evolution of the Marriage Archetype" (R. Stein); "Fee-less Practice and Soul Work" (Vasavada); "Reassessing Femininity and Masculinity" (Whitmont); "Festival, Communion, and Mutuality" (Willeford); and "The Hydrolith: On Drinking and Dryness in Archetypal Medicine" (Ziegler).

The Owl Was a Baker's Daughter: Obesity, Anorexia Nervosa, and the Repressed Feminine, by Marion Woodman. Toronto: Inner City Books, 1980p* (Studies in Jungian Psychology by Jungian Analysts, 4) (139, incl. 5-p. index, 2-p. bibl., 2-p. gloss. of Jungian terms, 9 illus.).

Woodman explores the meaning of the feminine and suggests practical ways women can learn to listen to its authentic voice and discover and love the goddess lost within her own rejected body. She discusses the problems of obesity and of anorexia nervosa in terms of the repressed feminine and the need for the women to come to grips with their femininity. Following her presentation of the experimental background of primary and secondary obesity, Jung's association experiment and its application to obesity, and the nature of complexes and personality traits, she analyzes the relationships of body and psyche, including body metabolism; some contemporary views on obesity; how stress influences obesity; pathological effects of fear and rage; clinical approaches to obesity; and Jung's concept of psyche and body. She interprets three case studies and then concludes with an analysis of the loss of the feminine by considering the father complex, the mother complex, and food, sexuality, and religion complexes.

(Bk.revs.: Choice '81/18:1165; SFJInstLib '81/3n1:17–36; Harvest '82/28:164–6; Quad '82/15n1:85)

Psyche and Substance: Essays on Homeopathy in the Light of Jungian Psychology, by Edward C. Whitmont. Richmond, Calif.: North Atlantic Books, 1980; Berkeley: North Atlantic Books, 1983* +p* (208, incl. 4-p. index).

Writing from many years of experience as a Jungian analyst and practicing homeopath, Whitmont examines analogies in homeopathy and analytical psychology and presents synchronicity or meaningful non-causality as a unifying principle in psychosomatics. Following an overview of the practice of homeopathy, psychic and somatic interrelationships, the law of similars in analytical psychology, and nature and symbol and imaginal reality, he discusses homeopathic remedies and their archetypal forms. In putting homeopathy into practice, he analyzes the problem of soul-body relationship in prescribing and the problems of chronic prescribing, psychosomatics, and surgery. He concludes with case studies (allergic diathesis; new or forgotten indications of tuberculin; intestinal nosodes; and the chronic miasms).

(Bk.revs.: Quad '81/14n1:92–3; Resurg N–D'85/n113:38)

A Secret Symmetry: Sabina Spielrein between Jung and Freud, by Aldo Carotenuto. (It.: *Diario de una Segreta Simmetria.* Rome: Astrolabio, 1980.) New York: Pantheon Books, 1982; 1984p; London: Routledge & Kegan Paul,

1984p* (250, incl. 10-p. index, 21-p. ref. notes, 3 illus. 2-p. bibl. of Spielrein, 4-p. foreword by William McGuire).

Drawing on a diary (1909–12) of Sabina Spielrein (one of young Dr. Jung's patients in Burghölzli mental hospital in 1904) and on her letters to Jung and to Freud and Freud's letters to her, Carotenuto examines the very complex love-hate situation that saw the three principals struggling in a "trapped" predicament. He examines the story of Spielrein, who was born in the Ukraine in 1885, wrote her thesis on schizophrenia for a Zurich medical diploma, became a psychoanalyst in Freud's establishment, and practiced in Geneva and in the USSR after the Revolution.

(Bk.revs.: Atl Jn'82/249:100–1; BkRDig '82:213; Bklist '82/78:988–9; Choice '82/ 20:182 +; KirkR '82/50:314; LATimesBkR 4Jy'82:9; NYRevBks 13My'82/29:3 +; NYTimesBkR 16My'82:1 +; Newswk 21Jn'82/99:68; PubW 19Mr'82/221:61–2; SFJInstLib '82/3n3:33–6; TimesLitSup 10D'82:1351–2; VillVoice Oc'82/29:12–15; Commonw 25F'83/110:124; IntRPsy-An '83/10:241–2; JHistBehSci '83/19:240 +; PsyPersp '83/14:89–99; Quad '83/16n1:89–92; Harvest '84/30:128–9; JAmAcPsyan '84/12:141–2; PartisR '84/51:473–80; PsyanQ '84/53:135–7; PsyMed '84/14:954–5; ClinSocWkJ '85/ 13:91; Econ 18My'85/295:17; JAnPsy '85/28:73–5)

Analysis, Repair, and Individuation, by Kenneth Lambert. London and New York: Academic Press for Society of Analytical Psychology, 1981* (The Library of Analytical Psychology, vol. 5) (234 + xiv, incl. 10-p. index, 7-p. bibl., 16-p. gloss.).

In considering the matter of chaos, disintegration, and the conflict of opposites out of which various kinds of integration can arise, Lambert demonstrates the way in which clinical activities are being used by modern Jungians to help the psychological movement of patients into individuation. Following his discussions on individuation and the mutual influence of psychoanalysis and analytical psychology, as well as personal psychology and the choice of analytic school, he analyzes the topics of relationships of individuation and the personality of the analyst; resistance and counter-resistance; archetypes, object relations and internal objects; reconstruction; transference, countertransference and interpersonal relations; dreams and dreaming; and the individuation process.

(Bk.revs.: BrBkN '82:216; BrJPsychi '82/141:109; Harvest '82/28:169–70; JAnPsy '82/ 27:285–8; ContemPsy '83/28:317; AusJPsy '85/20:105)

Sandplay Studies: Origins, Theory, and Practice, coordinated by Gareth Hill. (An anthology of original papers by Katherine Bradway, Karen A. Signell, Geraldine H. Spare, Charles T. Stewart, Louis H. Stewart, and Clare Thompson.) San Francisco: C. G. Jung Institute of San Francisco, 1981; Boston: Sigo Press, rev. 1990 +p (238 + xiii, incl. 10-p. index, 22-p. bibl., 76 illus., foreword by Dora Kalff).

In this collection of nine papers by six authors who use sandplay therapy in connection with their practice of Jungian analysis, the contributors demonstrate the broad range of applications of the "pictures" or "worlds" revealed by the miniature figures placed by a patient in a sand tray. There are two papers by Bradway ("Developmental Stages in Children's Sand Worlds"; "A Woman's Individuation Through Sandplay"); two by Signell ("The Use of Sandplay with Men"; "The Sandplay Process in Men's Development"); one by Spare ("Are There Any Rules?—Musings of a Peripatetic Sandplayer"); one by Charles Stewart ("The Developmental Psychology of Sandplay"); two by Louis Stewart ("Play and Sandplay"; "Sandplay and the C. G. Jung Institute of San Francisco"); and one by Thompson ("Variations on a Theme by Lowenfeld—Sandplay in Focus").

(Bk.revs.: JAnPsy '82/27:294–5; Quad '82/15n2:68–70; SFJInstLib '84/4n4:42–6)

Addiction to Perfection: The Still Unravished Bride; A Psychological Study, by Marion Woodman. Toronto: Inner City Books, 1982p* (Studies in Jungian Psychology by Jungian Analysts, 12) (204, incl. 5-p. index, 3-p. bibl., 2-p. gloss. of Jungian terms, 20 illus.).

Suggesting that many men and women are addicted in one way or another because the patriarchal culture emphasizes specialization and perfection, Woodman proposes the recognition of the Jungian ideal of wholeness rather than perfection as the goal of psychological development. She examines the rituals of compulsive consumption and the split between body and spirit, whose healing requires the recovery of a feminine ground of being in which the language of the body itself must be heard. Her topics include sacred and demonic ritual; addiction to perfection; obesity and anorexia; assent to the goddess (the Great Mother); rape and the demon lover; and the ravished bride (on the integration of unconscious contents and the acceptance of one's own biological and spiritual identity). The nature of the feminine is explored through case histories, dreams, mythology and literature, food rituals, body imagery, sexuality, and creativity.

(Bk.revs.: CanBkRAn '82:385–6; Harvest '82/28:159–60; JAnPsy '83/28:284–5; PsyPersp '83/14:210–12; QuillQuire My'83/49:35; Chiron '84:195–8)

Alcoholism and Women: The Background and the Psychology, by Jan Bauer. Toronto: Inner City Books, 1982p* (Studies in Jungian Analysis by Jungian Analysts, 11) (140, incl. 4-p. index, 2-p. bibl., 2-p. gloss. of Jungian terms).

Recognizing that there are important general traits in backgrounds and symptoms that are shared by all alcoholics, and having been impressed during the years of her training in analytical psychology by the similarities between the individual approach of Jungian analysis and the collective approach of

Alcoholics Anonymous, Bauer writes about the problem of alcoholism from the point of view of the woman drinker. Using case material, sociological studies, dream analysis, and archetypal patterns from mythology, she discusses the topics of the medical background and theoretical models of alcoholism; Jungian concepts of alcoholism; archetypal patterns of alcoholism; the woman alcoholic (four case studies); psychological factors; and archetypal motifs. Appended are the twelve steps and the twelve traditions of AA, along with the letters between Jung and "Bill W.," cofounder of Alcoholics Anonymous.

(Bk.revs.: CanBkRAn '83:422–3; JAnPsy '83/28:283–4; QuillQuire Mr'83/49:66)

Echo's Subtle Body: Contributions to an Archetypal Psychology, by Patricia Berry. Dallas: Spring Publications, 1982p* (198 pp.).

Berry groups these ten essays, written between 1972 and 1982, under the headings of "Woman" ("What's the Matter with Mother?"; "Neurosis and the Rape of the Dogma of Gender"); "Dream" ("An Approach to the Dream"; "Defense and Telos, or Ultimate End"); "Poetics" ("Virginities of Image"; "Echo's Passion"; "Hamlet's Poisoned Ear"; "Stopping: A Mode of Animation"); and "Shadow" ("Reduction"; "The Training of Shadow and the Shadow of Training"). She provides insights gained by her clinical experience as a Jungian analyst, dream interpretation, and references to mythology as well as feminine studies. The collection's title is taken from a 1979 conference on poem, myth, and soul, at which she presented the paper on Echo, whose passionate love grief causes her body to waste away, leaving only her voice, a "body in air."

(Bk.revs.: Harvest '83/29:155–7; JAnPsy '83/28:392–5)

Jungian Analysis, edited by Murray Stein. LaSalle, Ill.: Open Court Publishing Co., 1982* (Reality of the Psyche Series, vol. 2); Boston and London: New Science Library/Shambhala Publications, 1984p* (411 + xvi, incl. 7-p. index, ref. notes, 5-p. gloss., editor's preface).

Intentionally limited to the practice of analytical psychology, this book consists of nineteen essays by twenty-two American analysts. Following a contribution on the history and practice of Jungian analysis (Henderson) and the editor's discussion of the aims and goals of Jungian analysis, the essays are grouped under four sections, namely, "The Structure and Dynamics of Analysis" ("Establishing and Maintaining the Analytical Structure" (Alexander McCurdy); "Transference/Countertransference: A Jungian Perspective" (Ann Ulanov); "Countertransference/Transference" (Harriet Machtiger); "Termination" (Joseph Wheelwright)); "Methods of Analysis" ("The Use of Dreams and Dream Interpretation in Analysis" (James Hall); "The

Use of Psychological Typology in Analysis" (Alex Quenk and Naomi Quenk); "Active Imagination in Practice" (Janet Dallett); "Dance/Movement and Body Experience in Analysis" (Joan Chodorow); "Sandplay and Jungian Analysis" (Louis Stewart); "Group Therapy and Analysis" (Thayer Greene)); "Special Topics in Analytical Practice" ("Treatment of Children in Analytical Psychology" (Edith Sullwold); "Analysis with the Aged" (Bruce Baker and Jane Wheelwright); "Gender Identity and Gender Roles: Their Place in Analytic Practice" (Katherine Bradway); "Psychopathology and Analysis" (Donald Sandner and John Beebe); "Recent Influences on the Practice of Jungian Analysis" (Whitmont)); and "The Education and Training of Jungian Analysts" ("The Education of the Analyst" (Singer); "Analysis in Training" (Thomas Kirsch)).

(Bk.revs.: CrossCurr '83–84/33:498–9; ContemPsy '84/29:334–5; IndivPsy '84/40:104–5; JAnPsy '84/29:201–2; PerkSchTh Sum'84/37:35; PsyPersp '84/15:108–12; Quad '84/17n2:76–84; SFJInstLib '84/5n1–2:1–13; BulBrPsySoc '85/38:223–4; Harvest '85/31:144–5)

Masochism: A Jungian View, by Lyn Cowan. Dallas: Spring Publications, 1982p* (137 + x, incl. 7-p. ref. notes).

Characterizing masochism as essential reality, before it is anything else, Cowan views it as a reflection of the soul in its tormented, most inarticulate moments—not a mere perversion, distortion, or deviation. Her psychological task is to find meaning and value in masochism as a symbol representing intense activity in the psyche, viewing masochism as an experience of humiliation and pleasure at roughly the same time. Following a discussion of the possibilities of perversion and a summary of masochism and modern American psychotherapy, she presents a Jungian view of the topics of humiliation (getting down to basics); pleasure ("the play's the thing"); Eros as sadist; mortification (alchemical masochism); the contract as sadist (the purpose of a masochistic contract being to ensure the unfairness of power); martyrdom (the mania of misery); Prometheus (a mythological case study); Dionysus (the madness of masochism); the fateful move in masochism; and masochistic exhibitionism.

(Bk.revs.: JAnPsy '83/28:285–6; PsyPersp '84/15:241–3; Quad '84/17n2:99–101)

Narcissism and Character Transformation: The Psychology of Narcissistic Character Disorders, by Nathan Schwartz-Salant. Toronto: Inner City Books, 1982p* (Studies in Jungian Psychology by Jungian Analysts, 9) (190, incl. 5-p. index, 4-p. bibl., 2-p. Jungian gloss., 14 illus.).

Combining both Jungian and psychoanalytic points of view (particularly Freud and Kohut) in the field of clinical depth analysis, Schwartz-Salant broadens the clinical perspective on the issue posed by narcissism and the problem of identity. Following an introductory discussion of narcissism and the problem of identity, he presents stage one of transformation in terms of clinical issues and of the mythology of transformation of the masculine and then analyzes modes of relating with an emphasis on body awareness in the relationship of the somatic and psychic unconscious. He concludes with an interpretation of the mythology of stage two (emergence of feminine power) and clinical issues of this stage of transformation.

(Bk.revs.: CanBkRAn '82:384; PsyPersp '82/13:204–10; ContemPsy '83/28:228–9; Harvest '83/29:157–9; JAnPsy '83/28:75–6; Quad '83/16n1:98–100; PsyanR '87/74:436–8)

Rape and Ritual: A Psychological Study, by Bradley A. Te Paske. Toronto: Inner City Books, 1982p* (Studies in Jungian Psychology by Jungian Analysts, 10) (157, incl. 6-p. index, 3-p. bibl., 2-p. gloss. of Jungian terms).

In confronting such a pressing and omnipresent contemporary problem as rape, Te Paske begins with the mundane facts of criminal rape in order to pave the way to consider adequately each angle of approach to the problem with the individual personality in mind. He analyzes the psychology of rape under the topics of the crime of rape; the victim of rape; a review of theories; the psychology of the rapist; archetypal background of rape; rape fantasy and individuation; the homosexual component; and ritual and sacrifice. Combining theory, mythology, and clinical material from his Jungian practice, he interprets the role of the Great Mother, the archetype of the masculine, of anima and Eros, and of ego and shadow.

(Bk.revs.: CanBkRAn '82:384–5; JAnPsy '83/28:191–2; Harvest '84/30:139–40; SFJInstLib '86/6n3:33–41)

St. George and the Dandelion: Forty Years of Practice as a Jungian Analyst, by Joseph B. Wheelwright, edited by Audrey Hilliard Blodgett. San Francisco: C. G. Jung Institute of San Francisco, 1982* (109 + xiii, incl. 5-p. index, preface by Erik Erikson, foreword by Gregory Bateson).

From his long experience as a Jungian analyst who trained with Jung himself, Wheelwright presents a casual yet serious account of his life and work, acknowledging indebtedness to Jung, Freud, Henry Stack Sullivan, and Erik Erikson. He provides anecdotal accounts of his experience with a delightful sense of humor. Following his introductory "Imprimis," he examines his beginnings and then his understanding of Jungian psychological concepts, as well as comments on attitudes and values in therapeutic practice (screening, patient fees, analyst-patient relationship, diagnosis, training analysis, and lay analysis). He also includes a discussion of anima-animus, a 25-page essay on psychological types (published in 1973 by the San Francisco

Jung Institute), a 10-page article on marriage in the second half of life (with the same husband or wife with whom one started), along with accounts of three selected encounters with Jung.
(Bk.revs.: PsyPersp '83/14:99–102; Quad '83/16n1:108–9; JAnPsy '84/29:83–5)

The Differing Uses of Symbolic and Clinical Approaches in Practice and Theory: The Proceedings of the Ninth International Congress for Analytical Psychology, Jerusalem, 1983, edited by Luigi Zoja and Robert Hinshaw. Zurich: Daimon Verlag, 1986* (369 + viii).

Reflecting one of Jung's most basic tenets that a therapist must find his or her own individual way of working, the twenty-five papers in this volume (including opening and closing addresses and two review papers on the Congress) vary widely. Seven are contributions by authors whose books are in this annotated bibliography: "Images of the Inferior Analyst" (Bosnak); "Depressed Patients and the Coniunctio" (Hubback); "Cultural Anxiety" (López-Pedraza); "Jerusalem: The Age of Plastic" (Newman); "The Winning of Conscious Choice: The Emergence of Symbolic Activity" (Redfearn); "The Symbolic Life of Man" (Sandner); and *"Horroris Morbus,* Unit of Disease and Image of Ailing" (Ziegler).
Bk.rev.: Quad '87/20n2:84–7; JAnPsy '88/33:85–9)

Healing Fiction, by James Hillman. Barrytown, N.Y.: Station Hill Press, 1983* +p* (145 + xii, incl. 13-p. ref. notes, 4-p. publisher's preface).

In revising the act of therapy into an imaginative act, in which imagination embodies the faculty of transformation itself, Hillman presents the psyche's mode of operation as fiction and emphasizes the primary psychological problem as that of "reading" the story as visionary literature. His three essays on the subject are: a round with Freud ("The Fiction of Case History"), Jung's contribution to "Know thyself" ("The Pandaemonium of Images"), and Adler's imagination of inferiority ("What Does the Soul Want?"). He offers as Jung's outstanding contribution to Western culture a psychological method that responds to the most persistent psychological need from Oedipus and Socrates through *Hamlet* and *Faust,* the need for self-knowledge. He speaks of poetics in the context of psychology and projects a two-way connection between psychology and literature that leads to soul-making.
(Bk.revs.: LibJ '83/108:504; SFJInstLib '87/ns7:17–21)

Images of the Self: The Sandplay Therapy Process, by Estelle L. Weinrib. Boston: Sigo Press, 1983* +p* (172 + xvii, incl. 5-p. index, 2-p. bibl., 27 illus.).

Considering sandplay as a nonverbal, nonrational form of therapy that reaches a preverbal level of the psyche, Weinrib believes that a patient's creation of "pictures" with miniature figures in a sand tray will enable the autonomous tendency deep in the unconscious for the psyche to heal itself. The first part is devoted to a discussion of sandplay therapy theory and practice, in which Weinrib presents eight basic concepts and characterizes sandplay as a way of transformation and a safe outlet for aggression, feeling, and creating. She makes a comparison of verbal analysis and sandplay. In the second part, she provides a detailed analysis of a case study, whose phases include penetration to the personal unconscious; actuation of instincts; beginning of father-complex resolution; appearance of the nascent ego; centering; resolution of paranoid inflation; differentiation and movement toward connection of masculine and feminine elements in the personality; constellation of the self; separation from father and reconciliation; appearance of symbols of renewal; and the emergence of the anima and the birth of a new consciousness.

(Bk.revs.: AmJArtTh '83/23:35–8; Quad '83/16n2:85–6)

Inter Views: Conversations with Laura Pozzo on Psychotherapy, Biography, Love, Soul, Dreams, Work, Imagination, and the State of the Culture, by James Hillman. New York: Harper & Row, 1983; New York: Colophon Books/Harper & Row, 1984p (198 + viii, incl. 4-p. index).

Hillman characterizes this lively interview/conversation as an Italian journey of the Northern imagination in that he views his orientation toward psychology as "Mediterranean" or "Southern" (mythical, passionately intellectual, aesthetic, urban). The topics are pathologizing and soul; psychoanalysis and schools; therapy and dreams and the imaginal; a running engagement with Christianity; on being biographical; old and new: Senex and Puer; writing; working; and loving.

(Bk.revs.: Commonw '83/110:540–1; Harvest '83/29:160–3; KirkR '83/51:225; LibJ '83/108:402–3; LATimesBk 5Jn'83:11; PubW 18Mr'83/223:56; BkRDig '84/716: StAnth Mr'84/91:51; Thought '86/61:172–3)

Starving Women: A Psychology of Anorexia Nervosa, by Angelyn Spignesi. Dallas: Spring Publications, 1983* (138 + xii, incl. 4-p. index).

Resting on assumptions (from the works of Freud, Jung, and Hillman) that the underlying psychic realm permeates everyday sense-perceptions, thoughts, emotions, values, attitudes, and behaviors, Spignesi explores the theme of a woman's relation to the psychic underworld. She tells the story of the anorexic-bulimic "from within the recesses of this psyche," beginning with data from literal anorexics and then going deeper to examine imagery

and metaphor that are produced spontaneously and affect their bodily existence. Her analyses and interpretations come under imaginative headings of mother and oppositionalism (the anorexic and methodology; cadaverous female); female of borders (ritual sacrifice; deficient ego: polymorphous child of soul); tyrant of fat (hyperactivity: tyrant's drive; bulimia and stealing); mother of skeletal lady; the gaping mouth; Gaia's sickle; and imaginal therapy.
(Bk.rev.: JAnPsy '85/30:108–9)

The Windows of the Soul, by Robert Kugelmann. Lewisburg, Penn.: Bucknell U. Press, 1983*; London and Toronto: Associated University Presses, 1983* (Studies in Jungian Thought) (258, incl. 7-p. index, 11-p. bibl.).

Kugelmann aims to restore metaphor to scientific language in order to bring the body back into awareness by means of an imaginal consciousness that perceives the body in its soulful entirety. His theme is the eye, organ of insight, whose imaginal anatomy reveals the soul at the core. He provides historical reflections on glaucoma and discusses primary glaucoma, that common pathology of the eye which refuses to stay within the eye and thereby affects various areas of the patient's life. By identifying archaic personages (Glaucus, Old Man of the Sea, Athena Glaucopis, Perseus, and Medusa of the Stony Eyes, among others) through whom psychological healing can become possible, he suggests that clarification of the experience of glaucoma enables patients, physicians, and therapists to bring healing to the person and not just to the eye.
(Bk.revs.: JAnPsy '85/30:395; LitMed '85/4:168–9)

Words as Eggs: Psyche in Language and Clinic, by Russell A. Lockhart. Dallas: Spring Publications, 1983p* (233, incl. 5-p. index).

Placing the thirteen essays in this book in chronological order, Lockhart forms a deliberate path, from his first essay, "On the Forgotten Psyche of Behavior Therapy" to the most recent, "Some Strange and Weird Experiences." In between are the essays "Myths Alive"; "Listening to the Voices of Psychosis"; "Cancer in Myth and Dream" (archetypal relation between dreams and disease); "What Whale Does America Pursue?"; "Words as Eggs"; "Eros in Language, Myth, and Dream"; "Psyche in Hiding"; "Eros at the Well"; "Coins and Psychological Change"; and "Metaphor as Illness." He views the essays as stepping stones in his symbolic life that is being pushed for realization by the self, not the ego.

The Analytic Encounter: Transference and Human Relationship, by Mario Jacoby. Toronto: Inner City Books, 1984p* (Studies in Jungian Psychology by Jungian Analysts, 15) (125, incl. 5-p. index, 2-p. bibl., 2-p. gloss. of Jungian terms, 8 illus.).

In these essays originally presented as lectures on the psychological subtleties involved in the transference and countertransference relationship between patient and therapist in the analytic encounter, Jacoby discusses the everyday problems of analytic practice and the archetypal depth-dimension (discovered by Jung) that lies behind personal involvements. Following an introduction to the analytic encounter (Freud's view on transference, Jung's contribution, and a case example), he examines the topics of transference and countertransference; narcissism and transference; transference and human relationship; human relationship in analysis; countertransference and the needs of the analyst; and erotic love in analysis.
(Bk.revs.: CanBkRAn '84:467; Harvest '85/31:141–4; JAnPsy '85/30:103–4; PsyPersp '85/16:110–11; Quad '86/19n1:69–71)

Archetypal Consultation: A Service Delivery Model for Native Americans, by Eduardo Duran. New York: Peter Lang Publishing Co., 1984p* (American University Studies, Series VIII, Psychology, vol. 2) (157 + xi, incl. 7-p. bibl., 1-p. notes, 3-p. gloss. of analytical terms).

Utilizing some of the ideas proposed by Jung, Duran attempts to solve some of the problems facing Native Americans in the field of mental health. He begins with a literature review, including dream phenomena and their relevance to Native Americans, and dreams in orthodox approaches to therapy, followed by a discussion of analytical psychology and its relevance to the Native American psyche. He proposes a theoretical approach that considers previous difficulties with the delivery of mental health services; and he presents a model of archetypal consultation that addresses Native American customs, concepts of illness, and healing.

A Casebook: Applications of the Myers-Briggs Type Indicator in Counseling, by Judith A. Provost. Gainesville, Fla.: Center for Applications of Psychological Type, 1984p* (86 + ii, incl. 2-p. bibl.).

This casebook is written for counselors and therapists who already have had an introduction to the Myers-Briggs Type Indicator (MBTI) and Jung's theory of psychological types. In it, Provost demonstrates the applications of the MBTI in individual counseling and psythotherapy with eighteen cases from actual counseling experiences that include people of various ages, though primarily college-age (18–24), with above-average intelligence and representing all sixteen types of personality. Following a discussion of the relationship of type development to counseling and the use of the MBTI, she makes observations on the types of clients in counseling, client-counselor relationships, therapies, and conclusions about psychological type and the counseling relationship, concluding with a summary of the value of the MBTI.

Hags and Heroes: A Feminist Approach to Jungian Psychotherapy with Couples, by Polly Young-Eisendrath. Toronto: Inner City Books, 1984p* (Studies in Jungian Psychology by Jungian Analysts, 18) (184, incl. 6-p. index, 4-p. bibl., 4-p. ref. notes).

Bringing together the archetypal theory and practice of Jungian psychotherapy with the interpersonal perspective of Henry Stack Sullivan and integrating them with a feminist viewpoint, Young-Eisendrath focuses on an understanding of how individual complexes interfere with harmonious relationships. She draws upon clinical experience with many couples in collaboration with co-therapist Ed Epstein to provide guidelines and practical techniques to revitalize love relationships. She writes within the context of the story of Sir Gawain and Lady Ragnell, a story about power, weakness, heroics, and conflict from the era of the Knights of the Round Table, in which each cherished the other's autonomy as if it were his own and cared for the other's needs in the same way. She emphasizes a revaluing of the feminine principle and a reassessment of feminine authority.
(Bk.revs.: CanBkRAn '84:469; Quad '85/18n2:105–7; Adoles '86/21:500; SFJInstLib '86/6n2:18–19)

Living in Two Worlds: Communication Between a White Healer and Her Black Counterparts, by M. Vera Buhrmann. Capetown: Human & Rousseau, 1984; Wilmette, Ill.: Chiron Publications, 1986p* (108, incl. 4-p. bibl., 2-p. gloss., 8 illus.).

Based on an experiential research method carried out among indigenous Xhosa healers in South Africa, this work by Jungian analyst Buhrmann shows that what is called "magic" in the healing systems is not "magical" in the usual sense of the word but is based on sound principles of depth psychology, especially those of Jung. She shares her experience in order to give some understanding of the meaningfulness and the effectiveness of native methods, including aspects of the treatment of emotional disturbances, the interpretation of dreams, ritual healing dances, and river ceremonies. She provides a background analysis of the concepts of depth psychology, Xhosa cosmology, and categories of illness.
(Bk.revs.: Chiron '86:217–20; JAnPsy '87/32:188–90)

Psychological Types and Psychotherapy, by Alex T. Quenk. Gainesville, Fla.: Center for Applications of Psychological Types, 1984p (54, incl. 3-p. bibl.).

Using a dynamic-process model of Jung's psychological typology, Quenk relates it not only to patterns of adaptation but also to psychotherapy. Following an introductory discussion on typology and character, he discusses the topics of the auxiliary function; type and adaptation; relationships of type to transference and to countertransference and the analytic process, and psychological type in relation to individuation. He presents many clinical examples from individual, group, and marital therapy to show the effects of typology on the choice of therapy and therapists and on procedures within the therapeutic process.

Transference/Countertransference, edited by Nathan Schwartz-Salant and Murray Stein. Wilmette, Ill.: Chiron Publications, 1984p* (206 + iv, incl. end-chapter bibl. notes, 2-p. editors' preface).

Consisting of nine essays on the subject of the transference and countertransference, this first issue of *Chiron: A Review of Jungian Analysis* contains the following contributions: "Psychological Types in Transference, Countertransference, and the Therapeutic Interaction" (John Beebe); "Successful and Unsuccessful Interventions in Jungian Analysis" (William Goodheart); "Dreams and Transference/Countertransference: The Transformative Field" (James Hall); "Reflections on the Transference/Countertransference Process with Borderline Patients" (Harriet Machtiger); "Transference/Countertransference Between Woman Analyst and Wounded Girl Child" (Betty DeShong Meador); "Archetypal Factors Underlying Sexual Acting-out in the Transference/Countertransference Process" (Nathan Schwartz-Salant); "Power, Shamanism, and Maieutics in the Countertransference" (Murray Stein); "Transference/Countertransference Issues with Women in the First Stage of Animus Development" (Florence Wiedemann); and "Transference and Countertransference in Analysis Dealing with Eating Disorders" (Marion Woodman). (Bk.revs.: JAnPsy '85/30:101–3; SFJInstLib '86/6n2:1–12)

Abandonment, edited by Nathan Schwartz-Salant and Murray Stein. Wilmette, Ill.: Chiron Publications, 1985p* (237 + iv, incl. end-chapter bibl. notes, 4 illus.).

The second issue of *Chiron: A Review of Jungian Analysis* contains nine essays on the subject of abandonment. These are "Dream Motifs Accompanying the 'Abandonment' of an Analytic Practice" (Berry-Hillman); "Symbol and Ritual in Melancholia: The Archetype of the Divine Victim" (Tristan Cornes); "Abandonment in Infancy (Michael Fordham); "Birth's Cruel Secret" (Gilda Frantz); "Abandonment and Deintegration of the Primary Self" (Renaldo Maduro); "Perilous Beginnings: Loss, Abandonment, and Transformation" (Harriet Machtiger); "Abandonment and Restitution in Psychosis and Psychotic Character" (Jeffrey Satinover); "Abandonment, Wish, and Hope in the Blues" (William Willeford); and "Abandonment in the Creative Woman" (Woodman).

Anatomy of the Psyche: Alchemical Symbolism in Psychotherapy, by Edward F. Edinger. LaSalle, Ill.: Open Court Publishing Co., 1985* +p* (Reality of the Psyche Series, vol. IV) (260 + xix, incl. 20-p. index, 8-p. bibl., 100 illus.).

Published first as a series of articles in *Quadrant* between 1978 and 1982, these essays by Edinger continue Jung's study of alchemy by examining certain experiential modes of the individuation process that appear in alchemical symbolism. Drawing upon Jung's discovery of the reality of the psyche, Edinger explores religion and literary scriptures as well as the "gropings" of the protosciences, such as alchemy, astrology, and pre-Socratic philosophy, in order to understand the phenomenology of the objective psyche. His goal is to present an anatomy of the psyche that is as objective as the anatomy of the body, an ordering of psychic facts. He throws new light on the basic patterns of increasing consciousness in the psychotherapeutic process by means of amplification of the alchemical opus in its operations of *calcinatio, solutio, coagulatio, sublimatio, mortificatio, separatio,* and *coniunctio* which make up the alchemical transformation and symbolize the process of individuation.

(Bk.revs.: PsyPersp '86/17:249–52; Chiron '87:209–18; ContemPsy '89/34:799)

Beyond the Brain: Birth, Death, and Transcendence in Psychotherapy, by Stanislav Grof. Albany: State U. of New York Press, 1985* +p* (466 + xviii, incl. 12-p. index, 10-p. bibl., 11-p. ref. notes, 45 illus.).

Grof considers Jung to be the "first modern psychologist." He distinguishes Jung's methods from Freud's psychoanalytic approach of finding rational explanations for all psychic phenomena by tracing them back to biological roots in linear causality. Grof cites Jung's scientific procedures as penetrating deeply into the transpersonal realm to formulate a system of psychology different from any of Freud's followers. He supports Jung's concept of synchronicity as an awareness that linear causality is not the only mandatory connecting principle in nature. His own approach to psychotherapy involves deep experiential processes, such as psychedelic therapy and holonomic integration. His thesis moves from the nature of reality to the dimensions of the human psyche and then to the topics of integration of psychotherapeutic approaches; the architecture of emotional disorders; dilemmas and controversies of traditional psychiatry; a new understanding of the psychotherapeutic process; and new perspectives in psychotherapy and self-exploration.

(Bk.revs.: SciTechBkN Oc'85/9:20; Choice '86/23:927; SFRBks Apr'86/11:11)

Forms of Feeling: The Heart of Psychotherapy, by Robert F. Hobson. London: Tavistock Publications, 1985* +p*; New York: Tavistock with Methuen, 1985; New York: Ark Paperbacks/Routledge, Chapman & Hall, 1988p* (318 + xvi, incl. 9-p. index, 10-p. bibl.).

Hobson presents his autobiography as a psychotherapist along with a method he has developed for learning how to relate to oneself and others. He describes the heart of the matter as a two-person relationship in which one hears the "true voice of feeling" (as the first part of the book is called). In the second part he discusses a model of psychotherapy, love and loss, and needs, conflict, and avoidance. He concludes with a section on "the heart of a psychotherapist."

(Bk.revs.: KirkR '85/53:1178; BkRDig '86/753–4; BrBkN '86:233–4; BulBrPsySoc '86/39:174; Harvest '86/32:158–61; NewSoc '86/75:293; NewStates 11Ap'86/111:26; NYTimesBkR 26Ja'86/91:37; PsyMed '86/16:933; Readings Jn'86/1:30; Chiron '87:218–23; JAnPsy '87/32:151–3; BrJPsychi '88/152:589)

The Pregnant Virgin: A Process of Psychological Transformation, by Marion Woodman. Toronto: Inner City Books, 1985p* (Studies in Jungian Psychology by Jungian Analysts, 21) (204, incl. 7-p. index, 7-p. ref. notes, 29 illus.).

Using the concept of the process of psychological pregnancy (the virgin forever a virgin, forever pregnant, forever open to possibilities), Woodman examines ways of restoring the unity of body and soul, suggesting that immortality is a reality contained within mortality. Drawing on her Jungian analytic practice with its analysis of hundreds of dreams, she explores the search for personal identity and relationships, including celebration of the feminine both in women and men. She begins with the symbolism of the chrysalis, then discusses abandonment in the creative woman, psyche-soma awareness, the ritual journey, further thoughts on addiction, and yin, yang, and Jung. She concludes with a section on modern initiation.

(Bk.revs.: CanBkRAn '85:404–5; ContemPsy '86/31:816–17; Gnosis '86/n2:42; JPsyTheol '86/14:246; Quad '86/19n2:90–4; SFJInstLib '86/6n2:13–17)

The Wise Old Man: Healing Through Inner Images, by Pieter Middelkoop. (Dutch: *Oude wijze man.* Rotterdam: Lemniscaat, 1985) Boston and Shaftesbury: Shambhala Publications, 1989p* (184 + x, incl. 4-p. bibl., 3-p. ref. notes, 2-p. intro. by Robert Bosnak).

Linking his ideas on inner images to Jung's personality model, whose center Middelkoop calls the core of the Self, Middelkoop develops his "imagination therapy" with the symbolic personification of the archetypal

Wise Old Man as inner source of wisdom to guide the individual to healing and wholeness. Using inner images as the starting point of therapy, he describes and explains several sequences of imagination by different people with different backgrounds. The first sequence deals with the processes of the ego and the unconscious, at first following divergent courses but eventually moving together; and the second involves the conflict of the different unconscious forces in the imaginal world from which the ego at first seems to be isolated. But gradually the ego begins to take part in bringing about an integration within the whole person. The third sequence concerns difficulties sometimes shared by the individual with large numbers of people. He concludes with a discussion of theoretical and technical aspects of the world of the Self.

Working with the Dreaming Body, by Arnold Mindell. Boston and London: Routledge & Kegan Paul, 1985p* (133, incl. 7-p. index, 8-p. ref. notes, 1 illus.).

Writing for the layperson as well as the professional in the search for meaning behind physical disease, Mindell introduces a single theoretical framework that concentrates on the relationship between dreams and body problems, using case reports, communication theory, dream and body work, Jungian psychology, and even a "smattering" of physics. Asserting that body therapies are split off from dream therapies and that dream therapy normally is done without reference to body feelings, he presents experiences from his work with normal, as well as psychotic, physically ill, and dying patients in training seminars, mental clinics, hospitals, and his own analytic practice. Among the topics covered are "flashes of insight"; from illness to inner development; illness and projection; the dreambody in a fairy tale; the dreambody in relationships; the world as a dreambody; cultural change; and working alone on one's self.

(Bk.rev.: RelStudR '86/12:45)

The Body in Analysis, edited by Nathan Schwartz-Salant and Murray Stein. Wilmette, Ill.: Chiron Publications, 1986p* (The Chiron Clinical Series) (220 + iv, incl. end-chapter ref. notes, 14 illus.).

Consisting of eight essays on the subject of the body in analysis, this third issue of *Chiron: A Review of Jungian Analysis* contains contributions by Jungian analysts on "The Body in Child Psychotherapy" (John A. B. Allen); "The Body as Symbol: Dance/movement in Analysis" (Joan Chodorow); "Body Language and the Self: The Search for Psychic Truth" (Hubback); "Getting in Touch and Touching in Analysis " (Jacoby); "Ceremonies of the Emerging Ego in Psychotherapy" (Perera); "The Subjective Body in

Clinical Practice" (Sandner); "Bare Bones: The Aesthetics of Arthritis" (Ronald Schenck); and "The Subtle-body Concept in Clinical Practice" (Schwartz-Salant).

Carl Jung and Soul Psychology, edited by E. Mark Stern. (Orig. publ.: Voices: The Art and Science of Psychotherapy. American Academy of Psychotherapists, 1986.) New York and London: Haworth Press, 1986 (192, incl. end-chapter references, 20 photos of authors).

Containing twenty-four essays and comments by twenty-two collaborators, most of which are less than nine pages in length, this collection consists of seven contributions by Jungian analysts, including essays on "When the Spirits Come Back" (Dallett); "Soul-loss and Restoration: A Study in Countertransference" (John Haule); "Soul and Spirit" (Hillman); "Creativity and the Healing of the Soul" (Phillip McGowan); "The Wandering Uterus: Dream and the Pathologized Image" (Stanton Marlan); "The Lumen Naturae: Soul of the Psychotherapeutic Relationship" (Marilyn Nagy); and "The Incest Wound and the Marriage Archetype" (Robert M. Stein).
(Bk.rev.: JPsyChry Fall'87/6:76)

A Critical Dictionary of Jungian Analysis, edited by Andrew Samuels, Bani Shorter, and Fred Plaut. London and New York: Routledge & Kegan Paul, 1986* +p* (171, incl. 3-p. index, 6-p. bibl.).

Considering Jungian terminology to be unfamiliar to many readers, the editors have created a dictionary of Jungian terms containing 192 entries arranged alphabetically, from "abaissement du niveau mental," "abreaction," and "acting out" to "word association test" and "wounded healer." The dictionary contains (a) terms and ideas introduced or developed primarily by Jung; (b) terms and ideas in general usage in psychodynamics but used in a particular way by Jung; (c) ordinary words used by Jung in a particular way; (d) major terms introduced and developed by other analytical psychologists; and (e) psychoanalytic terms which were adapted or extended by Jung.
(Bk.revs.: Harvest '87/33:223–5; JAnPsy '87/32:185–6; JMindBeh '87/8:359–60; Psy-Persp '87/18:447; Quad '87/20n2:93; TimesEdSup 22My'87:33; AmRefBksAn '88/19:303–4; ContemPsy '88/33:165–6)

Emotional Child Abuse: The Family Curse, by Joel D. Covitz. Boston: Sigo Press, 1986* +p* (162 + xii, incl. 2-p. bibl.).

Covitz believes that psychological child abuse often occurs because there is a lack of equality in the family system and lack of respect for the "genuine self," which results in a destructive chain of narcissistic disorders that is perpetuated through the generations. He looks behind the unhealthy narcissistic, egotistical, "me-first" behavior of the adult to find that this person's *healthy* narcissistic needs were not met as a child. Presenting a kind of guidebook for the development of a well-adjusted child-parent bond that is free from the most blatant to the most subtle forms of abuse, he first discusses the roots of narcissism (the disturbance of our time; setting the stage for narcissistic disorders), then abusive styles of parenting (the inadequate parent; the devouring parent; the tyrannical parent), repeating the family curse from generation to generation (money matters; sexuality and the incestuous style of parenting; abandonment; illness and death; discipline), and breaking the chain (motivation and expectation; methods of transformation; looking to the future).

(Bk.revs.: LibJ Ag'86/111:157; SmallPr S–Oc'86/4:84; BkRDig '87:396; Choice '87/ 24:824; JAnPsy '87/32:196–7; PsySch '87/24:296–8; CommBoun Jy–Ag'88/6:22–3; PsyPersp '89/21:210–13)

The Jungian Experience: Analysis and Individuation, by James A. Hall. Toronto: Inner City Books, 1986* (Studies in Jungian Psychology by Jungian Analysts, 26) (171, incl. 6-p. index, 4-p. bibl., 7-p. ref. notes, 2-p. gloss., 10 illus.).

Aiming to guide the person seeking Jungian analysis as well as to help therapists of other backgrounds to understand the clinical application of the classical Jungian approach, Hall illustrates theoretical points with clinical examples, weaving together theory and practice to avoid the pitfall of excessive symbolism. He demonstrates how to translate concepts into practice by means of a topical sequence, starting with "the troubled person" and moving to the topics of the mind and the body; diagnosis; the structure of analysis; process of analysis; dreams and techniques of enactment; variations of analysis; the individuating ego; and "beyond analysis," concluding with scientific and religious implications of Jungian theory. Appended is a description of the structural elements of the personality, along with a guide of how and where to find Jungian analysts.

(Bk.revs.: CanBkRAn '86:218–19; BksCan Mr'87/16:24–5; ContemPsy '87/32:756; Harvest '87/33:217–19; PsyPersp '88/19:169–71)

The Psychobiology of Mind-Body Healing: New Concepts of Therapeutic Hypnosis, by Ernest Lawrence Rossi. New York: W. W. Norton, 1986*; 1988p* (Professional Books) (231 + xv, incl. 11-p. index, 16-p. bibl., 7 illus., foreword by Norman Cousins).

This book is a result of the author's quest for personal health and desire to understand new texts about mind-body relationships, stress, psychoneuroimmunology, neuroendocrinology, molecular genetics, and neurobiology of memory and learning. Rossi offers a broad frame of reference and a language for understanding the natural processes of healing, using his experience as a Jungian analyst and his training in hypnosis under Milton Erickson. He discusses at length the psychology of mind-body communication, including the topics of placebo response (a rejected cornerstone of mind-body healing); mind-body healing and hypnosis; stress and psychosomatic phenomena; and the new language of mind-body communication. The second part deals with the psychobiology of mind-body healing, including an overview of mind-body communication and healing, and a discussion of mind modulation of the automatic nervous system and of the neuropeptide system.

(Bk.revs.: LibJ N'86/111:102; BkRDig '87:1610; Choice '87/24:1153; ContemPsy '87/32:1042)

The Scapegoat Complex: Toward a Mythology of Shadow and Guilt, by Sylvia Perera. Toronto: Inner City Books, 1986p* (Studies in Jungian Psychology by Jungian Analysts, 23) (126, incl. 5-p. index, 3-p. bibl., 2-p. gloss. of Jungian terms).

Drawing on her own experience and on material shared by friends and by analysands in her clinical practice, Perera examines the widespread scapegoat complex. In this, someone is found who can be identified with wrong-doing or evil, blamed for it, and cast out of the community so that the remaining members may be left with a feeling of guiltlessness. She examines the phenomenology of such scapegoat-identified individuals from the complex down to the original archetypal image and discusses how to heal those who are caught in the scapegoat complex. Her topics include the riddance of evil and guilt; the structure of the scapegoat complex; exile in the wilderness; scapegoating within the family; the scapegoat complex and ego structure (including distortions of perception, enduring painful experience, and problems of self-assertion); the scapegoat-messiah image; the feminine element; healing the scapegoat complex; and the meaning of the scapegoat archetype.

Withymead: A Jungian Community for the Healing Arts, by Anthony Stevens. London: Coventure, 1986p* (254 + vi, incl. 7-p. index, 3-p. bibl., 4 illus.).

A pioneer residential community composed of staff as well as patients using art therapy and Jungian analysis in a family setting in Devon, Withymead is presented by Stevens as a unique sanctuary of healing for people in mental distress. Established by Irene and Gilbert Champernowne during the Second World War, it functioned until overtaken by hard times and inner dissensions in the 1960s. Stevens, who trained with Jungian analyst Irene

Champernowne and subsequently became a colleague, describes and interprets the historical and social context of Withymead and discusses the topics of the human factor, the therapeutic community, creativity, therapy through the arts, family matters, and finally "a house divided."
(Bk.rev.: Harvest '87–88/33:213–15)

Archetypal Processes in Psychotherapy, edited by Nathan Schwartz-Salant and Murray Stein. Wilmette, Ill.: Chiron Publications, 1987p* (The Chiron Clinical Series) (228 + iv, incl. end-chapter bibl. notes, 8 illus.).

Containing nine essays on archetypal processes in psychotherapy, this fourth issue of The Chiron Clinical Series (entitled *Chiron: A Review of Jungian Analysis* until 1986) consists of contributions "On the Theory of Complexes" (Hans Dieckmann); "Archetypes on the Couch" (Rosemary Gordon); "Emerging Concepts of the Self: Clinical Considerations" (Charles Klaif); "An Extended Model of the Infant Self" (Joel Ryce-Menuhin); "Looking Backward: Archetypes in Reconstruction" (Murray Stein); "Affect and Archetype in Analysis" (Louis Stewart); "The Archetypal Foundation of the Therapeutic Process" (Barbara Sullivan); "Chiron's Wound: Some Reflections on the Wounded Healer" (Michael Whan); and "Archetypal and Personal Interaction in the Clinical Process" (Whitmont).

The Dreambody in Relationships: Dreambody, Anthropos, and Hologram Aspects of Couples, Families, and Groups, by Arnold Mindell. London and New York: Routledge & Kegan Paul, 1987p*; New York: Penguin, 1988p* (146 + x, incl. 9-p. index, 2-p. bibl.).

Convinced of the applicability of his earlier studies in physics to family therapy in the sense that groups behave in some respects like single systems, Mindell builds on his earlier experience in dream and body work as an aid in understanding group dream patterns (1982) and on the challenge to find out more about the relationship of the individual to the collective (1985). He begins with a discussion of dreambody language, followed by perspectives on family studies and analyses and the topics of working with local information processes, communication structures, channels and signals, working with couples, typical relationship processes, the universal dreambody, and the therapist's attitude. He concludes with the subject of planetary psychology.
(Bk.revs.: BrBkN '87:211; Quad '89/22n1:73–5)

The Dreambody Toolkit: A Practical Introduction to the Philosophical Goals and Practice of Process-Oriented Psychology, by Joseph H. Goodbread.

New York and London: Routledge & Kegan Paul, 1987p*; New York: Penguin, 1988p* (240 + viii, incl. 5-p. index, 2-p. bibl., 2-p. ref. notes).

Growing out of a course taught at the Research Society for Process-Oriented Psychology in Zurich, this work by Goodbread provides a "basic set of tools" to enable one to build one's own version of process-oriented psychology, a technique developed by Arnold Mindell. He presents first the philosophical basis and goals of process-oriented psychotherapy and then devotes most of the book to practical process work, in which he analyzes the discovery of process structures and the relationships of process structures to language, to paralinguistic signals, and to non-verbal signals. He then moves from signals to structures (identification and personification) and dynamics, concluding with process dynamics and the large patterns.

Female Authority: Empowering Women Through Psychotherapy, by Polly Young-Eisendrath and Florence L. Wiedemann. New York and London: Guilford Press, 1987p* (242 + xiv, incl. 5-p. index, 5-p. bibl.).

Basing their work on Jung's psychology and Jane Loevinger's concepts of ego development and the stages of animus development, Young-Eisendrath and Wiedemann propose a model of female development that articulates basic conflicts in female identity between consciously claimed gender (as female) and unconsciously excluded animus (as the authority of the male "other"). They define female authority as the ability of a woman to validate her own convictions of truth, beauty, and goodness in regard to her self-concept and self-interest, which involves body image, self-confidence, social functioning, occupational functioning, sexual pleasure, and subjective self-assessment. They discuss the topics of conflict as identity, competence, feminism and Jung, a model for psychotherapy for women, the animus as an alien outsider, the animus as father, God, or king, romancing the hero, restoration of female authority, and identity relationship in adulthood.

(Bk.revs.: Choice '87/25:392; SciTechBkN D'87/11:26; PsyPersp '88/19:181–3; PsyWomQ '88/12:372–3; Quad '88/21n1:93–6; PsythTheor '88/25:604; WomRBks My'88/5:20; ContemPsy '89/34:37–8; JAmAcPsyan '89/17:680–2)

Practical Jung: Nuts and Bolts of Jungian Psychotherapy, by Harry A. Wilmer. Wilmette, Ill.: Chiron Publications, 1987* +p* (279 + xiii, incl. 4-p. index, 3-p. bibl., 46 illus., nearly 100 drawings by author, 1-p. foreword by Joseph L. Henderson).

Drawing on forty years of experience in psychiatry and medicine (early Freudian training and later, extensive, Jungian training), Wilmer presents a how-to book of thoughtful and intuitive ways to integrate and implement both his own psychology and that of Jung. He describes interactions between therapists and their patients as well as the subtle, dynamic, illogical, non-mechanical, and irrational psyche with all of its power for healing as well as destruction. His humorous nuts-and-bolts approach deals with transference and countertransference, archetypes, outer manifestation of things, psychotherapy, the meaning and function of dreams, and symbolism and creativity. (Bk.revs.: Choice '88/25:1480; ContemPsy '88/33:728; PsyPersp '88/19:171+; Quad '88/ 21n2:102–4)

Touching: Body Therapy and Depth Psychology, by Deldon Anne McNeely. Toronto: Inner City Books, 1987p* (Studies in Jungian Psychology by Jungian Analysts, 30) (125, incl. 5-p. index, 4-p. bibl., 6-p. notes, 2-p. gloss., 2 illus.).

McNeely studied body therapy before undergoing Jungian training, and she integrates her knowledge of the body into her style of analysis, which reflects Jung's own interest in finding a way in which mind-body dualism could be overcome and opposites integrated. She views body therapy as any approach that focuses on the somatic expression of complexes with the intention to reveal and transform the complex and so to extend the ego-Self interaction. Following an introductory section on physiological origins of depth psychology (Freudian psychoanalysis; Jungian complex theory), she discusses body therapy in historical perspective (cultural background; pioneers; therapists of later influence; contributions of dance movement; contemporary body therapists; personal influences), followed by a section on integrating body therapy and depth psychology, in which she examines the topics of touch and the analytic model; the meaning of touch; gratification in analysis; touch and transference; touch and timing in analysis; body therapy and dream interpretation; touching and analytic training; and body therapy and Jungian typology. (Bk.rev.: PsyPersp '88/19:353–6)

The Borderline Personality: Vision and Healing, by Nathan Schwartz-Salant. Wilmette, Ill.: Chiron Publications, 1988* +p* (242 + x, incl. 8-p. index, 8-p. bibl., 20 illus.).

Schwartz-Salant states that it is essential to discover the spirit in matter in dealing with the borderline person, whose personality he defines as involving states of mind that move within and around a border between personal and archetypal, so that aspects of each are interwoven in an often bewildering way. Following an introductory chapter on experiences commonly found in treating the borderline patient, he contrasts the borderline personality and the narcissistic character, and then he discusses the topics of

the borderline personality's distortions of reality; the central significance of projective identification in treatment; the subtle body and dynamics of imaginal experiences in the interactive field between therapist and patient; and the borderline personality's splitting into normal/neurotic and psychotic parts. He concludes with a chapter using the tale of Apuleius' *Golden Ass* to reflect on the possibility of healing borderline conditions through imaginal awareness and body consciousness.
(Bk.rev.: Quad '90/23n1:141–2)

The Borderline Personality in Analysis, edited by Nathan Schwartz-Salant and Murray Stein. (The Chiron Clinical Series) Wilmette, Ill.: Chiron Publications, 1988p* (276 pp.).

Consisting of eight essays on the subject of the borderline personality in analysis, this fifth issue of The Chiron Clinical Series contains the following contributions: "Primary Ambivalence Toward the Self: Its Nature and Treatment" (Beebe); "Lines and Shadows: Fictions from the Borderline" (Randolph Charlton); "Formation and Dealing with Symbols in Borderline Patients" (Dieckmann); "Subject-Object Differentiation in the Analysis of Borderline Cases: The Great Mother, the Self, and Others" (Susanne Kacirek); "Transference and Countertransference Mirrored in Personal Fantasies and Related Fairytale Motifs in the Therapy of a Patient with a Borderline Structure" (Kast); "Ritual Integration of Aggression in Psychotherapy" (Perera); "Gender and the Borderline" (Samuels); and "Before the Creation: The Unconscious Couple in Borderline States of Mind" (Schwartz-Salant).

The Cassandra Complex: Living with Disbelief; A Modern Perspective on Hysteria, by Laurie Layton Schapira. Toronto: Inner City Books, 1988p* (Studies in Jungian Psychology by Jungian Analysts, 36) (155, incl. 5-p. index, 3-p. bibl., 2-p. gloss. of Jungian terms, 21 illus.).

Relating the occurrence of two clients dreaming about Cassandra (the princess of Troy who refused Apollo's advances after accepting his gift of prophecy) to the fact of her analysands having the shared pattern of a strong hysterical component in their personalities, Schapira presents her interpretation and analysis of the subject of hysteria both historically from a feminist point of view and constructively in its modern significance. She identifies the Cassandra complex as exhibiting a specific hysterical pattern, including a marked split in personality; and she characterizes the Cassandra woman as a person well adapted in an extraverted way whose persona at times suddenly falls apart, leaving a frightened, needy little girl. Following her examination of the myth and tragedy of Cassandra, its manifestations in today's feminine psyche, and its relevance to hysteria, Schapira offers a psychological profile of the modern Cassandra woman and discusses therapeutic implications and clinical phases of the analytic process.

Inscapes of the Child's World: Jungian Counseling in Schools and Clinics, by John Allan. Dallas: Spring Publications, 1988p* (235 + xxv, incl. 9-p. ref. notes, 8-p. foreword by James Hillman).

Basing his book on more than twenty years of clinical work with children (both "normal" children in classrooms and abused, neglected, or ill children), Allan describes different ways to utilize art as therapy, using spontaneous or directed drawing, guided imagery, and active imagination. In eleven essays written between 1977 and 1987, analyst Allan focuses on a Jungian approach to children in which the therapist provides the "safe and protected space" for treatment, along with appropriate materials, so that problems are expressed, traumas enacted, pain felt, and reparation experienced. He first discusses art and drawing, including emotional and symbolic communication, drawings in counseling sexually and physically abused children and seriously ill children, and common symbols used by children in art counseling. He follows this with discussions on fantasy and drama, including fantasy enactment in the treatment of a psychotic child, creative drama with acting-out, serial story writing as a therapeutic approach with a physically abused adolescent, and sandplay.

(Bk.revs.: Choice '89/26:1601; PsyPersp '89/21:213–14; SmallPr Ap'89/7:80–1)

Jung and Reich: The Body as Shadow, by John P. Conger. Berkeley, Calif.: North Atlantic Books, 1988* +p* (222 + xi, incl. 14-p. index, 5-p. bibl., end-chapter ref. notes).

Inspired by a fantasy about how Reich and Jung might have affected each other if they had had a long and deep association, Conger presents the thesis that both effectively exposed denied elements of spirit and body, emphasizing that the symbolic and energetic processes are profoundly related. Stating that people often are offended by the knowledge they need most, he discusses Reich's "offending" emphasis on genitality and his claims concerning orgone, and Jung's emphasis on psychological investigations of spiritual experience as well as his "mysticism." He points out that attention to images and attention to energy are both aspects of Jungian-Reichian therapeutic work, since one experiences the psyche in its outpouring of images and experiences the body through the flow and interruption of energy. Together they form a functional identity.

(Bk.rev.: PsyPersp '90/22:202–5)

Jungian Analysts: Their Visions and Vulnerabilities, edited by J. Marvin Spiegelman. Phoenix: Falcon Press, 1988p* (181, incl. autobiographical notes of authors).

A dozen experienced Jungian analysts (Swiss, English, American, Israeli, and Indian) share how they have approached their work and what they have learned from their experience. Contributors are Fritz Beyme ("How I Do It"); Gustav Dreifuss ("How I Do It"); Michael Fordham ("How I Do Analysis"); Adolf Guggenbühl-Craig ("How I Do It"); Mario Jacoby (What the Hell Am I Doing While Sitting with Analysands in My Office?"); Sonja Marjasch ("My Three Offices"); Spiegelman ("The Impact of Suffering and Self-disclosure on the Life of the Analyst"); Robert Stein ("Reflections on Professional Deformation"); Arwind Vasavada ("Therapy: How I Do It"); Baroness Vera von der Heydt ("How I Do It"); Joseph B. Wheelwright ("How I Do It"); and Alfred Ziegler ("Archetypal Medicine, or Archetypal Psychology Made Flesh").

(Bk.rev.: Harvest '88–89/34:173–5; PsyPersp'90/22:171)

Jungian Child Psychotherapy: Individuation in Childhood, edited by Mara Sidoli and Miranda Davies. London: Karnac Books for the Society of Analytical Psychology, 1988p* (The Library of Analytical Psychology, vol. 8) (286 + xvii, incl. 14-p. index, end-chap. bibl. ref., 2 illus.).

Paying tribute to Michael Fordham's creative and pioneering work in the field of Jungian child psychotherapy and introducing new developments, the editors present three essays by Fordham (on the emergence of child analysis; the principles of child analysis; and acting out as a management problem) and twelve papers by Jungian child psychotherapists who base their clinical work on Fordham's ideas. Sidoli offers two papers (on deintegration and reintegration in the first two weeks of life; and analysis and separation) and Davies shares a case study of the psychotherapy and management of a severely deprived boy. Other essays deal with individuation and management problems, children with autistic features, sandplay therapy, and working with adolescents.

(Bk.rev.: JAnPsy '89/34:305–6)

People Who Do Things to Each Other: Essays in Analytical Psychology, by Judith Hubback. Wilmette, Ill.: Chiron Publications, 1988* +p* (217 + xi, incl. 8-p. subject index, 3-p. people index, end-chapter bibl.).

Focusing on the concept of the wounded healer at work, Hubback offers descriptions of attempts to come to terms with the problems of personal life and the human condition by taking as full account as possible of the

unconscious forces at work that are distorting the patient's conscious life and relationships. Other topics presented are the symbolic attitude in psychotherapy; reflections on concepts and experiences; manipulation, activity and handling; acting out; uses and abuses of analogy; envy and the shadow; depressed patients and the *coniunctio;* reflections on the psychology of women; the assassination of Robert Kennedy (patients' and analysts' reactions); body language and the self; and change as a process in the self.
(Bk.rev.: Harvest '89–90/35:221–3; JAnPsy '89/34:192–4; ContemPsy '90/35:275–6)

The Secret World of Drawings: Healing Through Art, by Gregg M. Furth. Boston: Sigo Press, 1988* +p* (150 + xx, incl. 2-p. index, 15-p. bibl., 95 illus., 2-p. foreword by Elisabeth Kübler-Ross, 2-p. preface by Paul Brutsche).

Acknowledging insights gained from the teachings of Jung, Jacobi, Susan Bach, and Kübler-Ross, Furth presents a practical approach toward understanding certain psychological and somatic events within the individual in connection with the unconscious content manifested in pictures. He offers some basic focal points on how to decipher drawings, along with numerous illustrations of these points, collected over a period of sixteen years. His topics include drawings as expressions of the unconscious (aspects of a complex; psychic energy and redistribution of psychic energy; theory of opposites; theory of composition; role of the symbol in healing; art versus pictures in the unconscious); premises in which art therapy is grounded; collecting drawings; focal points to understand drawings (diagnostic and therapeutic aids); advice and precautions; and three case studies.
(Bk.rev.: PsyPersp '89/21:192–4)

When the Spirits Come Back, by Janet O. Dallett. Toronto: Inner City Books, 1988p* (Studies in Jungian Pyschology by Jungian Analysts, 33) (157 pp.).

Interweaving her own story with the stories of those who come to her for help as a Jungian analyst, Dallett demonstrates the concept that native people know that in telling one's personal story one becomes connected to the larger tale which the spirits are trying to bring into the world. She explains her rediscovery of the integrity of the healing process, as well as her own shamanic gifts. Her chapter titles give the flavor of her story: "Foundations of Madness," "Shaman, Artist, Lunatic, Thief"; "Telling the Truth"; "The Way of the Wilderness"; "The Two-headed Serpent"; "A Fragile Covenant"; "My Daughter the Doctor"; "A Time for Thieves"; "If I Were a Golden God"; and "When the Spirits Come Back" (rewritten from her paper in *Carl Jung and Soul Psychology,* 1986.)
(Bk.revs.: PsyPersp '89/20:207–8)

The Analytic Life: Personal and Professional Aspects of Being a Jungian Analyst, by The New England Society of Jungian Analysts. Boston: Sigo Press, 1989p* (78, incl. end-chapter ref. notes, 7–p. intro. by Sidney Handel).

Consisting of six papers presented at the 1985 National Conference of Jungian Analysts held in Boston, this collection on "The Analytic Life" is composed of three papers on the identity question ("Are analysts shamans, artists, and priests, or are they physicians, psychologists, and diagnosticians?") and three papers on the effects of aging, personal relationships, and the analyst's connection to suffering. These are *"Solutio* and *Coagulatio* in Analytical Psychology: One Man's View of Where Our Field is Today" (Murray Stein); "Jungian Psychology and Science: A Strained Relationship" (Dennis Merritt); "Voodoo: Our Link with the Occult" (Esther Leonard de Vos); "Stages of Life as Levels of Consciousness in the Analyst" (June Singer); "Jungian Analysis: The Impossible Profession" (Thomas Kirsch); and "The Impact of Suffering and Self-disclosure on the Life of the Analyst" (Marvin Spiegelman).

Coma: Key to Awakening, by Arnold Mindell. Boston and Shaftesbury: Shambhala Publications, 1989p* (121 + x, incl. 3-p. bibl., 3-p. ref. notes, 5-p. gloss. of terms).

Having witnessed the astonishing awakening of persons from comas, Mindell offers verbatim bedside reports of comatose experiences and discussions of theory along with practical exercises to demonstrate his techniques of communicating with the comatose person, based on process-oriented psychology (Jungian-derived therapy that he has developed using dreamwork and bodywork). He deals in the first half of the book with "The Key of Life" (introduction to working with the dying; transition issues of the last three weeks of a man dying of leukemia; how final dream and body states react to and ignore medical predictions of death; sudden awakening out of a profound coma to experience the key to life; dreamwork, bodywork, and the disappearance of symptoms on the final day of life; death and personal myths; practicing dying, grieving, and the meaning of death in life). He devotes the second half to theory and training (altered states and coma; working with comas; coma and shamanistic experience; dreambody and mythbody; immortal you; brain death and thanatos ethics).

Dreaming with an AIDS Patient, by Robert Bosnak. Boston & London: Shambhala Publications, 1989* (174, incl. 1 illus.).

Fulfilling his task to "write this book together" with Christopher, who moved from Texas to Boston to enter Jungian analysis, Bosnak presents in conversational-analytical style the story of Christopher's last year of dying with AIDS. In the sixteen untitled chapters he illustrates the way Jungian dream work provides access to the healing power within the unconscious, using forty-six dreams reported in analytic sessions and from Christopher's own dream book. The experience demonstrates the patient's journey from his struggle to make sense of his life in the context of alienation from the church he loved and weariness of the gay life, along with feelings of fear, guilt, and self-blame, to self-acceptance and spiritual healing. Bosnak also expresses the transforming effect of the relationship on the analyst.

Dreams, a Portal to the Source, by Edward C. Whitmont and Sylvia Brinton Perera. London and New York: Routledge, 1989* (200, incl. 4-p. index, 3-p. index of dreams, 3-p. bibl., 8-p. ref. notes).

Representing the accumulated fruit of many years of evolving analytical work and teaching, Whitmont and Perera provide an extensive guide to dream interpretation, aimed primarily at therapists who want to integrate dreams into their clinical practice. They support Jung's view that dreaming processes are undistorted and purposeful with the goal of synthesizing experience into images in meaningful and creative ways, assisting in individual development. Following introductory chapters on clinical dream interpretation, working with the dream in clinical practice, and developmental possibilities through dreamwork, they discuss the topics of the language of dream images; various relations between the dream and the dreamer's conscious positions; the dream's dramatic structure; mythological motifs; technical points; prognosis from dreams; body imagery; dream images of the analyst; and analysis as material revealing the relationships of transference and countertransference.

Dreams in Analysis, edited by Nathan Schwartz-Salant and Murray Stein. Wilmette, Ill.: Chiron Publications, 1989p* (The Chiron Clinical Series) (236, incl. 20 illus.).

Consisting of ten essays on the subject of dreams in analysis, the sixth issue of The Chiron Clinical Series contains contributions by Jungian analysts on dreams and dreaming (Whitmont); dreams and history of analysis (Stein); dream design: some operations underlying clinical dream appreciation (Perera); pedestrian approach to dreams (Thomas Kirsch) with comments on "knowing" by Caroline Stevens; dream experience (Elie Humbert); re-emergence of the archetypal feminine (Betty De Shong Meador) with response by Lionel Corbett; dream and psychodrama (Helmut Barz); and dreams of nuclear warfare (Redfearn).

Drugs, Addiction, and Initiation: The Modern Search for Ritual, by Luigi Zoja. Boston: Sigo Press, 1989* +p* (133 + ix, incl. 9-p. index, 3-p. foreword by Adolf Guggenbühl-Craig).

Having worked intensively in therapy with drug addicts while using his Jungian background as a depth psychologist, Zoja investigates the unconscious models which lead one to drugs despite the dangers involved. He views the use of drugs as unconsciously echoing the structure of initiation, which is fundamentally an archetypal process—a bipolar theme based on the opposition of life and death. He recognizes the deeper motivations and unfulfilled needs of drug addicts (including alcoholics) and seeks to understand the complex psychological process that is playing itself out in them. Following an introductory chapter of reflections on the problem, he analyzes archetypal fantasies underlying drug addiction and the relationship of drugs and society. He then discusses addiction in terms of death and rebirth and the death of rebirth, the story of "Carlo," and the relationship of initiation to consumerism, concluding with the prospect of rebirth today.
(Bk.rev.: Quad '90/23n1:142–3, 1945)

Hypnosis: A Jungian Perspective, by James A. Hall. New York and London: Guilford Press, 1989* (Guilford Clinical and Experimental Hypnosis Series) (179 + x, incl. 7-p. index, 5-p. bibl.).

Hall opens areas of cross-fertilization between traditional Jungian analysis and hypnotherapy, between "the skilled practice that is hypnosis and the vast vision of the human psyche brought by Jung." Following an introductory discussion of Jung and hypnosis, he examines the topics of complex psychology and dissociation; the place of theory in hypnosis; Jungian theory, hypnosis and the psychostructural emphasis; the transcendent function; dreams; active imagination; transference/countertransference in hypnotherapy; and working with imagery from the unconscious through typical induction protocol. He concludes with a chapter on clinical integration, the applications of hypnotherapy within a Jungian model.

The Living Psyche: A Jungian Analysis in Pictures, by Edward F. Edinger. Wilmette, Ill.: Chiron Publications, 1989p* (232, incl. 3-p. index, 3-p. bibl., 119 pictures/15 in color).

Expressing the need for published case histories which illustrate Jung's unique approach to the human psyche, Edinger presents the case of a middle-aged artist (age 36–46 during analysis) who had lost his sense of purpose in life in spite of a successful career. The unifying thread in this analytic effort is a series of more than 100 paintings done over a period of five years that touch on all the major themes of the analysis. Edinger provides a brief description and psychological commentary for each painting on the facing page, in some instances accompanied by a significant illustration from classical or other sources. He aims to demonstrate graphically the reality of the living psyche and to demonstrate Jung's statement that there is a process in the psyche that seeks its own goal independently of external factors.

Mourning Unlived Lives: A Psychological Study of Childbearing Loss, by Judith
   A. Savage. Wilmette, Ill.: Chiron Publications, 1989p* (Chiron Monograph
   Series, vol. 3) (126 + xiv, incl. 4-p. index, 5-p. bibl., 5-p. gloss. of Jungian
   terms, 3 illus., 2-p. foreword by Sherokee Ilse).

Savage examines the meaning gained from the loss of a child before or during childbirth, drawing on her own loss, along with the experience of others. She looks at the intrapsychic, symbolic role of the unconscious in bereavement, describing that imaginative relationship as the projections of the Self onto the unborn child and analyzing the influence of the symbolic, archetypal image upon attachment and separation. She begins with a long chapter entitled "When Nature Is Not a Mother," in which she deals with topics of the social context and models of bereavement of perinatal and reproductive losses; the vow never to forget; the wish to die; revitalization of religious orientation; change of values; greater tolerance; and shadow grief. She then discusses the Annunciation and the meaning of progeny; ethnological and archetypal motifs governing the structure of mourning; and archetypal patterns of mourning (the search; the recovery; rebirth; the resolution of mourning; and the expansion of consciousness). She concludes with a discussion of the implications of this subject for clinical practice.

The Plural Psyche: Personality, Morality, and the Father, by Andrew Samuels.
   London and New York: Routledge, 1989* +p* (253 + xiv, incl. 12-p. index,
   10-p. bibl., 4 illus.).

Reflecting on his book *Jung and the Post-Jungians* and on the way the apparently opposed developmental and archetypal schools have reacted similarly to the "tenets of classical analytical psychology," Samuels posits a pluralistic approach, showing how it can be used as an instrument to make sure that diversity need not lead inevitably to splits. He relates such pluralism to psychological theories by examining how the various parts of the personality relate to the psyche as a whole without losing their distinctiveness and how the individual has to reconcile the many internal voices in order to, when needed, speak with one voice. Starting with the idea of pluralism as a metaphor for and an approach to psychological processes, he then attempts to devise a pluralistic model of personality development, which leads to a

look at nonliteral meanings of parental imagery as it appears in analysis. He focuses on the father as crucial to the hindering or fostering of psychological pluralism, explores whether there are sex-specific psychologies, ponders whether or not "masculine" and "feminine" are valuable as metaphors, and considers the concept of gender and borderline personality disorders. He discusses analysis itself with a clinical emphasis on the countertransference.
(Bk.revs.: Harvest '89–90/35:214–16; JAnPsy '90/35:81–3; Quad '90/23n1:137–9)

Psychopathology: Contemporary Jungian Perspectives, edited by Andrew Samuels. London: Karnac Books, 1989p* (The Library of Analytical Psychology, vol. 9) (355 + xii, incl. 9-p. index, end-chap. bibl., 4 illus., 21-p. editor's intro.).

This volume of papers on psychopathology from a Jungian perspective is a resource book for analysts and psychotherapists. Samuels has selected fifteen papers from the *Journal of Analytical Psychology* and two from other sources. Papers deal with depressed patients and the *coniunctio;* overstimulation and depressive defense; anorexia nervosa; narcissistic disorder and its treatment; introversion and/or schizoid personality; borderline personality; treatment of chronic psychoses; problems of the psychotic patient and the therapist; delusional transference; masochism; fetishism and transvestism; and analysis and the old.

Psychotherapy Grounded in the Feminine Principle, by Barbara Stevens Sullivan. Wilmette, Ill.: Chiron Publications, 1989p* (205 + xiii, incl. 3-p. index, 5-p. bibl., 12 illus.).

Expressing "greatest appreciation" to her patients, Sullivan develops the thesis that the devaluation of the feminine principle has had a severely negative impact on therapeutic work. She addresses the subject of procedures that enable the patient to reach into inner psychic depths—the unconscious—in powerful ways, recognizing that the patient, like the therapist, offers constructive energy to the work as well as destructive tendencies. Beginning with a discussion of the feminine principle, she then analyzes the art of psychotherapy, the archetypal foundation of the therapeutic process (Campbell's monomyth, Jung's monograph on the transference, Sandner's patterns of symbolic healing, Perera's use of the myth of Inanna, and the theories of Michael Balint, Winnicott, and Kohut), and psychotherapy grounded in the feminine principle, after which she interprets the role of the masculine principle. She concludes with a chapter on a perspective of Jung's concept of archetypes, a chapter on two clinical examples of disrespect for the feminine principle in therapeutic work, and one on the dilemma of "the disliked patient."

Recovering from Incest: Imagination and the Healing Process, by Evangeline Kane. Boston: Sigo Press, 1989* +p* (232 + xiii, incl. 12-p. index, 16-p. bibl., 22-p. end-chapter ref. notes, 4-p. foreword by Russell Lockhart).

Using case studies from her own practice as well as mythology, religion, and literature on incest, Kane examines the potential for healing from the effects of incest, sexual abuse, and the basic demise of feminine consciousness in our society. She cites Jung's discovery that loss of imagination and denial of the feeling function are the result of the abandonment of the incest taboo, which causes the victim to retreat into fantasy and unrelatedness and ironically leaves her open to further exploitation. The victim becomes frozen in the mute witness to the crimes of failed masculinity. Following introductory chapters on the soul abandoned and on psychotherapy and incest, she discusses the need to move toward an imaginal therapy, exploring the topics of hysteria, epilepsy of the victims, and the absence of masculine spirit, and she analyzes the seduction of Little Red Riding Hood. She concludes with a chapter on "embracing the good news of the fish tail" (a woman's reclaiming of her body from numbness and terror).

Witness to the Fire: Creativity and the Veil of Addiction, by Linda Schierse Leonard. Boston and Shaftesbury: Shambhala Publications, 1989*; 1990p (390 + xviii, incl. 16-p. indexes by subject, title, name, 18-p. ref. notes).

Continuing her "dark and fiery journey" from being born into a family of alcoholics and co-addicts and struggling to undergo a spiritual transformation, Leonard examines the relationship between addiction and creativity as various archetypal figures of addiction arise in her dreams and in her waking life. The "witness" image in the title refers to the survivor of the fire who descends into the unknown underworld of the unconscious to find meaning from the chaos and then returns to life and society, a process that occurs in the psyches of both the addict and the creative individual. In each chapter she presents a portrait of the archetypal figure through a literary work, drawing heavily on Dostoevsky as well as O'Neill, London, and numerous other authors. She starts with "The Flight" (with archetypal figures of the Moneylender, Gambler, Romantic, Underground Man, Outlaw, and Trickster) and then moves to "The Fall" (Madwoman, Judge, Killer, and the World's Night of adoration of technology) and ends with "The Creation" (the Abyss, the Dark Night of the Soul, the Battleground, the Soul on Fire, the Work of the Heart, the Healing Fields, and the Dwelling). She concludes by discussing the "gift" of creating each day anew.

Circle of Care. Clinical Issues in Jungian Therapy, by Warren Steinberg. Toronto: Inner City Books, 1990p (Studies in Jungian Psychology by Jungian Analysts, 46).

Crossing the Bridge: A Jungian Approach to Adolescence, by Kaspar Kiepenheuer. Peru, Ill.: Open Court Pub. Co., 1990 +p.

Cultural Anxiety, by Rafael López-Pedraza. Einsiedeln, Switzerland: Daimon Verlag, 1990p.

Healing and Transformation in Sandplay: Creative Processes Become Visible, by Ruth Ammann. Peru, Ill.: Open Court Pub. Co., 1990 +p.

Jungian Psychiatry, by Heinrich Karl Fierz. Einsiedeln, Switzerland: Daimon Verlag, 1990p.

Kant's Dove: The History of Transference in Psychoanalysis, by Aldo Carotenuto. Wilmette, Ill.: Chiron Publications, 1990p.

Personal and Archetypal Dynamics in the Analytical Relationship: Proceedings of the Eleventh Congress for Analytical Psychology, Paris, 1989, edited by Mary Ann Mattoon. Einsiedeln, Switzerland: Daimon Verlag, 1990.

The Ravaged Bridegroom: Masculinity in Women, by Marion Woodman. Toronto: Inner City Books, 1990p (Studies in Jungian Psychology by Jungian Analysts, 41) (223, incl. 4-p. index, 2-p. bibl., 8 illus.).

Focusing on evolving masculinity and femininity as two energies within each individual, both striving toward an inner harmony, Woodman aims to understand what liberated masculinity and liberated femininity can be. She uses strong images from myth, poetry, dream analysis, and personal experience to show the needed confidence in one's own inner world that may set one free psychologically to be responsible for one's own strengths and weaknesses. She begins with "dragon slaying" (the murder of feminine identity under patriarchy or the sacrifice which leads to transformation), followed by discussions of masculinity in addictions; mother as matriarch (demanding perfection); images of ravaged masculinity in women's dreams; and the bride and bridegroom in dreams.

Symbols Come Alive in the Sand, by Evalyn Dundas. Boston and London: Coventure, 1990 +p.

12 Civilization in Transition

The final subject category of this classification of Jungian works includes those involved with the largely "outer" aspects of Jung's psychology that deal with social, political, and economic meanings in psychic life. Although most of Jung's writings are concerned with personal or individual psychology and the differentiation of consciousness in the individuation process, he also discusses significant aspects of "collective" or social psychology, in which society is faced with the problem of a general moral backwardness and the failure of our morality to keep pace with scientific, technical and social progress. He advises society to give thought to the question of human relationships from the psychological point of view, for in this resides its real cohesion and consequently its strength—adding that, where love stops, power begins, as well as violence and terror. He emphasizes the need for self-knowledge and for the discovery of the undiscovered self in the unconscious depths of the psyche. He asserts that the value of a community depends on the spiritual and moral stature of the individuals composing it.

Other than the categories of psychological types and the life of Jung, this is the least extensive of the twelve subject categories in this annotated bibliography. It is comprised of twenty-six titles, plus nine that are cross-referenced from other subjects. More than half of these works have been published since 1979.

Jung: *Civilization in Transition* [p. 355]
_____: *Essays on Contemporary Events* [p. 354]
_____: *Flying Saucers* [p. 355]
_____: *Modern Man in Search of a Soul* (See chapter 2, "Collections of Jung's Writings") [p. 22]
_____: *The Undiscovered Self* (See chapter 6, "Human Development and Individuation") [p. 80]

Abt: *Progress Without Loss of Soul* [p. 361]
Aldrich: *The Primitive Mind and Modern Civilization* [p. 356]
Baynes: *Germany Possessed* [p. 357]
Beebe (ed.): *Money, Food, Drink, Fashion, and Analytic Training* (See chapter 11, "Jungian Analysis") [p. 320]
Bernstein: *Power and Politics: The Psychology of Soviet-American Partnership* [p. 365]
Bertine: *Jung's Contribution to Our Time* [p. 358]
Borenzweig: *Jung and Social Work* [p. 362]
Czuczka: *Imprints of the Future* [p. 364]
Garrison: *The Darkness of God* (See chapter 9, "Religion and Jung's Psychology") [p. 225]
Greene: *The Outer Planets and Their Cycles* [p. 361]
Head (ed.): *A Well of Living Waters* [p. 360]
Henderson: *Cultural Attitudes in Psychological Perspective* [p. 362]
_____: *Shadow and Self* [p. 366]
Kirsch, H. (ed.): *The Well-Tended Tree* [p. 359]
Kirsch, J.: *The Reluctant Prophet* (See chapter 7, "Symbolic Life and Dreams") [p. 142]
Knapp: *Machine, Metaphor, and the Writer* (See chapter 10, "Creativity and Jung's Psychology") [p. 284]
Lockhart et al.: *Soul and Money* [p. 361]
Mattoon (ed.): *The Archetype of Shadow in a Split World* [p. 363]
Meier, et al.: *A Testament to the Wilderness* [p. 363]
Mindell: *The Year 1* [p. 366]
Neumann: *Depth Psychology and a New Ethic* [p. 357]
Odajnyk: *Jung and Politics* [p. 359]
Paris: *Pagan Meditations* (See chapter 8, "Feminine and Masculine Psychology") [p. 184]
Perry: *The Heart of History* [p. 363]
Progoff: *Depth Psychology and Modern Man* (See chapter 6, "Human Development and Individuation") [p. 86]
_____: *Jung, Synchronicity, and Human Destiny* (See chapter 6, "Human Development and Individuation") [p. 93]
_____: *Jung's Psychology and Its Social Meaning* [p. 358]
Saayman (ed.): *Modern South Africa in Search of a Soul* [p. 366]
Steuernagel: *Political Philosophy as Therapy* [p. 360]
Stevens: *The Roots of War* [p. 365]

Essays on Contemporary Events, by C. G. Jung. (Ger.: *Aufsätze zur Zeitgeschichte.* Zurich: Rascher Verlag, 1946.) (Subtitle 1989: *The Psychology of Nazism.*) London: Kegan Paul, Trench, Trubner, 1947; London: Ark Paperbacks, 1989p*; Princeton, N.J.: Princeton U. Press/Bollingen, 1989p* (93 + xvi, incl. 7-p. foreword by Andrew Samuels in 1989 edition).

Having felt obliged, from time to time, to step beyond the usual bounds of his profession as physician and psychologist, Jung gave his reactions to actual events, particularly during the period 1936–46. The introductory essay ("Individual and Mass Psychology"), whose original title was "The Fight with the Shadow" (a broadcast talk in a BBC program in 1946), deals with the susceptibility of the German mentality to mass psychology. Other essays are a 1936 article on Wotan (ancient god of storm and frenzy); a 1941 lecture and 1942 article on psychotherapy today (on the relationship of psychotherapy and the state of mind in Europe); a 1941 address and a 1943 article "after the catastrophe" as a sequel to his article on Wotan (by which time the myth had been fulfilled and the greater part of Europe lay in ruins); and an epilogue on the "German psychopathy and the mass psychosis of National Socialism."

(Bk.revs.: BksAbroad '47/21:47; BrBkN '48:116–17; NewStates '48/35:439; Sower Ap'48/ n167:40–2; TimesLitSup '48:178; PsyPersp '90/22:190–3)

Flying Saucers: A Modern Myth of Things Seen in the Skies, by C. G. Jung. (Ger.: *Ein moderner Mythus: Von Dingen, die am Himmel gesehen werden.* Zurich: Rascher Verlag, 1958.) London: Routledge & Kegan Paul, 1959; 1977p; New York: Harcourt, Brace, 1959; New York: Signet Books/New American Library, 1969p; Princeton, N.J.: Princeton U. Press/Bollingen, 1978p; London: Ark Paperbacks, 1987p* (138 + viii, incl. 8 illus.).

Considering himself not qualified to contribute anything useful to the question of the physical reality of UFOs, Jung concerns himself only with their undoubted psychic aspect, which he views as "visionary rumors" and projections of unconscious psychic contents—whether a primary perception was followed by a phantasm or whether, conversely, a primary fantasy originating in the unconscious invaded the conscious mind with illusions and visions. His analysis deals with UFOs as rumors, UFOs in dreams, UFOs in modern painting, previous history of the UFO phenomenon (including four illustrations from the twelfth to seventeenth centuries), and UFOs considered in a nonpsychological light.

(Bk.revs.: AmSchol '59–60/29:122; Bklist '59/56:47; ChrSciMon 10Ag'59/51:11; Econ '59/191:34; NewStates '59/56:162–3; NYHerTrib 2Ag'59:4; SatR 8Ag'59/42:17; Spec '59/212:447; TimesLitSup '59:44; 20Cen '59/165:298–9; BkRDig '60:718; IntJPsy-An '60/41:83–4; Spring '60:149–50; JAmAcadRel '79/47:700–1)

Civilization in Transition, by C. G. Jung. New York: Pantheon Books (Bollingen Foundation), 1964; London: Routledge & Kegan Paul, 1964; ed.2 1973*;

Princeton, N.J.: Princeton U. Press/Bollingen, ed.2 1970* (CW 10) (609 + xii, incl. 27-p. index, 9-p. bibl., 8 illus.).

Taking as its keynote Jung's 1918 essay on the role of the unconscious, in which he interprets the conflict in Europe as basically a psychological crisis originating in the collective unconscious of the individuals who form groups and nations, this collection contains twenty-three other writings, including the books *The Undiscovered Self* (59 pp.) and *Flying Saucers* (125 pp.). Extracted from *Essays on Contemporary Events* are the preface, epilogue, and the articles on Wotan; the fight with the shadow; and after the catastrophe. Others include a 1922 lecture and 1928 article on the love problem of a student; and articles on woman in Europe (1927); the Swiss line in the European spectrum (1928); the rise of a new world (1931); the complications of American psychology (1931); archaic man (1931); mind and earth (1931); meaning of psychology for modern man (1933); and the state of psychotherapy today (1934); a review of the book *La Revolution Mondiale* (1934); articles on the dreamlike world of India (1939); what India can teach us (1939); a psychological view of conscience (1958); good and evil in analytical psychology (1959); and the introduction to Toni Wolff's "Studies in Jungian Psychology" (1959). An appendix contains editorials, letters, and presidential addresses by Jung to Medical Congresses for Psychotherapy.

(Bk.revs.: LibJ '64/89:4812; NYTimesBkR 8N'64:3; BkRDig '65:658; BulMennClin '65/ 29:173; Choice '65/2:339; Spring '65:142–4; TimesLitSup '65:11; VaQR '65/41:xxiv; AnnAmAcad '66/366:199–201; JAnPsy '66/11:69–74)

*   *   *   *   *

The Primitive Mind and Modern Civilization, by Charles Roberts Aldrich. London: Kegan Paul, Trench, Trubner, 1931 (International Library of Psychology, Philosophy, and Scientific Method); New York: Harcourt, Brace, 1931; New York: AMS Press, repr. 1969*; Westport, Conn.: Greenwood Press, repr. 1970 (249 + xvii, incl. 13-p. index, 3-p. intro. by Bronislaw Malinowski, 3-p. foreword by Jung).

Expressing fascination with all the ways of the primitive, whether occurring "among savage tribes or in cultured Christian homes," Aldrich views the psychology of the primitive as essential in the course of studying human nature before the variations of behavior can be grasped and understood. Jung states in the foreword that Aldrich has made use of his studies in analytical psychology, which has yielded "sane and balanced" opinions. Aldrich discusses first the topics of instincts and complexes; the unconscious and the conscious; time and the psyche; the primitive; and "savages." He then examines perception; representations; mystic causation and mystic participation; individual, group, and totem; how fear consolidates the group; ritual sharing of desirable things; primitive socialism; and education and some orthodox views. He concludes with discussions on mana and sacred things, mana and taboo, tabooed persons, and confessions and rebirth.

(Bk.revs.: BkRDig '31:152; BrJPsy '31/22:182; JMentSci '31/77:834–5; NewStates '31/ 2:24; NYTimesBkR 8N'31:16; TimesLitSup '31:540; AmMer Ja'32/24:xx–xxii; PsyanR '33/20:457–9)

Germany Possessed, by H. G. Baynes. London: Jonathan Cape, 1941; New York: AMS Press, repr. 1972* (305, incl. 3-p. index, 4 illus., 4-p. intro. by Hermann Rauschning).

Baynes speaks of Germany under Hitler as a country participating in a mythological madness that affected people from deep within the unconscious. He makes use of Wotan and early Teutonic paganism in his psychological interpretation of the mad dream of an archaic mythological state with Hitler as a great medicine man with magical power, bolstered by his complete belief in himself and his mission. He begins with the topics of personal and daemonic analyses of Adolf Hitler; Wotan, god and devil; the god criminal; Hitler as symbol; and the messianic possibility (and betrayal); concluding with discussions of acceleration and destruction; the source of Hitler's ideas (especially Wagner); the Hitler disease; and factors governing morale.

(Bk.revs.: BulAnPsyNY D'41/3:9–12; Punch '41/201:172; Spec '41/167:111–12; Times-LitSup '41/330:447–8; BrJPsy '42/32:263)

Depth Psychology and a New Ethic, by Erich Neumann. (Ger.: *Tiefenpsychologie und Neue Ethik.* Zurich: Rascher Verlag, 1949.) London: Hodder & Stoughton, 1969; New York: G. P. Putnam's Sons for the C. G. Jung Foundation for Analytical Psychology, 1970; New York: Torchbooks/Harper & Row, 1973p; Boston and Shaftesbury: Shambhala Publications, 1990p (A C. G. Jung Foundation Book in association with Daimon Verlag) (168, incl. 8-p. index, forewords by Jung, Gerhard Adler, and James Yandell).

Against the background of the specter of a third world war in which the shadow side of the human race towers over all, Neumann proposes a new ethic whose nature is the maintenance of a painful conscious balance of opposing inner forces rather than the old ethic of repression of the negative forces that eventually erupt from the unconscious with devastating force. Following an introductory discussion of the disintegration of values in the modern world and the problem of evil, he examines the old ethic (denial of the negative; suppression and repression; persona and shadow; ego-influence and "good" conscience; suffering and suppression; guilt feelings and projection of the shadow and the scapegoat) and then discusses stages of ethical development before presenting the new ethic (experiences of the shadow in depth psychology; dethronement of the ego and of its value system; acceptance of the shadow and relationship with the negative side; and the new ethic as a total ethic).

(Bk.revs.: BksAbroad '49/23:289; AmJPsy '50/63:150–1; Frontier '69/12:234–6; Harvest '69/15:90–1; NewBlackf '69/50:665; AmJPsychi '70/127:550; BkRDig '70:1040–1; Choice '70/7:947; ChrCen '70/87:119; JAnPsy '70/25:196–7; JOttoRank D'70/5:52–72; LibJ '70/95:1572; LibJBkR '70:536; ModChman '70/ns13:291–2; PastorPsy Oc'70/ 21:65–6; RforRel '70/23:122; ScotJTheol '70/123:122; Theol '70/73:469–70; Times-LitSup '70:203; BrJMedPsy '71/44:187; InwLight '71/n/79–80:61–2; Quad '71/n10:26–7)

Jung's Psychology and Its Social Meaning, by Ira Progoff. (Subtitle 1985: *A Comprehensive Statement of C. G. Jung's Theories and Interpretation of Their Significance for the Social Sciences.*) New York: Julian Press, 1953; ed.2 1969; London: Routledge & Kegan Paul, 1953; New York: Evergreen Books/Grove Press, 1955p; Garden City, N.Y.: Anchor Books/Doubleday, 1973p; New York: Dialogue House, ed.3 1985p* (299 + xx, incl. 3-p. index, 6-p. bibl.).

Originally written as a doctoral dissertation applying Jung's concepts of depth psychology to a sociological study of history and civilization, Progoff's book offers a contribution to the social understanding of our time by interpreting new directions in psychological thought as related to the field of social study. Following an interpretation of the basic core of Jung's psychology (the historical situation; psyche and layers of consciousness; persons with the person; introvert, extravert, and psychological types; function and meaning of neurosis; and dreams and integration of the psyche), he then discusses Jung's social concepts and their significance (the pysche in society and history; historical implications of Jung's thought). Appended are notes and bibliography for use in Jung's psychology in social sciences and humanities and an analysis of the power of the archetypes in modern civilization.

(Bk.revs.: AmMer S'53/77:138–9; BkRDig '53:758; CathWorld '53/177:478; KirkR '53/ 21:94; PsychiQ '53/27:525; SatR 15Ag'53/36:15–16; Blackf '54/35:125; BrJPsy '54/ 45:317; SocR '54/2:139–40; Tabl '54/203:548; TimesLitSup '54:489; BulMennClin '55/ 19:72; JPastorCare '55/9:56–7; PastorPsy F'55/6:63–4; ContemPsy '56/1:198–200; RMeta '57/11:351)

Jung's Contribution to Our Time: The Collected Papers of Eleanor Bertine, edited by Elizabeth C. Rohrbach. New York: G. P. Putnam's Sons for the C. G. Jung Foundation for Analytical Psychology, 1967; Toronto: Longmans Canada, 1967; London: Barrie & Rockliff, 1968 (271 + xvi, incl. 3-p. bibl., 2-p. ref. notes, 3-p. foreword by Edward Edinger, 4-p. intro. by Alma Paulsen).

Consisting of fourteen papers written during nearly forty years of practice as a Jungian analyst, this work illustrates Bertine's consistent concern for the individual human being and the belief in the centrality of the Self as center and motivating force in the psyche. Most are papers read at the Analytical Psychology Club of New York and published in the journal *Spring*. The first group (on general themes in analytical psychology) includes Jung's greatest contribution to his time (1947), Jung's approach to religion (1958), the perennial problem of good and evil (1959), and the psychological meaning of initiation (1950). The second group (on men and women) consists of papers on some aspects of the problems of modern women (1949), the individual and the group (1938), and men and women (1937). The third group (on psychological issues during World War II) contains papers concerning Nazi dynamism (1939), some positive aspects of the times in which we live (1940), the great flood archetype (1944), and men and bombs (1945).

(Bk.revs.: BkRDig '68:113; Choice '68/5:1046; GuardW 12S'68/99:14; LibJ '68/93:561; LibJBkR '68:507; Quad '68/n1:26; Spring '68:134–5; TimesLitSup '68:1151; BrJPsy '69/60:272–3; JAnPsy '69/14:194–5; BrJMedPsy '70/37:407–8)

The Well-Tended Tree: Essays into the Spirit of Our Time, edited by Hilde Kirsch. New York: G. P. Putnam's Sons for the C. G. Jung Foundation for Analytical Psychology, 1971 (392 + xix, incl. 2-p. bibliography of James Kirsch's writings, 33 illus.).

Written in honor of Jungian analyst James Kirsch's seventieth birthday, this collection consists of thirty contributions by colleagues and friends, including ten written by authors whose works appear in this annotated bibliography, namely, "The Question of Meaning in Psychotherapy" (Adler); "The Shadow Revealed in the Works of Nietzsche" (Frey); "Religious Experience in Childhood" (Fordham); "The Burning Bush" (Harding); "Symbolism of the Unconscious in Two Plays of Shakespeare" (Henderson); "Jung as Philosopher and Theologian" (Kelsey); "Psychological Parameters of the Examination Situation" (Meier); "Analytical Psychology: Science or Religion?" (Sanford); "A Tribute and Some Comments on the Etiology of the Animus and Anima" (Joseph Wheelwright); and "Sickness, Suffering, and Redemption in the Human and Archetypal World: Dream Interpretation" (Zeller).

(Bk.revs.: AmJPsyth '72/26:448; IsrAnPsychi '72/10:279–81; JAnPsy '73/18:78–9)

Jung and Politics: The Political and Social Ideas of C. G. Jung, by V. Walter Odajnyk. New York: New York U. Press, 1976*; New York: Colophon Books/Harper & Row, 1976p (190 + xv, incl. 3-p. index, 4-p. foreword by Marie-Louise von Franz).

Feeling that Jung's conception of human nature is more satisfying than that of Freud, Odajnyk compiles, by means of lengthy quotes, Jung's ideas that have political and social implications for the future of humanity. After an introduction on the origin of culture and politics, he discusses the topics of psychic inflation; mass psyche and mass man; the individual and the state; and politics and the unconscious. He then deals with the German case and the end of politics, concluding with an analysis of the future of humanity, a comparison of Jung and Freud, and some thoughts about democracy.

(Bk.revs.: Quad '76/9n2:62–3; PolTheory '77/5:425–9; AmPolSciR '78/72:1383–4; ContemPsy '78/23:449–50; JAnPsy '79/24:163–6; PolStud '79/27:343; RPol '81/43:302–4)

A Well of Living Waters: A Festschrift for Hilde Kirsch, edited by Rhoda Head, Rose-Emily Rothenberg, and David Wesley. Los Angeles: C. G. Jung Institute of Los Angeles, 1977p* (283 pp.).

Honoring the life and work of Jungian analyst Hilde Kirsch on the occasion of her seventy-fifth birthday, sixty contributors (colleagues, analysands, and family) present mostly very short writings, including sixteen poems and three drawings. The longest contribution is an essay on "The Ecstatic Healer," by Jack Sanford (26 pp.), followed by an essay by Shirley Taft on "Shakespeare's Dreams" (16), Sallie Nichols in "The Star: Ray of Hope" (14), Glen McCormick on "The Three Marys" (13), and Gail Rheingold on "The Masks of Eugene O'Neill" (12), along with an introductory essay by analyst-husband James Kirsch on "New Wine in Old Bottles."

Political Philosophy as Therapy: Marcuse Reconsidered, by Gertrude A. Steuernagel. Westport, Conn. and London: Greenwood Press, 1979* (Contributions in Political Science Series, 11) (147 + xi, incl. 7-p. index, 10-p. bibl.).

Considering Jung's ideas to be more compatible than Freud's with the tasks of political philosophy, Steuernagel has chosen contemporary political philosopher Herbert Marcuse to demonstrate the therapeutic power of political philosophy and to show that Marcuse's thought is closer to Jung's than to Freud's. She explores the therapeutic relationship between the self and the political dimension, and between internal and external reality, using psychoanalytic concepts in the application of how the unconscious relates to politics. Following an examination of political philosophy as therapy, she considers Marcuse in depth and presents a therapeutic vision as regeneration toward a Marcuse-Jung synthesis, concluding with a Marcuse-Jung thesis as the feminization of political thought.

(Bk.revs.: LibJ '79/104:1462; LibJBkR '79:308–9; BkRDig '80:1165; Choice '80/16:1457; JPol '80/42:902–3; AmPolSciR '80/74:1068–70)

Soul and Money, by Russell A. Lockhart, James Hillman, Arwind Vasavada, John Weir Perry, Joel Covitz, and Adolf Guggenbühl-Craig. Dallas: Spring Publications, 1982p; 1986p* (89 pp.).

Consisting of six papers on the subject of money extracted from *The Proceedings of the 8th International Congress for Analytical Psychology, San Francisco, 1980,* this collection of essays on the psychological aspects of money in terms of depth psychology includes a study on "Coins and Psychological Change" (Lockhart); "Contribution to Soul and Money" (Hillman); "Fee-less Practice and Soul Work" (Vasavada); "Psyche, Wealth, and Poverty" (Perry); "Myth and Money" (Covitz); and "Soul and Money" (Guggenbühl-Craig).

The Outer Planets and Their Cycles: The Astrology of the Collective, by Liz Greene. Reno: CRCS Publications, 1983p* (Lectures on Modern Astrology Series) (182, incl. 14 illus., of which 11 are birth charts).

Consisting of seven untitled lectures given in 1980, this work by Greene combines her experience as astrologer and Jungian analyst to present the thesis that the outer planets (the ones farthest from the sun) and their cycles represent the realm of the collective unconscious, the repository of the archetypal images. Following her introduction, she discusses the significance of the planetary conjunctions of Saturn-Uranus, Saturn-Neptune, and Saturn-Pluto and then interprets the relationship of birth charts of famous persons (Hitler, Marx, Lenin, Freud, and Jung) to the outer-planets' keys of influence. She also interprets the zodiacal signs which outer planets rule with reference to the birth charts of John F. Kennedy, Salvador Dali, the Islamic Republic of Iran, the U.S.A., and Israel, following which she discusses approaching conjunctions of the outer planets with reference to the horoscope of the U.S.S.R. She concludes with the significance of individual configurations (relative positions or aspects) involving outer planets and an analysis of astrological maps that demonstrate the beginnings of the Piscean Age and the Aquarian Age.

Progress Without Loss of Soul: Toward a Wholistic Approach to Modernization Planning, by Theodore Abt. (Ger.: *Fortschritt ohne Seelenverlust: Versuch einer ganzheitlichen Schau gesellschaftlicher Probleme am Beispiel des Wandels im ländlichen Raum.* Bern: Hallwag Verlag, 1983.) Wilmette, Ill.: Chiron Publications, 1989* +p* (389 + xxii, incl. 9-p. index, 13-p. bibl., 28 illus., 1-p. intro. by Marie-Louise von Franz, 6-p. foreword by Laurens van der Post).

Jungian analyst Abt uses his experience as project director for a comprehensive economic development plan for two Swiss mountain regions as well as a series of noteworthy dreams that related to his work and made him aware of the spiritual-emotional realm, to demonstrate that Jung's discovery of the collective unconscious paved the way for the examination of the issue of the technological progress that threatens to take over our souls. He starts with the problem of malaise in rural areas and the disturbed relationship between the country and the city and then discusses at length the change in the relationship between humanity and the environment (including the milieu as symbol) along with the change in interpersonal relationships (including fundamental characteristics of the primordial manner of thought and behavior). He concludes with reflections on contemporary rural development policy in Switzerland and posits a guiding image for the support and promotion of rural independence and a vision of social planning that will consider the whole person along with his or her spiritual-emotional needs.

Cultural Attitudes in Psychological Perspective, by Joseph L. Henderson. To-
   ronto: Inner City Books, 1984p* (Studies in Jungian Psychology by Jungian
   Analysts, 19) (124, incl. 5-p. index, 5-p. bibl., 6-p. ref. notes, 2-p. gloss. of
   Jungian terms, 24 illus.).

After exploring some examples of four traditional cultural attitudes (social, religious, aesthetic, philosophic), Henderson presents a psychological cultural attitude as his dominant theme, using his experience as a psychotherapist to describe what it is and how it functions. He examines anthropology, art, mythology, literature, the history of ideas, and personal analysis for archetypal sources and uses the Jungian individuation process as a model for psychological development. He provides clinical illustrations to show how a given cultural attitude affects a person's life and the analytic process and suggests how the psychological attitude may enrich and modify the patient's traditional attitude. His discussion of the psychological attitude includes qualities of the Self, and psychology in its historical context and its modern context, concluding with comments on nature and psyche.

(Bk.revs.: SFJInstLib '84/5n3:1–7; CanBkRAn '85:402; JAnPsy '85/30:393–4; Quad '85/
18n1:116–18; ContemPsy '86/31:621–2)

Jung and Social Work, by Herman Borenzweig. Lanham, Md. and London:
   University Press of America, 1984 +p (215 + x, incl. 11-p. index).

Regarding Jung as one of the great thinkers of our time and Jung's psychology as championing the individual, Borenzweig considers it time for Jung's work to be incorporated into the profession of social work in order to compensate for the profession's current one-sidedness of Freudian, materialistic, and scientific social work theory and practice. Starting with ego and self, he then discusses psychology and alchemy (persona-shadow, anima-animus, psychological types, the psychology of the transference, alchemical processes, stages of the *coniunctio*); dreams and dream symbolism (myth, number symbolism, color symbolism); astrology (synchronicity); paranormal phenomena (the psychoid, *I Ching*, telepathy, psychokinesis, life after death); concluding with an analysis of the ideas of Jung and social work values (social action) and groups and families.

A Testament to the Wilderness: Ten Essays on an Address by C. A. Meier. Zurich: Daimon Verlag with Santa Monica: Lapis Press, 1985* +p* (142 + xiii, incl. 7-p. foreword by Robert Hinshaw).

Following Meier's address on the wilderness and the search for the soul of modern man at the 1983 World Wilderness Congress, nine selected colleagues responded with essays on the same topic in honor of Meier's eightieth birthday. In addition to Meier's paper are essays on nature, psyche and a healing ceremony of the Xhosa (Buhrmann); nature aphoristic with an excerpt from Goethe (Sam Francis); the four eagle feathers (Henderson); the arts of Mr. Hun Tun (Miyuki); Nduma to Inverness: the story of a personal journey (Ian Player); wilderness and a way of truth (van der Post); appointment with a rhinoceros (van der Post), the wilderness (Weaver); and the ranch papers (Jane Wheelwright).
(Bk.revs.: Harvest '86/32:163–4; JAnPsy '88/33:196–7)

The Archetype of Shadow in a Split World: Proceedings of the Tenth International Congress for Analytical Psychology, Berlin, 1986, edited by Mary Ann Mattoon. Zurich: Daimon Verlag, 1987* +p* (456 pp.).

Among the twenty-five papers by thirty-four authors delivered at the Congress for Analytical Psychology in Berlin, itself at that time a symbol of a split world, are nine by authors whose books appear in this annotated bibliography: "Planning Without Shadow" (Abt); "Jung's Shadow Problem with Sabina Spielrein" (Carotenuto); "Masochism: The Shadow Side of the Archetypal Need to Venerate and Worship" (Gordon); "The Structure of Collective Shadows: Why They Endure" (James Hall); "Original Morality in a Depressed Culture" (Samuels); "The Split Shadow and the Father-Son Relationship" (Sandner); "Archetypal Foundations of Projective Identity" (Schwartz-Salant); "The Shadow Between Parents and Children" (Sidoli); and "The Singer/Loomis Inventory of Personality" (Singer).
(Bk.rev.: Chiron '88:273–6)

The Heart of History: Individuality in Evolution, by John Weir Perry. Albany: State U. of New York Press, 1987* +p* (249 + ix, incl. 11-p. index, 10-p. bibl., 19-p. ref. notes, 12 illus.).

Examining the myth and ritual forms that reveal the evolution of individuality in various societies, Perry views history as finding its heart through these mythic visions. With myth at the heart of history, he explores the source and psychological dynamic of the principle of compassionate social concern and sees a parallelism in the processes of transformation in the psyche and in society, citing historical examples of the unbalanced assertion of individuality and dominance. In the first part of the book he deals with myth, ritual, and visions (the psyche and the evolution of culture; world images in turmoil and transition), followed by a section on cultural transitions (a legacy of pharaohs; sages and sons of heaven; kingship and compassion; agape and anointed ones; quests and a kingdom of the heart; revolution and world regeneration). He ends with a section of conclusions for our times, discussing individuality in evolution, modern myth and nuclear nemesis, and the future.

(Bk.revs.: JSciStudRel '88/27:456–8; SFJInstLib '88/8n1:33–53)

Imprints of the Future: Politics and Individuation in Our Time, by George Czuczka. Washington, D.C. and Zurich: Daimon Verlag, 1987p* (112 + xiii, incl. 4-p. index, 7-p. bibl., 3-p. foreword by Ann Belford Ulanov).

Seeking to demonstrate the relevance of Jungian psychology to the political process and to international relations, Czuczka explores the premise that the Jungian approach can contribute to healing the split and bridging the gap that separates nations, ideologies, and religions. He emphasizes the important distinction between individualism and Jung's concept of individuation as a natural process which unfolds in order for individuals to fulfill their own particular design and purpose. He examines the political history of Germany and the psychological damage caused by the exposure to the collective evil of Hitlerism that continues to affect us all as we experience an emptiness in our souls and the temptation to turn to totalitarian prescriptions. He then moves on to the American Dream with its ups and downs on a course of empire that tries to conquer the void within one's self by pursuing power without, and the "salvation bazaar" of marketing religious ardor warmed by "patriotism of an almost chosen people." He presents the challenge of the Jungian concept of individuation and the role it might play in bringing about significant social and political change, whereby the individual task of restoring the archetypal connection between the ego and the self also has a bearing on collective concerns of human rights, equitable distribution of wealth and resources, global rivalries, and nuclear dangers.

(Bk.rev.: Harvest '88–89/34:178–80)

Power and Politics: The Psychology of Soviet–American Partnership, by Jerome S. Bernstein. Boston and Shaftesbury: Shambhala Publications, 1989* (A

C. G. Jung Foundation Book) (231 + xxiii, incl. 5-p. index, 16-p. bibl., 5-p. ref. notes, 4 illus., 3-p. foreword by Edward C. Whitmont, 2-p. foreword by Senator Claiborne Pell).

Recognizing powerful forces in the collective unconscious that are moving both superpowers toward a single objective, Bernstein uses Jungian theory to reinterpret the superpower relationship and to analyze the major collective dynamics influencing both nations to facilitate a new world order for preservation of life. He emphasizes that psychology must play a dramatic role in analyzing the dynamics of the conflict between the Soviet Union and the United States, identifying archetypal forces that impel them simultaneously toward conflict and cooperation. He points out that the advent of the threat of nuclear weaponry is forcing the superpowers to examine the powerful underlying psychological dynamics that perpetuate the conflict. Following an introduction to Jung's theory of the collective unconscious and archetypes, he discusses the archetype of the shadow; the hero dynamic; power; war; primary cooperation; and paranoia between groups and nations. He concludes with a discussion on the potential for transformation. Appended is a case history of the U.S. Institute of Peace and a hypothetical structure for a Soviet-American Institute for War-Peace Research and Technology Development.
(Bk.rev.: PsyPersp '90/22:209–12; Quad '90/23n1:121–7)

The Roots of War: A Jungian Perspective, by Anthony Stevens. New York: Paragon House, 1989* +p* (237 + xvi, incl. 5-p. index, 7-p. bibl., gloss. of Jungian terms, 2 illus.).

Growing out of lectures given at the C. G. Jung Foundation for Analytical Psychology in New York in 1985 on the archetypes of war, Stevens' book employs Jungian psychology to rectify deficiencies in the literature of war, which ignores the unconscious, relies too heavily on rational explanations of national conduct, and attaches too little importance to human biology. He incorporates the premises of depth psychology that human behavior is motivated by the unconscious rather than consciousness and that extra-rational or irrational factors are involved in the "reasons" for war. He proceeds from a discussion of war and peace (universality of war; inevitability of conflict; war as an archetypal phenomenon) to the topics of warlike and peaceful behavior (attachment and hostility; conviviality versus aggression; the neurophysiology of "fight" or "flight;" biological factors; the archetypes of war), basic war (weapons; functions; war as homeostasis), and making warriors (rites of passage; why men enlist; basic training; in-group loyalty). He concludes with discussions on making love (women and war); making war (authority and obedience; going to war; symbols of war);

making peace (genetic engineering; inactivation and inhibition; alternatives to war; the positive shadow of the bomb); and finally on transcending war.

Shadow and Self: Selected Papers in Analytical Psychology, by Joseph L. Henderson. Wilmette, Ill.: Chiron Publications, 1989p* (333 + xii, incl. 5-p. index, end-chap. bibl., 3 illus., autobiographical chronology).

Henderson's thirty-five essays are arranged under the subjects of analytical psychology (origins and recent developments in Jungian psychology; the self in review; Self and individuation; analysis of transference; countertransference; unity of the psyche; philosophy of analysis), cultural attitudes (cultural unconscious; origins of a theory of cultural attitudes), religious thought (introduction to *Jung and Eastern Thought;* religious dilemma in a multicultural society; psychology of numbers; four eagle feathers; reviews of *Psychotherapy East and West* and *The Glorious Cosmology*), the American Indian (a Jungian orientation to the culture of the American Indian; a Sioux shaman), art and literature (review of *American Characteristics of Classical American Literature;* Goethe's initiation; psychology and the roots of design; drama of love and death; a space of consciousness; the picture method in Jungian psychotherapy), and film reviews (from twelve articles in *Psychological Perspectives,* 1970–83).

Modern South Africa in Search of a Soul: Jungian Perspectives on the Wilderness Within, edited by Graham Saayman. Boston: Sigo Press, 1990 +p.

The Year 1: Global Process at Work, by Arnold Mindell. London: Arkana/ Penguin, 1990p.

Part Two

Works Arranged by Author

More than 400 authors comprise this part of the bibliography, of which more than 350 are sole authors of books and 50 others are co-authors; 43 others are editors. Most are members of the International Association for Analytical Psychology, which indicates Jungian training. Others have had Jungian training in varying degrees or have developed special interests in various aspects of Jung's psychology so that they have Jungian orientation. Considering that this bibliography is restricted to works published in English, it is understandable that 90 percent are written by English-speaking authors and a few by bilingual authors, the remainder being translated into English. More than fifteen nationalities are represented.

Along with each title is given the page number in Part One where each book may be found. Complete bibliographic information is located in Part One, whereas only basic data are indicated in Part Two (author, title, dates of issues).

Listed first are the collected works of Jung, followed by other writings by Jung and then other authors.

The Collected Works of C. G. Jung. 1953 + [see p. 20]

CW 1	Psychiatric Studies. 1957; ed. 2 1970; 1983p [p. 293]
2	Experimental Researches. 1973; 1981p [p. 295]
3	The Psychogenesis of Mental Disease. 1960; 1982p [p. 294]
4	Freud and Psychoanalysis. 1961; 1985p [p. 294]
5	Symbols of Transformation. 1956; ed. 2 1967; 1976p [p. 127]
6	Psychological Types. 1971; 1976p [p. 67]
7	Two Essays on Analytical Psychology. 1953; ed. 2 1966; 1972p [p. 32]
8	The Structure and Dynamics of the Psyche. 1960; ed. 2 1969 [p. 55]
9i	The Archetypes and the Collective Unconscious. 1959; ed. 2 1968; 1980p [p. 55]

9ii   Aion: Researches into the Phenomenology of the Self. 1959; ed. 2 1968; 1979p [p. 199]
10   Civilization in Transition. 1964; ed. 2 1970 [p. 355]
11   Psychology and Religion: West and East. 1958; ed. 2 1969 [p. 200]
12   Psychology and Alchemy. 1953; ed. 2 1968; 1980p [p. 129]
13   Alchemical Studies. 1967; 1983p [p. 131]
14   Mysterium Coniunctionis. 1963; ed. 2 1970; 1977p [p. 130]
15   The Spirit in Man, Art, and Literature. 1966; 1971p; 1984p [p. 253]
16   The Practice of Psychotherapy. 1954; ed. 2 1966; 1985p [p. 293]
17   The Development of Personality. 1954; 1981p [p. 79]
18   The Symbolic Life: Miscellaneous Writings. 1976 [p. 26]
19   General Bibliography of C. G. Jung's Writings. 1979 [p. 33]
20   General Index to the Collected Works of C. G. Jung. 1979 [p. 21]
A   The Zofingia Lectures. 1983; 1984 [p. 27]

OTHER WRITINGS BY JUNG

Analytical Psychology: Its Theory and Practice. 1968; 1970p; 1976p; 1986p [p. 33]
Analytical Psychology: Notes of the Seminar Given in 1925. 1989 [p. 32]
Answer to Job. 1954; 1955; 1960p; 1965p; 1979p; 1984p (Ger.: 1952) [p. 199]
Aspects of the Feminine. 1982p; 1983p; 1986p [p. 160]
Aspects of the Masculine. 1989p [p. 160]
The Basic Writings of C. G. Jung (ed. de Laszlo). 1959 [p. 23]
C. G. Jung: Letters (ed. Adler & Jaffé). 1973–76 [p. 24]
C. G. Jung Speaking: Interviews and Encounters (ed. McGuire). 1977; 1978; 1980p; 1986 + p [p. 26]
Collected Papers on Analytical Psychology. 1916; ed. 2 1917; 1920 [p. 21]
Contributions to Analytical Psychology. 1928 [p. 21]
Critique of Psychoanalysis. 1975p [p. 296]
Dictionary of Analytical Psychology. 1987p [p. 67]
Dream Analysis: Notes of the Seminar Given in 1928–1930. 1984 [p. 292]
Dreams. 1974p; 1982p; 1985p [p. 132]
Essays on a Science of Mythology (with Kerényi). 1949; 1963p; 1969 + p (Ger.: 1941) [p. 161]
Essays on Contemporary Events. 1947; 1989p [p. 354]
The Essential Jung (selected by Storr). 1983 + p [p. 27]
Flying Saucers: A Modern Myth of Things Seen in the Skies. 1959; 1969p; 1977p; 1978p; 1989p [p. 355]
Four Archetypes: Mother, Rebirth, Spirit, Trickster. 1970p; 1971p; 1986p [p. 56]
The Freud/Jung Letters (ed. McGuire). 1974; 1979p; 1988p [p. 25]
The Integration of the Personality. 1939; 1940 [p. 78]
The Interpretation of Nature and the Psyche (with Pauli). 1955 (Ger.: 1952) [p. 79]

Introduction to a Science of Mythology (with Kerényi). 1950; 1985p [p. 161]
Jung: Selected Writings (ed. Storr). 1983; 1986p [p. 27]
Man and His Symbols. 1964; 1968p; 1975p; 1978p; 1981p [p. 130]
Mandala Symbolism. 1972p [p. 132]
Memories, Dreams, Reflections (ed. Jaffé). 1962; 1963p; 1965p; 1967p; rev.
    1973; 1983p; 1989p [p. 8]
Modern Man in Search of a Soul. 1933; 1955p; 1961p; 1970p; 1984p [p. 22]
Nietzsche's Zarathustra: Notes of a Seminar (ed. Jarrett). 1988; 1989p [p. 128]
On the Nature of the Psyche. 1969p; 1988p [p. 56]
The Portable Jung (ed. Campbell). 1971 + p; 1976p; 1985p [p. 24]
Psyche and Symbol: Selection from the Writings of Jung (de Laszlo). 1958p
    [p. 23]
The Psychoanalytic Years. 1974p [p. 296]
Psychological Reflections: Anthology (ed. Jacobi). 1953; 1961p: 1970; 1971 + p;
    1973p; 1986p (Ger.: 1945) [p. 22; 23]
Psychological Types; Or, Psychology of Individuation. 1923; 1959; 1971; 1976p
    (Ger.: 1921) [p. 67]
Psychology and Education. 1969p [p. 80]
Psychology and Religion (Terry Lectures). 1938; 1960p [p. 198]
Psychology and the East. 1978p; 1982p; 1987p [p. 201]
Psychology and the Occult. 1977p; 1982p; 1987p [p. 132]
Psychology and Western Religion. 1984p; 1988p [p. 201]
The Psychology of Dementia Praecox. 1909; 1936; 1974p (Ger.: 1907) [p. 291]
The Psychology of the Transference. 1969p; 1983p [p. 295]
Psychology of the Unconscious. 1916; 1925 [*Symbols of Transformation*]
    [p. 127]
The Secret of the Golden Flower (with Wilhelm). 1931; 1962; 1970p; 1975;
    1984p (Ger.: 1929) [p. 127]
Selected Letters of C. G. Jung, 1901–1961 (ed. Adler). 1984 [p. 28]
Studies in Word-Association. 1918; 1919; 1969 (Ger.: 1906–1909) [p. 291]
Synchronicity: An Acausal Connecting Principle. 1972 to 1985p [p. 79]
The Theory of Psychoanalysis. 1915; 1971 (Ger.: 1913) [p. 292]
The Undiscovered Self. 1958p; 1959p; 1971p; 1974p (Ger.: 1957) [p. 80]
The Visions Seminars. 1976p; 1983p [p. 128]

*   *   *   *   *

Abrams, Jeremiah (Sausalito, Calif., therapist; Mt. Vision Inst. dir.)
    (ed.) *Reclaiming the Inner Child.* 1990p [p. 122]
Abt, Theodor (Ph.D.: Zurich J. Inst. dipl.; Fed. Inst. Tech. planning prof.)
    Progress without Loss of Soul. 1989 + p (Ger.: 1983) [p. 361]
Adler, Gerhard (1904–88; Ph.D.; studied with Jung 1931–34; London
    Jn. analyst)

(co-ed.) *C. G. Jung: Letters.* 1973–1976 [p. 24]
(ed.) *Current Trends in Analytical Psychology.* 1961 (1958 Congress) [p. 39]
Dynamics of the Self. 1979p; 1989p [p. 62]
The Living Symbol: A Case Study in the Process of Individuation. 1961 [p. 87]
(ed.) *Selected Letters of C. G. Jung, 1901–1961.* 1984 + p [p. 28]
Studies in Analytical Psychology. 1948; rev. 1966; 1967; 1968; 1969 + p [p. 35]
(ed.) *Success and Failure in Analysis.* 1974 (1971 IAAP congress) [p. 306]
Aldrich, Charles Robert (1877–1933; Am. writer)
The Primitive Mind and Modern Civilization. 1931; 1969; 1970 [p. 356]
Alexander, Irving E. (1922–; Ph.D; Duke U. psy. prof.)
(co-author) *The Experience of Introversion.* 1975 [p. 61]
Allan, John (1941–; Ph.D.; Jn. analyst; U. Brit. Columbia psy. prof.)
Inscapes of the Child's World: Jungian Counseling in Schools and Clinics. 1988p [p. 343]
Amman, Ruth (studied with Dora Kalff; Kindhausen, Switzerland, Jn. analyst)
Healing and Transformation in Sandplay. 1990 + p [p. 352]
Analytical Psychology Club of New York
Catalog of the Kristine Mann Library. 1978 [p. 45]
Argüelles, José A. (1939–; Ph.D.; artist & art hist. prof.)
(co-author) *Mandala.* 1972 + p; 1985p [p. 142]
Argüelles, Miriam (1943–; M.A.; artist & art historian)
(co-author) *Mandala.* 1972 + p; 1985p [p. 142]
Armstrong, Thomas (Ph.D.; San Francisco educ. counseling serv. dir.)
The Radiant Child. 1985p [p. 110]
Aronson, Alex (1912–; Tel Aviv U. Engl. prof.)
Psyche and Symbol in Shakespeare. 1972 [p. 261]
Arraj, James (writer near Crater Lake, Ore.)
(co-author) *A Jungian Psychology Resource Guide.* 1987p [p. 52]
(co-author) *A Practical Guide to C. G. Jung's Psychological Types, Sheldon's Body and Temperament Types, and Their Integration.* 1988p [p. 73]
St. John of the Cross and Dr. C. G. Jung. 1986p [p. 238]
(co-author) *A Tool for Understanding Human Differences.* 1985p [p. 72]
Arraj, Tyra (writer near Crater Lake, Ore.)
(co-author) *A Jungian Psychology Resource Guide.* 1987p [p. 52]
(co-author) *Practical Guide to Jung's Psychological Types, Sheldon's Body and Temperament Types, and Their Integration.* 1988p [p. 73]
(co-author) *A Tool for Understanding Human Differences.* 1985p [p. 72]
Arroyo, Stephen (M.A. psy.)
Astrology, Psychology, and the Four Elements. 1975 + p [p. 310]
Atwood, George E. (Ph.D.)
(co-author) *Faces in a Cloud: Subjectivity in Personality Theory.* 1979 [p. 70]
Avens, Roberts (1923–; Ph.D.; Iona C. philos. prof.)

Imaginal Body: Para-Jungian Reflections on Soul, Imagination, and Death.
1982 + p [p. 227]
Imagination: A Way toward Western Nirvana. 1979p [p. 222]
Imagination Is Reality. 1980p (rev. of *Imagination: A Way toward Western Nirvana*) [p. 222]
Aziz, Robert (London, Ontario, Jn.-oriented therapist)
C. G. Jung's Psychology of Religion and Synchronicity. 1990 + p [p. 248]
Babcock, Winifred
Jung, Hesse, Harold. 1983 [p. 231]
Baker, Ian F. (Ph.D.; Zurich J. Inst. dipl.; Zurich Jn. analyst)
(ed.) *Methods of Treatment in Analytical Psychology.* 1980 (1977 IAAP congress) [p. 314]
Barker, Culver M. (1891–1967; M.D.; studied with Jung; London therapist)
Healing in Depth. 1972 [p. 307]
Barnaby, Karen (1944–; New York U. doct. study; *Quadrant* asst. ed.)
(co-ed.) *C. G. Jung and the Humanities.* 1990 [p. 282]
Barton, Anthony (1934–; Duquesne U. psy. prof.)
Three Worlds of Therapy: An Existential-Phenomenological Study of the Therapies of Freud, Jung, and Rogers. 1974 + p [p. 310]
Bates, Marilyn (Fullerton, Calif., State U. prof.)
(co-author) *Please Understand Me: Character and Temperament Types.* 1978p [p. 69]
Bauer, Jan (1943–; M.A.; Zurich J. Inst. dipl.; Montreal Jn. analyst)
Alcoholism and Women: Background and Psychology. 1982p [p. 323]
Baynes, Helton Godwin (1882–1943; M.D.; Jung's asst.; London Jn. analyst)
Analytical Psychology and the English Mind. 1950 [p. 36]
Germany Possessed. 1941; 1972 [p. 357]
Mythology of the Soul. 1940; 1949; 1955; 1969 [p. 298]
Becker, Raymond de (1916–; Vezelay, France)
The Understanding of Dreams. 1968 (Fr.: 1965) [p. 139]
Beebe, John (1939–; M.D.; San Francisco J. Inst. dipl.; San Francisco Jn. analyst)
(ed.) *Money, Food, Drink, Fashion, and Analytic Training.* 1983 (1980 IAAP congress) [p. 320]
Begg, Ean C. M. (M.A.; Zurich J. Inst. dipl.; London Jn. analyst)
The Cult of the Black Virgin. 1985p [p. 181]
Myth and Today's Consciousness. 1984p [p. 108]
Bell, Robert E. (1930–)
(ed.) *Dictionary of Classical Mythology.* 1982 + p [p. 148]
Bennet, E. A. (1888–1977; M.D.; Sc.D.; London psychiatrist; friend of Jung)
C. G. Jung. 1961; 1962p [p. 9]
Meetings with Jung. 1982; 1985p [p. 15]
What Jung Really Said. 1966; 1967 + p; 1983p [p. 41]
Berger, Merrill (Boston clin. psychologist)
(co-author) *The Wisdom of the Dream: The World of C. G. Jung.* 1989; 1990p [p. 18]

Berne, Patricia H. (Ph.D.; Washington, D.C., psychologist)
(co-author) *Dreams and Spiritual Growth.* 1984p [p. 232]

Bernstein, Jerome S. (1936–; M.A.; N.Y. J. Inst. dipl., Washington, D.C., Jn. analyst)
Power and Politics: The Psychology of Soviet-American Partnership. 1989 [p. 365]

Berry, Patricia (Ph.D.; Zurich J. Inst. dipl.; Cambridge, Mass., Jn. analyst)
Echo's Subtle Body. 1982p [p. 324]
(ed.) *Fathers and Mothers.* 1973p; 1977p; ed.2 1990p [p. 168]

Bertine, Eleanor (1887–1968; M.D.; studied with Jung; N.Y. Jn. analyst)
Human Relationships. 1958; 1963 [p. 86]
Jung's Contribution to Our Time. 1967; 1968 [p. 358]

Bianchi, Eugene C. (1930–; Ph.D.; Emory U. relig. prof.)
Aging as a Spiritual Journey. 1982; 1984p [p. 103]

Bickman, Martin (1945–; Ph.D.; U. Colorado Engl. prof.)
American Romantic Psychology. 1988p (rev. of *The Unsounded Centre*) [p. 267]
The Unsounded Centre: Jungian Studies in American Romanticism. 1980 [p. 267]

Birkhäuser, Peter (1911–72; Basel artist; analysand of von Franz)
Light from the Darkness: Paintings. 1980 [p. 268]

Birkhäuser-Oeri, Sibylle (d.1971; Jn. analyst; wife of Peter Birkhäuser)
The Mother: Archetypal Image in Fairy Tales. 1988p (Ger.: 1977) [p. 264]

Blackmer, Joan Dexter (1931–; Zurich J. Inst. dipl.; Concord, Mass., Jn. analyst)
Acrobats of the Gods: Dance and Transformation. 1989p [p. 282]

Bly, Robert (1926–; M.A.; poet)
A Little Book on the Human Shadow. 1988p [p. 118]

Boa, Fraser (1932–; M.A.; Zurich J. Inst. dipl.; Toronto Jn. analyst)
(co-author) *The Way of the Dream.* 1987 [p. 155]

Bolander, Karen (Ph.D.)
Assessing Personality through Tree Drawings. 1977 [p. 263]

Bolen, Jean Shinoda (M.D.; San Francisco Jn. analyst; UCSF psy. prof.)
Gods in Everyman: A New Psychology of Men's Lives and Loves. 1989; 1990p [p. 189]
Goddesses in Everywoman: A New Psychology of Women. 1983; 1984; 1985p [p. 177]
The Tao of Psychology: Synchronicity and the Self. 1979; 1980p; 1982p [p. 98]

Borenzweig, Herman (1930–; U. Sn. Cal. social work prof.)
Jung and Social Work. 1984 + p [p. 362]

Bosnak, Robert (J.D.; Zurich J. Inst. dipl.; Cambridge, Mass., Jn. analyst)
Dreaming with an AIDS Patient. 1989 [p. 346]
A Little Course in Dreams. 1988p (Dutch: 1986) [p. 153]

Branson, Clark (1939–; UCLA psy. study; Pasadena writer)

Howard Hawks: A Jungian Study. 1987 + p [p. 279]
Breaux, Charles
  Journey into Consciousness: Chakras, Tantra, and Jungian Psychology. 1989p
    [p. 120]
Brennan, Anne (Sister of St. Joseph; Seton Hall U. educ. prof.)
  (co-author) *Celebrate Mid-Life: Jungian Archetypes and Mid-Life Spirituality.*
    1988; 1989p [p. 242]
  (co-author) *Mid-life: Psychological and Spiritual Perspectives.* 1982; ed.2
    1987p [p. 228]
  (co-author) *Mid-life Directions.* 1985p [p. 235]
Brewi, Janice (Sister of St. Joseph; Seton Hall U. educ. prof.)
  (co-author) *Celebrate Mid-Life: Jungian Archetypes and Mid-Life Spirituality.*
    1988; 1989p [p. 242]
  (co-author) *Mid-life: Psychological and Spiritual Perspectives.* 1982; ed.2
    1987p [p. 228]
  (co-author) *Mid-life Directions.* 1985p [p. 235]
Brivic, Sheldon R. (1943–; Ph.D.; Temple U. Engl. prof.)
  Joyce between Freud and Jung. 1980 [p. 268]
Broadribb, Donald R. (1933–; Ph.D.; Zurich J. Inst. dipl.; Austral. Jn. analyst)
  The Dream Story. 1987p; 1990p [p. 154]
Brome, Vincent (1910–; London biog. writer)
  Jung: Man and Myth. 1978 + p; 1980p; 1981p [p. 14]
Brown, Clifford A. (Ph.D.)
  Jung's Hermeneutic of Doctrine. 1981p [p. 224]
Brownsword, Alan W. (Ph.D.)
  It Takes All Types! 1987p [p. 72]
Brunner, Cornelia (Zurich Jn. analyst)
  Anima As Fate. 1986p (Ger: 1963) [p. 165]
Bryant, Christopher, (1905–85; Anglican Cowley Father)
  Depth Psychology and Religious Belief. 1972p; rev. 1987p [p. 215]
  Jung and the Christian Way. 1983p; 1984p [p. 230]
  The River Within: The Search for God in Depth. 1978p; 1983p [p. 97]
Bührmann, M. Vera (M.D.; London Jn. training; Capetown Jn. analyst)
  Living in Two Worlds. 1984; 1986p [p. 331]
Burt, Kathleen (1943–; Solano Beach, Calif., astrologer; Jn. student)
  Archetypes of the Zodiac. 1988p [p. 116]
Campbell, Joseph (1904–87; Ph.D.; Sarah Lawrence C. lit. prof.)
  The Hero with a Thousand Faces. 1949; 1950; 1956; ed.2 1968; 1972p;
    1975p; 1988p [p. 84]
  The Inner Reaches of Outer Space. 1986; 1988 + p [p. 153]
  The Mythic Image. 1974; 1981p [p. 143]
  Myths to Live By. 1972; 1973p; 1978p; 1984p; 1985p [p. 216]
  (ed.) *The Portable Jung.* 1971 + p; 1976p; 1985p [p. 24]
  (co-author) *Tarot Revelations.* 1980p; ed.2 1982p; ed.3 1987p [p. 100]

Caprio, Betsy (M.A.; L.A. minister; L.A. J. Inst. member)
The Woman Sealed in the Tower. 1982p [p. 176]
Carlson, Kathie (M.A.; N.Y. J. Inst. study; Connecticut psychotherapist)
In Her Image: The Unhealed Daughter's Search for Her Mother. 1989 [p. 189]
Carotenuto, Aldo (Ph.D.; Rome Jn. analyst; U. Rome lecturer)
Eros and Pathos: Shades of Love and Suffering. 1989p (It.: 1987) [p. 113]
Kant's Dove. 1990p [p. 352]
A Secret Symmetry: Sabina Spielrein between Jung and Freud. 1982; 1984p
(It.: 1980) [p. 321]
The Spiral Way: A Woman's Healing Journey. 1986p (It.: 1979) [p. 318]
The Vertical Labyrinth: Individuation in Jungian Psychology. 1985p (It.:
1981) [p. 103]
Carroll, L. Patrick (1936–; Tacoma Jesuit priest)
(co-author) *Chaos or Creation: Spirituality in Mid-Life.* 1986p [p. 236]
Champernowne, Irene (1901–76; Ph.D.; Jn. training; Exeter Center founder)
A Memoir of Toni Wolff. 1980p [p. 147]
Chapman, J. Harley (1940–; Ph.D.; Harper C. philos. prof.)
Jung's Three Theories of Religious Experience. 1988 [p. 244]
Chetwynd, Tom (1938–; Brit. writer)
Dictionary of Symbols. 1982p [p. 148]
Chinen, Allan B. (1952–; M.D.; San Francisco Jn. analyst; U. Cal. prof.)
In the Ever After: Fairy Tales and the Second Half of Life. 1989p [p. 283]
Christou, Evangelos (1922–56; Zurich J. Inst. dipl.; Alexandria, Egypt, Jn.
analyst)
The Logos of the Soul. 1963p; 1987p [p. 301]
Cirlot, J. E. (1915–; Spanish poet)
A Dictionary of Symbols. 1962; ed.2 1971; 1972; 1983p; 1988 (Span.: 1958)
[p. 136]
Clark, Robert A. (1908–; M.D.; Zurich J. Inst. study; U. Pitt. psy. prof.)
Six Talks on Jung's Psychology. 1953p [p. 37]
Clarke, Thomas E.
(co-author) *From Image to Likeness.* 1983p [p. 106]
Clift, Jean Dalby (Ph.D.; Zurich J. Inst. study; Denver pastoral counselor)
(co-author) *The Hero Journey in Dreams.* 1988 [p. 117]
(co-author) *Symbols of Transformation in Dreams.* 1984; 1986p [p. 151]
Clift, Wallace B. (1926–; Ph.D.; Zurich J. Inst. study; U. Denver relig. prof.)
(co-author) *The Hero Journey in Dreams.* 1988 [p. 117]
Jung and Christianity: The Challenge of Reconciliation. 1982; 1983;
1986p [p. 227]
(co-author) *Symbols of Transformation in Dreams.* 1984; 1986p [p. 151]
Cobb, Noel (Ph.D.; London Jn. training; London Jn. analyst)
Prospero's Island: Secret Alchemy at the Heart of The Tempest. 1984p [p.
275]
Cohen, Edmund D. (J.D.; Ph.D.; Zurich J. Inst. study)

C. G. Jung and the Scientific Attitude. 1975; 1976p [p. 44]
The Mind of the Bible-Believer. 1986; 1988p [p. 237]
Colegrave, Sukie (1948–; studied Jn. psy. in London & Boston; Santa Fe psychotherapist)
By Way of Pain: A Passage into Self. 1988p [p. 116]
The Spirit of the Valley: Androgyny and Chinese Thought. 1979 + p; 1981 [p. 170]
Uniting Heaven and Earth. 1989p (reissue of *Spirit of the Valley*) [p. 171]
Colman, Arthur D. (1937–; M.D.; San Francisco Jn. analyst; U. Cal. psy. prof.)
(co-author) *Earth Father/Sky Father.* 1981 + p (earlier ed. of *The Father*) [p. 172]
(co-author) *The Father: Mythology and Changing Roles.* 1988 + p [p. 172]
Colman, Libby Lee
(co-author) *Earth Father/Sky Father.* 1981p (earlier ed. of *The Father*) [p. 172]
(co-author) *The Father* (reissue of *Earth Father/Sky Father*). 1988 + p [p. 172]
Conger, John P. (1935–; Orinda, Calif., Kennedy U. psy. prof.)
Jung and Reich: The Body as Shadow. 1988 + p [p. 343]
Cooper, J. C.
An Illustrated Encylopaedia of Traditional Symbols. 1978; 1979; 1987p [p. 145]
Corrie, Joan (Brit. writer)
ABC of Jung's Psychology. 1927 + p [p. 34]
Coudert, Allison (1941–; Ph.D.; San Francisco writer)
Alchemy: The Philosopher's Stone. 1980p [p. 147]
Coukoulis, Peter P. (Ph.D.; L.A. J. Inst. dipl.; Long Beach Jn. analyst)
Guru, Psychotherapist, and Self. 1976 + p [p. 311]
Coursen, H. R. (1932–; Ph.D.; Bowdoin C. Engl. prof.)
The Compensatory Psyche: A Jungian Approach to Shakespeare. 1986 + p [p. 278]
Covitz, Joel D. (1943–; D.D.; Zurich J. Inst. dipl.; Brookline, Mass., Jn. analyst)
Emotional Child Abuse: The Family Curse. 1986 + p [p. 336]
Visions of the Night: A Study of Jewish Dream Interpretation. 1990p [p. 156]
Cowan, Lyn (1942–; Ph.D.; Inter-Reg. Jn. dipl.; Minneapolis Jn. analyst)
Masochism: A Jungian View. 1982p [p. 325]
Coward, Harold G. (1936–; Ph.D.; U. Calgary Inst. Humanities dir.)
Jung and Eastern Thought. 1985 + p [p. 234]
Cox, David (1920–; Cambridge U. theol.; Zurich J. Inst. visiting lect.)
History and Myth: The World Around Us and the World Within. 1966 [p. 86]
How the Mind Works: Introduction to the Psychology of C. G. Jung. 1963; 1965; 1968p; 1978p [p. 40]
Jung and St. Paul. 1959 [p. 209]
Curatorium of the C. G. Jung Institute, Zurich
(ed.) *Conscience.* 1970 (Ger.: 1958) [p. 208]
(ed.) *Evil.* 1967 (Ger.: 1961) [p. 211]

Custance, John (pseudonym)
  Wisdom, Madness, and Folly: The Philosophy of a Lunatic. 1951; 1952 [p. 299]
Czuczka, George (For. Serv. Officer ret.)
  Imprints of the Future: Politics and Individuation in Our Time. 1987p [p. 364]
D'Acierno,Pellegrino
  (co-ed.) *C. G. Jung and the Humanities.* 1990 [p. 282]
Daking, D. C.
  Jungian Psychology and Modern Spiritual Thought. 1933 [p. 202]
Dale-Green, Patricia (d.1968; London An. Psy. Club member)
  The Archetypal Cat (orig. *Cult of the Cat*). 1963; 1970p; 1983p [p. 138]
Dallett, Janet O. (1933–; Ph.D.; L.A. J. Inst. dipl.; L.A. Jn. analyst)
  (ed.) *The Dream: The Vision of the Night,* by Max Zeller. 1975p [p. 144]
  When the Spirits Come Back. 1988p [p. 345]
Davies, Miranda
  (co-ed.) *Jungian Child Psychotherapy.* 1988p [p. 344]
de Castillejo, Irene Claremont (1896–1973; London Jn. analyst)
  Knowing Woman: A Feminine Psychology. 1973; 1974p; 1990p [p. 168]
de Laszlo, Violet S. (M.D.; London med. analyst; Zug, Switzerland, Jn. analyst)
  (ed.) *The Basic Writings of C. G. Jung.* 1959 [p. 23]
  (ed.) *Psyche and Symbol.* 1958p [p. 23]
de Vries, Ad (Litt.D.)
  Dictionary of Symbols and Imagery. 1974; ed. 2 1976; 1984 [p. 143]
Desteian, John (J.D.; Zurich J. Inst. dipl.; Minneapolis Jn. analyst)
  Coming Together/Coming Apart. 1989 + p [p. 189]
Dieckmann, Hans (1921–; M.D.; Zurich & Berlin J. Inst. dipl.; Berlin Jn. analyst)
  Twice-Told Tales: The Psychological Use of Fairy Tales. 1986p (Ger.: 1978) [p. 266]
Dione, Arthur (North England astrologer)
  Jungian Birth Charts. 1988p [p. 118]
Donington, Robert (1907–; Brit. musicologist)
  Wagner's Ring *and its Symbols.* 1963; rev. 1969 + p; 1974 + p [p. 257]
Donn, Linda (Ph.D. psy.)
  Freud and Jung: Years of Friendship, Years of Loss. 1988 [p. 52]
Doran, Robert M., (1939–; Ph.D.; Jesuit priest; Toronto Regis C. relig. prof.)
  Subject and Psyche: Ricoeur, Jung and the Search for Foundations. 1977 [p. 220]
Douglas, Claire (Ph.D.; N.Y. psychotherapist with Jungian training)
  The Woman in the Mirror; Analytical Psychology and the Feminine. 1990p [p. 193]
Dourley, John P. (Ph.D.; Cath. priest; Zurich J. Inst. dipl.; Ottawa Jn. analyst)
  Goddess Mother of the Trinity: A Jungian Implication. 1990 [p. 248]

The Illness That We Are: A Jungian Critique of Christianity. 1984p [p. 233]
Love, Celibacy, and the Inner Marriage. 1987p [p. 240]
The Psyche as Sacrament: C. G. Jung and Paul Tillich. 1981p [p. 223]
Downing, Christine (1931–; Ph.D.; San Diego State U. relig. prof.)
    The Goddess: Mythological Images of the Feminine. 1981; 1984p [p. 173]
    Journey Through Menopause: A Personal Rite of Passage. 1987; 1989p [p. 185]
    Myths and Mysteries of Same-Sex Love. 1989 + p [p. 191]
    Psyche's Sisters: Re-Imagining the Meaning of Sisterhood. 1988 [p. 187]
Dry, Avis M. (Zurich J. Inst. training)
    The Psychology of Jung: A Critical Interpretation. 1961 [p. 40]
Dundas, Evalyn T. (Zurich J. Inst. study; N. Calif. child psychologist)
    Symbols Come Alive in the Sand. 1990 + p [p. 352]
Dunne, Carrin (Rice U. relig. prof.; Houston Jung Center lect.)
    Behold Woman: A Jungian Approach to Feminist Theology. 1988; 1989p [p. 245]
Duran, Eduardo (1949–; Ph.D.)
    Archetypal Consultation: A Service Delivery Model for Native Americans. 1984p [p. 330]
Dyckman, Katherine Marie
    (co-author) *Chaos or Creation: Spirituality in Mid-Life.* 1986p [p. 236]
Edinger, Edward F. (1922–; M.D.; L.A. Jn. analyst)
    Anatomy of the Psyche: Alchemical Symbolism in Psychotherapy. 1985 + p [p. 333]
    The Bible and the Psyche: Individuation Symbolism in Old Testament. 1986p [p. 111]
    The Christian Archetype: A Jungian Commentary on Life of Christ. 1987p [p. 112]
    The Creation of Consciousness: Jung's Myth for Modern Man. 1984p [p. 107]
    Ego and Archetype. 1972; 1973p [p. 92]
    Encounter with the Self: A Jungian Commentary on William Blake's Illustrations of the Book of Job. 1986p [p. 278]
    Goethe's Faust: *Notes for a Jungian Commentary.* 1990p [p. 284]
    The Living Psyche: A Jungian Analysis in Pictures. 1989p [p. 348]
    Melville's Moby-Dick: *A Jungian Commentary.* 1978 + p [p. 265]
Eliade, Mircea (1907–86; Ph.D. Bucharest; U. Chicago relig. prof.)
    The Forge and the Crucible: The Origins and Structure of Alchemy. 1962; 1971p; ed.2 1978p (Fr.: 1956) [p. 135]
Ellenberger, Henri F. (1905–; Montreal psy.)
    The Discovery of the Unconscious. 1970; 1981p [p. 42]
Engelsman, Joan Chamberlain (1932–; Ph.D.; Drew U. Women's Center dir.)
    The Feminine Dimension of the Divine. 1979p; 1987p [p. 222]
Evans, Elida
    The Problem of the Nervous Child. 1920; 1921 [p. 297]
Evans, Richard I. (1922–; Ph.D.; U. Houston psy. prof.)

Conversations with Carl Jung. 1964p [p. 40]
Dialogue with C. G. Jung (repr. of *Jung on Elementary Psychology*). 1981 [p. 40]
Jung on Elementary Psychology. 1976p; 1979p [p. 40]
Evans-Wentz, W. Y. (1868–1965; Oxford U.)
   (ed.) *The Tibetan Book of the Dead.* 1927; ed.2 1949; ed.3 1957; 1960p; 1973; 1980p [p. 201]
   (ed.) *The Tibetan Book of the Great Liberation.* 1954; 1968p; 1978p [p. 207]
Fierz, Heinrich Karl (d.1984; Dr.Med.; Zurichberg Clinic dir.)
   Jungian Psychiatry. 1990p [p. 352]
Fierz-David, Linda (1891–1955; pupil of Jung; Zurich J. Inst. docent)
   The Dream of Poliphilo. 1950; ed.2 1987p (Ger.: 1947) [p. 134]
   Women's Dionysian Initiation. 1988p (Ger.: 1957) [p. 164]
Fodor, Nandor
   Freud, Jung, and Occultism. 1971; 1972 [p. 141]
Fordham, Frieda (1902–88; London Jn. analyst)
   An Introduction to Jung's Psychology. 1953; ed.2 1959p; ed.3 1966p [p. 36]
Fordham, Michael (1905–; M.D.; London Jn. analyst; co-ed. of Jung's *Collected Works*)
   (co-ed.) *Analytical Psychology: A Modern Science.* 1973; 1980 [p. 43]
   Children as Individuals (orig. *The Life of Childhood*). 1969; 1970 [p. 82]
   (ed.) *Contact with Jung.* 1963 [p. 9]
   Explorations into the Self. 1985 [p. 108]
   Jungian Psychotherapy. 1978; 1986p [p. 316]
   The Life of Childhood. 1944 [p. 82]
   New Developments in Analytical Psychology. 1957 [p. 38]
   The Objective Psyche. 1958 [p. 58]
   The Self and Autism. 1976 [p. 312]
   (ed.) *Technique in Jungian Analysis.* 1974; 1981; 1989p [p. 309]
Foster, Genevieve W. (1903–; M.A.; studied with Harding; Bryn Mawr C. lect.)
   The World Was Flooded with Light: A Mystical Experience Remembered. 1985 [p. 152]
Foster, Steven
   (co-ed.) *Betwixt and Between: Patterns of Masculine and Feminine Initiation.* 1987+p [p. 184]
Frey-Rohn, Liliane (D.Psy.; Dr.Phil.; Zurich Jn. analyst)
   Friedrich Nietzsche: A Psychological Approach to His Life and Work. 1988p [p. 107]
   From Freud to Jung. 1974; 1976p (Ger.: 1969) [p. 60]
Fried, Jerome
   (co-ed.) *Funk & Wagnalls Standard Dictionary of Folklore, Mythology, and Legend.* 1949; 1951; 1975; 1984p [p. 134]
Fritz, Donald W. (1933–; Ph.D.; Miami U. Engl. prof.)
   (ed.) *Perspectives on Creativity and the Unconscious.* 1980p [p. 269]

Fry, Ruth Thacker (Ph.D.; Houston J. Educational Center founder)
(co-author) *The Symbolic Profile*. 1976 [p. 312]

Furth, Gregg M. (Ph.D.; Zurich J. Inst. dipl.; N.Y. Jn. analyst)
Secret World of Drawings: Healing through Art. 1988 + p [p. 345]

Gallant, Christine (1940–; Ph.D.; Virginia Commonwealth Engl. prof.)
Blake and the Assimilation of Chaos. 1978 [p. 265]

Gardner, Robert L. (Zurich J. Inst. dipl.; Toronto Jn. analyst)
The Rainbow Serpent: Bridge to Consciousness. 1990p [p. 122]

Garrison, Jim (1951–; Ph.D.; Brit. writer)
The Darkness of God: Theology after Hiroshima. 1982p; 1983p [p. 225]

Gay, Volney P. (Ph.D.; Vanderbilt U. relig. prof.)
Reading Jung: Science, Philosophy, and Religion. 1984p [p. 50]

Gillette, Douglas (Chicago Inst. for World Spirituality cofounder)
(co-author) *King, Warrior, Magician, Lover*. 1990 [p. 192]

Globus, Gordon G. (1934–; M.D.; U. Cal. at Irvine psychi. & philos. prof.)
Dream Life, Wake Life. 1987 + p [p. 154]

Glover, Edward (1888–; London psychoanalyst)
Freud or Jung? 1949; 1950; 1956p; 1958p [p. 35]

Godard, Jerry Caris (1936–; Ed.D.; Guilford C. psy. & lit. prof.)
Mental Forms Creating: William Blake Anticipates Freud, Jung, and Rank.
1985 + p [p. 276]

Goldbrunner, Josef (Ph.D.; Cath. priest; U. Regensburg theol. prof.)
Individuation: A Study of the Depth Psychology of Carl Gustav Jung. 1955;
1956; 1964p [p. 37]

Goldenberg, Naomi R. (Ph.D.; Zurich Inst. study; Ottawa U. psy. of relig. prof.)
The Changing of the Gods: Feminism and the End of Traditional Religions.
1979 + p [p. 221]
*The End of God: Important Directions for a Feminist Critique of Religion in
the Works of Freud and Jung*. 1982p [p. 226]

Goodbread, Joseph H.
The Dreambody Toolkit. 1987p; 1988p [p. 339]

Gordon, Rosemary (Ph.D.; London Jn. analyst; *Journal of An. Psy*. ed.)
Dying and Creating: A Search for Meaning. 1978 [p. 315]

Goss, James (1939–; Ph.D.; Cal. State U. at Northridge relig. prof.)
(co-ed.) *Essays on Jung and the Study of Religion*. 1985 + p [p. 234]

Grant, Toni (Ph.D.; L.A. psychotherapist; radio commentator on women)
Being a Woman. 1987; 1989p [p. 184]

Grant, W. Harold (1933–; Ph.D.; Cath. lay missionary)
(co-author) *From Image to Likeness*. 1983p [p. 106]

Greene, Liz (Ph.D.; London Jn. analyst & astrologer)
The Astrology of Fate. 1984; 1984p; rev. 1985p [p. 107]
(co-author) *The Development of the Personality*. 1987p [p. 113]
(co-author) *Dynamics of the Unconscious*. 1988p [p. 116]
The Outer Planets and Their Cycles: Astrology of the Collective. 1983p [p.
361]

Relating: Astrological Guide to Living with Others. 1977; ed.2 1978p; 1986p [p. 95]

Saturn: A New Look at an Old Devil. 1976p; 1977p [p. 94]

Griffin, David (Ph.D.; Claremont philos. of relig. prof.)

(ed.) *Archetypal Process: Self and Divine in Whitehead, Jung, and Hillman.* 1989+p [p. 247]

Grinnell, Robert (d.1984; Ph.D.; Santa Barbara Jn. analyst)

Alchemy in a Modern Woman. 1973p; 1989p [p. 167]

Grof, Stanislav (1931–)

Beyond the Brain: Birth, Death, and Transcendence in Psychotherapy. 1985+p [p. 333]

Guggenbühl-Craig, Adolf (M.D.; Zurich Jn. analyst)

(ed.) *The Archetype.* 1964 (1962 IAAG congress) [p. 59]

Eros on Crutches: Reflections on Psychology and Amorality. 1980p; 1986p [p. 319]

Marriage: Dead or Alive. 1977p; 1981p; 1986p [p. 314]

Power in the Helping Professions. 1971p; 1979p; 1985p (Ger.: 1971) [p. 305]

Gustafson, Fred (Ph.D.; D.D.; Zurich J. Inst. dipl.; Watertown, Wis., Jn. analyst)

The Black Madonna. 1990+p [p. 192]

Guzie, Noreen Monroe

(co-author) *About Men and Women.* 1986p [p. 182]

Guzie, Tad W. (U. Calgary educ. prof.)

(co-author) *About Men and Women.* 1986p [p. 182]

Haddon, Genia Pauli (minister & therapist; Zurich J. Inst. study)

Body Metaphors: Releasing God-Feminine in Us All. 1988 [p. 241]

Hall, Calvin S. (1905–85; Ph.D.; Santa Cruz Inst. of Dream Research dir.)

(co-author) *A Primer of Jungian Psychology.* 1973p [p. 43]

(co-author) *Theories of Personality.* 1957; ed.2 1970; ed.3 1978 [p. 39]

Hall, James A. (1934–; M.D.: Zurich J. Inst. dipl.; Dallas Jn. analyst)

(co-ed.) *The Book of the Self: Person, Pretext, and Process.* 1987; 1988p [p. 64]

Clinical Uses of Dreams: Jungian Interpretation and Enactments. 1977 [p. 313]

Hypnosis: A Jungian Perspective. 1989 [p. 348]

Jungian Dream Interpretation. 1983p [p. 150]

The Jungian Experience: Analysis and Individuation. 1986p [p. 337]

(co-author) *Jung's Self Psychology.* Forthcoming in 1990 [p. 122]

Hall, Joyce

(co-author) *The Symbolic Profile.* 1976 [p. 312]

Hall, Nor (Ph.D.; St. Paul therapist)

The Moon and the Virgin: Reflections on the Archetypal Feminine. 1980+p [p. 171]

Those Women. 1988p [p. 188]

Hamaker-Zontag, Karen (Amsterdam astrologer & psy. counselor)

Astro-Psychology: Astrological Symbolism and the Human Psyche. 1980p
  (Dutch: 1978) [p. 96]
Elements and Crosses. 1984p (Dutch: 1979) [p. 97]
The Houses and Personality Development. 1988p (Dutch: 1981) [p. 102]
Planetary Symbolism in the Horoscope. 1985p (Dutch: 1980) [p. 100]
Hanna, Charles Bartruff
  The Face of the Deep: The Religious Ideas of C. G. Jung. 1967 [p. 213]
Hannah, Barbara (1891–1986; studied with Jung; Zurich Jn. analyst)
  Encounters with the Soul: Active Imagination as Developed by C. G. Jung.
    1981p [p. 148]
  Jung: His Life and Work: A Biographical Memoir. 1976; 1977; 1981p [p. 13]
  Striving towards Wholeness. 1971; 1973; 1987 + p [p. 91]
Harding, M. Esther (1888–1971; M.D.; studied with Jung; N.Y. Jn. analyst)
  The "I" and the "Not-I": A Study in the Development of Consciousness.
    1965; 1970; 1973p [p. 89]
  Journey into Self: An Interpretation of Bunyan's Pilgrim's Progress. 1956;
    1958; 1963 [p. 85]
  The Parental Image: Its Injury and Reconstruction. 1965; 1990 [p. 302]
  Psychic Energy: Its Source and Transformation. 1948; ed.2 1963 + p;
    1973p [p. 57]
  The Way of All Women: Psychological Interpretation. 1933; rev. 1970; 1971p;
    1975p; 1983p [p. 161]
  Woman's Mysteries: Ancient and Modern. 1935; ed.2 1955; 1970p; 1972;
    1975p; 1982p; Forthcoming in 1990p [p. 162]
Haule, John R. (Ph.D.; Zurich J. Inst. dipl.; Newton Centre, Mass., Jn. analyst)
  Divine Madness: Archetypes of Romantic Love. 1990 [p. 192]
Havice, Doris Webster (1907–)
  Personality Typing: Uses and Misuses. 1977p [p. 69]
Head, Rhoda
  (co-ed.) *A Well of Living Waters: A Festschrift for Hilde Kirsch.* 1977p [p.
    360]
Heisig, James W. (1944–)
  Imago Dei: A Study of C. G. Jung's Psychology of Religion. 1978; 1979 [p.
    220]
Henderson, Joseph L. (1903–; Ph.D.; studied with Jung; San Francisco Jn.
    analyst)
  Cultural Attitudes in Psychological Perspective. 1984p [p. 362]
  Shadow and Self: Selected Papers in Analytical Psychology. 1989p [p. 366]
  Thresholds of Initiation. 1967; 1979p [p. 90]
  (co-author) *The Wisdom of the Serpent.* 1963; 1971p; 1990p [p. 88]
Henke, James T.
  The Ego King. 1977p [p. 264]
The Herder Symbol Dictionary. 1986p (Ger.: 1960) [p. 144]
Herzog, Edgar (psychotherapist)

Psyche and Death. 1966; 1967; 1980p; 1983p (Ger.: 1960) [p. 137]
Heyer, Gustav Richard (M.D.)
   The Organism of the Mind: An Introduction to Analytical Psychology. 1933; 1934 (Ger.: 1932) [p. 297]
Hill, Gareth (Ph.D.; Berkeley Jn. analyst)
   (coord.) *Sandplay Studies: Origins, Theory, and Practice.* 1981; rev. 1989+p [p. 322]
   (ed.) *The Shaman from Elko: Papers in Honor of Joseph L. Henderson.* 1978p; 1990p [p. 316]
Hillman, James (Ph.D.; Zurich J. Inst. dipl.; Thompson, Conn., Jn. analyst)
   Anima: Anatomy of a Personified Notion. 1985p [p. 180]
   Archetypal Psychology: A Brief Account. 1983p [p. 62]
   A Blue Fire: Selected Writings. 1989 [p. 245]
   The Dream and the Underworld. 1979+p; 1983 [p. 146]
   Emotion: A Comprehensive Phenomenology of Theories and Their Meanings for Therapy. 1960; 1961 [p. 300]
   (ed.) *Facing the Gods.* 1980p [p. 223]
   Healing Fiction. 1983+p [p. 327]
   Insearch: Psychology and Religion. 1967p; 1970p; 1979p; 1984p [p. 213]
   Inter Views. 1983; 1984p [p. 328]
   (co-author) *Lectures on Jung's Typology.* 1971p; 1979p; 1986p [p. 68]
   Loose Ends: Primary Papers on Archetypal Psychology. 1975p; 1978p; 1986p [p. 61]
   The Myth of Analysis. 1972; 1978p; 1983p [p. 308]
   (ed.) *Puer Papers.* 1979p [p. 170]
   Re-Visioning Psychology. 1975; 1977p [p. 44]
   Suicide and the Soul. 1964; 1973p; 1976p; 1978p; 1985p [p. 302]
Hinkle, Beatrice M. (1872–1953; M.D.; Jn. analyst)
   Re-Creating of the Individual: A Study of Psychological Types and Their Relationship to Psychoanalysis. 1923 [p. 297]
Hinshaw, Robert (Ph.D.; Zurich J. Inst. dipl.; Zurich Jn. analyst)
   (co-ed.) *Differing Uses of Symbolic and Clinical Approaches in Practice and Theory.* 1986 [p. 327]
   (ed.) *A Testament to the Wilderness.* 1985+p [p. 363]
Hobson, Robert F. (M.D.; Manchester Jn. analyst)
   Forms of Feeling: The Heart of Psychotherapy. 1985+p; 1988p [p. 334]
Hochheimer, Wolfgang (Berlin Jn. analyst; Berlin Sch. Educ. psy. prof.)
   The Psychotherapy of C. G. Jung. 1969 (Ger.: 1966) [p. 303]
Hoeller, Stephan A. (L.A. U. of Oriental Studies relig. prof.)
   The Gnostic Jung and the Seven Sermons to the Dead. 1982+p; 1989p [p. 226]
   Jung and the Lost Gospels. 1989+p [p. 247]
Hogenson, George B. (1948–; Ph.D.; Yale U. pol. philos. prof.)
   Jung's Struggle with Freud. 1983 [p. 49]

Homans, Peter (1930–; Ph.D.; U. Chicago relig. & psy. prof.)
Jung in Context: Modernity and the Making of Psychology. 1979; 1982p [p. 46]
Hopcke, Robert H. (1958–; M.A.; M.S.; Berkeley Jn.-oriented psychotherapist)
A Guided Tour of the Collected Works *of C. G. Jung.* 1989 [p. 52]
Jung, Jungians, and Homosexuality. 1989 [p. 190]
Men's Dreams, Men's Healing. 1990p [p. 192]
Hostie, Raymond (1920–; D.Th.; Zurich J. Inst. study; Louvain U. theol. prof.)
Religion and the Psychology of Jung. 1957 (Dutch: 1954) [p. 207]
Howell, Alice O. (analytical astrologer; Jung Inst. lect.)
The Dove in the Stone: Finding the Sacred in the Commonplace. 1988p [p. 243]
Jungian Symbolism in Astrology. 1987p [p. 114]
Jungian Synchronicity in Astrological Signs and Ages. 1990p [p. 122]
Howes, Elizabeth Boyden (1907–; San Francisco Jn. analyst; Guild Psy. Studies founder)
(co-author) *The Choicemaker* (orig. Man, the Choicemaker). 1973; 1977p [p. 92]
Intersection and Beyond. 1963; 1971p; 1986p [p. 212]
Jesus' Answer to God. 1984 + p [p. 108]
Hubback, Judith (M.A.: London Jn. analyst; Soc. of An. Psy. training analyst)
People Who Do Things to Each Other. 1988 + p [p. 344]
Hull, R. F. C. (1913–74; translator of Jung's *Collected Works*)
(co-ed.); *C. G. Jung Speaking.* 1977; 1978; 1980; 1986p [p. 26]
Humbert, Elie G. (Ph.D.; Paris Jn. analyst; French Soc. for An. Psy. founder)
C. G. Jung: Fundamentals of Theory and Practice. 1988 + p (Fr.: 1983) [p. 48]
Hurwitz, Siegmund (Zurich J. Inst. lect.)
Lilith—the First Eve. 1990 [p. 192]
(co-author) *Timeless Documents of the Soul.* 1968 (Ger.: 1952) [p. 135]
Hyer, Mary W.
(co-author) *Archetypal Patterns in Women's Fiction.* 1981 + p [p. 270]
Jacobi, Jolande (1890–1973; Ph.D.; studied with Jung; Zurich Jn. analyst)
(ed.) *C. G. Jung: Psychological Reflections.* 1970; 1971 + p; 1973p; 1986p [p. 23]
Complex/Archetype/Symbol in the Psychology of Jung. 1959; ed.2 1965; 1971p (Ger.: 1957) [p. 59]
Masks of the Soul. 1976; 1977p (Ger.: 1967) [p. 90]
(ed.) *Paracelsus: Selected Writings.* 1951; ed.2 1958; 1988p (Ger. 1942) [p. 82]
(ed.) *Psychological Reflections: Anthology of Jung.* 1953; 1961p (Ger.: 1945) [p. 22]
The Psychology of C. G. Jung: Introduction. 1942; ed.8 1973p (Ger.: 1940) [p. 34]
The Way of Individuation. 1967; 1983p (Ger.: 1965) [p. 89]

Jacobs, Hans (1902–; studied with Jung; Australian psychiatrist)
Western Psychotherapy and Hindu-Sadhana. 1961 [p. 301]
Jacobsohn, Helmuth (Ph.D.; U. Marburg Egyptology prof.)
(co-author) *Timeless Documents of the Soul.* 1968 (Ger.: 1952) [p. 135]
Jacoby, Mario (1925–; Zurich J. Inst. dipl.; Zurich Jn. analyst)
The Analytic Encounter: Transference and Human Relationship. 1984p [p. 329]
Individuation and Narcissism: The Psychology of the Self in Jung and Kohut. 1990 [p. 109]
The Longing for Paradise: Psychological Perspectives on an Archetype. 1985 + p (Ger.: 1980) [p. 319]
Jaffé, Aniela (Jung's pers. secr. 1955–61; Zurich Jn. analyst)
Apparitions: An Archetypal Approach to Death Dreams and Ghosts. 1963; 1979p (Ger.: 1957) [p. 136]
(co-ed.) *C. G. Jung: Letters.* 1973–1976 [p. 24]
(ed.) *C. G. Jung: Word and Image.* 1979; 1983p (Ger.: 1977) [p. 13]
From the Life and Work of C. G. Jung. 1971 + p; 1972; 1989p (Ger.: 1968) [p. 41]
Jung's Last Years and Other Essays. 1984p [p. 15]
(ed.) *Memories, Dreams, Reflections,* by C. G. Jung. 1962; 1963p; 1967p; rev. 1973; 1983p [p. 8]
The Myth of Meaning. 1970; 1971; 1975p; 1984p (Ger.: 1967) [p. 90]
Was Jung a Mystic? and Other Essays. 1989p [p. 121]
Jaffe, Lawrence (1931–; Ph.D.; S.F. J. Inst. dipl.; Berkeley Jn. analyst)
Liberating the Heart: Spirituality and Jungian Psychology. 1990p [p. 248]
Jarrett, James L. (Ph.D.; U. Cal. at Berkeley educ. prof.)
(ed.) *Nietzsche's Zarathustra: Notes of the Seminar Given in 1934–1939 by C. G. Jung.* 1988 [p. 129]
Jensen, Ferne
(ed.) *C. G. Jung, Emma Jung, and Toni Wolff: A Collection of Remembrances.* 1982p [p. 15]
Jobes, Gertrude
Dictionary of Mythology, Folklore, and Symbols. 1961 [p. 138]
Johnson, Buffie (N.Y. artist; 1954 meeting with Jung)
Lady of the Beasts. 1988; 1990p [p. 244]
Johnson, Robert A. (1921–; Encinitas, Calif., Jn. therapist)
Ecstasy: Understanding the Psychology of Joy. 1987; 1989p [p. 113]
Femininity Lost and Regained. 1990 [p. 192]
He: Understanding Masculine Psychology. 1974; 1977p; 1986p; 1989p [p. 168]
Inner Work: Using Dreams and Active Imagination for Personal Growth. 1986; 1989p [p. 112]
She: Understanding Feminine Psychology. 1976; 1979p; 1986p; 1989 + p [p. 170]

We: Understanding the Psychology of Romantic Love. 1983; 1984p; 1985p; 1987p [p. 178]

Jones, Joyce Meeks (Arkansas State U. at Jonesboro Engl. prof.)
Jungian Psychology in Literary Analysis: A Demonstration Using T. S. Eliot's Poetry. 1979p [p. 267]

Jung, Emma (1882–1955; Zurich Jn. analyst)
Animus and Anima. 1957; 1969p; 1981p; 1985p (Ger.: 1934; 1955) [p. 163]
(co-author) *The Grail Legend.* 1970; 1971; ed.2 1986 + p (Ger.: 1960) [p. 256]

Kalff, Dora M. (1904–90; analysis with Emma Jung; Zurich J. Inst. lect.)
Sandplay: Mirror of a Child's Psyche. 1971p (Ger.: 1966) [p. 303]
Sandplay: Psychotherapeutic Approach to the Psyche. 1981p (rev. of 1971 ed.) [p. 303]

Kane, Evangeline (Ph.D.; Edmonton psychologist & counselor)
Recovering from Incest. 1989 + p [p. 351]

Kaplan-Williams, Strephon (Berkeley Jn. psychologist; Jungian-Senoi Inst.)
(co-author) *Dreams and Spritiual Growth.* 1984p [p. 232]
Jungian-Senoi Dreamwork Manual. 1980p; 1989p [p. 147]

Kast, Verena (1943–; Ph.D.; St. Gallen Jn. analyst; U. Zurich lect.)
The Nature of Loving: Patterns of Human Relationship. 1986p (Ger.: 1984) [p. 180]
A Time to Mourn: Growing through the Grief Process. 1988p (Ger.: 1982) [p. 105]

Kaufmann, Walter A. (1921–80)
Discovering the Mind. Vol. 3: *Freud versus Adler and Jung.* 1980 [p. 46]

Kawai, Hayao (1928–; Ph.D. analysand of Spiegelman; Kyoto analyst; U. prof.)
The Japanese Psyche: Major Motifs in the Fairy Tales of Japan. 1988p (Japan.: 1982) [p. 272]

Keirsey, David (Calif. State U. at Fullerton training therapist)
(co-author) *Please Understand Me: Character and Temperament Types.* 1978p; 1984p [p. 69]

Kelsey, Morton T. (1917–; B.D.; visited Jung; writer, lecturer & counselor)
Caring: How Can We Love One Another? 1981p [p. 101]
Christianity as Psychology. 1986p [p. 236]
Christo-Psychology. 1982; 1983p; 1984p [p. 225]
God, Dreams, and Revelation. 1968; rev. 1974p [p. 140]
The Other Side of Silence. 1976p; 1977p [p. 219]
Prophetic Ministry: Psychology and Spirituality of Pastoral Care. 1982 [p. 229]

Kerényi, Karl/Carl (1897–1943; Hung. classics prof.; Bollingen fellow)
Asklepios: Archetypal Image of Physician's Existence. 1959; 1960; 1967 (Ger.: 1947) [p. 205]
Athene: Virgin and Mother. 1978p; 1988p (Ger.: 1946) [p. 203]
Dionysos: Archetypal Image of Indestructible Life. 1976 [p. 218]

Eleusis: Archetypal Image of Mother and Daughter. 1967; 1977p (Dutch: 1960) [p. 210]
(co-author) Essays on a Science of Mythology. 1949; 1963p; 1969p (Ger.: 1941) [p. 161]
Hermes: Guide of Souls. 1976p; 1986p (Ger.: 1944) [p. 203]
Prometheus: Archetypal Image of Human Existence. 1963 (Ger.: 1946) [p. 204]
Zeus and Hera: Archetypal Image of Father, Husband, and Wife. 1975 (Ger.: 1972) [p. 216]
Keyes, Margaret Frings (1929–; San Francisco psychotherapist)
Inward Journey: Art as Therapy. 1974p; rev. 1983p; 1985p [p. 261]
Khan, Pir Vilayat Inayat
(co-author) Sufism and Jungian Psychology. 1990p [p. 249]
Kiepenheuer, Kaspar (1942–; Ph.D.; Zurich Jn. analyst)
Crossing the Bridge: A Jungian Approach to Adolescence. 1990 + p [p. 352]
Kirsch, Hilde (d.1978; L.A. psychotherapist; L.A. J. Inst. training analyst)
(ed.) The Well-Tended Tree: Essays into the Spirit of Our Time. 1971 [p. 359]
Kirsch, James (1901–89; M.D.; Berlin psychiatrist; L.A. Jn. analyst)
The Reluctant Prophet. 1973; 1990 [p. 142]
Shakespeare's Royal Self. 1966 [p. 258]
Kluger, Rivkah Schärf (d.1987; Ph.D.; L.A. Jn. analyst; Haifa Jn. analyst)
The Gilgamesh Epic. 1990 [p. 122]
Psyche and the Bible: Three Old Testament Themes. 1974p [p. 217]
Satan in the Old Testament. 1967 (Ger.: 1948) [p. 205]
Knapp, Bettina L. (1926–; Ph.D.; Hunter C. French & comp. lit. prof.)
Archetype, Architecture, and the Writer. 1986 [p. 277]
Archetype, Dance, and the Writer. 1983p [p. 273]
Dream and Image. 1977 [p. 263]
A Jungian Approach to Literature. 1984 [p. 275]
Machine, Metaphor, and the Writer: A Jungian View. 1989 [p. 284]
Music, Archetype, and the Writer: A Jungian View. 1988 [p. 280]
Theatre and Alchemy. 1980 [p. 270]
Women in Twentieth-Century Literature: A Jungian View. 1987 [p. 280]
Word/Image/Psyche. 1985 [p. 277]
Knipe, Rita 1926–; (L.A. J. Inst. dipl.; Honolulu Jn. analyst)
The Water of Life: A Jungian Journey through Hawaiian Myth. 1989 [p. 284]
Koltuv, Barbara Black (Ph.D.; N.Y. J. Inst. dipl.; N.Y. Jn. analyst)
The Book of Lilith. 1986p [p. 183]
Weaving Woman: Essays in Feminine Psychology from the Notebooks of a Jungian Analyst. 1990p [p. 193]
Kraemer, William (1911–82; M.D.; London Jn. analyst)
(ed.) The Forbidden Love: The Normal and Abnormal Love of Children. 1976 [p. 311]
Kranefeldt, Wolfgang Muller (1892–?; M.D.)

Secret Ways of the Mind: A Survey of the Psychological Principles of Freud, Adler, and Jung. 1932; 1934 (Ger.: 1930) [p. 34]

Kroeger, Otto (authoriz. MBTI prof. training; consulting firm founder)
(co-author) *Type Talk.* 1988p [p. 73]

Kugelmann, Robert (1948–; Ph.D.; Seattle U. psy. prof.)
The Windows of the Soul. 1983 [p. 329]

Kugler, Paul K. (Ph.D.; Zurich J. Inst. dipl.; Buffalo Jn. analyst)
The Alchemy of Discourse: An Archetypal Approach to Language. 1982 [p. 271]

Kunkel, Fritz (1889–1956; M.D.; Berlin psychiatrist; L.A. psychotherapist)
Creation Continues: A Psychological Interpretation of the Gospel of Matthew. 1947; rev. 1973p; 1987p [p. 83]
Fritz Kunkel: Selected Writings (ed. John Sanford). 1984p [p. 232]

La Dage, Alta J.
Occult Psychology: Comparison of Jungian Psychology and Modern Qabalah. 1978 [p. 220]

Lambert, Kenneth (d.1986; Litt.D.; Cambridge, England, Jn. analyst)
Analysis, Repair, and Individuation. 1981 [p. 322]

Laughlin, Tom
Jungian Theory and Therapy. 1982p [p. 48]

Lauter, Estella (1940–; Ph.D.; U. Wisconsin at Green Bay humanities prof.)
(co-ed.) *Feminist Archetypal Theory: Re-Visions of Jungian Thought.* 1985 [p. 182]

Lawrence, Gordon D. (1930–; Ph.D.; U. Florida at Gainesville educ. prof.)
People Types and Tiger Stripes. 1979p; ed.2 1982p [p. 70]

Layard, John (1891–1975; D.Sc.; anthropologist; Oxford Jn. analyst)
The Lady of the Hare. 1944; 1977 [p. 298]

Leach, Maria
(co-ed.) *Funk & Wagnalls Dictionary of Folklore, Mythology, and Legend.* 1949; 1951; 1975; 1984p [p. 134]

Lee, M. Owen (1930–; Cath. priest; Toronto U. classics prof.)
Death and Rebirth in Virgil's Arcadia. 1989 + p [p. 283]

Leichtman, Robert R. (M.D.; psychic consultant)
Jung and Freud Return. 1979p [p. 46]

Leonard, Linda Schierse (Ph.D.; Zurich J. Inst. dipl.; San Francisco Jn. analyst)
On the Way to the Wedding: Transforming the Love Relationship. 1986 + p [p. 183]
Witness to the Fire: Creativity and the Veil of Addiction. 1989 + p[p. 351]
The Wounded Woman: Healing the Father-Daughter Relationship. 1982; 1983p [p. 176]

Lindzey, Gardner (1920; Ph.D.; Stanford behavioral sci. dir.)
(co-author) *Theories of Personality.* 1957; ed.2 1970; ed.3 1978 [p. 39]

Little, Meredith
(co-ed.) *Betwixt and Between: Patterns of Masculine and Feminine Initiation.* 1987 + p [p. 184]

Lockhart, Russell A. (1938–; Ph.D.; L.A. J. Inst. dipl.; Port Townsend, Wash., Jn. analyst)
Psyche Speaks: A Jungian Approach to Self and World. 1987 + p [p. 155]
(co-author) *Soul and Money.* 1982p; 1986p [p. 361]
Words as Eggs: Psyche in Language and Clinic. 1983p [p. 329]

Long, Constance E. (M.D.; Brit. Educ. Fund med. officer)
(ed.) *Collected Papers on Analytical Psychology.* 1916; ed.2 1917; 1920 [p. 21]

López-Pedraza, Rafael (Zurich J. Inst. study; Caracas Jn. therapist; U. lect.)
Cultural Anxiety. 1990p [p. 352]
Hermes and His Children. 1977p; 1989p [p. 313]

Lough, George (Ph.D.; Sherman Oaks, Calif., Jn.-oriented psychologist)
(co-author) *What Men Are Like.* 1988p [p. 188]

Lowen, Walter (1921–; D.Sc.; SUNY at Binghamton Sch. Adv. Tech. dir.)
Dichotomies of the Mind: A Systems Science Model of the Mind and Personality. 1982 [p. 71]

Lowenstein, Andrea
(co-author) *Archetypal Patterns in Women's Fiction.* 1981 + p [p. 270]

Luke, Helen M. (1904–; M.A.; London & Zurich Jn. studies; Jn. retreat founder)
Dark Wood to White Rose: A Study of the Meaning of Dante's Divine Comedy. 1975p [p. 262]
The Inner Story: Myth and Symbol in the Bible and Literature. 1982 [p. 272]
Old Age. 1987 + p [p. 114]
The Voice Within: Love and Virtue in the Age of the Spirit. 1984p [p. 233]
Woman, Earth, and Spirit: The Feminine in Symbol and Myth. 1981; 1986p [p. 174]

Mahdi, Louise Carus (M.A.; Zurich J. Inst. dipl.; Chicago Jn. analyst)
(co-ed.) *Betwixt and Between: Patterns of Masculine and Feminine Initiation.* 1987 + p [p. 184]

Mahoney, Maria F. (Springfield, Mass., journalist)
The Meaning in Dreams and Dreaming: The Jungian Viewpoint. 1966p [p. 140]

Malone, Michael
Psychetypes: A New Way of Exploring Personality. 1977; 1978p; 1980p [p. 69]

Mamchur, Carolyn Marie (1943–; Simon Fraser U. educ. prof.)
Insights: Understanding Yourself and Others. 1984p [p. 71]

Mankowitz, Ann (Ph.D.; Santa Fe Jn. analyst)
The Change of Life: A Psychological Study of Dreams and the Menopause. 1984p [p. 178]

Martin, Luther H. (1937–; U. Vermont relig. prof.)
(co-ed.) *Essays on Jung and the Study of Religion.* 1985 + p [p. 234]

Martin, P. W. (1893–1971); Intl. Study Center of Applied Psy. founder)
Experiment in Depth: A Study of the Work of Jung, Eliot, and Toynbee. 1955; 1976p; 1982 [p. 37]

Mattoon, Mary Ann (Ph.D.; Zurich J. Inst. dipl.; Minneapolis Jn. analyst)
(ed.) *The Archetype of Shadow in a Split World.* 1987 + p (1986 IAAP Congr.)
[p. 363]
Jungian Psychology in Perspective. 1981; 1982; 1986p [p. 47]
(ed.) *Personal and Archetypal Dynamics in the Analytical Relationship.* 1990
[p. 352]
Understanding Dreams (orig. *Applied Dream Analysis*). 1978; 1984p [p. 145]
McCaulley, Mary H.
(co-author) *Manual: A Guide to the Development and Use of the Myers-Briggs
Type Indicator.* 1985p [p. 68]
McCully, Robert S. (1921–; Ph.D.; N.Y. J. Inst. dipl.; Charleston, S.C., Jn.
analyst)
Jung and Rorschach: A Study in the Archetype of Perception. 1971; ed.2
1987p [p. 305]
McDonald, Phoebe (Long Beach counselor)
Dreams: Night Language of the Soul. 1985; 1987p [p. 151]
McGann, Diarmuid (M.S.; Bay Shore, N.Y., parish priest & counselor)
The Journeying Self: The Gospel of Mark through a Jungian Perspective.
1985p [p. 109]
*Journeying within Transcendence: A Jungian Perspective on the Gospel of
John.* 1988p [p. 117]
McGuire, William (1917–; M.A.; exec. ed. of Jung's *Collected Works*)
(ed.) *Analytical Psychology: Notes of the Seminar Given in 1925.* 1989 [p. 32]
(co-ed.) *C. G. Jung Speaking: Interviews and Encounters.* 1977; 1978; 1980p;
1986 + p [p. 26]
(ed.) *Dream Analysis: Notes of a Seminar Given in 1928–1930.* 1984 [p. 292]
(ed.) *The Freud/Jung Letters.* 1974; 1979p; 1988p [p. 25]
McNeely, Delton Anne (Ph.D.; Inter-Reg. J. dipl.; Lynchburg, Va., Jn. analyst)
Touching: Body Therapy and Depth Psychology. 1987p [p. 341]
Meckel, Daniel J. (M.A., U. of Chicago Div. School doct. cand.)
(co-ed.) *Jung and Christianity in Dialogue.* 1990p [p. 248]
Meier, C. A. (1903–; Zurich Jn. analyst; Swiss Fed. Inst. Tech. psy. prof.)
Ancient Incubation and Modern Psychotherapy. 1967 (Ger.: 1949) [p. 299]
Consciousness. 1989 + p; 1990p [p. 94]
Healing Dream and Ritual (reissue of *Ancient Incubation and Modern Psycho-
therapy*). 1989p [p. 299]
Jung's Analytical Psychology and Religion. 1959; 1977p [p. 209]
The Meaning and Significance of Dreams. 1987; 1990p (Ger.: 1972) [p. 142]
Soul and Body: Essays on the Theories of C. G. Jung. 1986 + p [p. 51]
A Testament to the Wilderness. 1985 + p [p. 363]
The Unconscious in Its Empirical Manifestations. 1984; 1990p (Ger.: 1968)
[p. 60]
Michael, Chester P. (Cath. monsignor)
(co-author) *Prayer and Temperament.* 1984p [p. 233]

Middelkoop, Pieter (1929–; Arnhem, Netherlands, psychotherapist)
The Wise Old Man: Healing through Images. 1989p (Dutch: 1985) [p. 334]
Miller, David L. (1936–; Ph.D.; Syracuse U. relig. prof.)
Christs: Meditations on Archetypal Images in Christian Theology. 1981 [p. 224]
Hells and Holy Ghosts: A Theopoetics of Christian Belief. 1989p [p. 246]
The New Polytheism: Rebirth of the Gods and Goddesses. 1974; ed.2 1981p [p. 217]
Three Faces of God: Traces of the Trinity in Literature and Life. 1986p [p. 239]
Miller, William A. (1931–; Ph.D.; Minneapolis pastoral counselor)
Make Friends with Your Shadow. 1981p [p. 102]
Mindell, Arnold (1940–; Ph.D.; Zurich J. Inst. dipl.; Zurich Jn. analyst)
Coma: Key to Awakening. 1989p [p. 346]
Dreambody: The Body's Role in Revealing the Self. 1982 + p; 1984p [p. 149]
The Dreambody in Relationships. 1987p; 1988p [p. 339]
River's Way: The Process Science of the Dreambody. 1985 + p [p. 152]
Working with the Dreaming Body. 1985 + p [p. 335]
The Year 1: Global Process at Work. 1990 [p. 366]
Miyuki, Mokusen (Ph.D.; Zurich J. Inst. dipl.; Montebello, Calif., Jn. analyst)
(co-author) *Buddhism and Jungian Psychology.* 1984; 1985p [p. 231]
Moacanin, Radmila (Ph.D.; L.A. psychotherapist; USC Med. Center therapist)
Jung's Psychology and Tibetan Buddhism. 1986p [p. 236]
Mogenson, Greg (1959–; M.A.; Calif. Family Study Center)
God Is a Trauma: Vicarious Religion and Soul-Making. 1989p [p. 246]
Monick, Eugene (1929–; Ph.D.; Zurich J. Inst. dipl.; N.Y./Scranton Jn. analyst)
Phallos: Sacred Image of the Masculine. 1987p [p. 186]
Monk, Patricia (1938; Ph.D.; Dalhousie U. Engl. Prof.)
The Smaller Infinity: The Jungian Self in the Novels of Robertson Davies. 1982 [p. 273]
Moon, Sheila (1910–; Ph.D.; Berkeley Jn. analyst)
Changing Woman and Her Sisters. 1985 + p [p. 180]
(co-author) *The Choicemaker* (orig. *Man, the Choicemaker*). 1973; 1977p [p. 92]
Dreams of a Woman: An Analyst's Inner Journey. 1983 + p [p. 105]
A Magic Dwells: A Poetic and Psychological Study of the Navaho Emergence Myth. 1970; 1985p [p. 215]
Mooney, Lucindi Frances
Storming Eastern Temples: A Psychological Exploration of Yoga. 1976 + p [p. 95]
Moore, Robert L. (Ph.D.; Chicago J. Inst. dipl.; U. Chicago relig. prof.)
(ed.) *Carl Jung and Christian Spirituality.* 1988p [p. 241]
(co-ed.) *Jung and Christianity in Dialogue.* 1990p [p. 248]
(co-ed.) *Jung's Challenge to Contemporary Religion.* 1987p [p. 239]

(co-author) *King, Warrior, Magician, Lover.* 1990 [p. 192]
Moore, Thomas W. (1940–; Ph.D.; Dallas psychotherapist)
   The Planets Within: Marsilio Ficino's Astrological Psychology. 1982 [p. 104]
Moorish, Ivor
   The Dark Twin: A Study of Evil—and Good. 1980p [p. 223]
Moreno, Antonio (1918–)
   Jung, Gods, and Modern Man. 1970; 1974+p [p. 214]
Morley, Patricia (1929–; Ph.D.; Concordia/Montreal Engl. prof.)
   Robertson Davies. 1977+p [p. 264]
Mudd, Peter (Chicago J. Inst. dipl.; Chicago J. Inst. exec. dir.; Evanston Jn.
   analyst)
   (ed.) *International Abstracts in Analytical Psychology:* 1986 (annual) [p. 51]
Murr, Priscilla (1942–; Ph.D.: Zurich J. Inst. dipl.; Austin, Tex. Jn. analyst)
   Shakespeare's Antony and Cleopatra. 1988p [p. 281]
Myers, Isabel Briggs (1898–1980; writer)
   (co-author) *Gifts Differing.* 1980+p [p. 70]
   (co-author) *Manual: A Guide to the Development and Use of the Myers-Briggs
   Type Indicator.* 1985p [p. 68]
Myers, Peter B.
   (co-author) *Gifts Differing.* 1980+p [p. 70]
Neumann, Erich (1905–60; M.D.; Ph.D.; studied with Jung; Tel Aviv Jn. analyst)
   Amor and Psyche: The Psychic Development of the Feminine. 1956; 1962p;
   1971p (Ger.: 1952) [p. 162]
   The Archetypal World of Henry Moore. 1959; 1965p; 1984p [p. 255]
   Art and the Creative Unconscious. 1959; 1961; 1971+p (Ger.: 1954) [p.
   254]
   The Child: Structure and Dynamics of the Nascent Personality. 1973; 1976;
   1988p (Ger.: 1963) [p. 87]
   Creative Man. 1979; 1982p [p. 266]
   Depth Psychology and a New Ethic. 1969; 1970; 1973p; 1990p (Ger.:
   1949) [p. 357]
   The Great Mother: An Analysis of the Archetype. 1955; ed.2 1963p; 1972p
   (Ger.: 1956) [p. 163]
   The Origins and History of Consciousness. 1954; 1962p; 1970+p; 1982p
   (Ger.: 1949) [p. 84]
   The Place of Creation. 1988 [p. 281]
New England Society of Jungian Analysts
   (ed.) *Analytic Life: Personal and Professional Aspects of Being a Jungian
   Analyst.* 1989p [p. 346]
Newman, Kenneth D. (M.A.; Zurich J. Inst. dipl.; Jerusalem Jn. analyst)
   The Tarot: A Myth of Male Initiation. 1983p [p. 106]
Nichols, Sallie (Zurich J. Inst. study; Santa Monica therapist)
   Jung and Tarot: An Archetypal Journey. 1980; 1984p [p. 99]
Nicoll, Maurice (1884–1953)

Dream Psychology. 1917; ed.2 1920; 1979p [p. 133]
Nordby, Vernon J. (U. Cal. at Santa Cruz prof.)
(co-author) *A Primer of Jungian Psychology.* 1973p [p. 43]
Norrissey, Marie C. (*The Open Door* ed.)
(co-author) *Prayer and Temperament.* 1984p [p. 233]
Oakes, Maud (1903–90; anthropologist & artist)
The Stone Speaks: The Memoir of a Personal Transformation. 1987 + p [p. 115]
(co-author) *The Wisdom of the Serpent.* 1963; 1963p; 1971p; 1990p [p. 88]
O'Connor, Peter (1938–; Ph.D.; Melbourne, Australia, psychotherapist)
Dreams and the Search for Meaning. 1986; 1987p [p. 155]
Understanding Jung, Understanding Yourself. 1985; 1986p [p. 51]
Understanding the Mid-Life Crisis. 1981; 1988p [p. 102]
Odajnyk, V. Walter (1938–; Ph.D.; Zurich J. Inst. dipl.; N.Y. Jn. analyst)
Jung and Politics: Political and Social Ideas of C. G. Jung. 1976 + p [p. 359]
Olderr, Steven
(comp.) *Symbolism: A Comprehensive Dictionary.* 1986 [p. 154]
Olds, Linda E. (Ph.D.; Linfield C. psy. prof.)
Fully Human: How Everyone Can Integrate the Benefits of Masculine and Feminine Sex Roles. 1981 + p [p. 173]
Olney, James (1933–; Ph.D.; Lousiana State U. Engl. prof.)
Metaphors of Self: The Meaning of Autobiography. 1972 + p [p. 11]
The Rhizome and the Flower: The Perennial Philosophy—Yeats and Jung. 1980 [p. 47]
O'Neill, Timothy R. (1943–; Ph.D.; U.S. Mil. Acad. behavioral sci. prof.)
The Individuated Hobbit: Jung, Tolkien and the Archetypes of Middle-earth. 1979; 1980 [p. 98]
Oppenheim, James (1882–1932; writer)
The Psychology of Jung. 1925p [p. 34]
Papadopoulos, Renos K. (Ph.D.; London Jn. analyst; NHS clin. psychologist)
(co-ed.) *Jung in Modern Perspective.* 1984 [p. 49]
Paris, Ginette (1946–; Ph.D.; U. Quebec soc. psychologist)
Pagan Meditations: The Worlds of Aphrodite, Artemis, and Hestia. 1986p [p. 184]
Parker, Thomas E. (Ph.D.; S.F. J. Inst. dipl.; Cardiff-by-the-Sea, Calif., Jn. analyst)
Return: Beyond the Self. 1979p [p. 98]
Parsifal-Charles, Nancy (M.A.; Chapel Hill, N.C., ed.)
The Dream: Four Thousand Years of Theory and Practice; A Critical, Descriptive, and Encyclopedic Bibliography. 1986 [p. 152]
Pauli, Wolfgang (1900–58; Nobel Prize physicist)
(co-author) *The Interpretation of Nature and the Psyche.* 1955. [p. 79]
Pauson, Marian (Ph.D.; Zurich J. Inst. study; Old Dominion U. philos. prof.)
Jung the Philosopher: Essays in Jungian Thought. 1989 [p. 120]

Pearson, Carol S. (1944–; Ph.D.; U. Maryland prof.)
The Hero Within: Six Archetypes to Live By. 1986p [p. 111]
Peat, David (1938–; Ph.D.; Queen's U. physics prof.)
Synchronicity: The Bridge between Matter and Mind. 1987p [p. 115]
Perera, Sylvia Brinton (1932–; M.A.; N.Y. J. Inst. dipl.; N.Y. Jn. analyst)
Descent to the Goddess: A Way of Initiation for Women. 1981p [p. 172]
(co-author) *Dreams, A Portal to the Source.* 1989 [p. 347]
The Scapegoat Complex: Toward a Mythology of Shadow and Guilt. 1986p [p. 338]
Perry, John Weir (1914–; M.D.; Zurich J. Inst. study; San Francisco psychoanalyst)
The Far Side of Madness. 1974 + p; 1989p [p. 309]
The Heart of History: Individuality in Evolution. 1987 + p [p. 363]
Lord of the Four Quarters: Myths of the Royal Father. 1966; 1970p [p. 165]
Roots of Renewal in Myth and Madness. 1976 [p. 311]
The Self in Psychotic Process: Symbolization in Schizophrenia. 1953; 1954; 1987p [p. 300]
Philipson, Morris H. (1926–; Ph.D.; U. Chicago Press dir.)
Outline of a Jungian Aesthetics. 1963 [p. 257]
Phillips, Dorothy Berkley (1906–85; counselor; student of Jung's psychology)
(ed.) *The Choice Is Always Ours.* 1948; rev. 1960; 1975p; 1989p [p. 83]
Philp, Howard L.
Jung and the Problem of Evil. 1958; 1959; 1974 [p. 209]
Plaut, Fred C. (M.D.; London Jn. analyst)
(co-ed.) *A Critical Dictionary of Jungian Analysis.* 1986 + p [p. 336]
Poncé, Charles (Ph.D.; San Francisco psychotherapist)
The Archetype of the Unconscious. 1990p [p. 65]
Papers toward a Radical Metaphysics: Alchemy. 1983 + p [p. 150]
Working the Soul: Reflections on Jungian Psychology. 1988p [p. 150]
Pratt, Annis (Ph.D.; U. Wisconsin Engl. prof.)
(co-author) *Archetypal Patterns in Women's Fiction.* 1981 + p [p. 270]
Progoff, Ira (1921–; Ph.D.; studied with Jung; N.Y. psychotherapist)
The Death and Rebirth of Psychology. 1956; 1964p; 1973p; 1983 [p. 38]
Depth Psychology and Modern Man. 1959; ed.2 1969; 1973p; 1983 [p. 86]
Jung, Synchronicity, and Human Destiny. 1973; 1975p; 1987p [p. 93]
Jung's Psychology and Its Social Meaning. 1953; 1955p; ed.2 1969; 1973p; ed.3 1985p [p. 358]
The Symbolic and the Real. 1963; 1973p; 1977 + 3; 1983 [p. 88]
Provost, Judith A. (1942–; Ed.D.; college personal counselor)
A Casebook: Applications of the MBTI in Counseling. 1984p [p. 330]
Qualls-Corbett, Nancy (Ph.D.; Zurich J. Inst. dipl.; Birmingham, Ala., Jn. analyst)
The Sacred Prostitute: Eternal Aspect of the Feminine. 1988p [p. 187]
Quenk, Alex T. (Ph.D.; Albuquerque Jn. therapist; U. New Mexico psychi. prof.)

Psychological Types and Psychotherapy. 1984p [p. 331]
Radin, Paul (1883–1959; Ph.D.; anthropologist)
   The Trickster: Study in American Indian Mythology. 1956; ed.2 1972p (Ger.:
   1955) [p. 58]
Raine, Kathleen (1908–; M.A.; London poet)
   The Human Face of God: William Blake and the Book of Job. 1982 [p. 227]
Rathbauer-Vincie, Margreta
   (co-author) *C. G. Jung and Analytical Psychology: A Comprehensive Biblio-
   graphy.* 1977 [p. 45]
Read, (Sir) Herbert (1893–1968; M.A.; poet & art historian; co-ed. of Jung's
   Collected Works)
   The Forms of Things Unknown: Essays toward an Aesthetic Philosophy. 1960;
   1965p [p. 256]
   *Icon and Idea: The Function of Love in the Development of Human Conscious-
   ness.* 1955; 1965p [p. 255]
Redfearn, J. W. T. (London Society of Analytical Psy. dir. of training)
   My Self, My Many Selves. 1985 [p. 110]
Reed, Jeannette Pruyn (clin. psychologist; studied with Dora Kalff)
   *Emergence: Essays on the Process of Individuation through Sand Therapy, Art
   Forms, and Dreams.* 1980p [p. 99]
Reid, Clyde H. (Ph.D.; Zurich J. Inst. study; Colorado pastor and therapist)
   Dreams: Discovering Your Inner Teacher. 1983p [p. 149]
   The Return to Faith: Finding God in the Unconscious. 1974 [p. 218]
Ribi, Alfred (Dr.Med., Meilen, Switzerland, Jn. analyst)
   Demons of the Inner World. 1990p [p. 65]
Richards, David G. (1935–; Ph.D.; SUNY at Buffalo mod. lang. and lit. prof.)
   The Hero's Quest for the Self: An Archetypal Approach to Hesse's Demian
   and Other Novels. 1987 + p [p. 278]
Roberts, Richard (1941–)
   From Eden to Eros: Origins of the Put Down of Women. 1985p [p. 182]
   The Original Tarot and You. 1971; 1987p [p. 91]
   Tales for Jung Folk. 1983 + p [p. 274]
   (co-author) *Tarot Revelations.* 1980p; ed.2 1982p; ed.3 1987p [p. 100]
Robertson, Robin (1944–; Ph.D.; L.A. psychologist)
   After the End of Time. 1990p [p. 122]
   C. G. Jung and the Archetypes of the Collective Unconscious. 1987 [p. 64]
Robertson, Seonaid M. (London psychologist)
   Rosegarden and Labyrinth: A Study in Art Education. 1963; 1982p [p. 257]
Rohrbach, Elizabeth C.
   (ed.) *Jung's Contribution to Our Times: Collected Papers of Eleanor Bertine.*
   1967 [p. 358]
Rolfe, Eugene
   Encounter with Jung. 1989 + p [p. 17]
Rollins, Wayne Gilbert (Ph.D.; Assumption C. relig. prof.)

Jung and the Bible. 1983p [p. 230]

Rossi, Ernest Lawrence (Ph.D.; L.A./Malibu Jn. analyst)
Dreams and the Growth of Personality. 1972; ed.2 1985 [p. 307]
The Psychobiology of Mind-Body Healing. 1986; 1988p [p. 337]

Rothenberg, Rose-Emily (M.A.; Pacific Palisades Jn. analyst)
(co-ed.) *The Well of Living Waters.* 1977p [p. 360]

Rothgeb, Carrie Lee (1925–; Nat. Clearinghouse for Mental Health Info. chief)
(ed.) *Abstracts of the Collected Works of C. G. Jung.* 1978p [p. 27]

Rudhyar, Dane (1895–1986; Calif. astrologer, composer, artist & poet)
Astrology and the Modern Psyche. 1976p [p. 94]

Rudin, Josef (1907–; Jesuit priest; Innsbruck pastoral psy. prof.)
Psychotherapy and Religion. 1968 + p (Ger.: 1960) [p. 210]

Rupprecht, Carol Schreier (Ph.D.; Hamilton C. lit. prof.)
(co-ed.) *Feminist Archetypal Theory.* 1985 [p. 182]

Ryce-Menuhin, Joel (M.Phil.; London Jn. analyst; *Harvest* ed.)
The Self in Early Childhood. 1988 + p [p. 118]

Saayman, Graham S. (Ph.D.; Sudbury, Ontario, hosp. psy. serv. head)
(co-ed.) *Jung in Modern Perspective.* 1984 [p. 49]
(ed.) *Modern South Africa in Search of a Soul.* 1990p [p. 366]

Saliba, David R. (Ph.D.; U. Texas at San Antonio Am. lit. prof.)
A Psychology of Fear: The Nightmare Formula of Edgar Allen Poe. 1980 + p [p. 269]

Samuels, Andrew (1949–; London Jn. analyst)
(co-ed.) *A Critical Dictionary of Jungian Analysis.* 1986 + p [p. 336]
(ed.) *The Father: Contemporary Jungian Perspectives.* 1985 + p; 1986; 1988p [p. 181]
Jung and the Post-Jungians. 1985; 1986p [p. 50]
The Plural Psyche: Personality, Morality, and the Father. 1989 + p [p. 349]
(ed.) *Psychopathology: Contemporary Jungian Perspectives.* 1989p [p. 350]

Sandner, Donald R. (M.D.; S.F. Jn. analyst)
Navaho Symbols of Healing. 1979p [p. 318]

Sanford, John A. (1930–; B.D.; Zurich J. Inst. study; San Diego Jn. analyst)
Dreams: God's Forgotten Language. 1968; 1982p; 1986p; 1989p (Ger.: 1966) [p. 140]
Dreams and Healing. 1978p [p. 315]
Evil: The Shadow Side of Reality. 1981; 1987p [p. 224]
(ed.) *Fritz Kunkel: Selected Writings.* 1984p [p. 232]
Healing and Wholeness. 1977 + p [p. 313]
The Invisible Partners: How the Male and Female in Each of Us Affects Our Relationships. 1980p [p. 171]
King Saul, the Tragic Hero: A Study in Individuation. 1985p [p. 110]
The Kingdom Within: A Study of the Inner Meaning of Jesus' Sayings. 1970p; 1980p; rev. 1987p [p. 214]
The Man Who Wrestled with God: Light from the Old Testament on the Psychology of Individuation. 1974; 1981p; 1987p [p. 93]

The Strange Trial of Mr. Hyde: A New Look at the Nature of Human Evil.
1987 [p. 240]
(co-author) *What Men Are Like.* 1988p [p. 188]
Santa Maria, Maria L. (D.Min.; St. Petersburg, Fla., psychotherapist)
Growth through Meditation and Journal Writing. 1983p [p. 230]
Sasportas, Howard (London astrologer & therapist)
(co-author) *The Development of the Personality.* 1987p [p. 113]
(co-author) *Dynamics of the Unconscious.* 1988p [p. 116]
Savage, Judith A. (St. Paul Jn. analyst)
Mourning Unlived Lives: A Psychological Study of Childbearing Loss.
1989p [p. 349]
Savary, Louis M. (Ph.D.; S.T.D.)
(co-author) *Dreams and Spiritual Growth.* 1984p [p. 232]
Schaer, Hans (1910–68; U. Bern church hist. & psy. of relig. prof.)
Religion and the Cure of Souls in Jung's Psychology. 1950; 1951; 1966 (Ger.:
1946) [p. 204]
Schapira, Laurie Layton (1949–; M.S.; N.Y. J. Inst. dipl.; N.Y. Jn. analyst)
The Cassandra Complex: Living with Disbelief. 1988p [p. 342]
Schectman, Jacqueline M. (Boston J. Inst. dipl.; Boston Jn. analyst)
The Step-Mother in Fairy Tales. 1990p [p. 193]
Schellenbaum, Peter (1939–; Dr. theol.; Zurich Jn. analyst)
How to Say No to the One You Love. 1987 (Ger.: 1984) [p. 179]
Schultz, Duane (Ph.D.; U. South Florida adjunct psy. prof.)
Intimate Friends, Dangerous Rivals. 1990+p [p. 53]
Schwartz-Salant, Nathan (1938–; Ph.D.; Zurich J. Inst. dipl.; N.Y. Jn. analyst)
(co-ed.) *Abandonment.* 1985p [p. 332]
(co-ed.) *Archetypal Processes in Psychotherapy.* 1987p [p. 339]
(co-ed.) *The Body in Analysis.* 1986p [p. 335]
The Borderline Personality: Vision and Healing. 1988 + p [p. 341]
(co-ed.) *The Borderline Personality in Analysis.* 1988p [p. 342]
(co-ed.) *Dreams in Analysis.* 1989p [p. 347]
Narcissism and Character Transformation. 1982p [p. 325]
(co-ed.) *Transference/Countertransference.* 1984p [p. 332]
Scott-Maxwell, Florida (1883–1979; studied with Jung; Scot. psychologist)
Women and Sometimes Men. 1957; 1971p [p. 164]
Segaller, Stephen (documentary writer/producer)
(co-author) *The Wisdom of the Dream: The World of C. G. Jung.* 1989 [p.
18]
Seifert, Theodor (1921–; Ph.D.; Stuttgart Jn. analyst)
Snow White: Life Almost Lost. 1986p [p. 274]
Serrano, Miguel (1917–; Chilean diplomat)
C. G. Jung and Hermann Hesse: A Record of Two Friendships. 1966; 1968p;
1971p [p. 9]
The Visits of the Queen of Sheba. 1960; 1972; 1973p; 1974 [p. 138]

Shapiro, Kenneth Joel (Ph.D.; Bates C. psy. prof.)
(co-author) *The Experience of Introversion.* 1975 [p. 61]
Sharp, Daryl (1936–; M.A.; Zurich J. Inst. dipl.; Toronto Jn. analyst; ed.)
Dear Gladys: The Survival Papers, Book 2. 1989p [p. 120]
Personality Types: Jung's Model of Typology. 1987p [p. 72]
The Secret Raven: Conflict and Transformation in the Life of Franz Kafka. 1980p [p. 100]
The Survival Papers: Anatomy of a Midlife Crisis. 1988p [p. 119]
Shelburne, Walter A. (San Jose, Calif.: Applied Philos. Inst. founding member)
Mythos and Logos in the Thought of Carl Jung. 1988 + p [p. 64]
Shorter, Bani (M.A.; Zurich J. Inst. dipl.; London Jn. analyst)
(co-ed.) *A Critical Dictionary of Jungian Analysis.* 1986 + p [p. 336]
An Image Darkly Forming: Women and Initiation. 1987p [p. 185]
Sibbald, Luella (1907–; Zurich J. Inst. study; Berkeley analyst & astrologer)
The Footprints of God: The Relationship of Astrology, C. G. Jung, and the Gospels. 1988p [p. 117]
Sidoli, Mara (London Soc. An. Psy. child-analysis training; Santa Fe analyst)
(co-ed.) *Jungian Child Psychotherapy: Individuation in Childhood.* 1988p [p. 344]
The Unfolding Self: Separation and Individuation. 1989 + p [p. 121]
Signell, Karen A. (Ph.D., San Francisco Jn. analyst)
Wisdom of the Heart. 1990p [p. 156]
Singer, June (Ph.D.; Zurich J. Inst. dipl.; San Francisco/Palo Alto Jn. analyst)
Androgyny: The Opposites Within. 1976; 1977p; 1989p [p. 169]
Boundaries of the Soul: The Practice of Jung's Psychology. 1972; 1973p; 1975 [p. 306]
Energies of Love: Sexuality Re-Visioned. 1983; 1990p [p. 177]
Seeing Through the Visible World. 1990 [p. 249]
The Unholy Bible: Blake, Jung, and the Collective Unconscious. 1970; 1972p; 1986 + p [p. 260]
Slusser, Gerald H. (1920–; Ph.D.: Eden Theol. Sem. theol. & educ. prof.)
From Jung to Jesus: Myth and Consciousness in the New Testament. 1986p [p. 111]
Smart, Frances (1909–68; Zurich J. Inst. dipl.; London Jn. analyst)
Neurosis and Crime. 1970 [p. 304]
Smith, Curtis D. (Ph.D.)
Jung's Quest for Wholeness: Religious and Historical Perspective. 1990 [p. 248]
Spiegelman, J. Marvin (1926–; Ph.D.; Zurich J. Inst. dipl., L.A. Jn. analyst)
(co-author) *Buddhism and Jungian Psychology.* 1984; 1985p [p. 231]
(ed.) *Catholicism and Jungian Psychology.* 1988p [p. 242]
(co-author) *Hinduism and Jungian Psychology.* 1987p [p. 239]
(ed.) *Jungian Analysts: Their Visions and Vulnerabilities.* 1988p [p. 344]
The Knight: The Theory and Method of Jung's Active Imagination Technique. 1982p [p. 149]

The Nymphomaniac. 1985p [p. 276]
The Quest. 1984p [p. 276]
(co-author) *Sufism and Jungian Psychology.* 1990 [p. 249]
The Tree: A Jungian Journey; Tales in Psycho-Mythology. 1974; ed.2. 1982+p [p. 262]
Spier, Julius
    The Hands of Children: Introduction to Psycho-Chirology. 1944; ed.2 1955 [p. 133]
Spignesi, Angelyn (Ph.D.; N.Y. J. Inst. lect.)
    Lyrical-Analysis. 1990p [p. 285]
    Starving Women: A Psychology of Anorexia Nervosa. 1983p [p. 328]
Spoto, Angelo (Tampa therapist; Jung Libr. & Info. Center founder)
    Jung's Typology in Perspective. 1990+p [p. 73]
Staude, John-Raphael (Ph.D.; Zurich J. Inst. study; Proteus Inst. dir.)
    The Adult Development of C. G. Jung. 1981 [p. 14]
Steele, Robert S.
    Freud and Jung: Conflicts of Interpretation. 1982 [p. 48]
Stein, Charles (1944–)
    The Secret of the Black Chrysanthemum. 1987 [p. 279]
Stein, Murray (1943–; Ph.D.; Zurich J. Inst. dipl.; Wilmette, Ill., Jn. analyst)
    (co-ed.) *Abandonment.* 1985p [p. 332]
    (co-ed.) *Archetypal Processes in Psychotherapy.* 1987p [p. 339]
    (co-ed.) *The Body in Analysis.* 1986p [p. 335]
    (co-ed.) *The Borderline Personality in Analysis.* 1988p [p. 342]
    (co-ed.) *Dreams in Analysis.* 1989p [p. 347]
    In MidLife: A Jungian Perspective. 1983p [p. 106]
    (ed.) *Jungian Analysis.* 1982; 1984p [p. 324]
    (co-ed.) *Jung's Challenge to Contemporary Religion.* 1987p [p. 239]
    Jung's Treatment of Christianity. 1985; 1986p [p. 235]
    (co-ed.) *Transference/Countertransference.* 1984p [p. 332]
Stein, Robert (1924–; M.D.; Zurich J. Inst. dipl.; Beverly Hills Jn. analyst)
    Incest and Human Love: Betrayal of the Soul in Psychotherapy. 1973; 1974p; ed.2 1984p [p. 308]
Steinberg, Warren (1944–; Ph.D.; N.Y. J. Inst. dipl.; N.Y. Jn. analyst)
    Circle of Care: Clinical Issues in Jungian Therapy. 1990p [p. 351]
Stern, E. Mark (1929–; Ed.D.; Iona C. counseling prof.)
    (ed.) *Carl Jung and Soul Psychology.* 1986 [p. 336]
Stern, Paul J. (1921–; Cambridge, Mass., psychotherapist)
    C. G. Jung: Haunted Prophet. 1976+p; 1977p [p. 12]
Steuernagel, Gertrude A. (Kent State U. pol. sci. prof.)
    Political Philosophy as Therapy. 1979 [p. 360]
Stevens, Anthony (M.D.; London psychotherapist)
    Archetypes: A Natural History of the Self. 1982; 1983p [p. 63]
    On Jung. 1990 [p. 53]

The Roots of War: A Jungian Perspective. 1989 + p [p. 365]
Withymead: A Jungian Community for the Healing Arts. 1986p [p. 338]
Stolorow, Robert D. (Ph.D.)
(co-author) *Faces in a Cloud: Subjectivity in Personality Theory.* 1979 [p. 70]
Storr, Anthony (1920–; M.D.; Oxford psychiatrist; Oxford U. psychi. lect.)
The Art of Psychotherapy. 1979; 1980p; 1989p [p. 317]
C. G. Jung (orig. *Jung*). 1973 + p; 1986p [p. 11]
(ed.) *The Essential Jung* (orig. *Jung: Selected Writings*). 1983 + p; 1986p [p. 27]
The Integrity of the Personality. 1960; 1963p; 1970p [p. 301]
Solitude (Brit.: *The School of Genius*). 1988; 1989p [p. 119]
Streatfeild, D.
Persephone: A Study of Two Worlds. 1959 [p. 137]
Stroud, Joanne
(co-ed.) *Images of the Untouched: Virginity in Psyche, Myth, and Community.* 1982p [p. 175]
Sullivan, Barbara Stevens (1943–; S.F. J. Inst. dipl.; Berkeley Jn. analyst)
Psychotherapy Grounded in the Feminine Principle. 1989p [p. 350]
Suzuki, Daisetz (1870–1966; D.Litt.; Otahi U. Buddhist philos. prof.)
An Introduction to Zen Buddhism. 1949; 1959p; 1964p; 1969p; 1974; 1983p; 1986p; 1987p (Japan.: 1934) [p. 202]
Szemborski, Chester P.
The Wisdom of Jung; A Theory of Personality. 1978p [p. 45]
Taub-Bynum, E. Bruce (1948–)
The Family Unconscious: An "Invisible Bond". 1984p [p. 63]
Te Paske, Bradley A. (1951–; M.F.A.; Sante Fe Jn. analyst)
Rape and Ritual: A Psychological Study. 1982p [p. 326]
Thomas, Gail
(co-ed.) *Images of the Untouched: Virginity in Psyche, Myth, and Community.* 1982p [p. 175]
Thompson, Helen (relig. prof.)
Journey toward Wholeness: A Jungian Model of Adult Spiritual Growth. 1982p [p. 104]
Thompson, Magdala (Ph.D.; Sister of Mercy; Auburn U. career counselor)
(co-author) *From Image to Likeness: A Jungian Path in the Gospel Journey.* 1983p [p. 106]
Thornton, Edward (1907–; Yorkshire merchant; visited Jung irreg. 1947–51)
The Diary of a Mystic. 1967 [p. 213]
Thuesen, Janet M. (MBTI authoriz. trainer; counselor)
(co-author) *Type Talk.* 1988p [p. 73]
Toor, Djohariah (artist; marriage & family counseling center dir.)
The Road by the River: A Healing Journey for Women. 1987; 1990p [p. 186]
Tuby, Molly (London Jn. analyst)
(ed.) *In the Wake of Jung: A Selection from Harvest.* 1983p [p. 49]

Turner, Dixie M. (M.A.; Olivet Nazarene C. Engl. prof.)
  A Jungian Psychoanalytic Interpretation of William Faulkner's As I Lay Dying.
  1981+p [p. 271]
Ulanov, Ann Belford (Ph.D.; Union Theol. Sem. rel. & psy. prof.; N.Y. Jn.
  analyst)
  (co-author) *Cinderella and Her Sisters: The Envied and the Envying.* 1983p [p.
  176]
  The Feminine in Jungian Psychology and in Christian Theology. 1971;
  1980p [p. 166]
  Picturing God. 1986p [p. 238]
  (co-author) *Primary Speech: A Psychology of Prayer.* 1982p; 1985p [p. 228]
  Receiving Woman: Studies in the Psychology and Theology of the Feminine.
  1981p [p. 173]
  (co-author) *Religion and the Unconscious.* 1975; ed. 2 1985p [p. 218]
  The Wisdom of the Psyche. 1988p [p. 245]
  (co-author) *The Witch and the Clown: Archetypes of Human Sexuality.*
  1987p [p. 187]
Ulanov, Barry (1918–; Ph.D.; Barnard C. Engl.prof. arts chair)
  (co-author) *Cinderella and Her Sisters: The Envied and the Envying.* 1983p [p.
  176]
  (co-author) *Primary Speech: A Psychology of Prayer.* 1982; 1985p [p. 228]
  (co-author) *Religion and the Unconscious.* 1975; ed.2 1985p [p. 218]
  (co-author) *The Witch and the Clown: Archetypes of Human Sexuality.*
  1987p [p. 187]
van der Hoop, Johannes Germanus (1887–?; Amsterdam U. lect.)
  *Character and the Unconscious: A Critical Exposition of the Psychology of
  Freud and Jung.* 1923 [p. 57]
van der Post, (Sir) Laurens (1906–; S. African explorer-writer; friend of Jung)
  Jung and the Story of Our Time. 1975; 1976; 1977p; 1978p [p. 12]
  A Walk with a White Bushman. 1986; 1988p [p. 17]
van Meurs, Jos (1925–; U. Groningen Engl. & Am. lit. prof.)
  *Jungian Literary Criticism 1928–1980: An Annotated, Critical Bibliography
  of Works in English.* 1988 [p. 280]
van Waveren, Erlo (studied with Jung; N.Y. Jn. analyst)
  Pilgrimage to the Rebirth. 1978p [p. 96]
Vasada, Arwind U. (D. Litt.; Zurich J. Inst. dipl.; Chicago Jn. analyst)
  (co-author) *Hinduism and Jungian Psychology.* 1987p [p. 239]
Vincie, Joseph F. (Ph.D.)
  (co-author) *C. G. Jung and Analytical Psychology: A Comprehensive Bibliography.* 1977 [p. 45]
von der Heydt, (Baroness) Vera (1899–; London Jn. analyst)
  Prospects for the Soul: Soundings in Jungian Psychology and Religion.
  1976 [p. 219]
von Franz, Marie-Louise (1915–; Ph.D.; studied with Jung; Zurich Jn. analyst)

Alchemical Active Imagination. 1979p [p. 146]
Alchemy: An Introduction to the Symbolism and the Psychology. 1980p [p. 146]
(ed.) *Aurora Consurgens.* 1966 (Ger.: 1957) [p. 136]
C. G. Jung: His Myth in Our Time. 1975; 1977p (Ger.: 1972) [p. 10]
(co-author) *The Grail Legend.* 1970; 1971; ed.2 1986p (Ger.: 1960) [p. 256]
Individuation in Fairy Tales. 1977p; 1982p [p. 95]
An Introduction to the Interpretation of Fairy Tales. 1970p; 1972p; 1987p [p. 259]
(co-author) *Lectures on Jung's Typology.* 1971p; 1979p; 1986p [p. 68]
Number and Time. 1974 + p (Ger.: 1970) [p. 61]
On Divination and Synchronicity. 1980p [p. 99]
On Dreams and Death. 1986; 1987p (Ger.: 1984) [p. 150]
The Passion of Perpetua. 1980p (orig. 1949) [p. 206]
Patterns of Creativity Mirrored in Creation Myths. 1972p; 1986p [p. 260]
Problems of the Feminine in Fairy Tales. 1972p; 1976p; 1986p [p. 167]
Projection and Re-Collection in Jungian Psychology. 1980; 1985p (Ger.: 1978) [p. 96]
Psychological Interpretation of The Golden Ass *of Apuleius.* 1970p; 1980p [p. 259]
Psychological Meaning of Redemption Motifs in Fairy Tales. 1980p [p. 269]
Puer Aeternus. 1970p; ed.2 1981 + p [p. 166]
Shadow and Evil in Fairy Tales. 1974p; 1987p [p. 262]
Time: Rhythm and Repose. 1978p; 1983 [p. 62]
(co-author) *Timeless Documents of the Soul.* 1968 (Ger.: 1952) [p. 135]
(co-author) *The Way of the Dream.* 1987 [p. 155]
Wallis, Jack H. (Brit. marital & psy. counselor)
Jung and the Quaker Way. 1988p [p. 243]
Washbourn, Penelope (1944–; Union Theol. Sem. study; Jn. analysis)
Becoming Woman: Quest for Wholeness in Female Experience. 1976; 1979p [p. 169]
Watkins, Mary M. (1951–; Ph.D.; Zurich J. Inst. study; Cambridge, Mass., psychologist)
Invisible Guests: Development of Imaginal Dialogues. 1986; 1990p [p. 153]
Waking Dreams. 1976; 1977p; 1984p; 1986p [p. 144]
Weaver, Rix (1902–?; W. Australia Jn. analyst)
The Old Wise Woman: A Study in Active Imagination. 1964; 1973; 1991p [p. 139]
Weber, Christin Lore (D.Min.; relig. counselor)
WomanChrist: A New Vision of Feminist Spirituality. 1987p [p. 241]
Wehr, Demaris S. (Ph.D.; Cambridge, Mass., Episc. Theol. Sem. relig. & psy. prof.)
Jung and Feminism: Liberating Archetypes. 1987; 1989p [p. 185]
Wehr, Gerhard (1931–; Rummelberg bei Nürnberg Diocesan Sch. teacher)

An Illustrated Biography of C. G. Jung. 1989 [p. 18]
Jung: A Biography. 1987; 1988p (Ger.: 1985) [p. 16]
Portrait of Jung: An Illustrated Biography. 1971 + p (Ger.: 1969) [p. 10]
Weinrib, Estelle L. (M.S.W.; N.Y. J. Inst. dipl.; N.Y. Jn. analyst)
  Images of the Self: The Sandplay Therapy Process. 1983 + p [p. 327]
Welch, John (Ph.D.; Carmelite; Washington Theol. Union relig. prof.)
  Spiritual Pilgrims: Carl Jung and Teresa of Ávila. 1982p [p. 229]
Werblowsky, R. J. Zwi (1924–; Jerusalem, Hebrew U. humanities dean)
  Lucifer and Prometheus: A Study of Milton's Satan. 1952; 1977p; 1978 [p. 254]
Wesley, David
  (co-ed.) *The Well of Living Waters: A Festschrift for Hilde Kirsch.* 1977p [p. 360]
Westman, Heinz (1902–86; N.Y. Jn. analyst)
  The Springs of Creativity: The Bible and the Creative Process of the Psyche. 1961; ed.2 1986p [p. 212]
  The Structure of Biblical Myths. 1983p; 1984 [p. 231]
Wheelwright, Jane Hollister (studied with Jung; San Francisco Jn. analyst)
  The Death of a Woman. 1981 [p. 102]
  For Women Growing Older: The Animus. 1984p [p. 179]
Wheelwright, Joseph B. (1906–; M.D.; studied with Jung; San Francisco Jn. analyst)
  (ed.) *The Analytic Process: Aims, Analysis, Training.* 1971 (1968 IAAP Congress) [p. 304]
  (ed.) *The Reality of the Psyche.* 1968 (1965 IAAP Congress) [p. 59]
  St. George and the Dandelion: Forty Years of Practice as a Jungian Analyst. 1982 [p. 326]
White, Barbara
  (co-author) *Archetypal Patterns in Women's Fiction.* 1981 + p [p. 270]
White, Victor (1902–60; Dominican priest; Oxford U. theol. lect.)
  God and the Unconscious. 1952; 1953; 1960p; 1961p; 1967p;1982p [p. 206]
  Soul and Psyche: An Enquiry into the Relationship of Psychotherapy and Religion. 1960 [p. 211]
Whitman, Allen (D.D.; Episc. rector; Zurich J. Inst. study)
  Fairy Tales and the Kingdom of God. 1983p [p. 274]
Whitmont, Edward C. (1912–; M.D.; Jn. training with Harding; N.Y. Jn. analyst)
  (co-author) *Dreams, a Portal to the Source.* 1989 [p. 347]
  Psyche and Substance: Essays on Homeopathy in the Light of Jungian Psychology. 1980; 1983p [p. 321]
  Return of the Goddess. 1982; 1983p; 1984p; 1986p; 1987p [p. 175]
  The Symbolic Quest: Basic Concepts of Analytical Psychology. 1969; 1973p; 1978 + p [p. 42]
Wickes, Frances G. (1874–1967; studied with Jung; N.Y. child psychotherapist)

The Inner World of Childhood: A Study in Analytical Psychology. 1927; 1930; rev. 1966; 1968p; 1977p; 1978 + p; 1988 + p [p. 81]

The Inner World of Choice. 1963; 1976p; 1977p; 1988p [p. 88]

The Inner World of Man. 1938; 1948; 1950; 1959; 1988p [p. 81]

Wiedemann, Florence L. (Ph.D.; Inter-Reg. Jn. dipl.; Dallas Jn. analyst)

(co-author) *Female Authority: Empowering Women through Psychotherapy.* 1987 [p. 340]

Wilhelm, Richard (1873–1930; Munich Sinologist)

(tr.) *The I Ching.* 1950; 1951; ed.2 1965; ed.3 1967; 1968; 1988p [p. 85]

(co-author) *The Secret of the Golden Flower.* 1931; rev. 1962p; 1970p; 1975; 1984p (Ger.: 1929) [p. 127]

Willeford, William (Ph.D.; Zurich J. Inst. dipl.; Seattle Jn. analyst)

Feeling, Imagination, and the Self: Transformations of the Mother-Infant Relationship. 1987 + p [p. 113]

The Fool and His Scepter. 1969 + p [p. 141]

Williams, Donald Lee (1943–; Zurich J. Inst. dipl.; Boulder Jn. analyst)

Border Crossings: Carlos Castaneda's Path to Knowledge. 1981p [p. 101]

Wilmer, Harry A. (1917–; M.D.; Ph.D.; mil. psychiatrist; Salado, Tex., Jn. analyst)

(ed.) *Mother/Father.* 1989p [p. 190]

Practical Jung: Nuts and Bolts of Jungian Psychotherapy. 1987 + p [p. 340]

Wilson, Colin (1931–; Brit. writer)

Lord of the Underworld: Jung and the Twentieth Century. 1984; 1988p [p. 16]

Wilson, Katherine M.

The Nightingale and the Hawk: A Psychological Study of Keats' Ode. 1964; 1965 [p. 258]

Wing, R. L.

The I Ching Workbook. 1979p; 1983 [p. 97]

Winski, Norman

Understanding Jung. 1971 [p. 43]

Witcutt, William P.

Blake: A Psychological Study. 1946; 1966; 1974; 1977 [p. 253]

Catholic Thought and Modern Psychology. 1943 [p. 203]

Wolff, Hanna (1910–; Dr. theol.; Zurich J. Inst. dipl.; Waldbronn Jn. analyst)

Jesus the Therapist. 1987 + p (Ger.: 1978) [p. 316]

Wolff-Salin, Mary (Sacred Heart religious; psychotherapist)

No Other Light: Points of Convergence in Psychology and Spirituality. 1986; 1989p [p. 237]

The Shadow Side of Community and the Growth of the Self. 1988 [p. 119]

Woloy, Eleanora M. (M.D.; InterReg. dipl.; Virginia Beach, Va., analyst)

The Symbol of the Dog in the Human Psyche. 1990p [p. 65]

Wood, Douglas K. (1938–)

Men Against Time: Berdyaev, Eliot, Huxley, and Jung. 1982 [p. 104]

Woodman, Marion (Zurich J. Inst. dipl.; Toronto Jn. analyst)
Addiction to Perfection. 1982p [p. 323]
The Owl Was a Baker's Daughter: Obesity, Anorexia, and the Repressed Feminine. 1980p [p. 321]
The Pregnant Virgin: Process of Psychological Transformation. 1985p [p. 334]
The Ravaged Bridegroom: Masculinity in Women. 1990p [p. 352]
Woolger, Jennifer Barker (teacher; psychotherapist)
(co-author) *The Goddess Within*. 1989p [p. 192]
Woolger, Roger J. (Ph.D.; Zurich J. Inst. dipl.; New Paltz, N.Y., Jn. analyst)
(co-author) *The Goddess Within*. 1989p [p. 192]
Other Lives, Other Selves. 1987; 1988p [p. 114]
Wyly, James (1937–; Ph.D.; Chicago J. Inst. dipl.; Chicago Jn. analyst)
The Phallic Quest: Priapus and Masculine Inflation. 1989p [p. 191]
Young-Eisendrath, Polly (1947–; Ph.D.; Bala Cynwyd, Penn., Jn. analyst)
(co-ed.) *The Book of the Self: Person, Pretext, and Process*. 1987; 1988p [p. 64]
(co-author) *Female Authority: Empowering Women through Psychotherapy*. 1987 [p. 340]
Hags and Heroes: A Feminist Approach to Jungian Psychotherapy with Couples. 1984p [p. 331]
(co-author) *Jung's Self Psychology*. 1990 [p. 122]
Yungblut, John R. (B.D.; Jn.-oriented psychotherapist)
Discovering God Within. 1979p [p. 221]
The Gentle Art of Spiritual Guidance. 1988p [p. 243]
Zaehner, Robert Charles (1913–)
Mysticism: Sacred and Profane. 1957; 1961p [p. 208]
Zeller, Max (1904–80; D.Jur.; Zurich J. Inst. study; L.A. Jn. analyst)
The Dream: The Vision of the Night (ed. Janet Dallett). 1975p; ed.2 1990 [p. 144]
Ziegler, Alfred J. (1925–; M.D.; Zurich Jn. analyst)
Archetypal Medicine. 1983p (Ger.: 1979) [p. 317]
Zoja, Luigi (Dott.; Zurich J. Inst. dipl.; Milan Jn. analyst)
(co-ed.) *Differing Uses of Symbolic and Clinical Approaches to Practice and Theory*. 1986 [p. 327]
Drugs, Addiction, and Initiation: The Modern Search for Ritual. 1989 + p [p. 348]
Zweig, Connie (Topanga Canyon, Calif., writer & editor)
(ed.) *To Be a Woman*. 1990p [p. 193]

Part Three

Works Arranged by Title

More than 780 titles comprise this part of the bibliography. Also included are nearly 400 subtitles, in view of the fact that some searchers may know the subtitle but not the title of a book. Moreover, many authors select a provocative or a symbolic title and then attach a subtitle that reveals more specifically the nature and content of the book.

Key words, other than the first word of the title or subtitle, are included to help the reader search for precise topics. Thus, Part Three serves as an index as well as a listing of titles. The inclusion of key words allows the searcher to locate a book when maybe only one word is known and provides an opportunity to encounter books dealing with particular topics. For example, the topic of "the unconscious" appears only once as the first word of a title but thirteen times as a secondary word. "Analytical psychology" appears four times as the first word and eighteen times secondarily.

Complete titles (in most instances with a subtitle) are italicized and accompanied by the author's name, whereas subtitles and key words are indicated by Roman type. Bibliographic information (publisher, date, etc.) for a book may be found in Part One on the page number indicated in brackets.

Appendixes

Appendix A

Abbreviations Used in This Book

Abbreviations of periodicals are provided in Appendix B.

Ag	August	ed.2, ed.3, etc.	second edition, third edition, etc.
Am	American		
An.Psy.Club	Analytical Psychology Club	educ.	education
		Engl.	English
Ap	April	F	February
asst.ed.	assistant editor	Fr.	French
Au	Autumn	Ger.	German
bibl.	bibliography	hist.	history
Bk.revs.	Book reviews	illus.	illustrated, illustrations
C.	College		
Cath.	Catholic	incl.	including
chron.	chronology	Inst.	Institute
clin.	clinical	Inter-Reg.	Inter-Regional Society of Jungian Analysts
co.-ed.	coeditor		
comm.	commentary		
corr.	corrected, corrections	intro.	introduction
CW	*Collected Works* of C. G. Jung	It.	Italian
		J.	Jung
D	December	J.Inst.	Jung Institute
dipl.	diplomate	Ja	January
dir.	director	Jn	June
doct.	doctoral	Jn. analyst	Jungian analyst
ed.	editor	Jn.-oriented	Jungian-oriented
edn.	edition	Jy	July

lec.	lecturer	Span.	Spanish
lit.	literature	Spr	Spring
Mr	March	subj.	subject
My	May	Sum	Summer
N	November	sup	supplement (in
n	number in		book review
	volume		data)
ns	new series	supp.	supplement,
Oc	October		supplementary
orig.	original (edition)	theol.	theology
p	paperback	U.	University (as in
	(edition)		Princeton U.
p.	page		Press)
+p	paperback	U.Brit.Columbia	University of
	edition as well		British
	as hardback		Columbia
philos.	philosophy	U.Cal.	University of
prof.	professor		California
psy.	psychology	U.Sn.Cal	University of
psychi.	psychiatry		Southern
ref. notes	reference notes		California
relig.	religion	v.1, vol.1	volume 1
ret.	retired	Wint	Winter
rev.	revised	*(following a year,	
S	September	e.g., 1986*)	in print as of
serv.	service		1989

Appendix B

Book Review Periodicals

More than 570 periodicals comprise this list in which book reviews of books in this annotated bibliography appear, thereby indicating the wide range of coverage of Jungian writings. Included are professional journals in psychology and psychotherapy, as well as professional journals in other fields, along with popular journals, magazines, and newspapers.

More than 4,000 book reviews are listed in Part I (Books Arranged by Subject, with descriptive annotations and with book-review sources for each book, ranging from short notices to long, critical reviews— whose presence may be noted by the kind of periodical and by the number of pages devoted to the review.

The largest number of reviews appear in the *Journal of Analytical Psychology* (222) of London's Society of Analytical Psychology; *Library Journal* (181) of the American Library Association; *Book Review Digest* (158) of H. W. Wilson Company; *Choice* (153) of the Association of College Research Libraries; *Quadrant* (152) of New York's C. G. Jung Foundation for Analytical Psychology; the *Times Literary Supplement* (112) of the *Times* of London; *Contemporary Psychology* (108) of the American Psychological Association; *Psychological Perspectives* (101) of the Los Angeles Jung Institute; *Harvest* (97) of London's Analytical Psychology Club; *Booklist* (58) of the American Library Association; *New York Times Book Review* (57); *San Francisco Jung Institute Library Journal* (56); and *American Journal of Psychiatry* (48) of the American Psychiatric Association.

Adoles	Adolescence	AmArtist	American Artist
AgeingSoc	Ageing and Society	Ambix	Ambix
AmAnth	American Anthropologist	AmBkColl	American Book Collector

AmCathSocR	American Catholic Sociological Review	AnnSci	Annals of Science
		AntiochR	Antioch Review
		AppalJ	Appalachian Journal
Amer	America	Archaeol	Archaeology
AmHistR	American Historical Review	ArchGenPsy	Archives of General Psychiatry
AmJArtTh	American Journal of Art Therapy	ArizQ	Arizona Quarterly
		ArtActiv	Arts and Activities
AmJClinHyp	American Journal of Clinical Hypnosis	ArtJ	Art Journal
		ArtPsyth	Art Psychotherapy
AmJOrthopsy	American Journal of Orthopsychiatry	ArtsPsyth	Arts in Psychotherapy
		AsbSem	Asbury Seminarian
AmJPsy	American Journal of Psychology	Atl	Atlantic [Monthly]
		AUMLA	A.U.M.L.A. [Australian Us.]
AmJPsyan	American Journal of Psychoanalysis	AusJPsy	Australian Journal of Psychology
AmJPsychi	American Journal of Psychiatry	AusNZJPsy	Australian & New Zealand Journal of Psychiatry
AmJPsyth	American Journal of Psychotherapy		
AmJSoc	American Journal of Sociology	AusPsyist	Australian Psychiatrist
AmLib	American Libraries	AveMaria	Ave Maria
AmLit	American Literature	BehInfTec	Behavior Information & Technology
AmMerc	American Mercury		
AmNotes&Q	American Notes and Queries	BehResTh	Behaviour Research and Therapy
AmPoetR	American Poetry Review	BestSell	Best Sellers
		BibSocAm	Biblical Society of America
AmPolSciR	American Political Science Review	Biog	Biography
AmRefBksAn	American Reference Books Annual	BioSci	BioScience
		BkFor	Book Forum
AmR	American Review	Bklist	Booklist
AmSchol	American Scholar	Bkman	Bookman
AmSocR	American Sociological Review	Bkmark	Bookmark
		BkMClubN	Book of the Month Club News
Americas	Americas		
AnglTheolR	Anglican Theological Review	BkRDig	Book Review Digest
		BkRep	Book Report
Anima	Anima	BksAbroad	Books Abroad
AnnAmAcad	Annals of the American Academy of Political and Social Science	BksBkmen	Books and Bookmen
		BksCan	Books in Canada
		BksRel	Books and Religion
		BksTrial	Books on Trial

BkWorld	Book World [Washington Post]	BulMennClin	Bulletin of the Menninger Clinic
Blackf	Blackfriars	BurlMag	Burlington Magazine
Blake	Blake: Illustrated Quarterly	CalvTheolJ	Calvin Theological Journal
BloomR	Bloomsbury Review	CanArt	Canadian Art
BrBkN	British Book News	CanAuthBk	Canadian Author and Bookman
BrJAddic	British Journal of Addiction	CanBkRAn	Canadian Book Review Annual
BrJAesth	British Journal of Aesthetics	CanCathR	Canadian Catholic Review
BrJCrim	British Journal of Criminology	CanForum	Canadian Forum
BrJDevPsy	British Journal of Developmental Psychology	CanJPsychi	Canadian Journal of Psychiatry
		CanJTheol	Canadian Journal of Theology
BrJEdStud	British Journal of Educational Studies	CanLit	Canadian Literature
BrJ18Cen	British Journal of Eighteenth Century Studies	CanMentH	Canada's Mental Health
BrJMedPsy	British Journal of Medical Psychology	CanPsychiJ	Canadian Psychiatric Association Journal
BrJPhilSci	British Journal for the Philosophy of Science	CanRAmStud	Canadian Review of American Studies
		CanRCompLit	Canadian Review of Comparative Literature
BrJPsy	British Journal of Psychology	CanTheatreR	Canadian Theatre Review
BrJPsychi	British Journal of Psychiatry	CathBibQ	Catholic Biblical Quarterly
BrJSocClin	British Journal of Social and Clinical Psychology	CathCharis	Catholic Charismatic
		CathEdR	Catholic Educational Review
BrJSocWork	British Journal of Social Work	CathLib	Catholic Library World
BulAnPsyNY	Bulletin of the Analytical Psychology Club of New York	CathNewTimes	Catholic New Times
		CathWorker	Catholic Worker
BulBrPsySoc	Bulletin of the British Psychological Society	CathWorld	Catholic World
		CaudaPav	Cauda Pavonis
		ChingFeng	Ching Feng [Christian Study Center]
BulHistMed	Bulletin of the History of Medicine	Chiron	Chiron

ChiSunTrib	Chicago Sunday Tribune	ContemPsy	Contemporary Psychology
Chman	Churchman	ContemPsyan	Contemporary Psychoanalysis
Chman(L)	Churchman [London]	ContemSoc	Contemporary Sociology
Choice	Choice		
ChrCen	Christian Century	ContLearn	Continuous Learning
ChrScholR	Christian Scholars' Review	CovenantQ	Covenant Quarterly
		CrimLawR	Criminal Law Review
ChrSciMon	Christian Science Monitor	Criterion	Criterion
		Critic	Critic
Chry&Lit	Christianity and Literature	Criticism	Criticism
		Cross&Crown	Cross and Crown
ChryToday	Christianity Today	CrossCurr	Cross Currents
Church	Church	CrozerQ	Crozer Quarterly
ChurchQR	Church Quarterly Review	CurrPsy	Current Psychology
		DalhousieR	Dalhousie Review
CistStud	Cistercian Studies	DeathEd	Death Education
ClassBul	Classical Bulletin	DenverQ	Denver Quarterly
ClassJ	Classical Journal	Diacrit	Diacritics
ClassPhilol	Classical Philology	Dial	Dial
ClassR	Classical Review	Dialog	Dialog
ClassWorld	Classical World	Dialogue	Dialogue
ClergyR	Clergy Review	DickStud	Dickinson Studies
ClinSocWkJ	Clinical Social Work Journal	DoctLife	Doctrine and Life
		Domin	Dominicana
CollLit	College Literature	DownR	Downside Review
Colloq	Colloquium	DrewGate	Drew Gateway
CollResLib	College Research Libraries	DublR	Dublin Review
		EAsPastorR	East Asian Pastoral Review
Columbia	Columbia		
CommBound	Common Boundary Between Spirituality and Psychotherapy	EastWorld	Eastern World
		Econ	Economist
		EdLeader	Educational Leadership
Commonw	Commonweal	EdStud	Educational Studies
CompLit	Comparative Literature	Encoun	Encounter [Indianapolis]
Composer	Composer	Encoun(L)	Encounter [London]
ConcordiaTh	Concordia Theological Monthly	Engl	English
		EnglHistR	English Historical Review
ConradG	Conrad Grebel Review	EnglR	English Review
ConsJud	Conservative Judaism	EnglStud	English Studies

EnglStudCan	English Studies in Canada	HumSyst	Human Systems Management
Epiph	Epiphany	IllifR	Illif Review
Esq	Esquire	IndivPsy	Individual Psychology
EssCanWrit	Essays on Canadian Writing	Integ	Integrity
Etc	Et Cetera	Intell	Intellect
Ethics	Ethics	Interp	Interpretation
EurStudR	European Studies Review	IntJAmLing	International Journal of American Linguistics
ExposTimes	Expository Times	IntJEth	International Journal of Ethics
FarEQ	Far Eastern Quarterly	IntJGroup	International Journal of Group Psychotherapy
FilmQ	Film Quarterly		
Folk	Folklore		
Found	Foundations	IntJParapsy	International Journal of Parapsychology
FriendsJ	Friends Journal		
Frontier	Frontier	IntJPhRel	International Journal for the Philosophy of Religion
FrR	French Review		
FrStud	French Studies		
Furrow	Furrow	IntJPsy-An	International Journal of Psycho-Analysis
GaR	Georgia Review		
GerLifeLet	German Life and Letters	IntJSocPsy	International Journal of Social Psychiatry
GerQ	German Quarterly		
GerStudR	German Studies Review	IntJSymb	International Journal of Symbology
Gnosis	Gnosis		
GuardW	Guardian Weekly	IntlAff	International Affairs
Harper	Harper's	IntRPsy-An	International Review of Psycho-Analysis
HarvDivBul	Harvard Divinity Bulletin	InwLight	Inward Light
Harvest	Harvest	IrEcclRec	Irish Ecclesiastical Record
HeythJ	Heythrop Journal		
HibbJ	Hibbert Journal	IrTheolQ	Irish Theological Quarterly
HispAmHistR	Hispanic American Historical Review	Isis	Isis
Hist	History	IsrAnPsychi	Israel Annals of Psychiatry
HomPastorR	Homiletic and Pastoral Review	JAbnPsy	Journal of Abnormal Psychology
Horiz	Horizons		
HudsonR	Hudson Review	JAbSocPsy	Journal of Abnormal & Social Psychology
HumContext	Human Context		
HumDev	Human Development		

JAdol — Journal of Adolescence

JAesthArt — Journal of Aesthetics and Art

JAltState — Journal of Altered States of Consciousness

JAmAcadRel — Journal of the American Academy of Religion

JAmAcPsyan — Journal of the American Academy of Psychoanalysis

JAmFolk — Journal of American Folklore

JAmOrSoc — Journal of the American Oriental Society

JAmPsyan — Journal of the American Psychoanalytic Association

JAmSocPsy — Journal of the American Society for Psychical Research

JAmStud — Journal of American Studies

JAnPsy — Journal of Analytical Psychology

JApplBehSci — Journal of Applied Behavioral Science

JApplSoc — Journal of Applied Sociology

JArtDesEd — Journal of Art and Design Education

JAsianStud — Journal of Asian Studies

JAssnPerc — Journal of the Association for the Study of Perception

JBibRel — Journal of Bible and Religion

JBibLit — Journal of Biblical Literature

JBioPsy — Journal of Biological Psychology

JBlackSacM — Journal of Black Sacred Music

JBSP — Journal of the British Society for Phenomenology

JChildPsy — Journal of Child Psychology

JChinPhilos — Journal of Chinese Philosophy

JCommun — Journal of Communication

JContemPsy — Journal of Contemporary Psychology

JCounsPsy — Journal of Counseling Psychology

JEcumStud — Journal of Ecumenical Studies

JEdPsy — Journal of Educational Psychology

JEdSoc — Journal of Educational Sociology

JEGP — Journal of English and Germanic Philology

JEmplCouns — Journal of Employment Counseling

JEurStud — Journal of European Studies

JHighEd — Journal of Higher Education

JHistBehSci — Journal of History of the Behavioral Sciences

JHomeEc — Journal of Home Economics

JHumRel — Journal of Human Relations

JIndivPsy — Journal of Individual Psychology

JInterdHist — Journal of Interdisciplinary History

JLegalEd — Journal of Legal Education

JMarFamTh — Journal of Marital

	and Family Ther-apy	JRelAging	Journal of Religion and Aging
JMentSci	Journal of Mental Science	JRelHealth	Journal of Religion and Health
JMindBeh	Journal of Mind and Behavior	JRelPsyRes	Journal of Religion and Psychical Re-search
JModHist	Journal of Modern History	JRelThought	Journal of Religious Thought
JModLit	Journal of Modern Literature	JRoyalSoc	Journal of the Royal Society of Arts
JNABI	Journal of the Na-tional Association of Biblical Instruc-tors	JSciStudR	Journal for the Scien-tific Study of Reli-gion
JNervMent	Journal of Nervous and Mental Dis-ease	JTheolStud	Journal of Theologi-cal Studies
JOttoRank	Journal of the Otto Rank Association	JTranspPsy	Journal of Transper-sonal Psychology
JParapsy	Journal of Parapsy-chology	Jubilee	Jubilee
		Judaism	Judaism
JPastorCare	Journal of Pastoral Care	KenyonR	Kenyon Review
		KirkR	Kirkus Review
JPersAssess	Journal of Personal-ity Assessment	Kliatt	Kliatt Paperback Book Guide
JPhenPsy	Journal of Phenome-nological Psychol-ogy	LATimesBkR	Los Angeles Times Book Review
		Leon	Leonardo
JPhilos	Journal of Philoso-phy	LibJ	Library Journal
		LibJBkR	Library Journal Book Review
JPhilosStud	Journal of Philosoph-ical Studies	Life	Life
JPol	Journal of Politics	LifeLtrsToday	Life and Letters To-day
JPopFilmTV	Journal of Popular Film and Televi-sion	LifeSpir	Life in the Spirit
		Listen	Listener
JPsyChry	Journal of Psychol-ogy and Christian-ity	LitEW	Literature East and West
		LitMed	Literature and Medi-cine
JPsysomRes	Journal of Psychoso-matic Research	LitPsy	Literature and Psy-chology
JPsyTheol	Journal of Psychol-ogy and Theology	LivLigh	Living Light
		LondMag	London Magazine
JRel	Journal of Religion	LondMerc	London Mercury

LondQHolb	London Quarterly & Holborn Rev.	NathCathRep	National Catholic Reporter
LondRBks	London Review of Books	Nation	Nation
		NatR	National Review
LATimesBkR	Los Angeles Times Book Review	Nature	Nature
		NewAge	New Age
LumenVitae	Lumen Vitae [Brussels]	NewBlackf	New Blackfriars
		NewCath	New Catholic World
LuthForum	Lutheran Forum	NewDirWom	New Directions for Women
LuthQ	Lutheran Quarterly		
LuthTheolJ	Lutheran Theological Journal	NewEnglQ	New English Quarterly
LuthWorld	Lutheran World	NewIdeas	New Ideas
Manus	Manuscripta	NewMexQ	New Mexico Quarterly
Marriage	Marriage		
MexLife	Mexican Life	NewRBksRel	New Review of Books and Religion
Midstream	Midstream		
MidWFolk	Midwest Folklore		
Mind	Mind	NewRep	New Republic
Mission	Mission Bell	NewScholas	New Scholasticism
ModAge	Modern Age	NewSci	New Scientist
ModChman	Modern Churchman	NewSoc	New Society
ModDrama	Modern Drama	NewStates	New Statesman [and Nation]
ModFictStud	Modern Fiction Studies		
		NewStatSoc	New Statesman and Society
ModLangJ	Modern Language Journal		
		Newswk	Newsweek
ModLangQ	Modern Language Quarterly	NICM	NICM Journal [National Institute of Campus Ministries]
ModLangR	Modern Language Review		
ModPhilol	Modern Philology	19CenFict	Nineteenth-Century Fiction
ModSchman	Modern Schoolman		
Monist	Monist	19CenFrStud	Nineteenth-Century French Studies
Month	Month		
Mosaic	Mosaic	Notes&Q	Notes and Queries
Ms	Ms.	Novel	Novel
MusEdJ	Music Education Journal	NYHerTrib	New York Herald Tribune Book Review
MusR	Music Review		
MusJ	Music Journal	NYorker	New Yorker
MusOpin	Music Opinion	NYRevBks	New York Review of Books
MusTimes	Musical Times		
Mythlore	Mythlore	NYTimesBkR	New York Times Book Review

Observ	Observer	PsychiAn	Psychiatric Annals
OregHistQ	Oregon Historical Quarterly	PsychiForum	Psychiatric Forum
		PsychiJOtt	Psychiatric Journal of the University of Ottawa
PacAff	Pacific Affairs		
Parab	Parabola		
ParMag	Parents Magazine	PsychiQ	Psychiatric Quarterly
PartisR	Partisan Review	PsyMed	Psychological Medicine
PastorPsy	Pastoral Psychology		
Pax	Pax	PsyPersp	Psychological Perspectives
PerfArtsJ	Performing Arts Journal		
		PsyRec	Psychological Record
PerkJ	Perkins Journal	PsySch	Psychology in the Schools
PerkSchTh	Perkins School of Theology Journal		
		PsysomMed	Psychosomatic Medicine
Person	Personalist		
PersRelStud	Perspectives in Religious Studies	PsythTheor	Psychotherapy Theory, Research and Practice
Philo	Philosophia [Bar-Ilan U., Israel]		
		PsyToday	Psychology Today
Philos	Philosophy	PsyWomQ	Psychology of Women Quarterly
PhilosLit	Philosophy and Literature		
		PubW	Publishers Weekly
PhilosPhen	Philosophy and Phenomenological Research	Punch	Punch
		QJSpeech	Quarterly Journal of Speech
PhilosQ	Philosophical Quarterly	Quad	Quadrant
		QueensQ	Queen's Quarterly
PhilosSocSc	Philosophy of the Social Sciences	QuillQuire	Quill and Quire
		R&Expos	Review and Expositor
Playboy	Playboy		
PoeStud	Poe Studies	RBksRel(C)	Review of Books and Religion [Cincinnati]
Poetry	Poetry		
PoetryR	Poetry Review		
PolStud	Political Studies	RBksRel(W)	Review of Books and Religion [White River]
PolTheory	Political Theory		
PrincSemBul	Princeton Seminary Bulletin		
		Readings	Readings
ProseStud	Prose Studies	ReformR	Reformed Review
PsyanQ	Psychoanalytic Quarterly	ReformThR	Reformed Theological Review
PsyanR	Psychoanalytic Review	RefResBkN	Reference and Research Book News
PsyBul	Psychological Bulletin	RefServR	Reference Services Review
Psychi	Psychiatry		

ReligEd	Religious Education	SciTechBkN	SciTech Book News
ReligHum	Religious Humanism	ScotJTheol	Scottish Journal of
ReligLife	Religion in Life		Theology
ReligStud	Religious Studies	Scrut	Scrutiny
RelIntell	Religion and Intellec-	SewaneeR	Sewanee Review
	tual Life	SexRoles	Sex Roles
RelStudBul	Religious Studies	SFChron	San Francisco Chron-
	Bulletin		icle
RelStudR	Religious Studies Re-	SFJInstLib	San Francisco Jung
	view		Institute Library
RelStudTh	Religious Studies and		Journal
	Theology	SFolkQ	Southern Folklore
REnglStud	Review of English		Quarterly
	Studies	SFRBks	San Francisco Review
ReprBulBkR	Reprint Bulletin		of Books
	Book Reviews	ShakesQ	Shakespeare Quar-
ResRefBkN	Research Reference		terly
	Book News	ShakesStud	Shakespeare Studies
Resug	Resurgence	SHumR	Southern Humanities
Review	Review		Review
RforRel	Review for Religious	Signs	Signs
RMeta	Review of Metaphys-	SisToday	Sisters Today
	ics	SmallPr	Small Press
RockyMtR	Rocky Mountain Re-	SmallPrBkR	Small Press Book Re-
	view of Language		view
	and Literature	SnR	Southern Review
RofRel	Review of Religion	Soc	Society
RPol	Review of Politics	SocAn	Sociological Analysis
RQ	RQ [Chicago]	SocForc	Social Forces
RRelRes	Review of Religious	SocOrder	Social Order
	Research	SocR	Sociological Review
SAtlQ	South Atlantic Quar-	SocSciMed	Social Science and
	terly		Medicine
SAtlR	South Atlantic Re-	SocSciR	Social Science Re-
	view		view
SatNight	Saturday Night	SocServR	Social Service Review
SatR	Saturday Review	SocSocRes	Sociology and Social
SchArts	School Arts		Research
SchLibr	School Librarian	SocThought	Social Thought
SchSoc	School and Society	SocWork	Social Work
SciAm	Scientific American	Sojour	Sojourners
SciBkClubR	Science Book Club	Sower	Sower
	Review	Spec	Spectator
SciBksFilm	Science Books and	SpecLib	Special Libraries
	Films	Specul	Speculum

SpirLife	Spiritual Life	TimesHighEd	Times (London) Higher Education Supplement
SpirToday	Spirituality Today		
Spring	Spring		
StAnth	St. Anthony Messenger	TimesLitSup	Times (London) Literary Supplement
StLukeJTh	St. Luke's Journal of Theology	TorJTheol	Toronto Journal of Theology
StMarkThR	St. Mark's Theological Review	TrinSemR	Trinity Seminary Review
StudAmFict	Studies in American Fiction	TSF	TSF Bulletin [Theological Student Fellowship]
StudComRel	Studies in Comparative Religion		
StudForm	Studies in Formative Spirituality	TulsaStud	Tulsa Studies in Women's Literature
StudIrQR	Studies: Irish Quarterly Review	20Cen	Twentieth Century
		UCLALawR	UCLA Law Review
StudNovel	Studies in the Novel	UHartStud	University of Hartford Studies in Literature
StudRel	Studies in Religion		
StudRom	Studies in Romanticism		
StudShFict	Studies in Short Fiction	UnionSemQR	Union Seminary Quarterly Review [N.Y.]
SubStance	Sub-Stance	UnionSemR	Union Seminary Review [Richmond]
Surv	Survey		
SurvMidM	Survey Midmonthly	UPrBkN	University Press Book News
SWJTheol	Southwestern Journal of Theology		
SWRev	Southwest Review	USCath	U.S. Catholic
Sympos	Symposium	UTorQ	University of Toronto Quarterly
Syst	Systematics	VaQR	Virginia Quarterly Review
Tabl	Tablet		
Teilhard	Teilhard Review	VillVoice	Village Voice Literary Supplement
Tempo	Tempo		
TheatResInt	Theatre Research International	WallStJ	Wall Street Journal
		WaltWhitR	Walt Whitman Review
Theol	Theology		
TheolLife	Theology and Life	WAmLit	Western American Literature
TheolStud	Theological Studies		
TheolToday	Theology Today	WCoastR	West Coast Review
Thom	Thomist	WCoastRBks	West Coast Review of Books
Thought	Thought		
Time	Time	WFolk	Western Folklore
TimesEdSup	Times (London) Education Supplement	WHumR	Western Humanities Review

WilsonLibB	Wilson Library Bulletin	WorldAff	World Affairs Interpreter
WilsonQ	Wilson Quarterly	World Lit	World Literature Today
Wingspan	Wingspan		
WomRBks	Women's Review of Books	WorldLitEngl	World Literature Written in English
WomStudIntQ	Women's Studies International Quarterly	WorldView	World View
		YaleR	Yale Review
WordWorld	Word and World	Zygon	Zygon

Appendix C

Publishers of Jungian Literature

More than 300 publishers figure in this annotated bibliography of books on Jungian thought published in English; more than half of these publishers are represented by one or two books. The largest number of titles have been published by the London firm of Routledge (formerly Routledge & Kegan Paul, which was preceded by Kegan Paul, Trench, Trubner), which has issued nearly 100 Jungian books, including the volumes of Jung's *Collected Works*. Princeton University Press, chiefly through its connection with the Bollingen Foundation (whose early volumes were published by Pantheon Books), has published 80 Jungian books, also including the *Collected Works*. The other of the "big three" is Spring Publications (formerly of New York's Analytical Psychology Club and taken to Dallas by James Hillman in 1977), which has published 60 books included in this annotated bibliography.

Other major publishers of Jungian works are Harper & Row (53); Inner City Books (46 in its series of Studies in Jungian Psychology by Jungian Analysts); Sigo Press (35); Chiron Publications (35); Shambhala Publications (28); Paulist Press (27); Putnam Publishing Group (26), principally for the C. G. Jung Foundation for Analytical Psychology; and Crossroad Publishing Company (21). These figures include books scheduled for publication in 1990.

Listed are twenty-six publishers with ten or more books in this bibliography.

Allen & Unwin Publishers, 40 Museum St., London MC1A 1LU (01-405-8577);
    8 Winchester Place, Winchester, MA 01890 (800-547-8889)
Analytical Psychology Club of New York, 28 E. 39th St., New York, NY 10016
    (212-697-7877)
Ark Publications, 11 Fedder Lane, London EC4P 4EE (01-583-9855)
Chiron Publications, 400 Linden Ave., Wilmette, IL 60091 (312-256-7551)

Crossroad Publishing Co., 370 Lexington Ave., New York, NY 10017 (212-532-3650; 800-638-3030)

Daimon Verlag, Am Klosterplatz, Hauptstrasse 85, Einsiedeln CH-8840 Switzerland (4155-532266)

Doubleday & Company, Inc., 245 Park Ave., New York, NY 10017 (212-953-4561; 800-645-6156)

Fitzhenry & Whiteside Ltd., 195 Allstate Parkway, Markham, Ontario L3R 4T8 (416-477-0030)

Harcourt Brace Jovanovich Inc., 1250 Sixth Ave., San Diego, CA 92101 (619-231-6616)

Harper & Row Publishers, 10 East 53rd St., New York, NY 10022-5299 (212-107-7000); Icehouse One-401, 151 Union St., San Francisco, CA 94111-1299 (415-477-4400)

Hodder & Stoughton Ltd., London WC1B 3DP (01-636-9851)

Inner City Books, Box 1271, Station Q, Toronto, Ontario M4T 2P4 (416-927-0355)

Kegan Paul, Trench, Trubner & Co. Ltd. (combined with Routledge in 1950)

McClelland & Stuart Ltd., 25 Hollinger Rd., Toronto, Ontario M4B 3G2 (416-751-4520)

Northwestern University Press, 625 Colfax St., Evanston, IL 60201 (312-491-5313)

Pantheon Books (div. of Random House), 201 E. 50th St., New York, NY 10022 (212-572-2346)

Paulist Press, 997 Macarthur Blvd., Mahwah, NJ 07430 (201-825-7300)

Penguin Books Ltd., Wright's Lane, London W8 5T2 (01-938-2200); 299 Murray Hill Parkway, East Rutherford, NJ 07073 (800-631-3577)

Princeton University Press, 41 William St., Princeton, NJ 08540; 3175 Princeton Pike, Lawrenceville, NJ 08648 (609-452-4122)

Putnam Publishing Group, 200 Madison Ave., New York, NY 10016 (212-576-8900; 800-847-5515)

Routledge Ltd., 11 New Fedder Lane, London EC4P 4EE; Routledge, Chapman & Hall Inc., 29 West 35th St., New York, NY 10001-2291 (212-244-3336)

Shambhala Publications, Inc., 300 Massachusetts Ave., Boston, MA 02115 (617-424-0030)

Sigo Press, 25 New Chardon St., no. 8748, Boston, MA 02114 (617-526-7064; 800-338-0446)

Spring Publications, Inc., P.O. Box 222069, Dallas, TX 75222 (214-943-4093)

University Press of America, Inc., 4720 Boston Way, Lanham, MD 20706 (301-459-3366)

Weiser (Samuel) Inc., P.O. Box 612, York Beach, ME 03910 (207-363-4393; 800-423-7087)

Appendix D

Jungian Organizations

Jungian organizations include professional and lay associations, societies, foundations, clubs, centers, and "friends of Jung," some of which maintain book stores, libraries, and training programs and clinics. Listed below are some of these organizations.

International Association for Analytical Psychology (IAAP), Postfach 115, 8042 Zurich, Switzerland

Founded in 1956, the IAAP provides members with a newsletter and a periodic list of members and holds international congresses every three years. The first of these was held in Zurich in 1958 (on current trends in analytical psychology), followed by ones in Zurich in 1962 (on the archetype), in Montreux in 1965 (on the reality of the psyche), in Zurich in 1968 (on the analytic process: aims, analysis, training), in London in 1971 (on success and failure in analysis), in Rome in 1977 (on methods of treatment in analytical psychology), in San Francisco in 1980 (on money, food, drink, fashion, and analytic training), in Jerusalem in 1983 (on symbolic and clinical approaches in theory and practice), in Berlin in 1986 (on archetype of shadow in a split world), and in Paris in 1989 (on personal and archetypal dynamics in the analytical relationship). The proceedings of these congresses are published.

IAAP memberships number approximately 1,450, nearly sixty-five percent of whom live in Europe and nearly thirty percent in North America. Countries having the greatest number of members in 1989 are the United States (395), West Germany (254), Great Britain (226), Switzerland (216), Italy (133), France (54), Brazil (40), Belgium (30), and Israel (26). Other members reside in Canada, Australia, Austria, Japan, Venezuela, Spain, New Zealand, Denmark, Korea, South Africa, Finland, Sweden, Mexico, Uruguay, and the Bahamas. The greatest concentration of members are in the metropolitan areas of London (152), San Francisco (93), Zurich (86), Berlin (73), Rome (62), New York (56), Stuttgart (34), Los Angeles (30), Milan (28), São Paulo (28), Paris (24), Chicago (18), Boston (17), and Brussels (17).

Within the United States, the distribution of Jungian analysts (according to the 1989 directory of IAAP members) includes: West Coast, 163; Northeast, 133; Southwest, 38; and Southeast, 19.

The over-all distribution by countries in 1989 was as follows.

NORTH AMERICA = 411		EUROPE = 935				ASIA = 35		
U.S.A.	= 395	Germany	= 254	Austria	= 9	Israel	= 26
Canada	= 14	Great Britain	= 226	Spain	= 6	Japan	= 7
Bahamas	= 1	Switzerland	= 216	Denmark	= 1	Korea	= 2
Mexico	= 1	Italy	= 133	Finland	= 1	AFRICA = 2	
SOUTH AMERICA = 46		France	= 54	Greece	= 1	South Africa	= 2
Brazil	= 40	Belgium	= 30	Netherlands	= 1	AUSTRALASIA = 16	
Venezuela	= 5			Sweden	= 1	Australia	= 12
Uruguay	= 1					New Zealand	= 4

Professional societies within IAAP exist for the following countries:

AUSTRALIA AND NEW ZEALAND
  Australian and New Zealand Society for Jungian Analysts
AUSTRIA
  Österreichische Gesellschaft für Analytische Psychologie
BELGIUM
  Société Belge de Psychologie Analytique
BRAZIL
  Sociedade Brasileira de Psycologia Analitica
FRANCE
  Société Française de Psychologie Analytique
GERMANY
  Deutsche Gesellschaft für Analytische Psychologie
GREAT BRITAIN
  Society of Analytical Psychology
  Association of Jungian Analysts
  Independent Group of Analytical Psychologists
  British Association of Psychotherapists: Jungian Section
ISRAEL
  Israel Association of Analytical Psychology
ITALY
  Associazione Italiana per lo Studio della Psicologia
  Centro Italiano di Psycologia Analitica
SWITZERLAND
  Schweizerische Gesellschaft für Analytische Psychologie
UNITED STATES
  Chicago Society of Jungian Analysts
  Inter-Regional Society of Jungian Analysts
  New England Society of Jungian Analysts
  New York Association for Analytical Psychology

Pacific Northwest Society of Jungian Analysts
Society of Jungian Analysts of Northern California
Society of Jungian Analysts of San Diego
Society of Jungian Analysts of Southern California

Association of Graduate Analytical Psychologists of the C. G. Jung Institute, Zurich (many members of which also belong to local associations)

In addition to the IAAP's member societies, there exist numerous local groups interested in promotion of the study of Jung and analytical psychology. In the United States and Canada, information on such groups is provided by The Centerpoint Foundation (33 Main St., Suite 302, Nashua, NH 03060) through its thrice-yearly newsletter *In Touch*. Seventy-two such groups are listed below.

ALABAMA
Friends of Jung South, Birmingham
ARIZONA
Phoenix Friends of Jung, Scottsdale
Southern Arizona Friends of C. G. Jung, Tucson
CALIFORNIA
Analytical Psychology Club of Los Angeles
Analytical Psychology Club of San Francisco
C. G. Jung Club of Claremont
C. G. Jung Club of Orange County
C. G. Jung Institute of Los Angeles
C. G. Jung Institute of San Francisco
Central Coast Jung Society, Los Osos
Friends of Jung, San Diego
CANADA
C. G. Jung Foundation of the Analytical Psychology Society of Ontario, Toronto
C. G. Jung Society of Montreal
C. G. Jung Society of Ottawa
C. G. Jung Society of Vancouver
Friends of Jung, Edmonton
COLORADO
C. G. Jung Institute, Denver
C. G. Jung Society of Colorado, Denver
C. G. Jung Society of Colorado Springs
CONNECTICUT
Connecticut Association for Jungian Psychology, North Haven
DISTRICT OF COLUMBIA
Washington Society for Jungian Psychology
FLORIDA
C. G. Jung Society of Northeast Florida, Jacksonville

Center for Jungian Studies for Southeast Florida, Palm Beach
Jungian Society of Daytona Beach

Georgia
C. G. Jung Society of Atlanta

Hawaii
C. G. Jung Center of Hawaii, Honolulu

Illinois
C. G. Jung Institute of Chicago, Evanston
Friends of Jung/Quad Cities, Moline

Indiana
Central Indiana Friends of Jung, Indianapolis
Friends of Jung, Fort Wayne

Iowa
Iowa City Friends of C. G. Jung

Louisiana
Acadiana Friends of Jung, Lafayette
C. G. Jung Society of New Orleans

Maine
Brunswick Jung Center

Maryland
Baltimore Jung Working Group

Massachusetts
C. G. Jung Institute, Boston
Friends of Jung in Boston, West Newton

Michigan
Center for Jung Studies of Detroit, Grosse Pointe
Northern Michigan Friends of Jung, Harbor Springs

Minnesota
Minnesota Jung Association, Minneapolis

Missouri
Friends of Jung of Greater Kansas City
Friends of C. G. Jung, St. Louis

Montana
Montana Friends of C. G. Jung, Missoula

New Mexico
Inter-Regional Society of Jungian Analysts, Santa Fe

New York
Analytical Psychology Club of New York
Analytical Psychology Society of Western New York, Buffalo
C. G. Jung Society of Central New York, Syracuse
Jungian Society of Rochester

North Carolina
C. G. Jung Society of the Triangle Area, Chapel Hill
Cape Fear Jung Society, Wilmington
Charlotte Friends of Jung

OHIO
C. G. Jung Association of Miami Valley, Dayton
Greater Cincinnati Friends of Jung
Jung Educational Center of Cleveland
Toledo Center for Jungian Studies
OREGON
Oregon Friends of Jung, Portland
PENNSYLVANIA
C. G. Jung Center of Philadelphia
C. G. Jung Educational Center of Pittsburgh
Jung Society of Scranton
Pittsburgh Jung Society
TENNESSEE
C. G. Jung Society of Knoxville
TEXAS
Analytical Psychology Association of Dallas
C. G. Jung Educational Center of Houston
Jung Society of Austin
UTAH
Provo Friends of Jung
Salt Lake City Jungian Study Group
VERMONT
C. G. Jung Society of Vermont, Montpelier
VIRGINIA
C. G. Jung Society of Tidewater, Norfolk
Jungian Venture, Richmond
WASHINGTON
C. G. Jung Society, Seattle
WISCONSIN
Lake Superior Friends of Jung, Hurley

Other C. G. Jung Foundation Books
from Shambhala Publications

Absent Fathers, Lost Sons: The Search for Masculine Identity, by Guy Corneau.

*The Child, by Erich Neumann. Foreword by Louis H. Stewart.

*Depth Psychology and a New Ethic, by Erich Neumann. Forewords by C. G. Jung, Gerhard Adler, and James Yandell.

*Dreams, by Marie-Louise von Franz.

*From Freud to Jung: A Comparative Study of the Psychology of the Unconscious, by Liliane Frey-Rohn. Foreword by Robert Hinshaw.

A Guided Tour of the Collected Works *of C. G. Jung*, by Robert H. Hopcke. Foreword by Aryeh Maidenbaum.

Individuation in Fairy Tales, Revised Edition, by Marie-Louise von Franz.

In Her Image: The Unhealed Daughter's Search for Her Mother, by Kathie Carlson.

Knowing Woman: A Feminine Psychology, by Irene Claremont de Castillejo.

Lingering Shadows: Jungians, Freudians, and Anti-Semitism, edited by Aryeh Maidenbaum and Stephen A. Martin.

The Old Wise Woman: A Study of Active Imagination, by Rix Weaver. Introduction by C. A. Meier.

Power and Politics: The Psychology of Soviet-American Partnership, by Jerome S. Bernstein. Forewords by Senator Claiborne Pell and Edward C. Whitmont, M.D.

The Way of All Women, by M. Esther Harding. Introduction by C. G. Jung.

The Wisdom of the Dream: The World of C. G. Jung, by Stephen Segaller and Merrill Berger.

Woman's Mysteries: Ancient and Modern, by M. Esther Harding. Introduction by C. G. Jung.

*Published in association with Daimon Verlag, Einsiedeln, Switzerland.